Prof. Dr. Karl-Heinz Nassmacher

The Funding of Party Competition

Political Finance in 25 Democracies

Nomos

Die Deutsche Nationalbibliothek verzeichnet diese Publikation in
der Deutschen Nationalbibliografie; detaillierte bibliografische
Daten sind im Internet über http://www.d-nb.de abrufbar.

Die Deutsche Nationalbibliothek lists this publication in the Deutsche
Nationalbibliografie; detailed bibliographic data is available
in the Internet at http://www.d-nb.de .

ISBN 978-3-8329-4271-7

1. Auflage 2009
© Nomos Verlagsgesellschaft, Baden-Baden 2009. Printed in Germany. Alle Rechte,
auch die des Nachdrucks von Auszügen, der fotomechanischen Wiedergabe und der
Übersetzung, vorbehalten. Gedruckt auf alterungsbeständigem Papier.

This work is subject to copyright. All rights are reserved, whether the whole or part of
the material is concerned, specifically those of translation, reprinting, re-use of illus-
trations, broadcasting, reproduction by photocopying machine or similar means, and
storage in data banks. Under § 54 of the German Copyright Law where copies are
made for other than private use a fee is payable to »Verwertungsgesellschaft Wort«,
Munich.

To the memory of

Khayyam Z. Paltiel

1922-1988

Preface

The cross-national study of political finance is a time-consuming process. Information and data for this analysis have been collected during more than 25 years. Financial support on a total of five different projects by Deutsche Forschungsgemeinschaft and Volkswagen Stiftung is once more acknowledged.[1] My his own field research in Canada, the U.S., Sweden, Italy and Austria was supplemented by the work of research assistants, who have completed doctoral dissertations on Canada, the U.S., Sweden, Austria and the Netherlands.[2] On Australia, Britain, France, Israel, Japan, the Netherlands and Spain I was involved in a joint effort during the preparation of the International IDEA Handbook.[3] Even for Germany scholarly work done by two graduates and a Ph.D. candidate [4] has been most helpful as was my membership in the Presidential Commission on Party Financing appointed by President Herzog.[5]

For other countries this study relies mostly on the available literature. The communication with experts from a variety of countries during my tenure on the board of the International Political Science Association's Research Committee on Political Finance and Political Corruption (1985-2006) has helped to bridge the gap between information from the literature and empirical findings of long-standing observers in their own country.

I gratefully appreciate that my work has greatly benefited from earlier drafts on individual countries prepared by Dima Amr, M.A. (on Canada), Mareen Bergemann, M.SocSc. (on Japan), Mareike Finck, M.A. (on Israel), Dr Rainer Lisowski (on Australia), Christian Thode, M.A. (on Italy), all of them graduates of Carl-von-Ossietzky University, Oldenburg (Germany), and joint chapters partly written by my colleagues Dr Ingrid van Biezen (Birmingham), Dr Verena Blechinger (Tokyo/ Berlin), Dr Gullan Gidlund (Örebro) and, last but not least, Dr Ruud Koole (Leiden). Other country experts have kindly added data for their country and pointed out errors, which were included in earlier drafts of chapter III. I am obliged to Tania Martinez, M.A. (Mexico), Dr Enrico Melchionda (Salerno), Dr Karina Pedersen (Copenhagen) and Dr Hubert Sickinger (Vienna) for data, suggestions and improvements.

As a German author who insisted to write his final contribution to the subject in a language, which is not his own, I am most grateful to Dr Claire M Smith, formerly of Notre Dame University, now of Wildeshausen (Germany), who read the whole manuscript, greatly improved my style and revised some of the contents with her superb knowledge of the subject. All remaining German idiosyncracies must have been added

---

1 The most important of these projects resulted in: Nassmacher et al. 1992.
2 Kreutz-Gers 1988; Wawzik 1991; Klee-Kruse 1993; Cordes 2001.
3 Austin/ Tjernström 2003.
4 Brunken-Bahr 1990; Ringena 2000; Boyken 1998.
5 Deutscher Bundestag, *Drucksache* (Parliamentary Paper), no. 13/ 3574.

after she had given the book her final touch. For all mistakes, which the meticulous reader will find, I bear sole responsibility.

Data processing for chapter IV was a major responsibility of Manuela Kulick, M. SocSc., who did a perfect job in providing the statistical knowledge that I missed so much. The many years of consecutive library research were excellently covered by Mareike Finck, M.A., Alina Puczylowski, M.SocSc., and Annegret Kunde, M.A., who all graduated in Oldenburg during the time of researching, writing and re-drafting. Renate Kettmann, Sibylle Künnert and Elisabeth Wiese provided secretarial assistance, not least the printing of an endless sequence of new drafts. I have thanked all of them for their individual contribution during the various stages, but happily repeat this after completion of the manuscript.

During the whole process of production my companion of a lifetime, Dr Hiltrud Nassmacher (Carl-von-Ossietzky University, Oldenburg, Germany), has been (as she always is) much more than a permanent source of encouragement and support.

This book is **dedicated to the memory of Khayyam Z. Paltiel**, Carleton University in Ottawa, Canada, the **leading scholar of comparative political finance,** who has set so many precedents and who has introduced me to the community of international scholarship.

Oldenburg, in the autumn of 2008   Karl-Heinz Nassmacher

Table of contents

List of tables and graphs	15
List of abbreviations	17

CHAPTER ONE – Money in Democratic Politics (Introduction)   19

A)	Scholarly analysis of political finance	20
	1. Areas of interest: issues in political finance	20
	2. Desiderata of political finance research	26
B)	Approaches to political finance	30
	1. Definition of the subject: political finance	30
	2. Demarcation of the subject of this study: party funding	34
C)	Research questions and overview	37
	1. Party spending	38
	2. Sources of revenue	40
	3. Impacts of funding	43

CHAPTER TWO – Factual Pattern of (Party) Expenditure   47

A)	Cost centres (units of party organisation)	48
	1. National, regional and local tiers (levels of party organisation)	50
	2. Groups of party activists	54
	3. Party penumbra (ancillary bodies and affiliated organisations)	56
	a) Intra-party organisations	56
	b) Party institutes	57
	4. Parliamentary party groups (caucuses)	58
B)	Types of cost (elements of expenditure)	60
	1. Paid labour	61
	a) Wages and salaries	61
	b) Professional fees	64
	2. Offices (rent of premises etc.)	64
	3. Communication	66
	4. Publicity	68
	5. Other goods and services	71
	a) Polling/ research, interest and fundraising	71

		b) Peculiar types of cost	72

    b) Peculiar types of cost — 72
    c) Residual costs — 72
- C) Cost objects (purposes of spending) — 73
    1. Election campaigns (campaign spending) — 74
    2. Organisation maintenance — 79
    3. Policy development (research and training) — 84

CHAPTER THREE – Costs of 18 Party Democracies — 87

- A) Establishment of data for spending totals — 89
    1. Costs of the biggest democracies: USA, Japan, Germany, Mexico — 90
    2. Costs of major democracies: Italy, Britain, France, Spain, Poland — 96
    3. Costs of medium sized democracies: Canada, Australia, the Netherlands, Sweden — 101
    4. Costs of small democracies: Austria, Switzerland, Israel, Denmark, Ireland — 105
- B) Adjustment for election cycle, country size and economic performance — 109
- C) Comparison of spending levels — 115

CHAPTER FOUR – Causes of Spending Levels — 121

- A) Features of the democratic polity — 121
    1. Stages of political and economic development — 121
        a) Economic development — 122
        b) Democratic tradition — 123
    2. Size of the electorate (economies of scale) — 124
    3. Routines of conflict resolution — 128
        a) Plural societies and federal systems — 128
        b) Competitive vs. consociational decision-making — 129
        c) Anglo-Saxon vs. other traditions of polities — 131
- B) Framework of party politics — 132
    1. Capital-intensive campaigning vs. labour-intensive party apparatus — 133
    2. Modes of party competition — 135
        a) Ideological warfare — 136
        b) One-party dominance — 137
        c) Intra-party competition (individual candidates, factions and primaries) — 138

C)	Consequences of public policy	141
	1. Unlimited sources of funding	142
	a) Unrestrained political graft (corruption)	142
	b) Generous public subsidies	144
	2. State intervention in the economy	146
	a) Share of government expenditure	147
	b) State regulation of the economy	148
D)	Interaction of causal factors	149

CHAPTER FIVE – Cost Explosion: Fact or Fantasy?   155

A)	Background variables for the spending spree	155
	1. External influences (electorate and inflation)	156
	a) Growth of electorate	157
	b) Impact of inflation	158
	2. More comprehensive data	162
	3. Intensified competition	164
	a) Parliamentary election cycle	164
	b) Other competitive factors	165
B)	Causes of increased party spending	167
	1. Paid TV advertising	167
	2. New technology	172
	3. Professional politics	177
C)	Cost push or demand pull?	183

CHAPTER SIX – Grass-Roots Revenue   193

A)	Cornerstone of democracy or demand from never-land?	194
B)	Roads to voluntary contributions (Soliciting money in small amounts)	199
	1. Membership dues	199
	a) Number of party members (including member-to-voter ratio and trends)	200
	b) Average contribution per party member	206
	c) Revenue from membership dues (by party families and by countries)	208
	2. Small donations	215
	3. Fundraising events (social activities)	222

C)	Public incentives (for small political contributions)	224
	1. Energising fundraisers (matching funds)	224
	2. Stimulating contributors (tax add-on, tax deduction, and tax credit)	225
D)	Intra-party transfers	230
	1. Association quotas	231
	2. Equalisation transfers	233
	3. Revenue sharing	234

CHAPTER SEVEN – Plutocratic Funding (Interested Money and Graft) — 239

A)	Moral hazard of democracy?	240
B)	Contributions from interested money	244
	1. Institutional fundraising	245
	a) Collective membership (affiliation fees)	246
	b) Conveyer organisations	249
	c) Political action committees (PACs)	251
	2. Donations by wealthy individuals (contributions from personal wealth)	254
	a) Fat cat contributions (without or with strings attached)	255
	b) Buying honours and offices	257
	c) Paying for campaigns from personal wealth	258
	3. Corporate contributions (money from the business community)	260
	4. Public disincentives to discourage interested contributions	269
	a) Bans	269
	b) Contribution limits	270
	c) Disclosure of donors' identity	271
	5. Income from foreign funds	272
C)	Returns on investment: dividends and interest (parties as entrepreneurs)	274
D)	Party income from political graft	276
	1. Abuse of public resources	277
	2. Graft from business sources	279
	3. Assessment of party/ political officeholders (graft from public office)	284

CHAPTER EIGHT – Public Subsidies — 289

A)	Stop-gap, life-saver or white knight?	290
	1. Developing a case for public funding	290
	2. Problems of public funding	292
	3. Means to increase the legitimacy of public subsidies	294

B)	Types of subsidies	296
	1. Subsidies-in-kind	297
	a) Access to media	297
	b) Other support options	299
	2. Reimbursement of costs incurred	300
	3. Earmarked funds	300
	4. General grants	302
C)	Recipients of cash subsidies	303
	1. Candidates (for parliament or the presidency)	303
	2. Party organisations	304
	3. Party caucuses (parliamentary groups)	306
	4. Organisations of the party penumbra	308
D)	Allocation of national party subsidies	310
	1. Access to public funding	311
	a) Minimum of votes polled	311
	b) Minimum of seats held	311
	c) Other options (fixed amount, successful fundraising)	312
	2. Distribution of subsidies	314
	a) Allocation of matching funds	314
	b) Distribution by party size (number of seats held or votes polled)	315
	c) Distribution of base amounts	316
E)	Significance of public funding	317
	1. Contribution to party revenue (Income situation of parties)	317
	2. Level of the taxpayers' contribution	322
F)	Politics of public subsidies	324
	1. Influence of party competition on funding rules	324
	2. Public funding as a result of government structure	326
	a) Level of public funding in consensus democracies	327
	b) Level of public subsidies in majoritarian democracies	331
	c) Countries, which do not fit (either the categories or the hypothesis)	331
	3. Public funding in (comparative) perspective: parties and other organisations	332

CHAPTER NINE – Impacts on Party Systems — 335

A)	Spend and win? – Money as a means of success	335
	1. (Campaign) Spending by individual candidates	336
	2. Skewed competition between individual parties	341

B)	Ossification of the party system?	346
	1. Access for new parties: Openness of the party system?	347
	2. Room for changing weight of individual parties: Freezing of the party system?	352
	3. Changing roles of political parties: Arrested distribution of power?	356
C)	Summary of findings for party competition	360

CHAPTER TEN – Impacts on Party Organisation 363

A)	Linkage between parties and their grass-roots	364
	1. Changes of grass-roots linkage via membership dues and small donations	366
	2. Approaching members and supporters by direct mailings	370
	3. Measurement of and incentives for grass-roots linkage	372
B)	Distribution of power within party organisations	374
	1. Parties and their candidates	375
	2. Different levels of the party organisation (headquarters, branches and chapters)	378
	3. Party organisation and party penumbra	387
C)	Summary of findings for party organisation	389

CHAPTER ELEVEN – Money as a Political Resource (Conclusion) 393

A)	Summary of major findings	393
	1. Spending/ expenses	393
	2. Revenue/ income	393
	3. Impacts of political funding	397
B)	Consequences for the debate on party type(s)	398
	1. Catch-all parties	398
	2. Cartel parties	402

Bibliography	407
Index	451

List of tables and graphs

Graph 2-1:	Dimensions of cost accounting applied to party spending	48
Table 2-1:	Federal, state and local party expenses in Germany, 1994-2004	53
Table 2-2:	Salaries, wages and benefits (in percent of total expenses)	62
Table 2-3:	Staff costs by party family and country (in percent of total expenses)	63
Table 2-4:	Costs of premises for parties in Europe (Britain and France) (rent and maintenance in percent of headquarters' total expenses)	65
Table 2-5:	Operating expenses for major Canadian parties (in percent)	67
Table 2-6:	Costs of communication and publicity for parties in France (in percent of headquarters' total expenses)	69
Table 2-7:	Election expenses in Canada (by type of cost), 1997-2006 (reported as a percentage of total election expenses)	70
Table 2-8:	Campaign expenses of national campaigns, election years 1971-2000 (in million CAD, DEM, GBP, USD)	77
Table 2-9:	Operating expenses of Canadian parties, non-election years 1985-2005 (in million CAD)	79
Table 2-10:	Annual routine spending by British national party headquarters for non-election years only (in million £; 1952-91 annual averages)	81
Table 3-1:	Costs of party competition in comparative perspective, late 1950s and early 1980s	88
Table 3-2:	Campaign and party expenditure totals (per year and eligible voter)	110
Table 3-3:	Currency equivalents of per capita spending	113
Table 3-4:	Averages of party and campaign expenses per eligible voter and year (Index of Political Spending)	115
Graph 3-1:	Different measures/ indicators for per capita political spending	116
Table 3-5:	Costs of party competition in comparative perspective, late 1950s and late 1990s	118
Table 4-1:	Party spending, development and size of democracies	125
Graph 4-1:	Scattergram of IPS values by size of democracy (in three clusters)	126
Table 4-2:	Party spending and Lijphart's indicators of decision-making routines	130
Table 4-3:	Levels of party spending, corruption and public subsidies	143
Table 4-4:	Political spending and government intervention in the economy	147

Table 4-5:	Regression analysis for level of politicial spending (IPS)	150
Table 4-6:	Factor analysis of variables explaining spending levels	152
Table 5-1:	Political spending in the United States, 1952-2004	158
Table 5-2:	Political spending per citizen, CPI adjusted, 1971-2000	160
Table 5-3:	Campaign spending per elector, CPI adjusted (U.S., U.K. and Canada)	173
Table 5-4:	Details of party spending in Germany, 1984-2001	182
Table 5-1:	U.S. Presidential campaign spending, 1912-2000	185
Table 5-5:	Political spending per citizen, GDP adjusted, 1971-2000	188
Table 6-1:	Levels of party enrolment, 1950-2000	202
Table 6-2:	Average membership dues by party family and country	207
Table 6-3:	Annual average of membership dues for German parties	208
Table 6-4:	Average party income from membership dues (in percent of total)	210
Table 6-5:	Membership funding of party headquarters, averages	213
Table 6-6:	Association quotas as a source of national party revenue; the case of the U.K. Conservatives (1950-1997)	232
Table 7-1:	Corporate donations to selected party headquarters, 1968-2002	263
Table 8-1:	Public funding of party headquarters, by country and party family	319
Table 8-2:	Public funding of party headquarters, by country and time period	321
Table 8-3:	Party subsidies and type of democracy	328
Table 9-1:	Party revenue in Britain and Germany, 1970-2005	344
Graph 9-1:	Model of analysis (most relevant variables)	347
Graph 9-2:	Access to party systems (new parties since 1980)	350
Graph 9-3:	Composition of party systems (change of fragmentation)	355
Table 9-2:	Fragmentation of party systems (and the influence of public funding)	356
Table 9-3:	Changes of government composition (transition of power)	358
Graph 10-1:	Selected impacts of funding strategies on party activity	364

List of abbreviations

AEC	Australian Electoral Commission
ATS	Austrian shilling
AUD	Australian dollar
BEF	Belgian franc
BJP	Bharatiya Janata Party (India)
B.Q.	Bloc Quebecois (Canada)
CAD	Canadian dollar
CD	Centrum Demokraterne (Denmark)
CDA	Christen-democratische Appel (Netherlands)
CDS	Centre des Démocrates Sociaux (France)
CDU	Christlich-Demokratische Union (Germany)
CHF	Swiss franc (Switzerland)
CPC	Conservative Party of Canada
CPI	Consumer Price Index
CSU	Christlich-Soziale Union (Germany)
CVP	Christlich-demokratische Volkspartei (Switzerland)
DC	Democrazia cristiana (Italy)
DEM	German mark
DFP	Dansk Folkeparti (Denmark)
DKK	Danish kroner
DKP	Deutsche Kommunistische Partei (Germany)
ESP	Spanish peseta
EUR	Euro, single currency of many European (EU) countries (€)
FDP	Freie Demokratische Partei (Germany)
FDP	Freisinnig-demokratische Partei (Switzerland)
FEC	Federal Election Commission (USA)
FECA	Federal Election Campaign Act (USA)
FN	Front National (France)
FPÖ	Freiheitliche Partei Österreichs (Austria)
FPTP	First-past-the-post (= plurality electoral system)
FRF	French franc
GBP	British pound (sterling, £)
HDI	Human Development Index
IDEA	Institute for Democracy and Electoral Assistance, Stockholm (Sweden)
IEP	Irish punt
ILS	(new) Israeli shekel
IPS	Index of Political Spending (see chapter III)
JPY	Japanese yen
KF	Konservative Folkeparti (Denmark)
LDP	Liberal Democratic Party (*Jimintô*, Japan)

MMP	Mixed member proportional (= electoral system in Germany)
MP	Member of Parliament
MXP	Mexican peso
N.D.P.	New Democratic Party (Canada)
NLG	Netherlands (Dutch) guilder (Dfl., nfl.)
NOK	Norwegian kroner
NZD	New Zealand dollar
ÖVP	Österreichische Volkspartei (Austria)
PAC	Political Action Committee (USA)
P.C.	Progressive Conservatives (Canada), now: CPC
PCE	Partido Communista de Espana (Spain)
PCF	Parti Communiste Français (France)
PCI	Partido Comunista Italiano (Italy)
PDS	Partei des Demokratischen Sozialismus (Germany), now: Die Linke
PNV	Partido Nacionalista Vasco (Spain)
PP	Partido Popular (Spain)
PPP	purchasing power parity
P.Q.	Parti Quebecois (Canada)
P.R.	Proportional representation (electoral system)
PR	Public Relations
PR	Parti Républicain (France)
PRI	Partido Revolucionario Institucional (Mexico)
PS	Parti Socialiste (France)
PSI	Partido Socialista Italiano (Italy)
PSOE	Partido Socialista Obrero Espanol (Spain)
PvdA	Partij van de Arbeid (Netherlands)
RPI	Retail Price Index (see also CPI)
RPR	Rassemblement pour la République (France)
RV	Radikale Venstre (liberal party in Denmark)
SAP	Socialdemokratiska Arbetareparti (Sweden)
SD	Socialdemokratiet i Danmark
SF	Socialistik Folkeparti (Denmark)
SPD	Sozialdemokratische Partei Deutschlands (Germany)
SPÖ	Sozialdemokratische Partei Österreichs (Austria)
SPS	Sozialdemokratische Partei der Schweiz (Switzerland)
SVP	Schweizerische Volkspartei (Switzerland)
UDF	Union pour la Démocratie Francaise (France)
U.K.	United Kingdom (of Great Britain and Northern Ireland)
U.S.	United States (of America)
USD	U.S. dollar (US-$)
V	Venstre (liberal party in Denmark)
VAP	voting age population
VVD	Volkspartij voor Vrijheid en Democratie (Netherlands)

CHAPTER ONE

Money in Democratic Politics (Introduction)

Starting with the days of Aristotle, property or economic power have been regarded as a fundamental element in politics. The results of empirical research, however, are still limited; important aspects of political money are hidden and thus cannot be accessed easily. In the 1920s Max Weber emphasised that party funding belongs to the least transparent chapters of party activity, although it may be one of the most significant.[1] Since the 1920s the role of money in politics has been researched for quite a while. Pollock (1926), Overacker (1932), Heard (1960) and Heidenheimer (1963) were the pioneers. Khayyam Z. Paltiel, to whom this book is dedicated, contributed major enlargements of scope and perception to this field of study.[2] Because money affects political competition, scholars try to establish the consequences of this interaction, which can be foreseen for sustainable democracy.

Many will agree that money is an important resource in politics. "Money ... can be converted – through its power to buy goods and services – into other kinds of political activity."[3] It can acquire skills to compensate for shortcomings of specific parties or candidates. It can be employed to pay agents, who act on behalf of other people. A lobbyist, a politician, an advertiser or a journalist will help to voice interests in a society. People who lack the time or the skills to participate personally can use such agents as an efficient means to influence politics.

Dahl argued that an individual's political resources include (among others) time, money, information and the right to vote.[4] Heard stated, that donating "is a meaningful act of political participation," although such contributions are "but one *form of participation in politics*."[5] In a similar way donating money is only one type of political activity that may affect the outcome of elections. Spending large amounts of money in a political campaign matters, although it can even be counterproductive. The use of too much money may destroy the impression of trustworthiness and competence, which are major prerequisites for a successful election campaign. Moreover money may in-

---

[1] Weber 1925, p. 169.
[2] Paltiel 1966; Paltiel 1967; Paltiel 1970a; Paltiel 1970b; Paltiel 1976; Paltiel 1979; Paltiel 1980; Paltiel 1981.
[3] Alexander 1992b, p. 369.
[4] Dahl 1972, p. 226.
[5] Heard 1960, pp. 3 and 38 respectively (*emphasis* added). Some theorists of democracy view cheque-book participation as minimalistic, because it lacks important functions, e.g. educating in trust, reciprocacy, accomodation or tolerance. Nevertheles they accept that such participation may reduce entry barriers (Maloney 1999, pp. 112, 113, 115). Moreover this activity supplies an increasing number of participants.

fluence access to political actors and, directly or indirectly, political decisions. Although it is only one means among others, money remains a very flexible resource of access, influence and power.

However, there is a line between participation and abuse, which is not easily determined. Time and again the independent media in developed democracies reveal corrupt transactions. Scandals indicate that the line between acceptable and intolerable use of money has been crossed. In the past, politicians bought the votes of individual citizens by using all sorts of small gifts. Today party patronage and benefits granted by public policy are offered now and then. Party members sometimes buy membership cards to improve their own opportunities. Occasionally corporations bribe influential politicians or administrators. Where clientelism is commonplace,[6] it brings about a close connection between business and politics. Sometimes corruption is rife, as innumerable scandals, which arouse public opinion, indicate. However, as comparative analysis points out, there are great differences among the democracies.

A) Scholarly analysis of political finance

Although studies on money in politics contribute to our general knowledge, there is still a lack of information about the flow of money and its impacts on politics, as well as a shortage of theory. One common theory that most researchers refer to is a theory of resources. Within this paradigm, some political actors require resources, whereas others can dispose of them. Findings of incentive theory and exchange theory are useful in explaining the interrelations between those who provide money for political purposes and those who take it.[7] As a follow-up to the economic theory of democracy elaborated by Schumpeter and Downs, who see parties as entrepreneurs acting to maximise their votes, Ferguson has developed an investment theory of political competition. He identified the logic of money-driven politics and argued that the "real market for political parties is defined by major investors, who generally have good and clear reasons for investing to control the state."[8] Each theoretical paradigm highlights specific aspects of the complex flow of money as a participatory and power-generating resource. Prudent scholars assume that parties are vying for both, votes and funds. In democracies the affluent can employ money, whereas the masses have to rely on votes.

1. Areas of interest: issues in political finance

There are some general issues that are raised time and again. First, the rising *costs of political competition* were approached early but, due to data problems, neither frequently nor extensively. The first scholars in this field were Overacker and Pollock,

---

6 Piattoni 2001, pp. 195-198.
7 See Adamany 1972, p. v.
8 Ferguson 1995, p. 22; cf. Schumpeter 1950, pp. 269-283; Downs 1957, pp. 23-31.

although they did not have much impact on public debate or scholarly discourse.[9] Heard found, that "the costs of campaigning in the United States, ... are not extraordinarily high." Penniman recapitulated, that "American elections are usually less expensive than those of other countries."[10] Both compared the costs per eligible voter for various countries.[11] Heidenheimer was the first to explain why the level of expenditure in some countries was much higher than in others.[12] Klee-Kruse, who compared the costs of party democracy in Austria and Sweden, demonstrated that such comparisons have to include the different levels of the political system.[13] Until now research including the funding of political parties at the sub-national level is rare.[14]

The second field of interest is whether *money influences decision-making*. Although politics is washing cash into parties', candidates' or administrators' coffers, most policy studies simply neglect the financial aspect of influence. Years ago the pluralism debate focused on funds that special interest groups deploy in order to influence politics.[15] Studies of political power did not produce results that were widely accepted. The discourse ran aground, struggling with appropriate methods for the study of influence and power. This should remind scholars who study the problems of political finance that they have to employ qualitative and quantitative methods in a well-designed mix.

The media usually finds a great audience when publishing about the influence of money in politics. Time and again even scholars emphasise that money buys politicians.[16] A lot of researchers are interested in this improper use of money in politics. Fighting illegal funding practices and political corruption is one of the biggest challenges for established as well as emerging democracies.[17] Corruption is the clandestine exchange between two markets, the political or administrative market and the economic or social market.[18] Generally in established democracies pressure groups are widely involved as experts in legislation and implementation of policies, and therefore do not need to influence decision-making by providing cash. This is especially true in consociational democracies. However, even in such countries corruption scandals occur. Transparency International performs world-wide surveys and conducts training seminars to prevent corruption. However, a research report found knowledge about corrupt exchanges unsatisfactory. Only a few books or articles are available.[19]

---

9   Pollock 1926, pp. 170/171; Overacker 1932, p. 80. See below in chapter V, A 1 (electorates and inflation).
10 Heard 1960, p. 6; Penniman 1984, p. 51.
11 See below in chapter III, Table 3-1 (comparison of spending levels).
12 Heidenheimer 1963, pp. 797-800 (and Heidenheimer 1970b, pp. 9-12).
13 Klee-Kruse 1992, p. 462; Klee-Kruse 1993a, pp. 189, 197.
14 Pinto-Duschinsky 1981 and Sickinger 1997 are the major exceptions.
15 Dahl 1972, pp. 4/5, 241, 243/244; Polsby 1980 sums up the results of community power research.
16 For example Drew 1983.
17 Pinto-Duschinsky (2001b, pp. 5-7) offers recent examples.
18 Della Porta/ Meny 1997b, p. 4.
19 von Alemann 2005b, p. 14; Heywood 1997b; Burnell/ Ware 1998; Treisman 1998; Zovatto 2001.

Despite recurring scandals reported by the media it can be assumed that corruption is not a great problem in established democracies with a widely accepted rule of law. The strongest penalty in such countries is that, as a result of pressure by public opinion, some politicians have to resign public office, as events in Belgium, France and Germany indicate. Here, like in other established democracies, the major sanction is the danger to lose voting support after a series of scandals (as has happened to parties in Spain, in Britain and in Belgium) or to suffer an erosion of the dominant party (as has befallen Italy). Japan as a non-western democracy can be seen as an exception. Here the self-cleaning process may last too long, although there has been some change since the mid-1990s.[20] Because we deal mostly with established democracies, corruption will not be a focus of this book,[21] although it will be considered as an important source of political funding. In Western democracies highlighting scandals by the media often over-emphasises the importance of improper sources as compared to the overall amounts deployed in the political process.

Third, the *rules for the funding of parties, campaigns and candidates* are of major interest. Such rules, the political finance regime, are determined by policy decisions or non-decisions of politicians. Together with other institutionalised rules this output can be subjected to two major research strategies. The political finance regime can be examined as a dependent or as an independent variable of analysis. One perspective asks for the process that develops the rules of political finance; especially how specific programmes are hammered out. Do political finance regimes in specific political cultures, e.g. in the Anglo-Saxon orbit or in continental Europe, comprise particular policy programmes? Do typical strategies aim at specific challenges in the process of democratisation? A lot of case studies have pursued this avenue, trying to elaborate changes in legislation.[22]

Other analyses, which regard the political finance regime as independent variable, have discovered major impacts of legislation on parties. Ill-constructed or badly implemented rules of democratic competition create loopholes, where big money is able to override the principle 'one person, one vote' and thus to obstruct fairness. An important result is that bans do not work if private donors and political actors disregard them. Other studies describe changes in competition facilitated by new rules.[23] Some incentives for fundraisers and the specific modes to distribute public subsidies seem to have an impact on party systems or party structure.

---

20 Blechinger 1999, p. 60.
21 For a different approach see a total of 22 country by country analyses from 7 democracies and 10 political systems in transition in: Little/ Posada-Carbó 1996, Della Porta/ Mený 1997a and Williams 2000. In a similar vein: Heidenheimer/ Johnston 2002 and von Alemann 2005a, pp. 311-394.
22 Scarrow 2007, p. 194.
23 see Heidenheimer 1963, 1970a; Alexander 1989c and Alexander/ Shiratori 1994; Tsatsos 1992; Ewing 1999; Somes 1998 and books on specific countries, e.g. Doublet 1997, or areas, e.g. Wiberg 1991a.

Hiltrud Nassmacher and Claire Smith observe a direct connection between the design of political finance regulation and organisational change within parties. Other findings confirm that changes in funding rules shape party development. After all, the first priority of party building is improved access to sufficient funding.[24] A lot of scholars have neglected this aspect and focussed merely on changes in the environment, especially the growing importance of the media in political competition. It is assumed that the media will be "the new all-important set of vehicles for political campaigning."[25] Others provide catchy labels for the final outcome of this process. Panebianco, who saw electoral-professional parties emerge,[26] received much attention among scholars. All parties in all democracies have to face similar challenges by the media.[27] Certainly parties will need skills (and funds) if they want to communicate their message to the voters effectively. Therefore professionalisation is unavoidable. On the other hand, different political finance regimes may force parties to pursue particular strategies.

Many studies deal with the *public funding of political parties*. This leads to a more general remark. In 1986 Epstein observed a specific feature of American parties, and suggested that parties had become "public utilities." As long as "parties were regarded as private associations largely immune from mandatory legal regulation" they were "open to every abuse that unscrupulous men, ... incredible wealth and dictatorial power could devise."[28] The 19th and 20th century mass politics fired by unequal wealth and opportunities brought to the fore the many evils of participatory democracy without strictly enforced rules for political competition. The impact of a simple principle ('one person, one vote') proved to be too weak to check all abuses that human brains could possibly conceive. Much like the business world the political sphere of civil society required public regulation of competitive practices.

Attempts by individual countries initially seemed to be solitary efforts: British legislation against "Corrupt and Illegal Practices" (1883), dissemination of pre-printed publicly produced ballot paper with party labels (1888-92) and state-run party (nomination) primaries in the U.S. (late 19th century), constitutional recognition of and legal restrictions for political parties in Germany (1949, 1967), the party funding laws in Sweden (1969, 1972) and Austria (1975), the U.S. "Federal Election Campaign Act" (1971, 1974), official registration of political parties and official receipts for party donations in Canada (1974) and finally the British "Political Parties, Elections and Referendums Act" (2000). With hindsight all these individual measures were elements of a general process, the transformation of political parties from private associations to "public utilities."[29] No country has yet produced a comprehensive set of rules, which regulates all dimensions of intra-party operation (participatory rights and duties of individuals, organisational structure, decision-making procedure, funding) – but most democracies

---

24 Nassmacher, H. 2004b, pp. 95-106; Smith 2005, pp. 263, 265; Appleton/ Ward 1996, p. 137.
25 Lane/ Ersson 1996, p. 201.
26 Panebianco 1988.
27 Differences and similarities are discussed by: Kaid/ Holtz-Bacha 1995 and 2006.
28 Epstein 1986, p. 161; quotations in reverse order.
29 Epstein 1986, pp. 7, 155-157.

have stipulated statutory prescriptions for competitive behaviour. Among these the political finance regime, which combines public support and public control of party funding,[30] on average is the most developed part. However, in no major democracy it is the *only* statutory rule regarding inner-party affairs. In sum, the conversion into "public utilities" has made parties "to be perceived as key institutions performing a special service to democracy." More and more they are "seen as necessary and desirable institutions for democracy."[31]

However, in affluent societies the gap between the money needed to perform the competitive functions of political parties and political revenue from individual donations in small amounts is quite large. Politicians, who want to avoid public subsidies, have to make sure that "big money in small sums"[32] can spring up somewhere. The promoters of Britain's first major reform effort after more than a century, the "Political Parties, Elections and Referendums Act 2000," were among the most recent legislators who had to repent their generous neglect of this imperative when the next party funding scandals, the "cash-for-honours" crisis and the Abraham's affair, broke in 2006 and 2007.[33]

The continuous debate about public subsidies primarily relates to their amount. Which necessary functions do parties perform? Parties and candidates print campaign literature, organise meetings, produce election broadcasts and take up many other activities.[34] Because expenses for the selection of public officials "are simply necessary," scholars who argue in favour of appropriate funds, have stressed that governments "can encourage equal access to the electorate by subsidising and regulating…. The expenses for monitoring and electing public officials are among the inevitable financial costs of democracy."[35]

The impacts of public funding have been studied for a few countries only.[36] Because this new source of party revenue is widespread around the world differences among countries are so great, that for a start a smaller sample with specific hypotheses is more appropriate. Cordes researched the impact of public subsidies on political parties in three countries. She found that campaign spending has not been the major cause of increased financial needs but rather it is the costs of the party apparatus, especially driven by the salaries for full-time party staff.[37]

---

30 van Biezen 2004, pp. 706-707, 712-717.
31 van Biezen 2004, pp. 701, 713 (quotations in reverse order). This recent verdict is quite close to Hermens 1958, p. 162: "Political parties are the instruments of democratic government."
32 Heard 1960, p. 249.
33 "A sad, bad business." In: The Economist, 18 November 2006; "When the money machine blows up." In: *The Economist*, 29 November 2007.
34 Pinto-Duschinsky 2001a, p. 1.
35 Heard 1960; pp. 8, 10/11 (quotes in reverse order).
36 With the exception of Pierre/ Svasand/ Widfeldt 2000 and Casas-Zamora 2002; Casas-Zamora 2005a.
37 Cordes 2001.

Some expect unintended consequences after the implementation of new laws including public funding; especially that local parties may abandon their efforts to collect funds,[38] which would create a linkage problem. That is, parties will drift away from their grass-roots in general and their rank and file in particular. A comparison of the U.S., Canada and Germany identified efforts to prevent such effects and evaluated new strategies of participation.[39]

Other research deals with the impact of public funding on party systems. The petrification of the system is a major problem that scholars foresee. This would come along with the emergence of a new type, the cartel party.[40] Parties, which are characterised in this way, are accused of some sort of self-service as they try to provide enough public funds for themselves and to exclude competitors from access to parliament and subsidies. Preliminary analyses in 15 countries could verify neither the cartel party nor the petrified party system hypothesis.[41]

Currently the mainstream in the sub-field of political finance is searching for an adequate design of political finance regulation. The starting point for such efforts is descriptions and comparisons, which end up by identifying types of regulations. Since the issue became important in established democracies more than 30 years ago, some countries have developed highly sophisticated legislation. Canada, the U.S., the U.K. and Germany are among them. Their political finance regimes are composed of several regulative, distributive and incentive elements, including controls and enforcement strategies.[42]

Major differences between Western Europe and North America result in specific approaches toward public funding of party activity and public control of political money. Regulation of political finance in Britain is closer to that in North America, which emphasises limiting both expenses and contributions.[43] Campaign finance laws restrict the amount a candidate may spend on his or her campaign and the amount an individual or a corporate donor is allowed to contribute towards the competitor of her or his choice. American reform legislation follows the expectation that disclosing a donor's identity and the amount of the donation can help to control the flow of private funds into campaign coffers. Matching funds, campaign reimbursements and tax ben-

---

38   Pinto-Duschinsky 1981, p. 292; Neill report 1998, p. 92. It may be just a bit ironic that exactly this has happened to the U.K. Conservatives who have resisted all kinds of public subsidies for about three decades. For details see below in chapter VI, sub-sections B 3 (fundraising events) and D 1 (association quotas).
39   Nassmacher 1992a.
40   Katz/ Mair 1995.
41   Nassmacher/ Nassmacher 2001; Nassmacher, H. 2004a.
42   Nassmacher (2003a, pp. 10-13) presents four different types of regulation: an autonomy option (Sweden), a transparency option (Germany), an advocate for the public interest option (U.S.) and a diversified regulation (Canada). For a different systematic approach see Brändle 2002, pp. 41-48.
43   Pinto-Duschinsky (2001a, p. 19) identified "a Westminster model of political financing, which corresponds to the Westminster model of politics."

efits provide incentives for candidates (and parties) to co-operate with such programmes of public policy. In many European democracies flat grant public subsidies cover most of the financial needs for operating costs of permanent party headquarters. The reporting of major items of party income and expenses (occasionally debts and assets, too) was implemented in order to promote public confidence in political finance. Spending limits are rare, and effective contribution limits are unknown in continental Europe. Massive tax incentive plans for political donations exist in only a few countries. Until the late 1980s any kind of enforcement agency seemed to be anathema to European legislators. Now Britain, France and Germany have legislated their favourite solutions.[44]

Because political finance is a restless issue in politics with frequent amendments to relevant regulation, time and again new research efforts have to observe major changes and reveal weaknesses. Synopses of political finance laws (eventually in a worldwide approach) [45] contribute overviews towards detailed, but preliminary knowledge of public policy and political finance regimes only. There is no doubt that legislation provides the rules of the game. It imposes constraints on and offers opportunities for political actors. However, researchers have to be aware that formal arrangements (and their details) influence the behaviour of civil society (individuals, groups, corporations), regulatory agencies and party organisations. Enforcement agencies and public opinion may change the handling of a programme and the interrelation among its elements. In the long run this can bring about improved or deteriorated rules of the game; in short a new political finance regime, combined with new behaviour among politicians, organisations, agencies and citizens. This new behaviour in turn creates new opportunity structures within each polity. Because no one ever knows if a major change has taken place, constraints and ways to circumvent the rules have to be observed and analysed carefully. The behavioural aspect of regulation and its impact on party activity, party competition and party structure is the core subject of political analysis.

2. Desiderata of political finance research

Until now most research on the subject is descriptive, and has a certain *emphasis on legislation*. Scholars attempt to explain the efforts of political decision-makers to reform political finance regimes or to evaluate their major outcomes as compared to previous rules. This research reveals that as a result of long-standing traditions and power struggles countries have chosen different paths. Cross-national observations may have initiated institutional learning, depending on the political culture. Only occasionally are some impacts analysed more closely, for example the use of loopholes or changes within political parties. Frequently results were reached by chance; some-

---

44 An early attempt to evaluate the British PPERA is made by Ewing 2007.
45 E.g. Pinto-Duschinsky 2001a, pp. 1/10, 12; Pinto-Duschinsky 2001b, pp. 15-23; Pinto-Duschinsky 2002, pp. 75-77; Tjernström 2003, pp. 185-223.

times starting a new cycle of policy-making, ending up in revisions of former regulation or specific rules. In sum, more scholarly effort has been devoted to the input and output of political decisions than to their impacts. However, as the style of research that deals with the topic is changing, it is very difficult to compare case studies completed at different times, even if they concern the same country.

Moreover there is a *shortage in comparative approaches*. Only a few countries dominate academic discourse. This is equally true for longitudinal analyses of one country, as well as for cross-national comparisons of different countries. The first approach was preferred by Heard who covered the U.S. during the 1950s,[46] Pinto-Duschinsky with his outstanding work on Britain from 1830 until 1980,[47] Paltiel who was able to draw on the seminal work of a Royal Commission in Canada,[48] and Alexander who has analysed political finance in the U.S. for a total of nine presidential cycles (1960-92).[49] In addition to these senior scholars Schleth for Germany, Gidlund for Sweden, Sickinger for Austria and Walecki for Poland wrote one-country monographs.[50] Published (asynchronous) between 1960 and 2005 these books cover seven of the 25 countries, which are discussed in this study. Unfortunately three of the fundamental analyses are available in the author's language (which is not English) only.

To this day the typical procedure for "comparative" studies is an edited volume, which includes various countries.[51] It must be added that each expert writes about his own country. This happened in 1963 when Colin Hughes wrote on Australia, Martin Harrison on Britain, Emanuel Gutmann on Israel, Stefano Passigli on Italy, James Soukup on Japan, Ulrich Dübber and Gerard Braunthal on Germany. In 1970 Uwe Schleth presented Germany, Michael Pinto-Duschinsky Britain, Herbert Alexander the U.S. and Khayyam Paltiel Canada. However, articles by Nils Andren (Scandinavia), Stephen Milne (Southeast Asia) and Christian Anglade (Latin America) dealt with groups of countries.[52] The volumes edited by Herbert Alexander in 1979 and 1989 are much in the same fashion. The 1979 volume contains two comparative articles by Khayyam Paltiel and Dick Leonard, but over 70 percent of the text is dedicated to political finance issues as they prevail in the (exceptional) U.S.[53] The 1989 volume is more balanced although less comparative. Just one article concerns more than one country; the other chapters cover most of the G7-countries.[54] Articles on France were missing until 1993 when a German author published the first essay on that country in

---

46 Heard 1960.
47 Pinto-Duschinsky 1981.
48 Paltiel 1970; Paltiel 1966 and Barbeau report 1966.
49 Alexander 1962, 1966, 1971, 1976, 1979b, 1983, 1987; Alexander/ Bauer 1991; Alexander/ Corrado 1995.
50 Schleth 1973, Gidlund 1983, Sickinger 1997, Walecki 2005a.
51 Two tables provide overviews of the countries covered: Nassmacher 2001a, p. 20; Scarrow 2007, p. 196.
52 Heidenheimer 1963, Heidenheimer 1970a.
53 Alexander 1979a; on the "unique" status of U.S. parties (Epstein 1986, p. 156) see Ware 2006, pp. 270-277.
54 Alexander 1989a.

a comparative volume.⁵⁵ Generally it is quite rare that someone from Europe, say a Spanish, a British or an Italian scholar, works on North American political finance issues (or vice versa).⁵⁶

Exceptions are the contributions by Heidenheimer in a special issue of the "Journal of Politics," which was devoted to political finance, and in his edited book on "Comparative Political Finance."⁵⁷ The joint article by Schleth and Pinto-Duschinsky is more or less composed of two separate case studies (Germany and Britain). Alexander and Paltiel in the Malbin volume focus on the legislation.⁵⁸ Paltiel, in another volume that sums up the "At the Polls" series, provides a comparison of instruments although he does not develop the ideas laid out by Heidenheimer.⁵⁹ The volumes edited by Alexander (1989) and Alexander and Shiratori (1994) include early attempts at comparisons.⁶⁰ In Gunlicks (1993) a set of detailed categories for a comparison of income and expenditure was presented, and finally in Nassmacher (2001) this outline became the basis for comparisons of a total of 15 countries, mostly in a two by two format.⁶¹ More recently junior scholars have published monographs, which compare two to four countries. The most outstanding of them are Brändle and Casas-Zamora,⁶² only the latter is internationally accessible.

Some comparable information can also be drawn from material, which was provided by royal commissions or official committees of inquiry (in Canada, Germany and the U.K.), especially the Barbeau Commission in 1966, the Houghton Committee in 1976, the Fürst Commission (of Experts; *Sachverständigen-Kommission*) in 1983, the Lortie Commission in 1991, and the Neill Committee (on Standards in Public Life) in 1998.⁶³

General research on political parties has widely ignored the provision of financial resources as a basis for activity.⁶⁴ Party systems and party organisation, party platforms and party members, party activists and party elites have been the most frequent subjects. When Duverger presented his fundamental analysis of political parties in the 1950s, he dealt with party funding mostly in passing except for some detailed discussion of membership dues.⁶⁵ In the 1960s Epstein was more elaborate in presenting a

---

55 Drysch 1993, pp. 155-177; soon to be followed by Avril 1994, pp.85-95.
56 del Castillo 1985; Ewing 1992; Melchionda 1997.
57 Heidenheimer 1963, pp. 790-811 and 1970b, pp. 3-18.
58 Malbin 1980a, pp. 333-370. Contributions to Malbin 1984 cover the U.S. only.
59 Paltiel 1981, pp. 138-172.
60 Nassmacher 1989b, pp. 236-267; Nassmacher 1994, pp. 145-157.
61 Nassmacher 1993, pp. 233-267; Nassmacher 2001a, pp. 34-180.
62 Brändle 2002; Casas-Zamora 2002, 2005a.. - Klee-Kruse 1993a, Römmele 1995a, Cordes 2001 and Smith 2005 also belong to this group.
63 Barbeau report 1966; Paltiel 1966; Houghton report 1976; Fürst report 1983; Lortie report 1991 plus 23 volumes, among them Stanbury 1991, Seidle 1991a-d; Bakvis 1991 and Carty 1991; Neill report 1998.
64 Cf. Köllner 2000b, p. 147, note 2.
65 Duverger 1967, pp. 59, 63-65, 72-78, 80-81, 113-114.

variety of funding sources, although he did not offer too much detail.[66] In 1980 Janda proceeded towards a theoretical approach when he discussed funding as an indicator of two categories: autonomy and centralisation of power.[67]

For a while comparative research of political parties seemed to have lost interest or access to the resources of political organisations. The big comparative effort directed by Katz and Mair collected data on party funding for 12 democracies.[68] Although all country-by-country analyses include information on party funding, substantial coverage in the analytical chapters depends on the personal interest, which the individual author had for the subject.[69] Whereas most contributions make good use of the data, others either present the political finance regime or do not even mention funding details. The comparative article on party funds, which was written for a "third" volume that has never been completed, deals entirely with public funding of political parties. It nevertheless deserves high praise for its systematic and empirical approach.[70] In a more recent volume edited by Webb, Farrell and Holliday most contributions cover funding as an indicator of organisational strength.[71] The fragmentary information available emphasises the need for more comparable data.

In a comparative volume on elections and voting the chapter by Katz deals with party organisation first and with funding afterwards without ever linking both conceptually. The funding of political parties is just an incidental subject of party theory. Beyme is among the rare authors who cover the subject. Thus it seems to be quite telling that the recent "Handbook of Party Politics" touches upon funding issues mostly in passing. Detailed coverage is restricted to three of its 45 articles: "Party finance in the United States", "Party law" and "Regulations of party finance."[72]

All of the studies mentioned contribute to comparisons. However, most studies are one-shot-approaches only, because they do not combine long-term and cross-national comparisons. To this day there is neither a systematic overview for more than a few countries nor a longitudinal analysis for more than one country. Only the cross-national compilation of data from many countries under comparable conditions is an adequate starting point for the test of hypotheses, which thus far has been widely missing.

---

66 Epstein 1980, pp. 242-250.
67 Janda 1980, pp. 91/92, 111/112.
68 Katz/ Mair 1992, p. 18 and tables E1-6 for each chapter.
69 Katz/ Mair 1994, pp. 32-35, 53-55, 103-104, 174, 191-197.
70 Pierre/ Svasand/ Widfeldt 2000, pp. 1-24.
71 Webb et al. 2002.
72 Katz 1996, pp. 107-133; von Beyme 2000, pp. 127-144; Katz/ Crotty 2006, pp. 134-145, 435-445, 446-455.

B) Approaches to political finance

This study intends to be empirical and comparative. Scholars who believe in comparative studies observe a lot of similarities among the democracies. They consider the test of hypotheses by means of comparison an important step towards (more general) theory. Researchers of party funding still face Duverger's dilemma. That is, to develop a theory without a broad database or to collect (and analyse) more and more data in order to gather empirical evidence.[73] Some time ago Heidenheimer presented the dilemma: "Advances towards the more genuinely comparative study of political finance processes require on the one hand greater amounts of data and information, and on the other hand unifying concepts, which will help relate structures peculiar to various systems in terms of realistically conceived common denominators."[74]

Before we turn to a more detailed discussion of the subject and its demarcation some general remarks are appropriate. Democracy is a political system that settles conflicts by peaceful means established in constitutional principles and procedures. Among others each democracy needs rules for political parties, which organise the management of conflicts between freedom and equality,[75] participation and control. Parties are instruments of voluntary participation. In all democracies they compete for temporary control of government. Money can be used as a means of control and of participation.

Collecting money in small amounts is a fundraising strategy that does not interfere with equality. However, the freedom to use unrestricted amounts of money as a resource in politics transfers the unequal distribution of income and wealth among members of a modern society into the political process and therefore endangers equality (one person, one vote), an essential of all democratic politics.[76] Participation by the wealthy acquires additional importance, and the average citizens lose exclusive control of their democracy. Because parties are more loosely (pragmatic, leadership or policy-oriented parties) or very strongly (participatory, ideological or clientelistic parties) linked with different segments of society they will not have the same resources at their disposal. This may bring about unfair competition, especially during election times. Political differences between parties include their unequal appeal to voters and donors. Nevertheless all four principles (equality and freedom, participation and control) are part and parcel of our modern concept of democracy. Looking at the funding of party politics will bring all of them into focus at various stages of the analysis.

1. Definition of the subject: political finance

The major goal of any comparison is to learn from long-term experience in one country or from current experiences in various countries. Hypotheses have to be tested with

---

73 Duverger 1967, pp. xiii/xiv; see also Heard 1960, pp. 4/5 and Janda 1980, p. xi.
74 Heidenheimer 1963, p. 790.
75 For some details see Nassmacher 1992a, pp. 10-14, 153-155.
76 Paltiel 1981, p. 138.

data that are available either from the past or from a multitude of cases. This leaves us with three major tasks: the compilation of comparable data, the collection of testable hypotheses and the selection of a promising subject. We will start by identifying a realistically conceived topic of study before we advance to presenting data and testing hypotheses.

Even among long-standing scholars of political science and its specific sub-field ("political finance") there is an on-going debate, about how to define the subject. Some scholars neglect this problem by considering a wide range of possible influences of money in politics. As has been explained in the previous section, many complex items are worth studying in detail. "Speculative" considerations will end up in a principled treatise, a contemplative presentation or normative prescriptions. None of these is the purpose of this study, which aims at the analysis of accessible, cross-national and empirical information. Such data has to be compiled into systematic evidence, covering as many countries as possible.

Any empirical and comparative analysis needs to limit its scope to no more than a specific part of the whole subject. Because more variables enlarge the focus, research will become much more complicated or even impossible. Each piece of empirical study will advance general theory no more than just one small step. Therefore the focus of this effort has to be elaborated in detail.

Scholars of political finance are aware that each political system causes specific costs. Monarchies in the era of absolutism spent heavily on the building of magnificent castles and expenses for the royal household.[77] Likewise, a democracy needs to spend on mass entertainment and political contests.[78] This study monitors political competition in established democracies. The major actors in this field are the political parties. Thus Alexander Heard was perfectly right in calling their expenses the "costs of democracy."[79] Nonetheless many "extra-party actors and individuals are involved in political competition with clear political objectives like shaping public policy agendas, influencing legislation or even electoral debates and outcomes."[80] However, Robert Dahl has stated that probably no political institution shapes the competitive landscape of a democratic country more than its electoral system and its political parties.[81] All the processes of democratic consolidation have been party-dominated. Parties aggregate different interests and goals. Parties present candidates for public offices. Parties provide labels, which will serve as an orientation for the voters.[82]

---

77 As an impression of this it should be noted that German princes in the early 18th century spent more than half of their regular revenue on castle building and court maintenance – cf. Dipper 1997, p. 205.
78 Even if quite a bit of pork barrel legislation and all other patronage, expenses for ceremonial offices, remuneration of politicians and all of their privileges are included, any total of the current "costs of democracy" is much lower than the overall costs of other political systems.
79 Heard 1960, p. 8.
80 Walecki 2005a, p. 13.
81 Dahl 1971, pp. 221-225.
82 The debate on party functions is summed up by Wiesendahl 1980, p. 188.

Therefore the term "political finance" in scholarly analysis is frequently used as a synonym for party finance. However, it carries different connotations, integrating two important aspects of competition in democracies. Both are analysed in this study, the organisational and the electoral aspect. The term equally encompasses routine operations of political organisations and specific campaigns at election times. A lot of things look different after crossing the Atlantic Ocean. The political cultures of North America (U.S., Canada) are campaign oriented.[83] The term political finance is frequently substituted by campaign funds, i.e. money spent in order to influence the outcome of an election. In (continental) Western Europe the term political finance is often used as a synonym for party financing, emphasising the funding of inter-election routine activities. In Europe campaigns are run predominantly by parties, in America by candidates (and their specific committees). These candidates rely heavily on paid media advertising in their effort to reach the voting public. European parties face a financial burden unknown to their American counterparts: a permanent field organisation with full-time party agents at the grassroots ("on the ground"). In addition, European parties have to cope with a party press, which has been increasingly unable to maintain itself by sales in the newspaper market.

Political parties organise competition among themselves and they are (more or less) involved in the competition of candidates for public office. For both purposes they need organisations and funds. Accepting this brings the funding of political competition and party activity into the centre of scholarly investigation. Expensive competition could be a major cause for funding hazards and may de-legitimise the political system. The political finance regime has to ensure that people have confidence in their political parties.[84] A lack of confidence causes alienation between society and its political elite, which is frequently seen as a ruling class. Political finance literature time and again argues for more transparency, control and participation. In sum, political money is a substantial resource, which helps make democracies work. The major values of democracy should be guidelines for every study of political finance. Most important among these are:

- give parties *equal opportunities* to operate,
- make sure that parties are *grassroots-oriented* and
- encouraging parties to raise *revenue from different sources*.

The former are consistent with the basic values of democratic governance, the latter make parties independent from undesirable influence. Therefore the flow of funds (income and expenses) and its impacts (cost explosion, distorted competition, ossification of party systems, party bureaucracy, grass-roots based party activity) have to be analysed in detail.

---

83 As this is also true for Australia, India, Ireland, New Zealand and the U.K., „Anglo-Saxon orbit" may be a better point of reference. Cf. Nassmacher 2003b, pp. 33-52.
84 Nassmacher 1997a, pp. 37/38.

One limitation of this study must be mentioned, and that is the countries covered. Established democracies that have been subject of case studies and comparative efforts frequently will be discussed more closely in this book.[85] These are Australia, Austria, Belgium, Canada, Denmark, Finland, France, Germany, Ireland, Israel, Italy, Japan, the Netherlands, New Zealand, Norway, Spain, Sweden, Switzerland, the United Kingdom and the United States.[86] Of these 20 countries 14 belong to Western Europe and only two to North America. In addition to North America and Western Europe no more than four economically advanced countries with established democracies deserve attention: Australia, New Zealand, Israel and Japan. Furthermore, two non-affluent societies with long-standing democratic traditions (India, Costa Rica) and three recently transitioned democracies (Poland, Mexico and Uruguay) have been selected for this study, which covers a total of 25 countries.[87]

Despite obvious differences in size, tradition and culture, party and electoral systems, Israel and Japan are the only non-western examples of economically advanced, established liberal (mature) democracies. A long history of political corruption and scandals related to the funding of political parties has repeatedly brought about major political reform efforts in Japan, most recently in 1994. Any approach to political money in Israel has to pay attention to factors absent in other established democracies. That is, due to immigration, the number of citizens has increased more than 9-fold since 1949.[88] Additionally, the country has suffered periods of hyper-inflation,[89] and the influx of money from the Jewish Diaspora (especially in the U.S.) also has political implications. Costa Rica and India are examples of "second wave" (but well-established)

---

85 Two long-standing ("first wave") democracies (Iceland and Luxembourg) were not included in the initial sample because fragmentary information was expected for such small states of 100 to 200,000 citizens. Basic information is provided by Thorarensen/ Hardarson 2005, pp.153-168 (*Iceland*) and Wivenes 1992, pp. 309-331 (*Luxembourg*).
Three more recent ("third wave") democracies from Asia and two from Latin America cannot be covered in this book, but be traced in the literature. For *Argentina* see Sabsay 1998, pp. 1-31, Munné 2003, pp. 387-397; for *Brazil* see Aguiar 1994, pp. 77-84, Jardim 1998, pp. 53-67, Fleischer 2000, pp. 79-103, Vieira 2003, pp. 425-434; for *Korea* see Park 1994, pp. 173-186, Sung 2005, pp. 319-332; for *Taiwan* see Chang 2005, pp. 497-512; for *Turkey* see Genckaya 2005, pp. 613-530.
86 Two old EU members, which belong to the third wave of democratisation, Greece and Portugal, were dropped from the sample because information turned out to be too patchy. Interested readers may want to consult: Papadimitriou 1992, pp. 197-230 (Greece) or de Sousa 1992, pp. 399-419; de Sousa 1999, pp. 1-45 and van Biezen 2000, pp. 329-342; van Biezen 2003, pp. 53-76 (Portugal).
87 Two more democracies from Central Eastern Europe, the Czech Republic and Hungary, were considered to be included. However, at the end of the day information was not complete enough. Interested readers may want to consult the most comprehensive source: van Biezen 2003, pp. 105-156, 177-201. For party financing in Slovakia see Meseznikov 2005, pp. 439-448, and in the Baltic republics (Estonia, Latvia, Lithuania) see Winkelmann 2007, pp. 142-208.
88 International IDEA 1997, p. 65 and www.idea.int/vt/country_view/cfm.
89 Israel changed its currency twice, from 10 Israeli pounds to 1 shekel in 1981 and from 1,000 shekels to 1 New Israeli Shekel (NIS) in 1985.

democracies. However, economically they are quite apart from Israel and Japan. Mexico, Poland and Uruguay belong to the "third wave" of democratisation.[90]

When examining the institutional arrangements of our cases, we find that only the U.S., Mexico, Uruguay and Costa Rica have a presidential system, while parliamentary democracy prevails, sometimes with specific modifications. Among these are semi-presidentialism (France, Finland, Poland), federalism (Australia, Canada, Germany), one-party dominance over decades (Sweden, Norway, Denmark, Italy, Israel and Japan) as well as specific cleavages caused by class and religion (Switzerland, Netherlands, Austria) or ethnic and regional strife (Belgium, Canada, Spain). Switzerland, Austria, Belgium, the Netherlands, Sweden and Norway are democracies with a consociational tradition, while the other countries more or less belong to the majoritarian type.[91] Having identified the subject of the study and the cases that will be covered we can now turn to necessary clarifications.

2. Demarcation of the subject of this study: party funding

This study is unable to cover all participants of the political process that influence party competition. Many scholars of democratic politics focus on civil society and on non-governmental organisations (NGOs). These organisations are very important for each democracy. However, they cannot substitute political parties, which present candidates and mobilise voters, aggregate interests and manage conflicts. The role of organised interests (lobbies or pressure groups) also differs from that of parties. Because pressure groups do not strive for public office in an open competition, their actions to transform social or economic power into political power are mostly indirect. Pressure groups influence political competition via public opinion, by packages of votes, expertise and money. Among these groups labour unions and organised business, especially the funds they provide, deserve major interest. In the U.S. unions and corporations are banned from contributing directly to parties and candidates. As a consequence, numerous political committees have sprung up to collect contributions from interested money. Only as long as such funds go into party coffers or candidate campaigns, they should be included in this analysis. However, we will not use conveyor organisations as a stepping-stone to investigate the whole range of activities by interest groups.[92]

Whether the *media* influences the emergence of successful candidates is a question raised time and again. However, in democracies freedom of speech is an important constitutional principle, upon which the operation of independent media rests.[93] All political systems where the government controls the media are defect democracies at best. In established democracies newcomers or competitors receive a lot of the public attention focused by the media, whereas incumbents are merely safe in their positions

---

90 Huntington 1991, p. 16.
91 Lijphart 19999, pp. 34-41, 248, 307.
92 For details see below in chapter VII, sub-section B 1 c (political action committees).
93 On media see Kaid/ Holtz-Bacha 2006.

as long as they have no serious competitors. Messages communicated in favour of incumbents, candidates or parties, which are part of regular newscasts, are much more important than the expensive spots of political advertising. Such costs only partially support political competition because they mostly provide a high degree of entertainment. Because privately operated commercial media are common in nearly all democracies, even public channels have to air more entertainment. To separate the costs for specific items, like newscasts, sports, game shows or soaps, is impossible. Therefore the overall costs of the media have to be disregarded in this study of political finance.

The same is true for the costs of *public administration*, which is the most relevant institution that implements government policies. This activity may influence political competition in different ways. The most frequent is the general impact of public policy. A well-designed programme implemented efficiently may work in favour of the party in power. However, this advantage of governing over opposition parties will turn into a disadvantage as soon as cases of mismanagement or scandal are reported by the media. In post-authoritarian systems the government may use administrative resources (staff and procedures) to support one party and to harass others.[94] The impact of such activities on party competition cannot be assessed. Finally there is the issue of government advertising. Most governments distribute printed leaflets ("flyers") or produce announcements and spots in the media in order to propagate their services and policies among the citizens. This activity may increase during an election campaign.[95] For practical considerations most research on political finance (including this study) disregards these items, because the demarcation of government activities (information vs. propaganda) is not easy. Although there is little doubt about the potential influence on political competition, their precise impact is hard to establish.

To some extent, this is also true for financial support to *members of parliament*. Their personal income (remuneration, salary) may stimulate media outcries and occasionally stir up public debate. We can, however, neglect most of it whereas cash transfers from incumbents to their party organisation (i.e. assessments) are part of our subject.[96] Cash allowances to MPs (entitlements for incumbents), their perquisites of office and public grants to party caucuses pose more difficult issues of demarcation between public office and party work. In established democracies expenses for parliamentarians have increased considerably during recent decades. The amount of money given to parliamentary groups and to individual MPs seems to be independent of public subsidies to parties.[97] In some countries, where parties receive generous funding from the

---

94 Walecki 2001, pp. 412-413; Walecki 2005a, pp. 149-156.
95 Young and Tham (2006, pp. 79-94) offer a detailed analysis of the Australian case, where the "federal government has become the biggest advertiser in the country" (ibid., p. 80). In Belgium, Ireland and the U.K. per capita spending is assumed to be even higher (ibid., pp. 85, 87).
96 see below in chapter VII, sub-section D 3 (assessment of officeholders).
97 For details see below in chapter II, sub-section A 3 (parliamentary groups) and chapter VIII, sub-section C 3 (parliamentary groups); for Germany see Rudzio 2000, p. 244 and Borchert/ Golsch 1999, p. 134.

public purse, parliamentary groups and individual incumbents are also well equipped, as the cases of Germany and Austria demonstrate.

It is generally assumed that allowances given to individual MPs are used to support the local party organisation, e.g. to pay for a "constituency" office or to fund permanent staff at the local level. Travel funds for MPs strengthen the politicians' linkage to their constituents as well as their party's rank and file. Parliamentary caucuses are important for policy development. Thus scholars from the Netherlands (Koole), Austria (Sickinger) and Sweden (Gidlund) include their funds when analysing political finance. In most countries such funds are not available, because funding for parliamentary groups or individual incumbents is aimed at making parliaments, their caucuses and individual MPs serious counterparts of an enlarged and skilled administration.

In general, a line between the use of such funds in favour of an individual party and an abuse of public funds cannot be drawn. Sometimes parliamentary groups receive public grants, which are provided on behalf of their parties and the caucus is expected to forward the subsidy to the extra-parliamentary party organisation. Sometimes individual parliamentarians have to pay assessments to their caucus and all funds are spent on parliamentary work. In democracies, parties operate in the wider context of other political institutions. To include all of them in the analysis of political competition would render our subject unmanageable. On the other hand, focusing on competition among parties may be too narrow. However, as long as the suspicion prevails that behind an egalitarian facade money and economic interests are at work in democracies,[98] the flow of political funds will be a necessary focus.

In principle, a complete aggregate of money in political competition "would include: (1) Election campaign funds; (2) Political party funds; (3) Grants to elected officials; (4) Political organisation funds; (5) Pressure and interest group funs; (6) Political lobbying funds; (7) Litigation funds; (8) Partisan mass media funds; (9) Corrupt political funds; (10) Unofficial payments to elected officials; (11) Unofficial payments to civil servants; (12) Unofficial payments to the mass media; (13) Payments intended to improve the electoral process as a whole."[99] However, for the purpose of empirical research a narrow definition of political funds is the only way to make progress.

If the term "costs of democracy" is extended to include expenses incurred by NGOs, interest groups, public administrations, financial support to MPs, litigation funds, unofficial (i.e. corrupt) payments to elected officials, civil servants or media editors and the costs of operating partisan (or even non-partisan) mass media any figure given will be mere guesswork for quite some time. Including even the opportunity costs caused by specific political decisions (e.g. pork barrel legislation and patronage), which are taken to create a more friendly electorate,[100] would make the whole subject inaccessible to scholarly scrutiny. For such reasons this approach is limited, including all costs

---

98 Herz/ Carter 1964, p. 115.
99 Walecki 2005a, p. 13.
100 As considered by Schleth 1973, pp. 29/30, 64-70.

of party activity. Otherwise there would be room for endless argument. There is no doubt, that the "costs of democracy and the funding of democratic politics go far beyond just the financing of political competition. Similarly, economic power and finance can be politically potent in other ways than the funding of parties, candidates and election campaigns."[101] Nevertheless the funding of party competition is an essential issue of democracy.[102] Although only a segment of the whole democratic process can be studied here, it is an important one. Starting from our data and findings other researchers with more intimate knowledge of additional costs will have to continue at a later stage.

C) Research questions and overview

The general aim of this book is to assess the long-term impacts of party funding on the democratic process by empirical means. This general purpose can be subdivided into major research questions. As a comprehensive piece of cross-national research, the study will deal with simple questions, which have been asked before and will be asked in the future:[103]

- Who spends how much for which political purpose?
- Who gives how much to whom and why?
- How does political funding influence party systems and party organisation?

These general questions deal with three different areas: First, party spending, especially the causes for different levels, possible trends and effective checks to excessive spending. Second, sources of political revenue, especially strategies of party fundraising and their contribution towards "grassroots democracy" and equal opportunities of individual parties. Third, impacts of funding on the fairness of party competition, the development of party systems, and the structure of party organisation. Obviously all of these issues address important aspects of the subject. None of them is completely new and the existing literature is full of partial answers, which belong to "a set of widely held but unproven assumptions about general trends in the funding of political life."[104] Such assumptions have to be examined in the course of this research. Each of the three major topics that define the core of political finance analysis will be treated in several chapters: spending in chapters II to V, revenue in chapters VI to VIII and impacts in chapters IX and X. In order to give a more detailed outlook, it is important to take a quick look at the particular research questions that will guide individual chapters.

---

101 Burnell 1998, pp. 5/6.
102 Cf. Pinto-Duschinsky 2005, p. 67.
103 Cf. Scarrow 2007, p. 194.
104 Pinto-Duschinsky 2002, p. 81.

1. Party spending

Although modern democracies are run by political parties, the funds raised and spent for party activity remain a controversial subject. The simple question "How much money is needed to operate a party system?" will never find an easy answer. Most likely there will never be a consensus among citizens or scholars on "How much is enough?" On the one hand most media, some scholars and public opinion frequently feel that an awful lot of money is spent on party competition. On the other hand, each party will need more resources than those goods and services that are provided voluntarily and free of charge by its partisans.[105] Attempts to establish the *factual pattern* of political spending (chapter II) have to answer different questions:

- What are the costs of political competition?
- Is there a systematic approach to measuring and aggregating these costs?

Initially it seems obvious who spends: political parties. Yet, what is a party? Parties are multi-facetted types of organisation. The term may embrace the organisation proper (such as the national, regional and local units), the party's candidates (and their committees), groups of party supporters, the party penumbra including parliamentary groups, party institutes and party media (especially newspapers). Defining a precise line through the partisan complex may not be easy, but it is necessary. If there is no answer to the sub-question "who spends," then the sub-question "how much is spent (on partisan politics)?" poses even more problems. However, an answer is needed for the evaluation of political spending, its trends and their causes.

This task raises a question of methodology. An analysis of spending for political purposes has to be aware that party activity differs among the democracies. In order to facilitate a comparison, comprehesive totals for political spending have to be established. In some countries such costs may almost exclusively be campaign expenses, in others the emphasis is on the routine operation of party headquarters and field organisations. A reasonable comparison has to include both kinds of costs (routine and campaign), all spending units (be they part of the organisation or party candidates), and the whole range of goods and services required for politics.[106]

This procedure (chapter III) aggregates all the available data, supplements it by informed estimates and transforms both to a common format in order to prepare a *cross-national comparison*, which shall answer two questions:

- Does the considerable spread of political spending totals, which was established by Heard and Heidenheimer for a couple of countries and the mid-20th century, hold for a larger number of democracies and towards the turn of the century?

---

105 Heard 1960, p. 235.
106 For the Canadian case this process took many months of field research. See Nassmacher 1989c.

- If so, which democracies are the most excessive spenders? Where do parties compete on the most moderate terms? Which countries represent the intermediate level of the costs of democracy?

As soon as spending totals and a rank order of countries are established, a scholarly evaluation of trends and causes can be tried. This part of the study (chapters IV and V) will treat the funds spent on political competition as the consequence of social, political and economic factors. That is, political money is considered as the dependent variable.

Many scholars and media people believe that the current costs of party activity in some specific democracy, most likely their own, is exorbitant.[107] Political scientists have rarely tried to deal with this assumption because the necessary data are not readily available. For a serious test of the hypothesis a world-wide sample would be appropriate. However, due to many problems with the quality and availability of data this can not be achieved at present. Thus, for the time being a sample of 14 Western and 2 non-western democracies with affluent societies and many decades of experience in party competition (plus 2 more recent additions to the democratic fold) should be acceptable. For less demanding issues this sample will be supplemented by 7 other democracies selected from Europe, Asia and Latin America. Unfortunately a well-documented example from Africa was not available.[108]

Many approaches to spending totals seem to be driven by the assumption that political parties spend too much money on their activities. Empirical research may help answer vital questions. For example, is party activity in any one country more expensive now than it used to be in the same country decades ago? Is it more expensive in this country than it is in any other (comparable, similar) democracy in the world? Whereas the former question demands time series data, the latter can be answered by using a one-shot approach, i.e. data relating to a specific point in time.

In one first step (chapter IV) we shall neglect the dynamic aspects of political finance, use a one-shot approach and discuss possible *causes for different levels of political spending*.

- Do certain features of an individual polity, specific conditions of competitive politics or various impacts of public policy cause the impressive spread of spending levels, which has been identified in various studies?

Some causes of any difference in political spending will be due to the peculiar characteristics of individual polities, among them size of electorate, political tradition or stage of development. Other causes of a high or low level of party spending may be related to the peculiarities of national politics, e.g. intra-party competition, importance of a party apparatus or intensity of ideological conflict. Finally, decisions and non-

---

107 Von Alemann 1987, p. 210 (for Germany); Hofnung 1996a, p. 74; Hofnung 1996b, p. 132; Arian 1998, p. 155 (for Israel); Levit 1993, p. 473 (for the U.S.); Bouissou 1997, p. 133 (for Japan).
108 For details on some African countries see Kumado 1996 and Guthmann 2007, pp. 107-115.

decisions in the realm of public policy may contribute towards higher or lower levels of political revenue (and expenses). Ignoring corrupt exchanges or granting generous public subsidies generates additional party revenue. State intervention in the economy provides an incentive for interested money to get involved.

Looking at the development of political expenses over time (i.e. the dynamic aspect of political finance) will require time series data. Can we discover a trend for party spending during a few decades in any single democracy or even compare such trends for various democracies? In four decades (1956-96) campaign spending in the U.S. increased 27-fold.[109] In the U.K. the 1997 campaign expenses were more than nine times the outlay for 1983.[110] Both countries seem to be hit hard by an international trend. Namely, all over the world of democratic politics analysts observe a dramatic increase in political spending. Different hypotheses have been advanced to explain the causes of excessively growing amounts of political spending. Some scholars indicate that there has been a steep rise in expenses caused by general trends such as professional politics and commercialised campaigns. Other scholars argue that the impacts of extended electorates, inflationary trends and economic growth in modern democracies during the 20th century have to be taken into account.

Chapter V, which concludes the expenses section, looks into the alleged *"explosion" of political spending* and compares changes in spending patterns.

- Does an escalating use of paid media advertising or the recurrent implementation of new campaign technology or the unlimited expansion of a full-time paid organisation cause a "cost explosion" in party spending?

This attempt to pursue potential causes of increased political expenses requires specific data for as many democracies as possible. Although political finance in various democracies has been researched continuously for about four decades now,[111] long-term data of comparatively good quality are available for just a few cases.[112] These include four big, one medium-sized and one small democracy. After dealing with spending by parties and candidates at length, we will address the other big issue of political funding, the sources of party revenue.

2. Sources of revenue

Political debate and scholarly analysis currently emphasise a difference between private contributions and public subsidies as major sources of political funds. A traditional approach towards monetary resources for political parties (which is more appropriate in the 1950s than in the 2000s and more suitable in continental Europe

---

109 Alexander 1999, p. 15.
110 Neill report 1998, p. 43.
111 For an overview see Nassmacher 2001b, pp. 19/20.
112 Among the 25 established democracies covered in this study no more than six provide long-term data (of more or less quality and diverse coverage): Austria, Britain, Canada, Germany, Japan and USA.

than elsewhere) would look at membership dues and donations. Unfortunately the general term "donation" applies to different types of funding. Addressing this difference and rejecting conventional distinctions, Gidlund proposed to contrast "grass-roots" funding and "plutocratic" financing.[113] This alternative emphasizes the ambivalent nature of political donations. Whereas democracy is a political system based on equal participation by the multitude, plutocracy is a political system dominated by the riches of an affluent minority.

Party revenue from *grass-roots funding* includes all money in small amounts given by individuals who intend to support a party, a candidate or an issue of their personal preference. Because of its legitimising effect we turn to this source of political revenue first (chapter VI) and address three different aspects of grass-roots funding.

- How much funding for specific parties in different countries is provided by membership dues and small donations from the grass-roots of individual party supporters?
- Is grass-roots funding an important and reliable source of political revenue with no strings attached?
- Which of the various strategies to solicit small individual contributions is best suited to raise grass-roots revenue?

The income of individual parties is closely connected with the history of each party and thus the party family to which it belongs. Traditionally, parties of the left follow the mass-membership model and rely on members' dues as a major source of revenue, while those of the right (the former cadre parties as groups of notables) used to depend on donations from the upper strata of society. However, this funding model, which is oriented on party families, may not be important anymore. Some consider the age of individual parties to be more significant.[114]

Contributions to a political war chest represent a willingness to participate as well as a means to seek influence. H.E. Alexander recalls a continuing dialogue on this ambiguity with K.Z. Paltiel, "He thought I was naïve. I thought he was cynical. Of course, we were both right."[115] There are a variety of motives for political contributions. Some "people give because they share ideas and concerns." Others expect "favourable treatment from– or at least access to–... elected officials" and/or "a quid pro quo–..., a contract, or a policy."[116] The latter expectations contribute towards "a growing sense of unease among the voting public" about the funding of political parties from interested money. This unease demands that a line be drawn between "legitimate attempts to seek influence" (including influence on the outcome of a democratic election) and "illegitimate or corrupt attempts to buy influence and to sell it."[117]

---

113 Gidlund 1983, p. 42.
114 As suggested by Koole 1997, pp. 156-182 who used data from the comparative research conducted by Katz and Mair (cf. Katz/ Mair 1992).
115 Alexander 1992b, p. 356.
116 Quotes in: Alexander 1992a, pp. 49, 50 (in reverse order).
117 All three quotes from: Wilson 2004, p. 2.

What is the intention of wealthy individuals, business corporations and institutional donors (business associations and trade unions) who contribute to democratic politics? Do they intend to promote the smooth operation of their political system, to serve a general political cause or just to enhance some sort of special interest, or even to promote personal gain? "The familiar maxim that he who pays the piper calls the tune is widely believed to operate in the sphere of politics. Whether or not the suspicion is justified, the ordinary voter is apt to suspect that a very large gift to a political party must be made with some specific object in view."[118]

Whenever parties depend on donated funds they may want to reciprocate the generosity of their donors by granting access to politicians,[119] shaping specific policies or offering favourable deals. Because this opens the floodgate to corruption, *plutocratic financing* is the most "dangerous" source of funding. Some politicians have tried to palliate the inherent risk by calling the procedure collecting graft, instead of taking bribes. Party funds that originate from all sorts of interested money or political "graft," no matter whether the donor or the recipient is the initiator, threaten the legitimacy of a democratic system and will be treated jointly.

The analysis of plutocratic funding, i.e. interested money and graft, in chapter VII will cover three important questions.

- Is the free flow of money into politics a hazard for democratic government?
- How relevant are the different categories of interested money in political financing?
- Which kinds of political graft (corrupt exchanges) are most prevalent in party funding?

The scarcity of grass-roots funding and the hazards of plutocratic financing are often considered the most important among the problems associated with private sources of political funds.[120] Unfortunately both will not counterbalance each other. Thus in most established democracies the mix of different sources includes private funding as well as *public subsidies*. Public support for parties and candidates is the most important innovation in political finance during the second half of the 20th century. The resulting variety is expected to combine independence and linkage, adequate funding and fair competition. Moreover this aim is pursued by varying degrees of regulation.[121] A combination of "sticks and carrots" enhances the implementation of new rules. Sanctions help to enforce rules, benefits offer incentives to co-operate. A carefully designed political finance regime that combines public entitlement and transparency obligations is

---

118 Neill report 1998, p. 45.
119 According to Sorauf 1988, p. 331, this is the major benefit to political donors.
120 See below in chapter VI, section A (cornerstone of democracy) and chapter VII, section A (moral hazard).
121 Cf. Paltiel 1981, pp. 154-159; Pinto-Duschinsky 2002, pp. 74-77; Nassmacher 2006, pp. 450-452.

a practical device in promoting the diversification of political funding risks and enticing parties to co-operate voluntarily with regulation.

Party families traditionally differ in their share of grass-roots financing and plutocratic funding.[122] This may also be true for the share of total revenue collected from public subsidies. Their importance for parties and democracies varies considerably and possibly in different ways. Many scholars emphasise that new parties do not have the same access to public subsidies as major parties. The most pertinent questions will be raised in chapter VIII:

- Are public subsidies a problem-solving kind of political revenue?
- Does the variety of subsidies, recipients and allocation formulas recommend a best practice to policy-makers?
- How significant is public funding for parties and taxpayers?

Although it may be "almost impossible to calculate how much money the state ... spends on political parties,"[123] an effort has to be made to evaluate the level of subsidisation. The taxpayers' contribution to party funding can be measured either by the share that public subsidies contribute towards party revenue in a specific country or by the amount of cash the tax-paying citizen contributes to the funding of party activity. After discussing the major sources of party revenue, we shall evaluate the impacts of political funding.

3. Impacts of funding

Finally we will look at money spent on politics as an independent variable. There are two aspects to this analysis. First, competition under the rules enshrined in any political finance regime has to be open and fair. Parties in power may frame regulations exclusively for their own benefit. Second, the distribution of funds may influence intra-party power and links between parties and voters. The sustainable combination of fair competition and grass-roots democracy is a litmus test for good party government. The provision of public subsidies may foster or impede fairness and openness of a political contest as well as intra-party decision-making. The concluding chapters, which analyse the impacts of party funding, will deal with impacts on party systems and on party organisation separately.

First, we have to discuss whether or not *money* really matters *in political competition*, as it may be able to determine the outcome of an election. Frequently researchers focus on the role of money in campaigns. Whereas Heard argued that no "neat correlation is found between campaign expenditures and campaign results,"[124] other studies claimed

---

122 For details see below in chapters VI, sub-section B1c(2) (party families) and VII, sub-sections B1 (institutional fundraising) and B3 (corporate contributions).
123 Pierre/ Svasand/ Widfeldt 2000, p. 12.
124 Heard 1960, p. 16.

that a candidate with superior resources has an improved prospect of success at the polls.[125] This may also apply to competition among parties. The impact of such great potential of political funds in the real world of party competition (chapter IX) will be pursued in a stepwise process:

- Is the influence of money strong enough to make the competitor who can dispose of the most funds the likely winner of a political contest?
- Will competitors who hold a financial edge continuously or over a period of time be successful more often than those who have fewer resources?
- Does the availability of public subsidies obstruct change within party systems or infringe upon the opportunity of new and minor parties to compete?

Research on the third question has led to the widely accepted hypothesis that public party financing results in a petrification of party systems.[126] A closer look at the opportunities of change within party systems indicates that different variables have to be considered. The emergence of new parties should not to be confused with the performance of minor parties. Moreover neither may influence the distribution of power between parties in government and opposition. As a result, "ossification" can be viewed from three angles: "openness" (i.e. free access for new parties), the "freezing" of the party system (i.e. established parties stop growing or declining) and an "arrested" distribution of power between government and opposition parties. Each of these aspects should be considered separately.

After dealing with the impacts of party finance upon the party system, the emphasis of this study will shift to individual parties. Each *party organisation* has two faces. The first concerns the political machine; the mechanisms of its operation and the efficiency of its efforts. The other is directed towards the party's supporters, the accessible part of civil society that it represents in everyday politics. The specific sectors of a society that support a party are usually called its grass-roots. Parties are expected to provide a link between civil society and the political elite; more precisely between a part of civil society and a part of the political elite (hence the name political party). Among the environmental challenges parties have to face is a changing relationship with the electorate at large, which can be due to changes in communication technology, funding routines or finance regulations. In order to evaluate the impacts of such changes (chapter X) we have to consider various questions.

- Is money a means of or an obstacle to links with party supporters?
- Have specific routines of funding assisted parties in securing grass-roots linkage or have such routines contributed to alienation between civil society and political elite?

---

125 E.g. Alexander 1970, p. 104; Isenberg 1980, pp. 28, 38; Isenberg 1981, p. 5; Johnston/ Pattie 1995, pp. 269-271; for details see below in chapter IX, section A (spend and win?).
126 Andren 1970, p. 67; Paltiel 1979b, p. 38; Seidle/ Paltiel 1981, p. 279; Mendilow 1996, p. 346.

It is important for the sustainability of democratic government that grass-roots support and elite responsiveness do not whither away. One option to counteract the volatility of voting behaviour is an adequate party organisation.[127] As Robert Michels indicated, full-fledged party organisations can become bureaucratised or highly centralised, which has a significant impact on intra-party power.[128] Potential impacts of political funding on the internal operation of individual parties, more precisely their extra-parliamentary structure, will be discussed. Changes within individual party organisations can be caused (or enhanced) by political finance regimes and funding strategies. In this context the distribution of power between parts of the organisation, especially national headquarters, regional branches and local chapters, individual candidates and party affiliated bodies, comes to the fore.

In sum, among the nine chapters that follow this introduction four deal with political spending (chapter II to V), three with sources of party revenue (chapter VI to VIII) and two with impacts of political funding (chapter IX and X). Some concluding remarks (chapter XI) link our study to the general analysis of political parties. This book will not cover political finance regulation and its implementation, although they are quite important. The reason is that for the universe of established democracies each of these subjects has been exhausted elsewhere.[129]

---

127 Scarrow (1996, pp. 10-11) believes that party organisation makes a difference.
128 Michels 1962, pp. 129-148, 188-204, 254-270.
129 On political finance regulation see Pinto-Duschinsky 2001a; Pinto-Duschinsky 2002, pp. 74-80; Tjernström 2003, pp. 181-223 and Nassmacher 2006, pp. 446-455. On Implementation see Nassmacher 2003d, pp. 139-155 and Nassmacher 2003e, pp. 246-287. On restrictions see Cordes/ Nassmacher 2001, pp. 278-285 and Nassmacher 2006, pp. 446-448, 452-454.

CHAPTER TWO

Factual Pattern of (Party) Expenditure

Since the 1970s political parties have published a continuously increasing number of reports on campaign funds and/ or annual balances regarding income and expenditure. Financial reports reveal a lot of details about political spending for a considerable number of countries. Before a comparative evaluation of the spending by parties and their candidates can be attempted, this information has to be organised in a systematic fashion, supplemented by additional data on non-reported items and informed estimates for non-reporting countries.

This chapter attempts to establish the factual pattern of spending by political parties by answering two questions:

- What are the costs of political competition, in detail and in total?
- Is there a systematic approach to measuring and aggregating these costs?

In accounting terms, costs are "resources sacrificed ... to achieve a specific objective," especially monetary units paid for goods and services.[1] A standard procedure of cost accounting first records the amounts of particular expenses (*types of cost*), then allocates them to *cost centres* and finally charges various types of cost to *cost objects*, i.e. the units of a product or service, which created those costs. As parties "produce" regular campaigns and current operations (possibly including policy development), types of cost will be caused by either cost object and encountered in specific organisational nuclei, the cost centres. In Graph 2-1 the three sides of a cube adequately represent the combination of potential approaches by categories:

(a) **cost centres**: (1) party organisation, (2) party activists, (3) party penumbra, (4) party caucusses;
(b) **types of cost**: (1) paid labour, (2) offices, (3) communication, (4) publicity, (5) other goods and services;
(c) **cost objects**: (1) election campaigns, (2) organisation maintenance, (3) policy development (research and training).

Readers have to be aware that the purpose of political parties is not to operate a business. Thus unfortunately the complete set of data, which would be needed to draw up the whole "cube" of cost objects, cost centres and types of cost, is not avaiable, not

---

1   Horngren/ Foster 1987, pp. 20/21.

even for a single party, let alone for any complete party system.² Nevertheless the approach may improve the precision of political analysis.

A) Cost centres (units of party organisation)

In the language of business, a "cost centre" is any subunit of an organisation whose manager is responsible for a specified area or set of activities.³ The term "cost centre" is used to describe a location where costs are incurred, accumulated and then assigned to specific products or services (called "cost objects").⁴ "Cost centres are determined by individual organisations…"⁵

Graph 2-1: *Dimensions of cost accounting applied to party spending*

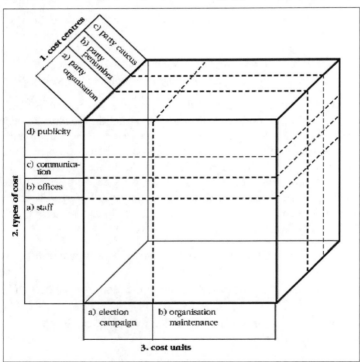

---

2   On cost centres German reporting is a good example, on types of cost Canadian campaign data is the most abundant. Data for cost units regularly lacks information on policy development, recruitment and training.
3   Horngren/ Foster 1987, p. 87.
4   Drury 2000, p. 51.
5   Dictionary of Business (www.xrefer.com).

Organisations that compete for political power in a democracy, i.e. parties, rarely establish a systematic collection of financial data. Party headquarters provide even less frequently data for their cost centres to the general public. Any approach to political spending, however, has to be aware of the full variety of party structures in the multitude of democracies.

Under U.S. law the basic unit of political organisation is a Political Action Committee (PAC).[6] Each PAC is a cost centre, which (raises and) spends money on (federal) elective politics. Any group of citizens supporting or opposing a candidate, an issue or a party may set up a PAC (and register with a public agency, the FEC). Legally even the two major parties are conglomerates of separate political organisations (PACs). In 2004 the core of the federal Democratic Party consisted of the Democratic National Committee (DNC), the Democratic Congressional Committee (DCC), the Democratic Senatorial Committee (DSC) and the Kerry-Edwards Committee, named after the party's presidential candidates. A similar combination of loosely coupled PACs represents the federal Republican Party. Beyond the federal level both parties are organised in each state, congressional district, county and further sub-units (e.g. townships and precincts).

An exact demarcation between party organisation and party penumbra is nearly impossible as all party candidates operate individual campaign PACs and many congressional leaders have set up their own leadership PAC.[7] To foreign observers, this variety of connected and unconnected, party and non-party PACs may just resemble the result of U.S. idiosyncrasies and an ill-begotten party finance legislation. Nevertheless it offers an important insight for the definition of cost centres. Any political party in any democracy may have a great variety of sub-units that are held together in a rather loose fashion by nothing but the common interest of using a specific label (the party name) for the purpose of political competition.[8] Thus it is just a little bit surprising that even the German SPD, previously the paragon of the highly centralised mass party, has been called a loosely coupled system.[9]

Any attempt to confront the financial dimension of party government runs into problems of definition and demarcation. That is, exactly which centre of political activity is part of a party? In order to establish the pattern of party financing, we must select reporting units. Many sub-units of parties have to be considered separately in order to present a complete picture of party activity. If we regard the party as a "holding company" or a "franchise organisation,"[10] then we must have data for all potential "subsidiaries" or "franchise" partners.

---

6 For details see Alexander 1992a, pp. 36-38.
7 For some details see below in chapter VII, sub-section B1c (political action committees).
8 Cf. Epstein 1980, pp. 9/10.
9 Lösche/ Walter 1992, pp. 77, 386; Lösche 1993.
10 Cf. Carty 2004, pp. 9-14.

For any political party this includes four different categories of cost centres:

- the *party organisation* proper (the "regular party structure") with national headquarters (federal/ central office), regional branches (state or provincial parties) and field organisations all over the country (including local chapters, the "party on the ground"[11]),
- ancillary organisations of the *party penumbra*, like separate groups for women and youth, or bodies for specific purposes, e.g. commercial enterprises, service institutes,
- the *parliamentary party* (caucus), which in federal systems will include caucuses in federation and states, probably party groups in municipal councils (for cities, counties, boroughs, townships and the like), and, finally,
- groups of *party activists*, which may spend money on behalf of the party in general, a specific intra-party cause or a candidacy for party office or public duty (leadership race, nomination contest, election campaign).

1. National, regional and local tiers (levels of party organisation)

Party structure is influenced by organisational need (as seen by individual parties) and statutory rules (set for political competition). In most countries it conforms to the levels and units of public administration (very much so in federal systems), although in FPTP systems there may be specific subdivisions to adapt to electoral districts. In Japan until the 1994 reforms, there were almost no *Jimintô* (LDP) chapters (*shibu*) at the local level due to factional infighting and strong intra-party competition. Support groups for individual MPs and parliamentary candidates (*kôenkai*) served as substitutes.[12]

Generally, national, regional (state, province, *Land, Kanton*) and local (municipal) organisations can be considered the relevant tiers of most party organisations.[13] Political finance regimes reflect the traditional practices of existing parties. Research may start with those units, for which the financial dimension of their activities is public knowledge. In Belgium, Denmark, Finland, France, Ireland, Israel, Italy, Japan, Mexico, the Netherlands, Poland, Spain, Sweden and the U.K. only the national party headquarters offer publicity on their funding. The data available vary considerably in detail, reliability and period of time covered.

Australia and Canada, Switzerland and Austria provide some data for the sub-national parties, too. In Canada details for federal and provincial headquarters and many local constituency (riding) associations are reported. However, such associations may be subdivided into branches and wards. Moreover Canadian parties operate two separate sets of riding associations, federal and provincial. The split between federal and pro-

---

11 Katz 1996, p. 121.
12 Köllner 2000b, pp. 149, 151/152.
13 For parties in EU member states supra-national party organisations and a caucus in the European Parliament should not be overlooked. (For some details see Ladrech 2006, pp. 492-498.)

vincial politics (each including one set of local ridings) has been estimated at about one third vs. two thirds of total spending.[14]

During the late 1980s Canadian federal riding associations of the three major parties spent an estimated total of CAD 5.5 to 7.4 million (about USD 4 to 5 million) between them.[15] In 1991 a more broadly based survey of 522 federal riding associations of five national parties provided more details: "Over three-quarters of the riding parties typically spend less than $ 5,000 a year between elections, just 11 percent more than $ 10,000." About 40 percent of the two major parties' local organisations spent more than CAD 1,000 and less than CAD 5,000 annually. A sitting MP makes the big difference to his or her local party. "Over half [of the riding associations with an incumbent] report annual expenditures of more than $5,000, while just 13 percent of those with no MP spend that much."[16]

Australian parties just report total expenses. Federal parties are less financially endowed than their state counterparts. For 1998/99 to 2005/06 the Labor Party spent 9 to 46 (on average 27) percent of its funds centrally, the Liberal Party 12 to 43 (on average 30) percent and the National Party only 4 to 14 (on average 9) percent. The bulk of all funds, in all years, was spent by the regional (state) party organisations.[17] Unfortunately local funds are included in the state party data and not presented separately. A rough estimate for the split between the three levels of party organisation may be a quarter of total spending each for federal and local, about half for the state parties.

Two studies of Swiss party financing include some data for state parties (*Kantonalparteien*). The figures given indicate that less then 30 percent of all party funds were spent federally, about 35 percent each by state and local parties.[18] In Austria according to Kofler's estimate for the late 1970s federal, state and local units spent 31, 58 and 11 per cent of the total ÖVP funds. However, data for other parties cannot be separated by tiers of the political system.[19] In India both leading parties, BJP and Congress, "raise and spend election funds in a major way at the constituency level."[20] More specific information is not available for that country.

Two other federal systems, the U.S. and Germany, are the odd couple of cases as far as the distribution of funds within party organisations is concerned. U.S. parties can hardly be isolated among the multitude of PACs. Nonetheless informed estimates (for 1952 and 1992) put the state level at just below half, the local level at around one third and the national level at about one fifth of total political spending.[21] German parties have to prepare and publish annual reports, which include details for federal headquar-

---

14   Nassmacher 1989c, p. 232.
15   Nassmacher/ Suckow 1992, p. 148.
16   Carty 1991, pp. 91/92 (more details in Table 4.12).
17   www.aec.gov.au/arwSummaryReturns (Summary of All Party Returns for 1/7/98 to 30/6/06). The highest shares for federal headquarters of the two major parties occur in national election years.
18   Ladner/ Brändle 1999, pp. 11/12; Ladner/ Brändle 2001, p. 163.
19   Kofler 1981, p. 383; cf. Sickinger 1997, pp. 243, 245, 249, 250, 252.
20   Sridharan 2006a, p. 328.
21   Heard 1960, p. 7; Alexander/ Corrado 1995, p. 5.

ters, state branches and summaries for local chapters. On average, each tier (federal, state, local) spends about one third of all party funds in Germany (Table 2-1 below).

Similar data are not available for the local level of other political systems. Two countries stand out as exceptions, the U.K. and Sweden. In Sweden the median for total expenditure of a Social Democratic *arbetarkommun* (workers' community, i.e. a local chapter of the *SAP*) was SEK 456,400 (about USD 49,600) in 1997 (a non-election year), SEK 555,000 (approximately USD 60,300) in 1998 (an election year). Spending by local Conservative chapters averaged SEK 70,300 (about USD 7,600) in 1997 and SEK 126,000 (USD 13,700) in 1998.[22] These figures reflect the size of the national parties, provided that local organisations cover about the same area.

Similar averages for the U.K. are available from the Houghton and the Neill reports. In regard to local party expenditures, a sample study estimated the average spending per constituency association in 1997 at £30,761 (USD 46,100) for the Conservative Party, £9,577 (USD 14,400) for the Labour Party, and £7,195 (USD 10,800) for the Liberal Democrats.[23] While the average local Conservative spending declined sharply in the decade before 1997, the average level of local Labour and Liberal Democrat spending increased, despite the fact that locally the Conservatives still spend much more than the other parties. An earlier study found that the average spending per constituency association in 1973 was £4,572 for the Conservative Party, £1,761 for the Labour Party, and £872 for the Liberal Party.[24] Over time the financial position of local Labour parties seems to have declined against both competitors. In his landmark study of British political finance, Pinto-Duschinsky estimated that around 1970 local expenses accounted for two thirds of total Conservative, less than 60 percent of all Labour, and almost three quarters of the Liberal outlay during a complete election cycle, whereas expenditure at the centre covered 28 to 43 percent of total spending.[25]

Time series data for cost centres are available for Germany only (Table 2-1 below). Since 1984 parties have to identify how much money was raised and spent on the federal, the regional and the local level of each party organisation in their annual reports. A tabulation for the major parties and the two years influenced by the 1987 campaign revealed that on average local chapters in West Germany spent less than 40 percent of the total whereas the federal parties and the state branches each spent slightly more than 30 percent of all party funds.[26]

This general impression seems to hold for the major parties of the united Germany, too. Only the federal FDP spends about 10 percentage points more than the 30 percent average share of national party headquarters. Whereas regional SPD branches spend significantly more than the 30 percent average, the shares of CDU and FDP state party

---

22 Gidlund/ Möller 1999b, pp. 101-103.
23 Neill report 1998, p. 41; US-$1 = £ .666; 1£ = US-$1.50.
24 Houghton report 1976, p. 181.
25 Pinto-Duschinsky 1981, pp. 150, 174, 208 (Labour and Liberals for 1970-74, Conservatives for 1966-70).
26 Nassmacher 1989d, p. 276.

organisations stay well below that level. Among the local chapters those of the CDU stand out with their relatively high spending potential (Table 2-1).[27] For all local parties, there are no spending peaks in the years of a federal election (1994, 1998, 2002, 2005). Those years, however, reveal the highest share of federal headquarters, which increase their spending by 5 to 15 percentage points as compared to non-election years.[28]

Table 2-1: *Federal, state and local party expenses in Germany, 1994-2004*

Level/Year	Party:	SPD	CDU	FDP	Grüne	PDS
Federal						
1994-1997	Range	27-36	27-36	38-41	28-36	22-40
	Average	31.5	30.2	40.0	30.8	27.4
1998-2001	Range	26-38	27-43	34-41	28-33	26-39
	Average	31.2	33.0	36.7	30.8	31.4
2002-2004	Range	30-36	25-35	34-45	19-37	25-35
	Average	33.6	28.2	38.7	26.1	29.8
Regional						
1994-1997	Range	30-42	20-28	22-33	27-37	28-36
	Average	35.3	25.1	27.8	31.9	32.9
1998-2001	Range	30-42	18-26	21-30	29-32	29-40
	Average	36.1	23.5	24.6	30.9	34.7
2002-2004	Range	33-35	21-26	19-22	27-36	37-41
	Average	33.9	23.5	20.7	32.1	39.5
Local						
1994-1997	Range	30-38	43-47	27-37	35-40	33-44
	Average	33.2	44.7	32.3	37.3	39.7
1998-2001	Range	28-36	39-50	33-44	35-41	32-38
	Average	32.7	43.5	38.7	38.3	33.9
2002-2004	Range	29-37	43-54	35-47	36-48	28-34
	Average	32.5	48.3	40.6	41.8	30.7

Notes: All data in percent of total expenses by individual party; data for 2005 not included because this year starts a new election cycle; CSU excluded because it does not run a federal headquarters.

Source: *Deutscher Bundestag*, parliamentary papers, no. 13/ 3390, 13/ 6472, 13/ 8923, 14/ 246, 14/ 2508, 14/ 5050, 14/ 8022, 15/700, 15/2800, 15/5550, 16/1270.

---

27 The deviation towards the federal FDP, the regional SPD and the local CDU organisations is mostly due to higher numbers of salaried staff at this tier, cf. Nassmacher 1989d, p. 277.
28 Readers are, however, advised to interpret the data cautiously. For the traditional parties (of the former West Germany) the average of internal transfers is below 10 percent for the SPD and FDP, and less than 3 percent for the CDU. The potential impacts of such transfer on the general distribution of funds can be neglected for these three parties. For the two other parties, which happen to be the most recent additions to the German party system, spending totals are heavily inflated by internal transfers and therefore should not be commented in more detail.

Some doubts notwithstanding, the financial means of the three tiers of German party organisation seem to be neatly balanced giving each tier enough resources for political activity. From 1994 to 2004 federal headquarters spent on average 32 percent of total SPD income and 31 percent of total CDU funds. Regional branches claimed 35 percent of annual SPD budgets and 24 percent of CDU cash totals respectively. The local organisations expended 33 percent (SPD) and 45 percent (CDU). The current distribution of funds within the two major parties in Germany does not support the hypothesis of a general trend towards centralisation of power and resources in modern political parties.[29] Quite to the contrary, each party boasts a variety of party-affiliated bodies, which in turn corroborate its character as a loosely coupled system. Another case in point is Canada, where the influx of public and private funds (caused by generous campaign reimbursements and tax credits) has added more to the resources of local riding associations than to those of federal party headquarters.[30] In many democracies some informal elements of the party structure are additional cost centres.

2. Groups of party activists

Some partisan activity beyond the formal party organisation may aim at the general public, especially people entitled to vote. This applies to all campaigns, which are partisan in nature, but not run by the party proper. We must first mention the support committees for presidential candidates (in Austria, Costa Rica, Finland, France, Ireland, Poland, Uruguay and the U.S.). A similar situation concerns the election agents of all constituency candidates in Australia, Canada, Ireland and the U.K., which are stipulated by national election law but not part of the formalised structure of a political party. As soon as any of the aforementioned partisan entities expends funds for the purpose of political competition as separate cost centres, they will be subjects of this study. (For each of them we will include expenses in our tabulation of party expenditures.) Under the German MMP system some constituency candidates run their own campaigns, whereas others rely completely on their local party organisation. As there is no general pattern of candidate vs. party campaign, we have to add all separate spending in the constituencies to the aggregate campaign outlay of party organisations.[31]

When partisan activity aims at intra-party decision-making the situation becomes a bit blurred. Canadian leadership contests within the federal, as well as most provincial, parties are expensive affairs (although this only concerns the Liberals and the Conservatives)[32] and they occur rather infrequently (once or twice in a decade).[33] Pre-

---

29 E.g. Panebianco 1988, p. 231; for a broader discussion see below in chapter X, sub-section B2 (levels of party organisation).
30 The opposite seems to be true for the U.K., see below in this chapter, sub-section B 1 a (paid labour).
31 For some details see Oldopp 2001, p. 281.
32 The N.D.P. holds leadership conventions, too, but they are far less expensive affairs; Archer 1991, pp. 39-44.
33 Cf. Stanbury 1986, pp. 468-469.

nomination campaigns ("primaries") for U.S. presidential and gubernatorial, House and Senate candidates,[34] which are more frequent and more expensive, are traditionally included in campaign spending data. Quite different from this, the pre-nomination campaigns of parliamentary candidates in other democracies are a blind spot of political finance. The first country to deal with such expenses systematically is Canada.[35] In other countries the amounts spent may be too modest or the number of electors involved may be too small to cause much spending. Nonetheless analysis has to be aware of the potential.

Right from the start, highly formalised internal *factions* structured the political activity of at least one party in four different countries (France, Italy, Japan and Uruguay). The *sublemas* of the Uruguayan *Blancos* and *Colorados*,[36] the *habatsu* of the Japanese *Jimintô* (LDP),[37] the *correnti* of the Italian *DC*,[38] and the *tendences (courants)* of the French *PS* [39] are well known to students of party politics. Within the process of intra-party competition, such factions operate their own networks of organisation and communication. They raise and spend their own money, which makes them a group of distinct cost centres. Unfortunately details of their funding are known to insiders only and thus cannot be discussed in detail.[40]

Finally, this group of cost centres also includes a different kind of institutions. In some countries (e.g. the U.K.) party leaders and senior politicians dispose of funds via a blind trust, which administers neither party nor personal funds. Nevertheless, such trusts expend political money that has been raised to support a politician and his (or her) politics. Donors ("undisclosed" to the beneficiary) have provided the funds, a politician's agent spends them for political ends. The existence of a blind trust is rarely known to the public, let alone the amounts (raised and) spent. This situation brings such trusts closer to a political reptile fund and introduces a "grey area" of considerable importance to the U.K.'s (and possibly other countries') political financing.[41] Because no party will know, how much is spent by groups beyond the formal organisation, we include such "informal" cost centres only if they concern constituency campaigns or reliable data are available. This is also true for auxiliary organisations.

---

34 For details see Oldopp 2001, S. 132-138 and Carty/ Erickson 1991, pp. 97-189.
35 For details see Carty 1991, pp. 91-98, 196-201; Heintzmann 1991, pp. 140-143.
36 Kerbusch 1971, pp. 21/22, 100-109; Janda 1980, pp. 567/568; Casas-Zamora 2005a, pp. 83, 91/92, 95, 179, 188, 214-216, 218.
37 Park 2001, pp. 433-447.
38 Epstein 1980, pp. 337/338.
39 Ladrech 1990, pp. 8/9; Kempf 1997, pp. 164-168; Kempf 2007, p. 184..
40 For some bits of information see Kevenhörster 1973, pp. 77-87; Bardi/ Morlino 1994, pp. 263, 265; Casas-Zamora 2005a, pp. 177-183.
41 Compared to a British blind trust the U.S. „leadership PAC" (see below in chapter VII, subsection B1c – PACs) is an icon of transparency.

3. Party penumbra (ancillary bodies and affiliated organisations)

A different group of potential cost centres of political activity may be called affiliated, ancillary, auxiliary, parallel and supporting bodies or organisations of the party periphery.[42] Most party-owned enterprises are income generating entities [43] rather than specific cost centres. In this sub-section, two types of partisan structures formally linked to a parent party shall be presented: separate organisations for specific groups (determined by certain social characteristics), and party institutes (created to deliver specific services).

a) Intra-party organisations

In contrast to informal factions special organisations for women and youth (occasionally students, too) are built into the formal structure of many parties. This pattern dominates in Canada, New Zealand and the U.K. as well as in Denmark, Finland, Norway and Sweden.[44] Starting from a Catholic (corporatist) view of society, only one party has based its whole organisation on two dimensions: area and social group. The conservative ÖVP in Austria combines regional and local chapters in states and municipalities with a set of six different leagues (*Bünde*) that organise farmers, small businessmen, workers, women, youth and senior citizens. Whereas the three latter leagues are more recent creations and financially unimportant, the three former date back to the 19th century and traditionally hold the reins of intra-party power, including the purse strings to party coffers.[45] Kofler estimated that in the late 1970s state and federal leagues accounted for 38 per cent of total ÖVP revenue and expenses.[46]

In a much looser fashion, the two major parties in Germany (CDU, SPD) have copied this model of additional intra-party associations (*Vereinigungen, Arbeitsgemeinschaften*), which are based on key groups (workers, small business, teachers, women, youth, municipal councillors) that they want to target. Such associations disburse separate funds, too, most of them, however, granted as public subsidies or as intra-party transfers. Current financial details for leagues and (non-territorial) associations are not available [47] and therefore significant cost centres for the three parties mentioned cannot be elaborated here.

---

42 In Italy, however, the latter term (*organizzazioni/ sedi periferiche*) is applied to local party chapters and thus refers to core parts of the party organisation. Pacifici 1983, pp. 60/61, 75/76, 103/104.
43 They will be covered below in chapter VII, section C (returns on investment).
44 Wiberg 1991c, p. 113; Svasand 1991, p. 126; Pedersen/ Bille 1991, p. 163; Kofler 1981, p. 383; Carty 1991, pp. 53-54; specific information for Sweden and the U.K. is not available; for Ireland see Mockler 1994; for New Zealand cf. Miller 2005, p. 89.
45 Müller 1994, pp. 56/57; Cordes 2001 and Smith 2005 offer no further details.
46 Kofler 1981, pp. 382/383.
47 Sickinger 1997, pp. 244/245.

b) Party institutes

In Germany, Austria and the Netherlands party institutes, which service their "parent" parties in the areas of research and training, have been created. All of them were set up as separate bodies in order to receive public grants and all of them have extended their mission to additional fields, e.g distribution of scholarships to college students and international aid for democratic transitions.[48] The German, Austrian and Dutch institutes (frequently called foundations) can be classified as separate cost centres of party activity as far as they serve a party.

In Denmark and Norway educational associations have a long tradition.[49] The German political foundations ("*parteinahe Stiftungen*") were the innovators in central Europe, and they still disburse the highest amounts of (public) money for "party purposes." Some British observers have misperceived the German foundations as "research" institutions and assigned them the role of "think tanks" covering "topics of current interest".[50] Others have, more realistically, summed up the whole range of activities and voiced serious doubts as to the partisan character and effectiveness of foundation activities.

The major areas of activity are "political education, research, student grants and international activities".[51] Dealing with party cost centres here, we must introduce two caveats. First, overseas operations constitute the largest area of activity as roughly two thirds of the foundations' funds are spent on such projects.[52] Because we only deal with the costs of party competition within Germany, this vast area of spending has to be ignored. Second, as far as their activity in Germany is concerned, party foundations provide additional jobs for a number of party faithful. However, this is just an opportunity for patronage besides public administration, and not an area of spending on party competition.

If we neglect international aid (which may have an impact on patronage opportunities) and scholarships (which possibly reinforce partisan commitment of future elites), political education and research *could* concern party competition in Germany. However, "research" is a heading, which contributes to confusion. Some of the topics, e.g.

---

48 The partisan endowments in the U.S. (NDI and IRI) and the all-party foundations (the British WFD and, more recently, the Dutch IMD) are confined to the latter purpose. Although these endowments were modelled after the earlier examples they do not meddle in the party competition of their own country. For details see Pinto-Duschinsky 2001c, pp. 299-302. For comparable institutions in other countries see Rich 2001, p. 49; Tadashi 2001, pp. 78/79; Stone 2004, p. 7; Radaelli 2004, p. 90; Fieschi/ Gaffney 2004, p. 212; Lucavelli/ Marsh/ Stone 2004, p. 262.
49 Svasand 1991, pp. 125/126, 139; Pedersen/ Bille 1991, p. 162.
50 Houghton report 1976, p. 325; cf. Leonard 1975, p. 13; Neill report 1998, p. 195; Stone 2004, p. 7. Occasionally even German observers repeat such myths: Thunert 2001, pp. 184/185; Thunert 2004, pp. 78-80.
51 Pinto-Duschinsky 1991b, p. 196; Thunert 2004, p. 79.
52 Pinto-Duschinsky 1991b, p. 210.

pre-campaign polls on voting behaviour,[53] are more important for politics than others. Most of the research does not concern current issues of public policy, but rather the maintenance of party archives and studies of "little immediate relevance – for instance, the history of the ... movement and problems of the Third World."[54] Parties have, on occasion, used their foundations as a "dumping ground" for staff, which they could no longer afford, or for activities that they had to discontinue due to lack of funds.[55] The initial field of the foundations has been political education, which in real life rarely equals the training of party activists. Some of the adult education may be adequately characterised by the quote: "When British workers are bored with their jobs, they go on strike; German workers report sick or take educational leave."[56] This leaves two major factors of importance for German party competition: an impressive budget and a pool of employment opportunities, both of which make the foundations "baronies" holding some power of patronage within the German party system.[57]

Whereas the German *Stiftungen* have grown into more separated political fiefs attached to their party's orbit of loosely coupled cost centres, their Dutch and Austrian equivalents (called *Stichting* or *politische Akademie*) have remained smaller, more controlled by their parent parties and more devoted to partisan services.[58] Even closer than the relationship between party and party institute, is the link between a party and its parliamentary caucus.

4. Parliamentary party groups (caucuses)

The inclination to identify the parliamentary group (caucus) as a cost centre of party activity creates various problems of demarcation. Is the caucus a part of the political party (the party in parliament) or is it part of a representative body (the partisan element of parliament)? Because the parliamentary party is a separate institution that administers its own funds, it should be treated as a separate cost centre. A federal political system and partisan politics in municipalities may even create a whole group of such cost centres besides or in competition with party headquarters, branches and chapters.[59] How much of the outlay of a parliamentary party belongs to party activity? How much of it to the operation of representative institutions?

---

53 For some examples see Landfried 1994a, pp. 105/106.
54 Pinto-Duschinsky 1991b, p. 207.
55 Pinto-Duschinsky 1991b, p. 217 gives an example: The *Friedrich Naumann Stiftung* bought for hard cash the FDP archives when the party was in need in the late 1960s; meanwhile the monthly or quarterly "theoretical" journal of each major party (*Die neue Gesellschaft, Die politische Meinung, Politische Studien, liberal*) is published by the respective foundation.
56 Pinto-Duschinsky 1991b, p. 201.
57 Pinto-Duschinsky 1991b, pp. 203, 207, 209/210, 215/216; in a similar vein for regional branches of Dutch parties: Koole 1999, p. 345.
58 Koole 1994b, p. 286; Lucardie/ Voerman 2001, pp. 325-333; Sickinger 1997, pp. 157-164; Sickinger 2001, pp. 342-349; Nassmacher, H. 2004b, p. 105.
59 Koole 1988, p. 214; Koole 1992a, pp. 213-214; Webb 1994, p. 123.

Regular contributions of its members (from their political salaries) and public subsidies (caucus grants[60] and/ or the pooling of members' allowances[61]) may cover the budget of an individual caucus. Such sources create additional problems of demarcation. Does the caucus just serve as a conduit for party revenue or does it spend a budget at its own discretion? If so, do these funds serve the needs of the caucus, its leaders or individual members? In Sweden caucus leaders control the purse strings and should be the major, if not the sole, beneficiaries.[62]

In Austria, Denmark, Germany, the Netherlands and the U.K. parliamentary groups have considerable budgets at their disposal.[63] Individual backbenchers rarely benefit from such spending on parliamentary routine, policy development and publicity. As a rule the caucus employs clerical and research staff whose work mainly supports the caucus leadership (frequently members of the party leadership) to perform duties in parliament and party. Swiss federal caucuses have small budgets (partially subsidised from public funds), which tend to be transferred to national party headquarters. Between 1987 and 1994 the aggregate amount rose from CHF 0.9 million (USD 560,000) to more than CHF 3 million (USD 1.9 million). Among the 26 states (*Kantone*), 17 provide additional grants, however, not to the Austrian level.[64]

Only in Austria do parliamentary groups spend large amounts of money on their own publicity, which supplements similar efforts by the party organisation. In 1998 a total budget of ATS 472 million (some USD 34 million) was expended by all caucuses in ten parliaments, which is about one fifth of the funds available to state and national headquarters of the major party organisations. Funded by public grants to the parliamentary caucus (*Klub*) and its individual members (and including staff directly hired by parliament but designated to serve with a specific caucus), the parliamentary group's apparatus has developed into the leading political nucleus of the smaller parties in Austria that lack similar resources for personnel.[65]

In the Netherlands, where parliamentary groups have always dominated the process of policy formation, the development of a "parliamentary party complex" composed of full-time MPs and large numbers of salaried staff employed by the caucuses has strengthened this role. The capacity of parliamentary parties to hire staff is based on two separate public grants to caucuses (since 1965) and to individual MPs (since 1974). The latter grants tend to be pooled as a staff fund of each parliamentary group.

---

60 see below in chapter VIII, sub-section C3 (parliamentary groups).
61 Koole 1999, p. 343.
62 Gidlund/ Koole 2001, p. 122.
63 In Britain this applies to parties in opposition only; for more details on the Short money and additional grants see below, chapter VIII sub-section C3 (parliamentary groups); for Canada see Nassmacher 1999, p. 271.
64 Weigelt 1988, pp. 140/141; Drysch 1998, pp.153-167.
65 Sickinger 1997, p. 189; Sickinger 2001, p. 341. - In Denmark the leading role of the parliamentary party is not only due to financing (Bille 1994, p. 149). In the U.K. the importance of the parliamentary party has been reduced although financing of opposition parties improved (Webb 1994, pp. 123, 125).

Ten years ago the four major caucuses employed a total of 121 full-time and 135 part-time staff between them.[66]

In the 1990s German federal caucuses jointly disposed of some DEM 100 million (about USD 50 million) annually. Their state counterparts were able to spend a total of DEM 117 to 136 million (approximately USD 65 million).[67] In addition municipal caucuses in many counties and all big cities enjoy their own funds. The consolidated budgets of all parliamentary and municipal caucuses are not much less than half the total outlay for their parent party organisation in an average non-election year.[68] In 2005 the parliamentary groups of the federal parliament (*Bundestag*) expended a total of € 60 million, about 50 percent of the aggregate amount spent by their parties' central offices in 2004 (a non-election year).[69] From 1995 to 2005 the five caucuses in the federal parliament (*Bundestag*) spent an average of 73 percent of their total budgets on salaries and related expenses.[70] The significance of staff hired by parliamentary party groups indicates that we should examine more details on salaries and other types of cost incurred by political parties.

B) Types of cost (elements of expenditure)

According to books on accounting, the term "type of cost" indicates the value of any item among a variety of goods and services that are used for the purpose of production. When we apply this concept to party activity, we target all items, which any unit of a party buys on any market in order to provide any service to its politicians, activists, members, supporters, voters or the general public. Operationalisation is a continuous problem in this area. How specific do categories for types of cost [71] have to be for the purpose of analysis? The data, which is available, uses rather broad categories, and even such distinction is rare.

Ever since political parties began to compete for a mass electorate, they have relied on goods and services provided by both volunteers and markets. The combination has been changing with parties, countries and periods of time. Even during the 19th century, parties needed some cash to pay for certain goods.[72] Over time such need has increased, as parties started to step up their advertising effort, to employ full-time staff, to require professional services and to order printed matter on a large scale. In this

---

66 Koole 1994b, pp. 291/292, 297/298.
67 von Arnim 1996, p. 142..
68 For some details see Kempf 1989, pp. 113-117.
69 *Deutscher Bundestag*, parliamentary papers, no. 15/ 5550 and 16/ 2465.
70 The range was 60-81 percent. Source: *Deutscher Bundestag*, parliamentary papers, no. 13/ 5473, 13/ 8456, 13/ 11264, 14/ 1391, 14/ 4040, 14/ 6652, 14/ 9943, 15/ 1511, 15/ 3646, 15/ 5946, 16/ 2465.
71 Examples are given by Horngren/ Foster 1987, pp. 28/29 and Drury 2000, pp. 22/23.
72 Pinto-Duschinsky (1981, p. 16) lists some types of costs for parliamentary candidates.

section we will try to present the *variety of goods and services that political parties buy*, i.e. acquire in exchange for cash.

Ignoring national peculiarities, some pieces of information can be gleaned from the standardised reporting forms used in various countries (mostly for national party headquarters). As the types of cost are extremely detailed, there is only one country (Canada) that provides data for a reasonable number of types of cost. For some countries (e.g. France, Germany, and the U.K.) selected data on individual types of cost are available on a regular basis. For other countries only bits of information may be drawn from the literature. The cost of employing *staff* and running *offices* is pertinent to all organisations. In addition, costs for *communication* arise from contacting people. Furthermore, the cost of *publicity* is a must in competitive situations of mass societies. Other costs may be specific to countries or parties.

1. Paid labour

The most important cost item of a full-time party apparatus is salaries, wages and benefits for party personnel. During the 19th century, working class parties in continental Europe started a new type of mass party with a permanent organisation based on the interlocking resources of membership dues and paid party workers.[73] Later, many competing parties copied this type of organisation. Duverger identified the process and called it "an interesting example of contagious organization."[74] Permanent party headquarters and a team of field organisers became the industry standard.

a) Wages and salaries

Today some reporting schedules (e.g. in Germany) require information on *salaries and wages* including all welfare taxes, social security charges and individual benefits provided by the employer.[75] This kind of expenditure is the result of a process that has substituted volunteer labour by professional service. Party staff need different skills for clerical, political and professional work. Various levels of training usually influence the pay schedule, which is, however, unknown in detail. Due to the process of party-building in most Western democracies *salaries and related expenditure* have become a major item among the costs of party democracy. In his comparative study Casas-Zamora finds that staff expenses have grown although there is no uniform trend.[76] We will demonstrate the importance of such costs for three countries, which provide data for about two decades: Britain (for party headquarters during the

---

73 Heidenheimer 1963, p. 791; Epstein 1980, pp. 131/132.
74 Duverger 1967, p. 25.
75 Some reports in France list such items separately. Canada terminated the specific category in 2001.
76 Casas-Zamora 2002, S. 67. - Krouwel 1999, p. 91, applies indicators, which are not based on spending data.

1960s/70s and 1990s), Canada (for federal parties from the 1970s to the 1990s) and Germany for all levels of the party organisation since 1984 (Table 2-2 below). Additional information for national headquarters in Denmark and France is available for less than a decade (1990s).

Table 2-2: Salaries, wages and benefits (in percent of total expenses)

	Years	Parties					
Britain		Labour	LibDem	Cons.			
Range	1967-75	51-62	25-56	47-69			
Average	1967-75	56.2	46.9	59.3			
Range	1992-97	48-59	50-67	69-71			
Average	1992-97	53.0	60.0	70.1			
Canada	*	N.D.P.	B.Q.	Liberal	P.C.	Reform	
Range	1975-90	n.a.	-	11-43	24-40	-	
Average	1975-90	n.a.	-	32.2	31.9	-	
Range	1994-00	34-39	19-40	22-31	25-39	23-40	
Average	1994-00	36.9	25.5	25.3	31.0	33.1	
France		PCF	Verts	PS	RPR	UDF	FN
Range	1993-01	22-33	12-27	24-30	7-29	14-23	3-25
Average	1993-01	28.6	20.9	26.9	22.5	17.4	15.7
Germany		PDS **	Grüne	SPD	CDU	CSU	FDP
Range	1984-89	32-42	9-21	28-35	27-37	19-29	16-23
Average	1984-89	36.6	15.4	31.6	30.5	23.2	19.2
Range	1991-99	20-55	20-33	24-39	24-39	17-31	14-29
Average	1991-99	36.8	27.5	33.4	32.7	24.5	23.5
Range	2000-05	32-42	24-35	27-35	26-36	16-31	11-21
Average	2000-05	36.3	30.1	31.0	29.2	24.6	14.5
Denmark	***	SF	Greens	SD	CD	RV	V	DFP
Range	1998-05	36-43	14-32	21-39	5-40	30-41	13-33	7-15
Average	1998-05	39.2	23.6	31.0	22.8	33.9	21.7	10.6

Notes: Reform Party, since 2000 Canadian Alliance;
* Since 2001 separate data for spending on salaries are not available;
** 1984-89 DKP (the West German Communist Party);
*** data for KFP reported by different format.
Sources: Houghton report 1976, pp. 100, 106, 113; Neill report 1998, pp. 36, 37; Stanbury 1991, S. 461, 476; www.elections.ca (Registered Political Parties Fiscal Period Returns, Table 5); Publication générale des comptes des partis et groupements politiques au titre de l'exercice 1993, in: *Journal Officiel*, annexe to no. 268 of 19 November 1994; Schurig 2006, pp.424-429; *Deutscher Bundestag*, parliamentary papers, no. 12/5575, 14/7979, 14/8022, 15/700, 15/2800, 15/5550, 16/1270, 16/5090; www.folketinget.dk (Folketingets partir/Parti- og grupperegnskaber).

From this diverse information for a total of 27 major parties no cross-national trend emerges. Only three general impressions are consistent with the data presented. First, in election years the share of expenses for personnel is lower than in non-election years because total expenditure increases more than staff size. Second, on average salaries and wages account for more than 20 and less than 50 percent of total spending. Third, the British average is below 60, the Canadian and the German about 30, the Danish and French around 20 percent of total spending.[77] Although these percentages are comparable only within each one of the five democracies individually, our best guess for the annual share of labour costs at a national party headquarters is 35 percent of total outlay in a non-election year.

Table 2-3: Staff costs by party family and country (in percent of total expenses)

Party Country	Communists/ Greens	Social Democrats	Liberals	Christian Democrats	Conservatives /Populist
Austria	22-38	24-52	-	13-39	10-24
Belgium	50	n.a.	n.a.	n.a.	-
Canada	-	26-37	25-32	-	31-33
Denmark	25-39	31	22-34	-	11-23
Finland	-	21-48	20-41	-	13-24
France	21-29	27	17	-	23
Germany	15-37	31-33	15-24	23-33	-
Ireland	-	39-51	20	24-34	33-41
Italy	5-10	12-18	-	16-32	-
Netherlands	-	30-47	-	35-48	-
Poland	-	-	30-45	-	36-41
Sweden	24-32	6-20	24-61	-	49-66
Switzerland	-	36	54	53	65
U.K.	-	53-56	50-60	-	59-70

Sources: Bardi/ Morlino 1992, pp. 604-606; Cordes 2001, pp. 133, 135, 140, 145, 179, 183; Deschouwer 1992, p. 191; Farrell 1992, pp. 449-451; Klee-Kruse 1993a, p. 174; Ladner/ Brändle 1999, pp. 10, 14/15, 25; Wiesli 1999, p. 423; Ladner/ Brändle 2001, p. 82; Pierre/ Widfeldt 1992, pp. 826-829; Schurig 2006, pp. 424-429; Sickinger 1997, p. 252; Smith 2005, pp. 113, 133/134; Walecki 2005a, pp. 206-207; Wiberg 1991c, pp. 85-87.

Scattered evidence from nine other countries [78] (Table 2-3 above) indicates a comparable range of labour costs in party budgets. Based on official reports and scholarly research for years that spread out from the 1970s to the 1990s the national party headquarters of the major parties show relatively stable shares of staff expenses. Overall

---

77 Their permanent organisation with salaried full-time local organisers is spread out over some 400 counties/ constituencies. In 1989 the number for the SPD was 335 (Poguntke/ Boll 1992, p. 338).
78 Austria (1980-95), Belgium, Finland (1960-89), Ireland (1973-90), Italy (1974-89), the Netherlands (1981-95), Poland (1997-2000), Sweden (late 1980s) and Switzerland (1990s).

averages for individual parties are presented by party families. In general the data fits in with the range and averages presented for the five democracies discussed earlier. Personnel (and offices) are needed in Australia and for U.S. campaign activities as well, albeit mostly on a temporary basis. Unfortunately no data on individual items of current spending, such as office expenses, staff salaries or consultancy fees, are available on the internet or in AEC respectively FEC publications.

b)   Professional fees

Some paid party workers, however, are not on the party's payroll although political activity increasingly depends on their services. There are two different types of self-employed professionals, who charge *fees* for their assistance: political consultants on the one hand, lawyers and auditors on the other.[79] The implementation of statutory nomination procedures and political finance regimes has created a need for the services of experts to ensure compliance with new rules, which were previously unknown to parties.[80] The most advanced political finance regimes stipulate that certified accountants must sign affidavits before a financial report can be filed with the agency designated by law. Professional campaigning requires the service of pollsters, fundraisers, public relations managers and media consultants, to name just a few of the most important experts that many parties regularly hire.

How much of a drain this type of outsourcing is on party coffers is solely known to the party treasurers. In the election years 1970 and 1974, the British Labour Party spent between 10 and 16 percent of its total budget on consultants' fees.[81] However, there is no schedule for public reporting of party spending, which itemises such fees separately.[82] Legal and audit fees are published in Canada only, and they are of minor importance there.[83] On average, the five national parties spend two to four per cent of their current expenses on this type of cost (cf. Table 2-5). As political finance regimes stipulate more specific tasks, *professional fees* for legal advice and accounting services will continue to grow in importance. A freelance consultant's fee will regularly include some overhead cost, e.g. office expenses.

2.   Offices (rent of premises etc.)

It is difficult to imagine modern democracies without established parties and their own headquarters. Few parties just have a central office located in the national capital. Regional (state, provincial) offices are quite common, not only in federal or devolution-

---

79   Cf. Newman/ Perloff 2004, pp. 23/24; Smith 2005, pp. 145-149.
80   This is a frequently ignored aspect of the parties' transformation to „public utilities" (see above in chapter I, sub-section A1 (areas of interest).
81   Houghton report 1976, p. 106. Details for the Conservative Party were not reported (ibid., p. 100).
82   However, Stanbury 1991, p. 477, reports some for the Liberal Party of Canada.
83   see Table 2-5 below and Stanbury 1991, pp. 462, 477.

ary systems. The litmus test, however, for a strong, permanent party organisation is the presence of local offices on the county or constituency (riding, district) level. Wherever a party employs permanent field organisers, they will set up shop within the area of their responsibility. Occasionally, a nucleus of volunteer party workers may even run a local office as the hub of party branch activity and organisational efforts. The chain of local offices and the size of national party headquarters depend on the financial resources available. Expenses for permanent offices include: *rent, heat, light and power, office supplies and stationery, furniture, equipment and machinery.* The technology revolution has raised expectations in the latter area as low-cost photocopiers, fax machines, printers and computers have become available. The costs of computer hardware, software, operation and maintenance are especially important.

In some democracies local offices for political parties are rare (e.g. Netherlands, Switzerland), and in many countries no information about these costs can be gleaned from the literature.[84] During the late 1980s the majority of party funds in Sweden were spent on offices, furniture, telephone, travel, etc. In 1997 and 1998 administration was still the most expensive item for *Socialdemokraterna*.[85] In Germany during the early 1990s detailed office expenses on average accounted for about 12 percent of the annual party budgets: 5 per cent for rent, 5 per cent for computers and IT and 2 per cent for office supplies. Some additional costs of offices remain hidden among "miscellaneous expenses" (13 percent).[86]

Table 2-4: Costs of premises for parties in Europe (Britain and France)
(rent and maintenance in percent of headquarters' total expenses)

	Years	Comm.	Greens	Soc. Dem.	Liberals	Conserv.	Populist
Britain		-	-	*Labour*	*LibDem*	*Cons.*	-
Range	1967-76	-	-	7-10	6-20	n.a.	-
Average	1967-76	-	-	8.2	16.3	n.a.	-
Range	1992-97	-	-	4-10	23-33	9-11	-
Average	1992-97	-	-	6.9	27.0	10.3	-
France		*PCF*	*Les Verts*	*PS*	*UDF*	*RPR*	*FN*
Range	1994-01	2.3-4.7	5.8-12.2	1.8-2.8	2.2-5.0	2.8-8.1	1.4-3.0
Average	1994-01	3.1	8.7	2.2	3.1	6.0	2.4

Source: Computed from official data as published by Houghton report 1976, pp. 106/107, 112/113; the Conservatives did not report such details (ibid., pp. 100/101); Neill report 1998, pp. 36-38; Schurig 2006, pp. 295, 297, 299.

---

84 For Austria, France, Israel, Italy, Australia and the U.S. such details are unknown.
85 Gidlund/ Koole 2001, p. 115.
86 *Deutscher Bundestag*, parliamentary papers, no. 13/7517, p. 2. For earlier estimates cf. Nassmacher 1989d, pp. 276/277; Landfried 1994a, p. 140.

For two other European democracies data on "rent, equipment, office services," "premises" or "rent and maintenance" for individual parties are available. Compared to staff expenses the cost of *premises* is a minor item. Depending on the definition of the category and the party, which is reporting, the information is rather divers. French parties spend less than their British counterparts, major parties less than minor ones (Table 2-4 above). In general 5 to 10 percent of annual spending seem a useful range for this type of cost. Once again more details are only available for Canada (see Table 2-5 below). This type of cost was listed among operational expenses and under two separate headings. Between 1994 and 2000 about 4 and 5 percent of the annual total was spent on "rent, heat, light and power" and between 8 and 14 percent on "printing and stationery", a category that partly relates to the cost of publicity or possibly communication.

3. Communication

As a voluntary organisation of civil society that provides political services for activists, supporters, voters and the political system at large, each and every party is involved in communication with groups and individuals. Doublet argues that "political party expenditures are mainly communication expenditures."[87] For the purpose of cost analysis, we separate intra-party communication (which is discussed in this sub-section) and communication as an element of political marketing (which under the heading of "publicity" is dealt with later).[88]

The most traditional means of communication for all organisations is face-to-face meetings. This requires that people get together, mostly in a meeting room (hall) after using some means of transportation. Cost accounting identifies various types of costs incurred during face-to-face communication: *travelling expenses* (including passenger fares and accommodation for participants), *rent of vehicles* (mostly cars, occasionally aeroplanes and helicopters), *rent of venue* (conference suites in hotels, public halls or convention centres), *catering* and adequate *conference equipment*. A problem of demarcation between publicity and communication arises because the spending on meetings, conferences, conventions and rallies is, in part, aimed at intra-party communication (including policy development), but is also caused by the public presentation of policies and politicians.

---

87 Doublet 2003, p. 12.
88 see below in this chapter, sub-section A1d (cost of publicity).

Table 2-5: Operating expenses for major Canadian parties (in percent)

Summary for 5 Parties	1994	1995	1996	1997	1998	1999	2000
Salaries, wages and benefits	33.1	33.7	31.1	28.6	33.3	32.9	26.4
Legal and audit fees	2.0	2.2	2.0	2.3	2.6	3.0	3.5
Rent, heat, light and power	5.4	4.1	3.6	4.1	4.3	4.6	4.1
Printing and stationery	8.0	8.8	13.8	13.7	9.6	10.6	10.3
Telecommunications	3.0	3.3	3.0	3.5	3.3	3.4	2.9
Travelling expenses	6.0	8.5	8.5	9.6	9.3	10.1	8.7
Party conventions and meetings	11.4	10.7	11.7	6.6	9.9	7.3	11.5
Advertising	7.4	8.0	7.9	7.1	4.9	4.1	7.3
Broadcasting	0.0	0.0	1.5	4.6	0.0	0.0	5.3
Miscellaneous expenses	23.7	20.7	16.9	19.9	22.8	24.0	20.0
Total percent	100.0	100.0	100.0	100.0	100.0	100.0	100.0
Total in million CAD	20.135	24.318	28.569	34.318	25.353	25.926	34.887

Source: www.elections.ca (Registered Political Parties Fiscal Period Returns, Table 5)
Comment:Since 2001 the data is no longer organised in this format.

The share of these costs in party budgets is rarely known to the public. Australia is no longer interested in spending details. The U.S. does not consolidate information on spending.[89] In Israel such particulars are not available in English, and other democracies (among them Austria, France, Italy, the Netherlands, Sweden and Switzerland) apply more general categories. The printing and distribution of a monthly newspaper for party members is a major item in the annual budget of Dutch parties. Danish parties spend rising amounts on membership services.[90] This piece of information leads our consideration to the costs of non-personal communication, traditionally *postage and freight*, increasingly *telecommunication fees* (especially telephone), and more recently charges by internet providers. The fragmentary evidence that can be gleaned for just a few countries suggests that 10 to 20 percent of total spending by party headquarters may be a reasonable range for the cost of intra-party communication.

In Britain the Houghton Commission has asked national party headquarters for annual totals of "printing, postage, telephone and stationery" and "travelling, conference, etc. expenses." Between 1967 and 1976 the Labour Party spent on average 4 to 5 percent of its central office funds on printing, postage etc. and 9 percent on travelling etc., whereas the Liberals spent 10 percent on the former and 3 percent on the latter. Conservative Central Office was either unable or unwilling to provide such details.[91] In Germany the Presidential Commision (based mainly on data for party headquarters) has estimated averages for travelling at 4 percent, use of vehicles at 2 percent, rent of

---

89   FEC data are itemised within the documents, but no summary is available for their more than 100 pages (cf. Smith 2005, p. 107).
90   Gidlund/ Koole 2001, p.115; Pedersen 2003, pp. 337/338.
91   Houghton report 1976, pp. 100, 106, 112.

halls (including conference equipment) at 5 percent, telephone charges at 4 percent and postage at 6 percent of total party expenses.[92]

Among all established democracies, only Canada provided the most detailed and most reliable regular information on individual items of party spending by type of political cost. The Canada Elections Act of 1974 gives the Chief Electoral Officer the mandate to prescribe categories for the reporting of expenses. The format applied between 1975 and 2000 provided interesting details for certain types of cost by party and year. Annual averages for *travelling* expenses range from 6 to 10 percent, *telecommunications* account for much less (around 3 percent) and *conventions and meetings* constitute 7 to 12 percent of the overall routine expenses (see Table 2-5 above). Part of the latter, however, relates to political publicity.

4. Publicity

When looking for spending on publicity, we are inevitably lead to election campaigns. In general, the idea of „permanent campaigning" suggests that there is no borderline between publicity (PR) and campaign. However, for the purpose of this study, "campaign" is defined as the aggregate of all activities to influence the outcome of an election,[93] and "publicity" is a group of costs that are incurred in order to buy some means of communication, which address the general public without identifying any specific purpose. Publicity costs may be divided into four broad categories: printing, advertising, broadcasting and direct marketing. The total of such costs differs widely (in all democracies) between election and non-election years.

The *printing* of material for publicity includes flyers and leaflets, brochures and other party literature as well as the design and production of posters. *Advertising* can be widely interpreted, and then it would be equivalent to publicity. Or it can have a more restricted meaning that is centred around non-party print media. The latter includes the acquisition of commercial poster space, the rent of billboards, and paid newspaper or magazine advertisements. More modern types of advertising, addressed here as *broadcasting*, use airwaves for spots on radio and TV or web-sites on the internet. For broadcasting, production costs are usually less than the broadcast fees. More recently parties have supplemented (and partially replaced) such impersonal PR with the more personalised techniques of *direct marketing*, such as direct mailing or phone banks.

From data reported by the six major parties in France (Table 2-6) there emerges no clear-cut impression for spending on publicity ("propaganda and communication"). As a percentage of total headquarters' expenses such costs indicate no general and extraordinary increase in election years (1995, 1997). Moreover, ranges and averages for individual parties demonstrate more diversity than congruence. At least, the two leading national parties offer a different approach. Whereas the RPR clearly identifies a

---

92 *Deutscher Bundestag*, parliamentary papers, no. 13/7517, p. 2.
93 see below in this chapter, section A3 (cost objects).

higher level of publicity costs, the PS spends a much lower share of annual expenses on this item.

Table 2-6: Costs of communication and publicity for parties in France
(in percent of headquarters' total expenses)

Year	PCF	Les Verts	PS	UDF	RPR	FN
1994	15.3	24.9	5.3	12.0	22.1	41.7
1995	8.0	3.2	6.1	13.9	26.9	17.4
1996	17.2	5.2	6.2	12.4	28.2	18.1
1997	15.8	2.4	16.2	10.2	24.7	9.9
1998	10.7	4.1	7.0	16.8	20.8	10.9
1999	4.4	4.8	5.8	11.0	13.5	12.2
2000	16.6	3.5	8.5	18.9	18.6	17.4
2001	10.6	8.7	9.3	15.9	16.5	8.4
Average	12.3	7.1	8.1	13.9	21.4	17.0

Source: Computed from official data as published by Schurig 2006, pp. 294-299.

The national parties in the U.K. spend most of their campaign money on outdoor *advertising* (about a third of total spending), rallies, and direct mail.[94] Paid advertising on television and radio is legally banned. The costs of party publications are less important items of expenditure for party headquarters. In constituency campaigns, the vast majority of 1983 expenditures were used on printing and stationery (GBP 3,856,704; about USD 5.8 million).[95]

In Germany the share of publicity cost (including the rent of halls for rallies, party congresses, conferences and meetings) amounts to 27 percent of the overall financial outlay of a party in a four-year-election cycle. The share of media expenses is exceptionally low. Of the 27 percent total just mentioned, only 5 percent are estimated for the rent of halls, 13 percent for the printing of brochures, leaflets and posters. This leaves a total of 9 percent for all advertising on billboards, in print media or on radio and TV.[96] Media time in publicly owned radio and TV networks is available free of charge.[97]

---

94 Neill report, 1998, pp. 36/37.
95 Johnston 1986, p. 468.
96 *Deutscher Bundestag*, parliamentary papers, no. 13/7517, p.2. For earlier estimates cf. Nassmacher 1989c, pp. 276/277; Landfried 1994a, p. 140.
97 Such costs are not specified for Austria, Israel, Italy, Sweden and Switzerland.

Table 2-7: Election expenses in Canada (by type of cost), 1997-2006 (reported as a percentage of total election expenses)

Type of Cost	All parties				CPC	Lib	N.D.P.	B.Q.
	1997	2000	2004	2006	2006	2006	2006	2006
Television and radio	41.8	39.7	37.9	43.2	50.9	46.6	35.6	31.7
Other advertising	13.2	16.9	12.1	6.2	0.0	7.6	8.0	18.7
Surveys or research	n.a.	n.a.	4.8	5.6	3.9	6.1	9.1	1.3
National office exp.	6.1	4.5	3.7	4.7	3.7	3.7	7.7	1.8
Professional services	3.6	1.4	8.7	5.8	15.2	0.8	0.4	3.2
Leader's tour	15.9	19.4	18.6	19.6	16.7	19.4	26.7	12.7
Other travel expenses	3.0	3.3	1.9	1.6	0,5	2.1	1.9	2.5
Salaries and wages	7.1	7.3	7.5	9.0	4.9	9.8	9.5	12.3
Fund-raising	2.3	1.8	n.a.	n.a.	n.a.	n.a.	n.a.	n.a.
Administration exp.	7.0	5.7	n.a.	n.a.	n.a.	n.a.	n.a.	n.a.
Other/ Miscellaneous	0.0	0.0	4.8	4.3	4.2	3.9	1.1	15.8
Total election expenses	100	100	100	100	100	100	100	100
Total in million CAD	34.92	34.97	50.99	54.55	18.02	17.45	13.52	5.76

Source: Elections Canada On-line, www.elections.ca (Election Expenses of Registered Political Parties), October 2000, November 2004, February 2005, July 2007.

In Canada, the important items of operating expenses (Table 2-5) are *advertising* (in most years 7 to 8 percent of the overall annual total) and *printing* (mostly 10 to 14 percent of total outlay). Considerable *broadcasting* expenses (13 percent) stand out among the expenses of the P.C. in 1997 only.[98] This indicates that the P.C. paid for pre-campaign advertising from their operational budget.[99] The election expenses of political parties offer a remarkably different pattern, as seen above in Table 2-7. During official campaign periods the bulk of Canadian party funds is applied to *advertising* and *broadcasting*. There are, however, significant differences in level and detail among the parties. In 2006 publicity expenses (advertising, radio, and television) ranged between 44 (N.D.P.) and 54 percent (Lib.). The share of TV spots was highest for the CPC (51 percent), and that of (old-fashioned) newspaper advertising for the B.Q. (almost 20 percent). Across the board travel cost for the leader's tour (a traditional feature of Canadian campaigns) accounted for about one sixth of total election expenses in 1997, one fifth in 2000 and 2006. Individually Conservatives and Liberals spent in this range, the N.D.P. more than a quarter and the B.Q. about one eight of the total in 2006.

---

98 Amr/Lisowski 2001, p. 58.
99 For details see Cordes/ Nassmacher 2001, pp. 281/282; Stanbury 1991, pp. 92/93, 388-391, 422.

The information, which has been presented, is too diverse to allow for generalisations. Even giving a range of percentages would be misleading.[100] A comparison of annual averages may be influenced by different approaches to fluctuating publicity expenses, which will be most important during campaign periods. Finally some residual issues need to be discussed.

5. *Other goods and services*

This item refers to costs that cannot be attributed to any other category (called *miscellaneous* expenses), costs that are due to *peculiarities* of competition in specific democracies and costs of *minor* importance.

a) Polling/ research, interest and fundraising

In 1997 the U.K. Labour Party recently spent heavily on surveys (£500,000, approximately USD 750,000) and focus groups (£180,000 about USD 270,000), too, while the Conservatives spent £400,000 (approximately USD 600,000) on private *polling*.[101] The cost of *research*, explicitly analysed by the Houghton and Neill committee, is less important for U.K. parties.[102]

If parties are indebted to banks and other financial institutions, as (according to rumours and media reports) many of them frequently are, their annual budgets have to cover *interest* on loans and mortgages. Data for interest paid by parties are available for Germany and France only. In their reports for 1993 the major parties in France showed considerable variance. Whereas the PCF, FN and RPR spent less than 0.5 percent of their total expenses on interest and similar cost, the PS approached a share of 3 percent, the CDS 5 percent and the UDF 8 percent.[103] For the most recent election cycle (2003-05) four of the six parties represented in German federal parliament reported just minor interest payments. Such expenses required between 0.1 (PDS in 2004 and 2005) and 3.3 percent (CDU in 2003) of the annual budget. The only exceptions were the SPD with a range of 6 to 17 percent (average 10 percent) and the FDP with a range of 5 to 10 percent (average 7 percent).[104] Most of this unusual burden was obviously caused by overdrafts from the 2002 campaign.

The costs of *fundraising* are considerable in the U.S. The Republicans spends more money than the Democrats, mainly on expensive direct mail. In 1996 the RNC spent $48 million targeting small donors.[105] These costs may include staff and offices to conduct the campaigns.

---

100 Transfers between reserves and current accounts as well as items prescribed by national reporting rules restrict a comparative approach to annual balance sheets.
101 Butler/ Kavanagh 1997, p. 223.
102 Contrasting the Houghton report 1976, pp. 98, 104, 110, to the Neill report 1998, pp. 36-38.
103 *Journal Officiel*, annexe to no. 268 of 19 November 1994.
104 *Deutscher Bundestag*, parliamentary papers, no. 15/5550, 16/5090.
105 Corrado 1999, pp. 80/81; Hrebenar et al. 1999, p. 145; Smith 2005, pp. 193/194.

b) Peculiar types of cost

Some costs stand out in the two non-western democracies. The major part (about 40 percent) of the total outlay incurred by Japanese politicians is expended on activities within the constituency, e.g. the cultivation of good *personal relations* with important local voters and members of personal support groups (*koenkai*). At the events in their followers' private lives (such as coming of age, wedding and funeral), politicians give generously (in cash or kind). The distribution of money or presents during or, to circumvent strict election laws, previously to the official campaign period must be seen as part of this strategy.[106]

On Election Day, Israeli parties continue to spend money on taxis to bring voters to the polls and to pay for party workers' food and time. "Such expenses add up to between 25 and 33 percent of campaign expenses."[107] Polling day costs, however, are by no means a special feature of Israeli politics. In Germany party activists participate in the operation of polling stations as a civic duty and receive some remuneration from the public purse. Other party workers volunteer their own cars, gas and time to bring voters to the poll at no cost for the party or the voter. In Canada such "election day expenses" are part of individual candidates' regular campaign expenses. Here this item, however, seems to be of minor importance only.[108]

c) Residual costs

Finally, it is remarkable that the category "*miscellaneous* expenses" makes up an important part of total operating expenditures in some countries. In France about 40 percent of the total expenses reported by individual parties stay unspecified.[109] Such shares of obscure spending lead to serious doubts about the quality of a reporting schedule stipulated by law. From 1994 to 2000 in Canada (see Table 2-5) between 17 and 24 percent of current operations could not be classified as a specific type of cost. Thus even the most developed transparency scheme of party spending does not provide an adequate separation of different categories. Significant items (e.g. spending on media *consultants* or on opinion *polling*) neither count as an election expense nor are they specifically identified in the breakdown of operating expenses.[110] These items, however, are extremely important costs for technologically advanced parties in modern democracies. This may indicate one of the difficulties in finding a practical, as well as a legal, definition of specific types of political spending.

Reviewing the scattered information, which was presented in this section, it appears

---

106 Blechinger 1998, pp. 133-144; Kerde 1998, pp. 182-185.
107 Peretz/ Doron 1997, p. 128. This was already true in the late 1950s (Gutmann 1963, pp. 713/714).
108 Stanbury 1991, pp. 351, 617.
109 For 1994 to 2001 the annual averages were 38.7 to 43.6 percent. Schurig 2006, pp. 425, 427, 429.
110 Stanbury 1991, pp. 69, 386, 422. - *Fundraising* is itemised for campaign spending only.

that an important area of cost analysis has rarely been covered for political parties. Political spending is rather incompletely organised by type of cost. Just one type (expenses on staff) stands out for more than half of our sample (see Tables 2-2 and 2-3 above). If the costs of party activity are high or rising,[111] as they are said to be, the precise origin of this situation or process cannot be identified. Customary election day expenses, traditional vote buying, prevalence of full-time party workers, and innovations in campaign technology may all be influential. However, political finance research can hardly put a price tag on any of them. The goods and services, which a political party buys at market prices, can reveal more details for a programme of cost control than the purposes, to which a party may deploy such resources.

C) Cost objects (purposes of spending)

In the language of business accounting a *cost object* can be a product, a group of products or a service rendered. When applied to political parties, the traditional Anglo-Saxon approach contrasts expenses for election campaigns to spending on organisation routine.[112] German legislation (1984 to 1993) distinguished between three categories of spending: current operations, intra-party bodies and information,[113] public relations and election campaigns.[114] According to Paltiel, "parties require funds for three purposes: to fight election *campaigns*, to maintain a viable inter-election *organisation*, to provide research and advisory *services.*"[115] A comparative study of political finance would have to focus on funds (raised and) spent in order to influence the outcome of elections by effective campaigning, to support the routine operation of political parties, and/ or to provide services for the party leadership. Among these are public opinion polls, research on policy issues, training and recruitment of party workers and candidates.[116] Each cost object is the equivalent of a specific service that parties render in the political process.[117]

This is most obvious when we consider the mobilisation of voters in a campaign as a contribution towards political decision-making of a mass public. Recruiting members

---

111 For spending levels see below, chapters III and IV; for causes of rising expenses see below, chapter V.
112 E.g. Canada Elections Act; Commonwealth Electoral Act; Political Parties, Elections and Referendums Act; Pinto-Duschinsky 1981, pp. 138, 140-145, 150, 163-167, 174, 190-193, 208; Stanbury 1991, pp. 61-76.
113 This category included conventions, conferences, committees and ad-hoc (policy) commissions.
114 § 24, 3 *Parteiengesetz* 1984. A revised approach (§ 24, 3 *Parteiengesetz* 1994) is based on a slightly deviating demarcation: spending on current operations, on political activity in general, on campaigns. Whereas the general idea of a third cost object is convincing, the latter demarcation is not.
115 Paltiel 1970, p. 8 – emphasis added.
116 Paltiel 1987, p. 455 and Paltiel 1988b, p. 1625.
117 Cf. Horngren/ Foster 1987, p. 21; Drury 2000, p. 21.

to the political elite, training party activists to perform efficiently or designing public policy are less manifest activities. Although such services are identified as specific cost objects of party activity, we will mainly look into two distinct cost objects, for which data are available: campaign spending and organisation maintenance. In addition, policy development (research and training) will be discussed briefly as a third cost object, however, without comparable data.

This set of three major cost objects is by no means complete. Spending in the nomination process, such as U.S. primaries,[118] their Israeli equivalents and British, Canadian or German constituency contests [119] is not included in the cost objects chosen. Neither is spending on other arenar of intra-party competition, e.g. Canadian leadership contests or the continuously operating intra-party factions (as in Japan, Italy and France). The costs of factional strife, candidate nominations and leadership contests can hardly be estimated as yet. Accepting the current restrictions for scholarly scrutiny we shall limit our presentation to the three cost objects that were suggested by Paltiel with special emphasis on campaign and routine spending, which are still the most important in financial terms.[120]

1. Election campaigns (campaign spending)

All attempts to treat the financial dimension of party government run into problems of demarcation. This is particularly true when the focus is on campaigns. In many countries a distinction must be made between political parties on the one hand, and individual candidates (or elected politicians) on the other. Parties (and politicians) spend money on routine activities, as well as on electoral campaigns. In addition, *individual* (party) *candidates*, of course, spend money on their constituency campaigns.[121] Independent (non-party) candidates for all legislative bodies must be included in the costs of campaigning. Moreover elections can be partisan in nature, but not in name. In some countries the popular election of a president is an important arena for party competition. *"Heads of state"* (no matter whether they hold an executive or a ceremonial office) cause campaign expenses in Austria, Costa Rica, Finland, France, Ireland, Mexico, Poland, the United States and Uruguay.

Due to data limitations, most studies of party financing focus on the national (federal) level. Data for the *supra-national*, e.g. the European Parliament, or the *sub-national* levels (state, provincial, *Land* or *Kanton* as well as municipal governments) are more

---

118 For details see Oldopp 2001, pp. 131-138; for the German equivalent ibid., pp. 138-147.
119 Carty 1991, p. 117; Carty/ Eagles 2005, pp. 56-67.
120 The distinction between "campaign" and "routine" looks promising because a high level of expenses may be caused by tight networks of overstaffed party organisations or by excessive publicity activities during election campaigns. There is no indication that the cost(s) of policy development (research and training) or intra-party competition can be expected to reach a similar level of spending.
121 Yet once elected, individual politicians may also spend money on 'routine' activities. Cf. Blechinger/ Nassmacher 2001, pp. 160/161.

sketchy and incomplete. The (partisan) campaigns run by candidates for mayor of a big city and other local elections rarely fall within the scope of political finance studies.

In most parliamentary systems, the Prime Minister may at any time decide to dissolve parliament.[122] By *calling an election* at an unexpected time, the ruling party aims for an advantage over opposition parties. As a consequence, however, both groups of parties may engage in more or less "permanent" campaigning. Governing parties will try to avoid public dissent towards their controversial policies. Parties in opposition have to stage events in order to gain media recognition. The costs of such PR activities will be covered by party coffers, but not necessarily completely. Government advertising or interest organisations (lobby groups) may partly pick up the tab,[123] thus rendering futile a precise estimate of the costs of democracy.

Despite a global change in campaign routines from spontaneous personal contacts between party leaders and voters to professional TV presentations and more subtle media like direct mail, phone banks or internet web-sites, the situation in various countries is still extremely different. Moreover, campaign and routine expenses are not easy to separate, because the analytical distinction between types of party activities may be somewhat blurred in practice.

Two Commonwealth countries represent opposite styles of campaigning. In India campaign "expenses are very high. It is estimated that the typical candidate spends 15-30 times higher than the limit prescribed by electoral laws."[124] Illegal expenses add to the cost of elections, e.g. parties and candidates spend on intermediaries to buy votes. "In some states, candidates are known to supply free liquor, blankets, silk sarees and stainless steel utensils to woo the voters." Moreover a basically rural and illiterate society with very large constituencies requires "an unavoidable amount of transport and visual publicity expenditure."[125] Such traditional means of electioneering are much in line with 19th century Britain and Canada. Sridharan reports that in the 1999 election serious candidates (winner and runner-up) for the national parliament spent Rs. 7-8 million (= USD 165,000 to 190,000) each.

Australian parties emphasise the most modern approach of media marketing and campaign spots.[126] In 1984 and 1996 almost 50 percent of all campaign spending was allocated to TV and radio advertising (*broadcasting*). The percentage increased slightly during that period.[127] *Publishing* expenses (i.e. the costs of advertising in print media)

---

[122] This does not apply to non-parliamentary democracies (USA, Switzerland, Costa Rica, Uruguay and Poland) as well as to Sweden, the Netherlands, Italy, Germany and Austria.
[123] For details of the demarcation see above in chapter I, sub-section B2 (demarcation of the subject).
[124] Sangita 2005, pp. 178/179. Jain's estimate (2003, p. 103) of 6-8 times the limit is lower but still impressive.
[125] Quotes by Sangita 2005, p. 179 and Sridharan 2006a, p. 329; see also Sridharan 2006b, p. 376.
[126] Cf. Chaples 1994, pp. 32-35; Australian Election Commission 1996, p. 38; Amr/ Lisowski 2001, p. 56.
[127] Australian Election Commission 1984, p. 100.

used to account for another 25 to 30 percent of total expenses. The importance of print media, however, declined during the 1990s as campaign techniques were changing, obviously in favour of direct mailing.

Of all political costs in the U.S. the spending for *public relations* is most important. Ads on television are notoriously expensive.[128] U.S. campaigns clearly indicate a shift among the dominant media for political publicity from newspapers in the 1920s to radio in the 1930s, to television in the early 1950s and to direct marketing since the 1980s.[129] However, the process of substituting old-fashioned modes of voter communication with more modern techniques is time-lagged. That is, campaigners are reluctant to drop tours and meetings, posters and leaflets, newspaper and radio advertising completely, just in case TV spots and direct marketing do not reach all potential voters.[130] Thus campaign budgets may increase even more than new equipment and professional services demand.

Although we are well aware of the difficulties an effort shall be made to present an approximate total of campaign costs for nation-wide campaigns. In all established democracies *election years* are characterised by high levels of party (revenue as well as) expenditure. The term "(extra) election spending" emphasises this pattern. In election years party headquarters spend considerably more, even on "routine operations"[131] in addition to special "campaign" expenses. A distinction between "routine" and "campaign" spending is most traditional and quite familiar in Britain. For many other countries, equivalent amounts have to be calculated to facilitate a comparison. A rough approach to *separate spending on campaigns* from expenses caused by the party apparatus is to identify the amounts of additional spending for the years of the politically most important nation-wide election.[132]

Based on such facts a practical approach can be made to determine the difference between average (that is routine) spending in non-election years and total spending in an election year. This difference can be considered a close estimate of the net amount of (additional) campaign spending for that specific year.[133] Data from this estimate help establish a time series for a few individual countries: Britain, Canada, Germany and the U.S. (see Table 2-8 below).

---

[128] Nonetheless, how much so cannot be gleaned from FEC publications. Research would have to consult all reports, which have been filed by individual committees. As a consequence studies on communication (e.g. Kaid 2004 and Kaid/ Holtz-Bacha 2006) do not mention the costs of communication.

[129] Pollock 1926, pp. 169, 172; Overacker 1941, p. 706; Heard 1960, p. 22; Godwin 1988, pp. 144-154; Alexander/ Corrado 1995, pp. 239-241.

[130] Fisher 1996b, p. 167.

[131] Examples are Britain and Canada (see Tables 2-10, 2-5 and 2-9 in this chapter).

[132] Reif (1983, p. 198) has suggested to call them major elections (*Hauptwahlen*).

[133] In a different approach Krouwel (1999, pp. 88, 89) offers "campaign expenditures as proportion of the total annual party income in Western Europe 1960-1990" by time periods, countries and party families.

The data, which have been estimated in this manner, give a more reliable impression of campaign costs than official reports for campaign spending because they are not influenced by statutory limits and an artificial separation of campaign from pre-campaign spending. As was to be expected total campaign expenses are increasing over time. In Canada and the U.K. cover spending by party headquarters related to the election of the House of Commons, the national parliament. U.S. data add up spending on presidential, congressional and senatorial races (including primaries). For Germany the double-digit figures (since 1979) relate to campaigning for the European Parliament, the three-digit figures cover federal elections (*Bundestag*). Whereas Belgian, U.K. and U.S. data offer a clear-cut trend of increased spending, Canadian and German campaign costs indicate a less consistent pattern.[134]

Table 2-8: Campaign expenses of national campaigns, election years 1971-2000 [135]

Year	million of CAD, DEM, GBP, USD				€ per person entitled to vote				
	Canada	Germany	U.K.	U.S.	Canada	Germany	U.K.	U.S.	Belgium
1971	-	-	-						
1972	4.0	85	-	215	0.21	1.00		1.56	
1973	-	-	-						
1974	3.0	-	2.0	88	0.15		0.08	0.61	0.85
1975	-	-	-						
1976	-	100	-	276		1.19		1.84	
1977	-	-	-						1.75
1978	-	-	-	195				1.24	
1979	9.0	n.a.	2.3		0.39	n.a.	0.08		(0.74)
1980	10.0	100	-	514	0.42	1.16		3.13	
1981	-	-	-						2.10
1982	-	-	-	342				2.02	
1983	-	210	8.0			2.38	0.28		
1984	30.0	40	-	699	1.19	(0.45)		3.99	
1985	-	-	-						
1986	-	-	-	451				2.53	
1987	-	125	14.0			1.38	0.49		
1988	29.0	-	-	958	1.10			5.28	
1989	-	75	-			(0.82)			
1990	-	n.a.	-	446		n.a.		2.41	

---

134 Details are discussed below in chaper V (cost explosion: fact or fantasy?)
135 Per capita data in € amounts; conversion rates: US-$ 1.00 = CAD 1.50 = DEM 2.00 = GBP 0.667 = € 1.00.

| | million of CAD, DEM, GBP, USD | | | | € per person entitled to vote | | | | |
Year	Canada	Germany	U.K.	U.S.	Canada	Germany	U.K.	U.S.	Belgium
1991	-	-	-						
1992	-	-	27.0	1,228			0.94	6.50	
1993	45.0	-	-		1.53				
1994	-	170	-	726		1.41		3.71	
1995	-	-	-						
1996	-	-	-	1,465				7.45	
1997	43.0	-	48.0		1.46		1.62		
1998	-	160		748		1.32		3.65	
1999	-	55				(0.45)			
2000	40.0	-		1,678	1.26			8.31	

Sources: Paltiel 1974, pp. 344-347; Paltiel 1975, pp. 192-197; Chief Electoral Officer 1980, 1981, 1985, 1989, 1993; Elections Canada on-line; *Deutscher Bundestag*, parliamentary papers, no. 10/4104 (neu) to 14/ 5050; Pinto-Duschinsky 1981, pp. 138, 163/164, 190/191; Pinto-Duschinsky 1985, pp. 330-337; Pinto-Duschinsky 1994, pp. 14-20; Neill report 1998, pp. 36-38; Webb 2000, p. 232; Alexander 1999, pp. 15, 19, 23; Nelson 2002, pp. 24, 29; Patterson 2006, p. 71; Dewachter 1987, pp. 327/328.

The earliest estimate for spending in an Israeli election by Gutmann put the total for 1961 at $10.20 per registered voter.[136] In the following elections, per capita campaign spending for parliament (*Knesset*), as declared by the parties and reported by the state auditor (State Comptroller), varied, but eventually increased: $10.76 in 1965, $3.24 in 1969, $4.61 in 1977, $15.49 in 1992, $19.85 in 1996, and $25 in 2001.[137] The most recent figures include the (additional) campaign for prime minister who was directly elected, three times between May 1996 and February 2001.

For Belgium the available information on campaign spending in municipal, national and European elections is a bit dated as it covers a period between 1968 and 1981 only. A project at the University of Louvain established total spending in municipal elections (1976) at BEF 383.4 million (= € 1.51 per voter) and in the election of the European Parliament (1979) at BEF 193.3 million. For the national parliament some time series is possible: BEF 213.0 million (1968), 218.2 million (1974), 440.4 million

---

[136] Gutmann 1963, p. 714. Because of runaway (triple-digit) inflation, amounts are given in US-$ equivalents.
[137] Doron 1986, p. 44; Mendilow 1989, pp. 144/145; Mendilow 1992, p. 110; Hofnung 1996b, p. 142; Mendilow 1996, pp. 336/337, 345; Peretz/ Doron 1997, p. 127; Library of Congress 2001 – I. General Information; Hofnung 2005b, p. 76. Data in ILS have been converted to USD (1 USD = ILS 3.20).

(1977) and 584.1 million (1981).[138] A comparison of the data presented in Table 2-8 reveals that campaign spending per capita is lowest in the U.K. and Canada, and highest in the U.S. In Germany and Belgium this cost object requires intermediate amounts. This indicates that in Germany and other continental European countries the other cost object (routine spending) may be more important.

2. Organisation maintenance

All parties fund routine activities, which involve the maintenance of permanent organisations at the local, regional and national level. This includes the salaries of party staff, the operation of party offices and extra-parliamentary activities with no direct electoral purpose. All of this may, not in the least, serve as a measure of campaign readiness by coaching potential party workers and attending to the flock of party faithful. It is also part of providing forums for general discussion and policy debates among a specific segment of civil society. Treating the party apparatus as a cost object must touch upon coverage in terms of the space, scope and reach of field offices, multilevel organisation, number of full-time staff, continuous and additional activity, the level of salaries (as compared to other branches of the service industry), equipment with modern technology (fax machines, computers).

During the inter-election period party offices (both at the centre and in the field) serve two different clienteles: party activists and citizens. For citizens, local offices are the functional equivalent of factory outlets. They distribute party literature if requested and they arrange contacts within the party network. (Both services are obviously under heavy pressure by the internet.) For party activists, such offices organise meetings, which carry on the routines of a civic organisation, and offer opportunities for political discussion whenever the leadership or local supporters feel that there is a need for it. Quite a variety of meetings (committees, conferences and conventions) creates a web linking party leaders and grass-roots supporters. Usually the cost of voluntary party activity is split between the party and the activist. In general, the party pays for invitations, postage and venue, and the participants cover travel, food and beverages. This renders part of the total cost invisible.[139] Some participants or delegates will even have to pay a registration fee at party conferences in order to cover their costs.[140]

According to conventional wisdom among political scientists, party organisations in Australia and the U.S. exist almost entirely to organise and execute election campaigns. Virtually everything parties do in both countries "is directed at winning the next national, state or local election."[141] However, recent financial reports filed with the AEC indicate that Australian parties spend considerable amounts in years without

---

138 Dewachter 1987, pp. 327/328. –The per capita amount is BEF 34.50 (= € 0.85) for 1968 and 1974. – Data by Gielen (1981, p. 19) are in line with this for 1974, but differ for 1977 (BÉF 48.45 per voter).
139 see below in chapter III, introduction to section A (establishment of data).
140 Carty/ Erickson 1991, p. 112.
141 Chaples 1988a, p. 31; cf. Young/ Tham 2006, p. 111.

a federal or state election.[142] On average AUD 5.00 (about USD 3.10) per voter can be estimated as the consolidated expenses for the current operations of state and federal parties. Of these funds Labor uses about AUD 30 million, the Liberals some AUD 25 million and the National Party no more than AUD 6 million annually for organisation maintenance.

As party organisations are still relatively weak in the United States, there is hardly any permanent staff below the state level.[143] Many autonomous bodies or branches are loosely coupled in a non-hierarchical party structure. Activities are largely centred on elections and routine spending is low. However, data is rare. The best approach towards current expenses on the federal level may be the DNC and RNC budgets in non-presidential years. According to Smith total outlay of the DNC was $ 5 million in 1993 and $ 30 million in 2003. For the RNC the total budget was $ 25 million (1993) and $ 75 million (2003).[144] This does, however, not include the (small) outlay of state parties for routine operations.

Table 2-9: Operating expenses of Canadian parties, non-election years 1985-2005 (in million CAD)

Party/ Year	P.C. (CPC)	Liberals	N.D.P.	B.Q.	Reform Party	Total	CAD per Voter
1985	9.9	7.3	6.3	-	-	23.5	1.40
1986	11.5	9.6	7.0	-	-	28.1	1.67
1987	11.5	7.6	6.8	-	-	25.9	1.54
1989	10.7	5.5	7.7	-	-	23.9	1.36
1990	8.8	9.9	8.1	-	1.7	31.0	1.76
1991	9.6	4.8	8.4	-	4.2	27.0	1.53
1992	9.3	4.6	8.4	-	4.7	27.0	1.53
1994	2.9	5.7	7.9	1.2	2.9	20.6	1.04
1995	3.6	5.0	10.0	2.0	3.6	24.2	1.22
1996	4.6	7.4	9.4	1.2	4.6	27.2	1.37
1998	3.9	7.1	9.2	0.6	3.9	24.7	1.25
1999	4.3	5.8	9.5	1.0	4.3	24.9	1.26
2001	3.1	4.6	3.7	0.9	4.2	16.5	0.78
2002	3.0	3.9	3.2	0.9	3.6	14.6	0.66
2003	4.1	5.7	6.4	1.1	3.7	21.0	0.94
2005	21.1	12.9	14.5	1.9	(see CPC)	50.4	2.23

Sources: Stanbury 1991, pp. 462, 477, 493; Contributions and Expenses of Registered Political Parties and Candidates (Elections Canada) 1993, pp. 16-18; www.elections.ca (Registered Parties Annual Reports).

---

142 www.aec.gov.au/arwSummaryReturns (Summary of All Party Returns for 1/7/98 to 30/6/06).
143 Hrebenar et al. 1999, p. 56; Katz/ Kolodny 1994, pp. 25, 43, 45; Kolodny/ Dryre 1998, p. 276.
144 Smith 2005, p. 108, chart 3.15.

Although campaign activities paid for by the party headquarters add up to impressive figures, there is a substantial amount of fixed costs for permanent party organisations, even in Anglo-Saxon countries like Britain and Canada. In the latter country electoral fortunes and financial outlays of individual parties have changed massively since 1974. However, a general pattern prevails. During the election cycle, Canadian parties increase their routine spending step-by-step. The spending peak is reached in the election year when parties and candidates spend at least 60 percent of their election cycle total.[145]

Table 2-10: Annual routine spending by British national party headquarters, non-election years only (in million £; 1952-91 annual averages)

Year/Party	Conservatives*	Labour	Liberal (Dem)	Total million £	£ per voter
1952-54	0.56	0.18	0.02	0.76	0.02
1956-58	0.74	0.28	0.02	1.04	0.03
1960-63	0.89	0.41	0.07	1.37	0.04
1967-69	1.16	0.57	0.12	1.85	0.05
1971-73	1.62	0.80	0.09	2.51	0.06
1975-78	2.90	1.73	0.12	4.64	0.11
1980-82	4.8	3.6	1.0	9.4	0.23
1984-86	6.2	5.1	1.4	12.7	0.30
1988-91	16.0	7.7	1.4	25.1	0.58
1993	8.4	9.9	0.8	19.1	0.43
1994	7.0	9.1	0.9	17.0	0.39
1995	7.2	11.9	1.1	20.2	0.46
1996	7.9	15.5	1.3	24.7	0.55

* For the Conservative Party the years should read: 1993= 1992-93, etc. (1997= 1996-97).
Sources: Pinto-Duschinsky 1981, pp. 138, 163/164, 190; Pinto-Duschinsky 1985, pp. 330, 333, 336, 337; Pinto-Duschinsky 1994, pp. 14, 17, 18, 20; Butler/ Butler 1994, p. 133; Webb 2000, p. 232; Fisher 1996b, pp. 164, 165; Neill report 1998, pp. 36-38; Fisher 1999, p. 523. Figures given in constant prices by Houghton report 1976, p. 92, are basically in line with these data.

During the non-election years, federal parties spend considerably on routine operations. From 1985 to 1989 the three major parties at the time (Liberals, P.C. and N.D.P.) spent a grand total of CAD 24 to 28 million, biased in favour of the P.C., on their operating expenses. From 1994 to 1999 the five major parties (active since 1993) spent an aggregate total of CAD 21 to 27 million, this time split in favour of N.D.P. and Liberals (Table 2-9). The average total of CAD 25 million, or CAD 1.20 (approximately

---

145 Smith 2005, p. 105, chart 3.13.

USD 0.80) per eligible voter, for the national (federal) party headquarters during the late 1990s is quite impressive.[146]

Information from the late 1960s demonstrates that the grand total for the federal offices of the four national parties (including Social Credit at the time) was less than CAD 1 million.[147] For the campaign and candidate-oriented political culture in Canada, data for the 1980s to 2000s indicate quite a change since the 1960s when campaign spending used to be dominant.

Routine spending by the three major British parties at the national level (central offices) is also considerable (Table 2-10). About 80 percent of Conservative Central Office spending is used for routine purposes.[148] Because of different accounting periods, direct comparisons between parties and between years should be made with some caution. Annual totals of GBP 17 to 25 million give the impression of permanent party apparatuses rather than temporary campaign machines. At least the annual average of GBP 0.52 (about USD 0.78) per voter on the permanent register for the 1990s indicates a lot of organisational routine and continuity, even if the balance between the centre and the field may be shifting.

Although British parties use much of their routine spending [149] to pay the salaries of central office staff, Conservative Central Office now pays for local agents, who used to be employed by constituency parties. In 1970 central offices employed a staff of 95 (Conservatives), 50 (Labour) and 16 (Liberals).[150] At that time the Conservatives had 399 agents in the constituencies. The number of Labour agents who were employed at the constituency level decreased from 296 in 1951 to 141 in 1970 and to about 68 or 95 around 1990.[151] Within each two decades the total number of agents was halved twice. We have no information how „New Labour" has dealt with that situation. However, it may be interesting to note that total spending at Labour headquarters has increased massively.

For Italian parties it is impossible "to determine the amount of money devoted to party activity." As early as 1979 a foreign observer advised that "the published financial accounts must be treated quizzically".[152] Routine expenses of party headquarters as reported officially by the national parties totalled an average of some ITL 275 billion annually during the late 1980s. After the break-up of the old party system annual routine spending was estimated at ITL 160 billion for a major party and at ITL 65 billion

---

146 The consolidated operating expenses of the five major national parties cover more than 90 percent, probably more than 95 percent of total routine spending by all Canadian (federal) parties.
147 Paltiel 1970a, pp. 39, 42, 57, 72.
148 Fisher 1996b, p. 163.
149 This is total spending minus campaign spending; see below in this chapter, section A3 (cost objects).
150 Rose 1976, p. 169.
151 Butler/ Pinto-Duschinsky 1971, pp. 269-271; Butler/ Kavanagh 1988, p. 228; Webb 1992, p. 849.
152 Quotes by Bardi/ Morlino 1994, p. 248 and Paltiel 1979b, p. 35.

for a medium sized party. These amounts add up to a total of ITL 450 to 550 billion.[153] Per eligible voter party routine expenses at the national level (party headquarters) may be around ITL 10,000 (roughly USD 4.00).

In financial terms, Spanish parties focus primarily on the routine activities of the extra-parliamentary party rather than on campaign spending. The evidence available should also be interpreted with caution. Between 1988 and 1992, the national parties established a quite extensive and costly extra-parliamentary structure, maintaining local offices with paid staff throughout Spain. A per voter average of about ESP 500 (roughly USD 4.00) for the national headquarters [154] indicates another similarity with Italy. Overall, Italian and Spanish parties spend much more money on their organisation than on campaigns.

Between 1973 and 1992, Mendilow assumes a relative decline of current expenses in Israel, as compared to the escalation of campaign spending. Between 1973 and 1984, existing operations of parties amounted to USD 2.80 and USD 7.00 million (i.e. USD 1.20 and USD 2.70 per registered voter). If we use data presented by Mendilow and Arian to calculate per capita spending, the routine operations of the national party headquarters cost USD 8.70 per eligible voter during the early 1990s and USD 7.25 during the late 1990s, an overall average of USD 8.00 for the 1990s.[155]

Routine spending (including some campaigns for state and municipal elections) of all German parties in a non-election year (i.e. a year without a nation-wide election) during the 1990s amounted to about DEM 650 million, i.e. DEM 10.74 (USD 5.37) per registered voter and year. This does, however, cover all levels of German parties, federal, state and local, each of which is responsible for about one third of the total.[156] At the federal level, the major parties spending on staff and the party apparatus at current prices increased during the 1980s and 1990s, whereas in real terms (i.e. deflated by the CPI) there has been a marked decline.[157]

Detailed information on the expenditures of parties in Switzerland is rare. An estimate for the 1980s offers an amount of CHF 21 million (USD 13 million) for all parties in an average year and at all levels. A more recent estimate presented a total budget of more than CHF 10 million for current operations of federal, no less than CHF 17 million for state and at least CHF 12 million for local parties in the 1990s.[158] On average this means that CHF 2.13 (USD 1.33) per eligible voter was spent federally, CHF 3.62 (USD 2.26) at the state level and CHF 2.55 (USD 1.60) locally.

In general routine spending includes organisational maintenance, which is the minimum amount needed to run a political party during non-election periods. The exam-

---

153 Bardi/ Morlino 1992, pp. 604-608; Melchionda 1997, pp. 206, 251.
154 Heywood 1996, p. 126; van Biezen 2000, p. 338.
155 Data from Mendilow 1989, p. 143; Mendilow 1996, p. 332; Arian 1998, p. 155; see also Kalchheim/ Rosevitch 1992, p. 227; exchange rates from Mahler 1990, p. 49.
156 For more precise details see above in this chapter, sub-section A 1 a (cost centres).
157 Cordes 2001, pp. 153, 159.
158 Weigelt 1988, p. 36; Ladner/ Brändle 1999, pp. 10-12.

ples just presented demonstrate that additional amounts are frequently spent on current operations, which may not be essential but useful for a party operating under uncertainty in a competitive environment. Such expenses may inseparably include spending on a third cost object, policy development, which is desirable but cannot be established independently.

3. *Policy development (research and training)*

Among the services, which are provided for the party leadership, public opinion polls (surveys), research on public policy issues, training and recruitment of party workers (and candidates) tend to be the most important.[159] The costs of current operations include expenses dedicated to research, education and training. Unfortunately only examples can be given as an illustration.[160] Due to specific rules for public subsidies. Dutch parties have traditionally made transfer payments to affiliated foundations, which carry out research or training activities on behalf of their parent party. In Austria heavily subsidised "party academies" serve as training systems for the parties represented in the national parliament.[161] Over decades the "political foundations" in Germany have performed similar functions. Nowadays most of their activities are geared towards the general public or to foreign aid ("democracy building").[162]

Organisations competing for support among a democratic mass public have to consider, which segments they want to address, which policies will best serve their purpose of winning votes, and which personalities shall be the standard bearers. Intra-party competition for leadership positions is the bread-and-butter of everyday politics. The development of policies may require some medium-range preparation and consulting apart from day-to-day operations. Scholarly analysis can prepare options; working groups will discuss and pre-select them. Finally, the party leadership and the party convention adopt such policies before they become part of the party programme or platform.

However, the process may also be reversed. Shortly before an upcoming election the party leaders will set out general policy intentions, propagate them and gather support. Afterwards consultations have to hammer out details before legislation can initiate the necessary steps of implementation. This procedure is the more traditional and it will harness either the public administration or the caucus bureaucracy [163] with research on and development of policy.

If a party leadership wants to re-position their party in the policy arena in order to attract additional voters, some sort of advisory body composed of researchers, party bureaucrats and politicians needs time and funds to prepare new concepts. If the party

---

159 Paltiel 1987, p. 455 and Paltiel 1988b, p. 1625.
160 For some details see above in this chapter, sub-section A 3 b (party institutes).
161 For details see Lucardie/ Voerman 2001, pp. 325-333; Sickinger 2001, pp. 344-347.
162 For details see Pinto-Duschinsky 1991b.
163 See above in this chapter, sub-section A4 (parliamentary party groups).

operates a "think tank" (party institute),[164] much of the work may be completed there. If not, staff employed by a ministry or the parliamentary party may be involved, occasionally some of the draft documents can even be produced by research institutes on a contract basis. Whichever strategy is applied some funds will be needed to pay for working papers, full-time staff and frequent meetings at locations shielded from current operations and media scrutiny. All of this adds up to the cost of policy development, an infrequent and mostly invisible cost object.

U.K. legislation has recently used this function to legitimise a small public subsidy distributed among all serious contenders (large or small) of British politics.[165] Perhaps, by tacit understanding among legislators, the British term "policy development" stands for more short-term tasks, like speech-writing, drafting policy statements, media consultancy and voter research (by sample surveys or focus groups). All of this would bring the new cost object quite close to Paltiel's third purpose, the provision of services to the party leadership.[166]

The highly selective examples given of very scattered information recommend a precise delineation for the scope of this study: The party penumbra will be mostly neglected (except for the service oriented party institutes in Austria and the Netherlands). The financial dimension of party factions and party enterprises will not be covered in full.[167] The parliamentary party groups will generally be treated as parts of the national parliaments, regional and local assemblies despite their role as political "fiefdoms" within their party. Most chapters of this study are restricted to the analysis of the formal party organisation. However, all estimates of the costs of democracy will include spending by candidates as well.

After completing this detailed inquiry, it is appropriate to sum up the items presented on cost centres, types of cost and cost objects of party activity:

- The concept of *political party* covers many facets of political competition. This unifying concept is useful in identifying the manifold orbit of political competitors. However, the complete costs of political competition cannot be given in full or in detail for any one party or democracy.
- The *categories of cost accounting* (cost objects, cost centres, types of cost) facilitate the presentation of various dimensions of political expenses. These three systematic approaches to measure the costs of democracy will help to aggregate total expenditure on party politics in a cross-national comparison. In order to gather such information spending by all cost centres involved (parties and candidates) must be added up.

---

164 Cf. Houghton report 1976, pp. 19-21, 325/326, 328-330 and Neill report 1998, p. 93.
165 See Ewing 2007, pp. 190-191. Cf. below in chapter VIII, sub-sections D1b (access) and D2c (distribution).
166 see above in this chapter, at the beginning of section C (cost objects).
167 For some details see above in this chapter, sub-section A2 (groups of party activists) and below in chapter VII, section D (returns on investment).

- Although most of these (a variety of campaigns, a party organisation with national headquarters and local chapters, voluntary party workers and paid staff, expenses for PR and communication) are *common to all democracies*, detailed features are quite specific and data are rather patchy.
- The *approach by cost centres* is more promising than any attempt to aggregate types of cost (e.g. for staff, offices, communication and publicity) or cost objects, especially the variety of election campaigns and the different patterns of organisation maintenance. Nevertheless all three approaches help to assess details of political spending and to pursue comparative research of its levels, trends and causes.

CHAPTER THREE

Costs of 18 Party Democracies [1]

The supposition that a particular country is the "most expensive political system on earth"[2] appears to be a traditional paradigm for the study of money in politics.[3] Many approaches seem to be driven by the assumption that political parties spend too much. What are the necessary costs of adequate party activity? What are the adequate costs of necessary party activities?[4] As these questions contain normative terms (that is, "adequate", "necessary"), they cannot be answered by empirical research. There "are no objective criteria, by which to measure whether 'too much' is spent on political campaigns"[5] and party organisations.

For a scholarly effort it is more appropriate to gather knowledge about the factual situation. Parties and candidates spend the amount that individuals [6] are willing to contribute, and which politicians consider effective.[7] Empirical findings may help answer pertinent questions. For example, is party activity in any one country more expensive now than it used to be in the same country? Is it more expensive in this country than it is in any other (comparable, similar) democracy in the world? Whereas the former question demands time series data,[8] the latter can be answered by using data relating to a specific point in time. This kind of comparison has been tried by three U.S. scholars: Heard (1960), Heidenheimer (1963/1970) and Penniman (1984). The data, which can be reported from the literature (see Table 3-1 below), support three observations: First, levels of political spending spread considerably among the democracies. Second, scholars agree about the rank of Israel (top) and Britain (bottom). Third, spending levels in Germany and the U.S. are controversial among scholars.

---

1   Due to lack of data Belgium (see Weekers/ Maddens 2007), Costa Rica (see Casas-Zamora 2005a, p. 158), Finland (see Wiberg 1991c, p. 57), India (see Sridharan 2006b, pp. 325-327), New Zealand (see Miller 2005, p. 100), Norway (see Svasand 1991) and Uruguay (see Casas-Zamora 2005a, p. 158), i.e. a total of 7 democracies, are not covered in this chapter.
2   Bouissou 1997, p.133 (on contemporary Japan).
3   Pollock 1926, pp. 174, 177; Overacker 1932, p. 81; Heard 1960, p. 371 (reporting on the pre-1960 U.S.).
4   This kind of phrasing – although limited to campaign expenses – has been introduced by the German supreme court (BVerfGE, vol. 20, 1966, p. 116).
5   Overacker 1941, p. 727.
6   For general application this term has to include party members, political donors, taxpayers and voters.
7   Smith 2001, p. 45.
8   For this approach see below chapter V (cost explosion).

Pursuing the same line of research this chapter will aggregate available data, supplement it by informed estimates and transform both to a common format. This comparison should enable us to answer the following questions:

- Does the considerable spread of political spending totals that was established by Heard and Heidenheimer for a few countries in the mid-20th century hold for a larger number of democracies at the end of the century?
- If so, which democracies are the most excessive spenders, which parties compete on the most moderate terms, and which countries represent an intermediate level of the costs of democracy?

First, this task raises a question of methodology. How can levels of spending for organisation maintenance (party routine) and election campaigns be measured and compared? Because party activity differs among the democracies, neither an individual country nor a specific activity can serve as a "natural" point of reference. Although all parties in all democracies are involved in campaigning, this activity may be of different importance to them as well as for their political system. Moreover there is no such thing as a "natural" campaign period of any set interval of time. Therefore, various steps have to be taken to facilitate a comparison.

Table 3-1: Costs of party competition in comparative perspective, late 1950s to early 1980s

Country	1960 a)	1963 b)	1984 c)	1986 d)	Rank order			
	Amount	Index	Amount	Amount	1960	1963	1984	1986
(1)	(2)	(3)	(4)	(5)	(6)	(7)	(8)	(9)
Venezuela	-	-	$ 26.35	-	-	-	-	-
Israel	$ 5.00+	20.50	$ 4.34	-	1.	1.	1.	-
Philippines	-	16.00	-	-	-	-	-	-
Italy	$ 0.50	4.50	-	-	3.	2.	-	-
Ireland	-	-	$ 3.93	-	-	-	2.	-
Japan	-	1.36	-	-	-	3.	-	-
India	-	1.25	-	-	-	-	-	-
USA	$ 0.90	1.12	$ 3.25	DEM 8	2.	4.	3.	5.
Germany	$ 0.25	0.95	$ 3.20	DEM 35	4.	5.	4.	1.
Sweden	-	-	-	DEM 24	-	-	-	2.
Canada	-	-	$ 1.43	DEM 14	-	-	5.	3.
Netherlands	-	-	-	DEM 9	-	-	-	4.
Britain (UK)	$ 0.16+	0.64	$ 0.50	DEM 6	5.	6.	6.	6.
Australia	-	0.45	-	-	-	7.	-	-

Sources: a) Heard 1960, pp. 373-375 (amounts in US-$);
          b) Heidenheimer 1963, pp. 798/799.; Heidenheimer 1970b, pp. 11-13;
          c) Penniman 1984, pp. 52-53 (amounts in US-$);
          d) Nassmacher 1986, p. 95 (amounts in DEM).
Legend: Countries in *Italics* are not in the current sample.

A) Establishment of data for spending totals

Step one for any comparative effort is to establish "the costs of democracy" (Heard), i.e. the total amounts of political *spending for routine and campaign purposes by parties and candidates* at all tiers of various political systems. In some countries this may almost exclusively be campaign expenses, in others the emphasis is on the routine operation of party apparatuses. This does not necessarily mean party headquarters alone, but also field organisations covering the whole country. "A study of ... political spending must ... take into account the total cost of campaigning [and party organisation] at all levels [of the political system] and not just the national one."[9] Reasonable comparisons have to include cost objects, routine and campaign spending, as well as all cost centres, be they party organisation, party penumbra or party caucus. Because this comprehensive approach would definitely abort the whole exercise,[10] we will limit our effort to parties and candidates. Data for the penumbra, parliamentary caucuses and all tiers of the party organisation are only partly available. Thus various elements of the complete picture will depend on some kind of carefully designed scholarly guesswork.[11]

Given the circumstances of inquiry, the results will systematically underestimate the actual amount of political spending. This is due to the fact that parties are voluntary organisations for political purposes and some local spending will not flow from party coffers. In everyday life, local party workers cover much of their own travel expenses, stationery, telephone charges and some postage from personal funds. A considerable amount of such spending will never show up in any (local or consolidated) party account and will thus be neglected as an in-kind-contribution by the democratic avantgarde, the voluntary army of local party workers.[12]

The total costs of party politics in individual democracies have to be measured on a country by country basis. In the early 1980s a "distinguished French political scientist gave up" covering the subject even for his own country because there was "scant hope of ascertaining the truth." That scholar felt that the task, possibly at the time, was "beyond the capacity of a single researcher."[13] Standing on the shoulders of so many scholars of political finance, this author feels that it can and should be done now. At this stage of inquiry it seems obvious that bigger countries will need to spend larger amounts of political funds than smaller ones. Thus we shall proceed by size of the democracies, measured by the number of eligible citizens.[14]

---

9   Pinto-Duschinsky 2002, p. 84.
10 This is all the more true where new trends in government communication and issue advocacy by interest groups (for details see Lisowski 2006, pp. 80-112) add to the costs of democratic politics.
11 For one federal system, the Canadian, this rather simple process already took a separate article. Nassmacher 1989b, pp. 217-243.
12 Carmen Theis, Ph.D. candidate and political activist, who has spent a lot of her time and money to keep democracy in Germany going, offers some examples. Theis 2007, pp. 72-77.
13 All three quotes taken from: Penniman 1984, p. 52.
14 For the data see below in this chapter, table 3-2. - The potential impact of size on the spending level will be discussed below in chapter IV, sub-section A 2 (economies of scale).

1. Costs of the biggest democracies: USA, Japan, Germany, Mexico

a) Because political finance in the **United States** is dominated by campaign expenditures, inter-election spending on routine activities by party organisations, which takes the lead in many other Western democracies, plays only a minor role in the most advanced democracy.[15] Although total spending on congressional elections is less than half of the amount Americans spend on potato chips each year, the U.S. may still "spend less on political activity than several other [yet unnamed] democracies, including some that are considerably poorer."[16]

The wealth of data collected and published by the FEC poses more problems than it helps to solve as far as comparative research is concerned. No foreign observer will learn much from figures given for PAC spending, soft money, issue advocacy or independent expenditures. Such categories, which are applied even in scholarly research, relate solely to the legal situation in one specific country. They do not assist anyone who tries to analyse political spending in any kind of cross-national approach. Each U.S. election entails spending on the *registration* and identification of voters, recruitment of volunteers and professionals, organisational set up, fundraising activities and *get-out-the-vote* drives.

According to an estimate by Herbert Alexander for the Citizens' Research Foundation, numerous political actors on national, state and local levels and competing organisations spent a total of $4.2 billion during the 1995/1996 election cycle. This includes spending on the highly competitive recruitment process (nomination via primaries and conventions). Spending on campaigns for Congress (House and Senate) has been estimated at $765 million for 1996. The cost of electing a president in 1996 was about $700 million. The extra cost for state election campaigns (all state offices including governors and state legislatures) was estimated at $650 million, the cost of local elections was $425 million. The total amount spent by parties and candidates for all offices was $ 3.45 billion in 1995-96.[17] For the 1997/1998 non-presidential cycle, about $ 2.6 billion have to be added. Political spending during a four-year election cycle may well add up to $6 billion.

Bradley Smith, a stimulating critic of U.S. political finance regulation and a member/chairman of the FEC, estimates the total "direct campaign spending for all local, state, and federal elections" for the 1997/1998 election cycle at $1.5 to $2.0 billion and possibly at $3.0 billion for the 1999/2000 cycle (including a presidential election).[18] For a four-year-period these estimates amount to more than USD 4.5 and less than USD 6.0 billion.

---

15   The same applies to the small presidential democracies of Costa Rica and Uruguay (Casas-Zamora 2002, p. 16; Casas-Zamora 2005a, p. 11). Due to lack of comprehensive data both cannot be included in this chapter.
16   Smith 2001, p. 42.
17   Alexander 1999, pp. 13, 15, 17, 23.
18   Smith 2001, p. 41.

b) The overall amount of money spent for party democracy in **Japan** includes spending by party organisations, by intra-party factions (*habatsu*) and by individual candidates and active politicians as well as by their personal support groups (*kôenkai*) and local party chapters (*shibu*). Despite the two week campaign time most of the money that is needed for political purposes in Japan is spent by MPs in their constituencies. MPs (and candidates) spend more than half of their total expenses for the whole election cycle (on average about JPY 130 million each) during the election year and less than one fifth in each of the non-election years. However, campaign and routine spending by most Japanese parties is more evenly split between election and non-election years.[19] The election cycle is no more than four years for the House of Representatives and six years for the House of Councillors, where half of the seats are up for re-election every three years. Despite such a precise framework, no practical distribution of costs between parties and politicians, campaign and routine purposes can be elaborated for Japan; not even a guess seems appropriate. Although reporting requirements have become more rigid in recent years, considerable problems remain. Slush funds expended by national parties, intra-party factions (especially of the LDP, *Jimintô*), and local bosses still require a careful interpretation of official information.

Blechinger's estimates for the years from 1991 to 1999 range between JPY 152 billion and 186 billion.[20] These figures are based on the political finance reports submitted to the Ministry of Home Affairs by political organisations active at the national level. There is still no overall information concerning the amount spent at the national and the local level. Thus the data available does not represent the total amount of money circulating in Japanese politics and may result in too conservative an approximation for party spending. Based on different calculations Bouissou presents a guesstimate of JPY 900 billion as an annual average spent on party politics around 1990.[21] A more reasonable approach is to use Blechinger's data as minimum and Bouissou's data as maximum estimate. However, some intermediate data are available from an article by Köllner based on reports in *Asahi Shimbun*.[22] This newspaper puts total expenses between 1994 and 1998 at JPY 308 to 345 billion. If we average all three estimates (Blechinger's JPY 170 billion, Köllner's JPY 330 billion and Bouissou's JPY 900 billion per year) the aggregate annual spending on Japanese politics may well have been around JPY 465 billion during the late 1990s.[23]

c) The total amount of annual expenses by all parties in **Germany** is now available for the years from 1984 to 2005. These (official, but pretty reliable) data include routine

---

19 Blechinger 1998, p. 153; Kerde 1998, p.184.
20 Blechinger/ Nassmacher 2001, p. 158.
21 Bouissou 1997, pp.133/134. Due to a long recession period there is no need to adjust this for inflation.
22 Köllner 2000, p.152.
23 The official data reported by Ferdinand (1998, p. 196) supports this estimate because a 30 per cent supplement (JPY 465 billion compared to JPY 357 billion) for unreported expenses seems rather moderate. For consequences of the difference on Japan's international ranking see below in this chapter, Table 3-4.

and campaign spending by all parties at all levels (national, regional and local) of the (extra-parliamentary) *party organisation*. The aggregate annual spending ranged between DEM 630 and DEM 700 million from 1995 to 1997 (non-election years), and totalled about DEM 900 million for the (European) election year 1999 and some DEM 1 billion for the (federal) election year 1998.[24] The total amount of spending by all party organisations (big and small) during the 1995/1999 election cycle adds up to DEM 3.9 billion.[25]

The almost perfect financial transparency of party organisations in Germany is considerably off-set by the obscured demarcation line between parties and their penumbra.[26] Thus an effort to establish the costs of party democracy (and the part of the bill, which is picked up by the taxpayer) has to rely on informed estimates of additional expenses. Party youth organisations and parliamentary caucuses are traditionally supported from state funds. Federal MPs, M.E.P.s and state legislators are granted an allowance for the employment of clerical staff and research assistants. In 1967 a party subsidy for civic education, i.e. the training of volunteers for the democratic process, was transferred to separate institutions, which have acquired a wider range of responsibilities. The most important common feature of all these items is that public funds are used for partisan purposes under a pretext, which is neither completely false nor adequately restricted. Thus a broad area of political finance has developed in the shade.[27]

Funding of party youth organisations is the easiest to estimate. The federation, all state budgets and a wide range of municipal governments provide public funds, which are distributed among the established parties' youth organisations. Based on a separate note in the parties' annual reports,[28] the total amount of such subsidies from 1995 to 1999 can be estimated at DEM 43 million. Federal budget data would suggest a total of roughly DEM 100 million for the whole cycle.

Party caucuses operate in a dual context; parliament on the one hand, party on the other.[29] Any borderline between party and parliamentary activity will be arbitrarily drawn. However, when caucuses claim publicity of their own and develop policy proposals for their parties or provide personal assistance to leading politicians, they perform tra-

---

24 *Deutscher Bundestag*, parliamentary papers, no. 14/7979, pp. 71, 91.
25 Because election cycles for the European parliament and many state legislatures cover five years, it is advisable to calculate a total amount of party spending for the years 1995 to 1999 (which include all major elections) and then to compute an annual average.
26 When the Constitutional Court banned public funding of party activity but allowed public "reimbursement" of campaign spending (BVerfGE, vol. 20, 1966, pp. 114/115), it triggered off a search for tricks, which help to avoid a clear-cut breach of constitutional law.
27 Critics simply subsume that all such funds are party financing by the public purse. Defenders argue (equally simply) that it all may be partisan, but that it is definitely not party political in a legal perspective.
28 *Deutscher Bundestag*, parliamentary papers, no. 13/6472, 13/8923, 14/246, 14/ 5050, 14/ 2508.
29 See above in chapter II, sub-section A4 (parliamentary party groups).

ditional party functions. In order to prepare a rather conservative estimate, we will ascribe less than one third of all staff expenses (15 to 25 percent, as compared to a total of 76.3 percent) and all expenses for conferences, meetings and publicity (10 percent) to party operations. This adds up to 25 to 35 percent of the caucus subsidy. For the years from 1995 to 1999 the federal grant totalled DEM 550.8 million.[30] The state budgets provided some additional DEM 690 million.[31] Municipal subsidies are harder to establish.[32] Depending on the size of the city, amounts ranging from DEM 0.5 to 8.0 million were allocated to council caucuses in some 430 cities during the 1995/1999 election cycle. The total outlay was approximately DEM 500 million; 30 to 50 percent of this may have been devoted to party (more likely than council) work. The party related share of federal, state and municipal caucus subsidies adds about DEM 460 to 684 million to party spending in Germany.

Although a specific group of entities called *politische Stiftungen* carry out work that is of benefit to their parent parties, it is neither possible nor "practicable to establish clear distinctions between some of the operations of the parties and of the party foundations ....[or]... an accurate breakdown of spending for domestic and for foreign purposes."[33] Nevertheless, a generous approach would consider all funds used for "research" (i.e. 4 to 8 percent of the annual budget) plus about half of the costs for adult education (which totals 13 to 22 percent of annual spending) to be related to party competition. During the 1990s with the *Friedrich Ebert Stiftung*, the SPD foundation, education and research represented about half of the annual block grant (*Globalzuschuss*) from the federal government.[34] An approximation would allow for different policies among the *Stiftungen* and thus consider a range of one third to two thirds of the block grant to be a fair equivalent of the foundations' outlay for German party politics. During the 1995/1999 election cycle block grants added up to DEM 936 million. Thus, DEM 312 to 624 million has to be included in the total costs of party activity.

Among the privileges of office that are available to parliamentary incumbents, there is an employment allowance for assistants (secretarial, clerical, and research). During the 1995/ 1999 election cycle the allowance from the federal budget totalled DEM 802.2 million.[35] Some DEM 1,200 million state and DEM 120 million EU funds have to be added to the federal grant. This brings the total employment allowances to DEM 2.12 billion. Provided that on average legislators split their allowance about equally be-

---

30 *Bundeshaushaltsplan* (Federal Budget) 1997 respectively 1999; *Deutscher Bundestag*, parliamentary papers, no. 13/5473, 13/8456, 13/11264, 14/1391, 14/4040.
31 Computed in accordance with von Arnim 1996, p. 142.
32 Cf. Kempf 1989, p. 115.
33 Pinto-Duschinsky 1991b, p. 190. For details see above in chapter II, sub-section A2d (party institutes).
34 Friedrich Ebert Stiftung, Jahresbericht 1998, p. 82; Jahresbericht 1999, p. 60; Jahresbericht 2000, p. 68. Figures given there are roughly compatible with Pinto-Duschinsky 1991b, pp. 194, 214/215. However, during the late 1980s the block grant was less important (a quarter of total spending) than during the late 1990s (35 per cent of the annual budget).
35 Data for both grants from *Bundeshaushaltsplan* (Federal Budget) 1997 resp. 1999, *Einzelplan* (title) 0602.

tween parliamentary work and constituency service half of the money is spent locally.[36] Depending on how much the local party is in need assistants of parliamentary incumbents may devote between 40 and 60 percent of their time to party business. Thus, of the total allowance 20 to 30 percent is a conservative estimate that takes into account the actual division of labour between parliamentary work, constituency service and party activity. DEM 420 to 635 million have to be added to the party spending total as a result of this approximation.

In general, campaign costs are covered by the party and included in its financial report. However, under the Mixed Member Proportional (MMP) electoral system individual candidates can run their own constituency campaigns. 1,000 to 1,500 serious contenders for 669 federal seats may have spent about DEM 24,000 each,[37] and 3,000 to 4,500 contenders for 1,943 seats in all state legislatures about DEM 16,000. Both amounts add up to a range of DEM 72 to 108 million for extra campaign spending by candidates in state and federal elections.

Campaigns for municipal councils are party affairs, as well as most of the popularly elected officers (mayors in townships and cities and county administrators). However, candidates for *Bürgermeister* and *Landrat* contest a salaried office and thus are made to pay for part of their campaign costs by the nominating and supporting party. This extra spending has to be estimated. Although mayoral campaigns have been researched for decades, information on campaign costs and their split between nominating party, individual or corporate donors or sponsors and the candidate's personal purse is scarce. Two publications provide starting points. In a survey in the state of North-Rhine Westphalia, extra donations are a source of about half of the candidates, those right of centre (CDU, FDP) more frequently than those left of centre (SPD, *Grüne*). Nine out of ten candidates for mayor are assigned a minimum amount from their own funds.[38] We apply an average of DEM 20,000 for two serious contenders in a total of 260 cities (with more than 50,000 inhabitants) and some 300 counties plus an amount of DEM 10,000 for 500 smaller cities. This would add DEM 32 million of extra spending on the popular election of municipal officers to the total costs of party politics.

A study of mayoral contests in the state of *Baden-Württemberg* revealed that campaign costs per citizen decline with size. Based on this study, we can assume that on average mayoral campaigns by two serious contenders in townships of less than 5,000 inhabitants cost DEM 4.00 per citizen. For municipalities in the range of 5,000 to 50,000 we estimate DEM 3.00 in per capita spending and for cities over 50,000, DEM 2.00 per

---

36 By 1991 M.Ps. employed a total of 4,008 assistants. More than 60 percent of them regularly worked in the constituency office (Schindler 1994, pp. 1282/1283.) and thus close to the local party organisation, for which they may double as local agents (for some details see Roland Nelles: Treue Helfer, in: *Der Spiegel* (news magazine), no. 13/2007, p. 46).
37 For the 1987 election, 112 respondents to a mail questionnaire reported an average of DEM 16,000 for their additional campaign costs. Landfried 1994a, pp. 121-125. For details see Oldopp 2001, pp. 281, 363-368.
38 Gehne/ Holtkamp 2002, pp. 98, 100, 112, 298.

voter.[39] Because campaigns in big cities are totally partisan affairs, our estimate is based on the assumption that in small towns and villages a candidate contributes half, in big towns and small cities about one third and in larger cities no more than a fifth of the total campaign outlay. This adds up to DEM 28 million for small municipalities, DEM 36 million for medium sized and DEM 11 million for cities with more than 50,000 inhabitants. The DEM 75 million total has to be complemented by DEM 12 million for 300 counties. Total support from candidates' pockets to campaigns for popularly elected municipal offices would be in the range of DEM 32 to 87 million.

All of these additional items of spending on party activity (mostly paid for by public funds) add up to a range from DEM 1.34 to 2.24 billion. When these amounts are combined with the total outlay for party organisations proper, it brings the total costs of party democracy in Germany to a range of DEM 5.24 to 6.14 billion for the 1995/1999 election cycle.

d) A political transition, which began in 1987 and was completed in 2000 when the first non-PRI president in seven decades was elected, has turned **Mexico** into a pluralistic multi-party democracy. Two pieces of information are available, which allow us to start an estimate of the total costs of party competition: the amount of public subsidies to political parties (at the federal level) and the estimated proportions of public and private funding.

The total amount of public subsidies for a complete election cycle (1994-99), which includes a presidential election (1994) and two congressional campaigns (1994, 1997), was MXP 5.89 billion.[40] The estimated percentages of public and private spending reveal amounts for individual years.[41] Adding up these estimates puts political spending (on the federal level) at MXP 7.7 billion for the 1994-99 cycle.[42] Data provided by Tania Martinez offer slightly different totals of MXP 5.22 billion for public subsidies and MXP 7.12 billion for overall spending.[43] Information for the state and local level is not available. However, based on the experience of other federations,[44] it should be safe to assume that the modal split of political spending during a complete election cycle in the late 1990s covered a similar range.

Federal party headquarters in Switzerland[45] and Germany[46] spend about one third (27 to 37 percent) of the parties' total budget. In Canada the provincial level accounts for considerably more than half (roughly 63 percent) of all political spending,[47] the local level in that country is mostly non-partisan. Australia seems to be a bit more de-cen-

---

39 Roth 1998, pp. 129, 142.
40 de Swan/ Martorelli/ Molinar 1998, pp. 163/164; additional data provided by Tania Martinez.
41 Lujambio 2003, p. 383.
42 More realistic estimates of MXP 9.6 billion for the 1995-2000 cycle and MXP 12.5 billion for 1997-2002 are beyond the scope of this comparison, which is limited to the late 1990s.
43 Martinez 2005, pp. 178-179 and personal communication to the author.
44 See above in chapter II, sub-section A1 (party organisation).
45 See below in this chapter, sub-section A3c (small democracies).
46 For details see below in chapter V, sub-section B3 (professional politics).
47 Nassmacher 1989c, p. 232.

tralised as 54 to 60 percent of all party spending is non-federal.[48] In the U.S. state and local level politics absorb slightly more than half of all identified political spending.[49] As Mexico's federalism is more centralised than any of the five other nations, it seems fair to assume that the federal level accounts for most of the party spending and covers a range between half and two thirds of total political outlay. Thus the consolidated spending by Mexico's local, state and national parties during the 1994-99 election cycle would probably have been between a higher range of MXP 11.6 to 15.4 billion and a lower range of MXP 10.7 to 14.2 billion. Using both sets of data, we can assume that an amount between MXP 11 and 15 billion is a fair representation of the total spending on political competition during the 1994-99 election cycle.

2. *Costs of major democracies: Italy, Britain, France, Spain, Poland*

a) Due to a lack of transparency of political funds, it is still impossible to compute the overall costs of democracy in **Italy**. Scandals and the systematic investigation of corruption have opened up opportunities to estimate the amounts spent by Italian parties, which appear to by-pass their official financial reports considerably. These contain information provided by the party headquarters, which should be taken with a pinch of salt.[50] From the limited evidence available, we can gather that the campaign expenses of Italian parties are unusually low. For the 1996 election campaign Italian parties spent about ITL 52 billion, i.e. ITL 1,064 per voter on list. *Forza Italia*, Berlusconi's new party spent 30 percent of the total alone (not counting large pre-campaign spending and subsidies to its allies *Lega Nord* and *Aleanza Nazionale*); over ITL 15.5 billion. Although the imbalance with other parties declined a little afterwards (but on a higher level), *Forza Italia* still has extraordinary resources (not only financial ones) set aside by its leader, Berlusconi, at its disposal.[51] The very serious crisis of Italian parties and changes in the electoral system have resulted in more candidate-centred politics. Thus future analysis of political finance in Italy will have to pay more attention to personalised campaigns. In recent elections, expenditures by all candidates (save those of *Rifondazione comunista*) have become more and more independent of their party and have surpassed campaign expenditures by parties.[52]

During the mid-1990s (i.e. after the break-up of the old party system) annual routine spending was estimated at ITL 160 billion for a major party and at ITL 65 billion for a medium sized party. These amounts add up to a total of ITL 450 to 550 billion. As reported officially by the national parties, headquarters' expenses totalled an average

---

48 See below in this chapter, sub-section A3b (medium sized democracies).
49 Estimate for the 1993-96 election cycle based on data from: Alexander 1999, pp. 13, 23 and Alexander/ Corrado 1995, p. 5.
50 Paltiel 1979b, p. 35.
51 For some details see Grasmück 2005, pp. 443-448.
52 Information provided by Enrico Melchionda, University of Salerno, who anticipated this trend in: Melchionda 1997, pp. 208/209.

of some ITL 275 billion annually for the late 1980s.[53] Ciaurro has suggested that this amount ought to be almost doubled in order to include local, provincial and regional branches.[54] Even adding the campaign expenses of some ITL 50 billion annually for any of the election campaigns for the national parliament, the European parliament, regional assemblies and municipal representatives does not provide a reliable figure.[55] Nevertheless this basis would suggest a ITL 600 billion minimum annual outlay. The *mani pulite* (clean hands) inquiry that was launched in 1992 led to revised estimates of some 3,400 billion lire for an average year during the 1980s.[56] Taken together both data indicate a range between ITL 600 and 3,400 billion for party political spending per year. Applying this range to the late 1990s would neglect the impact of a decade of ongoing inflation. However, as the range is so broad and just some rough estimate of the political spending level can be provided anyway this data will be used for further consideration.

b) Despite continuous efforts by Michael Pinto-Duschinsky and Justin Fisher, it is still difficult to assess the overall 'costs of democracy' for the **United Kingdom (Britain)**. This concept has to add up the totals of routine and campaign spending at the national and the local level.[57] Central office spending (on routine and campaign activities) by the major parties is documented quite well.[58] However, campaign expenses in Britain can be sub-divided into two categories: spending by national parties and spending by individual candidates. Separate campaigns for the national (Westminster) parliament, the European Parliament, the Scottish parliament, the Welsh assembly, the parliament of Northern Ireland and local councils in all regions of the U.K. are fought regularly. Their campaign costs are not available. Campaign spending by all parties for the 1997 Westminster parliament may be estimated at some £58 million.[59] Local campaign expenses incurred by parliamentary candidates in single member constituencies are tightly regulated and continuously reported. The grand total of all candidates' declared election expenses for the same year was between £12 and 13 million.[60] However, a reliable summary of (or a comprehensive figure for) all other campaign expenses and local routine spending by political parties is not known. As reported by the Neill Committee central office expenses of the three national parties for routine and campaign activities during the 1993-97 parliamentary cycle add up to £186.2 million. Allowing

---

53   Melchionda 1997, pp. 206, 251; Bardi/ Morlino 1992, pp. 604-608.
54   Ciaurro 1989, p. 157.
55   Bardi/ Morlino 1992, pp. 616-618.
56   Bardi/ Morlino 1994, p. 260, referring to *La Repubblica* (daily newspaper), 20 February 1993.
57   Pinto-Duschinsky 1981, p. 14.
58   See above in chapter II, section C (cost objects; Tables 2-8 and 2-10) and below in chapter V, sub-section B2 (new technology; Table 5-3).
59   Of this total, the Conservatives spent GBP 28.3 million, Labour GBP 25.7 million and the Liberal Democrats GBP 2.1-2.3 million (Neill report 1998, pp. 36-38, 41, 43). Our estimate in Table 2-10 is more moderate.
60   Butler/ Kavanagh 1997, p. 223. Because Pinto-Duschinsky (2003, pp. 327/328) claims that all constituency expenses are notoriously under-reported, this sub-total may give a too conservative amount.

for minor parties' expenditure and including parliamentary candidates' campaign spending, a subtotal of £205 million (except local routine expenses and spending on non-Westminster campaigns) emerges.

Both, the Houghton and the Neill committee have commissioned sample surveys of constituency parties and reported average data.[61] Justin Fisher (on behalf of the Neill committee) set the average of local party routine expenditure per constituency in 1997 (an election year) at £9,577 for the Labour Party, £30,761 for the Conservative Party and £7,195 for the Liberal Democrats. A rough approximation for non-election year totals would be 60 or 70 percent of these amounts. Based on such data, a conservative estimate for total routine expenses (1993-97) in the constituencies is £60 million. A more generous estimate may add up to £83 million. Thus the total amount spent by parties and candidates in the U.K. during the 1993-97 election cycle can be approximated at £265 to 288 million. Whereas in the early 1970s local spending accounted for 67 percent of the national total,[62] the combined share of central offices has now increased to more than two thirds of total political spending (campaign plus routine), which would indeed demonstrate a reverse split between both levels and a centralising effect. Adding £15 to 20 million for the 1994 European election, £20 million for all municipal campaigns and £5 million for a regional election in Northern Ireland would bring the U.K. spending total for 1993-97 to GBP 295 to 333 million.[63]

c) Although empirical data on **France** has improved considerably, it is still rather diverse,[64] and reliable information is scarce. Thus it is very hard to estimate with a certain degree of precision the overall costs of this established democracy, especially, due to the variety of political funds, which are expended. For the year 2001 Yves-Marie Doublet reports the annual total of public subsidies to political parties (and the party press) as FRF 938 million and an aggregate party income of about FRF 900 million.[65] The official reports by some 100 parties for 1993 (the year of a parliamentary election) added up to FRF 1.45 billion.[66] During the years 1994 to 1998 the six major parties spent between FRF 833.5 million and FRF 1.06 billion. This adds up to a total

---

61 Any interpretation of this information must reflect that in the 1960s and 1970s the income and expenditures fluctuated without a clear trend, but have increased considerably since the 1980s (Webb 2000, pp. 231-242).
62 Pinto-Duschinsky 1981, pp. 150, 174, 208; Neill report 1998, pp. 41/42.
63 Regional elections in Scotland, Wales and Greater London can be neglected for the particular cycle under study. However, they will have to be considered in any analysis of later years.
64 An estimate for the early 1990s revealed a total amount of FRF 866 million per annum just for public subsidies (Schmitt 1993, p. 93). – Limited to party organisations, a German newspaper reported total expenses of FRF 1.126 billion for an election year (1997) and of FRF 1 billion for a non-election year (1998) (*Frankfurter Allgemeine*, 3 December 1999).
65 Doublet 2003, p. 13. - The annual total for public subsidies (FRF 471 to 499 million) given by Knapp 2002, p. 127, is much lower and looks incomplete. – For 2001-03 Schurig (2006, p. 133) established an annual subsidy total of € 162.6 million (= FRF 1,065 million).
66 *Journal Officiel*, no. 268, 19/11/1994. 86 parties accounted for 176 million FF (= 12% of the total), 7 parties for FRF 230 million (= 16% of the total) and 7 major parties for FRF 1.04 billion (= 72% of the total).

of FRF 4.7 billion for a five year election cycle.[67] To this about FRF 100 million annually have to be added for minor parties.[68] Based on these data all parties may have spent a total of FRF 5.2 billion during a parliamentary cycle in the mid-1990s.

This amount includes neither routine spending by local and regional party branches, nor expenses for presidential campaigns and parliamentary campaigns at the constituency level, nor campaigns for European, regional and municipal elections, nor the cost of campaign services, which are covered by the Ministry of the Interior.[69] During an entire cycle (1998-2002) the ministry spent a total of FRF 980 million for election materials covering the European, presidential, parliamentary, regional and municipal elections.[70] Even if part of this covers the stationery used for elections (ballots, registration notices and the like) some FRF 600 to 700 million will be a fair equivalent of the in-kind services (costs of restricted publicity, mostly posters), which is allowed by the election law and was rendered free of charge to parties and candidates during the 1994-98 cycle.

For the 1988 presidential election, Fromont compares the official figures to estimates in *Le Monde*. According to the *Journal Officiel* eight candidates campaigned on FRF 342 million, all candidates declared a total amount of FRF 354 million. *Le Monde* estimated total campaign spending at FRF 800 million just for the four leading candidates. The presidential campaign in 1995 officially cost more than FRF 440 million.[71] A range of FRF 700 to 950 million should provide a fair estimate of actual spending.

In 1993 constituency candidates for parliament reported expenses that totalled some FRF 670 million. In the early 1990s *Le Monde* estimated an average campaign budget of FRF 1.5 to 2.0 million for each constituency candidate running for the national parliament.[72] As there are 577 single member constituencies, about 900 to 1,000 candidates have been serious contenders, which might have been willing and able to spend within that range. This would bring the local costs of a parliamentary campaign to a range of FRF 1.35 to 2.0 billion. Thus for the 1997 election of the national parliament a range of FRF 900 to 1,500 million solely for parliamentary candidates should be a fair assumption.

The European election cost more than FRF 250 million;[73] however, FRF 400 million may be more realistic. Regional and municipal campaigns may be estimated at FRF 300-350 million each. The interim total of FRF 8.1 to 9.1 billion for a full election cycle is still a very conservative estimate as it neglects routine spending by local and regional party organisations. Adding a sum of FRF 200 to 300 million per year for all

---

67 Schurig 2006, pp. 89, 424-427.
68 Knapp 2002, p 127. Unfortunately the summaries for spending totals in 1997 and 1998 have fallen victim to misprints. Nonetheless, the supplementary amount of FRF 100 million for minor parties should be adequate.
69 For details see below in chapter VIII, sub-section B1 (subsidies in-kind).
70 Schurig 2006, p. 113.
71 Fromont 1992, pp. 187/188; Camby 1995, p. 86; Kempf 1997, p. 32; Kempf 2007, p. 36.
72 *Journal Officiel*, no. 37-R, 27/04/1994; Fromont 1992, p. 188.
73 Camby 1995, p. 91.

party branches would increase the overall total of the complete election cycle in the mid-1990s to a range of FRF 9.1 to 10.6 billion.

d) We can begin to estimate the costs of party democracy in contemporary **Spain** from two bits of information. First, due to legal stipulations parties report on income and expenses annually, as well as after each national election. Second, public subsidies are distributed for current operations as well as for campaign expenses related to the European, the national, the regional and the local elections. The data on reported expenses for 1989 to 1992 add up to a total of ESP 60.35 billion.[74] Adjusted for inflation (by 30 or 40 percent), an election cycle in the late 1990s may have cost a minimum of ESP 78.45 billion and a maximum of ESP 84.48 billion in national operations.[75] This does not include regional branches and local chapters. An addendum of 40 to 60 percent for that purpose, and thus a total of ESP 109.83 to 135.17 million, should be appropriate.

In 1996 the six major parties reported aggregate expenses of ESP 6.83 billion for the election of the national parliament (*Cortes*).[76] An estimate of the costs for European, regional and local elections can only start with data for public subsidies. In the late 1990s these subsidies were ESP 1,992 million for the European parliament, ESP 4,654 million for assemblies in the 17 autonomous regions and ESP 3,234 million for some 8,000 municipal councils.[77] How much of the total campaign expenses did the aggregate subsidy of ESP 9.88 billion cover? The subsidy covered three quarters of reported campaign expenses for the national election of 1996; for earlier national campaigns the rate had been about half.[78] Thus, we assume that a fair minimum coverage may be 60 percent, a maximum, however, about 80 percent.[79] Due to this reasoning total campaign spending for European, regional and local elections ranges from ESP 12.35 billion to ESP 16.47 billion. After adding an extra 5 to 10 percent (i.e. ESP 617 to 1,647 million) for all expenses by minor parties, the total spending of Spanish parties for a complete election cycle in the late 1990s is estimated between ESP 123 and 153 billion.

e) Among the post-communist countries of Central and Eastern Europe **Poland** is the first, which provides data for a comparison with more established democracies. Based on officially declared spending, systematic press investigation and detailed interviews conducted by the researcher himself Marcin Walecki has presented an overall estimate of national and local, parliamentary and presidential, campaign and routine costs of party politics.[80] Data refer to 2001 in particular and the 1999 to 2002 election cycle.[81]

---

74 van Biezen 2000, pp. 334/335.
75 If this adjustment seems too high, it may also cover some of the shady area of party funding, which was revealed by the considerable number of scandals in the early 1990s. See del Castillo 1994, pp. 101/102; Heywood 1996, pp. 115-117, 125-127.
76 van Biezen 2000, p. 338; van Biezen/ Nassmacher 2001, p. 134.
77 Hofmann 1998, pp. 205, 210; 190-204; 60, 69/70, 93.
78 van Biezen 2000, p. 338; cf. van Biezen 2003, pp. 185-192.
79 The latter rate is given by Doublet 2003, p. 12.
80 Walecki 2005a, pp. 175-181.
81 Walecki 2005a, pp. 178 (Table 4.5) and 180 (Table 4.6).

As the 2001 data offer ranges for specific types of costs [82] and mainly illustrate the diversity of the real picture, we preferably refer to the overall estimate. This estimate is based on spending in presidential (PLN 120 million), parliamentary (PLN 150 million) and local elections (PLN 150 million) as well as annual routine expenses of PLN 100 to 120 million. The overall total given for the whole election cycle is PLN 880 million. If we apply this information to a cycle during the late 1990s the estimate will be less conservative than the data for other democracies. However, this exaggeration may just suffice to cover a major part of the non-accounted political spending by "trade unions, political foundations and associations, religious and advocacy groups," which Walecki puts at PLN 50 to 60 million a year.[83]

3. *Costs of medium sized democracies: Canada, Australia, the Netherlands, Sweden*

a) Parties and candidates in **Canada** report their federal campaign expenses to the Chief Electoral Officer, who publishes accounts of spending for routine operations and campaign purposes by federal parties and candidates. These reports provide an excellent basis for an estimate of the overall costs of Canadian democracy.[84] For the 1997 election year (federal) parties reported a total of CAD 35.7 million in operating expenses and CAD 34.9 million in campaign expenses. In addition to party headquarters, 1672 constituency candidates reported election expenses totalling CAD 39.2 million. Thus the grand total of declared spending on the 1997 federal campaign was CAD 74.1 million.[85] To this amount we have to add the expenditures by federal parties for the non-election years 1994 to 1996 (about CAD 20 to 28 million each). Thus the overall federal total of reported expenses is CAD 183 million for an election cycle during the late 1990s.

However, this amount includes neither separate campaigns for parliaments in the 10 provinces and 3 territories nor any of the (mostly non-partisan) municipal elections,[86] nor annual routine spending by provincial branches and both sets of local riding associations. If (despite the operation of more parties) there has been no major change in total expenses since the 1980s, then federal politics account for no more than 37 percent of the total costs of democracy whereas provincial parties and their candidates spend about 63 percent.[87] A range of 35 to 40 percent allows for the fact that federal parties during the 1980s passed through a high tide of political spending.[88] Thus the total reported spending for the four year election cycle of 1994 to 1997 would cover a range of CAD 455 to 520 million.

---

82 see above in chapter II, section B (types of costs).
83 Walecki 2005a, p. 181.
84 Michaud/ Laferriere 1991, p. 375.
85 Data from www.elections.ca.
86 For a rare exception, the quasi-partisan local elections in Vancouver, B.C., see Purcal 1993, esp. pp. 139-146.
87 Nassmacher 1989c, p. 232.
88 See below in chapter V, sub-section B2 (campaign technology).

This does not, however, include routine spending by riding associations and expenses for leadership campaigns. A rough estimate of all federal and provincial leadership contests would be no more than CAD 10 million. The net total of all unreported (non-receipted and not tax-credited) funds should have been no more than CAD 2 million annually, which adds another CAD 8 million to total spending. Based on research of local parties the annual expenses for some 900 federal riding associations may have totalled CAD 3 million in 1990.[89] This adds about CAD 12 million to total expenses for the election cycle. Much of this should be included among the funds receipted by federal offices. Nevertheless we add this amount to our spending total. A reasonable estimate of the current expenses of the more numerous provincial riding associations may be in the range of CAD 18 to 24 million. The total cost of Canadian democracy for a four-year cycle ranges from CAD 503 to 574 million, which includes all four minor sums.

b) Two different bits of information are available to the public for political spending in **Australia**: reported campaign expenses for federal elections and annual reports by registered parties. For the election years 1984, 1987, 1990 and 1996 Australian parties had to report their campaign expenses to the AEC. The total amount of reported campaign expenses in 1990, as well as 1996, was AUD 33 million.[90] Data on campaign expenditure pertains to national elections at the federal level only. An overview of election expenditure in all Australian jurisdictions (including states and territories) cannot be drawn from any source. Assuming that the amount spent on all state elections is on par with spending on a federal campaign, total campaign spending on one election cycle would be close to AUD 70 million during the late 1990s.

In the federal election year 1999 Australian parties reported extra spending of about AUD 70 million, more than twice the amount of campaign spending in 1996.[91] Of this total about AUD 30 million was extra spending in the state of New South Wales, which held both a state and a federal election during the reporting period. If we split this into AUD 16 million for the state campaign and AUD 14 million for the regional part of the federal campaign, some AUD 54 million may thus be considered the outlay of a federal campaign in the late 1990s.

This does not, however, include the costs of municipal campaigns and routine operations of federal and state parties. If we set an average amount of AUD 1.5 million each for the three national parties operating with full-time staff in a minimum of 5 jurisdictions,[92] then it adds up to AUD 22.5 million annually and AUD 67.5 million for the full election cycle. Municipal elections may have cost no less than AUD 26 million, increasing total spending during an election cycle to a minimum of AUD 162 million.

---

89 See Nassmacher/ Suckow 1992, p. 148; for details see Carty 1991, p. 92.
90 Amr/ Lisowski 2001, p. 54.
91 www.aec.gov.au (Summary of all Party Returns); Amr/ Lisowski 2001, p. 54.
92 Based on the fact that there are three big and two-medium-sized states plus the federation. Cf. www.abs.gov.au/ausstat.

A different approach starts with data that have become available due to new legislation. Registered parties report to the Australian Electoral Commission (AEC) all payments that they have made in each fiscal year. Individual state parties have to include spending by their local chapters. Recent reports for fiscal years 1998 to 2001 are available on the AEC web-site. For the three years total payments added up to AUD 256 million. This figure certainly overstates the costs of democracy because it includes all transfer payments made within a party organisation. Reducing the total by 20 percent for financial transfers, plus an additional 10 percent for inflation, may get us closer to the real amount of expenses during the late 1990s. AUD 186 million represents a fair estimate of all party spending during a three year election cycle. The two different approaches result in a range of AUD 162 to 186 million. This provides a reasonable bracket for the costs of Australian democracy during the late 1990s.

c) Because the total amount of routine expenditures by parties (and their affiliated organisations) in the **Netherlands** equals their current income, the amounts available for party activities indicate that the combined expenditures of the four major parties (*CDA, PvdA, VVD* and *D66*) increased from NLG 23.3 million in 1989 (an election year) to 30.4 million in 1995 (a non-election year).[93] Four other parties add NLG 8.9 million to the total. Allowing for some more minor parties could increase the 1995 total to NLG 42 million. During the 1990s party campaign budgets increased, but they are still very modest. For the 1998 national election campaign spending by the four major parties was estimated at NLG 3.3 million for the *PvdA*, NLG 2.1 million for the *CDA*, NLG 1.5 million for the *VVD*, NLG 1.4 million for *D66* and NLG 1.0 million for *GroenLinks*. The small SP had a campaign budget of NLG 1.6 million.[94] This adds up to a total of about NLG 12 million of extra spending.[95]

A conservative estimate for a whole election cycle would be next to NLG 170 and 180 million in total expenses by the national parties. Because regional branches and local chapters raise and spend modestly, an additional amount of 20 to 40 percent of the national total is adequate. This assumption increases the total outlay for Dutch parties during the 1995 to 1998 election cycle to a range of NLG 205 to 250 million. Spending on campaigns for the European Parliament, regional assemblies and municipal councils (unfortunately this data is not available) has to be added to total expenses. If all three of these campaigns cost about the same as one national campaign, then the minimum total would rise to NLG 217 million. If these campaigns are slightly more expensive, the maximum would be NLG 268 million.[96]

---

93 At the Documentation Centre on Dutch Political Parties (DNPP) of the University of Groningen a wealth of information is available for Dutch parties and their penumbra of affiliated bodies (including financial data), but most of this relates to national party organisations only (www.ub.rug.nl/dnpp/).

94 This exceptionally high campaign budget was funded from proceeds of the „party tax"; see below chapter VII, sub-section D3 (assessment of party officeholders) and Gidlund/ Koole 2001, p. 119.

95 Gidlund/ Koole 2001, pp. 115/116.

96 Koole (1994b, p. 291) has indicated an uncontrollable element in any cash calculation of political spending: The modest scale of party expenses can be caused by scarce resources. However,

d) No official data is available for political spending in **Sweden**. However, since 1976 annual reports for party headquarters are accessible, and public subsidies are allocated on different levels of the political system. Based on both pieces of information a reliable estimate is possible. Since 1970 elections for all three levels of the Swedish polity (national parliament, regional assemblies and local councils) are held on the same day. This offers an opportunity of cash economy for the competing parties.

An estimate of campaign expenses in 1988 indicated that the Social Democrats (*Socialdemokraterna, SAP*) spent SEK 26 million on the campaign, which was about one quarter of their national headquarters' annual budget at the time. The Conservatives (*Moderaterna*) then spent SEK 15 million on campaign purposes, almost half of their routine expenditure during that year.[97] Spending by party headquarters totalled almost SEK 300 million in 1988 (an election year). In 1991 the major parties (Social Democrats, Conservatives and Centre Party) spent SEK 97.2 million on total campaign expenditures. The minor parties spent SEK 35.7 million.[98] This means that in 1991 the national party headquarters spent a total of SEK 133 million on campaign related purposes.[99]

The routine operation expenses in an election year, as well as in two non-election years, and all political costs (campaign and routine) incurred by regional branches and local chapters have to be added to the campaign spending by the national party organisations. National parties spent an aggregate of SEK 130 million in 1979 and SEK 300 million in 1988, SEK 100 in 1978 and SEK 190 million in 1987.[100] Spending more than doubled between election years and it increased by 90 percent for non-election years during the same time span of nine years. Based on such information national parties may have spent up to SEK 750 million in 1998 and SEK 370 million each in 1995 to 1997. This would add up to a national total of SEK 1.86 billion for a four year election cycle. If the regional branches and local chapters covered about the same outlay between them, we can approximate a realistic figure of SEK 3.72 billion for the 1995-98 cycle.

Because the political finance situation has not changed much since the late 1970s, a different approach is possible and more reliable. Almost 70 percent of party income at all three levels of the political system is provided by public subsidies. Since public subsidies to national, regional and local parties totalled SEK 666 million in 1999 (a non-election year), we can estimate total funds available for party activities in Sweden

---

this may be compensated by "the availability of free expertise from (professionally qualified) party members" who donate their time without showing up in any party account.
97   Calculated on the basis of: Pierre/ Widfeldt 1992, pp. 824-836.
98   Klee-Kruse 1993a, p. 172; Gidlund/ Koole 2001, p. 114.
99   The separate campaign for the European parliament should be much cheaper (and can be neglected because Sweden participated for the first time in 1999). Personalised voting and multi-member constituencies were added to the election law in 1998. Their impact will be ignored here as our estimates are for the late 1990s.
100 Klee-Kruse 1993a, p. 172.

at some SEK 950 million per year.[101] For a period of four years this adds up to SEK 3.8 billion, which is pretty close to the amount based on vague expense data. To allow for some leeway we estimate the expense total for a complete election cycle at SEK 3.7 to 3.9 billion.

4. Costs of small democracies: Austria, Switzerland, Israel, Denmark, Ireland

a) **Austria** has been called a party democracy quite frequently, because the parties run everyday politics as well as election campaigns. The annual reports filed by the Austrian parties include income and expenditure for the federal level only and completely neglect the party penumbra (official trade union factions and ÖVP sub-organisations, called leagues or *Bünde*). In order to establish an overall picture, the financial situation of nine state branches of each party and all local parties has to be included. Sickinger estimates campaign costs for the federal parliament (*Nationalrat*) in election years 1990 to 1995 at some ATS 300 million and approximates a total of about ATS 500 million for the separately held nine state elections.[102] Separate data for municipal campaigns in eight non-city states plus those for the federal presidency and the European parliament are not available.

However, Sickinger provides estimates, which indicate that the total amount of money available to Austrian parties was ATS 2.176 billion in 1993 and ATS 2.398 billion in 1998.[103] These data refer to party income and include party organisation, as well as party academies but not parliamentary groups. Used as an indicator for annual expenses the data that are given for two non-election years represent a rather conservative estimate. Probably ATS 9.6 billion would be more appropriate for a complete election cycle in the late 1990s than ATS 9.2 billion or ATS 9.4 billion.

b) In contrast to Austria, **Switzerland** takes pride in being a "militia"[104] type of democracy, where parties are still cadre type organisations.[105] However, due to the opportunities of popular initiative and referendum, parties are under strong pressure by interest groups. Until the late 1990s information on political finance was scarce, but it has improved considerably since then. A study of party spending in Switzerland offers data on political activity at all three tiers of the political system. Campaign spending at all levels of elective politics was estimated at a total of CHF 40 million.[106] Spending data for federal parties requires the addition of minor parties, which account for one quarter of total spending at the state level. Based on the data, which Ladner and

---

101 Klee-Kruse 1993a, p. 151; Gidlund/ Koole 2001, p. 114.
102 Sickinger 1997, pp. 258, 259.
103 Sickinger 1997, pp. 242, 245, 248, 250, 252 (subtotal for parties only). Sickinger 2001, p. 341 (excluding caucuses); Sickinger 2000, pp. 320-322; Sickinger 2002, p. 75.
104 Weigelt 1988, pp. 79/80.
105 The financial consequences for this type of party have been named by Heidenheimer 1963, pp. 791/792.
106 Ladner/ Brändle 1999, pp. 10-12. Separate data for specific levels is not available.

Brändle reported more recently, spending totals during the 1996 to 1999 election cycle were CHF 58-60 million by the local parties, CHF 84-94 million by the state parties and CHF 46-52 million by the federal parties.[107] The overall total of party expenses in the late 1990s is thus estimated at CHF 186 to 206 million in four years.

A separate analysis of almost 2000 local party chapters found a total cash expenditure for the early 1990s at the local level for all Swiss parties of CHF 12 million in a non-election year and some CHF 24 million in an election year. Adjusted for inflation local spending during a four-year election cycle may have totalled some CHF 66 to 69 million. However, the study provided an additional clue. Many local party presidents process their party work through their business office. Thus printing and mailing is frequently paid by their employer or business. Some adjustment for the cash outlay of such private sponsoring has to be made.

A very conservative addendum for "sponsored" printing and mailing of CHF 2 to 3 million per year, i.e. CHF 8-12 million per election cycle, would bring total spending at the local level in the late 1990s up to CHF 74 to 81 million, which is roughly CHF 20 million more than the figures given above. Taking this private cash outlay into consideration we will add CHF 20 million to the total of CHF 186 to 206 million. This puts our estimate of total spending on party competition in the range of CHF 206 to 226 million. As it does not include spending by organised interests (lobby groups) on popular initiatives and referenda this is still a conservative estimate of the total costs of Swiss democracy.[108]

c) Although it is widely believed that **Israel** is still the "the most expensive democracy per voter in the world,"[109] authors rarely provide details or summaries of the overall political expenses. An estimate of political spending in Israel during the late 1990s can start from two pieces of information. First, in 1998 the annual public grant to political parties totalled ILS 114 million. Second, on average Israeli parties spent less than half of the annual limit on current operations in the early 1990s.[110] Based on both facts, parties' routine spending has been around ILS 75 to 80 million annually.[111] A moderate increase to ILS 310 to 330 million for a full election cycle may take care of two facts: Several parties run permanent offices in urban centres and all MPs are entitled to a liaison office in a town of their choice.[112]

As the financing unit was ILS 900,000 in 1994, the campaign expenditure limit for the 1996 *Knesset* election totalled some ILS 220 million. As major parties notoriously overspend and some clandestine support is part of Israeli election routine, the 1996

---

107 Ladner/ Brändle 2001, pp. 166, 169, 178.
108 Cf. Schaller 1994, pp. 228, 230/231; Ladner/ Brändle 2001, pp. 181/182.
109 Arian 1998, p. 155. For similar observations see Kalchheim/ Rosevitch 1992, p. 226; Hofnung 1996a, p. 74 and Hofnung 1996b, p. 132.
110 Mendilow 1992, pp. 101-103; Yishai 2000, p. 674; Mendilow/ Rusciano 2001, p. 229.
111 Annual per capita amounts were around USD 8.00 during the 1990s. Arian 1998, p. 155.
112 Personal communication from Menachem Hofnung (May 2005). I assume that local parties raise extra funding for their offices and that MPs use about half of their office allowance (ILS 21,000 per year) to support local party activity..

Knesset election may have cost some ILS 250 million.[113] This would be quite moderate when compared to the increased rate of campaign spending between 1977 and 1988, but well below an estimate of about ILS 400 million for 2001. Hofnung mentions a total of ILS 326 million campaign expenses by all parties.[114] These data seem to cover the (additional) campaign for prime minister who was directly elected, three times between May 1996 and February 2001. In 1996 a joint total of ILS 250 to 300 million is a reasonable amount for both campaigns.

The estimate does not include the costs of nominations by internal party primaries. Based on a total of 100 to 150 candidates (and 6 to 8 party leaders) and Hofnung's average of ILS 2 million per candidate, ILS 150 million in pre-nomination spending may be the minimum, ILS 250 million a maximum total for spending on "party primaries."[115] A public subsidy of ILS 52 million was available in 1989 for municipal elections. In line with previous increases this should have been around ILS 140 to 150 million by 1997. Because we have to add the mayoral campaigns, total spending on local government elections may have added up to approximately ILS 170 to 210 million.[116] This leaves just the *Histadrut* elections, which are contested by the major parties. A guess of ILS 50 million would be a conservative price tag for this important campaign, mostly funded by the "political tax" levied on trade union members.[117] Adding up the figures for the five different areas of political spending in Israel, the total amount for a whole election cycle during the late 1990s can be expected in the range of ILS 930 to 1,140 million.[118]

d) We can base an estimate of total party spending in **Denmark** on four different sources,[119] which provide for various pieces of relevant information: public subsidies, membership data, members' contributions and central office expenses. Since 1998 Danish party headquarters are required by law to submit annual financial reports, which cover income and expenditures, to the *Folketing* administration. According to these reports a total of 12-13 parties spent DKK 138.4 million in 1998, DKK 110.9 million in 1999 and DKK 131.0 million in 2000.[120] However, due to a national election in 1998, an election of the EU parliament in 1999 and a referendum in 2000 none

---

113 Mendilow 1992, p. 110; Hofnung 1996a, p. 85; Peretz/ Doron 1997, p. 127.
114 Library of Congress 2001 – I. General Information ; Hofnung 2005b, p. 76.
115 Hofnung 2005b, p. 68. The total depends on the number of candidates (50-100) who are willing and able to spend the average amount given per candidate. For a breakdown by types of cost see Hofnung 2006, p. 382.
116 Kalchheim/ Rosevitch 1992, pp. 218/219, 226/227. - Hofnung (1996b, p. 142) mentions a per capita amount for the national and municipal elections of 1992-93 of $ 54 per voter (= $ 37 per voter on list). This is twice the USD per capita amount given for 1988-89 by Kalchheim/ Rosevitch 1992, p. 227.
117 Kalchheim/ Rosevitch 1992, p. 226.
118 Earlier estimates for total annual spending during the 1990s amounted to US-$15 resp. US-$17 or NIS 195-225 per person entitled to vote. Cf. Blechinger/ Nassmacher 2001, p. 157.
119 Pedersen/ Bille 1991, pp. 158, 160, 161; Bille 1992, pp. 263-272; Annual Reports by National Party Organisations for 1998 to 2000 (see next note); Pedersen 2003, pp. 152, 329, 336.
120 www.folketinget.dk (Folketingets partir/Parti- og grupperegnskaber - "De politiske partiers regnskaber").

of these years was a non-election year. As we intend to estimate from these data central office spending during the 1996-99 election cycle, two discounts are necessary: one for the EU plebiscite in 2000 and the other for creeping inflation. Taking care of both we assume that all parties spent between DKK 90 and DKK 100 nationally in 1996 and 1997. Together with spending in 1998 and 1999 this adds up to a total of DKK 430 to 450 million for all party headquarters during the 1996-99 election cycle.

Routine spending by local parties and municipal campaign spending are not included in this data. Regional branches and local chapters of the Danish parties can spend the public subsidy for regional and local elections, their share of membership dues plus voluntary contributions solicited locally as well as assessments of local councillors ("party taxes") collected by sub-national branches. Taking into account a voter turnout of 60 to 70 percent the regional and local campaign subsidy equals DKK 15 to 18 million. An estimate of the other amounts is facilitated by the data, which Karina Pedersen has recently presented.[121] If her membership figures and her average contributions are multiplied, then the total annual income of all Danish parties from this source of revenue would be about DKK 75 million. However, accounting for a response rate of two thirds in the membership survey, DKK 45 to 55 million should be closer to the national total. Of this amount (according to official reports) DKK 17 million was transferred to the national level: Thus regional branches and local chapters could still expend a range of DKK 28 to 38 million annually from this source.

When municipal (1997) or national elections (1998) are held, the fundraising capacity of local parties should be slightly higher than in an EU election year (1999) or a non-election year (1996). Thus it seems fair to assume that for the latter years DKK 28 to 33 million is adequate whereas for the former years DKK 33 to 43 million may be more realistic. This brings sub-national spending to DKK 137 to 182 million for a four-year period. For a complete election cycle during the late 1990s, total spending adds up to DKK 570 to 630 million.

e) Different sets of data are available for political spending in **Ireland**, too. Unfortunately they are incomplete and only one of them is recent. Whereas Farrell covers party headquarters and campaigns up to 1990,[122] Holmes reports spending in the 1987 to 1997 parliamentary campaigns.[123] Marsh identifies spending on the 1997 presidential campaign while Benoit and Marsh cover the 1999 local elections.[124] All of these sources neglect the costs of European elections and routine spending by local party branches. From 1981 to 1985 the central offices of four major parties spent a total of IEP 5.79 million. Six national parties spent an aggregate of IEP 11.57 million on central routine operations from 1986 to 1990. Additional income and inflation may have

---

121 Pedersen 2003, pp. 152, 336. – I appreciate the improvements, which Lars Bille and Karina Pedersen suggested to my earlier estimates. However, as the final result has not been double-checked with them, I bear sole responsibility for the data presented here.
122 Farrell 1992, pp. 448-451, 457.
123 Holmes 1999, p. 51; additional information on local spending by Farrell/ Farrell 1987, p. 236.
124 Marsh 1999, p. 223; Benoit/ Marsh 2003, p. 568.

increased this aggregate amount to IEP 23 million for the 1993-97 election cycle. Judging by the development of campaign expenses, this estimate may be too generous. A more conservative approach would set the increase at 50 percent and the total amount spent centrally by national party offices at IEP 17 million.

National and local electioneering by these parties cost IEP 4.3 million for the 1987 parliamentary campaign and IEP 5.3 million for the 1997 parliamentary campaign. We must add to this the 1997 campaign expenses of presidential candidates (IEP 1.1 million) and the spending total of 1,837 candidates in 180 constituencies for 30 county councils (IEP 3.1 million in 1999).[125] In addition to these amounts we need estimates for the routine spending by local party branches and for the nation-wide campaign concerning the European parliament.[126] Because this campaign is usually less costly than that for the national parliament, expenditures ranging between IEP 2.5 to 3.5 million seem reasonable. A conservative estimate for routine expenses by local branches may add up to about half of the amount spent by central offices, whereas a more generous estimate should assume two thirds of their total, i.e. IEP 8.5 to 15.3 million. This would put total expenses for the 1993-97 cycle somewhere between IEP 37.5 and 51.3 million.

B) Adjustment for election cycle, country size and economic performance

As expenses by parties and candidates (for various offices) differ widely between election and non-election years, any comparison concerning the level of political expenses must establish an annual average (step 2). This requires data for an entire election cycle,[127] which may be

- two years (for the U.S. House of Representatives),
- three years (as for parliaments in Australia and Mexico, both until this day, or the Swedish *Riksdag* up to 1994),
- four years (for U.S. presidents or parliaments in Austria, Denmark, Germany, Israel, the Netherlands, Poland, Switzerland -traditionally- and in Sweden -since 1997),
- five years (as the European Parliament -since 1979- and the president in Poland and France -since 2007- as well as parliaments in Britain, Canada, France, Ireland or Italy, although for all these national parliaments five years is just the maximum term, whereas an individual parliament may sit for a variable period of time),

---

125 Holmes 1999, p. 51; Marsh 1999, p. 223; Benoit/ Marsh 2003, p. 568 (€ 3.964 million = IEP 3.122 million).
126 This approach assumes that local elections can be neglected because they are fought on a non-partisan basis.
127 The assumption of a one-size-fits-all "nine-month election year time span" (1963, p. 797) or "nine-month pre-election period" (Heidenheimer 1970b, p. 11) is not really helpful for a comparison of political expenses. See below in chapter III, section C (comparison).

- six years (as for individual U.S. senators or presidents in Austria and Mexico) or even
- seven years (for the presidents of Ireland and France, the latter before 2002).

For many countries the definition of an election cycle will demand some unpleasant decisions for any researcher. Only a few countries apply the same election cycle for all national, regional and municipal elections (most notably Sweden). Others like Japan, the U.S. (and most federal systems) will apply various cycles for different offices or bodies. All countries of the European Union (EU) have to cope with the fact that elections for the European parliament are not in tune with national election cycles. By dividing the total amount spent during an entire election cycle by the number of years that make up this cycle (see column 3 in Table 3-2), step two will finally result in an *annual average* for the comprehensive, yet individual national costs of political competition. If comprehensive data for an entire election cycle are not available (e.g. for Italy, Japan and Sweden), then a fair estimate has to be based on the distinction between election and non-election years.

Table 3-2: Campaign and party expenditure totals (per year and eligible voter)

Country	Spending during election cycle (in million)	Number of years in election cycle	Average spending per year (in million)	Voters on list (million)	Per capita spending (national currency)
(1)	(2)	(3)	(4)	(5)	(6)
USA	4,500-6,000	4	1,125-1,500	196.6	5.70-7.60
Japan	n.a.	3-5	465,000	97.9	4,750
Germany	5,240-6,140	(4-)5	1,050-1,230	60.5	17.35-20.35
Mexico	11,000-15,000	6	1,833-2,500	53.1	34.50-47.10
Italy	n.a.	4-5	600,000-3,400,000	48.8	12,300-69,700
Britain	295-333	4(-5)	73.9-83.3	44.0	1.70-1.90
France	9,100-10,600	5	1,820-2,120	37.9	48-56
Spain	123,000-153,000	(3-)4	30,750-38,250	32.0	960-1,200
Poland	880	4	220	27.7	7.95
Canada	503-574	4(-5)	126-144	19.9	6.35-7.25
Australia	162-186	3	54-62	11.7	4.60-5.30
Netherlands	217-268	4	54.3-67.0	11.5	4.70-5.80
Sweden	3,700-3,900	4	950	6.5	146
Austria	9,200-9,600	4	2,300-2,400	5.8	395-415
Switzerland	206-226	4	51.5-56.5	4.6	11.20-12.30
Israel	930-1,140	4	232-285	4.1	57.70-69.50
Denmark	570-630	4	142-158	4.1	34.65-38.55
Ireland	37.5-51.3	5	7.5-10.3	2.6	2.90-4.00

Sources: Spending data from this chapter, section A1-4; number of eligible voters from International IDEA 1997 (www.idea.in/vt/country_view.cfm) (for USA: Voting age population in presidential election); for Mexico average of IFE data for 1994 and 2000 as supplied by Tania Martinez.

Because the *size of democracies* varies considerably, all annual average data resulting from step two have to be adjusted for size in step three. For this a well-established routine of cross-national comparison is available, the use of per capita data.[128] However, the number that will serve this purpose is less obvious than it seems. The number of inhabitants, i.e. the population, and the number of actual voters are not useful measures for the cost of politics. In various countries the former will include foreign workers who are living in the country but not entitled to cast a vote there. The latter depends on political participation rates,[129] which differ extremely among the democracies.

Thus the number of persons entitled to vote, the number of registered voters or citizens on the voters' list, is more adequate;[130] even if the compilation of that list may cause specific problems related to the processes of registration, enumeration or maintaining a permanent register. The *number of registered voters* is a comparable figure only for countries, which apply a system of compulsory registration, be it the Canadian enumeration procedure or the German voting roll, which is derived from the permanent list of inhabitants. Because the USA relies on voluntary registration the voting age population of that country will be closer to the total number of people entitled to vote than any other figure. Data for all countries within this study (column 5 in Table 3-2) are available from the International IDEA.[131]

Dividing the total amount of political spending for an average year by the number of people entitled to vote in a democracy will produce the annual average *per capita of party* (and campaign) *spending in national currency* for a reasonable number of democracies (see column 6 in Table 3-2). Any comparison of such economic data, however, brings up the fact that countries have different national currencies. Per capita figures will serve the purpose of cross-national comparison only if in step four they can be converted into units of an identical "currency." For this procedure various options have been offered by researchers.

The first approach is conversion of individual amounts to figures given in just one currency. For example, Alexander Heard used the *current exchange rate* and computed USD equivalents in 1960.[132] This was no problem under the Bretton Woods accord, which established fixed exchange rates. However, nowadays the basic risk inherent in this strategy is that the exchange rate can influence the outcome of the comparison. Using the current rate of floating currencies produces additional variance, whereas using the same rate over a long period of time neglects all influence of inflation and economic growth.

---

128 Pinto-Duschinsky 2002, p. 83.
129 Compulsory voting may be a cause for this. It is, however, neglected here because of the countries studied only Australia, Belgium, Cost Rica, Italy and Uruguay apply this rule. Moreover they use different sanctions. For details see Massicotte et al. 2004, pp. 36-37.
130 This indicator has already been used above in chapter 2, section C (cost objects).
131 International IDEA 1997 (www.idea.in/vt/country_view.cfm).
132 Heard 1960, pp. 373/374.

To use an average rate, the rate of a specifically selected day (see Table 3-3 below) or a range for each currency is an arbitrary act of intervention with the data. As exchange rates are floating over time, any cross-national comparison using them will become dependent on factors beyond its own subject. Whichever exchange rate is selected, it will bring influences from international trade or currency speculation to bear upon political spending, which in political and economic reality is not the case. A good example of this problem is the volatility of the dollar-euro exchange rate. Between 1989 and 2008 the maximum rate was USD 1.59, the minimum rate USD 0.82 for € 1.00, the range almost equal to the minimum and about half of the maximum within two decades.

The same, although with a smaller risk, holds true for all attempts to provide a purchasing power parity (PPP).[133] This measure was developed in order to take into account price differences when economic statistics are compared across countries. Its main advantage is that it reflects people's standard of living within such a comparison. The impact of using PPP-$ instead of US-$ is quite obvious between columns 4 and 6 as seen in Table 3-3 below. Big spenders stay big spenders and moderate spenders continue to spend moderately irrespective of the exchange rate, which has been applied. However, within each of the three groups of democracies the rank order changes slightly. This demonstrates that results of the research effort partly depend on the exchange rate, which in real life they should not do.

A slightly different, although more vivid but less reliable approach is the "Big Mac" index, which is derived from the current price of a standard hamburger in different countries.[134] The "Big Mac Index" as developed by *The Economist* (just like the PPP-$ concept) is based on the notion of purchasing power parity. In the long run, the parity among currencies should equal the rate, which allows a person to buy an identical basket of goods and services in any country. For the purpose of this specific PPP index the "basket is a McDonald's Big Mac, which is produced in about 120 countries."[135] The Big Mac PPP exchange rate assumes that a hamburger costs the same everywhere in the world. For the democracies that are covered here, the spread of the price for a standard hamburger, USD 1.38 (Poland) to USD 3.97 (Switzerland), reveals a considerable difference in purchasing power, which is not adequately reflected in currency exchange rates. Although we prefer to rely upon more respectable approaches to the currency problem, the ranking of political spending per person eligible to vote as seen in column 8 of Table 3-3 above represents the number of Big Mac equivalents that are spent on competitive politics. In a group of five "big spender" countries the average citizen forgoes the equivalent of five and more Big Macs in order to cover the annual costs of party competition. Four democracies are run on about three "Big Macs" per capita. In eight countries parties spend about two Big Mac equivalents per voter and

---

133 Cf. Lijphart 1999, pp. 59/60.
134 More recently: "Sizzling", in: *The Economist*, 7 July 2007, p. 74.
135 „Big Mac Index", www.economist.com/markets/bigmac/about.cfm (with links to individual articles).

year. Only two democracies can do with far less, the U.K. and the Netherlands, which may represent the moderate spenders among the democracies.

Table 3-3: Currency equivalents of per capita spending

Country	Annual costs per capita (national currency)	Exchange rate (July 1,1999)	Annual per capita costs in US-$	Exchange rate in PPP-$ 2002	Annual per capita cost in PPP-$	Big Mac in US-$ 1999	Per capita costs in Big Macs
(1)	(2)	(3)	(4)	(5)	(6)	(7)	(8)
Japan	JPY 4,750	122.170	38.90	104.794	45.35	2.44	15.95
Italy	ITL 41 K	1,894	21.65	2,439	16.80	2.50	8.65
Austria	ATS 405	13.462	30.10	15.513	26.10	3.73	8.05
Sweden	SEK 146	8.511	17.15	8.233	17.75	2.88	5.95
Israel	NIS 63.60	3.200	19.90	3.957	16.05	3.44	5.80
Germany	DEM 18.85	1.999	9.45	2.254	8.35	2.72	3.45
France	FRF 52	6.418	8.10	7.181	7.25	2.87	2.80
USA	USD 6.65	1.000	6.65	1.000	6.65	2.43	2.75
Spain	ESP 1,080	162.788	6.65	218.873	4.95	2.43	2.75
Canada	CAD 6.80	1.471	4.60	1.904	3.55	1.98	2.30
Mexico	MXP 40.80	9.60	4.25	13.625	3.00	2.09	2.05
Australia	AUD 4.95	1.508	3.30	2.047	2.40	1.66	2.00
Switzerld.	CHF 11.75	1.568	7.50	1.283	9.15	3.97	1.90
Ireland	IEP 3.45	0.771	4.45	0.905	3.80	2.80	1.60
Poland	PLN 7.95	3.894	2.05	6.742	1.18	1.38	1.50
Denmark	DKK 36.60	7.275	5.05	6.995	5.25	3.58	1.40
Britain,UK	GBP 1.80	0.642	2.80	0.635	2.85	3.07	0.90
Netherlds.	NLG 5.25	2.158	2.45	2.426	2.15	2.66	0.90

Sources: Spending data (column 2 above) is the average of column 6 in Table 3-2; for $-prices (column 7) see „Big MacCurrencies". In: *The Economist*, April 1, 1999 (quoted from: www.economist.com/finance).

A second, more sophisticated approach, based on income data not on consumption, was used by Heidenheimer in 1963.[136] He avoided all problems related to exchange rates and their volatility when he applied statistical information about a real world indicator, the average hourly wage of a male industrial worker, to construct an "index of political expenditure." Most likely the international community of statisticians will ensure that national offices provide comparable data. However, this can apply only to most OECD countries; certainly not to all countries of the developing world and to all countries recently in transition to democracy. Thus the reach of this concept is not glo-

---

136 Heidenheimer1963, pp. 797-798; Heidenheimer 1970b, pp. 11-13.

bal. Furthermore, the rise of the service industries in advanced economies has introduced some doubts as to whether this concept is still as applicable as it obviously was in the 1950s. In post-industrial service economies, the hourly wage of a male industrial worker may not be a good indicator of average income. Nevertheless Heidenheimer's approach offered a practical solution to an important problem: How can we insure that floating exchange rates do not interfere at random with cross-national comparisons?

A similar, yet more generally acceptable, approach to average income in modern economies may start with more encompassing figures, such as the per capita gross national income (GNI), gross national product (GNP) or gross domestic product (GDP).[137] This time the reliability of economic statistical data becomes even more important. If the shadow (or black) economy amounts to some 50 percent of the official GDP in any economy, then data have to be used with care for the purpose of cross-national comparison.[138] As these data (per capita GNI, GNP or GDP) in developed countries will be much higher than annual per capita spending on party activities, a statistical assumption must bring both figures closer together.

If a year is assumed to comprise about 50 working weeks each containing 40 working hours, then the factor 2,000 can be used to compute an average amount that is economically close to the hourly wage.[139] Data for the per capita gross domestic product (GDP) divided by 2,000 will represent the *"hourly rate of national income per average person,"* a figure that may well be suited to substitute for the more traditional measure of the industrial worker's hourly wage.[140] The resulting figure will always be in the same national currency as is all political finance data. It will include the impacts of inflation and overall economic growth, without trying to tell them apart, and avoid all parity problems. As a result of this effort, relative positions of individual countries on the Index of Political Spending (IPS), i.e. a "world ranking order," can be identified (see column 5 in Table 3-4) by step five of our procedure.

---

137 Although the Gross National Income may be more appropriate, we have decided to use the Gross Domestic Product because the data is more readily available from UNDP and OECD statistics.
138 I am indebted to Marcin Walecki (Warsaw, Oxford and Florence) for this information resulting from the experience of post-communist countries. Even the (more traditional) German speaking countries have a notorious "shadow economy". Recent estimates for Germany (16 to 18 percent of the "official" GDP), Austria (over 10 percent) and Switzerland (less than 10 percent) demonstrate that it is quite considerable (cf. "Zunahme der Schwarzarbeit erwartet." In: *Frankfurter Allgemeine* (daily newspaper), 15 January 2007; Plickert, Philip: „Ein ganzes Bundesland arbeitet schwarz." In: *Frankfurter Allgemeine* (daily newspaper), 4 February 2008).
139 However, in the real world the suggested procedure is still a simplification because the average number of working hours may be less than 40, the active workforce may include different shares of the population and in most countries people will work less than 50 weeks per year.
140 Nassmacher 2002, p. 13.

*Table 3-4: Averages of party and campaign expenses per eligible voter and year
(Index of Plitical Spending)*

Country	Annual spending per capita average (national currency)	GDP 1996 per capita (national currency)	Per capita GDP times 0.0005	Index of Party Spending (IPS)*
(1)	(2)	(3)	(4)	(5)= (2) : (4)
USA	USD 6.65	28,791	14.40	0.46
Japan	JPY 4,750	4,075,367	2,038.00	2.33
Germany	DEM 18.85	43,793	21.90	0.86
Mexico	MXP 40.80	27,318	13.66	2.99
Italy	ITL 41,000	33,152,230	16,576.00	2.47
Britain (U.K.)	GBP 1.80	12,862	6.43	0.28
France	FRF 52	136,212	68.11	0.76
Spain	ESP 1,080	1,967,021	983.50	1.10
Poland	PLN 7.95	10,928	5.46	1.46
Canada	CAD 6.80	27,705	13.85	0.49
Australia	AUD 4.95	30,790	15.40	0.32
Netherlands	NLG 5.25	44,713	22.36	0.23
Sweden	SEK 146	198,661	99.33	1.47
Austria	ATS 405	303,927	152.00	2.66
Switzerland	CHF 11.75	51,662	25.83	0.45
Israel	ILS 63.60	40,211	20.11	3.16
Denmark	DKK 36.60	204,489	102.24	0.36
Ireland	IEP 3.45	12,575	6.29	0.55

Sources: Per capita averages of political spending from Table 3-2; GDP from National Accounts of OECD Countries, vol. II, 1988-1999, OECD 2001; population figures from Statistisches Jahrbuch für das Ausland, 1998, p. 39. Data for Israel from: www.cbs.gov.il/sidfilee.cgi.

* = Annual per capita spending average divided by 0.0005 (=1/2,000) times per capita GDP in national currency.

C) Comparison of spending levels

There are two systematic options to confront spending data. First, the data elaborated in this chapter can be balanced against each other. When contrasted to dollar equivalents (see columns 4 and 6 in Table 3-3 above), the IPS rank order (see column 9 in Table 3-5 below) shows a big change for Mexico, which moves from moderate spender to excessive spender, for Switzerland, which moves from a top rank among the medium level spenders to a more moderate position, for Sweden, which moves slightly from big spender to medium level spender and for the U.S., which is in a more moderate position on the IPS than on the dollar ranking. However, most democracies occupy a very similar station in all four rank orders, i.e. even including the Big Mac equivalents. Graph 3-1 presents an impression of all individual values of the IPS and each of the dollar equivalents.[141]

Graph 3-1:   *Different measures/ indicators for per capita political spending*

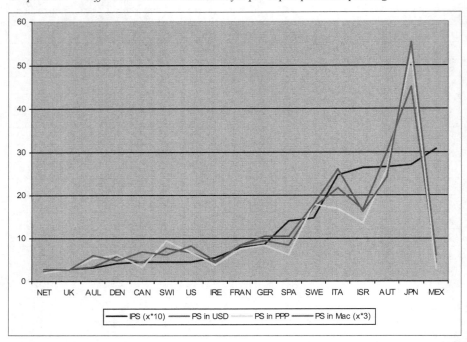

Data in Graph 3-1 (as well as in Tables 3-3 and 3-4, all above) demonstrate that there is a obvious spread for the levels of political spending among the democracies. However, in Graph 3-1 different indicators look very much in line with each other. Correlations between the IPS and the other measures are high and significant (Pearson's $r = 0.69$, $p=0.002$ for spending in USD; $r = 0.60$, $p=0.01$ for PPP-$ amounts and $r = 0.66$, $p=0.004$ for BigMac equivalents). The obvious outliers are Italy, Israel, Japan and Mexico. This seems to support our contention that the kind of measurement (partially) influences the result of the comparison. In general, however, there is no need to be too critical of actual findings.

---

141   In order to avoid the impression of big differences, which result from the overall ranges of the four indices (2 to 50 dollars for USD and PPP, 1 to 18 for Big Macs and 0.2 to 3.00 for the IPS) actual values have been multiplied by 3 (Big Mac based index) respectively 10 (IPS).

Thus we turn to the second comparative option. This is a comparison of data presented by different scholars (as reported in the beginning of this chapter).[142] Within five decades only four political scientists have tried to answer the question, "How much money is spent for the party apparatus and/or election campaigns?" The first was Alexander Heard who in his pioneering work presented the "cash costs of electioneering" per inhabitant for a total of five countries[143] (see column 2 in Table 3-1 above). Of these Israel was the big spender, whereas the level of political expenses in the U.S. and in Italy was much lower. Germany and Britain posed as "low cost" democracies. Other countries were not mentioned by Heard, because the data were not available.

In 1963 Arnold Heidenheimer, in a special issue of the *Journal of Politics*, estimated the per capita cost of party activities for "a nine-month election year time span" around 1960 to be 3s9d for Australia, 3s9d for Britain, DM 2.73 for Germany, $2.53 for the United States, Rs 0.75 for India, Yen 150 for Japan, Lit 1,000 for Italy, P. 12 for the Philippines and ISP 25.7 for Israel.[144] Heidenheimer's conclusion (repeated in 1970) was summed up by his "Index of Expenditure" based on the average hourly wage. This index (see column 3 in Table 3-1 above and column 2 in Table 3-5 below) placed Australia and Britain in the lower stratum, Germany, the United States, India and Japan about twice as high. Italy, the Philippines and Israel, although markedly different from each other, were at the high end. Austria, Canada, Denmark, France, the Netherlands, Sweden and Switzerland were not mentioned, Poland and Spain had not yet returned to the democratic fold.

Using information available for the late 1970s, this author calculated the per voter costs of national politics in 1986 during a full four-year election cycle (see column 5 in Table 3-1 above) for the U.K. (DEM 5), Canada (DEM 7), the U.S. (DEM 8), the Netherlands (DEM 9), West Germany (DEM 21) and Sweden (DEM 27).[145] The only conclusion drawn from this data was to label the U.K., Canada, the U.S. and the Netherlands as 'moderate expenditure' countries, Germany, Sweden plus Italy, Austria and Israel (the latter three countries, however, without a "price tag") as 'high expenditure' democracies. In that sample, Australia, Denmark, France, Ireland, Japan, Mexico, Spain and Switzerland were missing because no data was available then.

In 1984 Howard Penniman stated that "in most of the twenty countries with 1.5 million voters and twenty-five years of continuous democratic practice, there is neither adequate financing data nor recognised experts with the knowledge and experience to make informed and generally accepted judgements of costs."[146] Using data, for which he identifies the inadequacies, Penniman ended up with seven countries (see column

---

142 See above in this chapter, Table 3-1.
143 Heard 1960, pp. 373-375. Earlier attempts by Pollock 1926, pp. 175/176 and Overacker 1932, pp. 81-85 were less comprehensive in scope and outreach.
144 Heidenheimer 1963, pp. 797-798; Heidenheimer 1970b, pp. 11-13.
145 Nassmacher 1986, pp. 95-96.
146 Penniman 1984, pp. 52-53.

4 in Table 3-1 above).[147] Of these countries, the U.K. and Canada had exceptionally inexpensive party competition while Germany, Ireland, Israel and the U.S. displayed, more or less, a similar level of party spending; a range of USD 3.20 to 4.34. Venezuela had the most expensive politics ($26.35 per eligible voter) by far.

Table 3-5: Costs of party competition in comparative perspective, late 1950s to late 1990s

Country	1963[a]	1960/84[b]	2002[c]	Big Mac	Ranking			
	Index	Amount	IPS	Index	1963	1960/84	2002	BigMac
(1)	(2)	(3)	(4)	(5)	(6)	(7)	(8)	(9)
Venezuela	-	$ 26.35	-	-	-	1.	-	-
Israel	20.50	$ 5.00+	3.16	5.80	1.	3.	1.	5.
Mexico	-	-	2.99	2.05	-	-	2.	11.
Austria	-	-	2.66	8.05	-	-	3.	3.
Philippines	16.00	-	-	-	3.	-	-	-
Italy	4.50	$ 0.50	2.47	8.65	5.	15.	4.	2.
Japan	1.36	-	2.33	15.95	7.	-	5.	1.
Sweden	-	-	1.47	5.95	-	-	6.	4.
Poland	-	-	1.46	1.49	-	-	7.	15.
Spain	-	-	1.10	2.75	-	-	8.	9.
Germany	0.95	$ 3.20	0.86	3.45	13.	6.	9.	6.
France	-	-	0.76	2.80	-	-	10.	7.
Ireland	-	$ 3.93	0.55	1.60	-	5.	11.	14.
Canada	-	$ 1.43	0.49	2.30	-	11.	12.	10.
USA	1.12	$ 3.25	0.46	2.75	11.	7.	13.	8.
Switzerland	-	-	0.45	1.90	-	-	14.	13.
India	1.25	-	-	-	9.	-	-	-
Denmark	-	-	0.36	1.40	-	-	15.	16.
Australia	0.45	-	0.32	2.00	17.	-	16.	12.
Britain(UK)	0.64	$ 0.50	0.28	0.90	15.	15.	17.	17.
Netherlands	-	-	0.23	0.90	-	-	18.	18.

Sources: a) Heidenheimer 1963, pp. 798/799.; Heidenheimer 1970b, pp. 11-13;
b) Heard 1960, pp. 373-375 and Penniman 1984, pp. 52-53, combined (amounts in US-$);
c) Nassmacher 2002, p. 13 (revised, as above); d) column 8 in Table 3-3 above.
Legend: Ranking for 1963 and 1960/1984 with incomplete numbering to adjust for low number of cases. Countries in *Italics* are not in the current sample.

These data fit perfectly with the other efforts, because Britain, Canada, Venezuela and Israel finish at their "usual" ends of the spending continuum whereas Germany, Ireland and the U.S. hold an intermediate position in the ranking. Penniman's general proposi-

---

147 For the comparative table (columns 3 and 7 in Table 3-5 above) we have combined the highest $-amounts for the countries covered by Heard and Penniman.

tion that electoral campaigns are not "conducted at a much lower cost in all other democracies" than they are in the U.S. is very much to the point.[148] Between the 1960s and the 1980s the U.S. has not experienced much change.[149] However, this situation offers something of a paradox, because the cross-national impression contrasts markedly to findings of national research.[150]

The spending level given for Venezuela by Penniman is quite consistent with the level given for the Philippines by Heidenheimer. Both countries are neglected in this study because neither is an established democracy. Nonetheless, it seems fair to add the conclusion that competitive politics in Third World countries is extremely expensive.[151] Moreover, the observations, which result from all four efforts, seem to fit with the more recent country by country survey.

Based on information for the late 1990s, Britain, Australia, the Netherlands and Denmark belong to a group of 'moderate spenders,'[152] which now can be defined by an Index of Political Spending in the range of 0.2 to 0.4 (see column 5 in Table 3-5 above). Mexico, Italy, Austria, Israel and Japan are the 'big spenders,' now more precisely defined by an IPS range of 1.6 to 3.2.[153] The big spenders represent the "old" patronage-inclined type of electioneering rather than the "modern" type of media-centred campaigning.[154] Obviously this finding reiterates the "development theory" of political spending as advanced by Heidenheimer and Pinto-Duschinsky.[155] As a general trend, the spread among countries repeats their finding that the "old" (patronage oriented) politics is more expensive than the "new" (media based) politics. Countries with an IPS below 2.0 practice a less traditional (i.e. patronage oriented) style of politics and rely on the modern means of mass communications for their campaigns.

The intermediate range of 0.4 to 1.6 can be divided up into an upper (0.8 to 1.6) and a lower (0.4 to 0.8) medium group, each of which comprises four established democracies: Canada, Ireland, Switzerland and the U.S. vs. Germany, Spain, Poland and Sweden. France (with an IPS of 0.76, close to the dividing line), the ninth country in this group, is the median of the intermediates. The U.S. and Germany once again belong to the 'medium expenditure' democracies although both are separated by the artificial 0.8 demarcation line.[156]

---

148 Penniman 1984, p. 53.
149 Heard 1960, pp. 373-375.
150 Bloom 1956, p. 170; Crotty 1977, pp. 103-105; Sorauf 1988, p. 29; Alexander/ Corrado 1995, p. 178; Katz 1996, pp. 129, 132; Alexander 1999, p. 15; Scarrow 2007, p. 206.
151 See below in chapter IV, sub-section A1 (political and economic development).
152 Nassmacher/ Nassmacher 2001, p. 183 and Nassmacher 2002, p. 13.
153 Actually the range is even more narrow: 2.3 to 3.2.
154 Pinto-Duschinsky 2002, pp. 82/83. – The odd case seems to be Austria.
155 Heidenheimer 1963, pp. 800/801; Heidenheimer 1970b, pp. 11/12; Pinto-Duschinsky 1981, p. 15 – See below in chapter IV, sub-section A1a (stages of development).
156 Despite differences in analytical approach the European countries covered by Webb's (1995, p. 308) income data roughly follow the IPS rank order. The only exception (Italy) is due to Webb's reliance on official data.

The "perfect fit" of these results notwithstanding it may well be that "the relatively low costs of party politics" in the Netherlands[157] (and elsewhere) owes as much to a lack of data for all sub-national activities, as to a tradition of modest political spending. Another dose of caution should be added, too. Careful readers may recall that the data for Mexico depends very much on an assumption about the financial share of federal politics and estimates for Italy and Japan have been approximated roughly. Thus even the averages used in this study might be overblown. As a contrast, the data for Austria (along with Britain and Germany, which belong to different strata) are the most carefully researched and the most detailed among our sample. Thus they should not be precisely comparable to data of much lower quality. However, in general the edge of the most expensive democracies as compared to the rest of the sample is rather large. Even with a pinch of salt added to the IPS, the spending rank order among established democracies should be quite safe.

Summing up the evidence, which was presented in this chapter, four statements cover most of the findings:

- The considerable spread of per capita spending totals as observed by Heard, Heidenheimer and Penniman for party competition in the mid-20th century was still valid at the end of that century.
- Although data quality and reliability may in some respect be subject to doubt, high level spenders and low cost democracies can be identified, as well as countries that fall in-between the two extremes.
- Among the eighteen democracies, for which the costs of political competition can be established, five stand out as *excessive spenders* (Austria, Israel, Italy, Japan and Mexico). No more than four display a *moderate level of party expenses* (Australia, Britain/the U.K., Denmark, the Netherlands). A total of nine democracies operate at an *intermediate level of political spending* (Canada, France, Germany, Ireland, Poland, Spain, Sweden, Switzerland and the U.S.).
- Most countries have not changed their general position as far as the level of political spending is concerned in about five decades.

Two of the four modest spenders belong to the "Anglo-Saxon orbit," more precisely to the "Westminster tradition" of democratic government,[158] whereas two of the big spenders are the only examples of an established democracy with a non-western culture. Moreover, in Mexico for most of the 20th century, quite a few rigged elections do not support the idea of a western-style democracy. Do these observations indicate that the concept of political culture offers any explanation to the causes of largely different spending levels? That is, can comparative research in political finance now hope to elaborate causes for the different levels of political spending, which have been established in this chapter?

---

157 Daalder 1987, p. 271.
158 For the terms used here (Anglo-Saxon orbit, Westminster tradition) cf. Nassmacher 2003b, pp. 33, 51 resp. Pinto-Duschinsky 2001a, p. 19.

CHAPTER FOUR

Causes of Spending Levels

Looking at the total amounts of party (and candidate) expenditure not only demands an evaluation of the causes for the largely different levels of spending, but it also re-emphasises the need to follow the development of political expenses over time. Can we discover a trend of party spending for a couple of decades, either in a single democracy or even compare various democracies? Before we move to the dynamic aspects of political finance and a study of time series data,[1] we shall use a one-shot approach and discuss the possible causes for different levels of political spending.[2] This chapter intends to answer the question: Do features of a democratic *polity*, conditions of competitive *politics* or impacts of public *policy* cause the impressive spread of spending levels, which was identified in the previous chapter?

A)   Features of the democratic polity

We expect that some difference in political expense levels are due to peculiar characteristics of individual polities, such as size of electorate, political routines or stage of development. Among these, political scientists identify the most traditional cause for a high level of political spending as the stage of a specific country's political and economic development.

1.   Stages of political and economic development

When Heidenheimer published comparative volumes on political finance,[3] he argued that economic development helps decrease the cost of elective politics. That is, the more advanced a country is economically, the less cash has to be spent on its democracy. This relationship exists because "vote buying" and other traditional means of voter mobilisation have been substituted by more modern instruments like mass meetings, canvassing or media advertising. In his 1963 comparison, the Philippines and Israel ranked highest among the nine countries included in his "Index of Expenditure."

---

1   This is pursued below, in chapter V (cost explosion).
2   On Belgium, Costa Rica, Finland, India, New Zealand, Norway, Uruguay see note 1 in chapter III above.
3   Actually the first volume was the special issue of a journal, and the second was an edited book.

Italy, Japan and India were next, and outspent the economically more advanced countries (Australia, Britain, Germany and the U.S.).[4]

In his seminal case study of political funding in the U.K. Pinto-Duschinsky applied this theory to one of the "old democracies" in 1981. He identified three stages, through which British political finance has evolved: *the aristocratic, the plutocratic,* and *the modern era*. During the aristocratic era a candidate had "to bribe voters, to fund innkeepers for refreshments on polling day, and to ingratiate himself with the electors ... [by employing them] ... as cabdrivers, messengers, canvassers, clerks, agents, and poll watchers. ... On top of this, candidates were expected ... to give annual subscriptions to local political clubs and charities." Development of cohesive parties, which began in the late nineteenth century, shifted demands for political money to "the central party war chest. This soon led the Liberals and, ..., the Conservatives to seek these extra central funds from rich capitalists."[5] In the 1920s the "challenge of Labour led the Conservative party managers to invest heavily in propaganda campaigns and professional publicity techniques. ... These developments placed heavy demands on the national party's routine and campaign expenditure. ... In general election campaigns, the extra money for advertising was provided largely by the significant decrease (in real terms) in Central Office grants to parliamentary candidates."[6]

In 1986 Pinto-Duschinsky reiterated the general consequence from both early studies: "Money is most likely to be deployed for political purposes ... in *developing nations*, ..."[7] This term may embrace a political as well as an economic connotation. Both dimensions deserve to be considered because modern democracies have developed politically as well as economically.

a) Economic development

Because our sample essentially includes OECD countries only,[8] a high level of economic output in each country can be expected. In fact, most of the democracies that are discussed in this book are very likely to have extremely high per capita GDPs. However, any difference between individual countries or groups of countries may be mirrored in their level of political spending. A first test, which uses per capita GDP for the year 2002, indicates an inverse relationship between GDP and the Index of Political Spending.[9] That is, whereas moderate political spenders had a per capita GDP (PPP $ 28,613) above average, the big spenders' output (PPP $ 22,218) was well below av-

---

4   Heidenheimer 1963, p. 798; Heidenheimer 1970b, p. 12 – cf. above in chapter III, Tables 3-1 and 3-5. However, Heidenheimer expected political spending to rise again as a consequence of modern campaigning.
5   Pinto-Duschinsky 1981, pp. 15-16, 31.
6   Pinto-Duschinsky 1981, pp. 93, 101.
7   Pinto-Duschinsky 1986b, p. 32; emphasis added.
8   Israel – although a highly developed economy – is the only non-OECD country in our sample.
9   As developed above, in chapter III, section B (adjustment); major results see below in Table 4-1, column (2).

erage (PPP $ 26,068). A Pearson's r for IPS on the one hand, and GDP in PPP $ (r = –0.56; p=0.02) respectively GDP in USD (r = –0.49; p=0.04) on the other indicate a rather strong (inverse) correlation.

However, GDP can be an unreliable indicator. Even economists voice doubts as to the quality of measurement that can be achieved by GDP because it reveals nothing about how national income is distributed or spent. Therefore we also use a different indicator, which has become more widely used recently. The Human Development Index (HDI) is a composite index that measures a country's average achievements in three basic areas of human development: longevity of life, level of knowledge, and a decent standard of living. Of the 18 democracies that are studied in depth, 16 are among the 22 top ranking countries on the HDI in 1995 and 1999.[10] Only Mexico and Poland rank much lower. Values of the 1995 HDI range between 0.776 (Mexico) and 0.933 (Canada) among the democracies covered in this chapter. The average value is 0.901 (Italy), the median is 0.916 (Switzerland). Values for 1999 are not much different. The (inverse) correlation between IPS and economic development decreases slightly to r = –0.50 (p=0.03) for the mean of 1995 and 1999 HDIs (see column 3 in Table 4-1 below).[11] The level of economic development appears to have a strong impact on political spending. That is, the more a country can afford economically, the less likely it is to spend much on its democracy.[12] However, economic achievement seems to be less important than the length of democratic experience.

b)   Democratic tradition

The theory that modern democracies are less expensive than newly democratised systems connects neatly with more recent writings on various waves of democratisation. Reformulated the theory would read: Old democracies are less expensive than new democracies because they have already passed the most expensive preliminary ("aristocratic" and "plutocratic") stages and have reached the "modern era" of political finance. Among the democracies, which are included in the computation of spending levels (see above in Tables 3-2 to 3-5), nine countries (Australia, Britain, Canada, Denmark, Ireland, the Netherlands,[13] Sweden, Switzerland and the U.S.) have con-

---

10 There are only six other democracies, which score high on the HDI, but are not covered in this chapter. Iceland and Luxembourg are rather small. Belgium, Finland, New Zealand and Norway had to be excluded due to lack of spending data.
11 Human Development Report 1998, p. 20 (http://hdr.undp.org/reports/global/1998/en/) and Human Development Report 2001, p. 141 (http://hdr.undp.org/reports/global/2001/en/).
12 This refutes Heidenheimer's contention (mentioned above in this chapter) that rising expenses are due to modern campaign technology.
13 Unfortunately Huntington (1991, p. 15) does not distinguish between democracies that discontinued their democratic tradition between 1920 and 1940 (such as Austria, France, Germany, Italy) and countries where democratic government was interrupted by German occupation (such as Denmark, the Netherlands and Norway). We consider the former as part of the second wave of democratisation and the latter as part of the first wave. (Merkel 1999, pp. 175, 188 is inconsistent on this issue.)

tinuously been democratic since the first wave. Six countries (Austria, France, Germany, Israel, Italy and Japan) can be considered second wave democracies. Poland, Mexico and Spain are cases of a third wave democracy.[14]

For two of these groups the reformulated theory seems to hold. On average second wave democracies cost about four times as much as first wave democracies. For the latter the IPS ranges from 0.23 to 1.47, the median is 0.45, the mean 0.51 (with a standard deviation of 0.37). Eight of these democracies have an IPS below 0.6 (except Sweden, where the level of spending is much higher). For second wave democracies in our sample the IPS ranges from 0.76 to 3.16, the median is 2.40, the mean equals 2.04 (with a standard deviation of 0.98). Among these "retarded" democracies only France and Germany (both with an interrupted tradition) do not have extremely high levels of political spending. The three third wave democracies (Mexico, Poland, Spain) do not differ much from the second wave pattern.[15]

If democratic tradition is measured by years of popularly elected government and general (male) suffrage, the Pearson's r for IPS and democratic tradition equals –0.60 (p=0.01), a correlation comparable to other indicators describing the impact of development.[16] Thus it seems fair to conclude that increasing experience in popular government (as measured by years of democratic tradition or by wave of democratisation) reduces the level of political spending. However, various factors can pull the level of party spending into different directions. Now that we have discussed two of them (the level of economic development and the "age" of a democracy) we should turn to another obvious cause. Since democracies differ in size more than in wealth, it may well be that economies of scale are a decisive factor.

2. Size of the electorate (economies of scale)

The least sophisticated hypothesis that tries to explain different levels of spending on elective politics starts with a transfer of basic economics to party funding. As everywhere else in modern economies, larger quantities or units cause less overhead than smaller ones. For example, the costs to produce five home-made hamburgers in your own kitchen will be (relatively) higher than the costs of serving five billion burgers world-wide in a chain of fast-food restaurants. Thus, parties appealing to a small electorate of 2 million voters can be expected to need (relatively) more money than their counterparts serving 200 million citizens. Although small democracies will be rather inexpensive, this advantage is likely to disappear or even to be reversed into a disadvantage when compared to bigger political systems on a per capita basis. Because

---

14 Merkel 1999, p. 175 (Table 7), based on Huntington 1991, p. 15.
15 Measured by Somer's d (N=18) the correlation between IPS and wave of democratisation is 0.58 (p=0.00), which indicates a remarkable relationship.
16 Party spending per capita as measured by the IPS and other indicators is, not at all surprising, highly correlated (in USD r = 0.66, p = 0.003; in PPP $ r = 0.57, p=0.01; in BigMac equivalents r = 0.62, p=0.006).

fewer citizens have to put up with the basic costs of running an election campaign and/ or competing party organisations, small democracies may cause relatively more expenses per eligible voter.[17] This simple approach, however, does not explain the different levels of political spending among the cases presented in this study.

Table 4-1: Party spending, development and size of of democracies

Country	Index of Party Spending	Economic performance: HDI 1995/99 (average)	Democratic Tradition by wave	IPS decreasing with size of electorate
(1)	(2)	(3)	(4)	(5)
Israel	3.16	0.887	Second	Gently
Mexico	2.99	0.785	Third	Gently
Austria	2.66	0.917	Second	Gently
Italy	2.47	0.907	Second	Gently
Japan	2.33	0.926	Second	Gently
Sweden	1.47	0.932	First	Gently
Poland	1.46	0.810	Third	Steeply
Spain	1.10	0.906	Third	Steeply
Germany	0.86	0.916	Second	Steeply
France	0.76	0.922	Second	Steeply
Ireland	0.55	0.905	First	Gently
Canada	0.49	0.935	First	Gently
USA	0.46	0.930	First	Steeply
Switzerland	0.45	0.921	First	Gently
Denmark	0.36	0.917	First	Gently
Australia	0.32	0.934	First	Gently
Britain (U.K.)	0.28	0.922	First	Steeply
Netherlands	0.23	0.929	First	Gently

Sources: Party spending data (IPS) from Tables 3-4 and 3-5 in chapter III above; HDI from http://hdr.undp.org/reports/global/1998/en/; for other data: Huntington 1991, p. 15 (modified).
Comments: Outliers are indicated by *italics*.

Viewed more systematically, the smallest democracies in the sample (i.e. Ireland, Denmark, Israel, Switzerland, Austria and Sweden) should be among the big spenders. While Israel and Austria (plus Sweden in a way) behave as predicted, Ireland, Denmark and Switzerland do not.[18] Although "economies of scale" are available in much bigger democracies, the per capita comparison does not produce the anticipated re-

---

17 For a preliminary discussion cf. Nassmacher 2002, p. 14. For the first empirical test of the relationship between spending and size see the analysis of party funding in Swiss municipalities by Schaller 1994, p. 231.
18 See above in chapter III, Tables 3-2 (column 5), 3-3 and 3-4.

sults. Party competition in the U.S., Mexico, Japan and Italy should most certainly be much less demanding and be among the least expensive democracies, which in actual fact only the U.S., but none of the others really is.

Two tests confirm that the 18 democracies of our sample offer no statistical evidence supporting the "economies of scale" theory. First, the Pearson's correlation coefficient for IPS and millions of voting age citizens is $r = -0.02$ ($p=0.93$). Second, the same coefficient for IPS and logged size of the electorate equals -0.045 ($p=0.86$). Both coefficients indicate that no correlation can be established between IPS and a democracy's size.

Graph 4-1:   Scattergram of IPS values by size of democracy (in three clusters)

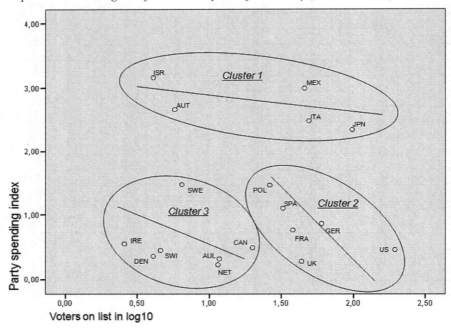

However, an inquisitive look at the scattergram of IPS values by size of democracy suggests that the sample includes three sub-groups (see graph 4-1 above). The first is located in the top half of the graph, and the second in its lower left corner and a third in the lower right quarter. A cluster analysis (with data for size and IPS) bears out the expected difference:

(1) Austria, Israel, Italy, Japan and Mexico (the countries with the highest spending levels) form the first cluster.
(2) France, Germany, Poland, Spain, the U.K. and the U.S. (all of them democracies with a high number of voters) belong to a second cluster.

(3) Australia, Canada, Denmark, Ireland, the Netherlands, Sweden and Switzerland (most of the smaller countries of our sample) compose a third cluster.

IPS averages indicate major differences between the three clusters. For cluster (1) the IPS average is 2.72, for cluster (2) 0.82 and for cluster (3) 0.55. If we run separate regression analyses for the subgroups they reveal different, yet declining regression lines (Graph 4-1): a gentle decline of spending levels for big spenders (cluster 1) and small countries (cluster 3), a steep decline for big countries (cluster 2). This finding leads to a more sophisticated interpretation of the data. It may well be that the sample consists of three subgroups. They operate at different spending levels, which are decreasing as the voting population increases, either

(1) gently for a first group of five (expensive) democracies (Australia, Israel, Italy, Japan and Mexico),
(2) steeply for a second group of six (big) democracies (France, Germany, Poland, Spain, the U.K. and the U.S.) or
(3) gently for a third group of seven (smaller) democracies (Australia, Canada, Denmark, Ireland, the Netherlands, Sweden and Switzerland).

The equations for the three different regression lines are:

(1) IPS = $3.021 - 0.357$ x log (voters on list / 10^6) (*gently* declining),
(2) IPS = $2.226 - 0.826$ x log (voters on list / 10^6) (*steeply* declining) and
(3) IPS = $0.722 - 0.200$ x log (voters on list / 10^6) (*gently* declining).

All regression lines for the three subgroups (see Graph 4-1 above) support the economies of scale theory that the level of party spending decreases with an increasing size of the electorate, although they also indicate that the impact is not equally strong for all countries.

In passing, it is interesting to mention that there is some notable overlap between two of the factors presented so far: size and tradition of democracy. A first, systematic approach to tackling the difference between steeply and gently declining costs of democracy reveals some fit between the categories. In seven old ("first wave") democracies (the third cluster), per capita costs of political competition decline gently by size, whereas in younger (second and third wave) democracies the decline is either steep or gentle. However, experience with democracy does not offer a clue to distinguish between the two other clusters. Moreover one of them includes two "first wave" democracies, the U.K. and the U.S. Besides economies of scale, length of democratic tradition and level of economic development, there must be other forces at work. Among these may be the fact that, as a political system, democracy comes in a variety of forms, which mould the process of conflict resolution within each party system.

3. *Routines of conflict resolution*

The basis of political conflict and the instruments of decision-making may also be driving forces for party spending. For example, Hiltrud Nassmacher has argued that coalition politics is expensive for the taxpayer because small parties demand high prizes at the expense of the public.[19] This may also apply to the costs of democracy. Thus the very nature and organisation of different political systems deserves attention. Potential indicators for the predominant pattern of conflict resolution and the structure of party competition are:

- Some formal institutions, e.g. *federalism* or electoral system, structure the political process.
- The established *routines of conflict resolution* used in a political system will influence the position of a country on the competitive-consociational continuum.
- The *segmented* ("plural") character of a *society* leads to deep-rooted conflicts between political camps, pillars and the like.

Any of these variables may cause different levels of political spending. Pluralism in modern societies will enhance their ability to resolve conflicts, segmentation may be counterproductive. Federalism has been designed to cope with this ambivalence by assigning separate political jurisdictions to distinct areas (and their predominant segment of society).

a) Plural societies and federal systems

In his recent comparative study, Lijphart classified democracies by their degree of societal division, i.e. the main organised sub-societies resulting from ethnic or linguistic differences and religious cleavages. According to his classification, our sample includes 5 plural, 6 semi-plural and 7 non-*plural societies*.[20] An average per capita spending of USD 5.88 for the plural societies (Canada, Israel, Mexico, Spain, Switzerland) as compared to USD 11.81 for the semi-plural and USD 12.60 for the non-plural societies (Australia, Britain, Denmark, Ireland, Japan, Poland and Sweden) indicates a considerable difference.[21] This clear distinction is repeated by the IPS, which averages 0.65, 1.49 and 1.34 respectively. However, each subgroup includes big as well as moderate spenders. Somer's $d = -0.07$ ($p=0.69$) confirms the assumption of statistical insignificance.

The framers of political systems organised plural societies as *federal systems*, and non-plural societies as unitary states. More recently some unitary democracies have recog-

---

19 Nassmacher, H. 2004a, p. 48; Nassmacher, H. 2006, pp. 77-78, 82-83.
20 Lijphart 1999, pp. 57/58. Mexico is a plural society and a federal system, Poland non-plural and unitary.
21 PSinPPP-$ is 5.36, 10.04, 12.98; PSinMac is 2.14, 4.09, 4.78 for non-plural, semi-plural and plural societies.

nised their semi-plural societies and devolved power to regional units (France, Italy, and Spain).[22] Thus we can distinguish between federal, devolved and unitary systems. Assigning political power to various levels in a multi-tier (e.g. federal) political system will duplicate party systems, party organisations and elections. This could possibly increase the costs of political competition. It can be anticipated that decentralised political systems are inversely related to the IPS. That is, the more centralised the political system the lower the level of political spending.

For federal systems, the median of party spending per capita was USD 6.65, which contrasts with USD 8.10 for devolved systems and USD 4.75 for unitary democracies. If the IPS is reviewed by groups of countries, the average for unitary democracies (1.23) is less different from the mean for federal democracies (1.18).[23] Somer's d=0.08 (p=0.97) underlines the suggested non-relationship. Social segmentation and federal systems do not influence the level of political spending. However, other routines of conflict resolution may have a different impact.

b)   Competitive vs. consociational decision-making

Long ago the comparative analysis of democracies shifted its emphasis from the institutional dichotomy of parliamentary versus presidential systems, to the procedural dichotomy of competitive versus consociational decision-making. In his recent study Lijphart prefers the terms 'majoritarian' and 'consensus' democracies. The latter "share, disperse and limit power in a variety of ways."[24] Austria and Israel are two examples of consociational democracies. Their IPS values are high and pretty close to each other (2.66 and 3.16). Australia and the U.K. offer obvious cases of competitive decision-making. Their IPS values are much lower and even less different (0.32 and 0.28). Party politics in both consociational countries costs almost ten times the per capita amount that citizens in the two competitive democracies have to put in. This proportion shrinks to roughly 8 times the amount spent in USD or PPP-$ and less than twice the number of Big Macs that citizens forgo to fund their democracy. By all these measures the difference between the two pairs remains obvious and considerable.

However, other individual examples leave room to question the obvious proposition that consensus politics increases the level of political spending. Both, competitive Mexico and consociational Japan, show extremely high costs of party competition. The strong consensus polities of the Netherlands and Switzerland operate at low costs of democracy. Therefore, details of a potential cause-effect relationship have to be elaborated.

---

22   The U.K. did not completely divide its territory into devolved units as the three other countries have done.
23   Lijphart's (1999, p. 189) index of "federalism" is very moderately correlated with the IPS (r=-0.14). However, this correlation is not statistically significant (p=0.6).
24   Lijphart 1999, p. 2.

During the process of his comparative studies Lijphart has identified the position of individual democracies on a competitive-consociational continuum.[25] Finally he developed a composite index (called the "executive-parties dimension") to locate each country. Five individual indicators ("variables") contribute towards the combined impact. They are the effective number of parliamentary parties, minimal winning one-party cabinets, executive dominance, electoral disproportionality and interest group pluralism.[26]

As suggested by the obvious difference between the two pairs of countries, most of Lijphart's scaled measurements relate to the IPS as well as to per capita political spending, however, at a medium level (Pearson's r between 0.3 and 0.4). The correlation is lower for two of his variables and higher for no more than one. These correlations indicate that party competition in competitive (majoritarian) democracies is less expensive than it is in consociational (consensus) democracies. Although none of the correlations is statistically significant (see Table 4-2), it seems remarkable that p approaches a relevant level as r increases.

Table 4-2: Party spending and Lijphart's indicators of decision-making routines [27]

Indicator of consociationalism	Pearson's r	Significance (p)
Executive dominance of the legislature	-0.180	0.505
Effective number of parliamentary parties	0.251	0.349
Interest group pluralism	-0.354	0.178
Disproportionality of electoral procedure	-0.359	0.172
Executive-parties dimension	0.388	0.138
Minimal winning one-party cabinets	-0.458	0.088

For this purpose it is advisable to consider the variables individually. Among the five subindices, which have been tested, cabinet dominance of the legislature is the indicator most moderately correlated to the IPS (r=-0.18). This may be due to specific problems of measurement.[28]

The number of competing parties can influence the intensity of political conflict. Contrasting a two-party and a multi-party system is a traditional approach towards the format of party competition. Laakso and Taagepera proposed an index (the effective number of parties), which transformed the dichotomous typology into a continuum.[29] After defining ways to handle twinned (i.e. closely co-operating) and factionalised parties, Lijphart presents values for the average number of parties operating in a coun-

---

25 Starting with Lijphart 1984 and leading to Lijphart 1999, pp. 246, 248.
26 Lijphart 1999, pp. 3, 312-314.
27 Mexico and Poland, which are not included in Lijphart's data set (1999, pp. 312-314), had to be excluded.
28 See Lijphart 1999, pp. 129-134.
29 Laakso/ Taagepera 1979, pp.3-27.

try's legislature.[30] The assumed relationship between the level of political spending and the format of the party system does not stand the statistical test ($r = 0.25$; $p=0.35$).

The role of interest groups within the political process invariably leads to a dichotomy between *pluralism and corporatism*. "The typical interest group system of majoritarian democracy is a competitive and uncoordinated pluralism of independent groups in contrast with the co-ordinated and compromise-oriented system of corporatism that is typical of the consensus model."[31] Lijphart's index of interest group pluralism is inversely correlated to the IPS. That is, the higher interest group pluralism, the lower the spending level. The overall correlation is moderate ($r = -0.32$), yet it is statistically not significant ($p=0.23$).

The transformation of popular support (votes) into parliamentary representation (seats) is regulated by the *electoral system*. The traditional dichotomy of plurality voting (first past the post; FPTP) and proportional representation (P.R.) is based on procedure rather than impact. Lijphart accounts for the disproportionality of each voting system via the accumulated average difference between votes and seats.[32] In 16 democracies (i.e. excluding Mexico and Poland) the correlation between Lijphart's index and political spending is inverse, i.e. political spending increases as electoral disproportionality decreases. However, the coefficient is less impressive than might be expected ($r = -0.34$) and not significant ($p=0.17$).

The fifth of Lijphart's variables refers to a prerequisite of the Westminster type of parliamentary democracy, the *minimal winning one-party cabinet*.[33] If the persistence of such cabinets is correlated to the IPS, the Pearson's coefficient increases to $r = -0.46$. Once again (due to Lijphart's indexing) the correlation is inverse, i.e. the more likely a one-party cabinet the less likely is a high level of political spending. Although the net value of r in this correlation is higher than for any other of the Lijphart variables, which have been tested, the correlation (once again) is statistically not significant, although it is closer to this ($p=0.09$) than before. A less sophisticated look at majoritarian democracy may hold a promising prospect.

c)   Anglo-Saxon vs. other traditions of polities

Comparing political finance in 171 democracies Pinto-Duschinsky has identified a "Westminster model of political financing" (read: political finance regulation).[34] Adding the campaign centred U.S., this would lead to an Anglo-Saxon view of political finance. If campaigns cause the problem, regulators will approach the issue from this

---

30   Lijphart 1999, pp. 69-74, 76/77.
31   Lijphart 1999, p. 171; cf. ibid., p. 177.
32   Lijphart 1999, pp. 158, 162, 313.
33   Lijphart 1999, pp. 10/11, 98, 110/111.
34   Pinto-Duschinsky 2001a, pp. 19/20.

perception.[35] This basically reflects the voting system that is applied in a democracy. However, voting system, effective number of parties, one-party cabinets and interest group pluralism are interrelated variables.[36]

Interest group corporatism, fragmentation of the party system and frequent coalition governments are joint characteristics of the polities of Western Europe. Thus it may well be that a difference in *political tradition* is among the potential causes for different levels of political spending. The relationship between less expensive *Anglo-Saxon* style party competition and the multi-party coalition governments of continental *Western Europe* becomes more visible. The IPS (representing the level of per capita spending on party politics) averages 1.24 for the whole sample of 18 democracies, 0.42 for five Anglo-Saxon polities, 1.18 for ten countries in continental Europe and 2.83 for the three non-western cases. Somer's d for the three categories of political tradition and the IPS equals 0.56 (p=0.00).

The obvious conclusion that political tradition has an impact on spending levels draws attention to the three *non-western* democracies in our sample, Mexico, Japan and Israel, which are among the big spenders. Adding the two big spenders in continental Europe (Austria and Italy) suggests another potential cause for unlimited expenses. There is a *clientelistic tradition* of politics in predominantly Catholic as well as non-western countries (Israel, Japan, Mexico, Poland, Austria, France, Ireland, Italy, Spain). An individualistic (Calvinist/ Puritan) tradition in other democracies, e.g. Britain, the U.S., Canada, and Australia, may contrast to this.[37]

Spending data for countries with a clientelistic tradition are 2.3 times (IPS values even 3.4 times) higher than those for democracies in a predominantly Protestant society. (Averages for democracies with a mixed tradition are even slightly below the Protestant level.) Somer's d of -0.56 (p=0.000) reveals a significant statistical relationship. This suggests that the more clientelistic (the less individualistic) the political tradition, the higher the costs of democracy. A different approach may be found in everyday practice of party politics. More precisely the instruments of voter mobilisation are frequently seen as a major cause of political spending.

B) Framework of party politics

All democracies regularly hold elections. However, beyond the principles of free and fair elections, rules and practices for this common procedure of political competition are rather diverse. This may have an impact on the specific "costs of democracy".

---

35 For details see Cordes/ Nassmacher 2001, pp. 280-282.
36 Cf. Lijphart 1999, pp. 112, 169, 182, 183.
37 The (unitary system of the) Netherlands as well as (the federal systems of) Switzerland and Germany represent a mixed tradition. Whereas Switzerland and the Netherlands seem to be predominantly Calvinist and belong to the latter group, Germany may end up on the Catholic side of the grand divide.

Among these are the particular features of party competition, e.g., intra-party factions, ideological warfare, one-party dominance, capital-intensive campaigning and a labour-intensive party apparatus.

1. Capital-intensive campaigning vs. labour-intensive party apparatus

Recently Carty has argued that capital-intensive campaigning, after dominating national campaign activity for quite a while, may be returning to the local level.[38] The observation is drawn from the democracies of the Anglo-Saxon orbit (Britain, Australia, Canada, Ireland, New Zealand), where it is good electoral politics to go for the marginal seat, not for the marginal vote in a nation-wide campaign. If the sophistication of capital-intensive campaigns were a major cause of political spending, then the fact that all expensive campaign technology is deployed in the U.S. first, should make this country the leading political spender, possibly followed by Britain and Canada, who are the most willing to implement such advances in their own campaigns. According to our findings (see Table 3-4 above) all three of these countries (together with Australia and Ireland) are in the lower half of political spenders. This indicates that the parties in high level spenders must expend their funds on something else.

Two aspects spring to attention when leaving the Anglo-Saxon orbit. First, under systems of P.R. parties and not candidates preferably compete with each other. The individual party's electoral success does not depend on marginal areas (constituencies), but on the marginal vote of target-groups that most likely do not cluster in any local environment.[39] Given such a competitive situation a second aspect of party competition comes to the fore, a permanent *party organisation* at the centre (party headquarters) and on the ground (in the field). Both can be, and some of them actually are, manned by numerous paid full-time staff.

In continental Europe parties spend a lot of their financial resources running central offices in national (and state) capitals, possibly adding a permanent field organisation. Does this different deployment of political money have an impact on the level of spending? The mass membership party of the late 19th and the early 20th century left its mark upon the concept of party organisation, in political analysis as well as in political practice. Although most writers seem to convey that the heyday of the mass party is over, few would argue that one of its major achievements, the full-time party apparatus, has completely disappeared. In all democracies studied more closely, all of the national parties operate a permanent party headquarters. Late in the 20th century size, staff and budget of such headquarters increased.[40]

As the country-by-country presentation of spending totals has shown,[41] information that permits a reliable separation of campaign and routine spending at the national and

---

38 Carty 2003, pp. 619-636.
39 As correctly observed by Denmark 2003, pp. 608-614.
40 Krouwel 1999, pp. 90-93.
41 See above in chapter III, section A (establishment of spending totals).

sub-national level is not available. Thus we will unfortunately have to postpone a detailed discussion of this factor until we can analysise time series data for a restricted number of cases.[42] However, a specific problem comes to mind when the U.S. and Sweden are compared to France, Germany, Italy, Austria, Australia, Canada, Switzerland and the U.K., namely the frequency and scope of election campaigns. Both former countries elect a variety of public officers all on the same day, the latter have many election days in each election cycle. (The Netherlands, Poland, Denmark, Ireland, Spain, Japan, Israel and Mexico hold less, yet separate elections, too.)

Unfortunately detailed information is only available for some countries. Doris Cordes found that the federal headquarters of German and Austrian parties (but not the national headquarters of the two major Dutch parties) spend an increasing proportion of their overall budget on the party apparatus.[43] Such data indicate that permanent headquarters are a major burden for party budgets and thus may be expected to influence overall spending levels.

In order to test both hypotheses (sophisticated campaigning and party apparatus respectively as major causes of spending), we have assigned democracies of our sample to three groups:

- campaign-centred party activity with no permanent paid staff in the field (Australia, Canada, Ireland, Japan, the Netherlands, Switzerland and the U.S.),
- central offices, frequent campaigns and a variety of election days (Denmark, France, Israel, Italy, Mexico, Poland, Spain) and
- permanent field organisations with paid staff (Austria, Germany, Sweden, U.K.).

Parties in Austria, Germany, Sweden and the U.K. probably spend most of their funds "oiling the party machine," because field offices with paid staff add to overall payroll, operating expenses and spending totals. This assumption seems to hold for all four cases. Austria and Sweden are examples of modern ("social democratic") party machines with central offices and local field organisations, which are run on paid labour. In Italy (and Japan) party field work means "vote-buying" (in a more or less traditional fashion).[44] Israel seems to combine a high level of national campaign spending with a medium level of routine expenses. Several parties have field offices in urban centres and *Knesset* members use some of the public allocation for liaison offices in their "hometown" to fund "substitutes" for local party offices. The average IPS (or per capita spending in USD) for the 7 campaign-centred democracies contrasts quite nicely to the averages for 4 countries with highly developed parties on the ground: 0.69 (USD 9.45) as compared to 1.32 (USD 14.86). However, the Somer's correlation is neither impressive ($d = 0.30/0.20$) nor significant ($p=0.08/0.30$).

---

42 See below in chapter V, sub-section B 3 (professional politics).
43 Cordes 2001.
44 For the traditional style of party competition (at the grassroots) see Pinto-Duschinsky 1981, pp. 15-16; for details on Italy and Japan see below in this chapter, sub-section B2b (intra-party factions).

The evidence discussed in this sub-section refutes the conventional wisdom on the causes of excessive political spending. Neither highly sophisticated (capital-intensive) campaigns for national parliaments (occasionally including a presidency) nor lavishly staffed (labour-intensive) central offices of the major parties will necessarily cause a high level of political spending. A number of separate campaigns (as in Spain) and an abundance of field offices (as in Sweden) are more likely to have this impact. Austria, Germany, Italy and Sweden combine high-tech campaigning with an elaborate party organisation.

Obviously the financial burden of a party organisation is reinforced if parties employ permanent organisers and other full-time staff in local and regional offices. In federal systems regional offices at the state level must also be considered. Permanent local offices contribute towards their party's payroll and budget. The staff and office expenses of a nationwide field organisation help create and sustain considerable spending levels in many countries. Australian, Canadian, Danish, Dutch, Irish and U.S. parties do not incur such costs, which helps to keep the spending level of these countries within the bottom half of our sample. In Australia, Canada, Switzerland and the U.S. the major parties' offices are moderately staffed.

British, French and Swiss party activity in the field deserves individual remarks. Local parties in Switzerland mostly operate via the professional offices of voluntary party officers, thus saving their party a lot of money ("militia democracy").[45] French local parties have been notoriously related to municipal spoils by putting party workers on the payroll of municipal agencies or enterprises.[46] In Britain the Labour Party has always operated a very loose network of constituency agents. Staff employed by municipal majorities and MEPs have partially filled the manpower gap at no cost to the party. The number of constituency agents for the Conservatives declined during the 1980s and 1990s. Central Office has tried to counteract this trend by putting such agents on its own payroll,[47] thus increasing its share of total Conservative outlay. This leads to a more systematic analysis of factors, which are based on details of intra-party as well as inter-party competition, in short the very essence of party politics.

2. Modes of party competition

Because the difference between (potentially) capital-intensive campaigning and a (paid) labour-intensive party apparatus cannot be identified as the most cost-relevant issue of actual politics, we have to continue the search for other variables. All available factors concern different modes of party competition, among them intra-party relations, the impact of one-party dominance and the role of ideology.

---

45 See above in chapter III, sub-section A 4 b (small democracies). – The same is true for the FDP in Germany, cf. Theis 2007.
46 See below in chapter VII, sub-section D 1 (abuse of public resources).
47 Webb 1995, pp. 310, 314; Webb 2000, pp. 243/244.

a)   Ideological warfare

An important means of party competition is *ideological warfare*. Ideology has a two-sided influence on political funding. On the one hand, it may help raise funds from loyal supporters of a political cause.[48] On the other hand, a determination to conquer the opponent may also increase the greed for resources, even if they are not easily available.

After pondering the relationship between ideology and funding, Pinto-Duschinsky offered an unexpected hypothesis: "Money is most likely to be deployed for political purposes ... where ideological conflict is least intense."[49] This hypothesis deserves some elaboration and explanation. It may well be true that ideology helps save money. First, leadership contests (be they a presidential primary, a leadership convention or a constituency nomination) can rely on the binding spell of ideology. Groups sharing common beliefs will vote for a candidate who is "one of us," not "one of them." This feature of democratic politics is quite likely to apply to party competition as well. The frequently proclaimed "end of ideology" may thus have created a new situation for political contests of all sorts. The need to manufacture identification and support will increase the cost of its production, i.e. campaigning. This reasoning may be sound, but empirical evidence is inconclusive at best.

The most convincing piece of evidence comes from Britain. In Pinto-Duschinsky's long-term analysis of campaign spending by the Conservative Central Office (at 1980 prices), the most expensive years were 1935 and 1964.[50] In both campaigns the party headquarters of the governing Conservatives spent GBP 7.7 and 6.1 million respectively (in real terms, i.e. at constant prices), which is more than twice the costs of most (other) election years. In financial terms 1935 and 1964 were obviously the peak years of class warfare. A Conservative majority and its financial backers were trying to fight-off the assault by Labour forces, which had recovered from a party split over the Great Depression (1935) and from 13 long years in opposition (1964).

In Germany the 1949 and 1972 campaigns seem to have been the most controversial ones, ideologically speaking. Whereas financial evidence for 1949 is not available, conservative expenses in 1972 appear to parallel British spending in 1935 and 1964. However, the ideological character of the 1949 election in Germany ("market economy") is more obvious than that of the 1972 campaign (featuring anti-Communism vs. end the "cold war").

In the U.K. evidence for the ideological heat of both fights (in 1935 and 1964) over a more traditional ("nationalisation of the means of production") or more modern ("economic planning") version of "socialism" is inconclusive. Do these examples suffice for a final refutation of Pinto-Duschinsky's hypothesis? Without additional supporting evidence the initial assumption about ideology as a cause (or shock absorber) of party

---

48   See below in chapter VI, section A (normative implications).
49   Pinto-Duschinsky 1986, p. 32 (emphasis added).
50   Pinto-Duschinsky 1981, p. 143.

spending should be dropped and the discourse can now proceed to factional or personal power struggles within a dominant party, which holds a leadership role that can be taken for granted.

b) One-party dominance

Some party systems are dominated by one major party, which seems bound to win each election, including the next one to be held in the near future and to retain government office despite much political discontent, which in other countries would drive the governing party from power. For many decades the Israeli *Mapai* (now the *Avodah*), the Italian *Democrazia cristiana* (*DC*; now dissolved), the Mexican *Partido Revolucionario Institucional* (*PRI*), the Swedish *Socialdemokraterna (SAP)* and the Japanese *Jimintô* (LDP) were major cases in point. With a pinch of salt the Liberal Party of Canada, the Irish *Fianna Fáil* and the French Rassemblement pour la Republique (RPR, earlier UNR, now RMP) can be added to that group. Party systems in Australia, Austria, Germany, Poland, Spain, the U.K. and the U.S. are more balanced between the major parties. Politics in Denmark, the Netherlands and Switzerland is so diverse that not even a balance between major parties can be expected.

The example of Sweden, where the *SAP* still holds a leading position, indicates that even a "natural government party" can occasionally lose an election. This happened in 1976, 1991 and 2006, followed by a quick recovery and a speedy return to power.[51] However, due to major changes of party systems (and individual societies) no situation of dominance is forever. The Israeli *Mapai*, the party that founded the country and ruled it (in changing coalitions) between 1948 and 1973, lost its dominance early. The same happened to the Mexican *PRI* in the process of transformation to democracy (i.e. after 1996), although much later in 2000. The leading role of the Italian *DC* lasted all the way into the 1990s, and to this day (after a short break during the 1990s and a menacing challenge in 2007) the Japanese *Jimintô* (LDP) is still in power. The Liberal Party governed Canada for most of the 20th century (1896-1911, 1921-1930, 1935-1957, 1963-1979, 1980-1984, 1993-2005)[52] and the role of *Fianna Fáil* in Ireland (after independence) and the Gaullist party (UNR, RPR) in the Fifth Republic of France is not much different.

We identify one-party dominant political systems by the period of time, during which a country has been governed by chief executives from the same party. Such phases are 1928-2000 (72 years) in Mexico, 1932-1976 (44 years) in Sweden, 1955-1993 (38 years) in Japan, 1945-1981 (26 years) in Italy, 1958-81 (23 years) in France,

---

51 Between 1932 and 2006 *SAP* governments covered a period of 65 of the total 74 years (= 88%).
52 The total of 80 in 110 years (73%) covers more than any other party in any democracy of our sample.

1963-1984 (21 years) in Canada,[53] 1932-1948, 1957-1973 (32 years in all) in Ireland.[54] Israel is not included among our "one-party dominant" countries because the 25 years of *Mapai* rule (1948-1973) ended long before the period covered by IPS data. This is also true for Austria despite 30 years under *SPÖ* chancellors (1970-2000) and 25 years under *ÖVP* leadership (1945-1970), because during most of each phase the parties governed in a "grand coalition." Neither do the 20 years of Democratic presidents in the U.S. (1932-1952) or *CDU* chancellors in (West) Germany (1949-1969) qualify for "dominance", as they were over long before the 1990s.

The impact on the costs of democracy may look strange. A dominant party makes the outcome of individual elections much more predictable for competitors and observers. Nevertheless it seems to increase the level of party spending.[55] On average democracies with a protracted dominance of one party spent USD 14.15 (IPS=1.58), much more than democracies with more balanced party systems (USD 8.66, IPS=1.03). However, a Somer's d of 0.29 (for IPS and one-party dominance) does not support this relationship statistically (p=0.08). Part of the additional costs may just be due to factional infighting.

c)   Intra-party competition (individual candidates, factions and primaries)

(1) Competition is a major feature of modern democracy. After a first glance at the competition of individual candidates, two dimensions come to mind. Candidates can compete with candidates of other parties, e.g. in single member constituencies, but also with other candidates of the same party, e.g. in nomination contests or in multi-member constituencies. If the latter occurs, the most likely cause is *factional strife*. Competition among parties is overshadowed by rivalries between intra-party factions, which maintain their own clientelistic networks. The Italian *Democrazia cristiana* (*DC*; now dissolved), and the Japanese *Jimintô* (LDP) are the major cases. The leading role of the *DC* and the LDP lasted all the way into the 1990s. Their internal factions (*correnti, habatsu*) fought for power within the party and needed money to compete for local support.

Occasionally intra-party competition may substitute for the competition between parties. In post-war Italy and Japan the dominant party was the only road of access to real political power. For both parties, organisation in the field did not mean salaries for full-time local party agents, but rather "presents" to cultivate contacts to loyal supporters across the nation. Spending was not limited to campaign periods. A permanent cam-

---

53   The short period of the Clark minority government (1979/80) notwithstanding.
54   The Irish Free State (*Éire*) has enjoyed 85 years of independence. During 54 years (64%) the Prime Minister (*Taoiseach*) has been the leader of *Fianna Fáil*.
55   At this point an analogy to campaign spending by incumbents comes to mind. They also spend more than they need to, possibly just because they can raise the funds and want to be on "the safe side," or secure a war chest to scare off challengers. For details see below in chapter IX, subsection A 1 (individual candidates).

paign of goodwill activities and "vote buying" sustained linkage to local clienteles.[56] The electoral systems (preferential voting, multi-member constituencies) reinforced this.[57] Because little is known about the costs of factional infighting in France, we will demonstrate the process for *Italy*.

The preference voting option of the pre-1991 electoral system provided a strong incentive for candidates to organise in factions (*correnti*). Local community networks demanded sophisticated organisation, which swallowed more and more funds. "The higher the cost of political activity, the more incentive to raise funds from *tangenti* [i.e. bribes]: the more funds raised from *tangenti*, the more could be spent on electoral and factional competition."[58] *Democrazia cristiana* and *Partito socialista italiana*, which formed a quasi-permanent coalition after 1962, were the co-operating holders of real power and "highly factionalised parties with deep personality-led divisions, ... running from leadership to rank-and-file. ... Those who controlled the membership controlled internal party elections, ... the allocation of ministerial portfolios, ... (and) politically appointed administrative posts."[59] The obvious consequences of this clientelistic machine politics were not only increasing costs of politics, but also ample incentives for political corruption.[60]

Initially there was no evidence that factional strife resulted in an increase in overall political costs in *Israel*. Instead of producing a burden, intra-party competition in nomination primaries in the beginning induced more people to join a major party, thus increasing party revenue after a long decline in party membership and income from that source.[61] More recently, an influx of corporate and foreign money into the unregulated area of political finance (which is intra-party competition and factional strife in Israeli "primaries") has motivated politicians to extensively use this new pathway to funds into political competition. "Furthermore, internal party primaries gave considerable leverage to 'vote contractors,' people who could deliver the votes of blocs of registered voters [i.e. party members] in the internal elections." Vote contractors involved in secular parties were able to register supporters of religious parties as members of non-religious parties and deliver the votes of their cohorts to specific nomination contests. More recently "vote contractors switched their attention from

---

56 In the context of clientelistic politics we should heed the observation by Pinto-Duschinsky (2002, p. 83) „that old-fashioned face-to-face politicking costs more than the new mass-marketing, media-heavy approach ... traditional patronage politics imposes far greater financial burdens than television-based campaigning."
57 Other factors like a top-down factional funding to "buy" votes of ordinary citizens (in Japan) or membership cards (and thereby delegates at national party congresses in Italy) reinforced a clientelistic system of high spending, which drove up the cost of party_politics. Rhodes 1997, p. 65; della Porta/ Vannucci 1999, p. 117.
58 Pujas/ Rhodes 1999, p. 49.
59 Hine 1996, p. 144.
60 See below in this chapter, sub-section C1a (political corruption).
61 Mendilow 1996, pp. 331-338; Mendilow/ Rusciano 2001, pp. 228/229. See below chapter VI, section B1 (membership dues).

mobilising large masses of voters in the primaries ... to arranging the election of members of the party's Central Committee." [62] Depending on the electoral system (fixed list P.R. in Israel, loose list P.R. in Italy or multi-member constituencies in Japan), power brokers offer their services to deliver the votes that they control to the "political market," which needs such assistance in order to ensure that specific candidates will become MPs.

(2) Besides Israel, Italy and Japan there are two other notorious cases where intra-party competition involves political spending: the *U.S. and Canada*. Whereas nomination in a Canadian constituency (riding) generally involves spending only a couple of hundred dollars,[63] the nomination of the political leaders of the major parties (federally as well as provincially) is achieved after *expensive leadership contests*, which sometimes costs a few million dollars.[64] Because this event is rare (in most cases once in a decade for each party) the overall impact on political spending is rather low.

The converse is true in the U.S. *Primaries* are a regular event and have always been included in data on political spending.[65] However, cost intensive intra-party competition does not stop once the candidates have been nominated. Because U.S. voting behaviour has changed since the 1940s, the competitive situation of the individual candidate also varies. U.S. citizens cast their ballot for many public offices on the same day. As long as most individuals (guided by the old-fashioned party machines) voted "straight ticket," then the leading candidate (for example the nominee for president) pulled his party's candidates for governor, senator, congressman and other offices either to defeat or to victory on his "presidential coattails."

When the majority of U.S. citizens started to split their ballots (for example, voting for a Republican president and a Democratic congress at the same time) each individual candidate had to fend for himself. Candidates running for different offices spend money on personal advertising in order to reach out to their specific constituency. Without such efforts they will not get heard by their voters because of the "noise" produced by all other candidates. Thus not only the personal opponent (i.e., the other party's nominee for the same office) but also many candidates of the *same party* running for *different offices* compete for the attention of a mass audience. These days this intra-party competition starts early due to the "expensive primary nominating system."[66] In sum, split ticket voting and candidate campaigns have contributed to media overkill.[67]

Unlike the clear-cut example of the U.S. (which is specifically troubled by media costs), it is still hard to tell whether demanding intra-party competition or an unlim-

---

62 Hofnung 2005b, pp. 72, 75, 77 (quotes on p. 72 and p. 75 respectively).
63 Carty 1991, pp. 117-118; Carty/ Erickson 1991, pp. 125-126, 138, 168.
64 Stanbury 1991, pp. 368-372. More details are available due to new reporting rules, which were introduced in 2001.
65 cf. Oldopp 2001, pp. 115-132.
66 Crotty 1977, p. 106.
67 Paltiel 1981, p. 142.

ited supply of funds has driven the spiral of exploding expenses in the Italian and the Japanese cases of clientelistic "vote buying.[68]

To sum up, we can organise our sample of 18 democracies into three groups according to the costs caused by intra-party competition.

- There is no substantial amount of such costs in Australia, Austria, Denmark, Germany, Ireland, Mexico, the Netherlands, Poland, Sweden, Spain, Switzerland and the U.K.
- Parties practise internal contests only (nomination, leadership), which cause some financial outlay in Canada, France and Israel.
- There is high-level intra-party competition for support among the general voting public in Italy, Japan and the U.S.

We expect that the costs as measured by the IPS will increase accordingly. However, a Somer's d of 0.20 (p=0.23) does not statistically support this assumption. When we discuss spending levels, the sources of party money should not be neglected. In no less than two democracies (Italy, Japan) there is a notoriously high level of corruption, which despite many other causes is a result of inactivity in the realm of public policy that has not made serious efforts to fight corruption effectively.

C) Consequences of public policy

The growing importance of public policy, whether for arms procurement or as a device for full employment and/ or social services, necessarily creates special interests, which either influence specific political decisions or the decision-makers. Because many of these are politicians, a new connection between parts of the general public and parts of the political elite is created. In addition, public subsidies for political activity are a consequence of public policy decisions. Another (potentially unlimited) source of political funding is the political manifestation of profiteering (conventionally called graft), which in certain ways results from a public policy of non-enforcement or non-intervention. If, in the realm of interpersonal relations, the rule of law and the market economy are not enforced, a specific "black market" of political bounty will spring up, which exchanges favours by public officials for money paid by those who benefit from their decisions.

---

68 Rhodes 1997, pp. 65-68. – See also below in chapter V, section C (push or pull?).

1. *Unlimited sources of funding*

Parties, which look for additional funding, will turn to sources of income that are within their reach. The options are either political graft (corruption) or the general revenue fund. Whereas public subsidies will be discussed next, we turn to the peddling of political influence first.

a) Unrestrained political graft (corruption)

Corruption creates additional political revenue, which readily can be deployed in political competition. Additional funds may increase the level of political spending just as additional income improves the standard of living. When parties or politicians decide to barter policy decisions (or access to political leaders) for contributions to their "war chest," this is undoubtedly a form of political corruption.[69] As we are unable to conduct research into details of this process,[70] we shall limit our discussion to two relevant items.

First, is there any indicator of corruption available that can be correlated with our Index of Political Spending (as presented in column 5 of Table 3-4)? Arnold Heidenheimer was the first to investigate systematically the potential link between party spending and the incidence of corruption. He compared his 1963 ranking of spending levels and a current index related to levels of corruption.[71] The Corruption Perceptions Index (CPI), as presented annually by Transparency International, is the best known and widely used indicator. The index attempts to measure "the degree to which corruption is *perceived to exist* among *public officials and politicians*." The index "relates to perceptions of the degree of corruption *as seen by business people, academics, and risk analysts*, and ranges between 10 (highly clean) and 0 (highly corrupt)" (italics added).[72] (Measurements for our cases are listed below in Table 4-3.)

---

69 For some examples see below in chapter VII, section D (income from graft).
70 Heidenheimer/ Johnston et al. 2002 have dealt at length with many facets (causes and consequences).
71 Heidenheimer 2002, pp. 767-768. We replicate this effort using more recent spending data and including more countries.
72 Both quotes from Press Release by Peter Eigen, www.transparency.org/cpi/2001. The *italics* (added in the quote) hint at limitations of reliability. The CPI indicates how various **observers** who are not necessarily involved in corrupt transactions with politicians **perceive** the situation in a specific country and includes the behaviour of people who are not relevant for our research (politicians and **public officials**).
For Germany, which has a medium level of perceived corruption and no major recent corruption cases, Eigen mentions that corruption is rife in the construction industry, distribution of pharmaceuticals and medical auxiliaries ("Weniger Korruption in Deutschland", in: *Frankfurter Allgemeine*, 21 October 2004). All of these industries depend heavily on public contracting by local governments and public sick-funds respectively.

Table 4-3: Levels of party spending, corruption and public subsidies

Country	Index of Party Spending (Table 3-4)	Level of corruption		Level of subsidy	
		Corruption Perceptions Index (TI) 2001	Corruption on record	Per capita subsidy amount in US-$	Subsidy in per cent of total costs
Israel	3.16	7.6	Medium	13.50	55
Mexico	2.99	3.7	High	1.90	85
Austria	2.66	7.8	Medium	19.00	40
Italy	2.47	5.5	High	1.20	35
Japan	2.33	7.1	High	3.00	35
Sweden	1.47	9.0	Low	11.00	60
Poland	1.46	4.1	Medium	0.75	20
Spain	1.10	7.0	Medium	1.50	40
Germany	0.86	7.4	Low	5.50	60
France	0.76	6.7	Medium	4.20	55
Ireland	0.55	7.5	Low	3.80	30
Canada ***	0.49	8.9	Low	1.20	25
USA	0.46	7.6	Low	0.30	5
Switzerland *	0.45	8.4	Low	0.80	10
Denmark	0.36	9.5	Low	0.60	25
Australia	0.32	8.5	Low	0.60	15
Britain **	0.28	8.3	Low	0.25	5
Netherlands	0.23	8.8	Low	0.40	20

Sources: Party Spending from Tables 3-2 to 3-4; Corruption Perceptions Index from the TI website: www.transparency.org/cpi/2001; subsidies from Nassmacher 2002, p. 16 (revised because of caucus and other grants; see below in chapter VIII, Tables 8-1 and 8-3).
Comments: Outliers are printed in *italics*.
* including federal and state caucus grants, because they are handed over to party headquarters
** policy research grant as of 2001 included already;
*** quarterly allowance as of 2003 included already.

Among the established democracies in our sample, Italy, France, Spain and Japan score the highest levels of perceived corruption, covering a range between 7.1 and 5.5, which is much less than the clean 9.5 of Denmark or 9.0 of Sweden, but considerably better than Poland's 4.1, Mexico's 3.7 or Nigeria's score of 1.0.[73] For the complete sample of 18 countries, the correlation between IPS and CPI is -0.56 (p=0.02).[74] The general level of correlation even surpasses those for all significant indicators for char-

---

73 www.transparency.org/cpi/2001.
74 The inverse correlation is due to the allocation of CPI values. Countries with a low level of perceived corruption are allocated high values and vice versa.

acteristics of the polity.[75] However, does perception correspond with reality? Indeed does the TI index raise doubts about methodology. Are the experts surveyed close enough to party funding?[76] Is the perception of observers an adequate indicator for the behaviour of social actors? Because of such grave doubts we need to add some more evidence. As we really want to test the hypothesis that a high level of corruption (as a relevant source of political funds) increases the level of political spending (and control for measurement problems) we turn to data from a more home-grown approach.

Second, are there reliable reports from individual countries that corrupt exchanges have been an important source of political funding? For Italy,[77] Japan[78] and Mexico there is a lot of scholarly work on this connection. For France[79] and Spain[80] similar processes, although on a smaller scale, have been frequently unveiled. Relying on this limited evidence, we can conclude that the democracies of Italy, Japan and Mexico can be expected to be among the top political spenders due to an extra-ordinary level of corruption, whereas France, Israel and Spain (most likely somewhat less in corrupt exchanges) take a more medium position as far as party spending is concerned. If we contrast a group of six corruption-prone countries (Italy, Japan, Mexico, France, Israel, Spain) with the other 12 democracies, averages for IPS and per capita spending vary considerably (an IPS of 1.85 vs. 0.94; USD 15.94 vs. 3.63; PPP-$ 13.09 vs. 8.67; BigMac equivalents 5.61 vs. 3.08). A Somer's d of 0.37 (for the IPS; p=0.01) bears out the difference. This additional evidence makes the correlation between IPS and CPI look more reasonable. Because corruption is not the only source of "unlimited" political funds we will have to pursue the other one, i.e. generous public funding of party activity, too.

b) Generous public subsidies

Just like political graft public subsidies provide additional revenue for political competitors. Parties are unlikely to save such funds in a bank account when the quest for political power demands their deployment. In regard to the impact of public funding on political spending, we can expect the level of overall spending to rise with the level of subsidisation.[81] Two indicators spring to mind for the level of subsidisation: the per capita subsidy and the subsidy's share of total outlay (see Table 4-3 above). Sur-

---

75 See above in this chapter, section A (polity).
76 The *perception of experts* may miss to measure the true level of corruption.
77 Ciaurro 1989, p. 153; della Porta 1997, pp. 35-48; Vannucci 1997, pp. 50-64; Hine 1996, pp. 137-152; Newell 2000, pp. 61-83.
78 Shiratori 1994, pp. 187-206; Bouissou 1997, pp. 132-146; Köllner 2000, p. 149.
79 Avril 1994, pp. 86-89; Mény 1996, pp. 159-171; Mény 1997, pp.7-20. The most recent case was Denis Gautier-Sauvagnac, who had to resign as president of an employers' association (UIMM) because he had clandestinely funded trade unions. See "Geld gegen Kompromissbereitschaft", in: *Frankfurter Allgemeine*, 18 October 2007.
80 Del Castillo 1994, pp. 100-102; Heywood 1996, pp. 115-132; Heywood 1997b, pp. 65-83.
81 Nassmacher 2002, pp. 15-17.

prisingly both indicators produce similar results, i.e. a group of highly subsidised countries and a group of countries with low subsidisation, which leaves **six** countries at a medium level of subsidisation. Comparing this to party spending produces a good fit. That is, all high subsidy countries spend big on party politics. Among the low subsidy countries, only Italy stands out as a big political spender. The source for exorbitant funding in this case (i.e. corruption) has already been discussed. The average for the IPS, as well as for the USD amount of per capita political spending, varies considerably between the groups of moderate and big spenders: from 13 to 50 percent for the share of public subsidies and USD 0.42 to 7.72 for the total per capita amount of all subsidies. Correlations establish a remarkable fit between IPS and per capita amount of subsidies ($r=0.57$; $p=0.01$), and an even closer fit between IPS and the percentage of subsidy ($r=0.64$; $p=0.005$).

Two different explanations may be able to account for the remarkable fit between these variables. First, parties have grown accustomed to high levels of spending and, after exhausting other sources of income, finally decided to ignore the general opposition to public funding, because they were unable to develop any alternative policy. This can be called a cost push inflation of political spending. (As this kind of reasoning also applies to corrupt sources, it indicates that a high level of spending will make parties more willing to turn to much riskier funding strategies. That is, risky in terms of disappointing voters or in terms of facing scandals.)

The second explanation is no less plausible. A rising level of subsidisation may have induced parties to behave like drug addicts.[82] That is, because effective opposition to public subsidies faltered early, parties could use a vast supply of funds to start or to continue an arms race of political competition. For example, they spent more and more money on organisation building and/ or campaigning because money was easily available. We call this the income pull theory for high levels of political spending.[83]

Judging from the cross-national information available, either of these interpretations may be true.[84] We must postpone a final decision regarding which explanation deserves preference until detailed time series data become available, especially for trends in staff deployment, office provision and campaign activity that can be related to the data for spending totals.[85] Nevertheless a close correlation can be established between the level of public subsidies and the level of political spending.

In passing it should be noted that first wave democracies seem to be less willing to provide public subsidies. An average per capita subsidy of USD 2.11 for nine first wave democracies compares favourably to an average subsidy of USD 7.73 for six

---

82 Cf. Nassmacher 1989e, p, 35.
83 Most findings by Smith 2005 ("Money to Burn") corroborate this interpretation. This does, however, not mean that parties waste money because they can spend it on items that are important for a party.
84 Cf. Nassmacher 2002, p. 17; Nassmacher 1992b, pp. 482/483.
85 See below in chapter V, section C (push or pull?).

second wave democracies. A brief look at the extent of financial support reveals an average subsidy of less than 22 percent of total party spending for first wave democracies and of almost 47 percent for second wave democracies.

For the time being we will have to stick to the multi-cause theory that has been advanced throughout this chapter. Various factors act together and influence the level of party spending; some of them will increase, while others will decrease the outlay of parties for political competition. Another factor that has been mentioned in scholarly analysis is the interaction between governments and economies.

2. State intervention in the economy

"Money is most likely to be deployed for political purposes ... where the *extent of government spending* and *economic regulation* is great."[86] This hypothesis contains two potentially different aspects of state involvement in the economy. First, each government is a buyer and consumer of goods and services. A high level of state expenditure may encourage all suppliers to influence those who decide the details of public demand [and public spending]. This applies especially to policy-makers, who hand out government contracts or grants to special interests, not least among them politicians and their parties. Second, any democratic state may for good *political* reasons decide to counterbalance market forces in general, or in detail, either in certain areas or on a large scale. Everyone who depends on measures of state regulation for their current income or economic activity will thus be induced to let their interests be known to their rulers, not least via contributions to party coffers.

Israel is an appropriate example for the need to counteract the „heavy involvement of the central government in many economic activities" by "personal contacts in government offices," which "can pave the way for grants, licenses and building authorizations."[87] Access to government departments is via politicians, who have amassed IOUs to all sorts of moneyed interests during their intra-party bid for nomination to the party list. Our analysis of influences on party spending will separate both angles of government intervention in the economy, the highly elaborated welfare state (including a large volume of tendered contracts) and the extent of non-market governance,[88] by discussing the reach of state regulation of the economy, as well as the magnitude of government expenses.

---

86 Pinto-Duschinsky 1986, p. 32; emphasis added.
87 Hofnung 2005b, p. 69 referring to Aharoni 1991, pp. 205-68 (unfortunately in Hebrew).
88 During the postwar era the immigrant society of Israel and the corporatist polity of Austria were perfect examples of this approach. For a later decade the large public sector of "tangenti" inclined Italy and the Swedish "people's home" (*folkhem*), a specific version of the "welfare state", may be mentioned.

a)   Share of government expenditure

The level of government spending is an important indicator of the economic weight of state activity within the economy. Two yardsticks come to mind when the public share of the economy must be measured: total government expenditure as expressed by the state budgets and government consumption as indicated by national accounting procedures. Both indicators are included in the Heritage Foundation's Index of Economic Freedom.[89]

However, when confronted with party spending, individual data from this index (see Table 4-4 below) seem to be inconclusive. A first indicator of government penetration into the economy, the level of *government consumption* (in percent of total consumption), is not correlated with the Index of Political Spending (Pearson's r=0.04). For the other measures of political spending the relationship looks closer [90] although none of the correlations are statistically significant.

Likewise, the other measurement of government share of economic output is no more indicative. The correlation between IPS and government spending (r=0.13, p=0.60) is not much higher than for government consumption. Thus the first half of the hypothesis (i.e. government spending increases party spending) does not hold.

Table 4-4:   *Political spending and government intervention in the economy*

Country	Index of Party Spending	Index of Economic Freedom	Government expenditure	Government consumption	Level of government regulation
	Score	Score	(in percent)		Score
(1)	(2)	(3)	(4)	(5)	(6)
Israel	3.16	2.45	54.5	29.7	3.0
Mexico	2.99	2.80	21.6	12.8	3.0
Austria	2.66	2.10	49.6	19.9	3.0
Italy	2.47	2.35	45.7	17.5	3.0
Japan	2.33	2.50	36.9	17.5	3.0
Sweden	1.47	1.90	52.5	23.6	3.0
Poland	1.46	2.85	44.5	16.0	2.0
Spain	1.10	2.35	38.5	17.3	3.0
Germany	0.86	2.10	45.9	19.4	3.0
France	0.76	2.55	48.6	23.3	3.0

---

89   A variety of indicators are available, which compare "competitiveness" among "free market economies" (e.g., by World Economic Forum, International Institute for Management Development, Fraser Institute and Bertelsmann Foundation). The major difference between these indicators is the mix of data from survey research and national accounting. Among the host of indices, the Heritage Foundation's IEF prefers statistics over opinions and therefore seems to be most suited for our purpose.

90   For political spending in PPP-$ **r=0.16**, in BigMac equivalents **r=0.18** and in USD **r=0.21**.

Country	Index of Party Spending	Index of Economic Freedom	Government expenditure	Government consumption	Level of government regulation
	Score	Score	(in percent)		Score
(1)	(2)	(3)	(4)	(5)	(6)
Ireland	0.55	1.75	30.6	12.4	2.0
Canada	0.49	2.05	40.6	21.2	2.0
USA	0.46	1.80	30.4	18.0	2.0
Switzerland	0.45	1.95	38.2	14.7	3.0
Denmark	0.36	1.80	54.3	33.7	3.0
Australia	0.32	1.85	33.1	18.7	2.0
Britain	0.28	1.85	38.3	18.7	2.0
Netherlands	0.23	1.90	41.7	22.9	3.0

Sources: Index of Political Spending see above, Table 3-4; Index of Economic Freedom (and details on sub-indexes) see Heritage Foundation, web-site: www.heritage.org/index.

b) State regulation of the economy

At first glance the Index of Economic Freedom (IEF, see Table 4-4) produced by the Washington-based Heritage Foundation, looks highly indicative of the level of state meddling in the economy, which in turn seems to contribute towards the level of political spending. The correlation between IPS and IEF ($r=0.67$; $p=0.003$) is higher than most other correlations presented in this chapter. Thus the second part of the hypothesis under study seems to hold. As government regulation of the economy increases, the level of political spending goes up.

However, a closer examination of the ten dimensions (sub-indexes) that compose the Heritage Foundation's IEF offers a slightly different impression. The ten dimensions include, among others, trade policy, monetary policy, foreign investment, property rights and black market activity.[91] These factors are quite important for a comparison between advanced economies and less developed third world countries, but they do not contribute much to an internal ranking of established democracies. The category in question here can only be tested by the sub-index on regulation (see column 6 in Table 4-4), which indicates some significant differences among the democracies included in the Index of Political Spending. Whereas the top half of the political spenders have a straight score of 3.0 on the level of state regulation of the economy,[92]

---

91 As measured by TI's index of perceived corruption; see above in this chapter, sub-section C1a (corruption).
92 Six variables contribute to the composition of this sub-index: „Licensing requirements to operate a business; ease of obtaining a business license; corruption within the bureaucracy; labour regulations, such as established work weeks, paid vacations, and parental leave, as well as selected labour regulations; environmental, consumer safety, and worker health regulations; regulations that impose a burden on business."
The grading scale translates 2.0 into "*Low* Simple licensing procedures; existing regulation

the bottom half behaves significantly different. Only three countries attain a high level of regulation (3.0), five others have a 2.0. A Somer's d of 0.25 indicates some correlation between spending and regulation, which, however, is not significant (p=0.18).

Nevertheless, it should be noted in passing that regulation of the economy and level of public subsidies [93] coincide. That is, for the low regulation economies the mean of total subsidies (per capita) is USD 0.32, while public subsidies average 5.2 percent of the total outlay for party politics. In high regulation economies both indicators are considerably higher (USD 7.03 and 37.4 percent respectively). As long as no other data is available to measure the level of government intervention in modern economies, the current evidence supports the second rather than the first part of the hypothesis that state meddling in the economy increases the costs of political competition.

D) Interaction of causal factors

After testing a variety of factors, which in theory may influence the level of political spending, we are now in a position to draw preliminary conclusions. Some factors have to be neglected until more reliable indicators become available. Others cause an impact across the board (with occasional outliers). Various aspects will influence only a few countries (as the specific element, which either increases or decreases political spending does not occur in all democracies). Two conclusions can be drawn from the evidence, which has been presented thus far. First, any one-dimensional approach at elaborating the causes of different levels of party spending is bound to fail. For the time being we have to stick to the multi-cause hypothesis, which was advanced earlier in this chapter.[94] Second, of the various factors at work, some will stimulate an increase of political spending, others will decrease it. Both types of factors position the costs of party democracy on a scale with considerable spread.

The interaction between the intervening variables that have been established as significant can be tested with more sophisticated statistics, especially *multiple regression*, *cluster analysis* and *factor analysis*. For the multiple regression a set of promising variables have to be selected, which meet the basic requirements. The variables must have potential relevance for the subject and possess a specific level of measurement. They ought to be statistically significant and independent of each other. These requirements reduce the maximum number of variables that can be run in a multiple regres-

---

relatively straightforward and applied uniformly most of the time, but burdensome in some instances; corruption possible but rare." and 3.0 into "*Moderate* Complicated licensing procedure; regulations impose substantial burden on business; existing regulations may be applied haphazardly and in some instances are not even published by the government; corruption may be present and poses minor burden on businesses."
(all quotes from: www.heritage.org/research/features/index/2003/chapters/chapter5, p. 13)

93   See above in this chapter, sub-section C1b (public subsidies).
94   See above in this chapter, sub-section A2 (size of electorate).

sion dramatically. All variables discussed in this chapter are potentially relevant. Only variables with a minimum coefficient (r or d between 0.3 and 0.6) indicate some statistical relationship with the level of political spending.

If statistically significant variables are based on continuously scaled data, a multiple regression can identify interrelations. Unfortunately some of our variables do not meet the latter requirement, continuous level of measurement. This leaves only a few variables, which can be run in a regression: Gross domestic product per capita in PPP-$, Human Development Index, years of popular government, Corruption Perceptions Index, party subsidies in USD per voter, party subsidies in percent of party spending. The level of political spending can be measured by the IPS or by party spending per capita, in USD or PPP-$ or BigMac equivalents.

For the multiple regression this leaves the problem of multicollinearity. Of the variables, which show a significant inter-correlation, only one can be included. Fortunately this does not apply to any of the pre-selected indices because most of these are by far not significant. A regression of six independent variables and one dependent variable (the IPS) reveals that some variables are of minor influence on the level of political spending: per capita GDP in PPP-$, Human Development Index, experience with democracy (measured by years of popular government and general male suffrage). Two variables stand out from the regression: perceived corruption (CPI) and level of public subsidisation. The public subsidy to political parties [95] (in USD rather than percent of total revenue) explains 61 percent of the total variance among our 18 democracies. In addition, the level of perceived corruption explains another 21 percent. All other variables, although some of them are correlated with political spending individually, do not contribute any more explanation (see table 4-5).[96]

Table 4-5: Regression analysis for level of political spending (IPS)
Summary of model (c)

Model	R	R square	Adjusted R square	Standard error
1	0.780 (a)	0.608	0.583	0.66043
2	0.848 (a)	0.719	0.681	0.57781

(a) independent variable: public subsidies in USD
(b) independent variables: public subsidies in USD, Corruption Perceptions Index
(c) dependent variable: Index of Political Spending

---

95 For details see below in chapter VIII (public subsidies).
96 For other indicators of political spending (per capita spending in USD, PPP $ or Big Mac equivalents) the multiple regression includes two more independent variables: public subsidies in percent of total revenue and Human Development Index.

Excluded variables

Model 2	Beta In	T	Significance	partial correlation
Gross Domestic Product	-0.061	-0.276	0.785	-0.074
Human Development Index	0.189	0.697	0.497	0.183
Years of democratic tradition	-0.148	-0.734	0.475	-0.192
Public subsidies in percent of total revenue	-0.007	-0.031	0.976	-0.008

The major consequence of this analysis reminds us of something that is easily neglected when political spending is discussed. When total amounts of expenses are discussed data for income should not be neglected. It may well be that the level of party revenue turns out to have a major influence on party spending, much more so than is expected in most discussions of political spending data.[97]

The variables that offer significant values of Somer's d are *categorical*, i.e. non-metric.[98] Some of them (e.g. level of corruption) are even dichotomous rather than scaled-continuous. Such variables cannot be included in a regression. As a substitute we will use a *cluster analysis* to indicate some interaction between these variables. Clustering can be based on wave of democratisation, Anglo-Saxon vs. other heritage, clientelistic tradition, high/low level of corruption and level of political spending (IPS). According to this analysis our sample of 18 democracies can be grouped into three clusters:

- Australia, Canada, Denmark, Ireland, the Netherlands, Sweden, Switzerland, the U.K. and the U.S.;
- Austria, Israel, Italy, Japan and Mexico;
- France, Germany, Poland and Spain.

The first cluster includes all countries characterised by an Anglo-Saxon style (Puritan) individualistic tradition, balanced party competition and a low level of corruption. In all but one of these countries the costs of party activity are low and in most of them these costs decline gently with the size of the electorate. The big exception among the group is Sweden, which due to its spending level we would expect in the third cluster.

The second cluster represents countries with the highest costs of democracy, which is most likely caused by a combination of non-western political heritage, clientelistic tradition, high level of corruption on record and one-party dominance. Moreover it is reasonable to assume that such features keep political spending from being overly affected by "economies of scale".

---

[97] This will be discussed below in chapter IV, section C (cost push or demand pull?).
[98] For details see Lijphart 1999, pp. 313/31.

For the third cluster of medium level spenders the second wave democracies in continental Europe (Germany and France) are less obvious candidates than the third wave democracies of Poland and Spain. Possibly all of them offer a mixed situation where clientelism, corruption and/ or public subsidies have pulled up political spending, which otherwise had been declining in line with the size of the electorate.[99]

A *factor analysis* can include metric and non-metric variables in order to evaluate the interaction between both sets of data. Among the eleven statistically significant variables that have been elaborated in this chapter nine stand out by high loads on factor 1 (see Table 4-6 below). Most of them represent important aspects of "western modernisation", e.g. many years of democratic experience, freedom of individual action, economic and social development. Even low levels of corruption and clientelism can be seen as features of an individualistic society and a market economy. Two other variables "define" factor 2. As both are related to public subsidies we call this the "party subsidy" factor. The factor of "western modernity" is highly and significantly correlated with the IPS ($r = 0.75$, $p = 0.000$). This result supports the major findings from our previous analysis. The level of political spending is low wherever democracy has been entrenched for many years and sources of extra funding are not available.

Table 4-6: Factor analysis of variables explaining spending levels

Variable	Factor 1	Factor 2
Index of Economic Freedom	**0.95**	-0.11
Wave of democratisation	**0.94**	-0.09
Years of democratic tradition	**-0.89**	0.02
Gross Domestic Product in PPP $	**-0.86**	0.14
Corruption Perceptions Index	**-0.86**	0.38
Human Development Index	**-0.79**	0.27
Intensity of corruption	**0.79**	-0.31
Anglo-Saxon vs. other political tradition	**0.73**	0.38
Intensity of clientelism	**-0.67**	-0.17
Public subsidies per citizen in USD	0.56	**0.69**
Public subsidies in percent of party revenue	0.40	**0.83**

In conclusion, some causes for the level of political spending can be identified:

- Among the features of a democratic *polity* a few have a specific impact. The more a country can *afford economically,* the less likely it is to spend much on its democracy. Increasing experience in popular government (indicated by *earlier wave of*

---

99 Closing the consideration of factors that pull/push political spending in different directions with a reminder of the different intensity of "economies of scale" rounds off the presentation in this chapter.

democratisation) reduces the level of political spending, which also decreases as the *size of the electorate* rises, although the intensity of this impact differs. Party competition is less expensive in highly individualistic ("Puritan") *Anglo-Saxon style* democracies than it is in the multi-party coalition governments of continental Western Europe and the clientelistic non-western democracies.

- The impressive spread of spending levels noted in all comparative analyses is mainly caused by the impacts of public *policy* and the absence thereof. A practice of *corrupt exchanges* and generous *public subsidies* (as relevant sources of an – unlimited – supply of political funds) boosts the level of political spending.
- Variables related to *politics* rarely apply to all countries in the sample. Nevertheless the most influential can be identified. Neither *campaign-centred* and *organisation-oriented parties*, nor *ideological warfare*, nor different forms and levels of *intra-party competition* [100] increase or decrease spending on party politics. However, *one-party dominance* of political contests during more than two decades inflates the costs of democracy well beyond those in more competitive situations.

In concluding this chapter we must point out an important outlier. In the U.S. all major causes of high political expenditure are absent. It is a big, first wave democracy with low levels of corruption and public subsidies (for political activity), yet with a high level of economic performance. However, the most important devices that were introduced to U.S. politics by "good government" reforms are nomination of candidates by primary and campaign finance laws. Both have dismantled the countervailing power of parties and reduced the major parties to an array of PACs. Clinging to the anti-party and anti-democratic concept of the founding fathers, who insisted on an ill-conceived model of representative, i.e. non-popular,[101] government makes the U.S. indeed "unique" among the universe of established democracies. Such measures increased political expenses well beyond the Anglo-Saxon average,[102] and gave it the highest ranking among the moderate political spenders (as defined by an IPS below 0.5).

A rising level of party expenses is the cause of much public alarm in the media and academia.[103] A traditional paradigm of political finance analysis is the assumption that the most recent campaign "may well have been the most expensive … election in

---

100 Both, clientelistic "vote buying" (whether Israeli, Italian or Japanese style) and the fight for name recognition (e.g. in the U.S.), constitute *intra-party competition,* which was expected to contribute towards a high level of political spending. The professional politics of an elaborated field organisation has to be dealt with later on. See chapter V, sub-section B 3 (professional politics).
101 Hermens 1958, pp. 430-451.
102 For Anglo-Saxon democracies the IPS averages 0.42, politicl spending per capita USD 4.36 or PPP-$ 3.85. Their citizens assign less than the equivalent of 2 BigMacs to fund democratic competition. For the U.S. all of these values are higher: 0.46 (IPS), USD and PPP-$ 6.65, BigMacs equivalents 2.75.
103 Surprisingly this alarmist news was already well known to Overacker 1932, p. 79, and Heard 1960, p. 371.

history"[104] or one of „the most expensive … contests in … history."[105] To a prudent observer such remarks indicate that systematic analysis requires more details than just a list of increasing dollar amounts. Time series data cannot stand alone. A sound interpretation has to link political spending data to concurrent economic indicators, e.g. inflation or average income. Political observers were predicting even beforehand that the 2008 presidential election, "a clash of titanic intensity, … will involve vastly larger sums than those spent on previous … campaigns."[106] Such alarm is a traditional feature of the campaign finance discourse.[107] It has to be put into perspective, both in space and in time. Therefore we will now turn to the analysis of time series data.

---

104 Paltiel 1974, p. 342. Quite in this line Alexander (1971, p. 3) had called the 1968 U.S. presidential election "the most expensive in American history."
105 Alexander/ Corrado 1995, p. 178. Still in this vein „*Der Wahlkampf in Amerika ist der teuerste aller Zeiten*", in: *Frankfurter Allgemeine* (daily newspaper), 29 October 2008 – based on a report by the Center for Respansive Politics (www.opensecrets.org/news/10/us-election-will-cost-5.3-billi.html).
106 „Money's Going to Talk in 2008", in: *Washington Post*, 11 March 2006.
107 As indicated by Walecki 2005a, p. 171.

CHAPTER FIVE

Cost Explosion: Fact or Fantasy?

In democracies all over the world the costs of party activity and election campaigns seem to be exploding. "Each year the cost of campaigning rises progressively to fantastic heights."[1] The leading scholar on U.S. campaign funds observed that in four decades (1956-96) campaign spending increased 27-fold. In less than three decades (1968-96) total expenditure for political purposes has multiplied by a factor of 14.[2] Similar trends were documented for France, Australia, Canada, Sweden, Austria and the U.K. "In absolute terms campaign expenditures have sky-rocketed almost all over Western Europe during the post-war period."[3] In short, political analysts observe a dramatic increase of political expenditures everywhere. It is not surprising that the U.S. experience seriously influences how the problem is perceived in other countries.[4] The "mother of elective government," Britain, and the biggest established democracy, the United States, seem to have been hit hardest by the international trend. In both countries excessively growing amounts of money are spent on political competition.

A) Background variables for the spending spree

After several decades political finance research should be able to test the hypotheses that have been advanced, and to open up comparative analysis into the alleged "explosion in the cost" of political competition.[5] The question guiding the next step of this

---

1   Bloom 1956, p. 170; still in this vein: Katz 1996, p. 132 and Scarrow 2007, p. 206.
2   Alexander 1999, p. 15; Alexander/ Corrado 1995, p. 178.
3   Quote by Krouwel 1999, p. 86. For details see Coignard/ Lacun 1989, p. 329; Amr/ Lisowski 2001, pp. 54, 57; Katz 1996, pp. 129/130; Neill report 1998, p. 43.
4   E.g. in New Zealand (Wilson 2004, p. 3). - The data for levels of political spending as presented above (chapter III, especially in Table 3-5) were not prepared for a comparison in time. Nevertheless it is tempting to try this approach contrasting the different studies. Heidenheimer (1963, p. 798/799 and 1970b, p. 11-13) ranked Israel and Italy among the big spenders, and they still are. He found that Australia and Britain spent moderately, which they still do. From his intermediate group (Japan, Germany and the U.S.), Japan has risen to a top rank whereas the latter two countries have held their intermediate positions. In roughly four decades the costs of party democracy – quite in line with conventional wisdom in academia and the media – have increased, but mostly at equal pace among the democracies. If earlier data presented by Heard (1960, pp. 373-375) are considered, too, Israel, Britain, Germany and Italy have not changed much. However, among medium level spenders the U.S. has declined from top rank to bottom.
5   Katz 1996, p. 129. Quite wisely Herbert Alexander (1999, p. 12) avoided to use this term. Instead he preferred "excessive" spending and "explosion of spending," both of which do not imply that "cost" was the cause.

comparative effort is:

- Does an escalating use of *paid media advertising* or the recurrent implementation of new *campaign technology* or the unlimited expansion of a *full-time paid organisation* cause a "cost explosion" for party spending?

Any attempt to investigate the potential causes of increased political expenses will require time series data for as many democracies as possible. Although political scientists have researched political finance in various democracies continuously for about four decades,[6] long-term data of comparatively good quality are available for only a few cases.[7] These include big countries (the U.S. and Japan, Germany and the U.K.), a medium-sized (Canada) and a small democracy (Austria). Four of the countries, which can be studied in depth, belong to the election oriented, two to the organisation centred group of democracies.

"Many commentators ... regard it as self-evident that the costs of politics have been rising [in most parts of the world] and that the cause of this upward trend has been the development of [television and of other] mass media as the main forms of modern electioneering."[8] In analysing the rise of U.S. campaign spending, Alexander and Bauer have suggested to look for various factors, which interact in causing the obvious outcome: increases reflect *inflation*, greater *availability of comprehensive data*, higher *levels of competition*, the *professionalisation of politics*, and the *application of more high technology*. Decades ago James K. Pollock mentioned two major causes for rising campaign costs: the increasing number of voters, and rising costs of labour, materials and supplies.[9] Because purchasing power is declining over time, the latter factor represents *inflation* that is already included in the Alexander-Bauer set of factors. Following Pollock's advice, we will add a considerable change in the *size of the electorate* due to population growth. A growth in the adult population (and thus the electorate) as well as declining purchasing power due to inflation of all currencies, and more comprehensive data represent non-political influences.

1. External influences (electorate and inflation)

As we are looking for political factors, which may cause a possible "cost explosion" among the democracies, we shall first consider the impact of the two general social

---

6   For an overview see Nassmacher 2001b, pp. 19/20.
7   Among the 25 democracies covered in this study no more than six provide long-term data of more or less quality and diverse coverage: USA (1912-2000), Britain (1952-1997), Germany (1968-2002), Austria (1976-2002), Japan (1976-99) and Canada (1971-2002). Five of these democracies are members of the economically leading Group of Seven (G7). Two countries are big spenders, two are medium level spenders and two are moderate spenders (for details see above in chapter III, Table 3-5).
8   Pinto-Duschinsky 2002, pp. 81/82.
9   Alexander/ Bauer 1991, p. 4; Pollock 1926, pp. 170/171.

and economic trends (creeping inflation and growing electorate). Then we will look into the impact of improved data quality before we pursue specifically political factors such as paid TV advertising, use of new technology and professional services.

a) Growth of electorate

The first intervening factor identified by Pollock, the *expanding electorate*, is neglected in most studies of political spending.[10] In one of his earlier studies Alexander mentioned the amount of campaign spending per vote from 1912 to 1968.[11] In computing this he obviously used the number of votes cast. With this procedure any change in voter turnout will influence per capita cost of campaigning, that is lower turnout translates into higher cost and vice versa. A more reliable figure to start with would be the total number of electors.[12] Between 1912 and 2000 the U.S. voting age population increased by a factor of 7.6, from 28.1 million to 214.0 million. Presidential campaign spending per citizen has risen 36-fold, from $0.08 (1912) to $2.84 (2000).[13] More comprehensive data is available for a shorter period of time only.

When Herbert Alexander was the director of the Citizens' Research Foundation, he compiled and published lots of detailed information on U.S. elections. This data is readily available for a time series analysis of about five decades. These estimates indicate a 28-fold increase of total political spending in a presidential year from $140 million (1952) to $3.93 billion (2000). However, as electorates have become larger "it is necessary to calculate costs-per-elector rather than total costs."[14] Between 1952 and 2000 the size of the U.S. electorate has more than doubled. Thus total spending on elective politics per elector rose from $1.45 to $18.36 (Table 5-1), which is less than 13-fold but still an impressive trend.

---

10 However, as a factor that determines the size of a polity, we have applied it in our cross-national approach already. See above in chapter III, section B (adjust for size).
11 Alexander 1971, p. 4. The data is also reported by Crotty 1977, p. 104. An earlier tabulation for 1912-28 by Overacker 1932, p. 80. A follow-up for 1912-80 in: Alexander 1983, p. 110.
12 In the U.S. the number depends on voter registration, a voluntary activity of the individual citizen. Thus the number of registered voters is regularly much lower than the voting age population, and the number of enfranchised citizens is somewhere in between. We will use the voting age population as the closest substitute.
13 Pollock 1926, p. 170; Nelson 2002, p. 24.
14 Pinto-Duschinsky 2002, p. 83.

Table 5-1: Political spending in the United States, 1952-2004

Year	No. of Voters (VAP) (million)	Total political expenses			Spending on federal candidates		
		Amount spent in million $	Spending per capita in $	Per capita increase per cycle in %	Total amount in million $	Spending per capita in $	Share of total in %
1952	96.4	140	1.45	-	-	-	-
1956	100.7	155	1.54	6.2	-	-	-
1960	105.3	175	1.66	7.8	-	-	-
1964	111.6	200	1.79	7.8	-	-	-
1968	117.4	300	2.55	42.5	-	-	-
1972	136.2	425	3.12	22.4	215	1.58	50.6
1976	146.2	540	3.69	18.3	276	1.89	51.1
1980	157.0	1,200	7.64	107.0	514	3.27	42.8
1984	165.8	1,800	10.86	42.1	699	4.22	38.8
1988	173.6	2,700	15.55	43.2	958	5.52	35.5
1992	189.5	3,220	16.99	9.6	1,228	6.48	38.1
1996	196.5	4,200	21.48	29.8	1,465	7.46	34.9
2000	214.0	3,812	17.81	- 6.5	1,678	7.84	41.1
2004	222.0	4,273	19.25	12.1	2,489	11.21	58.2

Sources: International IDEA 1997; www.idea.int/vt/country_view.cfm (VAP=voting age population); Alexander 1999, pp. 15, 19, 23; Nelson 2002, p. 24; Patterson 2006, p. 71.

In some countries the growth of the electorate has been equally striking. Canada, Japan and Germany (the latter mostly due to unification) are close to the U.S. In Austria and the U.K. this process has been more moderate. During the second half of the 20th century in these countries the number of citizens eligible to vote increased by about 25%. In Germany, the U.S., Japan and Canada the electorate almost doubled during that period.[15] If political spending data for all six countries were available, deflators of 1.25 for Austria and the U.K., 1.9 for Germany, 2.2 for the U.S., 2.3 for Japan and 2.5 for Canada would apply. On average an enlarged electorate caused about half of the increase in political spending since 1950. Unfortunately, only data for the U.S. and the U.K. cover such a lengthy period of time. Nevertheless the deflators mentioned above, indicate the impact of this frequently neglected dimension. The importance of purchasing power when making comparisons over time is more obvious.

b) Impact of inflation

Rising costs of labour, materials and supplies, i.e. a general trend of inflation, will necessarily increase the currency amounts spent by parties and candidates for a similar set

---

15 For details see International IDEA 1997; www.idea.int/vt/country_view.cfm.

of goods and services.[16] The Consumer Price Index (CPI) or the Retail Price Index (RPI) measure the decline of purchasing power of any currency. The problems of measurement, which accompany both indexes and their specifics, abound.[17] For all practical purposes the CPI/ RPI, "is the simplest and probably the best single measure of inflation".[18] "Examining politically relevant data over time using inflation-adjusted dollars [or other currency] often shows striking, and sometimes surprising, patterns."[19]

From 1952 to 2000, consumer prices in the U.S. increased by a factor of 6.5.[20] The number of potential voters has more than doubled. Total political spending, on the other hand, has risen 28-fold, which is definitely out of step with either trend. In general, previous comparisons match the increase of campaign costs against both trends separately.[21] However, growth of electorate and inflation of currency are not mutually exclusive trends, as both influence spending at the same time. They have a cumulative effect on the rise of political costs.

Therefore the rate of inflation has to be applied not to total campaign spending, but to per capita expenses on party politics. Deflated per capita figures are the only adequate indicator of the net increase of political spending over time. When adjusted for size of the electorate and inflation, U.S. per capita campaign spending has not even doubled in half a century. This result stands in stark contrast to all the overblown perceptions in the literature. Much smaller increases than discussed to date must be explained by political factors. For example, during almost the same period (1952-97), consolidated central office spending by the major U.K. parties per voter on list in constant pounds[22] has increased by a factor of 2.7, i.e. almost trebled, which is significantly more than the "explosion" of campaign costs in the U.S.

Table 5-2 (below) offers comparable data for all six countries studied in depth for three decades, which is a shorter period of time than the 50 years available for the U.S. Ranges of USD 1.00-4.00, GBP 0.04-0.20, CAD 0.20-2.40, JPY 1,500-2,300, ATS 45-157 and DEM 5.00-19.00 indicate considerable, although not continuous increases across the board. In Japan, the per capita amount of the financial outlay of political competitors at current prices more than doubled from the mid-1970s to around 1990. During the 1990s the per capita outlay for political purposes declined, mostly in years

---

16 Pollock 1926, p. 171. More recently this concept has been re-introduced in tth U.S. by Alexander (1999, pp. 16, 18, 20) and Nelson (2002, p. 26), in Britain by the Houghton (1976) and the Neill (1998) committee.
17 Among the distortions Sahr (2004, pp. 273/274) mentions the cost of home ownership, the prices of food and energy, components and weighting in the market basket, improved quality of goods and services, lagged reflection of changes in consumer preferences and supply options.
18 Pinto-Duschinski 1981, p. 288, note 21.
19 Sahr 2004, p. 275.
20 Data by U.S. Bureau of Labor Statistics (www.bls.gov/cpi).
21 E.g. Crotty 1977, pp. 103-105; Sorauf 1988, p. 29.
22 The precise averages are: 4.14p for the 1952/55 election cycle, 11.23p for the 1994/97 election cycle.

without a national election.[23] At constant prices the increase is less dramatic, from JPY 1,500 in 1976/82 to JPY 2,200 in 1986/89.

In the U.S. per capita expenses of federal candidates at current prices increased about five-fold almost continuously (Table 5-1 above). The pattern of the per capita outlay in CPI deflated dollars is less clear-cut. As might be expected in presidential years, all federal candidates together spend about twice the per capita amount of congressional candidates (in off-years). Over the years both averages have about doubled, in CPI deflated dollars. In other countries, especially in the U.K., Canada and Germany, the influence of parliamentary cycles is similar. Nevertheless per capita spending at constant prices increased significantly over time (Table 5-2). If we neglect some outliers, the range for Germany lowers to €3.60-6.10 (DEM 7.00-12.00) in three decades and does not exhibit any particular pattern.

Table 5-2: Political spending per citizen, CPI adjusted (1980=100), 1971-2000

Year	USA	GB	CDN	JPN	A	D
1971		0.0472	0.165			5.06
1972	**2.21**	0.0510	**0.786**			**9.72**
1973		0.0617	0.215			5.80
1974	1.02	**0.0877**	**0.685**			7.07
1975		0.0435	n.a.	n.a.		8.28
1976	**1.92**	0.0416	0.658	**1,482**		**9.79**
1977		0.0435	0.775	**1,463**		6.54
1978	1.47	0.0656	0.857	**1,489**		8.02
1979		**0.0819**	**1.455**	**1,777**	n.a.	19.15
1980	**2.74**	0.0589	**1.400**	**1,814**	56.50	**10.76**
1981		0.0541	0.846	1,534	44.51	6.55
1982	1.79	0.0561	0.832	1,635	64.74	5.34
1983		**0.0970**	0.936	**2,161**	**69.05**	**12.25**
1984	**3.09**	0.0534	**2.347**	1,675	53.85	9.65
1985		0.0536	1.093	1,936	56.48	8.45
1986	1.88	0.0675	1.267	**2,216**	**100.74**	10.42
1987		**0.1278**	1.082	1,905	58.14	**10.09**
1988	**3.89**	0.0691	**1.976**	2,258	53.99	8.39
1989		0.0780	0.819	**2,221**	69.16	11.04
1990	1.54	0.0896	0.911	2,166	**127.15**	11.18
1991		0.1206	0.796	2,112	78.47	7.39
1992	**3.58**	**0.1172**	0.770	**1,947**	109.81	7.09
1993		0.0639	**1.819**	**1,891**	93.84	7.00
1994	2.08	0.0679	0.538	1,627	**136.23**	**11.13**
1995		0.0722	0.627	**1,760**	108.16	7.01

---

23 Blechinger/ Nassmacher 2001, p. 158.

Year	USA	GB	CDN	JPN	A	D
1996	**4.05**	0.1094	0.726	**1,699**	112.42	7.26
1997		**0.1996**	1.724	1,565	101.14	6.44
1998	1.83	n.a.	0.621	**1,826**	90.54	**9.69**
1999		n.a.	0.607	1,491	156.73	8.91
2000	**3.16**	n.a.	1.292		63.30	6.68
Min.	1.02	0.04	0.16	1,463	44.51	5.06
Max.	4.05	0.20	2.35	2,258	156.73	19.15

Data sources: electors = www.idea.int/vt/country_view.cfm; CPI = Mitchell 2003a, pp. 79/80, 866-868, 921, 926; total spending = Alexander 1999, pp. 19, 23; Paltiel 1974, pp. 344-347; Paltiel 1975, pp. 192-197; Chief Electoral Officer 1980, 1981, 1985, 1989, 1993; Elections Canada on-line; Pinto-Duschinsky 1981, pp. 138, 143, 163, 164, 167, 190/191; Pinto-Duschinsky 1985, pp. 330, 333, 336, 337; Pinto-Duschinsky 1994, pp. 14, 17, 18, 20; Butler/ Butler 1994, pp. 133, 241; Neill report 1998, pp. 36-38; Webb 2000, p. 232; Fisher 1996b, pp. 164/165; Fisher 1999, p. 523; Blechinger/ Nassmacher 2001, pp. 158/159; data for Austria kindly provided by Doris Cordes, Claire Smith and Hubert Sickinger from official reports; *Deutscher Bundestag*, parliamentary papers, no. 10/4104 (neu) to 14/5050.
Comment: Data for presidential years/ parliamentary election years in **bold** face type.

Before we draw any kind of conclusion, we have to recall that campaign dollars, pounds or euros are not consumer dollars, pounds or euros. Political activity requires a different "basket" of goods and services than everyday life in a family of four (two adults, two children), which is what the CPI stands for. Unfortunately a "basket" of campaign goods and services is not available. No public agency has ever tried to establish a price index for the costs of campaigning.[24] Demand for campaign services is probably changing faster than for consumer goods. Thus the index applied here (as elsewhere) to measure the decline in purchasing power (i.e. the CPI) may not be too precise. However, as a general measure of inflation it should suffice.

Inflation has decreased the purchasing power of USD, GBP, CAD, JPY, ATS and DEM in the range of four- (DEM) to 23-fold (GBP), on average by a factor of 8.5 in the second half of the 20th century. During the three decades presented in Table 5-2, consumer prices rose about 4- to 5-fold. What is the combined impact of both general factors (continuous inflation and growing electorate) on the costs of democracy? On average a 17-fold (i.e. 2 times 8.5) increase in nominal political spending, in political and economic reality just about balances the 50 years impact of two social and economic trends. Neither of these trends is caused nor influenced by political competition. Any growth in political costs beyond that level must be explained by specific factors inherent in political activity. Before we discuss innovations in campaign technology and professionalised politics, we have to consider any impact, which may be hidden in the data that are available for comparison.

---

24 The only exception, which has come close to this goal, is the German Presidential Commission (*Parteienfinanzierungskommission*). See *Deutscher Bundestag*, parliamentary papers, no. 13/ 3574 and 13/ 7517.

2. *More comprehensive data*

Due to the efforts of scholarly investigation and the demands of public disclosure, more and more data concerning the costs of political competition is available. Whereas detailed knowledge for Austria, Canada, Germany and Japan has improved mostly because of transparency regulation, for the U.S. and the U.K. continuous research[25] has uncovered much data. The consequences of both processes for any long-term analysis require a note of caution. The U.S. case offers some important evidence. The total amount of spending on behalf of all federal candidates (presidential, senatorial and congressional) expanded from $215 million (1972) to $1,613 million (2000), which is less than 8-fold. Total campaign spending, on the other hand, grew more than 9-fold (Table 5-1above). This difference hints at the fact that total spending data for the same period may not present comparable information.

Over time additional campaigns (e.g. for ballot issues or by issue advocacy groups) as well as party-building activities ("soft money") have added to the total cost of democracy. Compulsory reporting by PACs, the activities of enforcement agencies and more experienced research have disclosed information, which hitherto was hidden. On the one hand, this process has contributed to additional spending on elective politics; but on the other hand it has also improved our knowledge about the true costs of democracy.

The increase in total campaign spending in 1988 over the 1984 figure may indicate a way to understand the impact of more precise knowledge. That is, additional expenses totalled $888 million (almost 50% of the 1984 total). An amount of $155 million (i.e. 17% of this increase) was caused by ballot issues, which had become more and more popular. $165 million (or 19%) was related to increased campaign spending for local offices and $215 million (or 24%) to campaigns for state offices.[26] Because state and local campaign spending was initially less precisely known, conservative estimates had to be adjusted in more recent years.[27] More than half of the total increase was due to the fact that more complete data had become "available at the state and local levels and regarding ballot issues."[28] Consequently the national estimate of total political spending has become more accurate. In sum, 60% of the 1984-88 increase is explained by various areas with improved data quality.

Similar effects may have caused some part of the other big increases of political spending. In 1980 22% of the gross increase was related to campaigns for state offices. In 1996, this applied to 14%. In 1984 about 17% of the extra cost was incurred by non-party groups, a new player in the political game. In 1996 such PACs contributed another 12% to the additional outlay. In the same year "soft money," a more recent

---

25 We owe most of this progress to Herbert E. Alexander (U.S.) and Michael Pinto-Duschinsky (U.K.).
26 Alexander/ Bauer 1991, p. 3 and Alexander/ Haggerty 1987, p. 83.
27 Problems related to the compilation of reasonably reliable estimates for spending on state and local offices as well as on ballot issue campaigns are presented in: Alexander/ Haggerty 1987, pp. 118-124.
28 Alexander 1983, p. 105.

strategy to avoid restrictions created by U.S. regulation, accounted for 29% of the extra dollars spent on politics.[29]

This approach does not indicate that all additional spending is due to improved knowledge. It especially leaves a big amount of the quite excessive 1980 increase unexplained. However, the details presented here do issue a warning against the perception of skyrocketing expenses. If we heed this warning, our search for the impact of changing campaign practices on the costs of U.S. democracy may be served better by selective data (for example on campaigns for federal candidates) than by overall figures.

Such unique impacts of improved knowledge about individual contests and specific (election) years are much less important in a large number of continuously covered races where specific influences are balanced against each other. The biannual competition for some 33 senatorial and 435 congressional seats offers this opportunity. The spending totals for federal candidates (see Table 5-1 above), which we use in our comparison, will be less prone to influence by different quality of data in specific years and more dependent on general trends.

In many respects the time series data, which is available for Japan differ from its U.S. counterparts. In Japan the period covered is much shorter. The data are based solely on official reports, which mean that they are far from comprehensive. Nevertheless it is useful in identifying a trend. The information available relates to the income of political actors, not to expenses. However, we assume that such data can be used to identify the long-term development of spending levels. There are two good reasons for this assumption. Separate data for income and expenses, which are available for individual parties (1995-99) show that most parties operate on a spend-as-you-raise basis.[30] This is reinforced by the aggregate data for individual years, which illustrates increases in election years and decreases in non-election years. As our sole intention in this chapter is to discuss trends in political spending levels, the necessary reservations should not preclude a use of the data, which are available.

For Germany time series on party financing can be established for any period starting in 1968 (due to compulsory reporting of data on party funding). However, early data concern party revenue only. They will be considered as substitutes for spending totals assuming that each party spent at least as much as it collected.[31] From 1984 to 2002 the six major parties (five of them represented in the national parliament during the entire period)[32] accounted for an average of 97.2 percent (between 94.6 and 99.6%) of

---

29 Data from Alexander 1979b, pp. 166/167; Alexander 1983, p. 104; Alexander/ Haggerty 1987, p. 83; Alexander/ Corrado 1995, p. 5; Alexander 1999, p. 13.
30 Blechinger/ Nassmacher 2001, p. 159.
31 Because debt incurred, which is listed as a source of funds, will be ignored, the data for funds raised represent a conservative estimate of spending totals. Thus data for the years 1968 to 1983 are rather rough estimates.
32 The parties included in the analysis are: *SPD, CDU, CSU, FDP, Grüne, PDS* (now: *Die Linke*). For all years before German unification (1968 to 1989) the West German Communist party (*DKP*), which was the major spender among the non-parliamentary parties, is included in our data.

total spending by all German parties. The data processed in detail for the period 1968 to 2002 will be limited to these parties.

Since 1984 German parties are obligated by law to publicly report their total expenses. The data processed for the major parties include all levels of the party organisation (federal headquarters, state branches and local chapters). Thus since 1984 the data is of very high quality, and its comprehensive character stands alone among Western democracies.[33] For the U.K., Austria and Canada information is still available for central (federal) office expenses only. Following these reservations caused by the different quality of available data we will now turn to the comparative analysis of party competition.

3. Intensified competition

Early in his study of U.S. elections Alexander distinguished two sets of causes for an extraordinary level of campaign costs. One group "includes factors, which must be considered continuing components of ... campaigns."[34] Such factors will be discussed as technological changes and professional politics. The other group of factors is unique to a specific year. In the American context this statement can be taken literally. For all parliamentary, democracies we will have to consider a cyclical difference between election and non-election years.

a) Parliamentary election cycle

In the lifespan of every parliament, party spending reaches a maximum when political competition is at its most fierce, i.e. during the election year. Campaign expenses add extra outlays to political spending totals (Table 5-2 above).[35] For the two campaign-centred examples of parliamentary government (Canada and the U.K.), the difference between election and non-election years is more marked than for the two continental European democracies (Austria, Germany). Because of its more traditional style of politics, Japan has to be considered separately.

Additional spending in election years (which is mostly campaign spending) has been more consistent in Canada than it was in the U.K. Independent of the actual length of the election cycle (which for the period under study is between one and five years), spending in election years expressed as a percentage of average spending in non-election years in Canada falls into two brackets. In four election years actual spending was less than 60% higher (55 to 59%), three times it was about twice as high as the (non-election year) annual average (92 to 100%). However, there is no obvious pattern,

---

33 Although the (reported) data used in this chapter are not comprehensive – see above in chapter III, sub-section A1 (major democracies) – they offer a pretty reliable base for time series analysis.
34 Alexander 1971, p. 4.
35 See above in chapter II, sub-section C 1 (election campaigns).

which election year belongs to which group. Among the five parliamentary democracies studied in depth, Canada represents the most modern capital-intensive campaign.

Japan is campaign centred, too, although in quite a different fashion. Working in a one-party dominated political system; clientelistic politicians favour an almost antithetical strategy of political spending. Their more traditional style of permanent campaigning ("vote-buying") is geared towards maintaining good relations with voters via local opinion leaders.[36] As a result, the spending difference between election and non-election years is much lower than it is in other liberal democracies (about 10 to 30% of annual routine spending – cf. Tab. 5-2).[37]

For Germany and Austria information on extra campaign spending is either not reliable or not available.[38] This leaves only three countries for the analysis of any financial impact of technology, the U.S., the U.K and Canada. In the latter countries we will apply CPI adjusted per capita campaign spending by central (federal) offices as indicator of a possible "cost explosion". For the U.S. we will use data on campaigns for all federal offices.

b)   Other competitive factors

Quite different from the U.K. (and the U.S.) two-party system, its Canadian counterpart has experienced considerable change since the 1970s. The federal three party system of the late 1970s and most of the 1980s has seen the almost total destruction of a governing party (the P.C. in 1988), in terms of parliamentary seats held, not necessarily in terms of funds available, and the rise of two new parties. One of them, the *Reform Party*, represented the Canadian West and is now part of the new CPC. The other is based solely in Quebec, the *Bloc Quebecois* (B.Q.), which is the federal arm of the separatist *Parti Quebecois* (P.Q.). Despite the major upheaval of the party system and a considerable drain on party coffers, there has been no permanent shift of federal parties' funds between campaign and routine purposes.[39]

The level of campaign spending in the U.K. (and elsewhere, however, not in Austria and Germany) can be estimated by comparing spending levels in election years to annual routine spending in non-election years. In election years the "routine" part of total spending should be near the average between the year before and the year after an election. The difference is a close approximation to extra campaign spending.

---

36 This type of campaign may be largely reminiscent of the aristocratic era of political spending in Britain. Cf. Pinto-Duschinsky 1981, pp. 15-16. Cf. above in chapter IV, sub-section A1b (political development).
37 Blechinger/ Nassmacher 2001, p. 158.
38 Computing averages (as applied to Canada and the U.K.) does not work here because state elections are scattered over the national election cycle and parties maintain a high level of spending on the organisation.
39 We will apply measurement as elaborated, see above in chapter II, sub-section C1 (election campaigns).

In Germany two new parties have entered the system. Both parties emerged because of new cleavages and could easily establish themselves under a P.R. voting system. The first is a post-materialist party (the Greens), which enlarged the party system in the early 1980s. The second is a post-communist sectional party for East Germany and was added after unification in 1990. In Austria a two-and-a-half party system was transformed into a three-and-a-half party system. The FPÖ increased its voting strength (by siphoning off support from the two major parties) and a Green party entered the system. Such changes may have an impact on the intensity of competition and party spending, which is similar to specific situations in the generally stable U.S. presidential contest.

Among the specific causes of exceptional spending in the U.S. are the presidential pre-nomination contests in both major parties, especially when neither of the presidential candidates is an incumbent or there is an occasional challenge by a third party presidential candidate. In 1952, 1968, 1980, 1988 and 1996 "the presidential nomination in one (or both) of the (major) parties was … seriously contested."[40] In 1988 "highly competitive campaigns in both parties"[41] increased pre-nomination spending by $106 million (almost 12% of the total increase in political spending).[42] Thus more than 70% of the total increase for the 1984-88 cycle ($888 million) had no specific link to media costs or technological innovations. In 1980 (as compared to 1976) total spending by federal candidates almost doubled (see Table 5-1 above). Candidates for Congress spent about 48% of the increase of these total expenses ($114 of 238 million).[43] In this context it is important to note that "in 1980, for the first time, more money from political action groups than from individuals financed senatorial and congressional races."[44]

A different approach to U.S. presidential spending also suggests caution with a cause-effect theory. Inflation adjusted presidential general election spending by the major party candidates peaked in 1896 (McKinley/ Bryan), 1936 (Roosevelt/ Landon) and 1972 (Nixon/ McGovern) and hit a low in 1912 (Wilson/ Taft/ Roosevelt), 1948 (Truman/ Dewey) and 1980 (Reagan/ Carter).[45] Neither the competitive situation (close contest, three-cornered contest, fringe vs. mainstream candidate) nor technical innovations help to explain any of these extremes.

In general, the influence of variations in presidential spending on the overall costs of U.S. campaigning should not be overestimated. From 1980 to 1996 the share of total funds spent on the presidential contest (including pre-nomination and general election spending) ranged between 16.7 to 22.9% of the overall total of political costs.[46] This

---

40 Alexander 1971, p. 5; cf. Alexander 1983, pp. 105, 107; Alexander 1999, p. 15.
41 Alexander/ Bauer 1991, p. 17.
42 Alexander/ Haggerty 1987, pp. 83, 85; Alexander/ Bauer 1991, pp. 3, 11/12.
43 Alexander 1979b, pp. 176/177; Alexander 1983, p. 104.
44 White 1982, p. 426. For some consequences see below in this chapter, section C (push or pull?), and in chapter VII, sub-section B1c (PACs).
45 Sahr 2004, p. 281 (graph M), who uses data from Alexander 1992a, p. 80.
46 Computation based on data in: Alexander 1983, p. 104; Alexander/ Haggerty 1987, p. 83; Alexander/ Bauer 1991, p. 3; Alexander/ Corrado 1995, p. 5; Alexander 1999, pp. 13, 15, 19, 23.

spread was about 6 percentage points, only 2 percentage points more than the spread for shares of congressional expenditures. Spending on all federal candidates for presidential years 1980-96 ranged between 35.1 and 42.8% of total U.S. campaign spending. The impact of individual years (e.g. the specific challenge by a significant independent candidate)[47] on total political spending is much lower than the impact of parliamentary election cycles or the difference between presidential and non-presidential years. As the financial impact of individual presidential years seems to be ambiguous, we now turn to the political causes of increased spending.

B) Causes of increased party spending

Although the competitive situation of each election campaign may differ in many respects from previous years, portions of increased spending can be attributed to changes in professional services, such as improvement of campaign technology or paid TV advertising. "The growing significance of media campaigning has entailed tremendous escalation of the costs of campaigns." "The cost of political broadcasting is the most measurable of these, ... Television is much more expensive than radio, and its use and cost are continually increasing."[48]

1. Paid TV advertising

"Political campaigning consists largely of communications – their preparation, production, and delivery. ... Communication costs – expenditures for television, radio, print media, and mass mailing – have taken a quantum leap in the last two decades, and consequently so has all political spending."[49] Modern campaigns, which use media advertising in radio and TV networks operated by commercial broadcasters, are frequently seen as a major cause of high (and probably increasing) levels of spending for political competition. "Television is the principal villain" for the rising costs of politics and the acceleration of campaign costs "parallels the increasing reliance on television as a medium of political communication".[50] Media, especially TV, play a crucial role "in modern political life ... Yet even in ... the United States ... the importance of televised political advertising easily lends itself to overstatement."[51] In general parties manage to reduce this impact by defining suitable rules for media access.[52]

---

47 E.g. Alexander 1983, p. 354.
48 Quotes by Pierre/ Svasand/ Widfeldt 2000, p. 4 and Alexander 1971, pp. 4/5 respectively.
49 Alexander 1983, p. 103.
50 Crotty 1977, pp. 107 and 103 respectively. At first glance arguing in this line identifies TV as a major problem in Costa Rica and Uruguay. This is, however, not due to high spending but to an addiction to extensive use, which has turned "network owners into ... powerful political donors" (Casas-Zamora 2002, p. 294; Casas-Zamora 2005a, p. 228).
51 Pinto-Duschinsky 2002, p. 82.
52 Nassmacher, H. 2006, pp. 511/512. In Europe only Italy seems to be a major problem (Holtz-Bacha/ Kaid 1995, pp. 14-18).

CPI adjusted per capita spending data in our sample of six democracies (Table 5-2 above) indicates, that in Austria, Germany and Japan annual party spending differs for years with or without a national election. However, no national trend of increased spending can be established for 1980-2000 in Austria, 1972-98 in Germany or 1976-99 in Japan. Given the role of commercial TV in these countries this is not surprising. Japanese campaigns are localised efforts, whereas German parties are reluctant to buy TV commercials [53] and Austria did not introduce commercial TV channels prior to 2002. This leaves the three Anglo-Saxon democracies (Britain, Canada and the U.S.) to be studied in detail.

In our sample of three, a first glance identifies the biggest increase of campaign spending for central offices in the U.K.[54] Within less than three decades total campaign expenses increased 53-fold in the U.K., 10-fold in Canada and by a factor of 7.5 in the U.S. (Table 5-3 below). At first glance, these figures indicate a cost explosion caused by modern campaigning. Controlling for the two non-political factors (which have been discussed above, i.e. size of electorate and inflation) changes the amounts, but not the rank order. Obviously the greater increase of electorates in Canada and the U.S. is balanced by the steep rise of the British RPI.

At first the British case seems to offer a clear-cut cause-effect-relationship. "Broadcasting provided the most talked-about innovations of the 1959 campaign. ... Between 1955 and 1959 the proportion of the electorate with a television set in their homes rose from under 40% to over 70% ... The advent of competitive television ... caused big changes."[55] Parties adapted to the new communication environment and learned the art of making news. The 1959 and 1964 campaigns together represent Britain's turn to a modern TV centred campaign using professional polling, publicity and advertising.[56] However, the bulk of spending was not for party broadcasting because the latter requires only production costs not purchased airtime.

Whereas in the U.S. paid TV spots seem to be the backbone of campaign spending in recent decades, the British case even outpaces continental Europe. Paid political advertising on radio and TV is legally banned in the U.K. "Under the BBC charter and the independent television legislation, no party is permitted to buy radio or television time, and free time is provided according to the allotment agreed on by broadcasters and parties."[57] For modern campaigning this "is an extremely important restriction on

---

53 They rely mostly on advertising via public networks, which provide airtime to all competitors free of charge.
54 In passing it should be noted that the U.K., which was the only case without public subsidies until 2001, has experienced the most impressive increase of political spending. On public subsidies see above in chapter IV, sub-section C1b (public subsidies) and below in chapter VIII (public subsidies).
55 Butler/ Rose 1960/ 1999, p. 75.
56 Butler/ Rose 1960/ 1999, p. 78. For some details see below in this chapter, sub-section B 2 (new technology).
57 Smith 1981, pp. 187/188; see ibid., p. 175 and Butler/ Rose 1960/ 1999, pp. 84-90, 96/97.

the national party organisations. It means that the most powerful advertising medium is not available for purchase, no matter how much money a party is prepared to pay."[58]

The Canadian example (Table 5-2 above) shows that party spending hit its high in 1984 and has declined ever since, albeit slowly at first and more massively later on. Under such circumstances a continuous rise in TV advertising at heavily increasing commercial rates is very unlikely. The development of political finance legislation probably indicates a different process. Direct public subsidies (introduced in 1974) were based on the idea of subsidised broadcasting time.[59] When in 1983 the N.D.P. demanded that the subsidy should not preclude any party's media mix, the subsidy rules were amended accordingly.[60] In 2003 an annual support grant (paid in quarterly installments) has become the backbone of direct subsidies for federal parties.[61] Obviously they feel no need to subsidise the purchase of airtime anymore.

U.S. campaigns are regarded as the most sophisticated and the most expensive in the world. Spending in a presidential year reached or surpassed a total of $ 4 billion. U.S. figures for amounts spent and rate of increase have significantly influenced perceptions in other countries. U.S. democracy is considered money-intensive because of its emphasis on campaigning and its use of TV spots for that purpose. Thus we finally turn to the U.S., which at this point of our discussion is the obvious starting point for any analysis of the long term impact of paid media advertising on the current costs of democracy. As early as 1968 "political broadcasting increased ..., ensuring its position as the largest single cost in political campaigns."[62]

The evidence presented by U.S. scholars on the importance of TV advertising for "excessive" campaign spending is inconclusive at best. Unfortunately, the "literature contains relatively few works categorising campaign expenditures."[63] Although TV became a staple in all U.S. households during the 1950s, and the aggregate charges for political broadcasts in the general elections quadrupled between 1956 and 1968, there was no significant shift in advertising from radio to TV during that time. In 1968 the modal split of such charges was two thirds (67%) for TV and one third (33%) for radio, just as it had been in 1956.[64] In 1952 the ratio in broadcasting expenses was roughly half and half with radio slightly in the lead. Finally, in 1988 TV stations won out among the broadcasters. In their general election campaigns the Republican nominee

---

58 Pinto-Duschinsky 1981, p. 253.
59 Barbeau report 1966, p. 37; Seidle/ Paltiel 1981, p. 234.
60 Amendment of Canada Elections Act (Bill C-169). For details see Paltiel 1989, p. 65; Stanbury 1991, p. 42.
61 Due to the amended Canada Elections Act (Bill C-24) an annual grant of almost CAD 24 million was adedd to a campaign reimbursement of about CAD 20 million (for the complete election cycle of four or five years).
62 Alexander 1999, p. 15; Nelson 2002, p. 24; quote in: Alexander 1971, p. 93.
63 Alexander/ Bauer 1991, p. 100.
64 Data base in: Crotty 1977, pp. 107, 109 and Alexander 1971, p. 95.

(Bush Sr.) spent $31.46 million on broadcasting (96% on TV), the Democratic presidential hopeful (Dukakis) $23.35 million (95% on TV).[65]

In 1968 political broadcasting (TV and radio) increased "to 19.6 percent (of $ 300 million) ..., ensuring its position as the largest single cost in political campaigns." The major parties' nominees spent 44% (Nixon) respectively 61% (Humphrey) of their total campaign budgets on media advertising, and at least half of this "went directly into television air time."[66] Of the $5.1 respectively $10.1 million spent on broadcasting about one fifth was expended on production costs, roughly four fifths were airtime charges.

A different approach supports the general impression: In 1952 the Democratic presidential candidate (Stevenson) spent 34 percent, the Republican (Eisenhower) 31 percent of the campaign budget on TV advertising. This share rose moderately for 1956 (42 resp. 40%) and 1984 (41 resp. 45%). Not until 1992 did TV absorb 59% of Democratic and 50% of Republican presidential spending. Consistently, campaign spending on behalf of all federal candidates rose by a factor 6.8 between 1972 and 1996. However, most of this increase was not caused by the presidential contest. Spending on congressional campaigns multiplied about 10-fold during this period. Among congressional campaigns, the costs of (state-wide) senatorial races, which are more inclined to TV advertising, grew more slowly (factor 9.4) than those of the house campaigns (factor 10.3).[67] Under the circumstances this is quite surprising.

"Usually, only serious candidates for major offices – presidential, senatorial, and gubernatorial – make substantial use of television advertisements. Probably only about one-half of the House candidates purchase television time," with just a small portion of their campaign budget. Based on selected campaigns analysed by the Congressional Research Service, it is fair to assume that almost half of all spending by senatorial candidates and less than one third of all spending by House candidates was designated for TV advertising. This distribution, however, does not explain the explosion of congressional campaign costs between 1972 and 1996. Presidential primaries in 1988 offer analogous evidence. "The intense competition in both parties resulted in a combined cost of about $ 212 million in presidential spending, twice that of 1984." However, "only 6 percent of presidential pre-nomination spending was devoted to television."[68] In light of the evidence presented, it seems fair to assume that media spending has not been the major cause of cost explosion in the U.S. in 1980 and 1988.

In addition, the British and Canadian experiences, which we presented already, offer an important insight that is frequently ignored in U.S. literature on the topic. In economic language, the price elasticity of campaign broadcasting is zero, because commercial providers of services (especially airtime on TV) successfully push for windfall

---

65 Heard 1960, p. 22; Alexander/ Bauer 1991, p. 36.
66 Quotes by Alexander 1971, p. 93 and Crotty 1977, pp. 107.
67 Heard 1960, pp. 390-393; Alexander/ Haggerty 1987, pp. 331, 345, 369; Alexander/ Corrado 1995, pp. 20, 235, 237; Alexander 1999, pp. 19, 23.
68 Alexander/ Bauer 1991, pp. 100/101; quotes on pp. 98, 11 and 26 respectively.

profits and politicians cannot postpone their campaign until lower rates are offered. However, parties are not will-less victims, which fall prey to social and economic developments and have to adapt to a general trend of increasing costs. They have (at least some) room for manoeuvre and can define their own strategies. Whereas some authors only use the term "higher campaign technologies" without going into details,[69] Snyder et al. elaborated that each U.S. campaign (committee) tries to substitute expensive advertising with more cost-effective methods. In a comparison of different data sets for House races, collected from the years 1970/72 and 1990/92, and advertising markets with the highest and the lowest prices, they conclude that "the increase in campaign spending ... has coincided with a significant increase in the cost of television advertising." However, "TV advertising expenditure accounts for less than one-third of the total growth in campaign spending in U.S. House elections."[70]

The inflationary effect of broadcast prices had only a moderate impact on total spending. Apparently the relationship between the cost of advertising and total campaign spending is unproven. Campaigns drastically cut their broadcast advertising expenditure and use direct mail advertising as a substitute for broadcasting. There are also other substitutes, including door-to-door canvassing, signs and pamphlets. "The presence of close substitutes weakens the inflationary pressure of TV advertising prices."[71] The increase of spending totals must be caused by other costs and not, as is stated usually, by broadcasting. The prices for direct mail and newspaper advertising grew more quickly than those for TV advertising.[72]

A more general conclusion to be drawn from these findings is that parties, politicians, candidates and campaigns are not just subjects to a modernising trend or force. In reality, some change their mix of campaign strategies, others work harder to improve their fundraising and increase their war chest.[73] The result of our reflection is that paid advertising in electronic media is not a general cause of exploding political costs. In the U.K. political spending has multiplied although paid TV advertising is not available. Canadian parties have framed political finance regulation to cover other costs. U.S. data, which are available, do not indicate the expected impact. Quite to the contrary, U.S. scholars have shown that campaigns react to overpriced media and structure their media mix accordingly. As a consequence, two other causes have to be addressed, campaign technology (especially in Anglo-Saxon democracies) and staff salaries (especially for Germany and Austria).

---

69 E.g. Adamany 1972, p. 63; Sorauf 1988, p. 342.
70 Ansolabehere/ Gerber/ Snyder 2001, p. 11 respectively 12.
71 Ansolabehere/ Gerber/ Snyder 2001, pp. 3, 14, 17-19; quote on p. 3.
72 Cf. Jacobson 1997 vs. Ansolabehere/ Gerber/ Snyder 2001, p. 24.
73 Paltiel (1970, p. 91) has indicated a similar resource-based practice of Canadian parties. This should remind us that in general income determines spending. See below in this chapter, section C (push or pull?).

2. New technology

Among political scientists, it is generally accepted that scientific and technological advances, "particularly in the areas of travel, polling, computers"[74] have "been associated with an explosion in the costs of political campaigns."[75] Modern campaign technology is helping parties, as well as candidates, to plan their efforts, fine-tune their messages and deploy their resources more efficiently to the marginal constituencies or swing states. The U.S. is the homeland of modern campaign technology, which is taking less and less time to export this technology. The campaigns of Tony Blair in Britain (1997) and Gerhard Schröder in Germany (1998) copied organisation and technology from Bill Clinton's campaigns in 1992 and 1996. Jacques Chirac in France and Junichiro Koizumi in Japan are also obvious examples of this global trend. High tech gimmicks are more expensive than traditional electioneering, and each innovation has meant yet another spin of spiralling costs. Thus recent campaigns may well have been the most expensive ordeal of elective politics in the history of any modern democracy.[76]

Until the 1950s, election campaigns relied on local activity and voluntary action. Party supporters rallied to mass meetings, party activists canvassed potential voters in their quarters and party workers dropped leaflets into the mailbox of people's homes. All of this was labour intensive, but less cost intensive than modern campaigning. Parties increasingly substitute those techniques, and "good campaign organization at the grassroots level and the personal contact ... that have marked" the old-style campaigns by TV spot advertisements.[77]

If modern technology and professional advertising substitute unpaid services rendered by voluntary party workers, the "principle of performance in exchange for money"[78] determines a high level of political spending.[79] Nowadays "political campaigning ... has become a highly professionalised undertaking, involving the employment of pollsters, media specialists, fund-raising consultants, and a host of other campaign experts whose services are expensive and ... essential."[80] Theodore White, observer of many campaigns, mentions that money "buys expertise, computers, organization, travel, visuals for the evening news".[81]

---

74 Alexander 1971, pp. 4/5.
75 Katz 1996, p. 129.
76 See above in chapter IV, section D (interaction of causal factors).
77 Crotty 1977, pp. 107 (quote), 109. Inflexible politicians caused extra charges by broadcasters.
78 Mayntz 1988, p. 41.
79 This process has been called "commercialisation" by Landfried 1990, p. 14; Landfried 1994b, p. 133.
80 Alexander/ Haggerty 1987, p. 82; see also Alexander/ Corrado 1995, p. 4 and Alexander 1999, p.12.
81 White 1982, p. 426.

Table 5-3: Campaign spending per elector CPI adjusted (U.S., U.K. and Canada)

Year	Total spending million	No. of electors million	CPI 1980= 100	Spending p. elector CPI adj.	Rates of increase (difference in per cent of total)			
					Total	electors	CPI	Spending
(1)	(2)	(3)	(4)	(5)	(6)	(7)	(8)	(9)
U.K.			*1970-1997*		*5230%*	*11%*	*740%*	*470%*
1955	0.25	34.85	16.6	0.0434				
1959	0.80	35.40	18.6	0.1215	220.0	..1.6	12.0	**180.0**
1964	2.10	35.89	21.3	0.2746	162.5	..1.4	14.5	**126.0**
1966	1.50	35.96	23.0	0.1813	- 28.6	..0.2	8.0	- 34.0
1970	0.90	39.34	27.7	0.0827	- 40.0	..9.4	20.4	- 54.4
1974	2.00	39.91	41.0	0.1222	122.2	..4.4	48.0	47.8
1979	2.30	41.10	84.8	0.0660	15.0	..3.0	106.8	- 46.0
1983	8.00	42.19	126.6	0.1498	227.8	..2.7	49.3	**127.0**
1987	14.00	43.18	149.6	0.2167	75.0	..2.3	18.3	44.7
1992	27.00	43.24	202.8	0.3079	92.9	..0.1	35.6	46.1
1997	48.00	43.78	232.7	0.4712	77.8	..1.2	14.7	53.0
Canada			*1972-2000*		*900%*	*65%*	*340%*	*39%*
1972	4.0	12.909	50	0.62				
1974	3.0	13.621	60	0.37	- 25.0	5.5	20.0	- 40.3
1979	9.0	15,235	91	0.65	200.0	11.8	51.7	**85.7**
1980	10.0	15.890	100	0.63	11.1	4.3	9.9	- 3.1
1984	30.0	16.701	138	1.30	200.0	5.1	38.0	**106.3**
1988	29.0	17.639	162	1.01	- 3.3	5.6	17.4	- 22.3
1993	45.0	19.907	194	1.17	55.2	12.9	19.8	15.8
1997	43.0	19.663	208	1.05	- 4.4	- 1.2	7.2	- 10.3
2000	40.0	21.243	220	0.86	- 6.3	8.0	5.8	- 18.1
U.S.			*1972-2000*		*649%*	*57%*	*312%*	*16%*
1972	215.3	136.2	50.7	3.12				
1976	275.5	146.2	59.0	2.73	28.0	7.3	36.1	- 12.5
1980	514.0	157.0	100.0	3.27	86.6	7.4	44.4	**19.8**
1984	699.1	165.8	126.1	3.34	36.0	5.6	26.1	2.1
1988	957.7	173.6	143.6	3.84	37.0	4.7	13.9	**15.0**
1992	1,228.3	189.5	170.3	3.81	28.3	9.2	18.6	- 0.8
1996	1,465.3	196.5	190.4	3.92	19.3	3.7	11.8	2.9
2000	1,613.0	214.0	209.0	3.61	10.1	8.9	9.8	- 7.9

Data sources: electors = www.idea.int/vt/country_view.cfm; CPI = Mitchell 2003a, pp. 79/80, 866-868, 921, 926; total spending = Alexander 1999, pp. 19, 23; Paltiel 1974, pp. 344-347; Paltiel 1975, pp. 192-197; Chief Electoral Officer 1980, 1981, 1985, 1989, 1993; Elections Canada on-line, election financing, Table 4, 19.10.2000; ibid., statement of revenues and expenses, 2001 and 2002; Pinto-Duschinsky 1981, pp. 138, 143, 163, 164, 167, 190/191; Pinto-Duschinsky 1985, pp. 330, 333, 336, 337; Pinto-Duschinsky 1994, pp. 14, 17, 18, 20; Butler/ Butler 1994, pp. 133, 241; Neill report 1998, pp. 36-38; Webb 2000, p. 232; Fisher 1996b, pp. 164/165; Fisher 1999, p. 523. Figures given in constant prices in Houghton report 1976, p. 92, are basically in line with these data.

Whereas total campaign spending has increased continuously in the U.S., this is not true for Canada and the U.K., where total outlay declined twice (U.K.), respectively three times (Canada). If we look at *CPI deflated per capita figures,* all three campaign-centred countries (which are studied in depth here) have experienced occasional declines (indicated by *italics* in Table 5-3). Quite like the similar experience of Japan (Table 5-2) this should warn us against assuming a continuous trend based on the implementation of new technology, which follows the pattern derived from U.S. trends (in Table 5-1 above).

A decline of spending per elector at constant price levels has occurred three times in the U.S. (1976, 1992, 2000) and in the U.K. (1966, 1970, 1979), five times in Canada (1974, 1980, 1988, 1997, 2000). This leaves specific years with considerable increases of campaign spending per elector at constant prices, which have to be discussed in detail: 1959, 1964 and 1983 in the U.K., 1979 and 1984 in Canada, 1980 and 1988 in the U.S. (column 9 in Table 5-3).

While the British Labour "party disliked the PR approach and refused to employ PR professionals to handle its publicity,"[82] the Conservatives in 1959 incurred an unprecedented increase of central campaign spending, which "relied heavily upon merchandising techniques."[83] They enlisted public relations men, who inserted the commercial concept of brand image into political warfare and switched the emphasis of the campaign effort from party pamphlets to pre-writ newspaper advertising, mostly in national Sunday papers, and nationwide posters, which were removed when the election was finally called. The use of professional PR by the Conservatives was the big innovation in campaign technology in 1959.[84]

The 1964 campaign in the U.K. saw no technical innovation. As in 1959, central office campaign spending was mainly driven by newspaper advertising, posters, production of broadcasting spots and polling (in this order). Increased per capita spending can be ascribed to three major factors. First, more newspapers (national and regional) were added to the advertising media. Second, the Conservatives kept up their high level of expenses because they were fighting an uphill battle. Third, the Labour party belatedly turned to commercial advertising and professional public relations for the first time.[85] Ever since 1964, parties have spent most of their central campaign budgets on newspaper advertising and posters, and much less on polling. Thus, it is not new technology, but the massive and systematic application of time-tested technology, which caused U.K. central offices to deploy more funds.

Once again, during the 1983 campaign there is no indication of any new technology, which may have had a major impact on total spending in the U.K. The main novelty

---

82 Butler/ Rose 1960/ 1999, pp. 27/28 – and once more produced a glossy pamphlet.
83 Rose 1965/ 1999, p. 373; cf. ibid., pp. 372, 374.
84 Butler/ Rose 1960/ 1999, pp. 17-21; Pinto-Duschinski 1981, p. 274, although he adds doubts on p. 275.
85 Data for 1964 (Rose 1965/ 1999, pp. 372, 374) and 1983 (Pinto-Duschinsky 1985, pp. 331, 335) do not indicate much change.

seemed to be that virtually all Conservative advertising was shifted away from pre-writ spending and "concentrated into the weeks before the poll." About half of the campaign budget was spent on press advertisements, a quarter on putting up posters, less than 10% on the production of broadcasts, less than 3% on polling and about 1.5% on the leader's tours. The Labour Party's headquarters spent considerably less (of a smaller total) on newspapers and posters and relatively more on polling and the leader's tour and spent about the same percentage on the production of broadcasts.[86] From this, a cause for the steep increase of per voter spending at constant prices does not emerge.

The cause, which scholars are looking for, is not additional costs but possibly increased revenue from donations, respectively trade union affiliation fees.[87] For the 1959 campaign Butler and Rose had already stated that the "Conservatives could not have attempted their advertising campaign without being able to raise large sums of money." Butler and King mention a considerable increase in union contributions to the Labour election fund in 1964.[88]

In Canada estimated campaign spending [89] (annual total minus estimated routine) by federal party headquarters increased from CAD 3-4 million (1972/74) to CAD 9-10 million (1979/ 80). The 1980s witnessed the expected cost explosion to CAD 30 million (1984), CAD 29 million (1988) and CAD 45 million (1993). The latter year, a year of political disaster for the P.C., saw a turn in the tide of campaign spending, followed by outlays of CAD 43 million (1997) and CAD 40 million (2000). It is interesting to note that (in CPI deflated funds) the high surge of campaign spending was reached in 1984 and 1993, the two contests, which both brought about a change of government.[90] Without the usual impact of inflation, 1984 marks the all-time high for election years, and 1993 turned the tide not only for the P.C. electorally but also for the party system financially.

The massive use of TV advertising, computers, fax machines, direct mail, surveys and media agencies in Canada began in 1972.[91] Nevertheless data for the exceptional years (1979, 1984) support the hypothesis that such tested campaign technology, not any innovative gimmick, was the major cause of rising expenses. The bulk of additional funds, in both years, were spent by the P.C. headquarters, which doubled its spending

---

86   Pinto-Duschinsky 1985, pp. 331, 335 (quote on p. 331). - Butler/ Kavangh 1984/ 1999, p. 271, indicate that the Conservative "campaign was the most media oriented yet seen in Britain."
87   As indicated by Pinto-Duschinsky 1985, pp. 330, 333, despite reservations due to inflation.
88   Butler/ Rose 1960/ 1999, p. 20; Butler/ King 1964/ 1999, p. 63.
89   It is not helpful to use the official data for campaign spending because the P.C. and the N.D.P. have used "creative accounting" in order to make their reported spending fit partisan aims: Stay within the legal limit by incurring pre-writ spending or maximise the public subsidy ("reimbursement") by reporting additional spending. For details see Paltiel 1989, p. 68 and Stanbury 1991, pp. 386-391.
90   This refers to the heyday of P.C. fundraising by direct mail. See below in this chapter, section C (push or pull?) and in chapter VI, sub-section B2 (small donations).
91   Paltiel 1974, pp. 343-345, 348.

total in 1979 as well as in 1984. The party surpassed others in radio and TV advertising as well as in printing and stationary. The latter category includes direct mail, polling and other professional services.[92]

For the U.S., a look at individual growth rates per election cycle (Table 5-1 above) reveals that the expansion of political spending was not a gradual process that proceeded at roughly an equal pace. In current dollars per capita spending more than doubled between 1976 and 1980, and grew by more than 40% in three other presidential cycles (1964-68, 1980-84 and 1984-88). It increased by 30% during the 1992-96 cycle. Among CPI adjusted data for presidential years (Table 5-2 above) 1980, 1984, 1988, and 1996 present the highest levels of per capita spending for all political purposes. Much of this may be due to improved data quality and non-federal activity. Data for federal candidates (column 9 in Table 5-3 below) indicates that only 1980 and 1988 (controlled for inflation and growth of electorate) demonstrate high rates of increase in political spending. Both election cycles should be checked for specific developments, favourably changes in the application of campaign technology. We have already refuted conventional wisdom, which generally ascribes extraordinary increases of spending to media spending, particularly to the cost of TV air time.[93] This leaves new technology as a potential cause for a "cost explosion." Important innovations in campaign technology have been (direct) mailing, (air) travel, (survey research) polling and (media) consultants.[94] Did the application of such technology cause the increases in 1980 and 1988? As U.S. scholars are fascinated by TV advertising, other dimensions of rising costs have never held centre stage in their research. Thus, it is a bit difficult to extract relevant information from the available literature.

However, it is obvious that the major innovations of the 1980 campaign resulted from new categories of exempt spending, which were established by the FEC, among them independent expenditures (on behalf of candidates) and legal and accounting fees (for FECA compliance). Such categories opened up new alleys of political spending. Total exempt spending for federal races equalled $ 50 million. Less than $ 17 million of it was spent for presidential candidates. The other innovation concerns the sources of political revenue. The number of corporate PACs almost trebled between 1976 and 1980, adjusted expenditures by PACs of all categories increased by $ 78 million (+148% of the 1976 total). Likewise their contributions to congressional candidates rose by 145%.[95]

A couple of conclusions can be drawn from the evidence, which has been presented so far:

(1) For the campaign centred Anglo-Saxon democracies, the massive application of new campaign technology (professional public relations, media advertising, and polling) has caused major increases of campaign spending.

---

92 Stanbury 1991, pp. 84, 86, 445, 453, 461.
93 See above in this chapter, sub-section B 1 (paid TV time).
94 Crotty 1977, p. 105.
95 Alexander 1983, pp. 122, 126/127.

(2) Such increases have been a discontinuous process. Its steep advances and occasional declines depend more on the competitive situation in individual countries and election years than on the availability of new technology (including new media).

(3) Among the factors affecting the factual use of campaign technology options are legal restrictions (as perceived by the competing parties), party leaders' willingness to apply modern technology and the availability of funds to pay for it.

(4) The U.S. case indicates that spending on political competition is impacted by a variety of individual factors. Among them the competitive situation in a specific year (within parties as well as between parties) and a shift from presidential to congressional campaigns, may be as equally important as technological innovations and the price of airing TV commercials.[96]

(5) The British case demonstrates that the impact of legal restraints on campaign expenses depends on precise phrasing (i.e. no paid political advertising on TV) as well as on accepted interpretation of the law (such as no limits on national campaigning prior to 2001). Labour leaders in 1959 and 1983 demonstrated that a party may refuse to make full use of modern technology (for a non-financial reason).

(6) The Canadian case proves that the rising costs of campaigning exhibit a technological as well as a funding aspect. If parties are unable to raise the money, which is needed for an expensive campaign, they will be unable to enter into a spending spree, which would be technologically feasible.

All of this indicates that there may be more to increased political spending than just technological options, the excessive use of which is deemed "necessary" by politicians who run campaigns or by scholars who study them. Besides political income, which provides basic funding,[97] the role of professional services comes into view.

3. *Professional politics*

"Good media performance ... relies on the skills of expensive media professionals, such as public relations experts, market researchers, advertising executives, media trainers, pollsters, stylists, and party press secretaries."[98] However, the idea of professional politics carries different connotations. First, professional people are taking over responsibilities in research, planning and management, which hitherto had been the duty of party "apparatchiks." This process, which involves growing numbers of experts serving the organisation, is called "professionalisation" by Panebianco. Second, salaried activity replaces voluntary work, as political organisations rely more and more on full-time (or part-time) employees, i.e. managers carry out the daily activities. This process emphasises the maintenance of the party as an organisation, which is

---

96 For the increased importance of PACs in 1976-84 see below in chapter VII, sub-section B1c (PACs).
97 This will be discussed below in this chapter, section C (push or pull?).
98 Wilson 2004, p. 3.

called "bureaucratisation". This trend towards the "electoral-professional party" is due to a general decline in voluntary involvement in advanced societies.[99] The former trend towards outsourcing of campaigns to consultants and advisers is a result of the successful experience of political innovators. In addition to the "rise of political consultants,"[100] the staff aspect of party building will be discussed now.

Political spending in Anglo-Saxon democracies is expected to be campaign centred, which means that permanent organisations are small. In principle, this is true for the U.S. (a medium level spender among the democracies) as well as for Australia, Britain and Canada, which belong to the group of „moderate spenders."[101] All of them have been rather reluctant in terms of party building and in activities involving organisational maintenance. In Canada, full-time party staff in the field is rare. In Britain constituency agents are less frequent than they were during the 1950s and 1960s.[102] Most Canadian parties, similar to their U.S. counterparts have never developed a full-time field organisation, although some field agents have been supplied by the federal and sub-national headquarters of the major parties.

Nevertheless, during the 1970s and 1980s developments in European style "party-building" could be observed in the U.S. and Canada.[103] Even for many of the low-spending countries in the Anglo-Saxon orbit (obviously except the U.S.), it is an important step towards reality to assume that "a large share of political spending goes to pay for the national and local offices and staffs of political parties."[104] We have already presented the major types of cost necessary for a full-fledged permanent party organisation ("on the ground") in detail.[105] The total amount of such expenses can be considered as the routine part of total costs. As time series data is patchy at best we will have to limit our comparison to central offices in the U.K. and federal parties in Canada. In both countries, the major parties have maintained national party headquarters for many decades and financial data for these cost centres is publicly available.

The downturn in financial fortunes for Canadian parties not only affected their campaign efforts, it also influenced opportunities to continue party-building (organisational development). Depleted party coffers led to shrinking routine spending, too, despite the fact that two more federal party headquarters had to be funded. However, the weight of salaries (as a percentage of total spending) between 1976 and 2000 remained remarkably constant, around 20% in election years (19.8 to 23.3), and around 35% in non-election years (33.4 to 36.9).

---

99   Panebianco 1988, p. 231.
100 Sabato 1985.
101 See above in chapter III, Table 3-5.
102 Pinto-Duschinsky 1981, pp. 154, 177; Webb 1995, p. 311.
103 Harmel/ Janda 1982, pp. 114-116; Nassmacher, H. 1992, pp. 122-128 and (more recently) Smith 2005, pp. 126, 130; also in Ireland see Benoit/ Marsh 2003, p. 565; Ward 2003, p. 596.
104 Pinto-Duschinsky 2002, p. 82.
105 see above in chapter II, section B (types of cost), especially paid labour and office maintenance.

An effort to elaborate on a trend for the U.K. can be based on the analysis of spending on staff. If party-building efforts have taken place, this would mean that spending on the party apparatus (especially on paid labour hired by central offices) has increased in relative importance. Evidence, however, is inconclusive. Between 1967 and 1997 Conservative spending on salaries, wages and benefits increased from 47 to 68% of Central Office expenses from 1967 to 1975, to 69-71% in 1992-96. Labour's outlay for staff was steadier as the party's Head Office spent 51-62% in 1967-76 and 48-59% in 1992-97. The trend for Liberal headquarters was closer to the Conservatives: 44-56% of the annual budget spent on staff in 1967-73, compared to 50-67% in 1992-97.[106]

Given the rising budget for Labour's central office and a declining budget for the Conservative Central Office, different trends in salary shares indicate that since the late 1960s the overall role of paid labour for central offices has remained unchanged with both major parties. As the share of labour costs in British party headquarters is more than half of the annual budget (even in most election years), total spending is driven more by growing gross income of party workers (i.e. the national income level) than by market prices for goods and services (i.e. inflation).[107] Nevertheless it should be noted that even in the U.K., which in 2001 finally capped national campaign spending, annual routine is 80% of central expense totals.[108]

The local organisations of Labour and the Conservatives deteriorated massively during the 1970s and the 1990s. In 1966 no less than 204 of the 242 constituencies held by the Conservatives and 181 of the 363 Labour held constituencies had a salaried party agent.[109] During the mid-1970s among the 618 "mainland" constituencies, more than half were served by a full-time Conservative agent, one sixth by a full-time Labour agent and 3% by a full-time Liberal agent, which adds up to a total of 350 to 440 party agents.[110] "While parties have consolidated their establishments of personnel at the central level ..., the local picture is one of substantial decline. ... Since the early 1960s ... the average number of local party employees has plummeted. ... The number of local party staff fell from 0.83 per elector to just 0.30 per elector."[111] However, British party headquarters may have increased their staff numbers at equal pace with the application of more expensive campaign technology (excluding TV airtime). If so, staff expenses as a percentage of total spending would not increase, even in election

---

106 Houghton report 1976, pp. 100, 106, 113; Neill report 1998, pp. 36, 37.
107 This, once again, may indicate that parties, just like consumers, are more likely to be subject to income pull than to cost push. For details see below in this chapter, section C (push or pull?).
108 Fisher 2002, p. 396.
109 Pinto-Duschinsky/ Schleth 1970, p. 34.
110 The conservative estimate (a total of about 350 constituency agents) is based on the response rate given – Houghton report 1976, p. 196.
111 Webb 1995, p. 310; Webb 2000, p. 243; Becker 1999, p. 65; details given by Pinto-Duschinsky (1981, pp. 154, 178) and Neill report (1998, pp. 41/42) support this impression of decline over time.

years. This has actually happened. Available data does not allow to separate both types of costs. As data are more detailed for Canada and Germany we will have to rely on these countries.

Building a political field organisation based on paid labour is a long-time practice of parties in continental Europe. A developed party headquarters located in the national capital and full-time staff in the field are well known features of European mass parties. Starting in the 19th century, labour parties pioneered this type of organisation and their conservative competitors in Britain, Austria, Italy, Germany, Sweden and finally France caught up with it during the second half of the 20th century. The continent of (Western) Europe, which encompasses a greater number of established democracies than the Anglo-Saxon orbit, has a different history of party politics and party activity.

Unfortunately among the organisation centred group of established democracies, just two countries provide long-term data of more or less good quality and diverse coverage, which are the prerequisites for time series analysis of political spending: Germany and Austria. Both democracies are particularly apt examples of organisation centred party activity. They combine an extended field organisation, which employs a lot of paid party workers, with many separate elections stretched out over the period of the national election cycle. Cordes observed that in both countries, the current expenditure of party headquarters devours much of the annual budgets of all the major parties, especially the Social Democrats and the Conservatives. Smith found that the *SPD* spends 18% of its annual budget on staff, the *CDU*'s share is 12%, the *FDP*'s 23% and the Greens' 13%. In Austria the *SPÖ* had the largest state offices, the *FPÖ* the smallest, both with tendencies of decrease.[112]

Thus, it seems fair to ask whether in two countries with such well-developed party organisations spending levels increase faster than in those democracies, which have been more reluctant in the process of party building and activities of organisational maintenance (e.g. Britain and Canada). Germany offers the most comprehensive set of comparable data for almost 20, some times for 35 years. Austrian data are less comprehensive because they are related to federal party headquarters and party academies only. As the latter are so close to their parties, their funds should be consolidated with party headquarters' funds in order to account for the complete financial outlay.

Restrictions, which result from the data base (especially the need for careful interpretation of estimates) notwithstanding, the available data offer some insights into the pattern of party spending. During a period of 15 years (1980-94), routine spending by central offices in Austria increased by a factor of 1.7, spending on staff by a factor of 3.5. Thus it can be identified as the real dynamic force. As a consequence, the five year average of expenses on staff rose from 31 to 40% of annual routine spending.[113]

---

112 Cordes 2001, pp. 217-233; Smith 2005, pp. 128, 135..
113 The ranges may be even more telling: 29-34% (1980-84), 34-42% (1985-89), 39-41% (1990-94). This neglects two outliers, one in the first group (1982), the other beyond the third one (1995).

The conclusion is obvious. As the weight of spending on staff increased, Austrian federal parties devoted more of their financial resources to salaries than to campaigns. If a cost push effect was at work, then its most likely cause has been the party apparatus and not improved campaign technology.[114]

This appears to be perfectly in line with an important result of Webb's comparison of the number of employees of party head offices in Western Europe in the late 1980s. Austria occupied not only the leading position among the smaller democracies, but also within the complete sample when the number of paid party workers at head offices was related to the number of electors. Among the large democracies, Germany (with an average of 140.5 employees at a national head office) was ahead of Italy (121.0) and outperformed the U.K. (65.3). Among the smaller democracies Austria (59.3) was ahead of Sweden (40.6), and better equipped than a group of four (Finland, the Netherlands, Ireland and Norway), which ranged between 23.4 and 16.0. Denmark had the smallest party staff (only 11.8 employees at a national head office).[115]

Fortunately, the data available for Germany (Table 5-4) allow us to carry this analysis a bit further in two directions. First, we can examine trends for overall party spending (national, regional plus local). We can also look at the relationship between the central offices on the one hand and state branches and local chapters on the other. About one third of the annual expenses of the complete party organisation (plus expenses for state and municipal campaigns) was spent on salaried party workers. The actual share of staff expenses for all parties (on all levels) rose slightly from 32% during the mid-1980s to 36% in the late 1990s. As the data can be broken down by levels of party organisation (federal offices vs. state and local parties), three other considerations are possible: trends for campaign and staff expenses at the federal level, a trend for staff expenses below the federal level and the overall distribution of funds between central offices and regional-local field operations.

Ignoring outliers, party federal headquarters' spending on staff ranged between 31 and 36% of its total expenses. The average was 32%, with marginal differences between the early and the late election cycle. The combined share of total funds spent by state and local parties ranged between 59 and 72%. The average share was almost exactly two thirds of total party spending.[116] The lower levels' spending on staff was slightly less than their share of the total budget. Most salaried party workers are employed by regional party branches, which means that they work for the field organisation rather than for central office. The sub-national share of expenses on staff ranges between 63 and 68% of all party staff expenses, and the average is one percentage point less than

---

114 However, a statistical relationship between rising staff expenses and increased public subsidies was indicated by Cordes 2001, p. 132.
115 Webb 1995, p. 310. Webb's average number of employees at party head offices per 100,000 electors for Austria is 1.14 compared to/ followed by Ireland (0.81) and Sweden (0.64). The Netherlands (0.20) and the U.K. (0.15) rank lowest in a sample of 10 countries.
116 Cf. Nassmacher 1989d, p. 277; Nassmacher 1997b, p. 174 and Nassmacher 2001d, p. 176.

for total spending. This is probably due to the fact that smaller parties rarely employ full-time salaried workers locally and even the two major parties have some local personnel on the payroll of either their municipal council or their local MP.[117]

Table 5-4: Details of party spending in Germany, 1984-2001

Year	Total spending	Annual routine	Staff expenses	Staff	Central campaign	Central staff	S&L* staff	S&L* expenses
	all parties, in million DEM			percent of total routine	million DEM	% of central routine	% of total staff	% of total expenses
1984	506.92	437	135.72	31.1	40	36.7	67.6	70.5
1985	456.11	456	144.58	31.7	-	38.2	66.5	72.3
1986	567.40	460	151.56	32.9	74	39.3	66.1	63.9
1987	553.08	460	154.46	33.6	51	38.0	66.8	66.3
1988	468.77	469	161.53	34.4	-	37.6	67.6	70.4
1989	638.63	481	166.97	34.7	75	39.6	65.6	67.2
1990	872.53	563	181.00	32.1	n.a.			
1991	598.23	598	192.55	32.2	-			
1992	585.32	585	215.50	36.8	-	39.3	65.0	67.1
1993	610.23	610	213.33	35.0	-	35.9	65.8	68.5
1994	997.52	628	220.70	35.1	170	37.8	65.6	62.8
1995	639.40	639	218.46	34.2	-	37.5	66.0	69.0
1996	672.30	672	220.35	32.8	-	40.3	65.4	65.6
1997	608.05	608	221.57	36.4	-	35.6	65.9	59.3
1998	925.67	626	238.15	38.0	160	40.3	62.8	68.9
1999	855.65	636	231.91	36.5	55	37.8	65.7	68.0
2000	646.04	646	219.78	34.0	-	34.7	67.3	
2001	758.29	758	221.22	29.2	-			

Sources: Computed by the author from data reported in *Deutscher Bundestag*, parliamentary papers, no. 10/4104 (neu) to 14/5050.

Notes: * S&L = state (regional) branches plus local chapters. – In percent of all staff respectively percent of total spending.

Data for 1990/91 are very conservative and incomplete approximations because the East German Post-Communist party (PDS) has been largely ignored. For 1990 this party reported total spending of DEM 1.1 billion; most of this was obviously due to „downsizing" efforts. For 1991 official reports (Drucksache 12/4475, p. 57 and Drucksache 14/7979, p. 73) give different spending totals.

---

117 Many county council groups (*Fraktionen*) (see Kempf 1989, pp. 112-121) and all European, federal or state MPs (see Boyken 1998, p. 28) receive extra public funds to employ research or constituency assistants who (partly, although illegally) double up as "agents" for their local parties.

Some conclusions emerge from the German data (Table 5-4). Despite adapting quickly to modern campaign technology, central office spending on campaigns is not a cause of increased party spending. Each of the three levels of a party organisation (federal, state and local) spend about one third of its total outlay on staff, with the higher tier spending a bit more than one-third of their expenditures on staff and the lower stratum spending a much smaller percentage. A centralisation of party funds at the national level (which is most likely a consequence of a potential gap between rising campaign expenses and declining fundraising potential) has not occurred in Germany. State branches and local chapters have held onto their own share of all party funds despite greater need at the centre.

In Germany, probably also in Austria, the paid labour of party staff is a drain on party coffers. As CPI adjusted total spending has not increased much in both countries, parties must have found ways to pay more for possibly fewer staff. Although new campaign technology is important in all the cases studied in-depth (including Japan), a single cause-effect relationship could not be established for any of them. Paid TV advertising may have become more expensive but parties have found ways to cope with bigger fees by mixing their media.

The evidence presented in this section indicates that there is a lot of alarmist noise in research, which observes something like a "cost explosion" in party (and/or campaign) spending. True, the total amounts of money spent for political purposes (parties, candidates or issues) have gone up considerably. This chapter identified two different causes for the possible rise, which depend on the specific approach to party competition in different democracies. Nevertheless the extent of actual increases in all countries studied in depth is less than expected at first glance. As political income seems to be the most efficient control towards more party spending,[118] we can apply a rather traditional finding of economic theory to this subject. Price fixing is a result of supply and demand. Consequently, inflation theory has identified demand pull as well as cost push to be the causes of a rising price level.

C) Cost push or demand pull?

This brings up the supply-side theory for consideration. Modern economies must not only deal with inflation, but they also experience economic growth. It may well be that political expenses rise as more money becomes available via an improved standard of living. In general, "average incomes have increased faster than the cost of living. Since party organisation and election campaigning are labour-intensive activities" the relevant index to measure any long-term trend "is per capita income rather than the cost-of-living index."[119]

---

118 For details see Cordes/ Nassmacher 2001, pp. 267-286.
119 Both quotes (in reverse order) from: Pinto-Duschinsky 2002, p. 84.

Louise Overacker, another senior U.S. scholar in the 1930s, tried this approach for the early 20th century. Taking economic growth as measured by (gross) national income into account, she found that for the period 1916-28 the level of U.S. campaign costs had "remained surprisingly constant."[120] This finding suggests that in a growing economy, political activities come at a price, which is not only influenced by purchasing power (as indicated by the cost of living) but also by the *standard of living,* which people can afford due to their rising income.[121] If we attempt to measure income levels by national averages, the gross domestic product (GDP) is a handy indicator. As GDP per capita (at current prices) increases it offers room for higher spending on political competition.

Between 1988-2000, the most recent 12 year period available (Table 5-1), per capita costs of U.S. democracy increased roughly by a factor of 1.3, per capita GDP by a factor of 1.7. This means that actual political spending per capita has increased less than the average income of U.S. citizens (both at current prices). In the late 20th century (1988-2000) parties and candidates, quite unlike their forebears early in the same century (1916-28), were unable to hold onto their share of people's income. At best the amount of money available for political causes (parties, candidates, issues) has shifted from parties (and party candidates) to issues, from the federal level to the state level. The worst case is not unlikely, either. Today American citizens are less willing to give to politics than their grandparents were 60 years ago (1936/40) and their great-grandparents 90 years ago (1912/16). Due to the joint efforts of Louise Overacker, Alexander Heard and Herbert Alexander data on the costs of U.S. presidential campaigns are available for most of the 20th century. This time series starts in 1912 and goes through 2000 (Graph 5-1). The long-term data prove that Pollock and Overacker were correct to suggest that three kinds of deflators be applied to current campaign spending data.[122]

The first step is to recall that the *voting age population* has increased by a factor of 7.6 since 1912. Thus, it is fair to account one part of the 209-fold increase in presidential campaign spending to the size of the electorate, which leaves some 28-fold long-term increase to be discussed by one of the next explanations. Two alternative approaches are feasible, which emphasise either declining purchasing power or advancing income levels.

The second step, as suggested by Pollock,[123] is to allow for the *consequences of inflation*. That is, dollars in the year 2000 were buying less "labor, goods and supplies" than 1912 dollars. An almost 18-fold increase of the Consumer Price Index during this period leaves an increase by a factor of 1.6 for presidential campaign costs per elector. We have elaborated the potential for this cost push already.[124]

---

120 Overacker 1932, p. 80.
121 For a similar process: „In reality ... prices drive costs. The more a company can charge for a drug, the more it will spend on developing and marketing it." (*The Economist,* 18 June 2005, p. 12).
122 Pollock 1926, pp. 170/171; Overacker 1932, p. 80.
123 And applied by Hrebenar et al. 1999, p. 141.
124 See above in this chapter, sub-sections B2 (new technology) and B3 (professional politics).

The third step, as proposed by Overacker, is the impact of economic growth (a potential "income pull" for political spending). National income is a more appropriate baseline "against which to measure the growth in campaign spending".[125] Per capita GDP in the U.S. economy has grown almost 85-fold between 1912 and 2000, and more than 74-fold between 1932 and 2000. Overacker's assumption in 1932 still holds in 2004. Presidential campaign spending is not outperforming *the nation's overall economic growth* (Graph 5-1). Quite to the contrary, GDP adjusted presidential campaign spending per citizen has decreased by two thirds.

Graph 5-1:   U.S. Presidential campaign spending, 1912-2000 (1960=100)

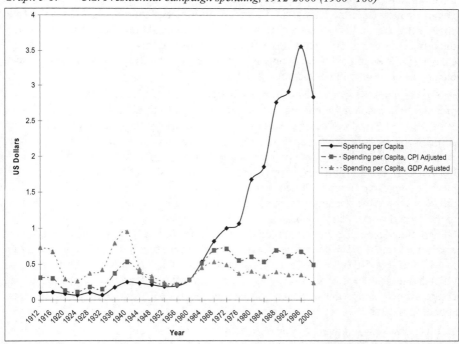

Sources for this graph: **Voting age population:** (1912-44) Estimates from data supplied by U.S. Bureau of the Census; (1948-96) International IDEA 1997, pp. 81, 97;
  campaign spending: Overacker 1932, p. 80; Overacker 1933, p. 770; Overacker 1937, p. 476; Overacker 1941, p. 713; Overacker 1945, p. 906; Heard 1960, pp. 7/8; Alexander 1999, p. 19; Nelson 2002, p. 24;
  consumer price index (CPI): U.S. Bureau of Labor Statistics (www.bls.gov/cpi) (1982-84= 100);
  gross domestic product per capita: (1912-28) Mitchell 2003b, pp. 61, 766; (1932-2002) U.S. Dept. of Commerce, Bureau of Economic Analysis (Table 8.7) (www.bea.gov); (1960-99) www.census.gov/statab/freq (no. 722);
  spending data refer to National Committee spending 1912-36; national level spending 1940-56; presidential spending 1960-96. Spending in 1948 has been estimated by the author.

---

125 Ansolabehere/ Figueiredo/ Snyder 2003, p. 119; see ibid., p. 120.

During the affluent 1980s and 1990s, U.S. citizens on average contributed to the election of a president the same small amount (a minimal part of their average annual income), which their grandparents paid during the worst economic crisis in 1932. As far as the presidency is concerned, no "explosion" of campaign costs took place if 1912 and 1936 or 1928 and 1976 or 1924 and 2000 are compared. Spending on presidential campaigns was exceptionally high 1936/40 and exceptionally low during the 1950s (see Graph 5-1).[126]

Political analysts (in the U.S. and elsewhere) who have observed a "cost explosion" may have fallen prey to their own neglect of the link between political and economic development. The application of cost intensive campaign technology is part of a more general pattern, i.e. the change in communication behaviour as observed during the change from an industrial society to a service economy. This aspect is neglected frequently in studies of political parties, their activities and their use of political resources. New ways of appealing to people may be a consequence of new technology, social change or economic development.[127]

A comparison of income (GDP) adjusted figures for 1912 and 2000 indicates that presidential campaign spending in real terms, receded to almost one third between 1940 and 1996 and between 1912 and 2000 respectively (Graph 5-1).[128] This is no surprise to any political scientist who is aware of the fact that U.S. campaign activity during that period shifted from presidential coattails to individual congressional races. Furthermore in 1912 and 1940 "party building activities" such as registration and get-out-the-vote drives were included in the national committee spending on the presidential race. Due to the impact of campaign finance regulation such efforts were transferred to the "soft money" category before 2000. In the presidential years from 1972 to 2000, GDP deflated spending per citizen on campaigns for federal offices (president, senate and house) remained fairly stable around $3 each, more precisely the range was $2.64 to $3.28 (Table 5-5 below). For the off-years 1974 to 1982, there was an increase of GDP deflated per capita expenses, which indicates that a shift between presidential and congressional campaigns has been quite obvious. This was followed by a more stable spending pattern.[129]

At this point we are unable to decide whether political spending is rising because the funds were needed (cost push) or because competitors were able to raise the money,

---

[126] The attentive reader on the subject will note that – of all years – 1952/1960 happened to serve as the starting point for most of Herbert E. Alexander's comparisons.

[127] Pollock 1926, p. 169.

[128] Neglecting differences in detail this finding is quite in line with the general statement by Snyder et al. (Ansolabehere/ Gerber/ Snyder, in: Lubenow 2001, ch. 2: rate of growth in campaign spending) that „contrary to the claims of reformers and the media, campaign spending has not exploded in recent years ... campaign spending ... has held relatively steady since 1912." (as cited by Pinto-Duschinsky 2002, p. 84).

[129] Here the other outlets for overflowing political war chests (ideological PACs, independent expenditures and soft money) come in. For details see Cordes/ Nassmacher 2001, pp. 280-283.

which they wanted to spend (demand pull).[130] A first attempt to support the income-pull theory of political spending is its application to the cases of extremely high or low spending in U.S. presidential contests.[131] The supporters of Presidents F.D. Roosevelt and R.M. Nixon, were willing to contribute massively to their favourite election outcome and thus made maximum spending in 1936 and 1972 possible. Likewise supporters of Presidents Taft and Truman may have been hesitant to exhaust their funding potential for either candidate. As income-pull theory applies to all of these cases, it can be considered the best explanation presented so far.[132]

If Japanese per capita figures are adjusted for GDP, the amount remains pretty stable, around some JPY 2,000 (1,800 to 2,200) for a period of 15 years. However, during the 1990s the per capita outlay for politics (in GDP equivalents) decreased massively from about JPY 1,900 to JPY 1,400 in national election years, and from JPY 1,800 to JPY 1,200 in non-election years (Table 5-5). In a stagnant economy, Japanese politicians lost financial support and thus were less able to spend, despite newly introduced public subsidies.[133] (Obviously traditional vote-buying is neither less nor more expensive than capital-intensive campaigning.)

When economic growth is taken into account, Canada offers the second example of a considerable decline in campaign spending (beside Japan). However, this decline cannot be ascribed to cultural peculiarities or economic crisis. It was, instead, the political crisis of a party system, which had lost the support of voters and donors. This was followed by the financial downsizing of party activity, despite all opportunities offered by innovation in campaign technology and all demands caused by increased rates for TV advertising. An important conclusion for party funding can be drawn from this case. In Canada the peak of party spending was reached during the late 1980s (in the heyday of P.C. fundraising by direct mail). Despite the usual impact of inflation, 1986 marks the all-time high for non-election years (Table 5-5), and the election of 1993 turned the tide not only for the P.C. electorally, but also for the party system financially. For election years GDP adjusted federal spending per citizen ranged from $0.77 to 2.36, excluding both outliers (1974, 1984) from $1.01 to $1.84. All non-election years (under the political finance regime of 1974) fall into a range of $ 0.54 to $1.20, the most recent years being among the more moderate.

Evidence from Japan and Canada suggests an important result. Campaign spending is income driven rather than cost driven. The use of modern technology and of paid TV advertising has not been the cause for constantly rising expenses, but an option for politicians and parties, which were able to raise more funds from their political clien-

---

130 See above in chapter IV, sub-section C1b (generous public subsidies).
131 For details see above in this chapter, sub-section A 3 b (intensified competition).
132 Ansolabehere/ Figueiredo/ Snyder (2003, pp. 120/121) report even higher outlays for "presidential campaigns in the 1880s and 1890s".
133 Another important factor may be that a series of political finance scandals and the end of the cold war induced *Keidanren* (the federation of Japanese industry) to retreat from its role as a conveyor for corporate donations in 1993. For details see below in chapter VII, sub-section A1b (institutional fundraising).

tele or the citizens at large (via public subsidies).[134] As the pressure of crisis reduced the politicians' potential for fundraising, they had to adapt expenses to their depleted party coffers.

Table 5-5: Political spending per citizen, GDP adjusted (1980=1.000), 1971-2000

Year	USA	GB	CDN	JPN	A	D
1971		0.20	0.22			6.41
1972	**3.28**	0.21	1.01			11.94
1973		0.24	0.26			6.81
1974	**1.05**	0.34	0.77			8.35
1975		0.17	n.a.			9.83
1976	2.78	0.16	0.69	2,036		11.05
1977		0.17	0.74	1,966		7.15
1978	1.47	0.24	0.89	1,903		8.33
1979		0.29	1.48	2,190		19.15
1980	3.27	0.21	1.40	2,252	56.50	10.76
1981		0.20	0.84	1,875	44.72	6.75
1982	1.71	0.21	0.88	1,964	64.05	5.62
1983		0.34	0.98	**2,566**	66.53	**12.80**
1984	3.11	0.18	**2.36**	1,897	51.54	9.60
1985		0.18	1.07	2,155	52.85	8.18
1986	1.66	0.22	1.20	2,389	**88.25**	9.49
1987		0.39	0.99	1,982	49.64	9.02
1988	3.25	0.20	1.74	2,223	**44.64**	7.20
1989		0.22	0.71	2,006	55.23	9.40
1990	1.30	0.26	0.82	1,884	75.53	7.77
1991		0.36	0.79	1,791	49.58	4.83
1992	3.23	0.34	0.77	1,641	57.43	6.11
1993		0.18	1.84	1,604	53.66	6.23
1994	1.71	0.16	0.54	1,377	70.15	9.84
1995		0.17	0.63	1,478	48.51	6.06
1996	3.11	0.25	0.74	1,395		6.28
1997		**0.44**	1.71	1,182		5.58
1998	???		0.61	1,527		8.25
1999			0.58	1,256		7.54
2000	2.64		1.22			**5.52**
Minimum	1.05	0.16	0.22	1,182	44.64	5.52
Maximum	3.28	0.44	2.36	2,566	88.25	12.80

Sources: Computed by the author from the data in Table 5-2 above.
Remark: The most extreme values (Germany 1979, 1991) are outliers created by specifics of the data base (rec notes 136 and to Table 5-4).

---

134 see below in chapter VIII (public subsidies).

During the small time period of 1980 to 1994, GDP adjusted per capita spending (by the federal party headquarters) in Austria ranges from ATS 69 to ATS 157 in election years and from ATS 45 to ATS 101 in non-election years. No trend can be observed, and no specific problems identified. However, the snap election of 1995 produced an exceptionally low amount of expenditure. This, at least, indicates that depleted party coffers were more important than technology based opportunities.

Looking at the German data for 35 years, our effort comes full circle. We can now apply the categories developed for an extremely campaign-oriented country (the U.S.) to an extremely party organisation centred polity, i.e. Germany, which has occasionally been called a "party state" or "party democracy."[135] How have political parameters like rising costs of political campaigns and party apparatus interacted with the economic trend of growing income? In the united Germany (1991-2000), GDP deflated party expenses per German citizen are considerably lower (range DEM 4.83-9.84)[136] than for West Germany (range DEM 5.62-12.80). The 1980s' average of DEM 8.88 contrasts markedly to the 1990s' average of DEM 6.85.

Using Overacker's approach the result resembles our findings for the U.S. In Germany (not least due to an excessive increase of public subsidies in 1979) the 1977-80 election cycle provided more money for political parties than any other during the period under review. Comparing a more recent cycle (1999-2002) to the earliest cycle available (1973-76) indicates that German parties, just like their U.S. counterparts, have not been able to solicit (or snatch from the taxpayer) an equal share of their citizens' rising income. Despite the financial needs caused by campaign technology innovations and expanded party organisations, which now also cover the ("new") eastern states, the 1990s saw an average per capita spending on party competition (in real terms) below the 1970s level. A least-square regression for Germany confirms a trend similar to U.S. experience.[137]

In general GDP deflated per capita expenses have increased exceptionally in the U.K. and Canada. This might easily confirm the hypotheses of rising campaign spending. The British maximum of 1997 was not repeated in 2005, and the Canadian maximum occurred long ago in 1984. In the U.S., Japan, Germany and Austria GDP deflated per

---

135 Leibholz 1965, p. 56.
136 There are two obvious exceptions, which have to be explained to the foreign reader: Per capita party income in 1979 (which substitutes for unavailable spending data) was higher than in 1980 because the full amount of subsidies for the first European election was distributed in 1979 whereas all other subsidies were paid in annual installments. Much of the outlay for the federal election in January 1987 was expanded in 1986 thus increasing respectively decreasing the spending levels for each individual year.
137 Based on per capita amounts of party spending totals at current prices for the years 1968 to 2001 the regression line ($y = 0.31x - 603$) indicates a considerable rise of average spending. At constant prices (based on the CPI) the slope is reduced ($y = 0.025x - 41$), which hints at a minor increase of political expenses. Deflated by annual per capita GDP the trend turns, the regression line ($y = -0.09x + 187$) indicates a moderate decrease (in real terms) of total amounts spent on party politics in Germany (Source: Computed by the author from official data).

capita expenses have developed more moderately. In some countries they have even recently declined.

If we neglect periods of (economic or political recession), the major finding is quite compatible with U.S. experience. In a growing economy, parties and politicians are able to expand their financial expenditures at roughly the same pace as the standard of living of their fellow citizens advances. The overall share of political spending has remained pretty stable when the general increase of income levels is taken into account. The "cost explosion" of political spending turns out to be a fair participation of political activity in the growing wealth of an economically advanced society. The demand-pull interpretation seems to explain the rise of political spending over time much better than any cost-push assumption.[138]

None of the six countries, which are available for an in-depth analysis of long-term trends, provides evidence that contradicts the income pull theory of political spending. In the case of Japan and Canada it is the only possible explanation, in the U.K. and Austria there are hints to support this explanation, and the U.S. and German cases indicate it the most strongly. In the U.S. and Canada, following party finance reforms, fundraising exploded in the 1970s.[139] For Germany Pinto-Duschinsky claimed that an "increased supply of funds has led to an even greater increase in parties' demands."[140] Probably the cause for a steep increase of per voter spending at constant prices in the U.K. in 1983 was not new costs, but increased income from donations, especially trade union affiliation fees.[141] After all this campaign pitted Michael Foot's class-conscious Labour Party against Thatcher's Conservative government, which was determined to fight British style trade unionism lock, stock and barrel. In 1963-64 the competition had been much calmer. During that campaign the U.K. "Conservatives faced considerable difficulty in raising funds for their political advertisements."[142] Both situations support the general hypothesis: Party revenue has the most decisive impact on party spending. In passing it should be noted that even in Israel, Hofnung supports the income pull theory. Money has been readily available in that country whenever it was needed for political competition.[143]

All of this evidence leads to a modified hypothesis, which may explain long term trends. If the average citizen's willingness to contribute to political competition (either voluntarily or by statute law) remains constant, an increased standard of living enables

---

138 If the cause for increased political spending is not cost push but income pull, the German Supreme Court (*Bundesverfassungsgericht* - BVerfGE 85, 264 (291), which limited party income (from public subsidies), has demonstrated more political wisdom than its U.S. counterpart, which in 1976 (Buckley v. Valeo 424 U.S. 1) decided to make unlimited spending for political causes a case of free speech, a civil liberty under the constitution, not to be restricted by law under any circumstance and thus "has encouraged greater spending" (Alexander 1999, p. 12).
139 Nassmacher, H. 2004, pp. 98/99.
140 Pinto-Duschinsky 1991b, p. 240.
141 As indicated by Pinto-Duschinsky 1985, pp. 330, 333, despite reservations due to inflation.
142 Pinto-Duschinsky 1981, p. 275.
143 Hofnung 2005b, pp. 64, 66/67, 74, 77.

political parties and candidates to implement modern campaign technology and to build or sustain a professional party organisation. Eventually **party income determines party spending**, not the need to keep (financially) abreast of technology. If parties are not able to raise the funds they consider to be politically necessary, they will be unable to spend as much as they would like to do.

Deep in their hearts, U.S. political scientists may have known the complete truth for quite a while. Despite public and academic hysteria about rising costs, Sorauf observed candidly, "the supply of available resources ... has until now seemed almost endless."[144] Nevertheless his scholarly attention was detracted from the multitude of willing donors to a minority of potential scoundrels, the incumbent politicians, when much later in his study the same author concluded that fundraising driven by the incumbents' quest for security and the fact that incumbents are funded affluently early on set the standard for the level of political spending.[145] Obviously the money was out there (among the general public and the PAC penumbra) and incumbents were simply better equipped to ask for it efficiently. In analytical terms such straightforward facts obscured that even two decades later in a four country comparison "money to burn"[146] is available and that competing politicians will always find ways to "burn" it.

Finally, innovation is not limited to items of spending. New sources of political funding have been developed since the 1970s. Corporate and ideological political action committees (PACs) solicit and spend millions of dollars, direct mail and the internet wash lots of money into party coffers, and the process of becoming "public utilities" provides a source of funding (i.e. public subsidies) unknown to parties before the 1960s. Whereas for decades the (national) U.S. debate was focussed on PACs, the international segment of scholarly debate was centred around public subsidies, which were first introduced in 1954/59, and up to 2001 proliferated to all established democracies (except Switzerland and India) and were massively expanded during the 1970s and 1980s.[147]

Pulling together the evidence, which has been assembled in this chapter, three clearcut answers to the initial question emerge:

- Although it is still limited to a few countries our knowledge of political spending has been greatly improved during recent decades. More and better data may be an important cause for spending totals, which have increased as time went by. Growth of electorates and inflationary trends have made many observers believe that a cost explosion has occurred. CPI adjusted per capita data show a less dramatic picture – all the more so, if more comprehensive data are taken into account.

---

144 Sorauf 1988, p. 185.
145 Sorauf 1988, pp. 342-345.
146 Smith 2005.
147 Alexander 1989b, p. 14; Nassmacher 1989b, pp. 238-239.

- Paid TV advertising, which is considered the principle villain far beyond the Anglo-Saxon orbit, may be a symptom for changes in political competition, but it is not the unavoidable cause for financial needs. Neither is new campaign technology, which is applied – wherever the funds to pay for it are at hand. Nor is the growing party apparatus staffed with highly skilled professionals and full-time personnel. Into both areas competing parties sink lots of money but this happens because – due to citizens' generosity, public subsidies or corrupt exchanges – parties can afford to do so.
- This supply-side theory of political spending is in line with earlier observations made by Pollock, Overacker und Heard. If GDP deflated per capita expenses for U.S. politics are compared for a period of some 90 years, they peak in 1912 and 1940. Following a trough between 1944 and 1964 political spending shows a lower and declining level since 1968. Similar trends can be demonstrated for four other countries. Only party headquarters in the U.K. happened to hit an all time high in 1997. Political spending peaked in Canada in 1984, in Germany and Japan in 1983. Current levels fall short of those peaks by far. Obviously it is not spending need but revenue potential, which determines the actual level of the "costs of democracy".

The pace of political spending in recent decades is not out of step with the general standard of living. Parties are spending more while the citizens whom they represent are enjoying the benefits of economic growth. Obviously political parties participate in this growth, either by employing more paid party workers (in order to compensate for a loss of voluntary activity) or by the use of new technology. Whichever they may choose will depend on the willingness of their citizens to provide funding for party activity.

CHAPTER SIX

Grass-Roots Revenue

A regular flow of funds from a variety of sources provides the essential revenue for any institutionalised party.[1] Currently, political debate and scholarly research emphasise the difference between private contributions and public subsidies[2] as major sources of political funds. In Europe private contributions are frequently divided into membership dues and donations. We will consider the first source of party revenue early in this chapter, and handle the latter category with care, because it hides more than it reveals. The general term "donation" applies to different kinds of funding. First, a donation may be some small amount given by an individual who supports a party, an issue or a candidate of her or his personal preference. This is a widely esteemed form of involvement, "a valid form of political participation."[3] Second, a donation may be much larger and given by a corporation or an interest group, which wants to "buy" general access to politicians or to influence specific policies. This is a form of interested money. Finally, a third "voluntary" donation may be given in exchange for political favours, such as a public office, an administrative job, a government contract or an official permit. The third form would of course be a clear case of bribery, but two of these examples are certainly important sources of income for any party in power (fundraising by graft).[4]

In a comparative analysis of 158 parties in 53 countries, Janda included information on the sources of party funds. Less than one third of the parties in the complete sample were operating in 14 established Western democracies.[5] During the 1950s only a minority of the 42 parties in advanced democracies (19) collected more than two-thirds of their total revenue „from party sources, including membership dues and income from party enterprises."[6] Due to their fundraising strategies, many parties were linked closely to a specific group of people, i.e. their signed-up, card-carrying party members. Some other democratic parties may have maintained close links and strong

---

1   Panebianco 1988, pp. 58/59.
2   See below in chapter VIII (public subsidies).
3   Scarrow 2007, p. 207.
4   For details see below in chapter VII, section B (interested money) respectively section D (graft/spoils).
5   Janda 1980, pp. 91, 93. His sample included Australia, Austria, Canada, Denmark, France, (West)Germany, *Greece, Iceland,* India, Ireland, *Luxembourg,* the Netherlands, New Zealand, Sweden, the U.K., the U.S. and Uruguay (countries in *italics* are not in our sample). He excluded Belgium, Costa Rica, Finland, Israel, Italy, Japan, Norway and Switzerland. Mexico, Poland and Spain were no democracies then.
6   Janda 1980, p. 92. Details computed from ICPSR data (Janda 1979, p. 149).

financial ties to their grass-roots supporters by raising small donations or constituency quotas.

Grass-roots revenue includes all money collected in small amounts by the rank-and-file of identified party supporters. It can be divided into (1) membership dues, i.e. regular subscriptions of party members; (2) small voluntary donations by large groups of individual citizens (either members or non-members), including those who contribute by means of internet solicitation, direct mail, fundraising events, auctions or lotteries. The legitimising effect of membership dues and small donations is emphasized frequently.[7] This source of political funding can be contrasted with interested money and corrupt payments for political purposes (plutocratic funding),[8] which will be covered in the next chapter. This chapter will solely discuss grass-roots funding of political activity (membership dues and small donations) and try to answer three questions:

- How much funding for specific parties in different countries is provided by membership dues and small donations from the grass-roots of individual party supporters?
- Is grass-roots funding an important and reliable source of political revenue with no strings attached?
- Which of the various strategies to solicit small contributions is best suited to raise grass-roots revenue?

A) Cornerstone of democracy or demand from never-land?

Many scholars (mostly European) assign a central role in democratic politics to parties, and as a result they give preferential treatment to dues-paying party members. For example, whereas Schumpeter emphasised competition and competing elites as the standard bearers of democracy,[9] Leibholz introduced the party organisation as a strategic unit of political competition and participation to democratic theory. Parties organise active citizens politically and serve "as the mouthpiece of the organised people".[10] Consequently party members are the voluntary political avant-garde of the democratic mass public. Starting with Duverger [11] this line of thinking has extremely influenced scholarly writing on modern democracy and party activity. The party member as a self-selected activist of democratic government pays a price for this privilege, which is a set fee, her or his regular membership dues. Political parties, like the working class parties of the late 19th century in Europe, are expected to operate on income from this source. If a party is not able to live up to this normative assignment, enthusiasts of grass-roots democracy expect it to double its efforts in recruiting members and collecting dues.

---

7 E.g. Sorauf 1988, pp. 49-51; Alexander 1992b, p. 356; Nassmacher 1992a, pp. 9-13, 154/155.
8 Gidlund 1983, p. 42.
9 Schumpeter 1950, pp. 269-273.
10 Leibholz 1965, p. 56; cf. ibid., pp.34-36, 82.
11 Duverger 1967, pp. 62-79, 109-116.

The ideal of participatory democracy demands that all citizens reinforce their privileged form of government by taking up individual responsibilities. These include participating in public affairs by contributing time, effort and, if need be, money. Furthermore, critics expect those that can afford it or take a specific (although not a special) interest in politics to contribute the funds, which are necessary to operate political competition in a democracy. Whereas parties can be expected to raise funds actively, people dedicated to a specific cause are prospective sources of voluntary political contributions. The funds may be forthcoming as regular membership dues or as occasional donations in moderate amounts.

Before we enter upon further considerations, it should be noted that "motivations for giving money are similar to those for participation in politics generally." People "have a mixture of reasons for making contributions ... Many people donate money to political campaigns simply because they are asked." Others contribute "out of a sense of civic duty or because they sympathize with a particular candidate", cause or party. Some "may give ... out of a sense of loyalty to ... a group with whom they identify ... others want favourable treatment ... some do want a quid pro quo – a job, a contract, or a policy."[12]

This variety of motives demonstrates that participatory democracy is a *normative ideal* rather than an empirical description of reality. Some implications deserve consideration. First, there is a massive contradiction between the normative ideal and an empirical approach to party democracy. A renowned scholar of democracy perfectly summed up the average citizen's feelings about party funding: "Parties cost money: but not mine, not from my taxes, and not from interest groups."[13] Most people are neither willing to become party members nor to give their own money nor to tolerate parties that receive public subsidies or seek funding from interested money. Opinion polls in Britain, Germany and Spain reflect the paradox that was mentioned. In all three countries about two thirds of the respondents rejected interested money as well as public funding.[14] No more than one fifth of them considered to make a contribution. From this (probably overstated) minority all grass-roots funding must be solicited.

A popular difference is made between political income, which is acceptable to everyone, and revenue, which incurs a lot of social costs. No money in politics, however, has ever been neutral.[15] Why should monthly, quarterly or annual dues paid by party members be an exception to the rule? With any other strategy of fundraising for party activity various social costs are involved. The same should be expected of grass-roots funding.

---

12 Alexander 1992a, pp. 49/50 (quotes in reverse order).
13 Linz 2003, p. 307.
14 Landfried 1994a, pp. 66, 68, 236; Linz 2003, p. 308; 'Taxes should not fund parties,' in: *BBC News* 2002 (news.bbc.co.uk/1/hi/uk_politics/1994874.stm).
15 The opposite belief that there can be "neutral" money, is mentioned for Sweden and Germany in Houghton report 1976, p. 51 (para. 8.32).

First, party members always have a partisan interest. "The decision to subscribe to a party need not indicate political commitment but may reflect more practical motives."[16] In a number of countries, e.g. Austria, Finland, Germany, Israel, some party members can have a specific *personal interest*, for example, access to jobs, housing, other services or public office.[17] Such aspirations link party membership in the ideal world of grass-roots democracy to the political reality of party patronage. Patronage can only be provided in restricted numbers and under favourable circumstances. Parties in opposition can hardly deliver benefits to their members. They may be able to disregard their members' expectations until a take-over of government positions becomes possible. *Governing parties* run the risk of crossing the line to corruption, if they give way to excessive demands of individual members. If governing parties disappoint support groups in terms of policy output, this comes at a price, too. Alienation of supporters by unpopular policies creates a crumbling willingness to continue membership and to pay appropriate dues. Cases in point are declining revenues of the *Parti Quebecois*, the Canadian *P.C.* and the German *SPD* from this source.[18]

The general character of party objectives creates a more specific problem. As far as donors and members are concerned, the returns available from smaller organisations are often more attractive for the individual than those offered by large organisations. Compared to political parties with goals and values, which are not very precise, single issue groups make it more clear what they stand for. Thus parties face even more problems than large interest groups, such as unions or business organisations. In addition, parties suffer the same problems as other big organisations. In fact, they are all losing support, while single issue groups and social movements find it easy to initiate spontaneous activity, which is more attractive to people. In any civil society, parties that strive for dues and donations compete with a lot of other organisations. Many collective actors, for example churches, political action committees and single issue groups, are supported by voluntary donations.

Olson's theoretical analysis of support for voluntary organisations clearly identifies the problems that emerge for all groups as a result of this competition. Any large organisation that seeks to advance a common interest, a collective or public good,[19] will have an acute problem of mobilising (monetary) support, unless it uses coercion or selective incentives for members. A public good is any commodity or service that is available to everyone, regardless of their participation. That is, nobody can be excluded from the benefit brought about by its achievement. "Though all ... members of the group ... have a common interest in obtaining this collective benefit, they have no common interest in paying the cost of providing that collective good."[20] Therefore

---

16 Pinto-Duschinsky 1991b, p. 226.
17 Cf. Paltiel 1981, p. 147; Sundberg 1994, p. 179; Sickinger/ Nick 1990, pp. 22, 59; Deschouwer 1994, p. 103.
18 Angell 2001, p. 258; Niedermayer 2002; Carty 2002, p 361.
19 Cf. Fisher in Neill report 1998, vol. II, p. 319.
20 Olson 1971, pp. 2, 14/15, 21, 51; quote on p. 21.

"individuals will have an incentive to *'free ride,'* and avoid the costs of contributing" to the provision of a public good.[21] This dilemma applies directly to parties, too.

Especially as far as political parties are concerned, citizens do not recognise a *personal value* of the "product" (the collective good), which the organisation stands for. Churches provide personal ceremonial services, which citizens do not want to miss. For trade unions (and the public good, which they supply, the collective wage agreement) free riding has become more and more common and many see the "product" of parties, organising political competition and selecting candidates, as available for all. Thus, paying taxes will do as a civic duty. It does not matter whether you consider that the operation of a political system (democracy), the presentation of candidates for public office or the support of an individual policy is the specific service delivered by an individual party or the party system. Each of these services is a public good, free for all who use it. Who can be expected to have an incentive to pay for it?

Quite similar to other sources of political funding, a wide base of small contributions has to be tapped at a price. Thus "big money in little sums"[22] may be most desirable in a democracy but it is not forthcoming without a streak of emotion and ideology.[23] Like trade unions and established churches,[24] political parties face this problem as well. In general ideological involvement decreases. Before the most recent (2008) campaign U.S. fundraising history offered four examples of presidential candidates who were able to attract large numbers of contributors (150,000 to 750,000) who gave considerable support in small amounts: Barry Goldwater (1964), Eugene McCarthy, George Wallace (1968) and George McGovern (1972).[25] All of them lost their bid for the presidency, which was to be expected. Successful appeals for grass-roots funding and for voters' support obviously require quite different political profiles. Whereas the low profile middle-of-the-road candidate will win a majority of voters more easily, the high profile ideological fringe candidate finds it easier to solicit big money in little sums.[26] "Donors naturally have a greater interest in promoting the success of a particular candidate if that candidate's position is significantly closer to the donor's ideal point than that of the other candidate. In settings where voters can be influenced by campaign expenditure, this in turn provides an incentive for candidates to consider both the preferences of the decisive voter and those of potential campaign contributors. ... If prospective financial support is not symmetrically distributed candidates

---

21 Whiteley 1983, p. 57.
22 Heard 1960, p. 251.
23 Godwin 1988, pp. 21-23, 27; Rieken 2002, pp. 129-150.
24 Presumably monetary considerations by individuals are relevant for long-term withdrawal from the Christian churches in Germany. Between 1968 and 1993 the protestant church lost 13 % of its members in Western Germany (Engelhardt et al. 1997, pp. 309/310, 327).
25 Crotty 1977, p. 121; Epstein 1986, pp. 281/282; Sorauf 1988, pp. 26/27.
26 In this context Verena Blechinger has offered interesting evidence: Former Prime Minister Koizumi was notorious for paying his respects to the Yasukuni shrine. Foreigners were appalled because war criminals are commemorated there, too. However, veterans' associations are big fundraisers for the *Jimintô* party (LDP).

may be pulled away ... from the median voter ... and political controversy may be forthcoming."[27]

A political party funded by ideologically committed members or donors will have to distance its policies from the beliefs of these contributors, because it needs voting support by many people who may be less dedicated to the cause. The leadership of a modern catch-all party [28] will balance its policies between the complacent majority (whose votes it needs to win in order to govern the country) and the militant minority of members (or small donors), which it needs to provide voluntary service and/ or funding for the election campaign (and the maintenance of some sort of party organisation). There is nothing wrong with this need to pursue a balance. However, much can be said to raise doubts about the preponderance of either group to determine party policies. The concept of the mass membership party has a political bias of its own. It favours the emotionally and ideologically committed fringe of any political movement over the less combative masses, which peacefully support the general ideas, the political goals or its popular leaders. Scholars have to be aware of this bias when they accept the notion of funding by membership dues.[29]

As we can see from the various aspects that were discussed the concept of grass-roots financing includes ambivalences and contradictions. These should be considered before the concept is idealised as a cornerstone of democracy (by way of normative prescription). There is no doubt that grass-roots funding provides a link between parties and parts of society. However, each contribution, be it a membership fee or a small donation, depends on an individual sacrifice for collective gain. The need for voluntary action will make the "free rider" a dominant figure in political fundraising. The financial basis for the public good of party activity through partisan action depends on militant supporters rather than pragmatic (rational) citizens. Any other expectation is a demand from never-land rather than a basis for political analysis.

Grass-roots funding may even have additional clandestine strings attached. Governing parties will run into more difficulties collecting contributions than opposition parties. The general appeal of political parties entrusts their funding to a minority of citizens. Although grass-roots financing is desirable for sustainable democracy this normative goal should not be overstretched. Otherwise the visionary may easily turn into romanticist. For all practical purposes other sources of political funding will have to supplement any amount, which possibly can be solicited from grass-roots sources.

---

27 Congleton 1989, pp. 114/115.
28 Kirchheimer 1966, pp. 188, 190, 192/193; see below in chapter XI, sub-section B1 (catch-all parties).
29 E.g. Duverger 1967, pp. 63-66, 73-77, 366 and Landfried 1994a, pp. 14, 356.

B) Roads to voluntary contributions (Soliciting money in small amounts)

Empirical evidence about the fundraising process will show that in all established democracies the contributing elite is a minority. The size of this minority may vary. It depends on the country, party or strategy used to contact potential contributors. This is true even if parties or candidates offer something in exchange for the contribution, e.g. by staging a *fundraising event*, which is then "sold" to the public. Other options include simply asking for a political donation or trying to recruit party members. In some countries, and for some parties, grass-roots funding means that "big money in little sums" is raised via *donations from individual citizens*. For a small number of parties in only a few countries (all of them in continental Europe), considerable funding is procured by way of *members' fees*.

1. Membership dues

A specific type of political party, the mass membership party or mass party, is expected to operate "a very strict system of individual subscriptions", which Duverger compared to the technique of public taxation.[30] At first glance this is a reasonable assumption as membership creates a formal obligation to pay on the part of the member and dues are a reliable source of revenue on the part of the organisation. However, the analogy misses two important points. First, no taxpayer becomes subject to taxation voluntarily. Second, no taxman solely depends on the co-operation of any taxpayer. The obligation to pay membership fees is a moral duty depending on the free will to value and to preserve the privileges of membership. No party treasurer can force an individual to submit his or her cash.

Like many right-of-centre parties the British Conservatives lack a clear definition of membership:[31] "individuals are expected neither to declare their attachment" to principles, "nor to pay a minimum level of subscription." Criteria for membership are loose, financial contribution is variable, and administration of members is decentralised. For individuals "membership of the party principally means giving money, and not much else." For the party finding local campaign volunteers and funding national headquarters are major reasons to recruit members.[32]

Parties tap members for their dues in various ways. Three strategies especially stand out:

- *Weekly or monthly collection* of dues by local party workers was the traditional way of the Social Democratic (Labour) parties in continental Europe.

---

30 Duverger 1967, p. 1.
31 The same is true for state parties (*Kantonalparteien*) in Switzerland; cf. Ladner/ Brändle 2001, pp. 151, 158.
32 Whiteley/ Seyd/ Richardson 1994, pp. 24-26, 77; two quotes on p. 24 and one on p. 77.

- Late in the 20th century personal collection was replaced by quarterly *pre-authorised checking* based on a computerised permanent register of party members.
- *Annual renewal of membership cards,* which are distributed in regular membership drives, is well known in Anglo-Saxon democracies but also in Italy.

Party income from membership dues ranges from large amounts to a small percentage of total revenue. Any attempt to compare the available information must take into account that in some countries and/or for some parties there is no data at all, and in other countries there are only figures for the national level and in just a few (like Germany since 1968 and Canada since 2005) a complete set of data is accessible. Some data may be only guesswork, which leads to results that are of extremely different quality. Sometimes only estimates of trends are available, e.g. in Latin America for Mexico, Costa Rica and Uruguay, where membership dues do not play a significant role in the funding of political parties and where, furthermore, this source is in decline.[33]

Party members as a source of revenue are by no means equally important across our sample of modern democracies. This is due to various factors. Traditionally the social democratic (workers') parties of western Europe are mass-membership parties.[34] Among their conservative counterparts (and non-European parties) some do not employ the concept of mass membership, which expects citizens to sign up voluntarily and to pay dues regularly. Where the concept is applied, people participate in party membership more or less frequently. The number of party members differs. More precisely, the levels of party enrolment and the member-to-voter ratios are different. Party enrolment ranges from one to 18 percent of the electorate, which gives a good impression of the diversity (see Table 6-1 below).

If the *member-to-voter ratio* is high, this does not mean that the members' contribution towards party income must be considerable. If a party sets low fees even a lot of members will not contribute much money. Only if the *average amount of annual membership dues* paid is substantial and the member-to-voter ratio is impressive, then the share of *party income from membership* fees will be as vital as can be expected under the concept of mass party. Finally, the distribution of income from dues among the different levels of an individual party has an impact on the significance of members as a source of funding for the party's central office.

a)   Number of party members (including member-to-voter ratio and trends)

In some countries party revenue from membership dues (or donations) is little, because there is only a limited number of members. Spain, France and Britain are examples of this.[35] Income from members and small donors are regarded as major indicators

---

33   Zovatto 2001, p. 376; Casas-Zamora 2005a, pp. 124, 168.
34   Membership figures for the first half of the 20th century are given by Duverger 1954, pp. 68/69.
35   Koole 2001, p. 78; Doublet 1997, p. 73; van Biezen 2000, pp. 334-335.

for linkages between parties and society. Nonetheless, in scholarly books only the development of membership numbers, more sophisticated as a percentage of the electorate (member-to-elector -M/E- ratio), is seen as an important benchmark.[36] Around 1990 M/E-ratios were exceptionally high with the Centre Party (55 percent) and the Swedish People's Party (30 percent) in Finland, the Social Democrats (46 percent) and the Centre Party (19 percent) in Sweden, the *ÖVP* (32 percent) and the *SPÖ* (30 percent) in Austria, the Centre Party (28 percent), the Conservatives (27 percent) and the Christian People's Party (26 percent) in Norway, the *Venstre* (21 percent) in Denmark and the Belgian Communists (20 percent).[37] Five of these 11 parties represent the agrarian interest in their country. One of the others is the party of an ethnic minority, one a workers' party with collective membership.

Sometimes membership figures as provided by the parties are blown up artificially, as is well known for the Austrian ÖVP and the former Italian DC. Sponsorship by some members paying for others and family memberships served that purpose. A lot of parties are not willing to correct their files. Thus membership without paying dues is a common feature of many parties, e.g. the U.K. Conservatives or most parties in Israel. Once a person is registered as a member, he or she is unlikely "to be dropped, even after prolonged non-payment of dues."[38]

Whereas social and political change has an impact on party enrolment, *incentives for members* may also cause a different outcome. In Israel the right to vote in intra-party nomination primaries helped (temporarily) recruit party members. In India membership is higher during election years. In Austria and Germany high numbers of members may be seen in the context of "petty corruption." That is, access to public or co-operative housing and jobs in the public sector are traditionally offered to party members in various countries. Such incentives are not available to Dutch citizens, "where party membership is by no means a prerequisite for a job in the public sector."[39] In Australia seeking public office seems to be the only incentive.[40]

Some countries experienced a more or less stable level of party enrolment (e.g. Australia, Austria, Switzerland), others saw drastic changes in their party membership totals (Denmark, Finland, France, Germany, Israel, Italy, Japan, the Netherlands, New Zealand, Norway, Sweden and the U.K.). For New Zealand, local sources reveal a considerably higher, but nonetheless declining, level of enrolment: While about 20 percent of the voting age population were members of a political party in 1960, this declined to 12.5 percent in 1981, 5-6 percent in 1996 and 3.5 percent in 2002.[41]

---

36 Krouwel 1999, pp. 69-71.
37 Katz 1996, p. 114.
38 Gutmann 1963, p. 704.
39 Andeweg 1999, p. 120. For Austria see Luther 1999, p. 54; for New Zealand see Miller 2005, p. 90.
40 Young/ Tham 2006, p. 111.
41 Vowles 2002, p. 416; Wilson 2004, p. 4.

Between the early 1960s and the late 1980s M/E-ratios declined to less than a third of the previous level in Denmark, Finland and the Netherlands and to almost one third of that in the U.K. In Sweden the level remained rather high (until the early 1990s). Decline in Austria, Italy and Norway was moderate, whereas in Belgium and Germany parties could even stage a small increase of membership levels.[42] However, this turned out to be temporary in the late 1990s, when all countries, except Spain, Canada and Australia, joint the declining trend.[43]

Table 6-1:   Levels of party enrolment, 1950-2000

Country	1950	1960	1970	1980	1990s	Late1990s	M/E ratio
Austria	1,041,000	1,262,000	1,308,000	1,321,000	990,000	1,031,052	17.66 %
Israel	-	230,000	320,000	250,000	350,000	440,000	10.30 %
Finland	396,000	485,000	531,000	579,000	428,000	400,615	9.65 %
Norway	-	324,000	399,000	456,000	276,000	242,022	7.31 %
Belgium	-	478,000	495,000	615,000	485,000	480,804	6.55 %
Switzerld.	-	367,000	357,000	367,000	391,000	293,000	6.38 %
Sweden	1,110,000	1,092,000	1,104,000	1,429,000	376,000	365,588	5.54 %
Denmark	597,000	599,000	489,000	276,000	202,000	205,382	5.14 %
Italy	3,698,000	4,280,000	4,620,000	4,078,000	1,867,000	1,974,040	4.05 %
Japan	205,000	404,500	741,500	2,175,000	3,648,000	-	3.60 %
Spain	-	-	-	-	-	1,131,250	3.42 %
Ireland	-	59,000	82,000	98,000	93,000	86,000	3.14 %
Germany	1,126,845	1,018,000	1,299,000	1,954,000	1,852,000	1,780,173	2.93 %
Netherlds	630,000	730,000	369,000	523,000	229,000	294,469	2.51 %
New Zeal.	288,000	246,000	228,000	167,000	50,000	-	2.00 %
U.K.	3,436,000	3,065,000	2,424,000	615,000	820,000	840,000	1.92 %
France	1,259,000	589,000	644,000	1,089,000	582,000	615,219	1.57 %
Australia	-	-	265,000	234,000	174,000	-	1.40 %
Poland	-	-	-	-	-	326,500	1.15 %
Mean	-	-	-	-	-	-	5.08 %

Sources: Scarrow 2000, p. 89; Mair/ van Biezen 2001, p. 9; Arian 1998, p. 161.

Since the founding days of post-war Italy, membership subscriptions were not a real source of funds for most parties. In 1970 almost 13 percent of the voters were allegedly affiliated with a political party. However, party membership never became an important financial source of the non-communist parties. DC party leaders especially "had little incentive to build a solid and autonomous organisation because the vital resources for its functioning were readily available from the external sponsor [i.e. the

---

42   Katz 1996, p. 121.
43   Knapp 2002, p. 121; Deschouwer 2002, pp. 162; Sundberg 2002, p. 197; Murphy/ Farrell 2002, p. 225; Bardi 2002, p. 57; Vowles 2002, p. 416; Holliday 2002, p. 257; Carty 2002, p. 355; McAllister 2002, pp. 389/390.

Catholic Church], including money and ideology."[44] Later, there was a sharp decline. In the 1990s the aggregate membership of all parties comprised about four percent of the electorate (Table 6-1). More than any other factor, the intensity of internal power struggles probably contributed to the "artificial inflation" of membership figures and the "see-saw fashion,"[45] in which they developed. The exposure of the *tangenti* scandal added a remarkable explanation. Within some parties, especially DC and PSI, clientelistic networks of intra-party factions used corruptly gained funds to buy membership cards and thus increase intra-party power in years of a party congress.[46] In the context of the parties' revenue from the grass-roots, it should be observed that factional leaders were able to launder "income from graft" into subscriptions "paid" in the name of non-existing party "members". The upheaval of the party system (1991) busted the overblown DC and PSI memberships.[47] The average party in Japan belongs to the cadre or elite type and (like the former Italian DC) displays a clientelistic structure. Citizens may identify with a party label by voting for individual MPs and by joining their (financial or organisational) support groups (*kôenkai*).

In former times Israel could be seen as a different kind of exception. For the Jewish immigrant society during the British mandate for Palestine (from 1920 until 1948) „grass-roots" financing was the most common way to fund all activities of a Zionist party. However, later on not all members paid up regularly. After statehood the electorate grew from 0.5 million in 1949 to 4.7 million in 2003. Even a soaring number of party members meant a sharp decrease in the M/E-ratio. Moreover the combined registered membership in all parties declined after 1970. Parties did not bother to collect dues because this source of income was no longer important.[48] Everything changed in the early 1990s when the major parties introduced internal primaries for the nomination of parliamentary candidates. Members, who did not resume paying their dues, were taken off the register. Afterwards, although the aggregate number of party members accounted for 10.6 percent of the electorate (Table 6-1), a „survey conducted in 1998 revealed that the proportion of respondents stating they were active party members amounted to a mere 4.9 percent."[49] In addition, it has to be noted that in the year after the nomination "primaries" participating parties consequently lost many of their new members.[50]

Early decline in partisanship in France during the 1960s coincided with the decay of the (unreformed, Stalinist) PCF. A similar trend during the 1980s lacks explanation. In general, the number of party members is estimated to be very low, although some parties report considerable figures. As one observer has stated, "French political parties are tiny organisations, not at all comparable to (German, English, Italian) parties

---

44 Mulé 1998, p. 65.
45 Bardi/ Morlino 1994, pp. 254/255; cf. Bardi 2002, p. 57.
46 Rhodes 1997, p. 71; Della Porta/ Vannucci 1999, p. 102.
47 For details see below in chapter VII, sub-section D 1 (abuse of public resources).
48 Mendilow 1989, p. 146.
49 cf. Yishai 2000, p. 675.
50 Hofnung 1996a, p. 81; Hofnung 2005b, p. 72. Just like the "jigsaw" pattern observed in Italy.

abroad."[51] In Germany party enrolment was about 1.0 to 1.3 million members between 1950 and 1970. Two steep increases (during a heated debate over foreign policy in the early 1970s and after unification in 1990) are currently wearing off, and the numbers have been declining ever since.

In Poland, as in other newly democratised countries of Central Eastern Europe, the member-to-voter ratio is very low (1.15 percent). When compared to other countries in the region (with an average of 2.8 percent) it is much lower. Apparently parties in the area are anything but mass parties. The low number of party members in Poland is especially striking. There is a remarkable contrast between the huge mobilisation by the Solidarity trade union and the failure of the post-Solidarity parties to take advantage of it. Probably the paradox is that Poland witnessed a political mass movement, but when the euphoria of 1989-90 disappeared, the membership base of its organised parties was particularly low.[52]

Despite a notable tradition of strong party membership, decline has afflicted all Scandinavian polities starting with Denmark in the early 1960s, where party membership dropped to one third of the previous level. This was the beginning of a pan-Scandinavian trend. "Aggregate membership peaked in Finland during the 1970s and 1980s, and a few years later in Norway and Sweden. Since then, however, membership decline has set in at an unprecedented rate. It has been most dramatic in Sweden" where the number of party members was relatively stable, but as a percentage of the population entitled to vote it decreased to 23 percent by 1990 and even more sharply since then. The abolition of collective memberships with the SAP in 1986 is the major cause for the striking drop of total party enrolment between 1980 and the late 1990s. In Finland, remarkable slides during the 1990s left "overall membership levels very similar to those in Sweden. ... Rapid decline in Norway has brought its membership level down nearly as far as Denmark's."[53]

De Hart and Dekker found that in the "rapidly modernized civil society" of the Netherlands women's organisations and political parties were the only organisations that declined. Between 1980 and 1994 the strongest growth (in members and donors) has taken place in single-purpose "organizations, which are concerned with moral issues (abortion and euthanasia), nature and the environment, and international solidarity (the Third World, human rights and refugees)." Dutch party enrolment suffered during the process of de-pillarisation. M/E ratios declined from 15% in 1946, 12.5 percent in 1956, 6.7 percent in 1967, 4.4 percent in 1977, 3.5 percent in 1986, 2.9 percent in 1994 to 2.5 percent in 2000.[54] Koole refers to this as "the exodus of members in the 1960s."[55] Popular enrolment in all Belgian parties was still beyond the European average in

---

51 Ysmal 1989, p. 162; cf. Schmitt 1993, p. 77; Kempf 2007, pp. 175/176, 178.
52 Walecki 2001, p. 397; Walecki 2005a, p. 115.
53 Sundberg 2002, p. 196.
54 de Hart/ Dekker 1999, p. 79, for the data referring to Voerman 1996, p. 199; Mair/ van Biezen 2001, p. 9.
55 Koole 1989, p. 205; cf. Koole 1994a, p. 126.

1999 (6.6 percent of the electorate). The "membership levels of the two major political families, the Christian Democrats and the Socialists, have declined much more slowly than has their electoral support."[56]

Obviously disenchantment with political parties in New Zealand started in the 1970s, however, party membership hit bottom when the electoral system changed (from FPTP to MMP) in the 1990s.[57] In the U.K. (Britain) individual party membership in both major parties must have declined extremely during the 1970s, which was a period of discontent for supporters (voters) and militants (members) alike as both left party ranks in droves due to political and organisational neglect. In the 1990s Labour headquarters encouraged constituency activists to collect regular dues from individual members. In 2001 media reports claimed that the Conservative Party had less than 320,000 members, the Labour Party about 280,000 (individual) members, while the Liberal Democrats was joined by 55,000 citizens.[58] This total of 655,000 is much less than the scholarly approximations of party enrolment. Scarrow claimed 820,000 members in 1997, Mair and van Biezen 840,000 in 1998.[59]

In India, as of 1992, there were 25 million members of the Congress party, i.e. five percent of the total electorate. However, this figure is variable. Before campaigns start, the number of party members increases. At that time candidates themselves are expected to make sizeable contributions to expand their influence.[60]

Although the data in Table 6-1 "largely confirm that enrolment within a political party is becoming a much less popular outlet for political participation,"[61] proceeds from membership dues do not always correlate with the number of members, as already indicated for Austria and the U.K. In Italy the number of party members was high and revenue from this source insignificant. Although both major parties in Germany have roughly the same number of members, the *SPD* collects more from this source than do *CDU* and *CSU*. In the Netherlands, with a high proportion of party income from this source, the M/E-ratio is extremely low.

Because our concern is membership as a reliable source of constant revenue, the striking difference of enrolment levels deserves attention. The extremely high M/E ratio (see Table 6-1) in just three countries (Austria, Israel and Finland) makes for a considerable difference between the two measures of centrality. In a sample of 19 democracies, old and new, the mean is 5.1 percent, the median 3.6 percent. Smaller democracies of continental Europe (Austria, Belgium, Finland, Norway) together with Israel belong to the first quartile (17.7 to 6.6 percent). A diverse group of old (mostly Anglo-Saxon) and new (Central European) democracies (New Zealand, the U.K., Australia,

---

56 Deschouwer 1994, p. 103.
57 Denmark 2003, p. 604.
58 Scarrow 1996, p. 120; Sturm 2003, p. 246.
59 Scarrow 2000, p. 89; Mair/ van Biezen 2001, p. 9.
60 Jain 2001, pp. 351, 352. - This looks like a practice, which was common in *Italy*, especially with the DC.
61 Scarrow 2000, p. 89.

Poland and France) represent the fourth quartile (2.0 to 1.2 percent), where only a small percentage of the electorate are party members.

In most countries with an enrolment level beyond average (Israel, Finland, Norway, Belgium, Sweden, Denmark, Italy), national party headquarters do not draw much revenue from their members. Among this group Austria and Switzerland are exceptions to the rule as parties in both countries (together with their counterparts in two countries with a low level of enrolment, the Netherlands and Germany) depend on party members for a significant portion of funding for national party organisations. The rest of the sample offers no surprises: low levels of enrolment accompany low levels of membership funding. Other sources of income, which are available to parties, especially high amounts of public subsidies,[62] seem to be very important in many countries (e.g. in Sweden). However, the revenue share of membership dues can be explained neither by the *number of members* nor by the *level of individual fees*.

b) Average contribution per party member

Unfortunately for inter-party comparisons of average membership dues, the data available is patchy (Table 6-2), and rarely current. Webb shows that most parties' headquarters between 1975 and (roughly) 1985 suffered a decline in revenue per party member.[63] Only Austria, Denmark, Ireland, the Netherlands and the U.K. are exceptions to this rule. During the 1950s membership dues in Israel "averaged 0.5 percent of the gross yearly salary." In the 1990s the annual fee for members of the *Likud* was NIS 24 (equivalent to US $9) whereas the Labour party (*Avodah*) required NIS 120 per year (about US $50).[64] The difference of average dues between the major right-of-centre and the major left-of-centre party seems to hold throughout the sample (except Austria).

Among Dutch parties (as of 1984) average annual membership dues were the "lowest for the small Orthodox Calvinist *SGP* (NLG 16/ €7) and the highest for the small left-wing *PSP* (NLG 105/ €48)."[65] The four major parties were closer to each other. Members of "bourgeois" parties paid about NLG 50 (€23), those of "progressive" parties NLG 86 (€39). In 1994 Austrian party members contributed at a similar level, except for the *ÖVP*. This (formerly Catholic) party collects dues via its major sub-organisations, literally called leagues (*Bünde*): the small-business league (*ÖWB*) solicits ATS 6,000 (€436) annually, the agrarian league (*ÖBB*) ATS 3,000 (€218) and the wage earners' league, mostly public employees (*ÖAAB*) ATS 3,120 to 14,400 (€226-1,046).[66] During the 1980s the average amount of dues per member per year ranged from ATS 60 (minimum) for the *ÖVP*, ATS 120 for the *FPÖ* to ATS 180 (minimum) for the *SPÖ*.[67]

---

62 see below in chapter VIII, sub-section E 1 (contribution to party revenue).
63 Webb (2000, p. 308), using for his calculations data from the Katz/Mair project (1992).
64 Quote from Mendilow 1989, p. 127; Data from Hofnung 1996a, pp. 77, 81.
65 Koole 1989, p. 205 (Dfl. amended to NLG; € amounts added).
66 Sickinger 1997, p. 38/39.
67 Houghton report 1976, p. 319; Kofler 1981, p. 366.

Table 6-2: Average membership dues by party family and country (all amounts converted to € per member and year)

Country	Voter-memb. Ratio	Year	Comm. / Left	Green/ Ecolo-gists	Social. Labour	Christ. Demo-crats	Liberal	Con-serva-tive	Popu-list	Coun-try Aver.
Austria	18	1994	-	44	30-40	436 218 226	-	-	26	35
Israel	11	1990s	-	-	50	-	-	9	-	30
Denmark	5	1989	-	-	33	-	7	4	-	15
Ireland	3	1990	-	-	?	-	?	6	-	?
Germany	3	2002	150	121	83	73 58	94	-	-	58
Netherld	2.5	1984	48	-	39	23 7	23 39	-	-	30
U.K.	2	1990s	-	-	5 -15	-	-	7 -13	-	10
France	1.5	1990	-	-	305-762	34	-	31	-	33
Family Average	-	-	99	82	48	39	41	14	26	50/30
Family range	-	-	48-150	44-121	30-83	23-73	7-94	4-34	26-26	10-58

Sources: Bille 1994, pp. 138, 145; Koole 1989, p. 205; Hofnung 1996a, pp. 77, 81; *Deutscher Bundestag*, parliamentary papers, no. 15/5550; Seyd/ Whiteley 1992, p. 27.
Voter-to-member ratio for the late 1990s: Average of data in Mair/ van Biezen 2001, pp. 15-16; (Israel) Mendilow 1996, p. 332.
Legend: - = data not available; *extreme outliers* have been neglected for range and average.

German parties traditionally demand (and collect) the highest membership subscriptions. The most obvious consequence, which can be drawn from the available data (Table 6-3), is that in four decades, despite a high level of public funding, German parties have been able to increase their average membership fees considerably. The (catch-all type) major parties raised a little less (CDU by a factor of 3.08, SPD by 3.56) than the more cadre type minor parties, which gathered much more (CSU by a factor of 4.14 and FDP even by 5.17). By German standards CSU membership has always been (and in a way still is) "cheap", but not so much today. The FDP, which once called itself (quite correctly) the "party of the prosperous few," did not care too much about members and dues during the early 1970s but it now does (due to amended subsidy rules). Average dues for the party, which represents the Communist tradition (DKP, PDS), have almost "exploded" (by a factor of 6.7). The party faithful are probably better off economically in the united Germany than were their West German "comrades" during years at the political fringe. During the period 1973 to 2003, the Consumer Price Index (CPI) increased by a factor of 2.3, and the gross national product (GNP) by a factor of 4.3.[68] On average, German parties have been able to hold onto

---

68 www.destatis.de/indicators.

their own in terms of membership fees, which have soared far beyond inflation and only slightly less than income.

Table 6-3: Annual average of membership dues for German parties

€ per year	DKP/PDS	SPD	Grüne	CDU	CSU	FDP
1973	22.24	23.26	-	23.62	13.98	18.15
1983	83.00	39.20	31.00	43.30	26.30	39.60
1993 *	52.00/ 46.80	43.00/ 31.00	178.00/ 106.80	55.00/ 39.60	43.00/ 30.50	61.00/ 49.40
2003	150.10	82.80	121.10	72.80	57.90	93.90

Sources: *Bundesanzeiger*, 7 January 1975; *Deutscher Bundestag*, parliamentary papers, no. 10/2172 and 15/5550; Rudzio 1987, 2nd ed., p. 159; Rudzio 2000, 5th ed., p. 186.
Comment: Data for DKP 1983 may include laundered cash support from East Germany.
* Data for 1993 have been adjusted for revenue from assessments.

Scattered data for other countries are less reliable. In 1990 membership dues were FRF 200 (€ 30.50) for the French Gaullists (RPR) and FRF 220 (€ 33.55) for the CDS. The Socialist Party (PS) collected much higher dues, between FRF 2,000 and 5,000 (€ 305 to 762) per year.[69] In Britain there are no set fees for members of the Conservative Party, and two percent of them pay nothing at all. Among those who pay, 80 per cent range between £1 and £20, 14 per cent between £20 and £50. Only 4 per cent of all Conservative members pay more dues regularly. The medium subscription is about £10-12 (€7-8) per year. Due to special fund-raising activities by Conservative constituency associations a member's average contribution was £20 in the 1990s. Some 40 per cent of the local party members contributed between £10 and £30, another 40 per cent more than £30 annually.[70] Individual members of the Labour Party pay £5 to 15 annually; for affiliated organisations the fee is £3 per member and year.[71] This is exceptionally low by continental European standards (see Table 6-2). In 1990 members of the Irish Fine Gael paid IEP5 (€6.35) each.[72] For U.S. state parties, which offer membership via their websites or by peer-to-peer contacts, dues for basic members are US-$15-25. More substantial payment entitles them to more access and privileges, e.g. tickets to social events.[73]

c) Revenue from membership dues (by party families and by countries)

Income from party membership is not equally important for all parties because they collect disparate amounts of money from dues. In fact, parties have different legacies

---

69 Schmitt 1993, p. 77.
70 Whiteley/ Seyd/ Richardson 1994, pp. 75-76.
71 Becker 1999, p. 80.
72 Mockler 1994, pp. 167-168.
73 Smith 2005, p. 226.

and concepts concerning their membership. Thus it may be expected that dues are a more significant source of revenue for some but not for others. Even the less recent percentages of total revenue indicate the variety and variable significance of this funding source for the *national headquarters* of individual parties. There are two good starting points for a useful comparison. One is by political tradition and general political orientation of individual parties (party families), and the other by national traditions (political culture). In some countries, parties are predominantly mass parties, which can be expected to rely on membership funding. In other countries, with a tradition of cadre parties or a complete transformation to catch-all parties, political organisations will depend on other sources of revenue. We shall start with differences related to *national tradition* and turn to *party families* later.

(1) National traditions/ political culture

In Anglo-Saxon democracies party members have always been relatively unimportant for party income. Even for the Australian Labour Party voluntary work of members is more important than their dues. Data for income from dues in Ireland are mere „guesswork".[74] As a source of political revenue party members have always been fairly inconsequential in Britain. During the 1980s shares of party income ranged from 0 to 14 %.[75] Although there are differences between parties and over time, local income for all British parties has declined. The Conservatives transfer some part of local revenue to Central Office via association quotas.[76]

Parties in the U.S. and Canada never relied on membership dues. Some U.S. state parties (e.g. Wisconsin) are documented exceptions.[77] In Canada only the N.D.P. and the provincial parties of Quebec came close to the mass-membership type.[78] More recently the B.Q. federally and the Reform Party (now part of the CPC) suit the new format. By using modern communication technology, however, the U.S. Republicans and the Canadian Progressive Conservatives (P.C.) have shown the world of democratic politics that there are (modern) ways and means to grass-roots funding beyond the search for party members.[79]

For different reasons more recent additions to the democratic fold display a similar pattern. Membership dues have always played a minor role in the funding of Japanese parties.[80] In Spain there existed neither individual responsibility nor a tradition "of associative mechanisms, which are central to the functioning of a party system."[81] Mem-

---

74 Laver/ March 1999, p. 159.
75 Pinto-Duschinsky 1994, pp. 14, 17; Johnston/ Pattie 1993, pp. 136, 140/141.
76 See below in this chapter, sub-section D 1 (association quotas).
77 Adamany 1969, pp. 24, 25.
78 Angell 1987, pp. 365/366; Carty 1996b, p. 200; Smith 2005, pp. 56, 99.
79 See below in this chapter, sub-section B2 (small donations). - The efforts by North American parties indicate that fundraising may be directly connected to incentives provided by political finance regimes.
80 Blechinger/ Nassmacher 2001, pp. 162/163.
81 Heywood 1997b, p. 73.

bership subscriptions have always constituted a practically irrelevant source of party income. Del Castillo reports a share between two to five percent for the 1980s, including assessments paid by party MPs. In the early 1990s membership fees contributed between three and five percent of the total funds of the three major parties (*PSOE, PP* and *PCE*).[82]

For a diverse group of democracies (mostly in Western Europe) the role of party members in the funding of party activities is rather ambivalent and changing (see Table 6-4). In Sweden revenue from dues as a percentage of national party income declined for some parties and increased for others during the 1980s. The *SAP*'s share of membership income had a maximum at 16.5, percent but shrank to 9.3 percent, whereas the Moderate Party managed to increase its share from 7 to 12 percent. On average Swedish parties depend on membership dues for less than 6 percent of their annual budget. Although the M/E-ratio is higher in Norway, there is no indication that members' contribution to party income is more important. In the late 1980s parties in that country on average raised 10-20 percent of their total revenue by dues. All Finnish parties have suffered from declining income from fees since the 1970s, which were extremely high for the National Coalition Party (a maximum of 33.3 percent), for the Christian League (a maximum of 10.1 percent) and for the Social Democratic Party (a maximum of 9.4 percent of total revenue). By the end of the 1980s, the maximum amount ranged between 3.9 percent and no income from this source.[83]

Table 6-4: *Average party income from membership dues (in percent of total)*

Country	Share of income		Country	Share of income	
	Krouwel	Casas-Zamora		Krouwel	Casas-Zamora
Finland	3%	4%	Germany	31%	20%
Spain	n.a.	1%	Austria	27%	41%
Sweden	7%	8%	Netherlands	75%	(35-61%)
France	n.a.	(9-10%)	Italy	17%	49%
Norway	34%	10%	Denmark	36%	63%
Ireland	33%	n.a.	Switzerland	n.a.	(2-60%)
			Britain	36%	n.a.

Sources: Krouwel 1999, p. 76; Casas-Zamora 2002, p. 64; Casas-Zamora 2005a, p. 47. Additional data (…) from Gidlund/ Koole 2001, p. 116; Ladner/ Brändle 2001, p. 180; Knapp 2002, p. 127.

In France, "the parties maintained that their resources came from their members' dues, with the candidates discreetly soliciting contributions from a few friends. These assertions have never been taken seriously, primarily because of the small number of party

---

[82] del Castillo 1989, pp. 186, 191-193; del Castillo 1994, p. 99. See van Biezen 2000, pp. 334-335.
[83] Wiberg 1991c, pp. 82-84, 92-97; Klee 1993b, p. 191.

members and the limitations of disinterested patronage."[84] Estimates assumed membership fees constituted 8 percent of total party income in 1995. Published reports from the 1990s present low, but significant, levels of members' share of party funds, which range from three to six percent of headquarters' budget for the UDF to 11 to 20 percent for the PS. No party has claimed more than 20 percent from dues, the average is about 10 percent.[85]

Only a minority of the countries in continental Western Europe display an important contribution of party members towards the funding of headquarters' activity. In Germany some 1.5 million ordinary citizens were party members and provided about one third of total party revenue. In Austria about 1.0 million citizens have signed up. Their dues cover no less than one third of SPÖ and ÖVP income at the federal level.[86] Casas-Zamora's estimates for Italy (48.5 percent) and Denmark (62.5 percent) should be used with care as Krouwel (based on the same data) offers much lower shares (see Table 6-4 above). An average of 20 percent for Denmark and a range of 15-20 percent for Italy seem closer to reality (see Table 6-5 below).

Only in the Netherlands membership fees constitute the main source of party income. In 1995, despite low enrolment, regular dues paid by members still contributed more than half of parties' total revenue. Figures for the 1980s even ranged from 80 to 75 percent. By 1989 members' contribution to national revenue of major parties was down to 60 percent. On top of regular fees, parties receive donations from their members, especially to fill the campaign chest.[87] In Belgium all parties collect membership dues. However, no amounts of income are available.[88]

In Switzerland, where more than six percent of the electorate are paid-up party members, income from this source is so different among political parties that general figures are not appropriate. As public subsidies are not available, membership dues and assessments from legislators provide 85 percent of the *SPS*'s income, while corporate and individual donations are more important for the *FDP*.[89] The Swiss example demonstrates that looking at individual countries is only one way to access the financial contribution of party members. Therefore similarities and differences related to party funding shall also be studied by *party families*.

(2) Party families

As a rule of thumb parties of the political left (Social Democrats and Communists) traditionally collect more funds from membership dues than do their bourgeois (Conservative and Liberal) competitors (Table 6-5). Even in countries within the Anglo-Saxon orbit, the Labour parties (where they exist) are more dependent on membership

---

84 Avril 1989, pp. 87/88.
85 Drysch 1993, pp. 156, 161; Doublet 1997, p. 73; Koole 2001, p. 78; Knapp 2002, pp. 126/127.
86 Müller 1992, p. 49; Sickinger 1997, pp. 37, 243, 245, 248, 250; Smith 2005, pp. 207/208.
87 Koole 1989, p. 203; Koole 1994a, p. 127; Koole 1999, p. 346; Gidlund/ Koole 2001, p. 117.
88 Deschouwer 2002, 163.
89 Wiesli 1999, p. 422 and Ladner/ Brändle 1999, pp. 19-22.

dues. However, data given by Krouwel for European parties in the late 1980s do not confirm this rank order. Social Democrats, Socialists and Christian Democrats covered more than a third of their revenue from dues, followed by Liberals, Greens and Conservatives (31-22%). The lowest shares (around 10%) he reported for Agrarian and Communist parties.[90]

Among the *Social Democratic* parties only two truly live up to expectations: the Swiss SPS (up to 90%) and the Dutch PvdA (60-70%) collect most of their headquarters' revenue from membership dues. The Austrian SPÖ, the German SPD and the Japanese Shakaitô just raise a substantial share (all about 25%) in this manner.[91] Many others deviate from the traditional pattern. Workers' parties in Denmark (11-14%), Sweden (6%) and Finland (4-9%) have seen their membership income decrease dramatically.[92] The Labour Party in Britain, which is still closely connected with trade unions via collective memberships, depended on (constituency) members' subscriptions for 10-17% of its annual revenue during the 1990s. Their Irish brethren collected 15-20% of total funds from members, the French PS raised 11-20% of declared party revenue from ordinary members, the Spanish PSOE only 5%.[93] In Italy the "socialist" PSI claimed to have increased income from membership fees during the 1980s (from 18% of total revenue in 1974 to 41% in 1984). However, it was gradually transformed from a party of sections and militants to a network of competing patrons and their clientelistic henchmen.[94]

For many *Communist* parties in western democracies membership dues were the most important source of sustaining funds.[95] For the PCI, the major party of opposition in Italy, members (including MPs) provided about 60% of total funds in 1989.[96] All membership dues were collected centrally and then (in parts) trickled down to lower tiers. Beginning in 1995 the PDS, the East German post-communist party suffered a decline to less than 50%.[97] The Socialist people's parties in Denmark and Norway collect about 30% of their total income from dues. Some Communist parties have much less income from dues, e.g. in France (10-12% of total revenue), in Japan (less than 5%), in Sweden (4%) and in Finland (3%).[98]

---

90   Krouwel 1999, p. 77.
91   Cordes 2001, p. 102; Sickinger 1999, p. 306; Blechinger/ Nassmacher 2001, p. 163; Smith 2005, p. 96.
92   Pedersen 2003, p. 338; Gidlund 1991a, p. 44; Wiberg 1991b, p. 82; Pierre/ Widfeldt 1994, pp. 346-347.
93   Fromont 1992, p. 157; Schmitt 1993, p. 77; Knapp 2002, p. 127; del Castillo 1989, p. 190.
94   Ciaurro 1989, p. 158; Della Porta/ Vannucci 1999, pp. 96, 100-102; Newell 2000, pp. 68/69.
95   Besides the financial support from the Comintern, which was channelled through export-import firms owned by the party. Bardi/ Morlino 1994, p. 248. – See below in chapter VII, sub-section B 5 (foreign funds).
96   Ciaurro 1989, p. 158; Bardi/ Morlino 1992, p. 600.
97   Neugebauer/ Stöss 1996, pp. 124/125; for membership figures cf. Niedermayer 2002, www.polwiss.fu-berlin.de/osi/dokumente/PDF/mitglied.pdf.
98   Wiberg 1991b, pp. 82, 93; Blechinger/ Nassmacher 2001, p. 162.

Table 6-5: Membership funding of party headquarters, averages (Calculated as a percentage of headquarters' annual revenue)

Country	M/E-ratio	Comm. Left	Green/ Ecolog.	Social. Labour	Centre	Chr. Dem	Liberal	Conservat.	Populist	Average
Austria	18	-	2	27-47	-	16-31	-	-	3-7	12
Denmark	5	32	-	11-80	11	43	19	-	5	20
Finland	10	3	-	5-9	1-2	-	3	5-6	-	4
France	2	10-12	1-3	11-20	-	-	3-6	7-12	5-15	9
Germany	3	50-76	3-6	23-24	-	17-21 13-14	2-5	-	-	21
Ireland	3	-	-	15-20	-	51	-	?	-	?
Italy	4	35-65 3	1 19	18-42	-	6-28	6 12	-	7	17
Japan	4	4-5	-	25	-	-	-	5-7 6-15	-	11
Netherlands	3	-	35	54-78	-	61-64	55-61 48-49	-	-	55
Norway	7	27	-	9	24	4-8	15	-	1	14
Spain	3	1-4	-	5	-	4-17	-	5-20	-	8
Sweden	6	4-5	12	6-30	1-3	-	6	6-10	-	9
Switzerl.	6	-	-	64-89	-	13	2-3	-	50	35
U.K.	2	-	-	10-17	-	-	23-40	3	-	16
Mean	5	22	8	25	10	26	22	13	4	
Median	4	10/27	2/3	20	3/11	20	15	10	5	
Range	2-18	1-76	1-35	5-89	1-24	4-64	2-61	3-20	1-50	

Sources: Casas-Zamora 2002, pp. 324/325; Nassmacher 2001c/d, pp. 116, 138, 162; van Biezen 2000, pp. 334-335; Deschouwer 1992, p. 191; Ladner/ Brändle 2001, p. 180.
Member-to-voter (M/E) ratio for the late 1990s based on Mair/ van Biezen 2001, p. 9.

In the 1990s members' share of total party funds was some 30% for the *Greens* in Germany.[99] For the Austrian Greens and the French Ecologistes much less (1-3%) originated from this source. The only exception from this general picture is the Netherlands. Members of *GroenLinks*, i.e. the former Communist party (CPN), contributed 35% of the annual budget to the national party in 1995.[100]

In general, critics expect *conservative parties* to make their members pay smaller fees (or to neglect dues collection) and as a result to be unable to raise substantial revenue from this source. Two significant exceptions stand out. First, the Dutch CDA received 61% of its national income from membership dues in 1995.[101] Second, the Irish Fianna Fail claimed to have raised 51% of its (central) budget from party members in

---
99 Raschke 1993, p. 723; Smith 2005, p. 207.
100 Müller 1992, p. 112; Fromont 1992, p. 157; Knapp 2002, p. 127; Gidlund/ Koole 2001, p. 116.
101 Koole 1994a, p. 205; Gidlund/ Koole 2001, p. 116.

1990.[102] The Italian DC publicly reported ups and downs in membership dues as a percentage of its central income: 13% in 1974, 8% in 1977, 27% in 1981 and 6% in 1984.[103] For CDU and CSU in Germany, the members' share of total funds was 26-29% in 2006. In the 1990s the Austrian ÖVP collected 16-29% of its total resources from dues.[104] It may be interesting to note that most of these parties belong to the Christian Democratic party family, which is heir to the mass party tradition. The average dues of such parties (see Table 6-2 above) indicate that this family may deviate from the general pattern of conservative parties, which have a cadre party tradition.

Conservatives in Sweden (*Moderaterna*) introduced membership dues as late as 1965. The party was able to increase members' contributions towards the national party budget from about 6% at the end of the 1960s to about 10% in the early 1990s.[105] The National Coalition Party in Finland, which drew about one third of its national revenue from party members in the early 1970s, suffered a decline of this source to about 5% in the late 1980s.[106]

In the 1990s proceeds from membership dues added up to seven to 12% of total revenue for the RPR in France.[107] When these figures are compared to Spanish data, grass-roots funding for the Alianza Popular, now part of the PP, was high. In 1983 it claimed to raise 20% of the total budget from membership dues. However, in 1992 the share was much lower, 12% (including assessments of officeholders).[108] Since decades the British Conservatives transfer part of their local income to fund Central Office. The share of grass-roots support was 12% in the 1950s, 20% in the 1970s and 3% in 1997.[109] Major conservative parties in Japan (*Jimintô, Kômeitô*) used to solicit only 5-15% of their total revenue from membership dues. This generally small share decreased even further for both parties during the 1990s.[110]

At the beginning of the 1960s the Centerpartiet, the former *Farmers'* Party, in Sweden received about half of its income from members. However, in the early 1990s no more than 1% of this party's budget depended on membership fees. For its counterpart in Finland, the Centre Party, the decline was much more moderate from 2-3% to 1.5%.[111]

For the *Liberals* in Switzerland income from this source is not important. The smaller parties in Italy (PLI, PRI, PSDI) never established a membership base, on which they

---

102 Farrell 1992, p. 447.
103 Ciaurro 1989, p. 158.
104 Sickinger 1997, pp. 39, 245; Smith 2005, p. 96.
105 Pierre/ Widfeldt 1994, pp. 339, 346/347; Klee 1993b, p. 191; Gidlund/ Koole 2001, p. 117.
106 Wiberg 1991b, pp. 82/83, 92/93.
107 Schmitt 1993, p. 77; Fromont 1992, p. 157; Knapp 2002, p. 127.
108 del Castillo 1989, p. 192; van Biezen 2000, p. 334/335.
109 Pinto-Duschinsky 1981, p. 139; Neill report 1998, p. 31. For details see below in this chapter, sub-section D 1 (association quotas).
110 Blechinger/ Nassmacher 2001, p. 163.
111 Wiberg 1991c, pp. 82/83, 92/93; Pierre/ Widfeldt 1994, pp. 346-347; Gidlund/ Koole 2001, p. 117.

could rely financially. The Austrian FPÖ, turned populist in the 1980s, collects much less from membership dues than its major competitors: either 3 or 20% of its financial resources.[112] In 2005 23% of the total income for the German FDP was from this source. [113] In France the UDF (which contains a liberal wing) raised 3-6% of its national budget by dues in the 1990s. For the Liberal Democrats in Britain a higher proportion of income from membership fees was reported during the 1990s (23-40%).[114] Among the liberal parties, the largest share collected from dues is by the Dutch, VVD members contributed 55-61% of the annual funding, and D66 members almost 50%.[115]

Only a few, traditionally smaller parties (as measured by voting strength or parliamentary seats) on the left seem to still be able to tap their traditional source of funds, i.e. party members. Some parties even show an occasional increase in membership income since the 1970s. The other data (see Table 6-5), when taken with a necessary pinch of salt, indicate that mass parties still exist, although the significance of income from membership dues for their funding has declined.

In sum, the major finding from a comparison of parties with a similar background is that historical differences in the role of membership dues among party families have waned.[116] A convergence of funding patterns has occurred as the membership of workers' parties has declined and conservative parties have recruited more members. Moreover, parties of the same country seem to converge, which may be due to the impact of social change and political finance regimes.[117] Some parties have tried very hard to rid themselves of dependence on big donors, which is the reverse side of low membership income. Some parties made only few attempts and some did nothing at all. Self-sufficiency as a result of other income (like in Sweden and Austria) or reluctance can lead an individual party to such a course of action. In order to fill the gap in grass-roots revenue, caused by low or decreasing income from membership dues, some parties have felt forced to go for small donations.

2. Small donations

Comprehensive information on grass-roots funding is not available for any democracy. The present German reporting format (in operation since 2003) brings us rather close to the subject, because it details the total amounts of membership dues for each party and for three different tiers of its organisation. However, for small donations the information is very limited, especially because a specific category is missing and the legal

---

112 Sickinger 1997, pp. 41, 248; Smith 2005, p. 96.
113 *Deutscher Bundestag*, parliamentary paper, no. 16/8400.
114 The largest proportion of their central income is raised by direct mail, although the technique is in steady decline (Fisher 1995b, p. 13).
115 Gidlund/ Koole 2001, p. 116.
116 cf. Krouwel 1999, p. 78.
117 This hypothesis is elaborated by Nassmacher, H. 2004b, pp. 94-114. For the Dutch parties Koole (1999, p. 350) mentions de-pillarisation and subsidisation as intervening variables.

definition of "small" (= €3,300) is rather inadequate. A lower threshold would have been more appropriate. No other country gets even close to such comprehensive information. In all other democracies statutory reporting does not even reach down to grass-roots organisations.

All parties, which collect membership dues, solicit additional voluntary contributions from their members and donations from non-member citizens, especially at election times. Like many other parties the National Party of New Zealand "has maintained a very low membership fee, while also soliciting higher donations from those of its members who can afford to contribute."[118] However, like membership dues, extra-money for political parties does not spring up easily. The same people who are quite willing to pay for individual services, sports and entertainment, are not equally prepared to donate to support their democracy including political parties.[119] Scholars often refer to civic culture when explaining differences in donations to charities and/or politics.[120] Collecting large numbers of individual donations in small amounts requires a lot of effort by parties and candidates, issue groups or conveyor organisations. In the course of some 15 decades, parties in different countries have creatively developed strategies of solicitation and adapted them to the opportunities of modern technology.

A modern and efficient strategy to raise small donations, *direct mail*, was developed in the U.S. However, Canadian parties soon adopted it. This fact points towards the innovative potential of parties. Other fundraising techniques include the annual distribution of *lottery* tickets, which is still a good source of income for Swedish national parties,[121] and mass solicitation via *telethons*, which was used on behalf of U.S. national committees during the 1950s and 1960s. A more traditional method is *individual solicitation* by local grass-roots activists. Voluntary party workers contact friends and neighbours whom they know or expect to sympathize with the party and ask for a donation, mostly quite small.[122]

More generally, parties as voluntary organisations rely on unpaid activity for various aspects of their service to the public at large. When party activists provide time free of charge to party work, they make a donation-in-kind to politics. However, local activities in parties are seen as less attractive than other hobbies or recreation activities. Only a minority of all citizens are willing and able to contribute time (unpaid service) to party activity. The general assumption is that such contributions are in decline.

---

118 Vowles 2002, p. 418.
119 Even non-profit-organisations for religious, health and social purposes. face fund-raising problems. On average only one tenth of total income is collected from private donations (including corporate donations). However, this percentage scatters from 2 in Japan and 4 in Germany to 19 in the U.S. Individual donations in the U.S. and France were much higher than in Germany (Anheier et al. 1997, pp. 165, 167, 199-201).
120 E.g. de Hart/ Dekker 1999, p. 78.
121 Gidlund/ Koole 2001, p. 118.
122 Casas-Zamora 2002, p. 229 (on Uruguay); Smith 2005, p. 186; Sridharan 2006b, p. 324 (on India).

Within the British Labour party "there has been a significant growth in the proportion of members who do no work at all for the party in the average month."[123] Any attempt to estimate the cash equivalent of such personal services would be futile. Some employers tolerate the use of office equipment, e.g. business telephones or computers, for party activities. Owners of small businesses may even be able to provide contributions-in-kind (such as franking vouchers, use of cars, billboards, pickets, banners).[124] As we discuss minor donations these have to be mentioned, too, although their value can scarcely be estimated adequately.

Cash contributions by individuals are the most important source of income for U.S. federal parties, i.e. the Republican National Committee (RNC) and the Democratic National Committee (DNC), and their respective Senatorial and Congressional Committees.[125] There was a great motivation among activists at the constituency level to raise funds in small amounts. Republicans often had no small gifts division. Democrats, frequently with no access to business, combed areas where Dollars for Democrats programmes had carried on.[126] After campaign finance reform in the 1970s, direct mail efforts replaced other drives for funds in small sums, e.g. telethons and fundraising dinners.[127]

Due to the efforts initiated by Bill Brock (1977-80) for the RNC and Charles Manatt for the DNC, the direct mail approach brought a lot of individual contributions into party campaign chests. The three national Republican committees (RNC, NRCC and NRSC) increased their donor base from 200,000 (in 1975) to 2.85 million contributors (in 1984). By the late 1980s the Republicans expected 80 percent of their donors to contribute less than $100, while the Democrats expected two-thirds of their donations to be in amounts over $100.[128] "The Democratic committees never matched the Republicans' direct mail fundraising record, but by 1984 they, too, had successfully raised substantial sums in small contributions."[129]

The better educated and the affluent provide these funds. This behaviour gives contributing financially an elite character and confines the approach to a limited proportion (10 to 12 percent) of the electorate. Survey research provides less reliable data but supports the general impression: Between 1952 and 2004 the number of adults who claimed to make a political contribution ranged between 4 and 16 per cent, the long-term average was 8.7 per cent of all respondents. Those who are willing to donate give

---

123 Seyd/ Whiteley 2002, p. 88; this also applies to Canada (Carty 2002, p. 356).
124 Theis 2007, pp. 72-76.
125 By European standards the consolidation of thsse committees each could well be called the financial core of a U.S. federal party. For recent the share of small individual contributions see Magleby 2006, pp. 12-13.
126 Alexander 1963, p. 34; Alexander 1999, p. 32.
127 See below in this chapter, sub-section B3 (fundraising events).
128 Clark 1980, p. 1617; O'Shaughnessy/ Peele 1985, p. 115; Alexander/ Haggerty 1987, pp. 99-101.
129 Herrnson 1993a, p. 24; Herrnson 1993b, p. 9.

frequently and the vast majority give more than $100 a year.[130] Donations from individuals accounted for almost two-thirds of the funds raised for all Senate races and over one-half of those for House races in the 1996 elections. For the presidential race, donations by individuals are very important during the primary stage because they are matched by public funds up to a certain maximum.[131] Moreover this source of funding contributes 60 to 90 percent of fundraising totals.[132] As in previous years, the Republicans out-raised the Democrats in 1996. Both parties received their funds primarily from individuals and PACs.[133] While the Democrats got 77 percent of their revenue from individual donors, the Republicans collected 87 percent from this source.

The widespread use of the direct mailing technique[134] by candidates and political organisations in the 1990s should have considerably increased the percentage of those who donate to candidates and parties. However, the participation rate has not changed much. Alexander reports that according to public opinion polls "from 1952 to 1996 between four and 12 percent of the total adult population said that they contributed to politics at some level."[135] Higher amounts of political income result from the fact that individuals who donate money, on average are giving more nowadays. "The bulk of general donors are probably givers of small contributions, [but] ... the majority of money contributed comes from a small number of citizens who make many large donations."[136] Since the 1990s over-prospecting has become a problem as different sub-organisations of parties plus many other organisations went for small donations using the direct mail approach.[137] The 2004 campaign added a new channel of access to potential donors. E-mails distributed via the internet have successfully replaced "good old snail mail". By the end of 2003, presidential hopeful Howard Dean had raised $41 million, "much of it in small donations from grass-roots activists".[138]

Although most donors in Canada pay no dues, many citizens are financial supporters of parties and candidates. In 1990 more than 200,000 individuals donated to a federal (or local) party. In election years involvement is even higher. Almost two percent of registered voters contributed to a federal party or candidate in 1984 and 1988, during the 1990s participation declined to 1 percent of the electorate. The importance of individual donations has increased over the years. About 90 percent of all party revenue is raised from donations. Larger and more competitive riding associations are better

---

130 Jones/ Hopkins 1985, p. 441; Jones 1988, p. 4; Jones 1990, p. 27; Patterson 2006, p. 79.
131 See below in this chapter, sub-section C1 (energise fundraisers).
132 Alexander 1983, p. 149; Hrebenar et al. 1999, p. 155.
133 Biersack/ Haskell 1999, pp. 158/159. – For PACs see below in chapter VII, sub-section B1c (PACs).
134 See Römmele 2001, p. 242; Godwin 1988; Rieken 2002, passim.
135 Alexander 1999, p. 27; Alexander 1963, p. 22. Data refer to national surveys of the University of Michigan since 1980, conducted every two years, in congressional as well as in presidential years.
136 Francia et al. 1999, p. 129. See also Hrebenar et al. 1999, p. 156, table 6.6; Alexander 1999, p. 25.
137 Herrnson 1999, p. 13.
138 "Money's Going to Talk in 2008", in: *Washington Post*, 11 March 2006.

funded.[139] Initially it was particularly the grass-roots organisations of the New Democratic Party (N.D.P.), which attracted the highest number of contributions by canvassing individuals during the annual membership drives. The contributions that individuals made directly to the federal wing of the N.D.P. declined from 77 to 80 percent "of all contributions between 1975 and 1978 to 39.5 percent in 1984".[140] However, the Progressive Conservatives were able to tap more individual donors by the end of the 1970s and throughout the 1980s.[141] The P.C. Canada Fund began to use structured mailing lists (the "house list") and electronically produced personalised letters from party leaders to contact citizens and ask for a donation. Although most donors gave less than CAD 100, the P.C. were able to obtain significantly more money each year. "This strategy has carved out a new class of givers among the young professionals and the bureaucracy of corporate business. Within three years direct mail had more than tripled the number of contributors."[142]

Within two decades (1978 to 1997) the P.C. experienced dramatic ups and downs in its political fortunes, which affected the overall income heavily.[143] The share of individual contributions peaked in 1983 (at almost two thirds of total income). Afterwards it stayed relatively stable at 50 to 60 percent for non-election years and about 40 percent for election years. Propensity to donate was strong during the early years of Mulroney's leadership and declined when he and his policies became unpopular.[144] This defection of donors still had an impact during the 1997 campaign. Fundraising potential deteriorated so much that the P.C. was unable to meet pre-campaign targets and ended up with a post-election debt of CAD 6 million.[145]

The N.D.P. depends on individual contributions for 70 to 80 percent of its federal income in non-election years, for about 60 percent in election years. Corresponding figures for the Liberals indicate that individuals provide 40 to 50 percent in non-election years and 25 to 35 percent in election years. The Liberals as the "natural governing party" felt little need to change the method of fundraising.[146] Their weakness in soliciting money from a large number of contributors was compensated by the larger size of individual contributions. "The contrast in the ... pattern in obtaining money from individuals can easily be seen in the ... average number of contributions from individuals in four-year intervals."[147] The Liberals more than doubled the number of individual donors from 14,200 in the mid-1970s to 29,800 in the early 1980s. The N.D.P. almost doubled their contributor base from 50,800 (1974-77) to 96,500 (1986-89). The

---

139 Stanbury 1993b, pp. 82/83; Sayers 1999, p. 6; Carty 2002, pp. 356/357; Smith 2005, p. 90.
140 Stanbury 1986, p. 803.
141 Rieken 2002, p. 88; Smith 2005, p. 185.
142 Paltiel 1989, p.70.
143 Smith 2005, p. 90.
144 Nassmacher 1992a, p. 90; Rieken 1993, p. 8/9.
145 Woolstencroft 1997, p. 88.
146 Stanbury 1993b, p. 80.
147 Stanbury 1993b, p. 82. For average size of contributions 1974 to 1990 see ibid., p. 85. – cf. Carty 1996b, p. 21; Smith 2005, p. 185/186.

number of P.C. donors peaked at an annual average of 80,100 in the early 1980s, but levelled-off to 46,500 in the late 1980s. The Reform Party, established in November 1987, finally merged with the P.C. to form the Conservative Party of Canada (CPC) in late 2003. At first the party depended very much on funds from its members, much more so than the three other parties.[148]

For many countries information on the total revenue share of (small and large) donations is scarce. In Australia small donations in any form do not appear in the public reports previously prepared by parties. In the Netherlands money to parties is donated mostly during campaign times. However, there are no precise figures (only the indication of other income).[149] In Austria no information on small donations is available, but they are not expected to be an important source of funds for any party.[150] In France donations (large and small) from individuals accounted for four to six percent of all parties' income during the late 1990s.[151] In 1992 (obviously small) donations from citizens supplied 12 percent of the revenue of French parties. This share dropped to six percent in 1996 and just three percent in 2002.[152] For the U.K and Germany more information is available but the situation is far from clear-cut.

In Britain members of the local Conservative associations contribute more than their regular subscriptions.[153] Both major parties have tried to become more independent of traditional sources of funds, especially institutional donations from interested money.[154] Since the mid 1980s both parties have started direct mail efforts. However, "direct mail fund-raising was still relatively undeveloped ... The profits of direct mail seem to have accounted for no more than 5 percent of the [Conservative] party's central income in the election year 1987-1988," less than the share raised by the Social Democratic Party's effort.[155]

In 1993 the Conservatives started a new effort to solicit donations, but Labour was more active this time. However, Labour was less successful in this activity than the Conservatives and the SDP. As Labour became more active in 'cultivating' its membership, the Conservatives targeted mainly wealthy financial backers.[156] In 1997 money from subscriptions and small donations accounted for 40 percent of the total income of the Labour party.[157] Thanks to modern fund-raising techniques (including direct mail and a fundraising credit card for members) the Conservatives brought about a re-

---

148 Stanbury 1996, p. 83.
149 Koole 1997, pp. 156-182.
150 Sickinger 1997, pp. 41-45; see also Smith 2005, p. 89.
151 Doublet1997, p. 73.
152 Doublet 2003, p. 12.
153 Details in: Whiteley/ Seyd/ Richardson 1994, p. 76; cf. Johnston/ Pattie 1993, pp. 136, 139, 140; Scarrow 1996, p. 104.
154 For details see below, chapter VII, sub-sections B 1 a (collective membership), B2a (fat cat contributions) and B3 (corporate contributions).
155 Pinto-Duschinsky 1994, p. 15.
156 Scarrow 1996, pp. 104, 123; Pinto-Duschinsky 1994, p. 16.
157 Koole 2001, p. 78.

emergence of individual donations. However, among these contributions, large donations from abroad were most important.[158]

Contributions from individual members (dues as well as donations, e.g. from fundraising activities) for the Labour party declined in the 1990s: "the medium amount dropped from £42 in 1992 to £28 in 1999. In other words in 1999 the average member gave about two-thirds of the amount he or she gave to the party in 1992."[159] The number of members who gave less than £20 more than doubled during this period. Party income from small donations is not quite clear for the Liberals as well as for their Alliance partner, the SDP.[160]

More recent data indicate that the role of small contributions in the U.K. is still small. In 2003-05 British parties raised almost GBP 58 million in donations. Parties solicited a total of less than GBP 8 million in amounts of less than GBP 5,000, and some GBP 4 million in amounts between GBP 5,000 and 10,000, some GBP 10 million in donations of GBP 10,000 to 50,000 and the breath-taking total of GBP 56 million in amounts of over GBP 50,000.[161] Despite many changes the small donor has by no means become the dominant player in British party funding.

Recently parties in Germany have begun to target direct mail at their centralised electronic membership registers. This has resulted in some additional income for federal and state party headquarters from individual donations. Not all donated income originates from grass-roots financing, which is limited to membership dues and small donations. 85 to 90 percent of all private political contributions are raised from individuals. However, this does not indicate a dominant role of small contributions. In the 1990s the two major parties professionalised their fundraising efforts via direct mail.[162] Unfortunately the legal threshold for separate reporting has been set at DEM 6,000 per donor per year, an amount which includes small as well as medium size contributions. Moreover the category includes membership fees, legislators' assessments and individual donations. Thus the relative weight of *small* donations among such contributions cannot be established.[163] Nevertheless two reasonable assumptions emerge. First, large donations are no longer important and the bulk of funds raised in (medium and small) donations ends up in local party coffers. Second, more than 95 percent of all individual contributions up to DEM 6,000, i.e. US $ 3,000, per person per year (which are solicited as donations, assessments or membership fees) are collected by the six (major) parties represented in the federal parliament.

In Norway the centralisation of computerised membership registration has enabled all major parties to address members via direct mail and thus to by-pass local and regional party units in a quest for additional contributions from the party membership.[164]

---

158 Fisher 1996b, p. 159.
159 Seyd/ Whiteley 2002, p. 87.
160 Pinto-Duschinsky 1994, pp. 18-20.
161 Electoral Commission 2004, paras. 5.51-5.53.
162 Rieken 2002, pp. 98-102.
163 Römmele 1999, pp. 191/192, 195; Smith 2005, p. 183.
164 Svasand 1994, p. 305.

Parties raise a specific form of very stable, most reliable grass-roots financing in Scandinavia by means of lotteries. This is also an expansive form of voluntary membership financing.[165] Especially Social Democrats in Sweden are successful in this respect. The agent acting on their behalf is a licensed public benefit organisation ("*A-lotteriet*"), which is jointly owned by the party/ SAP and its youth wing.[166] In 1986 they raised SEK 11.8 million from the proceeds of lotteries, in 1992 SEK 39.5 million, and in 1997 SEK 54.4 million, which accounted for 38 percent of the national party headquarters' total income.[167] This sort of income is also common in Norway and with Social Democrats in Finland.[168] In many countries parties obtain additional funds from various social activities such as events and festivals.

3. *Fundraising events (social activities)*

Since the 19th century, Anglo-Saxon democracies have used and developed a fundraising strategy, which benefits from the fact that a "party" is a place where people get together. Political parties organise social events in order to solicit contributions. "While a typical fund-raising event may still be the garden-variety round-up at a local club, some hold glitzy fund raisers aimed at garnering large contributions from members of elite groups and industries."[169] The formal approach to this kind of activity is selling tickets to a fundraising dinner. Procedure and price can be easily adapted to suit individual and local requirements. Usually the organiser offers two inducements, the presence of a significant political figure and a meal. People pay for the event on the tacit understanding that the commercial value offered is less than the price charged. "Buying a dinner ticket is both a purchase of food and a political contribution".[170] If such contributions do not exceed the amount, which an average citizen can afford, the event is a strategy of grass-roots funding. "Costs in promoting and staging the event may run an average of 10 to 20 percent".[171] A range of five to 25 percent of the gross amount will certainly cover all the out-of-pocket costs of any such dinner. During the 1950s proceeds from fundraising dinners "accounted for one-third of the total income of (U.S.) state party committees through the four year election cycle".[172] In 1968 a minimum of $ 43.1 million, i.e. almost one sixth of total spending "could be accounted for as receipts at political fund-raising events ... for candidates and committees at all levels".[173]

---

165 Gidlund 1991a, p. 44.
166 „Gierige Sozialministerin", in: *Frankfurter Allgemeine*, 9 August 2004; for details of the legal situation see www.lotteriinsp.se („The Swedish gambling market").
167 Gidlund 1991b, p. 44; Klee 1993b, p. 192; Gidlund/ Koole 2001, p. 118.
168 Svasand 1994, p. 324; Pesonen 1987, p. 11.
169 Alexander 1992a, p. 54.
170 Heard 1960, p. 237; see also Smith 2005, pp. 186-188.
171 Alexander 1971, p.189.
172 Heard 1960, p. 234; cf. ibid., pp. 238, 242.
173 Alexander 1971, pp.188/189.

Depending on the price of the ticket, the term fundraising dinner marks a broad variety of small and large contributions. For the 1950s Heard mentions a range between $ 5 and $ 2,500 per plate.[174] As a rule of thumb, the dinner is more likely to aim at grass-roots contributions if it is organised by the lower level of a political organisation, e.g. a constituency association or a local candidate. The higher the rank of the organiser or the guest of honour the more expensive the ticket and the more selective the group of potential donors that will be recruited. Demarcation between grass-roots and plutocratic funding will never be precise. Tickets sold at $100 may still indicate dedication to the cause rather than influence peddling. Demanding $500 for a chicken dinner most likely represents the opposite.[175]

In Ireland party headquarters traditionally try to persuade local activists to pursue small donations. However, sometimes the money solicited by means of a dinner must be categorised as large contributions, because only rich people are able to pay for the tickets.[176] In Germany fundraising dinners "only began to appear … in the late 1990s." However, the concept of "merchandising" seems to be more important for national headquarters of CDU and SPD.[177] In Italy and France additional income is raised from festivals, rallies, meetings and other events. In Australia fundraising efforts seek larger donations.[178]

In other countries local party organisations co-ordinate a variety of revenue-yielding events with less formality (and less cost to the organising party as well as the supporting participant) than the fundraising dinner. Such profit-generating entertainment includes teas, luncheons, breakfasts, cocktail parties, cash bars, picnics, yard or jumble sales and bazaars.[179] Low-priced social events raise rather modest sums. The "burden of patronising as well as arranging these affairs falls on the party faithful."[180] This type of activity keeps the organisation going, by providing opportunities for social interaction and helping to fill party coffers, a true strategy of grass-roots funding.

Heard reports different kinds of social gatherings among the constituency parties of Labour and the Conservatives in the U.K., as well as for urban political organisations in the U.S.[181] In his study of Canadian riding associations Carty found that Liberals and P.C., especially local parties with an incumbent MP, ranked social events as their most important fundraising activity.[182] For the 1980s there is some information about small amounts raised by local (constituency) party activities.[183] In 1974 political finance legislation introduced public incentives to stimulate popular fundraising.

---

174 Heard 1960, p. 235.
175 For details see below, chapter VII, sub-section B3 (corporate contributions).
176 Kelly 1992, pp. 262, 266, 267.
177 Smith 2005, pp. 184, 190 (quote on p. 184).
178 Young/ Tham 2007, p. 19.
179 Houghton report 1976, p. 35.
180 Heard 1960, p. 246, cf. ibid., p. 233.
181 Heard 1960, p. 245.
182 Carty 1991, pp. 85-87.
183 Smith 2005, p. 92 for German, Nassmacher/ Suckow 1992, p. 141, for Canadian parties.

C) Public incentives (for small political contributions)

Whenever carefully designed legislation was passed on the subject of political finance, it aimed to redress the imbalance between the principle of political equality in a democracy and the consequences of social and economic inequalities of modern capitalist societies.[184] As far as such regulation concerns private funds for political purposes, this intention may be pursued by encouraging small contributions or by discouraging large donations.[185] Public incentives to promote small contributions can target either potential donors or political fundraisers.

1. Energising fundraisers (matching funds)

In order to provide an incentive for candidates, campaign workers, party activists and political fundraisers, public funds can be distributed in addition to private funds after a party or candidate has solicited donations of a certain number and size (matching funds). The public programme needs to establish a match-able maximum (e.g. $ 250), the matching rate (e.g. 2:1) and a maximum amount for the public grant. In addition to a minimum number of donors a well-designed matching funds program may "treat in-district and out-of-district contributions differently, reward very small donations much more generously than larger donations, …".[186] This should be able to fend off "fat cat" favourites as well as self-financers.

The best known application of the matching principle is the primary stage of U.S. presidential elections and gubernatorial contests in some U.S. states.[187] Candidates for the Democratic or the Republican presidential nomination are entitled to matching funds provided their fundraisers have been able to collect no less than a total of $5,000 in contributions up to $250 from a minimum of 20 states.[188] Although foreign observers are still impressed by the principle, an informed observer recently concluded that in U.S. presidential contests "accepting matching funds is a thing of the past."[189] Still, experience at the state level may deviate from such harsh conclusion. The threshold for matchable donations differs widely between U.S. states, some of which use the matching principle, too. The matching rate varies between 2:1, 1:1 and 1:2, which means that a $100 donation can be matched by $50, $100 or $200.

The public reimbursement to parliamentary candidates (federal and provincial) in Canada has a similar impact. If contestants qualify for state aid, their campaign workers will have to raise exactly half of the total campaign outlay from corporate or indi-

---

184 Cf. Paltiel 1981, p. 138.
185 See below in chapter VII, sub-section B4 (public disincentives).
186 Steen 2006, p. 157.
187 Düselder 1992, pp. 108-113.
188 Wawzik 1991, pp.47/48; Alexander/ Corrado 1995, p. 18.
189 Steve Elmendorf, as reported in: "Money's Going to Talk in 2008", in: *Washington Post*, 11 March 2006.

vidual donors, small and large. There is no emphasis on small contributions, but a minimum of private funds has to be raised before a public subsidy can be claimed.[190]

Other attempts to operate the matching principle do not energise fundraising activity at the grass-roots. Matching funds in the Netherlands (until 1998) compelled parties (not individuals) to provide an adequate funding to their affiliated party foundations.[191] In Japan legislation was extremely short-lived (1994-95). In France the matching grant is not aimed at all competitors but rather a "consolation prize" for those who are not eligible for a general subsidy. In Germany national party headquarters alone will collect the matching benefit for all fundraising including that of local party chapters.[192] Only U.S. matching programmes encourage political competitors to seek small donations within the specific limit set by the applicable regulation.[193] As a result, matching funds have redirected fund-raising efforts to the broad mass of affluent, middle class citizens, a group of people who can afford to pay for their democracy. Tax incentives are aimed at these citizens more directly.

2. Stimulating contributors (tax add-on, tax deduction, and tax credit)

Traditionally states have not actively interfered in the relationship between potential donors and political "bagmen" who solicit funds for parties, candidates or causes. Whereas the donors appreciated privacy, most fundraisers could limit their contacting efforts to only a happy few. When democracies grow more and more aware of the hazards built into this clandestine operation (plutocratic influence, corrupt exchanges),[194] the need for mass contributions to fund sustainable democracy has become self evident. However, this has to be supported by tax incentives. "Voluntary funding [left on its own] simply does not generate sufficient income for modern political parties." The major reason for this is that "parties cannot enhance their income via good performance."[195] As in other areas where private activity is necessary to serve the public interest, tax legislation was used to stimulate mass behaviour. In order to encourage political contributions some democracies created a variety of tax measures, which offer a reward for good citizenship.[196]

In a global sample of 104 large and small, established and emerging democracies, only 19 provide some sort of tax relief for political donations, and 14 offer an income tax relief.[197] Among the 25 democracies studied in detail here about half do not provide

---

190 For details see below in chapter VIII, sub-sections B2 (reimbursements) and C1 (recipients, candidates).
191 Lucardie/ Voerman 2001, pp. 323, 333, 336.
192 For details see below in chapter VIII, sub-section D2a (allocation of matching funds).
193 Nassmacher 1992a, pp. 166/167; Nassmacher 1994, pp. 152/153.
194 For details see below in chapter VII, A (moral hazard).
195 Fisher 2002, p. 396 (quotes by inverse order).
196 Alexander 1961, p. 10.
197 Pinto-Duschinsky 2002, p.75; Pinto-Duschinsky 2001b, pp. 20-21; this includes 4 of 41 Commonwealth countries, Pinto-Duschinsky 2001a, p. 10.

any tax benefit for private donations to political parties.[198] Such instruments are expected to encourage party activists, candidates and incumbents to pursue small donations and thus make sure that political revenue is grass-roots supported. Because the benefit goes to the donor the individual citizen is the major target of public incentives. When (West) Germany in 1954 and the U.S. state of Minnesota in 1955 started to introduce tax benefits for political donations, they were miles apart from each other.[199] The Minnesota programme targeted small contributions, whereas the German legislation aimed at large amounts. Today German tax benefits are targeted at medium sized contributions, and the U.S. (federally and in most states) seems to be through with tax incentives for political donations. Previous federal tax benefits available to U.S. citizens were abolished as part of the Reagan tax cut package in 1986.

In order to avoid an incentive for extremely large donations from "interested money" tax benefit programmes should be restricted to individuals and stipulate a maximum amount. A regulation, which in addition to specifying a maximum amount also sets a minimum, tends to encourage donations by the well-off strata of wage earners and thus medium-sized political contributions. If the intention of political finance reformers is to reduce the influence of special interests [200] and to go for "big money in little sums", this type of regulation will be supplemented or replaced by incentives for small contributions. In general, tax incentives to stimulate political donations fall into three different categories: a tax add-on offers an easy procedure to make political contributions, a tax deduction reduces taxable income, and a tax-credit can to be claimed against tax.

The *tax add-on* gives taxpayers an opportunity to increase their tax liability by a small amount, which is then distributed among political parties or candidates. This programme uses the tax collection process as an additional path to solicit minuscule amounts for political purposes. In some U.S. states (e.g. Massachusetts, Virginia) this programme was an alternative to the limited distribution of general revenue funds via the tax check-off.[201] However, as people do not like to pay taxes, only few citizens choose to pay an extra tax to fund the political process voluntarily.[202] The participation rate is extremely low. Political contributions cannot be collected by public authorities.

A programme that aims at donations of considerable size is the *tax deduction*. Political contributions up to an amount specified in the tax law can be deducted from taxable income. As a consequence, the tax benefit for the donor (individual and/or corpora-

---

198 Details given by LeDuc/ Niemi/ Norris 1996, pp. 38-41 and Casas-Zamora 2002, pp. 39/40; Casas-Zamora 2005a, pp. 30/31).
199 Heard 1960, p. 445.
200 Boatright/ Malbin 2003, p. 2.
201 Whereas tax benefits and tax add-on are incentives for private donations to political purposes, the *tax check-off* mechanism uses the tax form as a "ballot" to legitimise public subsidies. For details see Alexander 1992a, pp. 100-102 and below in chapter VIII, sub-section A3 (means to increase the legitimacy).
202 Noragon 1981, p. 672; Nassmacher/ Wawzik 1992, pp. 43-45, 52, 158.

tion) will depend on the specific tax rate applicable for the specific taxpayer. Any income tax system that is not based on a flat tax rate will favour "fat cats" (large donations, high income, high tax rate) over "small guys" (small donations, low income, low tax rate). If the policy intention is to stimulate political contributions in small amounts, this will be counterproductive.

A more sophisticated programme of tax incentives takes care of the imbalance, the *tax credit*. Technically a specific percentage of a properly receipted political donation will reduce the tax liability, i.e. the political contribution will be considered as a (partial) advance payment on personal income tax.[203]

In the U.S. the federal tax credit is widely regarded as a failure. The participation rate was about five percent and the average benefit for a taxpayer was $50, too little to have much effect on the willingness of citizens to provide donations. Nevertheless, the U.S. treasury lost some $260 to $270 million in federal revenue on tax benefits for political donations annually.[204] Today only individual states (Arizona, Arkansas, Ohio, Oregon and Virginia) operate tax credit programmes. In Ohio contributions of $50 to state candidates are entitled to a hundred percent tax credit since 1995. This programme is potentially an important step towards expansion of the donor pool and change in the type of donors. If people knew more about the programme, they would contribute more. However, it takes a long time for citizens to use the tax credit effectively.[205]

For many countries detailed information is not available. In Switzerland nine states (*Kantone*), but not the federation, offer political donors the opportunity to deduct the amount of a contribution up to a legal maximum. This indirect support, however, is to be terminated due to an objection by the federal revenue service.[206] The majority of tax benefit programmes exclude corporate donors and favour individual taxpayers only. In Australia individual contributions made to registered political parties, including membership fees, up to AUD100 (€65)[207] per fiscal year may be claimed as an income tax deduction.[208] Pedersen and Bille report that membership dues are fully tax deductible in Denmark since 1954.[209] In France only contributions by individuals given to parliamentary and presidential candidates or parties (including membership fees) are deductible since 1995. The maximum contribution is FRF 30,000 (€4,573) to

---

203 For a systematic evaluation of the two major types of tax benefits (tax deduction and tax credit) see Alexander 1961, pp. 11-23 and Pappin 1976, pp. 299-301.
204 Adamany 1978, p. 4: Nassmacher/ Lemke 1992, p. 78; Alexander 1992a, pp. 30/31.
205 Boatright/ Malbin 2003, pp. 5, 9, 22.
206 Weigelt 1988, pp. 40-42, 180; Drysch 1998, p. 84; Ladner/ Brändle 1999, pp. 29/30.
207 As about half of the countries, which can be studied in depth, has introduced the single European currency we will give figures for cross-national comparison in € amounts. For purposes of general orientation all € amounts can be read as equivalents of US-$ figures. For the period 1999-2003 the parity between both currencies has ranged between 0.85 and 1.15, on average at 1:1.
208 www.ato.gov.au (08-03-04).
209 Pedersen/ Bille 1991, p. 154. Exactly the opposite is stated by Vesterdorf 1992, p. 69; Schefold 1996, p. 12; Casas-Zamora 2002, p. 39 and Casas-Zamora 2005a, p. 30.

a candidate and FRF 50,000 (€7,622) to a political party. The maximum tax relief is 40 percent of the donation, or up to five percent of taxable income.[210] An informed observer assumes that two thirds of all political contributions by individuals are tax deductible.[211]

Between 1985 and 1989 donors in Belgium were entitled to deduct up to BEF 2 million (€50,000) per party per year.[212] In 1989 the maximum was lowered to BEF 350,000 (€8,700), if the political donation is made to a non-profit organisation, which has been specifically designated by an eligible party.[213] As part of the 1994 political finance reform package, Japan introduced tax benefits for individual political contributions. Money may be contributed to a political party, a fundraising group or a support group (kôenkai).[214] In order to qualify for a tax benefit, the total amount per year has to exceed JPY 10,000 (€80), and the contribution has to be included in a report presented under disclosure provisions. The taxpayer may choose between a tax deduction (not exceeding 25 percent of his or her total income) and a tax credit of 30 percent.[215]

Current tax legislation in Germany limits tax benefits to individual contributions (including membership fees).[216] Donors receive a 50 percent tax credit (of up to €825) for a political contribution up to €1,650 per year per taxpayer. Another €1,650 per year per taxpayer for any donation in excess of the first €1,650 can be deducted from taxable income. The maximum contribution eligible for tax benefits is fixed at € 3,300 per year per individual donor. (Since 1992, following a supreme court ruling, no tax benefits are available for corporate donations). If an individual contributes €2,400 per calendar year either as membership fee, donation or assessment on his or her political income (Sonderbeitrag, Parteisteuer)[217] or any combination of these, the amount of the tax benefit will depend primarily on the marital status of the taxpayer. When filing a joint tax return, a contribution of € 2,400 earns a couple a tax credit of € 1,200 (the amount being considered as an advance payment on the final income tax due). If the contributor is single (and taxed accordingly), a party contribution of € 2,400 earns him/her a €825 income tax credit for the first €1,650 of the contribution (only donations to a party are eligible, not to a candidate or a caucus or any ancillary group). The rest of €750 (i.e. €2,400 minus €1,650) is available for a tax deduction. This amount is deducted from taxable income as established annually by the Internal Revenue Service (Finanzamt), and the income tax saved by the surplus contribution then depends

---

210 Fromont 1992, p. 166; Miguet 1999, p. 58; Doublet 1999, p. 70.
211 Information by Yves-Marie Doublet, Assembleé Nationale.
212 Schefold 1996, p. 12.
213 Suetens 1992, pp. 33/34.
214 Until January 2000 donations to an individual candidate were eligible for a tax benefit, too.
215 Levush 1997, p. 142.
216 The country has made various attempts to regulate the issue. Precedents applied 1920-21, 1955-58 and 1967-83. Since 1967 there are tax incentives for small donations (and membership dues). The current rules were created in 1984/88.
217 See below in chapter VII, sub-section B2 (assessment of officeholders).

on the personal tax rate applicable, e.g. 10 or 30 percent. There is no information about participation rates in Germany. However, a local case study found that in 1987 only seven percent of all taxpayers claimed a tax benefit.[218]

In no more than three countries tax benefits reach out to corporations and individuals alike: the Netherlands, Italy and Canada. In the Netherlands both individuals and corporate donations are tax deductible. Individuals may claim a tax benefit for donations in excess of NFL 120 (€55) and one percent of the individual's gross annual income. The maximum deduction is ten percent of the gross annual income. Membership fees are considered donations in fiscal terms. Corporations can deduct donations if they add up to more than NFL 500 (€227) per year and the maximum deduction is six percent of the annual profit made by the corporation.[219] However, as has been mentioned already,[220] this did not lead to a lot of fundraising activity. Any Italian individual or corporation may claim a 22 percent income tax benefit for a political donation between LIT 0.5 and 50 million (€258 to 25,826).[221]

The most sophisticated tax benefit for political contributions (by individual and corporate donors alike) is offered in Canada. Here, regulations calculate the (federal) tax credit [222] as follows:

- 75 percent of amounts contributed up to $400,
- 50 percent of amounts donated between $400 and $750,
- 33.3 percent of amounts exceeding $750, up to a total of $1,275 (€850).[223]

The maximum tax credit is $650 (the total of $300, $175 and $ 175), which can be claimed for a donation totalling $1,275 per year. (After an individual is nominated, the candidate's agent may issue receipts for tax credits. Registered parties, their provincial divisions and registered associations may issue receipts continuously.) In the 1980s the average amount of a federal tax credit claimed was $85, and the value of tax credits was equal to about 30 percent of the total income of federal parties[224] and no less than half of the government's total contribution to parties and candidates.[225]

Federal and provincial tax credits for political donations in Canada and the legal provisions for issuing tax receipts have supported efforts to collect small donations from individual citizens and small businesses. During the 1980s there was a steady increase

---

218 Brunken-Bahr 1990, p. 48-55.
219 Elzinga 1992, pp. 359, 361.
220 See above in this chapter, sub-section B1b (revenue from membership dues).
221 Melchionda 1997, p. 206; Newell 2000, p. 80.
222 In addition to the federal programme all Canadian provinces operate their own tax credits. The combination of both programmes increases the maximum tax credit, which is available to the individual taxpayer.
223 Subsection 127 (3) Income Tax Act (Compendium of Election Administration in Canada 2003, p. G81; www.elections.ca/loi/com2003).
224 Michaud/ Lafferiere 1991, p. 372.
225 Nassmacher 1989c, pp. 239-241; Stanbury 1993b, p. 87.

in use of this benefit, more by individuals than corporations. The number of individual donors soared and so did the average annual contribution from individuals.[226] "Big money in little sums"[227] for the Canadian parties became a political reality due to an innovative combination of public regulation and organisational effort. However, the portion of tax filers who actually claim the tax credit for political contributions is rising slowly.[228]

A comparison of the tax benefits offered by various democracies indicates that the Canadian tax credit has had and still has the most striking impact on fundraising practices in any democracy.[229] This is certainly not a surprising result for the best designed programme of public incentives. Quite a different approach to public impact on political donations is the idea to legislate disincentives for large contributions, which basically aim in the same direction. However, such programmes prefer to use a stick, rather than a carrot. Most countries have stayed aloof of tax benefits and restricted their legislative activity to discouraging "fat cat" donations.[230]

Using the instruments of specific incentives (e.g. tax benefits for donors) parties have to target affluent segments of society. This might provide an advantage for conservative or bourgeois parties. Is this unfair for their more progressive competitors, the left-of-centre parties? A question of fairness may not only arise for different parties but also among different elements of the same party. Therefore another topic related to grass-roots funding is the distribution of fundraising proceeds among different subsystems (sections, chapters or tiers) of a party.

D) Intra-party transfers

Mass membership parties traditionally maintain their national headquarters with funds collected at the grass-roots level and funnelled upwards within the party structure. In his sample of 42 parties in Western democracies, Janda found that during the 1950s 18 parties collected more than two-thirds of their total income „from party sources, including membership dues and income from party enterprises."[231] Roughly the same number of parties (19) combined decentralised fundraising with internal transfers to meet the headquarters' financial needs: „Funds are collected primarily on the local level but large amounts are transmitted upward for distribution by either the regional (state) or national organisations."[232] Certainly a lot of change has taken place since the 1950s. Due to public subsidies, the relevance of grass-roots funding for the mainte-

---

226 Nassmacher/ Lemke 1992, pp. 85-94.
227 Heard 1960. p. 249.
228 For details see Nassmacher/ Lemke 1992, p. 91; Boatright/Malbin 2003.
229 See above in this chapter, sub-section B2 (small donations).
230 See below in chapter VII, sub-section B 5 (public disincentives).
231 Janda 1980, p. 92; Janda 1979, p. 149.
232 Janda 1980, p. 112; Janda 1979, p. 190.

nance of party headquarters has decreased recently.[233] Nevertheless parties combining funding from membership dues with upward intra-party transfers can be easily identified as representing the mass membership party model, which was initiated by the 19th century working class parties. However, some parties, which were characterised as cadre parties, have tried to steer their organisation in this direction, as can be seen in the case of the British Conservatives. In addition, there are other kinds of intra-party transfers.

1. Association quotas

In Britain there is no membership of the national Conservative party. A modest number of members are spread out over the constituencies.[234] In the early 1990s there was an average of 1,200 members in a local association.[235] By and from these members some funds are raised and funnelled upwards to support the national organisation, which mainly depends on central fundraising. After Labour's election victory in 1945, the Conservative party implemented various measures to reverse its traditional pattern of top-down financing. Among the reforms emerging from the Maxwell-Fyfe committee was a (voluntary) quota for constituency associations.[236] "Local parties together were asked to pay £100,000 a year towards the upkeep of the party headquarters." In the early 1950s the quota supplied 16 to 21 percent of total income in non-election years for the Conservative Central Office, the party headquarters. The revenue share of constituency quotas peaked at more than 30 percent in 1966/67 and 1975/76 (see Table 6-6 below). Annual averages between 17 and 26 percent in non-election years indicate an important source of funding. Due to higher revenue totals in election years Conservative associations contributed a much lower share to Central Office income than in non-election years (8-16 percent). However, from the mid-1970s on transfers to the top level declined steadily. During the 1974-79 electoral cycle, constituency quotas provided 20 percent, in 1979-83 no more than 17 percent, and in 1983-87 barely 12 percent of Central Office's funds.[237] In more recent years, the party has neglected this option of grass-roots funding and has lost much of its potential. In 1992-97 the party headquarters received less than five percent of its total annual income from constituency quotas.[238]

"Every constituency association is assigned a ... 'target quota', which it is expected to send" to Central Office. In 1991-92, constituencies "contributed £ 1.3 million towards the ... total quota of £ 2.4 million," which is roughly half of the target.[239] In the 1980s

---

233 See below in chapter VIII, sub-section E1 (party revenue).
234 Webb 1994, p. 113; Becker 1999, p. 62.
235 Whiteley/ Seyd/ Richardson 1994, p. 24.
236 Gwyn 1962, p. 245; McKenzie 1963, pp. 653/654.
237 Pinto-Duschinsky 1981, pp. 130, 138 (quote on p. 130); Pinto-Duschinsky 1994, p. 15.
238 Neill report 1998, p. 31. There is no correlation between the number of members and the amount of money transferred to Conservative Central Office (Smith 1992, p. 240).
239 Whiteley/ Seyd/ Richardson 1994, pp. 26, 27.

the Maxwell-Fyfe initiative to establish association quotas as a reliable source of funding for Conservative Central Office fell victim to neglect. The long-term failure of a sensible reform effort may be caused by declining party income at the local level. In 1992 a cross-party sample of constituency associations averaged about £29,873, in 1997 about £20,267. This change is due to the substantial decrease of local income of the Conservative Party, for which local party funds have always been relatively important. The total income of a Conservative constituency association declined from an average of £44,304 to an average of £ 33,305 in the 1990s.[240]

There is, however, considerable variation in the amount, which the constituencies contribute to Central Office. Associations, which hold seats, return larger sums. The decline started in the early 1980s and with the lack of funds local associations lost importance. This took place despite an incentive programme to increase the quotas contributed by each constituency, which the Conservative Central Office had developed.[241] Nevertheless local Conservative income is still considerably higher than the average income of a local Labour Party.

Table 6-6: *Association quotas as a source of national party revenue; the case of the U.K. Conservatives (1950-1997) – in percent of total*

Year	share %	year	share %	Year	share %
1950	8.9	1965-66	n.a.	1984/85	22.7
1951	10.7	1967/68	32.9	1985/86	20.0
1952	18.1	1968/69	31.5	1986/87	13.3
1953	19.1	1969/70	28.6	**1987/88**	8.3
1954	20.8	1970/71	16.2	1988/89	13.8
1955	10.8	1971/72	27.4	1989/90	13.2
1956	21.2	1972/73	22.3	1990/91	9.1
1957	17.5	**1973/74**	13.3	1991/92	7.5
1958	16.0	**1974/75**	18.4	**1992**	5.6
1959	10.8	1975/76	30.4	1993	9.4
1960	27.5	1976/77	28.0	1994	5.0
1961	20.8	1977/78	23.7	1995	5.8
1962	19.6	1978/79	22.9	1996	3.7
1963	13.0	**1979/80**	17.1	**1997**	2.6
1964	8.1	1980-83	n.a.	1998	n.a.

Sources: Pinto-Duschinsky 1981, p. 138 (1950-80); Cahill et al. 1993, p. 42; Neill report 1998, p. 31.
Comment: Election years in **bold face type**.

---

[240] Cf. Houghton report 1976, pp. 178/179; Pinto-Duschinsky 1981, pp. 150, 154; Neill report 1998, p. 40.
[241] Pattie/ Johnston 1996, pp. 926-932; Fisher 1996b, pp. 161/162.

Another conservative party, the Austrian ÖVP, operates a different transfer system. This party is composed of three major and three minor sub-organisations (called leagues, *Bünde*), which collect membership dues. The bulk of income from this source is administered by the leagues, which then transfer part of their dues to the state and federal party headquarters. Formally the share of dues transferred to state and federal party organisations is determined by the respective party committee. Because these committees are dominated by representatives of the leagues, transfers to party headquarters at the federal as well as at the state level have to be negotiated in a fiscal compromise each year.[242] As a consequence just a small part of the total revenue from membership dues is handed over to state and federal party organisations.

2. Equalisation transfers

In cadre type parties the top-down distribution of funds for election campaigns was quite frequent. The U.K. Liberals (between 1910 and 1920) and the traditional parties (Liberals, P.C.) in Canada (up to 1974) are cases in point. Wherever there is a lack of income at the local level, top-down transfers are needed to win constituencies under a majority or plurality voting system. If central finances became tight these subsidies depended on the need of local parties and their prospect of electoral success. On the other hand (some) local parties may hold extensive reserves.[243] Such funds will not always be mobilized by party headquarters. During the 1980s the Liberal Party of Canada was a prime example for a centre in need and affluence in the field.

The Labour Party in Britain may serve as an example for both ends being in need. In the late 1980s there was a rise in constituency affiliation fees, representing the number of individual members. Consequently central party's share of total income from this source soared. Nevertheless constituency parties at election time depended financially on the central level. Local associations of the Labour Party and those of the Liberal Democrats are poor. Respectively, their average annual budget was £8,912 and £ 6,199 in 1997. Many Liberal associations have simply declined. Thus central office grants to the local party organisations are even more common with the Liberals.[244]

Due to extreme differences between strong and week provincial parties, the Canadian N.D.P. has long practised a system of fraternal aid. Stronger organisations send staff, volunteers and occasionally funds to support campaign efforts by weaker branches. This sort of subsidies-in-kind was also practiced by the Canadian P.C. provincial and the U.S. state parties when federal headquarters were overflowing with money from mass mailings.[245] Both U.S. parties (RNC, DNC) transfer part of their federal funds to state parties. "For example, while the DNC spent 10 percent of its federal dollars and

---

242 Sickinger 1999, pp. 306, 309.
243 Pinto-Duschinsky 1981, pp. 47-49; Paltiel 1970a, pp. 38/39, 41/42; Whiteley et al. 1994, p. 27.
244 Pinto-Duschinsky 1989, p. 31; Johnston/ Pattie 1993, pp. 139, 145 (for a different view Webb 1994, p. 118).
245 See above in this chapter, sub-section B2 (small donations).

31 percent of its non-federal funds in 1992 in direct support of state parties, the corresponding percentages for the RNC were one percent in federal funds and 15 percent for non-federal resources."[246] A large proportion of these transfers were made as subsidies-in-kind. Public subsidies to national headquarters have triggered off similar activities in European parties, including equalisation payments by German federal parties to their state and local party branches, especially in East Germany, whenever the traditional process of revenue sharing seemed insufficient.

If the top tier of a party (national headquarters) is the sole recipient of public funds and no partial transfer of that money takes place, this can enlarge centralised power but also may bring about loose contacts to local party supporters. Different parties have their own statutes regarding transfer funds to lower levels. In Finland national party organisations transferred more than half of their support from state funds to districts and local chapters. "Thus, the national party organisations had a good hold on the finances of the lower levels of the organisation."[247] Due to such transfers the sub-national level was able to employ staff. Only smaller parties with lower income did not transfer much.

3. Revenue sharing

In Germany transfers (up as well as down) are of great importance for intra-party life. The Greens share local income with their state and federal party, which in turn move most of their public subsidies to state branches and local chapters.[248] As conflicts occur quite frequently rules are set by negotiations among the treasurers. Some local treasurers are able to set aside bank accounts to be prepared for a campaign; others have to raise extra money to fund a campaign. The first case seems to be more common with the SPD and FDP, whereas CDU membership dues are collected at the county level and stay there without participation of local chapters or revenue sharing with party headquarters. Only small donations, which are collected at the local level, are partly transferred to constituency organisations.

SPD dues are collected centrally by pre-authorised checking of members' bank accounts. However, the traditional revenue sharing between national headquarters, regional chapters and local sections has never been discontinued. The federal treasury transfers a fixed share of membership dues to the regional branches (*Bezirke*), which then pass on part of their share to local chapters (*Unterbezirke, Ortsvereine*). The applicable rates are determined by party statute. In a similar fashion the federal level of the Austrian SPÖ collects all dues, and transfers a share to lower level party organisations. By contrast, membership dues in Spain are collected by provincial organisations of PSOE and PCE. Nevertheless both parties traditionally practise revenue sharing. The amount of membership dues that is transferred to the central level is small for the

---

246 Biersack 1996, p. 115.
247 Pesonen 1987, pp. 23-24.
248 Ringena 2000, pp. 46, 59.

Socialists (15 percent) and much higher for the Communists (25 percent).[249]

In Switzerland grass-roots financing is important for local parties, a bit less so (53 to 59 percent of total income in a non-election year) for state parties and a lot less important for three of the major federal parties (FDP, CVP, SVP).[250] In Sweden, due to small amounts, membership income is not important for transfers. In the Netherlands funds are probably concentrated at the top level; generally moderate party activities are performed by volunteers. However, there are fixed transfers from national headquarters to local chapters.[251]

For many emerging democracies, Italy is a case in point: Political life was dominated by notables who commanded their own political fiefdoms. Within the former DC the relationship of supporters to their party worked mostly in a top-down fashion. Factional leaders with clientelistic networks bought membership cards (and thus intraparty power). Intra-party factions „laundered" income from graft into subscriptions „paid" on behalf of non-existing members.[252] The statutory basis for this process was the procedure for collecting membership dues. Each year the DC party headquarters distributed packages of membership cards to its regional chapters and charged them a fixed amount for each individual card. The regional chapter then supplied as many membership cards to local sections as were in demand. Different chapters were entitled to set their own price and charge local sections accordingly. Local chapters were free to ask for dues at their own rate. If a local "godfather" decided to take out "foster" memberships on behalf of local citizens, this was accepted as long as the sponsor paid the price charged for a book of cards by the local chapter, which was the end of the dues collection chain. Obviously not too many questions were asked by anyone along the line of distribution.

In order to stimulate activities at the constituency level, Canadian parties offered to let their local organisations pocket a considerable share of income solicited in small donations. However, the figures for parties and provinces are different. The general impression is that membership dues are collected at the local level. This fits with the Canadian situation, however (as mentioned already) only a few parties have paid-up party members. Citizens join a party at the local level, which means either the provincial or the federal wing of a major party. Both wings are independent of each other and they have separate "war chests". Active constituency parties are able to hold bank accounts due to fund-raising activities and campaign subsidies.[253] In the 1980s most constituency parties were able to produce a surplus after elections. However, this is not only because of their ability to raise more funds but also because of their can-

---

249 del Castillo 1989, pp. 189, 194.
250 Ladner/ Brändle 1999, pp. 19, 22, 23; cf. Ladner/ Brändle 2001, pp. 160-163, 189-191.
251 Koole 1994b, p. 290 ; Cordes 2001, p. 54.
252 Hine 1996, pp. 142-143; Bardi/ Morlino 1994, p. 246. See above in this chapter, sub-section B1 (membership dues).
253 Nassmacher/ Suckow 1992, pp. 143, 145.

didate's public campaign reimbursement.[254] Within the N.D.P. this money, by party statute, has to stay at the local level.[255] A recent amendment to the Canada Elections Act offers federal candidates three options to dispose of a surplus: the general revenue fund, the federal party and the riding association. In 2001 the vast majority of all candidates opted for the latter.[256]

Following the Canada Elections Act of 1974 intra-party transfers were introduced both ways. The Liberal innovation of 1979 was that the party leader signed the nomination papers of a constituency candidate only if the candidate had formally agreed to transfer part of his or her campaign reimbursement to party headquarters.[257] The P.C. were much more successful with their procedure to process income tax receipts. As local candidates were entitled to issue such receipts only between their nomination and Election Day all donations solicited during the four to five years of a parliamentary cycle had to be receipted by the federal party. The P.C. Canada Fund, the official financial agent of the party, offered to issue such receipts for donations raised by local fundraisers, provided that a share of the donation was transferred to federal coffers in exchange for the administrative service. The Liberal Federal Agency soon followed suit. In order to surmount local resistance to direct mail efforts and to build up a federal register of members and donors, the principle of revenue sharing was even extended to donations raised by efforts of the federal party. Due to changes of political finance regulation (in 1974) revenue sharing between federal and local level has replaced top-down transfers, which were based on the central party's ability to provide funds.[258]

Summing up the evidence, which was presented in this chapter, some answers to the questions raised initially can be given:

- Experience from countries as diverse as Britain, Germany, the Netherlands, Sweden and the U.S. supports the conclusion that a considerable amount of grass-roots revenue is available for political purposes.
- On average individual donations in small amounts provide about half of the total revenue raised by federal parties in the U.S. and Canada.
- Only a few parties in Europe (most of them in the Netherlands and Switzerland) can collect a comparable share from signed-up party members. Even left-of-centre parties (Social Democrats, Socialists, Post-Communists) on average collect less than a quarter of their funds from grass-roots income.
- Popular financing can be an important source of political revenue, but it is not a constant and reliable one. Just like voters, individual contributors (party members and small donors) are a volatile sort of citizens.

---

254 See below in chapter VIII (public subsidies), sub-sections B2 (reimbursements) and C1 (candidates).
255 Nassmacher/ Suckow 1992, p. 145.
256 www.elections.ca.
257 Seidle/ Paltiel 1981, pp. 253, 255.
258 Paltiel 1970a, pp. 33, 37-39, 41/42.

- Thus grass-roots revenue will never suffice to cover all the costs of politics. However, this source of funding can supply large amounts if parties and candidates put in some organisational effort.
- There is no general approach, which will produce the best result under all circumstances. Various alleys have been explored successfully: recruiting party members, direct mail drives, neighbourhood and internet solicitation, lotteries, social events at the local level.
- Revenue sharing between different tiers of the same party will keep the local chapters happy. A quota system may provide local support for party headquarters.
- A public tax benefit programme (preferably matching funds or tax credits rather than tax deductions) can ensure that political fundraising will not fall victim to competing solicitation (by NGOs or charities) and stimulate political funding, which does not depend on flat grant (public) subsidies or plutocratic sources.

CHAPTER SEVEN

Plutocratic Funding (Interested Money and Graft)

A traditional approach towards the monetary sources of political parties would look at membership dues, assessments of office-holders, and (individual or corporate) donations. However, this approach is more appropriate in the 1950s than in the 2000s, and more suitable in continental Europe than elsewhere. Rejecting such distinctions, Gidlund has proposed to contrast *"grass-roots" funding* and *„plutocratic" financing*.[1] This alternative emphasises the ambivalent nature of political donations. Whereas democracy is a political system based on equal participation by the multitude, plutocracy is a system dominated by the riches of an affluent minority. Grass-roots financing, valued so dearly,[2] may be viewed as the participatory dimension whereas plutocratic financing can be called the capitalist dimension of party funding.

Obviously "capitalist financing of elections ... has survived the property franchise."[3] Contributions to a political war chest represent a willingness to participate as well as a way to seek influence. Alexander recalls a continuing dialogue on this ambiguity, Paltiel "thought I was naïve. I thought he was cynical. Of course, we were both right." There is a variety of motives for political contributions. Some "people give because they share ideas and concerns." Others expect access to or favourable treatment from elected officials, "a quid pro quo–..., a contract, or a policy."[4] The latter expectation is the floodgate for corruption. The ambiguity of the relationship can be explained by a few simple words: money rules, power solicits.

This contributes towards "a growing sense of unease among the voting public about the ... way financial support is provided to political parties" by unknown or unwanted sources. This unease demands that anyone who deals with interested money in politics needs to clarify the line of demarcation between "legitimate attempts to seek influence" (including impact on the outcome of an election) and "illegitimate or corrupt attempts to buy influence and to sell it."[5]

Whenever parties depend on donated funds, they may want to reciprocate the generosity of their donors by granting access to politicians,[6] shaping specific policies or offering favourable deals. Thus it is not surprising that scandals caused by plutocratic

---

1   Gidlund 1983, p. 42.
2   For details see above in chapter VI, section A (normative implications).
3   Duverger 1967, p. 65. - He was the first to indicate that the mass party replaced capitalist methods of funding by democratic fundraising (ibid., p. 63).
4   Quotes in: Alexander 1992b, p. 356; Alexander 1992a, p. 50 and p. 49 respectively.
5   All three quotes from: Wilson 2004, p. 2.
6   According to Sorauf 1988, p. 331, this is the major benefit to political donors.

financing ("money rules") have been instrumental in pushing regulatory reforms in the U.S. and Canada during the 1970s, in Germany and France during the 1980s, and in Japan and Britain during the 1990s.[7] Such reforms have added a new source of political funding for most established democracies, namely public subsidies to candidates and/or parties. In countries without such subsidies, e.g. India, New Zealand and the U.K., "the major proportion of a party's income is likely to come from wealthy individuals, business corporations, and interest groups."[8] As each source of political money has a specific impact on democratic politics, we discuss grass-roots funding and public subsidies in separate chapters.[9] This leaves the most "dangerous" sources of party funding to be treated jointly in this chapter. Because we are unable to establish the amounts paid to or solicited by parties in this manner, we aim to answer three more moderate questions:

- Is the free flow of money into politics a hazard for democratic government?
- How relevant are different categories of interested money in political financing?
- Which kinds of graft (corrupt exchanges) are most prevalent in party funding?

Party funds, which originate from all sorts of interested money or political "graft," no matter whether the donor or the recipient is the initiator, threaten the legitimacy of a democratic system and the acceptance of competitive politics.

A) Moral hazard of democracy?

Political competitors pursue both, votes and funds. Differences between parties and candidates include their unequal appeal to specific groups of voters and donors. The donor may buy time, energy or resources and thus influence the political decision.[10] The search for funds may induce a politician to pay more attention to those who give money to support a party, a policy or a campaign, than to those who simply vote for the party or its candidate.[11] As long as many people donate funds to different elites, the flow of money does no harm to the democratic process. A major problem is, however, that donors of large amounts are rare and often want more consideration. What is the intention of wealthy individuals, business corporations and institutional donors (such as, business associations and trade unions) who contribute to democratic politics? Do they want to assist the smooth operation of their political system or to serve a political cause or just to enhance some sort of special interest or to promote personal gain?

---

7 Cf. Alexander 1984b, pp. 31-54; Paltiel 1989, pp. 51-75; Schneider 1989, pp. 220-235; Doublet 1997, pp. 56-77; Shiratori 1994, pp. 187-205; Home Office Cm. 4413 [1999].
8 Miller 2005, p. 99; cf. Fisher 1996a, pp. 235-237, 240/241.
9 See above, chapter V (grass-roots funding) respectively below, chapter VII (public subsidies).
10 Hall/ Wayman 1990, pp. 84/85.
11 Paltiel 1981, p. 138; Scarrow 2007, p. 207.

"The familiar maxim that he who pays the piper calls the tune is widely believed to operate in the sphere of politics. Whether or not the suspicion is justified, the ordinary voter is apt to suspect that a very large gift to a political party must be made with some specific object in view." In reality this may be more innocent than a corrupt deal. "Access is the key to persuasion."[12] Most often donations buy "the opportunity to present information, explain a political position, or argue a case on a given issue". They will get people "a foot in the door to present a case", the opportunity to "tell their story".[13] In day-to-day politics this is more frequent, and thus more important than "the hope of special treatment in legislative or regulative matters."[14] A model, which assumes that "candidates [or parties] promise favours to interest groups in exchange for funds,"[15] is much too simple.[16]

The potential risk for the political system is linked to the practice of exchanging financial for political favours; this does not depend on who takes the initiative. Politicians may peddle their influence, and donors may parade their abundant resources. Plutocratic funding will have comparatively dire consequences whenever interested money does influence politicians and/or policies in favour of the donor's interest. If pressure groups apply money to promote political ends, this is plutocratic influence rather than democratic participation. Institutional donors (for example trade unions and other interest groups or associations) do not even have the right to vote. Compared to ordinary citizens, major pressure groups and business corporations are able to donate big money. Therefore, Etzioni ranks their donations close to plutocracy on a "democracy-to-plutocracy ladder".[17] Access to public contracts and licences may be an important motive of corporate and business donors. Quite often corruption seems to be the result, mainly brought about by a very close connection between politicians and business.

The use of money as a political resource necessarily brings into the political process the unequal distribution of income and wealth among members of a modern society. Any "large" donation counteracts the democratic principle of equality, which is enshrined in the formula "one person, one vote". Mature democracies open up different channels of political action according to their citizens' wealth: the lower strata can use their votes, the upper strata their money. If a supporting segment of society happens to be more affluent, its members will be able to donate freely from their personal income or wealth. If grass-roots supporters are less well off, they may need to organise effectively and to collect "big money in small amounts"[18] in order to promote their

---

12 Quotes from: Neill report 1998, p. 45; Sabato 1987, p. 127 (as cited by Austen-Smith 1995, p. 566).
13 Wilson 2004; p. 12 (first two quotes); Austen-Smith 1995, p. 566 (final quote).
14 Wilson 2004, note 50, referring to Ewing 2001, p. 188.
15 Ashworth 2006, p. 64; see also ibid., p. 55.
16 Ansolabehere/ Figueiredo/ Snyder 2003, pp. 110/111, confront the sums handled in different policy fields with the amounts given by PACs.
17 Etzioni 1984, pp. 227-231.
18 Paltiel 1981, pp.138, 171; quote from Heard 1960, p. 249.

political cause. This is what all working-class parties in Western Europe successfully did during the 19th and 20th century.

Party leaders strive for political success by reaching out to different audiences. They will listen to those who can vote for party candidates as well as to those who are able to contribute money. Financial contributions from a minority of voters help the party and its candidates to communicate with a majority of citizens. The risk of losing an election forces the governing parties to work and advertise for continuous support among the electorate. The hope of winning the next election helps the opposition to accept the powerless situation resulting from a minority position. Reliable links with groups in civil society are useful to any party in a sustainable democracy, be it the party in government or in opposition.

Donating money to a political organisation is a traditional means of establishing linkage in financial terms. Nevertheless the size of the contribution matters. For example in New Zealand, between 1996 and 2002 the average reported donation increased from NZD 10,828 to NZD 32,478 (US-$6,900 to 20,600), while the average named donation declined slightly and the average anonymous donation increased to NZD 40,000.[19] Large donations raise three questions. First, are the funds given without the expectation of a personal advantage or profit? Second, is a donation by someone who does not have the right to vote, an equivalent to speech and thus protected as a civil liberty? Third, is a donating organisation (e.g. a trade union or a corporation) legitimately spending money on behalf of its members or its shareholders respectively those who provide funds for a specific issue to an advocacy group?

Using money for political purposes is part and parcel of the logic of economic freedom. If an individual is entitled to engage in all sorts of socially acceptable action to maximise his or her fortune, then the realm of politics may be seen as an area where the principle of free access for all applies. Unfortunately the latter occasionally boils down to the rule of money. Political finance regulations try to balance equality and freedom. Some rules concerning contributions to parties, candidates and issues intend to promote a *level playing field* for parties and citizens (as pointed out by the German supreme court since 1958).[20] Others emphasise the *freedom of expression* for everybody (as stated by the U.S. Supreme Court in its 1976 Buckley v. Valeo verdict).[21] Unlimited freedom of expression ("free speech") and equality of opportunities (a

---

19　Wilson 2004, p. 4.
20　Starting in 1958 the court has upheld and refined this position in all rulings (including the one of 1992 – BVerfGE 8, pp. 51 to 85, 264). Details are summarised by Boyken 1998, pp. 56-59, 72-86, 158-162.
21　As long as money is not given for the election or defeat of a particular candidate, spending money is seen as a kind of free speech, and the freedom of communication is to be preserved (Biersack/ Haskell 1999, p. 176; Dwyre 1999, p. 202). Canadian courts dealing with initiatives by the National Citizens Coalition (see www. morefreedom.org) have handed down similar judgements.

level playing field, *Chancengleichheit*)[22] among all citizens, as well as among political contenders, are the major political and legal issues for a sustainable democracy.

The constitutional practice of countries, which ban all corporate donations because they endanger democracy, is most likely too strict.[23] Constitutional law, which ignores the inherent risk and allows the unregulated flow of corporate funds into party coffers, may be just too generous. Some political finance regimes aim to reduce inequalities among political competitors and limit the power of wealthy individuals and business corporations to influence political decisions.[24] Several researchers described the balance between equality and freedom, the target of any political finance regime, and placed a special emphasis on critical aspects:

- to avoid corruption, to limit the influence of moneyed interests, to provide equal opportunities for all competitors and to limit increasing costs (summed up by a "magic square:" enough money without corruption, dependence or unfair advantage), or
- to protect the functioning of the political system and the party system, to ensure that independent parties are closely connected and responsive to citizens, and to provide an adequate transparency of political funds, or
- to preserve the independence of politicians and parties, equal opportunities for competing parties, transparency of party finances and equal opportunities for all citizens.[25]

In order to reach these different but tightly related targets, political actors in established democracies choose different approaches. These often include trial and error, and they always depend on special paths, and eventually they result in specific types of programs and regimes. We can clearly see the different approaches towards the funding of politics and the disclosure of political money via a comparison between Western Europe and North America. In North America public regulation of political finance emphasises control of both campaign expenses and political contributions. Disclosure of the donor's identity and the amount of his or her donation is supposed to restrain the flow of interested money into party coffers.[26] In continental Europe spending limits are rare, and effective contribution limits are unknown. European legislators, unlike their North American counterparts, seem to detest any kind of enforcement mechanism for political finance regulation.[27]

---

22 Paltiel 1979, p. 17; Paltiel 1980, p. 355.
23 Sometimes it is simply partisan and intended to affect parties in opposition only, as in India. See Jain 1994, p. 162; Sridharan 2006b, p. 323.
24 For a detailed discussion see Nassmacher 2003a, pp. 9-17; Nassmacher 2003d, pp. 139-154:
25 Nassmacher 1981, p. 354; Nassmacher 1984, p. 34; Kreutz-Gers 1988, p. 9; Römmele 1995a, p. 175.
26 Non-disclosure of names in New Zealand emphasises this point; see Miller 2005, p. 99.
27 For details see Nassmacher 2006, pp. 446-454.

Democracy by itself does not prohibit any deployment of money, and quite rightly so. A variety of efforts to ban, limit or control the influence of money produced similar results in different political systems: they have all failed. The only option, which offers some remedy from the plutocratic hazard of democracy, is transparency.[28] Publicity of large donations and clear procedures for the continuous flow of funds reduce many of the hazards for democracy. Parties are competing organisations of civil society with a right to privacy, which is respected in some political systems more than others. The secret ballot and the private character of political parties, however, are enshrined in constitutional law in order to guard democracy from undue pressures, not in order to cover up shady dealings by plutocratic forces.

As (economic) freedom and (democratic) equality are opposing principles, the free-for-all use of money in politics has to be made subject to one important rule of democratic politics: transparency. To accept plutocratic influence does not imply keeping such influence clandestine. If the flow of funds into party or campaign coffers can be analysed by the democratic sovereign, the voter, at any time of his or her choice, especially at election times, the recipient will have to balance the need for funds against the risk of interested money. It is exactly this balancing act, which offers a safeguard for democracy.[29]

B) Contributions from interested money

A practical demarcation used to identify the plutocratic character of donations is based on size. As it seems very unlikely that small amounts of money will have any impact on politics, scholars' curiosity has been concentrated on large donations. This kind of political funding comes to mind when people assume that "money rules". Despite an academic consensus, a detailed and comprehensive account of the flow of large amounts of money into party coffers is very hard to obtain. Although transparency has improved in various countries since the 1970s, public reports do not reveal anywhere near all the facts of real life. The flow of interested money takes a variety of routes. No single democracy has tried all routes, but many countries have experienced several kinds of risky funding. Based on the available information we shall discuss the most frequent examples of large contributions by origin: business corporations, wealthy individuals and fundraising institutions.

---

28 For details see Cordes/ Nassmacher 2001, pp. 278-284.
29 As early as 1949 this kind of reasoning has prompted to incorporate a transparency clause into the German constitution: The parties „must disclose to the public the sources of their funds" (article 21, para. 1, clause 4 *Grundgesetz*). On the quick start towards inception see Titzck 1999, pp. 71/72; Adams 2005, pp. 49-54; for the long process of implementation see Nassmacher 1997a, pp. 44-61 and Adams 2005, pp. 57-60, 126-152.

1. Institutional fundraising

The flow of "interested money" is a long established routine, which is well known to every informed citizen. In his sample of 42 parties, Janda found that during the 1950s, 16 parties (i.e. two fifths) collected at least half of their total revenue from one sector of society, and 9 (i.e. one fifth) raised about two thirds from two different sectors. While agriculture and the professions provided the financial backbone for 5 parties, the business community and trade unions were more important financial sources.[30] Both still contribute to political competition. This flow of funds may be largely consistent with the sources of leadership and voting support. If so, the influx of cash simply reflects the political link between groups of citizens (be they workers or farmers, professionals or shopkeepers) and a party, which represents them. The recipient of institutional funding will support policies favourable to the common cause due to social links, not because someone has "bribed" them into such behaviour.

The origin of large donations traditionally corresponds to *party family*. In Japan the *Kômeitô* party draws most of its funding from *Sôka Gakkai*, a Buddhist lay organisation, which founded the party and is still closely attached to it.[31] In Denmark industrial associations traditionally donate to the Conservatives and farmers associations to the Agrarian Liberals (*Venstre*).[32] A special relationship between trade unions and workers' parties is common in all democracies, although empirical evidence indicates that such links have loosened up recently (such as in Britain or Sweden). Ideological ties do not provide a reliable source of revenue for all parties. For example, the ecological and peace movements were unable to secure cash for the Green party in Germany. A difference between the sources of votes and funding represents influence rather than linkage. In post-war Italy the Catholic Church mobilised voters for the *DC*, the Federation of Industrialists (*Confindustria*) provided generous funding for it.[33]

Neither the amount of money transferred, nor the source of such grants, nor the recipient of plutocratic funding is a reliable indicator of corruption. The regulatory problems are fairness of competition ("level playing field"),[34] a mismatch of social and economic clienteles, clandestine handling and, thus, the increased risk of shady dealings. Large donations mostly originate from a variety of organisations. This sub-section will elaborate the specific role of fundraising institutions that do not transfer their own funds, but rather donate the proceeds of their own solicitation.[35] Although con-

---

30 Janda 1980, pp. 91-93. – Details computed from ICPSR data (Janda 1979, pp. 148/149, 189/190).
31 Kevenhörster 1969, pp. 100-103; Kevenhörster 1993, p. 67.
32 Pedersen 1987, p. 41.
33 Mulé 1998, p. 65.
34 See below in chapter IX, section A (party competition).
35 Donations received without interference of a middling institution will be discussed below in this chapter, sub-sections B2 and B3 (individual and corporate donations). Deviating from British demarcation ("institutional sources", Pinto-Duschinsky 1981, pp. 126, 212) the latter sub-section will include all donations made directly by business enterprises, be they limited liability companies or partnerships.

veyer organisations have terminated their efforts and trade union affiliation is in decline, political action committees are still very much alive. All three strategies are presented in chronological order of their inception.

a) Collective membership (affiliation fees)

A close relationship between trade unions and (left-of-centre, social democratic) labour parties does not necessarily translate into union contributions to the party. The Netherlands and Germany are cases in point. Partisan factions within the Austrian trade union and a portion of union fees distributed among Israeli parties offer slightly deviating examples.[36] In Austria the trade union movement allows for partisan groups, which compete at internal elections and receive financial support from general union funds. Parts of this money may be transferred to the parent party if the partisan group decides to do so. In 1968 Israel introduced the Wage Protection Law, which created a compulsory political levy on trade union members. When Israeli parties were no longer able to function on membership dues only, they started party financing through the *Histadrut*, the only major trade union. Monthly deductions were to be made from wages and salaries of all union members. Israeli lawmakers intended that this „party tax" (not to be confused with its namesake in Austria),[37] still levied in the 1990s, would cover separate costs of trade union elections.

In Spain monetary transfers signal close ideological and organisational ties between workers' parties and trade unions (the Communist Party and *Comisiones Obreras*; the Socialist Party and *Unión General de Trabajadores*).[38] In Scandinavian and Anglo-Saxon democracies the traditional linkage with trade unions meant institutional funding for workers' parties.

In Denmark and Norway unions are entitled to make contributions to a labour party if individual members consent via not contracting-out. Sometimes Danish unions split their funds, which are earmarked for campaigns or newspapers, between left-wing parties.[39] Until the 1990s, local unions in Norway and Sweden affiliated with local chapters of the workers' party.[40] Although affiliation fees covered only a minor part of party income in the 1970s, the amounts of additional grants, which the national party received from unions in Norway, were close to those of the Danish Social Democrats (31 percent of total revenue in 1999). Swedish Social Democrats collected quite reasonable amounts from affiliated memberships at the local level, plus substantial union

---

36 Sickinger 1997, pp. 71/72; Boim 1979, p. 203.
37 See below in this chapter, sub-section D3 (assessment of office-holders).
38 van Biezen 2000, p. 340, note 7; van Biezen 1998, pp. 53-55; Gillespie 1990, pp. 47-62.
39 Elvander 1979, p. 17; Pedersen 1987, p. 41; Pedersen/ Bille 1991, pp. 164, 167; Svasand 1994, p. 305.
40 In 1971 collective affiliation accounted for half, in 1991 only for a fifth of the *Norwegian* Labour Party membership. Svasand 1992, p. 763; Pierre/ Widfeldt 1994, p. 337; Elvander 1979, p. 17. Although membership in Denmatk is direct (and local) considerable contributions go to the national party (Pedersen 2003, p. 338).

grants for national headquarters. Such contributions from the peak trade union (*LO*) and some individual unions (*fackförbund*) continue to this day. In a non-election year (1992) *LO* gave about SEK 6 million to *SAP* headquarters, in an election year they transferred considerably more (e.g. SEK 16.7 million in 1991).[41]

In Ireland trade unions are an important source of funding for the Labour Party and its candidates. In 1999 and 2000 ten to eight unions representing 44 to 41 percent of all union members were affiliated to the party, thus dwarfing the number of individual members. A decade earlier such funds had contributed 8 percent of Labour's total annual income.[42] In New Zealand union affiliates increase total membership of the Labour party. Unions continue to play a key role in the party despite an overall decline of union membership caused by the legal ban of closed shops.[43] The Australian Labor Party is heavily dependent on trade union contributions for its campaign funds. In 1987 it formed a front organisation to conceal such funds.[44] Canadian trade unions traditionally support the N.D.P.'s federal election campaign. They provide one third of all cash income in election years, and between 1975 and 1997 unions were, on average, responsible for about 15 percent of the party's revenue.[45] Union donations-in-kind (goods and services) usually exceed cash contributions. In the U.S. donations from labour unions are banned, but labour PACs help get around this ban. The bulk of all labour PACs disbursements (about 95 percent) go to Democratic candidates and committees.[46]

In Britain there have always been very close and mutually important monetary links between trade unions and the Labour Party. The party was run "like a joint stock company in which unions are given voting powers according to sums they are prepared to pay."[47] Some 30 to 50 individual unions, which comprise about half the union membership, are collectively affiliated to the national party and pay a regular affiliation fee from their political fund. Union members who have not 'contracted-out' pay an extra levy to support such political funds,[48] and national leaders of the union decide how they prefer to spend this revenue. Traditionally labour unions also sponsored parliamentary candidates, funding about 80 percent of their election expenses.[49] On top of this there was an annual grant for maintenance of constituency work (secretarial assistance), which should not exceed £600 in boroughs and £750 in counties.[50]

---

41 Gidlund/ Koole 2001, p. 118.
42 Farrell 1994, pp. 229/230; Holmes 1999, p. 51; Murphy/ Farrell 2002, p. 235.
43 Vowles 2002, p. 419.
44 Overacker 1952, p. 284; Chaples 1989, p. 76; Chaples 1988b, p. 6; for current details see Tham 2007, p. 5.
45 Paltiel 1970, p. 55; Seidle 1996, p. 8; Amr/ Lisowski 2001, p. 61.
46 Herrnson 1999, p. 108.- For details see below in this chapter, sub-section B2c (PACs).
47 Pinto-Duschinsky 1981, p. 307.
48 Fisher 1995b, p. 4; Becker 1999, p. 83; Ewing 2007, p. 101.
49 In 1979 there were 165 sponsored candidates (Bogdanor 1982, p. 369), in 1992 the number was 143 (Nassmacher/ Nassmacher 2008, Table 17). In1997 party by-laws terminated the procedure (Sturm 1997, p. 5).
50 Ewing 1982, pp. 82/83, 139.

Due to trade union legislation in 1984 all unions, which operate a political fund, are legally obliged to hold periodical membership ballots every ten years. Voting in the workplace and voting by mail made sure that people were able to participate. In both polls union members favoured political involvement. All unions (on average 80 percent in 1985/86, and 82 percent in 1994/96) voted to continue the financial support of the Labour Party.[51] During the 1980s affiliation fees totalled about £4 million, during the 1990s, despite a reduction in union membership, some £6 to 7 million, more recently £7 to 8 million, which is about twice the total of individual membership subscriptions. Nevertheless Labour's dependence on union funds declined from 80 percent in 1985 and 66 in 1992 to 40 in 1997 and below 25 percent in 2005.[52]

Traditionally union funds resulted in two kinds of institutional influence:

- First, the right of (affiliated) unions to vote en bloc on behalf of their members at party conferences.[53] This "bloc vote" was a moderating influence in the post-war years but it reduced policy options for the party during the 1980s.
- Second, decisive union power in the selection of candidates at the local level. Many constituency associations favoured a union sponsored candidate who brought in his "own" campaign funds.

However, as New Labour distanced itself from the unions, their influence decreased in the 1990s. In 1993, the party changed the rules for the nomination of parliamentary candidates and the election of the party leader. In 1996 the "Labour Party ended trade union sponsorship of individual MPs and replaced it with funding of constituency parties."[54] On the other hand in 2002 some unions "cut funding to Labour in protest at government policies."[55] To counteract such moves the leadership of the governing Labour party "negotiated a peace treaty with its traditional paymasters – the unions" in 2004.[56] This deal is publicly known as the "Warwick agreement". As a political price for "peace on the funding front" the Labour government made policy commitments concerning the NHS, pensions, job security for workers on strike and government procurements by British manufacturers.[57]

On the surface, affiliation fees and donations to parties by labour unions do not fit in with the category of 'plutocratic' financing, because such funds originate from small political levies paid by union members. Nevertheless there are different approaches to view trade union funding of workers' parties. On the one hand, both are the organisational offspring of the same social movement and both pursue similar policies to serve working class voters. On the other hand, however, the union leadership may decide to

---

51 Blackwell/ Terry 1987, pp. 623/624; Leopold 1997, p. 28.
52 Neill report 1998, pp. 30, 231; Leopold 1997, p. 34; Ewing 2007, pp. 261/262.
53 Webb 1992, pp. 851. 867; Webb 1994, pp. 109/110.
54 Leopold 1997, p. 35, cf. Seyd/ Whitely 2002, pp. 7, 42; Sturm 2003, p. 246.
55 „Treasury could match gifts to political parties", in: *The Times*, 9 July 2002.
56 „The real Labour funding crisis", in: *The Economist*, 10 February 2007, p. 40.
57 „The Warwick agreement", in: *The Guardian*, 13 September 2005 (http://politics.guardian.co.uk/print).

withhold contributions (institutional donations) if party policies tend to be less "class conscious" then expected. This "blackmail potential" (as applied by British and Swedish unions recently) uses money in a plutocratic fashion to achieve political ends – just as any other kind of interested money would.[58] Furthermore such influence may be institutionalised (as it was in the British Labour Party until 1993).[59] In former times union leaders cast a "bloc vote" at the annual party conference on behalf of their members who had paid the political levy. Thus collective affiliation of the millions was transformed into the plutocratic instrument of union leaders who influenced intra-party decision-making significantly. Although the sources of funds are different, some mechanisms are similar to a fundraising institution, which operates on behalf of business interests.

b)   Conveyer organisations

A more recent, though dated, support system used associational channels of communication among the business community as a tool of moneyed interest. Conveyer organisations raise cash from firms and distribute these proceeds among several non-Socialist parties. Thus, a cartel of donors acts as a crucial supplier of funds to competing parties (or factions). Conveyers establish a strong bargaining position, which permits them to press (policy or nomination) demands of business and to impinge on specific responsibilities of parties. Such organisations have operated only in a few countries; the post-war ("second wave") democracies in Germany and Japan are the most notorious cases.[60] Organisations of this type were formed to fight Socialist parties emerging under universal suffrage. They tended to be powerful in countries with multiparty systems and an ideological style of politics where non-Socialist parties lacked strongly institutionalised organisations. The "structure was similar …, but the aims, with regard to which it was utilised, were much more offensive" in Germany than in Japan.[61]

In Germany groups re-established conveyer techniques and utilised them in the 1950s.[62] In framing the major conveyer, called the Civic Association (*Staatsbürgerliche Vereinigung von 1954*), the Federation of Industry (*BDI*) assumed a leadership role. Its member associations included 75 percent of all German industrial enterprises in 1953. Goals of the conveyers, which operated federally and at the state level, were to prevent coalitions between bourgeois parties and Social Democrats, to form a cartel of non-Socialist candidates, to minimise "waste" of manpower and to influence candidate selection. At the state level smaller parties received financial support if they

---

58   The Warwick agreement (see above) provides perfect proof of such blackmail potential.
59   Becker 2002, pp. 170, 212/213; Seyd/ Whiteley 2002, p. 7.
60   *Libertas* in *Norway* never became politically important because businessmen were not willing to allow an association "to determine where their support should go" (Heidenheimer/ Langdon 1968, p. 98).
61   Heidenheimer/ Langdon 1968, pp. XVIII, 10; quote ibid. p. 50.
62   Adams 2005, pp. 68-104.

were willing to leave SPD-led cabinets. Architects of the conveyer structure "obviously reasoned that business, and especially industry's bargaining position vis-à-vis the parties, would be strengthened if funds from individual firms were channelled as completely as possible through" conveyers, and thus cumulated at the state and federal level.[63]

Conveyers raised funds by quotas that peak organisations set for member organisations, which in turn divided them up to call on individual member companies. Half of all employers and two thirds of the large corporations participated in the arrangement. The determinants of the quota included the number of employees and the amount of gross turnover or regular membership dues of a business association. Conveyers reached the climax of their support-channelling effectiveness between 1954 and 1958 when a change in the tax law made donations for "political purposes" as easily tax deductible as contributions to charities. In 1957 the major conservative party (*CDU*) covered about 40 percent of its campaign expenditure with this support. Income data for 1959 (non-election year) and 1961 (election year) indicate a similar level. Besides the conveyers' contributions both bourgeois parties, *CDU* and *FDP*, maintained their own fundraising efforts. Especially the *FDP* feared, and quite rightly so, that the strings attached to conveyer support eroded its freedom of action. During the 1960s institutional funding declined as the "parties took steps to free themselves from excessive dependence upon business."[64] The negative image of conveyer financing probably induced the *CDU* to support the introduction of public subsidies in 1959 and their increase in 1961.

Japanese business associations made a quick comeback after 1945, although a variety of top level organisations had only loose structures and weak power, due to the different interests of their members. After the influence of business had been questioned and divisions had developed among conservative factions, one peak organisation wanted to prevent a Socialist government and to contribute to the formation of a united conservative party. In 1955 the Federation of Economic Organisations (*Keidanren*) set up a separate conveyer to collect political funds, called the Economic Reconstruction Council (*Kondankai*). Although it was a giant version of various small sponsors and collecting agencies, its functions were different, larger and new. Substantial sums were turned over directly to endorsed candidates, which they spent on their own campaigns and personal networks of political support. In 1955 the sum that was provided, amounted to one-third or one-half, in 1958 to two-thirds of the reported headquarters expenditure of the conservative party (*Jimintô*, LDP).[65]

In 1961 the business controlled *Kondankai* was replaced by the Citizens' Association (*Kokumin Kyokai*), a fundraising arm of the party, because politicians "wished to retain the way of doing things." After termination of conveyer activity, business contri-

---

63 Heidenheimer/ Langdon 1968, pp. 45/46, 48/49, 63; quote ibid., p. 50.
64 Duebber/ Braunthal 1963, pp. 778/ 779; Heidenheimer/ Langdon 1968, pp. 51-55, 60, 71, quote ibid., p. 204.
65 Heidenheimer/ Langdon 1968, pp. 170, 176-178, 185/186, 190.

butions "have been forthcoming on a greater scale than ever."[66] Finally waves of scandal and reform produced new legislation and in 1993 *Keidanren*, the big business lobby, stopped "pooling campaign donations from its members on behalf of the LDP."[67] Institutional funding was replaced by direct business contributions to parties, politicians and factions. Whereas political revenue from institutional funding is decreasing almost everywhere, U.S. PACs are the major exception.

c) Political action committees (PACs)

Despite an entire century of legislative efforts, interested money has never been effectively eliminated from the funding of U.S. campaigns. Both, corporations and labour unions, learned how to deal with legal restrictions. At present Political Action Committees (PACs) are the major vehicle that channels pluralist diversity and plutocratic influence into the political process.[68] As an organised body for the support of an issue or a variety of candidates, a PAC collects money in small amounts from individuals. PAC's often use the technique of 'bundling.' For example, an intermediate, say a PAC, solicits contributions from individuals who make out their checks to a designated candidate who then receives the collection of individual contributions in a 'bundle'.[69] Under U.S. law PACs are allowed to use administrative resources (staff, computers, mailing lists) of their parent organisation, e.g. a trade union, a corporation or a lobby group, for their fundraising efforts. However, disclosure rules have made the funds raised and spent more transparent than they used to be in the past.

Changes were closely connected with the FECA, which introduced restrictions especially for solicitation. The significance of PACs rose from the 1970s to the 1980s. PACs have grown in numbers as well as in fiscal strength. The number of PACs increased more than six-fold between 1974 and 1989. PACs accounted for less than 1/5 of federal campaign spending in 1976, for about 1/4 in 1980 and for more than 1/3 in 1984. When compared to the previous presidential year campaign, related expenses by PACs more than doubled in 1976, 1980 and 1984. Between 1974 and 1986 PAC funds spent on candidates for the House of Representatives almost doubled. During the 1990s PAC donations accounted for 15 to 20 percent of contributions to Senate candidates and 30 to 35 percent of spending by House candidates.[70] In the U.S. (and quite rightly so) it has always been a big question, whether interested money (e.g. cash solicited by PACs) can buy politicians or influence the outcome of elections.[71]

---

66 Both quotes from Heidenheimer/ Langdon 1968, p. 205, cf. ibid., pp. 196/197.
67 „The end of donor fatigue?", in: *The Economist*, 18 September 2003.
68 Epstein 1976, p. 58; Epstein 1986, p. 285; Ansolabehere et al. 2003, p. 100.
69 Alexander 1992a, pp. 56/57; cf. Epstein 1986, p. 289.
70 Baker 1989, pp. 8, 10; Alexander 1984b, p. 94; Alexander/ Haggerty 1987, pp. 109-111; Sorauf 1990, pp. 207-224; Hrebenar et al. 1999, p. 155; Herrnson 1999, pp. 104-105, 109-110.
71 For details see below in chapter IX, section A (spend and win?).

Although PAC contributions for campaign purposes are given exchange oriented, interest groups do their own grass-roots lobbying.[72] Thus the flow of money into campaign chests is overemphasised. Whereas PACs disproportionately support safe winners, political parties are the most strategic givers. Moreover the connection between PAC money and congressional policy seems to be less significant than had been previously believed.[73] Further research finds close links between labour PACs and Democrats and business PACs and Republicans. As party policies and organised interests are close to each other this does not prove that politicians are for sale on specific decisions.

Select examples of corporate or labour PACs include the 'Connecticut Bankers Association PAC', the 'California Cotton Growers Association Inc. PAC', the 'Harley-Davidson Inc. PAC', the 'Procter & Gamble Co. Good Government Committee', the 'Staples Inc. PAC', the 'United Parcel Service of America Inc. PAC', the 'International Association of Fire Fighters Local 42 PAC' and the 'Sheet Metal Workers Local 100 PAC'.[74]

(1) *Labour PACs*: Labour union funds first became significant in national politics in 1936, and they have provided an important resource for the Democratic Party ever since. Congress extended restrictions on corporate giving to parties and campaigns (in existence since 1907) to labour unions in the 1940s. Because unions have long been prohibited from using membership dues to promote candidates in federal campaigns, they have developed expertise to solicit voluntary political contributions from union members. Such additional contributions can legally be used for direct assistance to federal candidates. Contributors to labour PACs outnumber by far those of the corporate PACs; however, corporate PACs are more numerous, receive much larger average contributions and raise more money.[75]

(2) *"Corporate PACs"* refers to all business related PACs, which have largely replaced the old strategy of fundraising from fat cats. Corporate PACs may use corporate treasury funds to solicit political money from shareholders or employees in small amounts and combine them into larger and meaningful contributions. Frequently they solicit executive and managerial personnel rather than non-executive, non-managerial employees or shareholders. To forward special interests, PACs transfer funds to the jurisdiction where the well-being of the company or industry is at stake. The partisan distribution of PAC money depends on the majority in Congress. In general, the corporate sector and trade associations have a closer affiliation to Republicans than to Democrats. The financial gap between these two major parties narrowed during the late 1990s.[76] Whereas the number of corporate PACs about tripled in 1976 and 1980, the prevalence of ideological and single-issue PACs followed suit in 1980 and 1984.

---

72 Welch 1980, p. 115; Epstein 1986, pp. 286, 290, 297.
73 Malbin 1979, pp. 21, 29, 39; Hall/ Wayman 1990, p. 814; Ansolabehere et al. 2003, p. 109.
74 www.fec.gov/pages/pacronym.htm
75 Alexander 1984, pp. 83, 89, 93; Alexander 1992a, p. 37.
76 Alexander 1983, p. 373; Alexander 1984, p. 89; Hrebenar et al. 1999, p. 159; Herrnson 1999, pp. 101/102.

(3) *Issue (ideological) PACs* enable all sorts of groups to promote a special interest by contributing money to politicians, who support specific issues. In 1980 (and probably later) ideologically "conservative PACs far outdistanced liberal PACs, as measured by receipts, expenditure, and contributions to candidates". Ideological and issue PACs disburse "about 30 percent of all PAC spending."[77] Some of it is needed for administration, because many of these PACs cannot expect an organisation (business or labour) to cover their overhead. They rely on direct mail solicitations with enormous fund-raising costs. Other adopted innovative activities, such as parallel campaigns, independent expenditures, negative advertising, and have become an important feature in the search for FECA loopholes.[78] Issue-oriented groups use independent expenditures as their primary means of electioneering. Among the independent expenditures spent on behalf of presidential candidates in 2000 three ideological PACs stand out: National Rifle Association Political Victory Fund ($2.3 million), National Right to Life PAC ($2.2 million) and National Abortion Rights Action League ($4.2 million). In total the NRA Victory Fund spent almost $6.5 million in independent expenditures, contributed $1.6 million in cash to individual candidates and disbursed more than $16.8 million by "sponsoring fund-raising and meet-and-greet events for candidates, as well as helping with candidates' research needs."[79] More recently, new types of PACs have grown in importance, such as "527s" or stealth PACs and leadership PACs.

(4) *Leadership (or personal[80]) PACs*: While junior politicians depend on funding from congressional and senatorial campaign committees, senior politicians (i.e. leaders of both houses and members of key committees) can become "like monarchs on royal barges afloat on a sea of dollars."[81] This creates new opportunities for machine building. Leadership PACs funnel money to other members on Congress, thus forming networks of mutual favours and strengthening hierarchical structures as well as independence from the parties. The 2006 race for Democratic Majority Leader offers a recent example of such influence.[82] Leadership PACs give money to relatively competitive races in order to maximise the number of seats controlled by their leaders or to candidates who are ideologically proximate. During the 1999-2000 cycle the amounts (in nominal dollars) handled by leadership PACs were roughly about ten times larger than those contributed during the 1983-1984 cycle.[83]

(5) *Stealth PACs*: Whereas some interest groups, like the AFL-CIO, the NAACP and the NRA have been traditionally active in electoral politics and their issue position as

---

77 Both quotes in: Alexander 1983, p. 129; cf. Alexander 1992a, p. 61.
78 Canada and the U.K. enacted pre-emptive measures against "third party advertising" (non-candidate campaigning). Cf. Stanbury 1986, pp. 471-474; Paltiel 1988a, pp. 143-145; Ewing 2007, pp. 157-160, 222/223.
79 Cigler 2002, p. 173. – Magleby 2002b, p. 7; Corrado 2002, p. 96.
80 Sorauf 1988, pp. 174-181; Alexander 1992a, pp. 62/63.
81 Baker 1989, p. 12. For some examples see Bedlington/ Malbin 2003, pp. 121/123, 125/126.
82 For details see Green 2008, pp. 63, 65, 66.
83 Bedlington/ Malbin 2003, pp. 130/133; Lowry et al. 2003, pp. 10, 14/15, 19.

well as their partisan orientation is well known to the general public, the 2000 election brought to the fore a new type of interested money: the "527s" or "stealth" PACs. The most important example was "Citizens for Better Medicine", a PAC that represented drug traders, drug producers, hospitals and healthcare providers.[84] Most of these groups operate under section 527 of the Federal Tax Code, which makes them non-profit organisations exempt from federal taxation and FECA transparency rules. The 527 committees, which became very popular in 2004, knocked a hole in the campaign-finance laws. "In fact, somebody was bound to find a loophole ... The Democratic Party ... has effectively outsourced its grass-roots operation."[85]

When considering the variety of PACs, two plutocratic impacts become obvious: Interested money impinges upon the political process, and access to funds provides additional opportunities for power politics. As competing parties need both, money and votes, this conflict will force them to strive for a dynamic balance.[86] For each left-of-centre party the support by a majority of voters is not enough, for each right-of-centre party monetary contributions will not suffice.[87]

Finally, it should be noted that PACs controlled by the party leadership [88] are a more formal and more transparent version of the Finance Committees, which used to raise funds for the Liberals or the P.C. in Canada. Up to the 1970s an informal group of party bagmen in the major economic centres (e.g. Toronto, Montreal, possibly Calgary) contacted their peers in business and the professions to solicit "adequate" amounts for the party campaign chest.[89] A general difference between fundraising by PACs and solicitation by finance committees is that control and initiative have shifted from party bosses to civil society. The most prosperous of its individual members are a long-known source of party funding.

2. *Donations by wealthy individuals (contributions from personal wealth)*

For bourgeois (right-of-centre) parties, individual contributions from personal income or wealth are a very traditional source of funds. Nowadays the media and public opinion almost automatically suspect that the donor intends to "buy" some sort of political

---

84 Cigler 2002, pp.176-181.
85 „The ersatz Democrats", in: *The Economist*, 22 May 2004. Legal treatment by Corrado 2006, pp. 54-58.
86 Cf. Hermens1958, p. 186.
87 Public incentives for small donations (see above in chapter VI, sub-section C2 – stimulating contributors) and public subsidies (see below in chapter VIII, section B – types of subsidies) as well as public disincentives for large contributions (see below in this chapter, sub-section B 5 – discouraging "fat cats") may help to redress an imbalance.
88 This includes national party committees (DNC, DCCC, DSCC; RNC, NRCC, NRSC), candidate committees for the presidential race, and leadership PACs, but not the bulk of labour, corporate or ideological PACs.
89 Paltiel 1970a, pp. 34/35, 40/41. Similar procedures are operated in India (Sridharan 2006b, pp. 322/323) and Costa Rica (Casas-Zamora 2002, p. 173).

or personal favour. However, such general suspicion may be grossly misleading. Some wealthy individuals have no other intention than to support a cause, which they happen to favour. Others may just want to "buy" their way into social acceptance. Quite recently *The Economist* has offered a motive to donate, which is rather innocent in political terms: a sense of arrival or belonging felt by those who have been rising economically but have not arrived socially (e.g. the descendants of poor immigrants).[90]

a) Fat cat contributions (without or with strings attached)

Because most North American parties do not collect sustaining amounts of membership dues, their revenue traditionally originated from large donations. The most striking example of a wealthy person who donated to a (left-of-centre party) without expecting any quid-pro-quo is Mrs. Irene Dyck, a Calgary widow, who has been the N.D.P.'s "top individual contributor for the entire period 1983-90." The amounts, which she contributed, ranged from CAD23,165 to CAD453,365. Despite such amounts, large donations from individual (or corporate) funds have not been "an important source of revenue for Canada's three largest political parties" during the period mentioned.[91]

The third wave democracies of Central and Eastern Europe offer evidence of the more traditional kind. Party funding by "oligarchs" and "businessmen" is frequent but not transparent. In the 1995 presidential election in Poland the former *Solidarnosc* leader, Lech Walesa, received one donation from a businessman (Aleksander Guzowaty), which constituted almost 72 percent of Walesa's total campaign funds. To date, this donation is the largest official donation in Polish politics.[92]

Although the United States has established strict rules to reduce plutocratic financing by big donors ("fat cats"), the country offers ample evidence on how to cope with restrictions. Because individual donations are limited to minor amounts, rich donors often give more than $1,000 to a candidate by way of a *'bundle'* of individual contributions by themselves, their aunts and uncles, in-laws and children on the same day.[93] Ever since entrepreneurial political consultants and politicians figured out ways of financing important parts of federal election campaigns with unregulated funds, *soft money* is a more important way to funnel unregulated funds into party competition. Soft money receipts totalled about $500 million in 2000.[94] Among the soft money raised for the 2000 election, fifty donors contributed $ 1 million or more, some of them to both parties. Finally, two entrepreneurs, Stephen Adams ($2.2 million) and Steven

---

90 "The meaning of Podge," in: *The Economist*, 8 December 2007, p. 48.
91 Both quotes in: Stanbury 1991, p. 224.cf. also Stanbury 1986, p. 459.
92 Walecki 2001, p. 399.
93 Another approach that "it is increasingly common for wealthy individuals", who have given the maximum under the statutory contribution limit to make sizable expenditures "independent" of the party or campaign organisation to assist candidates (Jones 1993, p. 54).
94 Nelson 2002, p. 24. The BCRA (the McCain-Feingold Act) was a failed attempt to fence in this process.

Kirsch ($1.3 million), stand out among the *independent expenditures* in favour of presidential candidates in 2000.[95]

Today the most important opportunity for contributions by wealthy individuals in the U.S. seems to be "seed money" to start off a pre-nomination campaign. Potential candidates without "national name recognition or a national fundraising network must ... build relationships with wealthy individuals in key donor states such as New York, California and Florida" to get their campaign off the ground.[96] This applies to presidential hopefuls as well as to Senate challengers in big states.

During the final years of the Conservative government in Britain damaging, although unproven, allegations about the party's funding practices received prominent coverage in the press. Problems had arisen from the party's increasing reliance on anonymous contributions of £1 million or more from a few wealthy backers, some of them living abroad.[97] For example in 1997 the party solicited ten separate donations beyond £1 million and 105 donations between £100,000 and £800,000 each.[98] Between 1979 and 1994 the Conservative party treasurer successfully exploited "the old-fashioned method of a personal approach to wealthy individuals".[99] In the 1990s personal donations have contributed about two-thirds of the total revenue of Conservative Central Office.[100]

Liberal Democrats had only one donation of more than £300,000. With the former SDP large individual donations had been more important.[101] Even Labour has turned to the mega-rich more recently. Within months of its landslide victory in 1997, the incoming government was accused of having received £1 million in exchange for allowing cigarette advertising at Formula One motor racing events in contradiction to Labour's anti-smoking policy. To clear itself from charges of impropriety, the party returned the donation.[102] Nevertheless the scandal served as a spur to new political finance regulation. Only a few weeks before the new rules came into force in 2000, three other donors (Paul Hamlyn, Christopher Ondaatje and David Sainsbury) contributed £2 million each to Labour coffers.[103] In 1997 the party received 134 donations (including sponsorships) of £5,000 or more; 21 of these were in excess of £50,000, six were over £1 million.

Personal wealth deployed for political gain is a traditional source of political funding. Some of it is used to promote business interests;[104] some of it is put to more personal

---

95   Corrado 2002, pp. 96/97.
96   "Money's Going to Talk in 2008", in: *Washington Post*, 11 March 2006.
97   Fisher 1996b, p. 159.
98   Pinto-Duschinsky 1998, p. 1. The donors can be looked up in the annual reports of the firms, connections of Conservative MPs in the 'Register of Member's interest'.
99   Pinto-Duschinsky 1994, p. 15; see also McAlpine 1998, pp. 212, 214/215.
100 Whiteley/ Seyd/ Richardson 1994, p. 219; Fisher 1996b, p. 159; Pattie/ Johnston 1996, p. 922.
101 Pinto-Duschinsky 1998, p. 1; Pinto-Duschinsky 1994, p. 19.
102 Ewing 2007, pp. 13-16; cf. also Osler 2002, pp.75-83.
103 "Cash for Labour", in: *The Economist*, 4 January 2001.
104 See below in this chapter, sub-section B3 (corporate contributions).

advantage. Among such quid-pro-quo is access to (elected or appointed) public office or the sale of (honours and) titles for hard cash.

b)   Buying honours and offices

The honours trade was quite common in Britain during the early 20th century for both governing parties. Business capital was given frequently to party bagmen in exchange for a title. The amounts raised were so high that "neither the Conservative nor the Liberal party managers could find ways of spending the sums that were coming" in. The funds were partly invested in newspapers, and to a smaller degree poorer but talented candidates were supported. "The un-political nature of the honours trade was particularly damaging to the Liberals."[105] From 1906, a progressive program brought them into political conflict with the commercial community. Big donations flowed to the party although political sympathies had disappeared, but the Liberals did not look for more popular sources. In 1922 the practice of peddling titles was suspended after Lloyd George's fall from office, which was partly stimulated by his honours' list. Businessmen were seeking to buy titles and Lloyd George's organisers had taken the opportunity to build up a Political Fund between 1916 and 1922. Officially, this money was given to combat socialism. Some businessmen made it to the honours' list, who had done wrong, been fined, traded with an enemy or avoided paying taxes in Britain.[106] Although the practice of raising money by selling titles was not terminated in the 1920s, it had passed the peak of political and monetary importance.[107] Some consider this a bit unfortunate because "it may be the least corrupt way for political parties to raise cash. Certainly, handing out medals and extra letters [i.e. titles] is preferable to handing out tax breaks and government contracts."[108]

In the U.S. comparable strategies survived longer. In the 1950s "a large number of political appointees to diplomatic posts show up as donors to campaigns." With some ambassadors "the contribution is but one item in a composite of political activities,"[109] with others it is the major one. When the qualification of some appointees to perform diplomatic responsibilities seemed questionable, financial generosity was obviously a decisive factor. Jimmy Carter was the first to pledge to "take the selection of envoys out of the realm of politics." In June 1977 no less than 25 percent of U.S. embassies were directed by non-career ambassadors. "The figure had been highest during the

---

105   Quotes in: Pinto-Duschinsky 1981, p. 54 and p. 56 respectively.
106   Pinto-Duschinsky 1981, pp. 87/88, 104, 116, 253.
107   Cf. Osler 2002, pp. 85-94. Alastair McAlpine (1998, pp. 256/257) claims that during his tenure as party treasurer the Conservative Party has not sold honours. A more recent example of "cash for honors" involving four different lenders of major "loans" was reported in 2006 ("Going, going, going", in: *The Economist*, 25 March 2006). For a detailed discussion see Ewing 2007, pp. 133-141.
108   As noted by Lloyd George, a shrewd practitioner (see „Honour killings", in: *The Economist*, 17 July 2004).
109   Both quotes in: Heard 1960, p. 147.

presidencies of Roosevelt (44 percent) and Kennedy (42 percent). It was 32 percent under Nixon,"[110] among them only a few campaign donors and fundraisers.

c) Paying for campaigns from personal wealth

It used to be quite common for wealthy people to employ their own resources to get into elected office or to gain an administrative position. This is true for countries in Western Europe and North America, as well as for those in Asia and Latin America. Pre-war Britain, where Conservative MPs had to run on their own funds, is a frequently cited example. "Only persons willing to pay all their election expenses ... had a really good chance of being adopted as candidates".[111] In Latin America it is harder to establish the facts, "because the candidates are reluctant to admit that they spent personal money."[112] In the U. S. there are only a few examples of wealthy people who were able to win an influential position using their own money in recent decades. The presidential campaign of Ross Perot in 1992 cost $67.3 million, 94 percent were funded by his own money.[113] Although Perot had the attention of the media and participated in the presidential debates, his bid was not successful. Money from personal wealth seems to wield its greatest influence during the pre-nomination period of a campaign. In 1960 John F. Kennedy, drawing on personal and family funds, was able to spend enough to discourage competition. However, much less wealthy candidates succeeded against Nelson A. Rockefeller in 1964.[114] The first presidential hopeful to forgo public funding was John Connally in 1976. Two decades on "two millionaire businessmen (Taylor and Forbes) sought the GOP nomination" without much impact.[115] The next pre-nomination campaign of Steven Forbes was a real threat to George W. Bush, although this bid also failed.[116]

A few candidates have made it on their own funds.[117] Rep. John Heinz (PA) in 1976, Sen. John D. Rockefeller (WV) in 1984, Herbert Kohl (WI) in 1988 and Jon Corzine (NJ), former chairman of the Goldman Sachs investment bank, in 2000. Although self-financers make serious challengers to incumbent senators, in 2000 no more than "two of the successful Senate challengers were heavily self-financed." In general, candidates are more willing to risk personal funds on a Senate campaign than in a House election. They are more likely to spend such funds in primary than in general elections.[118]

---

110 Quotes in: Alexander 1979b, p. 680 and p. 682 respectively; cf. Alexander 1992a, p. 70.
111 Heidenheimer 1963, p. 794; Harrison 1963, p. 664; quote by Gwyn 1962, p. 241.
112 Anglade 1970, p. 176.
113 Alexander/ Corrado 1995, p. 128.
114 Heard 1960, p. 323; Alexander 1984, pp. 24-26; Alexander 1992a, pp. 70/71.
115 Alexander 1983, p. 139; quote by Joe/ Wilcox 1999, p. 39.
116 "Money's Going to Talk in 2008", in: *Washington Post*, 11 March 2006.
117 Alexander 1984, p. 27; Alexander 1992a, p. 6.
118 Steen 2006, pp. 2, 4, 17, 23, 25, 29; quote on p. 4; cf. Nelson 2002, p. 27.

In 1970 six Senate and six House candidates each spent more than $25,000 of their own funds, five of each group lost. In 1976 half of the ten House candidates and four of the nine Senate candidates who spent more than $100,000 of their own money were defeated. "Personal wealth is obviously a useful asset, especially for candidates not blessed with the advantage of incumbency."[119] During the 1996 primaries one in three candidates funded more than 50 percent of his campaign with his own means. During the 1970s and 1980s candidates had to provide $20,000 or up to 10 percent of their own money. Especially candidates for open seats devote more cash sometimes, but frequently they are not successful.[120]

Self-financers may "swamp their opponents financially, they do not ... bury" them at the ballot box. Party label, incumbency, and political experience all have a massive influence on the outcome of an election, in most cases more than the amounts of campaign funds spent or self-financing by the candidate. Two major reasons for this small impact of self-financers on election outcomes relate to personal commitment by political activists: Self-financers miss the opportunity to build political support by fundraising activity. The more a candidate is self-financing the more she or he spends on media advertising and the less on all sorts of personal contacts with the electorate.[121]

In Canada campaign contributions by the candidate are reported as "other individual donations." For the late 1980s no examples of "buying" a nomination are available. However, eight percent of the potential candidates are expected to have invested more than CAD5,000 for their nomination.[122] The biggest amount from personal wealth came from Frank Stronach (Liberal), who spent CAD29,021 followed by Dennis Mills, who allocated CAD8,535, while the highest personal contribution by a P.C. candidate was CAD5,000, by an N.D.P. candidate CAD10,000.[123] Self-financing by wealthy candidates, in addition to corporate contributions, seems to be more influential in India.[124]

In Germany two SPD candidates sponsored their own campaigns with DEM65,000 each. A CDU candidate gave DEM40,000 from his personal wealth. These are exceptions, as the average expenditure of candidates seems to be lower than such amounts, namely between DEM5,000 and DEM20,000.[125] In Austria a scandal was helpful in promoting more transparency for private campaign funds.[126] Rabelbauer, an industrialist, proposed to pay for the right to nominate some candidates on the ÖVP party list for the national parliament. When the scandal exploded, the party returned the cash, which had been delivered in a briefcase.[127]

---

119 Jacobson 1980, pp. 97, 101 ; quote on p. 97.
120 Jacobson 1980, p. 97; Wilcox 1988, p. 278; Oldopp 2001, pp. 150, 186-189.
121 Steen 2006, pp. 19/20, 121, 143/144; quote ibid., p. 14.
122 Oldopp 2001, pp. 32, 149; Carty/ Erickson 1991, pp. 112, 117/118, 125.
123 Padget 1991, p. 325.
124 Sangita 2005, p. 180.
125 Oldopp 2001, p. 281; cf. also ibid., pp. 280-283, 363-368.
126 Wicha 1988, pp. 499, 500.
127 For details see Sickinger 1997, p. 63.

3. *Corporate contributions (money from the business community)*

During the 20th century, funds from the corporate world have been the most important source of political money. Right-of-centre parties and governing parties have been the favoured recipients.[128] As a consequence of corruption scandals, parties and politicians in most democracies watch their public reputation and shy away from dependence on corporate donors. Occasionally corporate donations have been banned (for more than a century in the U.S., since 1995 in France and temporarily in India) or their amounts have been capped (most recently in Canada 2004). Other countries have made large donations visible to the public via statutory disclosure of political money (Germany, Norway, Britain, Denmark, even Italy).[129] In the Anglo-Saxon orbit, where such rules are important elements of the political finance regime, potential donors and party bagmen have found ways to live with current restrictions. This has led to fundraising strategies, which are mostly questionable and frequently corrupt. A comparative study of four countries revealed that in Germany and Britain linkage between business and the conservative parties is closer than in Canada and the U.S., where incumbents and the governing parties are favourite recipients of corporate donations.[130]

Information for Spain indicates a different trend. Between 1987 and 1992 all kinds of donations (corporate and individual) amounted to a significant share of party income for just two minor parties, the PCE from 1987 to 1989 (13 to 18 percent) and the PNV from 1989 to 1992 (25 to 58 percent of total annual revenue).[131] On the face of it, this may demonstrate that business formally plays only a marginal role in party financing because efforts to forestall plutocratic financing have been successful. However, corporate funds have flown illegally into party coffers through clandestine channels.[132] Such strategies have also been mentioned for Australia and India.[133] By way of contrast, plutocratic funding really is a minor problem in the Netherlands. Although contributions are tax deductible (since 1954),[134] big donations from the business community hardly exist. However, parties are not required to disclose their financial sources, it is just considered a taboo since the 1960s. In Denmark Social Democrats deliberately abstain from corporate donations, while other parties accept them.[135]

Despite pressure from the media, dependence on large donations from the corporate sector of society prevails in some democracies, because candidates and/or parties feel that without such revenue, they will be short on funds. However, in various countries

---

128 Miller 2005, pp. 99/100, 103.
129 In New Zealand the name of the donor is not disclosed. For a detailed discussion see below in this chapter, sub-section B 5 (public disincentives).
130 Römmele 1995a, p. 172.
131 van Biezen 2000, pp. 334/335.
132 See below in this chapter, sub-section D2 (graft from business sources).
133 Tham 2007, pp. 5/6; Jain 1994, p. 162.
134 See above in chapter VI, sub-section C1b (stimulating contributions).
135 Elzinga 1992, p. 358; Koole 1989, pp. 206/207; Pedersen 2003, p. 327.

the dependence of party headquarters on large (corporate) donations has declined during recent decades due to:

- established links between governments and big business, which do not require backing via monetary means,
- the growing reluctance of the corporate world to donate triggered off by escalating costs of politics, political mishandling of funding scandals,[136] termination of tax privileges or statutory disclosure provisions,
- alternative sources of revenue found by political parties (be they public subsidies or individual donations), which can easily substitute corporate funds.

Any test of such hypotheses would face a multitude of intervening variables (such as, prevailing style of decision-making, wave of democratisation, type of political finance regime, frequency of election campaigns, relevance of party apparatus, intra-party innovations).[137] Reliable time series data on corporate donations as a source of party revenue are available for only a few established democracies. Information that can be given for other countries is patchy at best. Nevertheless some trends can be identified.

The first, and rather surprising, trend is the *transformed role of corporate funds* as a source of political money in the U.S. Despite legislation, which intended to restrict corporate donations, political practice has restructured them. The FECA sets contribution limits and explicitly prohibits corporations (as well as trade unions) from making political contributions. In presidential primaries candidates have aimed to raise small individual donations because these are matched by federal funds. This trend broke in 2004, when both major party candidates (Bush and Kerry) decided to forgo matching funds because they did not want to compete under the statutory spending limit.[138] In a way, dependence upon large donors had been reduced for three decades. Whereas most campaign funds came from this source in the 1970s, it was no longer true up to 2000. The real change has been just a shift in emphasis. In general, the funding of presidential campaigns has given way to soft money, independent expenditures and congressional races. During the 1978-90 elections, roughly one tenth of all funds spent in congressional campaigns originated from the corporate sector.[139] However, it is not the corporations proper, but corporate executives who contribute individual donations (made possible by extra pay) via corporate PACs.[140]

A second trend, the obvious *decline of corporate contributions* as a source of political funding, can be observed in Britain, Germany and Canada. In Britain corporate donations were a traditional source of party revenue. „Although companies are not formal-

---

136 For German examples see Adams 2005, pp. 157-166, 213-226.
137 As advanced by matching funds and tax benefits. See above in chapter VI, section C (public incentives).
138 Sorauf 1988, p.191; "Money's Going to Talk in 2008", in: *Washington Post*, 11 March 2006.
139 Adamany 1976, p. 22; Römmele 1995a, pp. 110, 122.
140 See above in this chapter, sub-section B1c (PACs).

ly politically affiliated to the Conservatives as some trade unions are to the Labour Party, the bulk of corporate political donations do go to the Conservative Party."[141] The reliance of Central Office on business contributions was evident until recently. During four decades (1950-88) donations contributed 60 to 90 percent of the annual budget. From the 1950s to the 1970s exactly four fifths of all donations originated from "companies, banks and partnerships".[142] Most of central office's total revenue was plutocratic funding (Table 7-1 below).

Between 1979 and 1994 the corporate share declined rapidly, from four fifths to one third of all Conservative donations. In the early 1980s plutocratic funding contributed 50 to 60 percent of national revenue. However, by 1992/93 this source provided less than 40 percent of Central Office's budget. By 1996/97 that share dropped to 20 percent. Party treasurer Alastair McAlpine had successfully applied both the personal approach to wealthy individuals and direct mail to a broader donor base. Among the 350 donations of more than £5,000 to the Conservative Party in 1996/97 almost a third (119) were larger than £50,000. Business contributions still outnumbered individual donations by 200 to 150.[143]

During the 1990s U.K. business may have withdrawn from politics. A pioneering study of contributing companies in the early 1990s revealed important details for the process. First of all, Labour successfully removed the traditional reasons for corporate contributions: fear of public ownership and the need to counterbalance trade union influence. Still relevant motives are a favourable environment for business and competent handling of the economy. Most important, however, seem to be personal support by the chairman of the company (obviously including his social networks) and "inertia" to continue making political donations.[144] None of these factors offers a promising outlook for any Conservative treasurer. All of this had already happened when the Labour government introduced a new regime for corporate donations, in which company boards now need to obtain the consent of their shareholders. In 2003/05 a total of 2,747 donors, who gave more than £50,000, contributed a sum of £46 million to all U.K. parties, which was more than two thirds of all revenue from donations.[145]

Whereas contributions by interest groups (except trade unions) are no great source of party funding in Canada,[146] the two major parties traditionally depended on contributions from large corporations for 75 to 90 percent of their income. For both the Liberals and the P.C. the principle source of funds were the business community in Toronto

---

141 Fisher 1996b, p. 162.
142 Pinto-Duschinsky 1981, pp. 138/139, quote on p. 139.
143 Pinto-Duschinsky 1994, p. 15; Fisher 1996b, pp. 158/159; Koole 2001, p. 79.
144 Fisher 1994a, pp. 691, 692, 697/ 698; Fisher 1996b, p. 162.
145 Electoral Commission 2004, para. 5.53.
146 Neither the N.D.P. nor the B.Q. nor the R.P. have ever raised significant amounts of corporate donations.

and Montreal, the regional financial centres of Western Canada and multinational (i.e. U.S.) corporations operating in the country.[147] Since 1974 the share of individual donations has increased considerably, the amounts of corporate contributions are smaller now and the bulk of them is made by small companies. The potential influence of large corporate contributions has been reduced.[148]

Table 7-1: Corporate donations to selected party headquarters, 1968-2002
(in the U.K., Canada and Germany, in per cent of total annual income)

Year	Conservative	P.C. (CDN)	Liberal	CDU (D)	CSU	FDP
1968	53.9			3.3	20.8	1.8
1969	53.5			25.4	50.8	79.9
1970	**64.8**			34.1	48.3	53.3
1971	53.6			16.3	11.2	40.5
1972	59.6			29.5	34.2	33.9
1973	**67.5**			58.9	37.0	76.3
1974	**59.8**	...	...	33.6	26.3	46.4
1975	48.2	49.5	44.8	20.6	14.5	51.4
1976	49.9	47.2	44.2	**29.6**	**38.7**	**61.8**
1977	55.7	45.7	49.9	42.9	38.9	75.2
1978	56.9	48.0	49.6	12.7	35.8	55.4
1979	**64.5**	**54.7**	**55.0**	4.0	7.8	18.0
1980	55.0	**51.1**	**44.6**	28.3	**42.1**	29.6
1981	53.0	37.0	48.4	13.1	31.9	77.1
1982	57.8	34.3	37.4	17.1	22.8	8.9
1983	**62.2**	14.8	45.8	5.3	**15.6**	32.0
1984	48.9	**47.0**	**41.0**	2.9	14.6	8.0
1985	56.0	44.4	39.5	4.5	17.8	17.6
1986	59.8	46.7	45.2	8.9	17.1	22.4
1987	59.0	51.3	60.2	**6.3**	**21.2**	**9.6**
1988	50.5	**53.2**	**47.2**	4.8	22.0	16.0
1989	50.4	47.8	61.5	9.3	19.3	10.9
1990	48.5	56.2	33.2	**11.4**	**17.5**	**10.8**
1991	51.3			12.7	18.2	8.0
1992	37.3			11.0	24.0	8.8
1993	**29.3**			10.6	21.4	8.9
1994	27.7	49.9	50.8	**4.7**	**10.6**	**5.9**
1995	27.7	51.3	56.8	3.9	12.4	4.2
1996	29.3	46.3	55.4	4.9	14.3	10.8
1997	**30.0**		**55.3**	5.4	15.6	17.2

147 For details of pre-1974 Liberal fundraising see Wearing 1981, pp. 59/60, 63/64, 173.
148 Paltiel 1970a, pp. 10, 34, 40; Stanbury 1986b, pp. 801, 814-816; Römmele 1995a, p. 138.

Year	Conservative	P.C. (CDN)	Liberal	CDU (D)	CSU	FDP
1998				**16.4**	**21.7**	**25.9**
1999				8.0	15.2	18.5
2000		**26.8**		10.9	16.4	8.9
2001		8.1		3.8	15.0	15.3
2002		12.9		**8.2**	**26.6**	**20.9**

Sources: Pinto-Duschinsky 1981, pp. 138-139; Pinto-Duschinsky 1989, p. 27; Pinto-Duschinsky 1994, p. 14; Fisher 1996b, pp. 158-160; Neill report 1998, p. 31; Stanbury 1991, pp. 457, 459, 469, 471; www.elections.ca; Bundesanzeiger 1969-83 (full documentation in Ebbighausen et al. 1996, p. 483 and *Deutscher Bundestag*, parliamentary paper, no. 10/2172, 10/4104, 10/6194, 11/977, 11/3315, 11/5993, 11/8130, 12/2165, 12/3950, 12/6140, 13/145, 13/3390, 13/6472, 13/8923, 14/246, 14/2508, 14/5050, 14/7979, 14/8022, 15/700, 15/2800.

Comments: Britain and Canada corporate donations; for Britain mostly estimates based on the above sources; Germany total donations (corporate share see text); data for election years in **bold face** type.

Between 1975 and 1997 business donors, on average, contributed about half of the Liberal and of the P.C. national revenue. In election years, significantly greater amounts are solicited from corporations than in non-election years. In the 1980s large (mostly corporate) contributions accounted for 5 to 26 percent of P.C. revenue and for 12 to 25 percent of Liberal income. During the same period the P.C. received 45 percent more large contributions from business than the Liberals. In the 1990s corporate donations ranged only between 10 and 20 percent of total income, which is a much more modest share of revenue than before 1974.[149]

After eliminating outliers for each party, the share of corporate contributions to national party coffers ranged between 34 to 55 percent for the P.C. and 37 to 60 percent for the Liberals (Table 7-1). This range, however, may suggest a misleading conclusion. All of the major 500 non-financial and the most important 155 financial (bank, insurance et al.) corporations together contributed no more than 8 to 16 percent of total P.C. funds.[150] This share may have been higher for the Liberals but nevertheless the old dependence of party headquarters on the big corporations is over.

The same trend applies to Germany. From the 1950s through the 1970s contributions from big donors and institutional fundraising was a major source of federal party income in Germany, at least for the right-of-centre parties in election years.[151] This influence decreased heavily during the 1980s.[152] For the right-of-centre parties (*CDU, CSU, FDP*) the revenue share of donations to party headquarters declined from 30 to

---

[149] Massicotte 1995, p. 386; Stanbury 1996, pp. 77-79, 83.
[150] Stanbury 1991, p. 465; comparable data for the Liberal party are not available.
[151] Landfried 1994a, pp. 121, 374; Ebbighausen et al. 1996, pp. 90, 93; Adams 2005, pp. 61-65.
[152] The statement that "direct public funding … was intended to replace donations but never actually did" (Schefold 1996, p. 12) is not a fair account of this important development.

10 percent of the total.[153] Between 1968 and 1990 donations have lost ground while public subsidies, membership dues and assessments of party office-holders have gained importance. During the 1970s and 1980s, the pre-direct mail era, donations to *CDU, CSU* and *FDP* headquarters were larger than average and they were made by the business community (individual businessmen, corporate executives, business associations and companies). Whereas donations (for all practical purposes large donations from business sources) on average contributed 25 percent to the CDU, 31 percent to the CSU and 47 percent to the FDP headquarters' revenue between 1968 and 1982, between 1983 and 2002 this share declined to 8, 27 and 21 percent respectively, i.e. much lower than the previous level (see Table 7-1 above).

After 1983 the range of income from donations for CDU headquarters was between three to sixteen percent, a far cry from the "golden age". For its Bavarian wing the change has been less dramatic. In 10 of 15 years (1968-82), they raised between 25 and 51 percent. During recent decades CSU headquarters raised 15 to 27 percent of its revenue in donations. For the federal FDP the wind of change has been particularly forceful. Donations have contributed over 15 percent in no more than 9 of 20 years (Table 7-1). Since 1994 the official reports tabled by the German parties list donations by legal entities (corporations and associations) and donations by individuals separately. Because donating organisations mostly are business associations, the category is the closest equivalent of corporate donations available in Germany. Detailed reporting for 1994 to 2002 reveals that corporate donations comprised between 3 to 8 percent of headquarters' revenue for the CDU, 5 to 19 percent for the CSU and 2 to 15 percent for the FDP. During the 1980s corporate donors may have contributed 3 to 5 percent of CDU, 10 to 13 percent of CSU and 5 to 20 percent of FDP headquarters' annual budget in elections years, which is more than in non-election years. Since that time neither of the three parties' headquarters has depended on corporate donors.

Nevertheless a recent study provided additional details on corporate giving in Germany. Legal entities (i.e. corporations etc.) contributed about 16 percent of total CSU revenue, 10 percent of FDP income and about 7 percent of the annual CDU budget in 2002. For donations in excess of €10,000 the highest correlations were for active involvement of corporate management with CDU/CSU and FDP and for corporations with a large number of shareholders and donations to CDU and CSU, whereas companies representing the motor car industry donated more heavily to the parties in government (SPD and *Grüne*).[154] Quite recently the sponsoring of party events, which is a traditional form of corporate contributions in the U.S., created some media hype in Germany. Scholarly debate dutifully followed suit and covers this "new" source of party funding.[155]

The third process of change has occurred in the north of continental Europe. In Finland and Sweden public subsidies have replaced corporate donations as a major source of

---

153 Römmele 1995a, p. 156.
154 Höpner 2006, pp. 297, 303.
155 Morlok/ von Alemann/ Streit 2006.

revenue for right-of-centre parties and helped them to gain more independence from interested money. Parties and donors have seized the opportunity. Until 1965, the national headquarters of the Liberals and the Conservatives in Sweden almost completely depended on business donations. In the 1970s the Liberal Party decided not to accept corporate donations anymore, first at the national level (1971) and later at all other levels (1976). Coalition pressures made the Conservatives reach a similar conclusion in 1977. Money from corporate sources then started to flow to issue advocacy groups, which do public relations work on behalf of conservative causes. In this way, corporate funds in Finland are now spent on independent advertising to promote specific issues, which are of interest to the business community.[156] Quite to the contrary "donations from interest organisations and industrial corporations" seem to have gained importance in Denmark and Norway.[157]

A different process has to be noted for a fourth group of countries. That is, legislation, which looks pretty precise, but has had *no significant impact* on real life. Despite (more or less detailed) disclosure rules practically no information is available about corporate donations in Italy, France, Israel, Japan and Australia. Although Italian legislation (since 1974) requires the publication of a corporate contribution in the company's annual report as well as in the party's balance sheet, not much disclosure has been forthcoming. Thus it is impossible to estimate the total amount of money, which parties raise from this source. It seems fair to assume that most donations are still given clandestinely.[158] According to official records in France, donations from the business community contributed 13 percent of parties' income in 1993. However, this figure is generally believed to be far too low. Since 1995 candidates and parties are no longer allowed to accept donations from private corporations and public sector companies. Nevertheless some observers expect that an increase of surreptitious donations to parties and candidates has just intensified a practice, which already existed before 1995.[159]

In order to avoid the legal ban on corporate donations in Israel businesses can provide in-kind-services. For example, an insurance company covers the publication costs of a political pamphlet, a newspaper publishes a party advertisement free of charge, a printer charges lower prices than market value, *kibbutzim* may hire extra workers and pick up their expenses (for travel, food etc.) while the workers "volunteer" for campaign activities. Between 1973 and 1994, parties found an obvious strategy to evade the disclosure of corporate donations. It was „a common practice among the Israeli parties to open bank accounts for private citizens, who happened to be the senior members of the party." Another avenue for business contributions opened up with the direct elections of mayors (since 1978). For all municipal campaigns between 1978 and

---

156 Gidlund 1994, p. 110; Nassmacher 1982, pp. 3-18; the opposite is claimed by Sundberg 2002, p. 199, based on Gidlund 1991, pp. 42-52 and Wiberg 1991c, pp. 80-98.
157 Svasand 1994, pp. 197-206; Bille 1997, pp. 163-191; as cited by Sundberg 2002, p. 199.
158 van Biezen/ Nassmacher 2001, p. 140.
159 Koole 2001, p. 80; Russ 2005, pp. 368-377.

1993, legal restrictions were absent. Thus „businessmen and corporations were able to give enormous contributions legally." The parties remained dependent on large donations. The business community preferred to donate to politicians who had proven their electoral appeal, a fact of life reported in Japanese politics as well.

Time and again the traditional dependence of the dominant party in Japan on business funding has caused scandals and has been subject to reform efforts. Traditionally corporate donations are given to individual politicians, to intra-party factions (*habatsu*) and to the formal organisation of the governing *Jimintô* (LDP). The introduction of contribution limits in the aftermath of the Lockheed Scandal in 1976 was not successful. The party switched to fundraising events, [160] and firms shifted their monetary backing to the support groups of individual MPs. Following the reform effort in 1994, corporate donations provided only 22 percent of LDP income in 1996, a sharp contrast to 50 percent in 1991. However, individual MPs continue to heavily solicit such funds. In 1998 LDP legislators got 45 percent, DJP legislators 54 percent and *Kômeitô* legislators 30 percent of their total funding from corporate sources. In order to strengthen the role of the political parties, MPs are allowed only one support group (*koenkai*) since 1994. Late in 1999 donations to individual politicians became illegal. Now local party organisations serve as a substitute for the traditional support organisations of MPs.[161]

In Australia party income from corporate donations is still effectively concealed from public scrutiny. Only in 1984 did reports offer a complete list of all contributions in excess of AUD1,000, disclosing name, amount and address of each donor. This detailed regulation was abolished after all three national parties had set up front organisations to prevent public disclosure of major donors' identity.[162] In the state of New South Wales an accounting firm scheduled fundraising functions for the Liberal Party, which it "viewed ... as a marketing expense" and which were attended by senior ministers. "Companies buying entire tables were able to choose, which Minister they would like to dine with."[163]

For other countries only illuminating [and amusing] details can be presented. Scarce data for Ireland indicate that *Fianna Fail* depended on the agricultural sector between 1987 and 1991. The funds donated by just three companies amounted to 10 percent of national party income during that period. Contributions to *Fine Gael* from the same source for the same period amounted to 7 percent of its total revenue. The Progressive Democrats revealed that this applied to 3 percent of their income.[164] *Fianna Fail* and

---

160 A company buying tickets for a fundraising party does not make a political contribution (subject to a legal limit) but incurs a business expense (without any such limitation). Blechinger/ Nassmacher 2001, p. 164.
161 Blechinger 1999, pp. 58/59; Blechinger/ Nassmacher 2001, p. 163; Köllner 2000b, pp. 151, 154.
162 Chaples 1988b, p.6.
163 Wilson 2004, p 12, quoting *The Age*, 14 September 2002 and *Sydney Morning Herald,* 13 June 2001.
164 Farrell 1993, p. 32; Farrell 1994, p. 234.

Fine Gael (as well as some of their politicians) had received generous payments from leading businessmen.[165]

In Austria only donations of ATS 100,000 (US-$ 7,000) and more must be disclosed. Financial reports show that different amounts flow from this source to major parties' federal headquarters. On average (for 1991 to 1994) the ÖVP raised more funds from this source (ATS 48.3 million) than the SPÖ (ATS 41.5 million). For the FPÖ large donations offer less reliable funding: ATS 10.7 million in 1991, none in 1994. The overall share of interested money contributed to Austrian parties is rather low, about 10 to 12 percent of total revenue.[166]

Traditionally the Swiss FDP solicits large donations.[167] Generally speaking big money seems to be important in Switzerland, but the public is informed only by means of an occasional scandal. For example, in the 1980s, when a high ranking civil servant and an employee of a mortgage bank were convicted of embezzlement in favour of governing parties. Just one important donor has disclosed party funding activity (Credit Suisse). This bank, which in former years contributed to the FDP and the CVP, pointed out that in the future no more donations would be forthcoming to either party because of a minor lobbying impact.[168]

Latin American democracies analysed by Casas-Zamora show similar patterns of fundraising among the business community: Politicians of all parties approach a small circle of wealthy people and these give to more than one party regularly.[169] However, in general (in Costa Rica possibly more so than in Uruguay) the process is "defined by *individual* links between donors and politicians, rather than by *collective* participation of social or economic sectors."[170]

Contributions of companies (and wealthy people) always played a major role for the Congress Party in India. The ban on corporate money (introduced in the 1960s) did not hinder the flow of this money, because the party received these funds in secret. When the ban on corporate donations was lifted in 1985, there were strong strings attached. However, the companies were able to circumvent them when financing parties and activities of parliamentarians, e.g. a party meeting as a donation-in-kind.[171] In 1996 corrupt practices forced a former prime minister and then leader of the opposition (Mr Rao) to resign.

The change of the political landscape in East Central Europe during the early 1990s created the need for financial support of political parties, which was matched by the need of bureaucrats to secure support from the new ruling class of post-communist politicians. In Poland corporate donations represented less than 40 percent of the total

---

165 Girvin 1999, p. 24; Murphy/ Farrell 2002, p. 220.
166 Sickinger 1997, pp. 67/68.
167 Weigelt 1988, p. 32.
168 *Frankfurter Rundschau*, 28 January 2000.
169 Casas-Zamora 2002, pp. 178-180, 227-235; Casas-Zamora 2005a, pp. 136-137, 174-179.
170 Casas-Zamora 2002, p. 180; Casas-Zamora 2005a, p. 136.
171 Jain 2001, p. 353.

revenue in the 1991 parliamentary campaign, compared to about 87 percent of the annual proceeds of the Freedom Union in 1997. Large donors play a special and disproportionately important role in East Central European political finance, which often overrides direct public funding.[172] Thus Poland recently decided to prohibit donations by all legal entities in a desperate attempt to limit the influence of plutocratic funding. More established democracies have devised a whole range of measures to counteract such potential.

4. Public disincentives to discourage interested contributions

Instead of stimulating small mass contributions via public incentives, a different regulatory approach that intends to influence the mix of donations from interested and non-interested money aims to actively discourage "unwanted" contributions. Public regulation can address the issue by levying additional taxes, stipulating shareholders' approval or prescribing more publicity.[173] Most popular is the heads-on approach. That is, the legal ban on corrupt sources of political funds and/or on donations by non-citizens, be they foreign individuals and governments or corporations of any nationality.

a) Bans[174]

In most countries anonymous contributions are banned. Parties in France, Spain and Israel may not accept money from foreign governments or institutions (except the European Parliament). However, virtually all parties in third wave democracies received ample financial support from abroad, especially during transition years. In order to prevent disguised contributions in Israel, loans can be negotiated from banks only.[175] Since 1995 candidates and parties in France are no longer allowed to receive funds from private corporations and public sector companies. In Italy, Spain and Japan donations from public or semi-public entities are banned. Moreover labour unions and other organisations in Japan may no longer donate to individual politicians. Do such bans prevent de facto financing by private business, usually through individuals or foundations as intermediaries?[176]

Although Germany and Austria do not apply such bans, there are practical restrictions. In Austria political donations by organised interests are subject to an income tax surcharge to be paid by the recipient party, and in Germany the Supreme Court has banned tax benefits for corporate donors.[177] In the Netherlands, traditional ethics inhibit par-

---

172 Walecki 2001, pp. 399, 402-403.
173 Ewing 2007, pp. 101/102, 110/111. For a complete overview see Nassmacher 2006, pp. 447-451.
174 On the variety of bans, which are on the statute book, see Tjernström 2003, pp. 197-203.
175 Mendilow 1996, p. 348.
176 India offers evidence for a clear-cut "no"; see Jain 1994, p. 162; Jain 2001, p. 351.
177 For details see Sickinger 1997, pp. 48, 52-54; Drysch 1998, p. 83 and Boyken 1998, pp. 56-59, 77-90.

ties from soliciting corporate donations.[178] Thus far experience shows that legal bans on specific donors are not effective. U.S. practice since the Chandler-Tillman Act of 1907 [179] demonstrates the limited impact of bans. Introducing a legal limit on the amount a specific donor may give and/or any political competitor may solicit, is a less strict approach.

b)   Contribution limits[180]

Spanish law limits donations and these limits tend to become stricter over time.[181] In Japan different contribution limits have been set for annual totals of donations given by individuals to parties and their fundraising bodies, to financial support groups of politicians and to other political organisations (e.g. *habatsu* or *kôenkai*). Since 1994 individual politicians are limited to one personal fundraising committee. Israel reduced the ceiling for contributions to parties. It now stipulates separate limits for contributions to internal party primaries for the nomination of candidates on the party list. Starting in 2004 individuals in Canada may contribute no more than CAD 5,000 per year to a party, to a leadership contestant or to a non-party candidate for the federal parliament. For corporations and trade unions the rule is much stricter.

In many countries (Britain, Australia, Germany, Austria, Switzerland, the Netherlands, Sweden) there is no statutory limit on the amount of political contribution that a person or corporation may give to a party or a candidate. If instituted as proposed by a U.K. Labour Party think-tank (the Institute for Public Policy Research), a cap on donations would have forced political parties to reject 3,002 donations, which represented 88 percent of the value of all donations made in Britain from 2003 to 2005.[182]

Sometimes such limits (just like bans) are no more than acts of symbolic politics. If anything else is intended politically, the flow of funds into party coffers demands monitoring and the rules need tough enforcement.[183] Since the 1970s, the U.S. law demonstrates the limited impact of contribution limits. The proliferation of PACs, the invention of "independent expenditures" and the bundling of donations are especially convincing cases in point.[184] Just like legal bans statutory contributions limits have been unable to eliminate the menace of plutocratic influence, especially from business sources. Time and again scandals have unleashed demand for more transparency of political funding.

---

178 Koole 1994a, p. 126.
179 Alexander 1992a, p. 24.
180 For the diffusion of such limits in 1998 see Casas-Zamora 2002, pp. 23/24; Casas-Zamora 2005a, p. 19.
181 van Biezen/ Nassmacher 2001, p. 148.
182 Cain/ Taylor 2002; Electoral Commission 2004, para. 5.51.
183 Cf. Paltiel 1976, pp. 108/109. For practical issues of enforcement see Nassmacher 2003d, pp. 139-154.
184 For details see Alexander 1992a, pp. 36-38, 56-60 and above in this chapter, sub-section B1a (PACs).

c) Disclosure of donors' identity

Although perfect transparency may not be achieved, the request for proper financial conduct is legitimate in each democracy. Limitations in action will result from the principle as well as from the technicalities of disclosure.[185] The most promising attempt to discourage large donations in general or by specific kinds of donors is publicity. The major aim of legal action is to make political money an issue of public policy, in which the public keeps a lasting interest. People have a right to know who the backers of a party are. If donations beyond a considerable threshold have to be disclosed to the public such funds may become subject to public debate. If a donor or a recipient wants to avoid this debate, their best bet is not to make or not to accept the donation. Once again, this all depends on the monitoring of political funds and on enforcing publicity rules effectively.[186] Canada, Germany and the U.K. offer some evidence of successful practice; even the U.S. FEC may be rather useful in this respect.

Nevertheless disclosure of donors' identity is ridden with contradictions. The very idea of the secret ballot suggests that a donor's privacy should be protected. Considerable influence by "fat cats", however, undermines democratic equality ("one person, one vote"). The practical solution may distinguish between different types of donors (i.e. individual, corporation, organisation) and look for cut-off points. The legislative task at hand is to find an enduring and reliable separation between contributing money (as a means of political participation) and buying access to decision-makers or a specific decision (as incidents of influence peddling).

While Swedish law still upholds the traditional view that donor's privacy has to be respected, Austria has found the "half-way" solution to gather information (for later inspection by the federal audit office in case of a scandal), but not disclose any donor's identity to the public.[187] Most democracies now operate disclosure rules, which separate individual donors from corporate donors and define a threshold amount that has to be disclosed. Germany, Britain and the Netherlands are at the high end in this regard (US-$ 10,000 to US-$ 5,000). The U.S., Canada, France and Japan represent the low end, with disclosure thresholds ranging between US-$ 400 and US-$ 100. In Australia the threshold for disclosure is AUD1,500.[188]

Furthermore, any disclosure regulation has to identify the legal procedure, a person or institution that is responsible and the kind of information, which has to be disclosed. The latter can be very different. For example, alongside the amount donated, the name (as in Canada and the U.K.) and address (as in Australia) can be required. Stricter rules may also stipulate the disclosure of an ID number (e.g. in Spain), the employer or oc-

---

185 Where blind trusts and other conduit bodies effectively shield donor's identity (e.g. in New Zealand; Miller 2005, 100), transparency is neither intended nor achieved.
186 For the diversity of current regulation see contributions in Nassmacher 2001a and Nassmacher 2003a-e; for an overview see Casas-Zamora 2002, pp. 30/31; Casas-Zamora 2005a, pp. 24/25.
187 Gidlund 1993, p. 108; Sickinger 1997, p. 134.
188 More details on this subject gradually emerge from a compilation of three (partially dependent) tables: Pinto-Duschinsky 2002, pp. 76/77; Tjernström 2003, pp. 193.195; Wilson 2004, p. 18.

cupation of the donor and the date of the donation (e.g. in France). For a policy to be effective the disclosed information should be accurate, timely, accessible and comprehensible to potential users.

Some countries have instituted additional provisions. In Britain donations must be reported quarterly between elections, and within seven days during a campaign period. (All of this obviously does not apply to loans, which have become a favoured loophole to get around the regulation.) In Japan disclosure also applies to individuals and corporations buying tickets for fundraising events. In Italy a corporate donation has to be approved by the board of directors and (according to statute law, but rarely in practice) be disclosed twice, i.e. in the donor company's annual report and in the recipient party's balance sheet. Full disclosure always places an administrative burden on the parties, and occasionally without really even improving their openness and accountability.[189] There is no easy solution at hand to this problem, quite like in any other combat zone of the continuing struggle for democratic politics, e.g. all attempts to counteract influence from foreign sources of political funds.

5. Income from foreign funds

From the start of Jewish settlement in Israel, the "National Foundation Fund," which collected cash in the diaspora and distributed it among the Zionist parties, supported parties according to the "party key", i.e. their share of the vote for national institutions. In the Yishuv years (and the early decades of statehood) it has „become axiomatic in Israeli politics that no election is possible without substantial assistance from ... abroad." It is hard to believe that this habit should have completely disappeared after public subsidies and contribution bans were introduced. Indeed, "parties receive a modicum of help from fraternal parties abroad, significant aid comes from organized groups and individual supporters in the Jewish diaspora, ..."[190]

In other new democracies political parties obtained money from abroad during the transition period. In post-war times this has happened in Germany, Italy and Japan when parties accepted American secret service funds to contain Soviet expansion and to support democracy building. Spain and Portugal were first among the third wave democracies, where "all sectors of society, apparently, have been willing to assist their friends abroad when necessity" dictated.[191] More recent examples are countries in Latin America, Southern Africa, South East Asia and Central Eastern Europe, where many established democracies via different NGOs provided support for party building and transition to sustainable democracy. Most notably British, German and U.S. foundations have actively promoted the transition process.[192]

---

189 Young 1991, p. 20.
190 Quotes from Gutmann 1963, p. 711 respectively Paltiel 1981, p. 150.
191 Breitling 1971, p. 475; Paltiel 1976, p. 52; Winkler 1978, pp. 475/476; quote in Paltiel 1981, p. 149.
192 For details cf. Pinto-Duschinsky 2001c, pp. 298-303. For early examples see Paltiel 1981, pp. 149/150.

Funding by aircraft manufacturers and other armament-makers or oil and other resource companies doing international business are cases of graft rather than foreign aid. Illegal funds, e.g. drug related money, are familiar in Latin America (including Mexico), where influence is wielded by the Gulf of Mexico drug cartel.[193]

A systematic analysis of foreign funding in Costa Rica and Uruguay was presented by Casas-Zamora. Although there have been incidents of multinational companies contributing to individual campaigns there is no evidence of continued interference. The same, in all likelyhood, is true for money from drug trafficking. Moreover, "the large funding role occasionally ascribed to German political foundations is, in Uruguay as in Costa Rica, simply a myth."[194]

Money from abroad seems of minor importance in the U.S., although the press mentioned it during the 1996 presidential campaign.[195] This is also true for Britain where such funds have been important occasionally, e.g. contributions from the Arab world. When Conservative party treasurer Alastair McAlpine successfully approached wealthy individuals in the 1980s, some of them were apparently living abroad.[196] In June 2001 Labour received a donation of £125,000 by Mr Lakshmi Mittal, the owner of a multinational steel company, which for tax purposes is registered in the Dutch Antilles. In July 2001 Prime Minister Blair sent a letter to his Romanian colleague in support of the firm's privatisation bid.[197] During the 1980s money from Iraq and Iran went into the campaign chests of governing parties in France as a reward for arms deals. After the Socialist party (PS) came to power, it got money from the SPD and German labour unions.[198]

In general, Communist parties in Western democracies are a special case. In India the Communists obtained funds from the Soviet Union; the Marxists are alleged to have once received money from China.[199] In France the PCF was frequently accused by its competitors of drawing monetary support from Moscow. The sums transferred have been quite relevant. For the French and the Italian Communist Party amounts were never clearly identified and only conjectures exist until the early 1970s. However, after the West European Communist parties were no longer in line with their East European "brethren," the flow of funds from this source declined sharply.[200] A frequently mentioned source of Communist party funding were businesses owned by the party,[201] among them import-export companies involved in foreign trade with COMECON countries. In West Germany the re-established Communist Party (DKP) received as-

---

193 Paltiel 1981, p. 149; Zovatto 2001, pp. 373-375.
194 Casas-Zamora 2002, pp. 183-186, 246-248; Casas-Zamora 2005a, pp. 140/141,186-188; quotes on p. 248 and p. 188.
195 Joe/ Wilcox 1999, p. 50.
196 Fisher 1996b, p. 159; Whiteley et al. 1994, p. 5.
197 "The Mittal way", in: *The Economist*, 23 February 2002; Osler 2002, pp. 146-149..
198 Schmitt 1993, p. 78.
199 Jain 2001, p. 352.
200 Timmermann 1971, pp. 2/3.
201 See below in this chapter, section C (parties as entrepreneurs).

sistance of DEM 10 million in 1970 and about DEM 20 million in 1971 from East Germany. The East German Communists covered nearly all financial needs of the West German party. For one year in the 1970s Winkler estimated this need at more than DEM 102 million.[202] The Communist parties indicate what applies to others as well. The borderline between foreign funds and entrepreneurship is crossed over frequently.

C) Returns on investment: dividends and interest (parties as entrepreneurs)

For the average political party, the accumulation of profit-yielding assets is not a regular activity. However, time and again parties have acquired real estate, business shares and monetary holdings. Some of these assets have been closely connected with party operations: office buildings house party headquarters or regional bureaus, printing shops produce newspapers, brochures, flyers and posters, campaign funds are set aside in a bank account. Any cash return on such investment is an incidental part of annual revenue. Occasionally party owned enterprises have rented surplus office space to others or marketed their printing capacity during non-campaign periods. Oversized financial reserves or funds held in a "blind trust" may carry considerable amounts of interest.

A significant distinction must be made between party-owned and *party-controlled* enterprises. From the latter a party will not yield a return on investment but these kinds of businesses open up ample opportunities for patronage, service at reduced cost or diversion of resources. Ownership of such enterprises may belong to trade unions, co-operatives, local, regional or (occasionally even) national governments, which collect the dividends, if there are any to be distributed. Party controlled enterprises have been notorious in Austria, Israel and Italy, where parties used to control (but not to own) banks, co-operatives and industrial companies.[203]

In some cases parties have set up commercial enterprises to serve as a conduit for political donations, which are disguised as payments for services rendered. *Party-owned* firms "sell" advertisements in publications, multiple subscriptions to newsletters, packages of research papers or consultancy meetings, all of them far beyond their commercial value, to individuals or corporations. The patron can either claim a tax exemption for a "business expense" or circumvent contribution rules (bans, limits or disclosure). Some of these transactions are outright illegal, and for some the party enterprise serves as a front organisation for an international transfer of funds. The party-owned enterprise makes a considerable profit that is turned over to the party either in cash or in extra service.

---

202 Breitling 1971, p. 474; Winkler 1978, pp. 101-103.
203 Paltiel 1981, pp. 147/148; Sickinger 1997, pp. 75/76.

Many political parties, mostly in continental Europe, actively run *commercial enterprises*. Party-owned companies include anything from newspaper publishers and printing plants to travel agencies, import-export companies and consulting firms, to name just the most frequent examples. During the second half of the 20th century the latter have mostly been used as front organisations to launder foreign or corporate donations into party coffers by a very diverse sample of parties including the German CDU and FDP, the French and Italian Communists, the French and Spanish Socialists.[204]

Of late computer services and retail distribution of "fan" merchandise have been subject to outsourcing. In addition, we have to consider printing and publishing houses, mainly for three reasons: If such enterprises make a profit, this can be used as a source of party income. If not, such enterprises can disseminate their parent party's ideology or advance its position in communications and propaganda. Finally, party owned establishments are a reservoir of manpower for all purposes a party wants to advance.

In general, party income from shareholding, interest on monetary assets and ownership of real estate property is of minor importance only. Even in Germany, where annual reporting gives a pretty good impression of party revenue, the returns on investment are rather modest. During the 1999-2002 election cycle return on investment was not a significant source of revenue for most German parties.[205] A range of 1.0 to 2.5 percent of the annual total includes most parties represented in the federal parliament (CDU, CSU, Greens and PDS). Only in 1999 the CSU collected more income from assets because it sold its headquarters, which yielded more than 1/6 of that year's income. The FDP made an above average gain (2.9 to 4.1 percent of annual revenue) regularly, with its federal party the share ranged between 5.4 and 9.2 percent of the total. The biggest owner of invested capital among German parties is the SPD, which earned 4.8 to 6.6 percent of its entire income in 1999-2002 from assets. A total of 20 printing and publishing companies [206] contributed 9 to 15 percent of the federal party's budget.

Publishing and printing houses (including party newspapers) are a traditional type of party owned enterprises. In earlier decades, parties received considerable income from the party press. More recently, party affiliated newspapers in Austria, Denmark, Germany, Italy, Norway and Sweden ran into problems. When the party press had become a drain on party funds, the newspapers were either closed down, de-politicised (e.g. in Denmark), sold to non-party publishers (e.g. in Germany) or their deficits were turned over to the public purse (as has happened in Austria, Italy, and Sweden).[207]

Other party-owned firms provide only small amounts towards party coffers. Some Communist parties in Western democracies did not fit into this picture. The Austrian

---

[204] Lösche 1984, pp. 49/50. For examples of the laundering process see below, chapter VII, section D (graft).
[205] *Deutscher Bundestag*, parliamentary paper, no. 14/5050, 14/8022, 15/700, 15/2800.
[206] *Deutscher Bundestag*, parliamentary paper, no. 15/2800, pp. 26-28.
[207] See Sickinger 1997, pp. 76/77; Pedersen 2003, pp. 246/247; Wewer 1987, pp. 11, 182, 185/186; Svasand 1991, pp. 126, 138; Gidlund 1991, p. 18 and Sundberg 2002, p. 208.

party (*KPÖ*) was the greatest capitalist of all, owning a petroleum company, which held the import monopoly for natural gas from the Soviet Union,[208] and businesses, which were involved in trade with Eastern Europe. In West Germany the Communist Party (*DKP*) owned printing shops, publishing houses, travel agencies and export-import agencies. In France and Italy import and export firms were important sources of funding for the Communist parties as well.[209] The Indian Communists are successfully operating a publishing house and selling newspapers, books and pamphlets. In Japan the Communist Party (*Kyôsantô*) is the only political party, which is able to draw most of its funds from a highly profitable printing business.[210]

At the beginning of economic transition in Central Eastern Europe (e.g. Poland), post-communist parties relied heavily on contributions from state enterprises, non-communist parties on foreign funds, because private contributors were few and potential donors lacked individual wealth. However, there is a major exception, the Polish Peasants' Party (*PSL*), which participated in the first non-Communist government and thus was very important for the final phase of the peaceful transition. This party, the *PSL*, a surviving satellite of the Communist regime, reported significant income (obviously from renting office space in its oversized headquarters building). Such income accounted for 77 to 91 percent of total revenue in 1997-2000.[211]

There seems to be a modern trend towards enlarging party revenue via "sundry income" from side businesses, often with affiliated but legally independent firms. The Conservatives in Britain tried to enlarge their funding base by commercial activities, e.g. financial services, conferences and sales.[212] Other parties started to sell fan merchandise, but the amounts raised in this manner do not match the income, which soccer clubs collect from the same effort. All Italian parties, even those which declined to splinter groups, own office buildings and other real estate.[213] Nonetheless graft has been a more important source of party revenue.

D) Party income from political graft

The ability to raise funds because someone exercises power is the substance of political graft ("power solicits"). When parties want to earn some revenue by using the spoils of office, they may target different groups. In the past, political parties in Western democracies successfully tapped various clienteles for financial contributions, given more or less voluntarily. The exercise of political pressure or mutual agreement on

---

208 *Frankfurt Allgemeine*, 20 August 1986.
209 Timmermann 1971, pp. 3, 5; Paltiel 1981, p. 148.
210 Jain 2001, p. 352; Blechinger/ Nassmacher 2001, p. 164. The latter may, however, be a fake similar to the use of membership dues to hide foreign funds in the 1950s (Soukup 1963, pp. 743/744).
211 Walecki 2005a, pp. 113, 125.
212 Fisher 1996b, pp. 159, 161.
213 *Das Parlament*, 18 February 2000.

clandestine exchanges may be the cause for a donation. The borderline to corruption is always close and sometimes has to be crossed in order to ensure the flow of party revenue from spoils. It goes without saying that politicians in power have easier access to funds than those in opposition. The use of state resources for the ruling party and practices rooted in clientelism by means of appointments to government positions or public works contracts are familiar in Latin America and beyond.[214]

Officials and MPs who want to promote their careers can be addressed easily and "asked" for a contribution to party coffers. This form of tithing is well known as *assessment* of office-holders. Members of the *business community* may offer or accept to pay a „voluntary" contribution in exchange for a political favour (e.g. a public contract). The demarcation between plutocratic financing, political graft and outright corruption is hard to observe where close (financial and personal) links between political parties and the business community exist. Expansion of the public sector has opened up new sources of graft, which 19th century U.S. bagmen could not even have dreamt of. Nationalised industries and corporations in public ownership offer a wealth of opportunities for the parties in power to obtain monetary advantages at the expense of *public property*.

Party coffers in France and Spain are also filled, besides donations from private firms working for a public administration, by expertise given just in pretence. The hypothesis of Della Porta and Meny that parties in opposition especially try to tap illegal money because they are excluded from the financial resources that the government parties have access to, could not be verified. In both countries there were efforts to get rid of illegal practices by providing public subsidies. There are doubts, whether the practice that publicly owned firms and private firms working on behalf of public administration, traditionally made to pay for parties' coffers, continues.[215] After all, according to an estimate of the 1980s this money contributed to party income up to an equivalent of 75 percent of the public subsidies.[216]

1. Abuse of public resources

Among the many abuses of power, the diversion of public funds for partisan advantage is an endless story frequently told by the media and criticised by parties in opposition. Advertising in favour of government policies has been an issue in many jurisdictions. Secret funds at the disposal of presidents or prime ministers, use of aircraft or helicopters, state visits planned as campaign events are the more serious abuses of executive privilege.[217] However, abuse does not stop with the options available to a government.

---

214 Zovatto 2001, pp. 374, 380.
215 Della Porta/ Meny 1997c, pp. 171/172; Mule 1998, pp.65-66; Newell 2000, p. 61.
216 As cited by Hine 1996, p. 138.
217 The appointment of Alan Milburn as Chancellor of the Duchy of Lancaster was a recent but minor incident. As a full-fledged member of Tony Blair's cabinet, his sole responsibility was the completely partisan task of coordinating the preparation of Labour's campaign effort for 2005.

Legislative privilege is another broad area for the abuse of public resources for partisan benefit. Incumbent legislators may use their franking or travel privileges, constituency offices, assistants and secretaries paid for by parliament funds to cover expenses of party competition, such as sending campaign mail or travel to campaign rallies, substitute for local party offices and party agents. All of these options are used at times, and public resources are thereby abused. Such abuses have to be prevented or contained by adequate measures, but they do not require closer consideration here.

Two options stand out as the most obvious examples, one of them outright illegal, the other somewhere between crude and tasteless. If there is no legal ban or contribution limit on corporate donations in general or donations by publicly owned corporations in particular, any such company may decide to make any number of donations of any size to any or all of the parties in power. Party notables will represent the public owner on supervisory boards and the appointment of managers will be a partisan decision. Small wonder, if managers are willing to make favourable donations on behalf of their corporation (and their own career).

Italian parties successfully tapped businesses of the public sector, which had expanded since the 1950s (especially IRI and ENI; later on ENEL was added).[218] An enormous financial fraud was related to a public-private joint venture (*Enimont* chemicals) that surprised even hardened observers by its size, audacity, and the many leading politicians and businessmen involved." By that time DC and PSI had become "highly southernised", i.e. even in the northern half of the country political life "acquired many of the characteristics originally most prevalent in the south."[219] Corporations in public ownership made a lot of political contributions during the 1950s and 1960s.[220] There is good reason to doubt that the 1974 legislation, which banned such contributions, stopped this flow of funds. For example it was public knowledge that managers of state owned companies expressed their "gratitude" towards politicians who had appointed them by donating large amounts to political parties. In a sense, managers simply "bought" their re-appointment with corporate funds.[221] Before 1974 such use of public resources for partisan benefit may not have been illegal, but certainly these cash contributions represent an extortionate use of political power.

The other strategy of extortion is illegal beyond doubt, putting party workers on the payroll of a public agency or public utility company without any work on behalf of their "employer". Four examples for this "subsidy-in-kind" strategy are public knowledge. In Italy the Milan underground paid some PSI party workers, who never showed up at their "workplace".[222] In Belgium some people are on the payroll of a national or

---

218 Mulé 1998, pp. 65/66; see also Rhodes 1997, pp. 57, 68-69; Newell 2000, pp. 64/65.
219 Hine 1996, pp. 138, 144/145.
220 cf. Passigli 1963, pp. 730/731.
221 Pasquino 1996, p.25.
222 Della Porta/ Vannucci 1999, p. 117.

a regional minister while being in practice a member of his party's study centre.[223] In Poland all major parties "use their position of [national, regional or municipal] power to nominate some of their mid-level party bureaucrats as 'political advisors' to ministers, ..., governors or city mayors, ... to cover the costs of routine party operation with public money."[224] In France some employees of public utility companies unofficially worked only for a party. The RPR headquarters used to employ staff who were paid either by the municipal government of Paris or by private enterprises that depended on public contracts with the city administration.[225]

In 1993 the State Controller's audit found that Israeli mayors had used their municipal authority's staff and budget for media advertising, publications, and presents (carrying the mayor's name) given to voters. Since the late 1980s the diversion of public resources (and trade union funds) has found a new focus, the intra-party competition for positions on the national party list. In their quest for a safe position on their party's slate of candidates, Israeli MPs have discovered an additional option. They use a perquisite of their public office, private members' bills, to obtain enough publicity to support their internal bid for re-election. In 1999-2003 "several politicians replaced spending on media airtime by getting considerable exposure through initiation and passing of expensive bills that gave certain benefits to targeted sections of the electorate."[226] There is no cash flow involved and there is nothing illegal about it. However, this creative use of public resources for personal gain is most likely not what an Israeli voter would expect his or her elected representative to do.

2. Graft from business sources

Political revenue can be extorted from the business community that is traditionally called graft in the U.S. „Graft has been defined as an abuse of power for personal or party profit." As personal profit is not a subject here, we limit the term to any enrichment of party coffers. It „usually involves a relationship between the official exercising the power, which is abused, and some other individuals" acting on behalf of an industry or a business.[227] The officials or the politicians in power "sell" political favours, e.g. contracts or licenses, and make sure that there is a response in cash to party coffers after a person or a company has received something valuable, such as, a permit or contract. Basically there are two broad categories of graft: kickbacks and toll-gating. *Toll-gating* is a system that depends on the ability of politicians to cut

---

223 Deschouwer 1994, p. 104.
224 Walecki 2005a, pp. 204/205.
225 Cf. Russ 2005, pp. 373-382. Prosecution of the former Prime Minister Alain Juppé; *Frankfurter Allgemeine*, 21 October 2004; "Korruptionsprozeß in Paris", in: *Frankfurter Allgemeine*, 22 March 2005. Similar allegations apply to Ex-Mayor (and Ex-President Jacques Chirac; see "Strafverfahren wegen Veruntreuung gegen Chirac", in: *Frankfurter Allgemeine*, 22 November 2007.
226 Hofnung 1996b, pp. 140/141; Hofnung 2005b, pp. 70, 71, 73; quote on p. 73.
227 Both quotes from: Key 1989, p. 39.

through the proper channels of bureaucratic decision-making. Short circuiting the process requires holders of government permits and concessions to make regular contributions to the war chests of incumbent parties. *Kickbacks* (slush funds, which are called *ristournes* in Quebec or *tangenti* in Italy) consist of a percentage of the value of all public contracts, which has to be made to the governing party.[228]

Underworld figures, who until the 1940s influenced party machines in big cities, like New York, Chicago and others, must not be taken into account nowadays, unless you suppose that crime goes undetected and certain amounts of money are still given for protection. However, Heard has already stated that there is no evidence of large sums being involved.[229]

Two factors seem to be most favourable for party income from graft based on the exchange of corrupt favours between businessmen and politicians: clientelistic structures in society and government involvement in a highly centralised and highly regulated economy.[230] Where state bureaucracy grants tax exemptions, material incentives and subsidies for food products, there are many opportunities for influence peddling. Elected office gives a politician significant advantage for toll-gating in exchange for permits and licenses, favourably a building permit, an excise or import license and kickbacks paid by public contractors, preferably by those who are involved in building projects (e.g. roads) or procurement of armaments. The Belgian Agusta-Dassault scandals provide the classic cases.[231]

After 1962 the DC and PSI, the real holders of power in Italy's *partitocrazia*, were firmly entrenched in office. They provided a low-risk environment to politicians and businessmen. Any entrepreneur, who wanted to land a contract for major public works, paid a pre-established kickback (about 5 percent of the project's value). The system of kickbacks (*tangenti*) exploded after the 1970s. The recipients were helpful in obtaining contracts from the national government, regional administrations and municipalities. Public construction works were the most obvious contracts related to the collection of bribes.[232] An estimate for the 1980s reveals the equivalent of 75 percent of all public subsidies paid to political parties. In 1988 an estimate of 12 trillion lire (about €6.2 billion) given as the net value of administrative corruption alerted the public.[233] Private persons partly pocketed kickbacks for public contracts, but a large part ended up

---

[228] Bloom (1956, p. 178) mentions „making payments by way of commissions, fees, gifts, entertainment, rebates, … and other forms of gratituities." Webster's dictionary refers to „a giving back of part of money received as payment, commission, etc., often as a result of coercion or a previous understanding."
[229] Heard 1960, pp. 155, 157, 165.
[230] For details see above in chapter IV, sub-section C 2 (state intervention in the economy).
[231] Weekers/ Maddens 2007, pp. 4, 7.
[232] Hine 1996, p. 146; Pujas/ Rhodes 1999, p. 49; Della Porta/ Vannucci 1999, pp. 102, 106, 108, 111, 115; Newell 2000, p. 71.
[233] Paolo Menghini: Tangenti e bustarelle: la corruzione costa 12 mila miliardi. In: *Corriere della Sera*, June 26, 1988, p. 7; quoted from Hine 1996, p. 138.

in party coffers.[234] In the Italian form of power-sharing, the parties distributed appointments as well as proceeds from graft proportionally among themselves (*lottizzazione*). Even the major party of opposition, the PCI, was willing and able to secure small slices of power, jobs and cash, most of all in local government.[235] Because public funds did not cover more than a decreasing share of party spending, the situation contributed to illegal funding. The long-time dominant party DC (including its *correnti* and regional branches) collected some €100 million in *tangenti* per year. When the scandal broke and the flow of slush funds stopped, the medium sized PSI accumulated an additional debt of €10 million in just one year and finally collapsed.[236]

The relationship between politicians and their „sponsors" from the corporate sector in Japan was and still is cemented by mutual obligations. While local interest groups expect their MPs to channel as many advantages as possible into that particular region, for example in the form of public works projects and government subsidies, corporations who financed individual politicians hoped for their backing in the central bureaucracy. The difference lay in the reward received for mediation. Whereas support groups in the constituency are able to mobilise great numbers of votes, sponsors from the private industry make political contributions. The fundraising practices of former Prime Minister Tanaka who was a long serving leader of the most important faction of the governing party included a kickback of three percent of the total value of any government contract. Major bribery scandals in Japanese politics, such as the Lockheed (1976), Recruit (1988), and Sagawa Kyûbin (1992) scandals show that MPs used the powers of their public office to promote the interests of their donors, for example in the bidding process for public construction projects. Thus, they have opened a channel for systemic corruption in Japanese politics.[237]

The problems of graft, kickbacks and toll-gating do not only concern the national but also the sub-national level of political systems. Especially in the field of town and country planning, industrial or commercial interests frequently coincide with the politicians' need for (financial) support. In France the parties of the right were able to stage ‚voluntary' collections. Because this did not work with parties of the left (when they were in power), they had to try illegal practices.[238] At times French parties seemed very much dependent on funding from graft. Corporations that wanted to sign contracts for the building of infrastructure had to pay to the party in power. Between 1988 and 1997 the (metropolitan) region of Paris (*Ile-de-France*) operated a slightly different scheme. By tacit understanding (if necessary enforced through power-brokers like the political lieutenants of Jacques Chirac, then Lord Mayor of Paris) contractors were

---

234 In the light of the *mani pulite* (i.e. clean hands) inquiry, starting in 1992, the amount illegally obtained summed up to some 3,400 billion lire a year, at least ten times the total official income of all Italian parties.
235 Hine 1996, pp. 136-137, quote on p.137; for details cf. Della Porta/ Vannucci 1999, pp. 112-116.
236 Trautmann 1997, pp. 524-525.
237 Blechinger/ Nassmacher 2001, pp. 166/167.
238 See above in this chapter, sub-section D1 (abuse of public resources).

expected to pay 2 percent of the commercial value of their contracts, 60 percent of it to the right-of-centre parties (RPR, PR), 40 percent to the left-of centre parties (PS, PCF).[239] As the local level is very much involved in the development of infrastructure, a bulk of political income may have come from that source, e.g. to promote urban development or commercial zoning. However, bogus enterprises subsidised by public expenditure are also well known. The PS even set up central agencies (Urba-Conseil, Urba-Technic) to collect these funds. This should hinder local functionaries or administrators from putting the graft money into their own pocket, but also keep the cash within the Mitterand wing of the party. This illegal practice should be dried up by public financing. However, observers doubt this would work.[240]

Despite efforts to forestall plutocratic financing in Spain, parties in need of money have found ways to approach big donors for kickbacks and license fees. A subtle strategy has been imported from abroad. Front companies affiliated with a party have charged businesses and banks (interested in buying access to politicians or favourable decisions) for bogus research papers, consultancy work or technical advice in exchange for favourable decisions. In the early 1990s Spanish police investigated the case of "Filesa",[241] a business group of Barcelona, which had laundered a total of about 5.8 million € for the PSOE. The responsible people were imprisoned for some years.[242] The Guerra, Naseiro, S.A.S and Ceres affairs revealed details. Quite obviously, shareholders did not know about the political donations given by their companies. Other cases of "insider trading" were related to property development and local government contracts.[243] Parties governing the nation, a region or a municipality are engaged in classic examples of pork-barrel graft by peddling their influence and selling their decision-making power over sources of patronage. Building companies, trash-collectors and other contractors pay kickbacks (commission fees) of 2 to 4 percent of the total value of a contract in return for many public works contracted with a government agency. For handling this "compulsory political tax", middlemen who sell such political favours to business interests pocket part of the commission paid in return for the contract and hand over most of the money to the party in power. This type of plutocratic fundraising seems to have assumed extensive proportions, particularly in Spain.

Israel has experienced the diversion of public and trade union funds to party coffers and payments that indicate a practice of kickbacks and toll-gating. For the municipal campaigns in 1993, a „significant number of the large donations were given by building contractors", some of them donated money to more than one contender.[244]

There are no recent reports of major scandals involving toll-gating or kickbacks from the Anglo-Saxon orbit. The "murky world of party fundraising" was mentioned among

---

239 „Korruptionsprozeß in Paris", in: *Frankfurter Allgemeine*, 22 March 2005.
240 Schmitt 1993, p. 78; Meny 1996, pp. 163, 167; Koole 2001, p. 80; Russ 2005, p. 374.
241 See del Castillo 1994; Pujas/ Rhodes 1999.
242 *Frankfurter Allgemeine*, 5 May 1995; *Frankfurter Allgemeine*, 30 October 1997.
243 Van Biezen/ Nassmacher 2001, p. 141.
244 Hofnung 1996b, pp. 140/141.

the causes of sleaze in Britain (e.g. "cash-for-questions"),[245] which brought the Major government down in 1997. However, the scandal involved personal bribes pocketed by politicians rather than monetary favours contributed to party coffers. An exception may be India, where governing parties barter licences, permits and import controls for revenue. During election time the corporate sector is forced to pay "protection money" in cash or kind. Sometimes this money does not fill party coffers but the pockets of individual politicians.[246]

Under German transparency rules[247] no major cases of kickbacks or toll-gating have occurred at the federal and state level in more than two decades, i.e. after the Flick affair.[248] During the final weeks of 1999, however, various shady dealings concerning the funding of the CDU, the major conservative party, came up for public debate. Criminal prosecutors (looking into a tax evasion case), media investigations and confessions by party leaders (past and present) revealed different slush funds administered on behalf of the federal party leader and a state party treasurer. For the bulk of these funds, the sources are still unknown. Some funds undoubtedly originated from interested money: an arms lobbyist, a big contractor of the national telecommunications monopoly and a businessman involved in the privatisation of a federal housing company.[249] Although a parliamentary committee of inquiry looked into other alleged sources, no reliable evidence emerged. The scandals concerned illegal handling of party funds rather than corrupt sources of political revenue.

Thus it seems fair to assume that kickbacks and toll-gating play no important role in the fundraising of German state and federal parties. The local level may still see cases of kickbacks from contractors and (disguised) toll-gating for zoning regulation and building permits. Construction companies are a likely source for both kinds of graft as some of them are public contractors; others are land developers (depending on zoning regulations set up by local governments). In 2001 two corruption cases involving local chapters of the German *SPD* in Cologne and Wuppertal have re-emphasised this potential.[250] Local politicians, who had taken the money, tried to circumvent the statute law that any "voluntary" donation larger than DEM 20,000 (US-$ 10,000) must be revealed publicly, and failed in their attempts.

This seems to be different in Austria, where it is a long-standing tradition that an agent (a firm) has to pay a sum to the principal (the parties in government) in recognition of services delivered. The same is true for Switzerland. Only occasional scandals point out that sometimes kickbacks may be of importance.

---

245 Dunleavy/ Weir 1995, p. 55 (MPs exchanged questions in parliament for money from entrepreneurs).
246 Jain 2001, p. 352; cf. Sridharan 1999, p. 237; Jain 1994, pp. 162/163; Sangita 2005, p. 180.
247 For details see Nassmacher 2001c, p. 106.
248 For details of the Flick affair see Landfried 1994a, pp. 149-153, 188-203; Pinto-Duschinsky 1991b, p. 189; Blankenburg et al. 1989, p. 926; Adams 2005, pp. 160-166.
249 See Nassmacher 2000, pp. 15, 19/20.
250 Nassmacher, H. 2003, pp. 158, 159, 160.

How much money from business goes directly to candidates is hard to establish. Some scholars see cultural tradition as important for the amounts. In Latin American, political tradition, which rallies the citizenry behind a leader (*caudillo*), has not only left its mark on the operation of political parties, but also on the way, in which private contributions for electoral purposes are channelled. The willingness of the donor to collaborate with a political party is often determined by ties of friendship or common interests shared with its candidate, which is, however, frequently separate from the ideological doctrine of political forces. This, again, allows for the majority of the contributions to go directly to the candidate, or to the candidate's inner circle of power, and not to the formal party structure. This creates serious obstacles to exercising any adequate control over the funding of political parties, be it devoted to campaign or organisation purposes.[251] A different kind of graft is not raised from outside the party, but rather from within.

3. Assessment of party/ political officeholders (graft from public office)

In the old days, under a spoils system, parties in power made public servants transfer part of their monthly pay cheque to party coffers if they wanted to preserve their jobs or to promote their careers. This *"macing"* of public servants (for periodic campaign contributions to the party in power) was common in the United States. In state and local governments contributions to political war chests by public employees were more common than at the federal level.[252] This created networks among the public service with the agency chiefs on top. Changes in the recruitment procedures created by civil service reform, combined with increasing professionalism, have restricted this practice of patronage and party revenue. It is expected to flourish only where patron-client relations are strong. For the early 1970s, Alexander mentions the case of Indiana where about one third of all state employees whose jobs were considered as patronage appointments had to pay two percent of their regular salary to the party of the current governor.[253]

The best documented example of "macing" was Puerto Rico. Between 1940 and 1957 this U.S. dominion established a quota system whereby the governing party forced public employees to contribute up to 2 percent of their salaries. This practice followed a period of completely plutocratic funding (by the sugar interest). The fundraising by macing of public servants was discontinued in 1957 when new legislation introduced public subsidies to political parties.[254] In Costa Rica the framers of the 1949 constitution felt compelled to state in article 96 that the state will not "permit any deduction to the salaries of public servants with the purpose of cancelling political debts," the

---

251 Cf. Zovatto 2001, pp. 374/375.
252 Heard 1960, p. 150.
253 Alexander 1972, p. 195; cf. Wawzik 1991, p. 26.
254 Wells 1961, p. 8.

euphemism for the practices between 1910 and 1948. Party taxes levied upon elected officials in Uruguay were quite close to full-fledged macing.[255]

In democracies of continental Europe this political tithe (i.e. macing) survives in the form of assessments, which are collected from public office-holders, especially MPs, regional legislators and municipal councillors. Most parties, both in government and in opposition, collect money from MPs and other office-holders, who received their appointment via patronage. Party members holding public offices (including board members and managers in state owned businesses) are expected to yield a certain percentage of their income to their party. Applying a more traditional term to a modern situation, this "assessment" may also be called a tithe, in which those who benefit from patronage pay their patron in order to support party activity. The Austrian term is most impressive: "party tax" ("party levy", *Parteisteuer*) indicates that all political income is taxed by the institution that can grant or withhold the patronage position, which is the source of this income. Professional politicians who want to continue in their appointment better pay the price that is being asked.[256] These funds are rarely reported. Thus revenue totals for this source of funding can only be given for a few countries.

All parties in Germany, France, Italy, the Netherlands, Belgium, Denmark, Finland, Austria and Switzerland assess their officeholders, especially (European, federal or state) legislators and regional or municipal councillors.[257] In India levies on MPs and assembly members are a common source. In Poland the party taxes are of "spectacular importance".[258]

Although a „party tax" is quite common differences remain. Compared to other countries Swiss parliamentarians pay very little, and revenue from party taxes is low. While Spanish MPs (representatives and senators) pay an equal amount of 10 percent of their salaries to both major parties, in most countries there are differences between party families. In Austria, France and Germany the bourgeois parties collect considerably less from their members of parliament, whereas left-of-centre parties have a tradition of higher assessments.

The Italian Communists (later: *Democratici di sinistra*) as well as their French comrades have been among the most efficient collectors of such funds. These parties used to compel their MPs to turn over the entire indemnities to the party and then receive the average salary of a skilled metalworker in exchange (the same practice is also applied by the United Left in Denmark) or of functionaries of the party, if the parliamentarian has no other income.[259] On average communist parties collected 70 percent of each political income. In 1983 the assessment of officeholders provided 5 percent of

---

255 Casas-Zamora 2002, pp. 91/92, 129; Casas-Zamora 2005a, pp. 73, 97.
256 An inquiry into causes and size of such „party taxes" is outlined by Bolleyer 2007, pp. 1-30.
257 Suetens 1990, p. 68; Pedersen 2003, p. 332; Pesonen 1987, p. 11. Unfortunately the comparative information provided by LeDuc/ Niemi/ Norris 1996, pp. 38-41 is not reliable.
258 Gidlund/ Koole 2001, p. 119; Somjee/ Somjee 1963, p. 693; Walecki 2001, p. 398; for details see Walecki 2005a, pp. 150/151.
259 Duverger 1967, pp. 194, 198; Timmermann 1971, p. 2; *Frankfurt Rundschau*, 28 January 2000.

PCI's total reported revenue. The party was even able to increase that share to 15 percent by 1991. In 1990s the French Communists collected 30 to 35 percent of their budget from assessments.[260]

Socialist and Social Democrats also levy this kind of income. The Belgian and the French Socialist Party require their MPs to pay a monthly assessment.[261] Amounts are set by the party congress. In the late 1980s it was FRF7200, about 30 percent of political income. In 1995 legislators provided 10 percent of total annual revenue to the French PS. In 1997 this share peaked at 19.5 percent and it was 14.4 percent in 1998.[262] Social Democrats in Sweden have a firm system of party taxation. MPs pay SEK 600 per month for office assistance. Members of the European Parliament and (preferably) office-holders at the local and regional level are also assessed a share of their political income.[263] In the Austrian SPÖ the party tax was 15 to 20 percent of gross income for parliamentarians, in addition 3.5 percent were paid to the parliamentary group up to the 1980s. In 1994 percentages were 12 to 25/ 30 percent of the gross salary (depending on the party caucus). More recent revenue estimates range between ATS 225 and 250 million (€16-18 million) per year.[264] State and local parties also assess members of state legislatures and local councillors.

Data available for Germany indicate that this source provides more than 10 percent of all parties' total revenue. Although many consider tithing to be illegal, and its abolition has been proposed, parties continue to levy assessments today.[265] During the early 1980s an average of 18.5 percent of the total income from SPD members was raised by assessing office-holders. For the mid-1990s this share had risen to 27.8 percent of the total revenue solicited from party members.[266] A transfer of solicitation from party caucus to party organisation (which could provide a receipt for income tax benefits since 1984) and post-unification effects (i.e. the opportunity to assess many more legislators and municipal councillors elected in East Germany) caused the increase. Of an annual total of DEM 43 million (€22 million) less than 3 percent go to federal SPD coffers and only 16 percent help fund the state party organisations. The unbelievable share of more than 80 percent of the assessments levied from SPD officeholders (about DEM 35 million) are raised and spent locally. SPD MPs and MEPs contribute about one fifth of their political income to party coffers. Local organisations of the Green party rely even more heavily on this kind of party revenue.[267]

For 2000 the treasurers of the five parties represented in parliament reported that about 20 percent (Grüne), 13 percent (SPD), 9 percent (PDS), 8 percent (CSU) and 3 percent (FDP) of their total revenue came from assessments ("tithing"). The CDU treasurer

---

260 Landfried 1994a, p. 366; Pulch 1987, p. 85; Miguet 1999, p. 47, note 8; Knapp 2002, p. 127.
261 Suetens 1990, p. 68; Schurig 2006, pp. 58-62.
262 Schmitt 1993, p. 76; Miguet 1999, p. 47, note 8; Knapp 2002, p. 127.
263 Gidlund/ Koole 2001, p. 119.
264 Drysch 1998, p. 90; Sickinger 1997, pp. 119-122.
265 Schneider 1989, p. 225; von Arnim 1993, p. 205.
266 Landfried 1994a, pp. 134/135; Nassmacher 1997b, p. 168.
267 Ringena 2000, pp. 50/51.

claimed that due to accounting procedure his party was unable to provide an estimate.[268] Statutory regulation makes precise data for each party available for years up to 1983 and since 2003. A comparison of both years reveals that most parties have increased their dependence on assessments as a source of revenue: the SPD from 7.0 to 12.5 percent, the CDU from 6.7 to 12.9 percent, the CSU from 5.4 to 6.9 percent and the Greens from 0.8 to 17.1 percent of each party's overall annual revenue. The PDS, non-existent as a democratic party in 1983, collected 5.1 percent in 2003 and only the FDP has neglected this source of revenue, which decreased its share from 4.9 to 4.6 percent. In 2006 both major parties raised similar shares of their total revenue. However, all minor parties reported increased income from assessments, almost 21 percent for the Greens, 7 to 8 percent for CSU, PDS and FDP.[269]

Green parties in other countries (e.g. Switzerland) follow this procedure. It is also common with Dutch left wing parties (PvdA and GroenLinks), where elected and appointed politicians pay a certain share of their political income into party coffers, but on a voluntary basis. An estimate is 29 percent in the PvdA. Payments to other parties tend to be lower. Today, the only party that obliges its MPs to hand over the total allowance to the party is the small SP. In exchange, SP parliamentarians receive a modest salary, which explains the exceptionally high percentage of 'other' income for this party.[270]

Some figures (e.g. for *Die Grünen*) include assessments of members of parliaments on all levels as well as municipal councils. Members and office-holders jointly contributed about 15 percent of party revenue in the 1980s, 37 percent in 1991. In the 1990s the *Les Verts* in France raised between 10 and 15 percent of their central income through assessments. Among the right wing parties in France, shares are lower: 3 to 6 percent for the UDF, 7 to 12 percent for the (Gaullist) RPR and 6 to 15 percent for the (populist) FN.[271] During the early 1980s in Austria incumbents paid 10 percent to the ÖVP and 7 percent the parliamentary group (*Klub*).[272] Other officeholders who benefited from party patronage are expected to pay as well, but frequently it is quite difficult for the ÖVP to collect the assessment.

In Switzerland state parties (*Kantonalparteien*) have different rules. Each person who got a position through party patronage has to transfer a share of 10 to 25 percent of the pay to party coffers. On average state branches of the major parties in Switzerland raise between 18 (FDP) and 33 (SPS) percent of their total funds from levies on officeholders.[273] In Italy the precise amount that an office holding party member has to contribute to his or her party depends on the income from office [274] and therefore on the level where the office is held.

---

268 *Deutscher Bundestag*, parliamentary paper, no. 14/6710, p. 39.
269 *Deutscher Bundestag*, parliamentary paper, no. 10/2172, 15/5550 and 16/8400.
270 Elzinga 1992, p. 355; Gidlund/ Koole 2001, pp. 116, 119.
271 Raschke 1993, p. 723; Schmitt 1993, p. 76; Knapp 2002, p. 127.
272 Kofler 1981, p. 368; Houghton report 1976, p. 322.
273 Weigelt 1988, p. 32; Drysch 1998, p. 91; Ladner/ Brändle 2001, p. 160.
274 Ridola 1992, p. 286.

In Poland "parties demand from members who hold an elective or appointed public office a fixed share of their salaries." The levies apply to most of the 560 members of the legislature, "hundreds of party members with governmental positions, members of supervisory boards and, above all, to thousands of local councillors. The amount depends on the party and in the case of councillors differs from 5 to 10 percent of their salaries or certain fixed quotas. Members of supervisory boards and other members with functional positions are compelled to contribute 10 percent of their salary."[275]

In conclusion, the analysis of plutocratic funding has produced important insights.

- First, the free flow of money into politics is both, *a hazard and a necessity* of democratic politics. The financial support of policies, politicians and parties is an expression of economic and political freedom, not necessarily the consequence of influence peddling or corrupt exchanges. However, as the latter may happen, the flow of funds into politics should be free, but transparent. Hence the democratic sovereign, the voter, can make informed choices.

- Second, among the various categories of *interested money,* contributions from personal wealth (i.e. by wealthy individuals) are the least dangerous if they are made in a manner, which is transparent to the general public. Although buying honours and offices (both an Anglo-Saxon tradition of fundraising) has not ceased, it is in decline. If a candidate for public office pays for his or her campaign from personal wealth, the voters can decide whether they want to elect that person or not.

- Third, money from the business community ("*corporate donations*" in most democracies) is no longer a real danger for democratic politics. Both alleys of raising such funds (direct contributions as well as institutional fundraising) have declined; mostly because their proceeds have been substituted by public subsidies. At the same time, public disincentives to discourage the flow of interested money into political competition (disclosure of large donations rather than limits or bans) have strengthened or preceded this trend.

- Fourth, however, there are still relevant cases of *political graft* (corrupt exchanges). One of them is the abuse of public resources for partisan purposes, another the extorsion of private business (toll-gating or kickbacks). The flow of such funds is always clandestine. Only investigative journalism that occasionally uncovers scandals can serve to interrupt such felonies for a while. Systematic assessments of political officeholders (macing) is a kind of graft that will be much harder to uproot, as parties will neither want to pass laws against any form of "party tax" nor to implement them completely if such laws have eventually made it into the statute book.

The elaborate forms of tithing have led supporters of public subsidies to expect that these clandestine forms of funding, quite like the progress made in Puerto Rico decades ago, should be replaced by more transparent and legitimate forms of state aid.

---

275 Walecki 2001, p. 398 (both quotes on this page).

CHAPTER EIGHT

Public Subsidies

For democratic polities around the world public funding, granted for partisan purposes by parliamentary decision, is a relatively modern phenomenon. In many countries it was introduced after scandals that revealed evidence of corruption and illegal financing. In other countries, the rising costs of politics stimulated the spread of party subsidies.[1] Costa Rica and Uruguay in 1954 were the first to introduce public funding, followed by Puerto Rico in 1957 and Germany in 1959.[2] In Quebec (1963), Sweden (1965), Finland (1967) and Israel (1969) parties entered the new "pasture" during the 1960s.[3] Norway (1970), Canada and Italy (1974), Austria (1975) and the U.S. (1976) were next. In Australia (1984), Denmark (1986), France (1988) and Belgium (1989) similar legislation became effective during the 1980s. The last to enact new rules were Japan (1994), Ireland (1997), the Netherlands (1999) and Britain (2000). Nowadays almost all first and second wave democracies make public funds available to parties and/or candidates.[4] Among the established democracies only India, New Zealand and Switzerland stand out as exceptions to the rule.[5]

In some third wave democracies, like Spain and Portugal, state aid to political parties has been available from the very beginning (1977), as no other reliable source of revenue could be expected to cover the costs of party democracy.[6] Public funding introduced in Mexico (1978/86) and reinstated in Uruguay (1984/89) was an element of the transition from authoritarian rule to democracy.[7] In Central Eastern Europe transformation was more difficult because communist tradition included public financing of politics. When the first Solidarity government in Poland revealed budget allocations to the communist party and its allies, this caused deep and widespread anger. The re-

---

1 Bardi/ Morlino 1994, p. 243; Houghton report 1976, pp. 321, 337, 340.
2 Casas-Zamora 2005, pp. 73, 98; Wells 1961, pp. 16-21; Schleth 1973, p. 232. – Alexander (1989b, p. 14) adds Argentina (1955) as a pioneer; Payne/ Zovatto et al. (2002, p. 167) claim that Uruguay (1928) was the first, while Costa Rica (1949) and Argentina (1961) followed later on.
3 Angell 1996, pp. 46/47;Walter 1966, pp. 396-397, 402-404; Pesonen 1974, p. 478; Mendilow 1989, p. 132.
4 Data given here are those the author considers to be the most reliable and comparable. Neglecting differences of one year (possibly between legislation and implementation) the years given are consistent with those mentioned in Alexander 1989b, pp. 14/15 for Australia, Canada, Costa Rica, Finland, Germany, Israel, Italy, Norway, Puerto Rico, Quebec, Spain, Sweden and the U.S. Years do not match for Austria, Denmark, France, Japan and the Netherlands.
5 Alexander 1989b, p. 14 and Casas-Zamora 2002, pp. 39/40; Casas-Zamora 2005a, pp. 30/31.
6 Greece, which is not covered in this study, took about a decade to follow this path in 1984.
7 Zovatto 2001, pp. 375/375; Casas-Zamora 2002, pp. 132/133; Casas-Zamora 2005a, pp. 99/100.

sulting mood of public opinion delayed direct subsidies until 1993. By now most postcommunist countries in Europe have come round to the standard set by their western neighbours.[8] While in continental Europe countries place some emphasis on private funding, Latin America seems to be heading in the opposite direction.

All the countries mentioned provide information to address the fundamental questions, which are the core of this chapter:

- How significant is public funding for parties and taxpayers?
- Does the variety of subsidies, recipients and allocation formulas recommend a best practice to legislators?
- Are public subsidies a problem-solving kind of political revenue?

A) Stop-gap, life-saver or white knight?

Need and scandal as major triggers for legislative reform suggest that the public subsidies for party activity are nothing but a stop-gap measure. As a matter of public policy it seems to lack any long-term perspective and any merit based on the values of democracy. However, this conclusion may be just a bit too obvious. A more sophisticated approach towards this source of party revenue should be urged by common sense and scholarly probity.

1. Developing a case for public funding

Two authors provide starting points for a general discussion about the intrinsic benefits of public funding, which do not relate to the recipient parties but rather to the democratic process. Paltiel has stated that a political finance regime without public funding as an important feature "is a formula for failure."[9] Panebianco has prescribed a mix of different funding sources in order to safeguard the operation of modern parties.[10]

Although Panebianco did not elaborate on the consequences of his recommendation, it is obvious that such a mix is supposed to balance the specific risks inherent in different sources of revenue, combine independence and linkage, as well as adequate funding and fair competition. Among the problems associated with private sources of political funds, the scarcity of grass-roots funding and the hazards of plutocratic funding are the most important.[11] Unfortunately these two problems do not counterbalance each other. Thus a mix of different sources must include private as well as public funding. Casas-Zamora adds another aspect to this point: "Even in the two most egalitarian

---

8   Winczorek 1990, p.13; Walecki 2001, p. 402 ; Ikstens et al. 2002, p. 25.
9   Paltiel 1976, p. 109.
10 Panebianco 1988, pp. 58/59.
11 See above, chapter VI, section A (cornerstone of democracy) and chapter VII, section A (moral hazard).

countries of Latin America [Costa Rica and Uruguay] subsidies prevent political finance from being totally controlled by an extraordinarily narrow set of interests."[12] Some kind of well-designed public funding programme (limited in amount, fair in access, adequate in distribution and participatory in allocation) has to be part of the funding mix, if party democracy is meant to persist.

Whereas this line of reasoning emphasizes a demand of the political system, Paltiel's formula for political finance regulation addresses an issue of public policy and a more recent one at that. As long as party competition per se was expected to provide fairness, reliability and linkage, any interference of public policy in the funding of political activity was unthinkable. However, the extension of the franchise demonstrated that the autonomy of political competitors can not be trusted. They needed rules to develop standards of competitive behaviour and thus to ensure free and fair elections. This type of legislation was implemented and continuously improved starting with a ban of corrupt and illegal practices in the late 19th century.[13] A more recent subject of this process is the quest for transparency of political funds.

Political finance regulation demands different degrees of disclosure and reporting. In all areas of public policy the implementation of new rules is enhanced by a combination of "sticks and carrots." Whereas fines and prosecution help to enforce rules, benefits offer incentives for those who are willing to co-operate. "Legal restrictions alone will neither eliminate group demands nor reduce the need of the parties."[14] In any legislative package, which intends to regulate the flow of money in politics, a certain dose of public funding may just be the proper kind of incentive for the parties to play by the rules – even if sometimes it is hard for them.

In arguing the benefits of subsidies, Alexander and Paltiel indicated two additional aspects. Public funds provide a floor for challengers and offer more fairness to opposition parties.[15] Governments use public resources for their own partisan purposes. An example from a "pre-democratic" age is the "reptile fund" that was used by the first German chancellor (Bismarck), as well as by many of his democratic successors, to influence public opinion. Secret funds at the disposal of a French president have survived into the present era.[16] No matter how much money is involved, these examples identify the unfair advantage of incumbency. The benefit of public subsidies is that the opposition receives at least a minimum of resources.

The case of floors provided for challengers recognises that an incumbent candidate enjoys automatic name recognition plus a fundraising edge if he or she decides to run for re-election. The challenger has to start from scratch, based on his or her own funds, plutocratic donors or an extremely efficient organisation. Public funding will not cre-

---

12   Casas-Zamora 2002, p. 293; Casas-Zamora 2005a, p. 228.
13   O'Leary 1962. This transforms private associations into "public utilities" (Epstein 1986, pp. 156/157).
14   Paltiel 1981, pp. 154-159; quote ibid., p. 171; cf, Nassmacher 2006, pp. 450-452.
15   Fisher 2002, p. 395 emphasizes adequate income and resolution of public disquiet.
16   Schurig 2006, pp. 168, 196/197.

ate a level playing field but it gives the challenger a head-start and thus improves democratic competition. Nevertheless this may be a specific problem of candidate-centred U.S. politics. In most democracies the party, which fields a candidate will have to organise and to fund the campaign (nationally as well as locally) and its own day-to-day operations.

Because political parties perform functions crucial for the political system the question arises, whether their routine operations as well as their campaign activity are a public service and hence should be supported by public funds. Perhaps this would avoid or decrease any dependency on private interests (e.g. party supporters or institutional donors), however, it also endangers the rootedness of parties in their society. As private funds do not spring up easily, public subsidies have become a necessity, for there seems to be no other way to bridge the gap between the expenses of political parties and the amounts provided by voluntary giving.

For all permanent party organisations, at national headquarters as well as in the field, a continuous flow of funds is a necessity. Given the well-known hazards inherent in fundraising from individual citizens and interested money, the concept of "floors" applies to government and opposition alike. Public subsidies provide a reliable source of funding that will keep some parties alive until the next election. Although survival of an individual party is not important beyond its own clientele, competition of more than two parties is needed for democracy to endure. However, quite like all other sources of political funding, public subsidies are by no means foolproof, risk-free or the only kind of party revenue with no strings attached.[17]

2. Problems of public funding

A "straightforward argument of principle against state aid [sic!] is that taxpayers should not be compelled to contribute to the support of political parties with whose outlook and policies they strongly disagree."[18] However, this line of reasoning is misleading in two respects. First, in a representative democracy no taxpayer has ever been asked to express a personal preference on items of government spending. Why should such logic apply to individual parties? Second, the taxpayer is not funding individual parties, some of which he or she may dislike, but supporting the operation of the party system, which in turn is a prerequisite of democracy. Despite all their partisan peccadilloes, parties are a necessary institution of democracy. Their activity contributes to the common good of modern societies.[19]

Many current theories of political parties identify two closely related hazards of public subsidies in party funding. Two frequently cited authors warn that parties become "part of the state apparatus" and dependent on the state.[20] Both suppositions emphasise

---

17 As has been suggested by some (cf. Houghton report 1976, p. 51, par. 8.32)
18 Neill report 1998, p. 91.
19 Hermens 1958, p. 162; Pierre/ Svasand/ Widfeldt 2000, p. 4.
20 Katz/ Mair 1995, p. 22; quote in Katz 1996, p. 122.

the role of parties as a part of civil society and the state as an independent entity, which the parties are supposed to oppose. Scholars who believe that parties may become part of the state itself or dependent on "the state," which more precisely means the state bureaucracy or the state budget (i.e. the public purse), neglect the parties' specific role as an instrument of linkage. However, in all forms of responsible government, it is the parties, which select the political class that ultimately calls the shots in all areas of public policy. The "state" in a modern democracy is no autonomous "Leviathan," but a synonym for the political system. If the authors intend to say that parties are a political institution, which is part of the political system, they are perfectly correct. But what is the consequence to be drawn from the obvious?

Is there a specific function to be assigned to parties among the ensemble of political institutions? Yes, there is. Parties "link people to the government,"[21] they are organisations that compete for power, nominate candidates for elections, campaign for specific elites and policies. All of these functions are public responsibilities performed by private voluntary organisations. As long as the private and the voluntary character of a party is preserved, there is nothing wrong with "dependence on the public treasury" to cover *part* of their costs.[22] However, the real hazard has been hit by a phrase, which was used in the Neill report. Parties may use "the state apparatus increasingly to further their own ends rather than those of the citizens."[23] This is inherent in the partisan character of this specific public utility, which is subject to transparency rules, media scrutiny, political opposition and regularly held elections, in short to a democratic culture of dissent, not a consequence of public or private funding.

A different approach to the matter may start with a different question. Who is the state? It may be the citizens, the parties or the bureaucracy. Depending on the point of view it can be the citizens, as the principle of "government of the people, by the people, for the people" legitimates all state activity. The state can also be the parties, because their leading representatives in various political institutions (government, parliament, judiciary; "the party in public office") make most political decisions. Or it can be the bureaucracy, which implements those decisions. Obviously the suggestive term "state" in the second quote from Katz and Mair connotes neither the citizens at large (parties depending on the citizens are no disaster, but an achievement; "the party on the ground") nor the bureaucracy (which would not try to subdue the parties at will). This leaves the parties themselves. The collective party system controlling the party system or parties controlling each other is a truism. The term "state" rather hides the real problem, which is that with public subsidies the governing majority controls the purse strings of all minority parties. This problem is real although it is not a problem of principle but of legislative detail, which must be taken care of by the procedure of entitlement and allocation in any public funding regulation.[24]

---

21 Sartori 1976, p. 25.
22 Pierre/ Svasand/ Widfeldt 2000, p. 2.
23 Neill report 1998, p. 92.
24 For details see below in this chapter, section D (allocation of subsidies).

This leads to another, possible intention of the authors. Do they mean to say (more precisely than their phrasing suggests) that parties can become dependent on the state budget?[25] This certainly is an important but specific issue and thus another problem of framing the subsidy programme. Indeed each subsidy provision should make sure that a funding mix is retained by combining public subsidies with incentives for party leaders and party activists to pursue additional sources of fundraising.

Decades ago Pinto-Duschinsky correctly observed that if parties are "artificially protected from the need to retain support and to encourage participation, democratic government ... will be damaged." The decline of party membership and the drop in the number of full-time local party agents cannot be cured by injecting money from the public purse. Less convincingly he went on to conclude, the "danger of public funding is that it makes popular backing unnecessary and creates a gulf between the professional staff and the ordinary members."[26] Emphasis on ordinary party members is misleading because membership can be direct or indirect, individual or collective, can imply a real flow of funds or just a token membership fee.[27] All of these will simply not have the same kind of impact.

Nonetheless the linkage of party organisations and party politicians to the financial support from the grass-roots of society are indispensable elements of participatory and responsive politics. In all modern democracies the politician, the party apparatchik as well as the elected representative, is a professional and the ordinary citizen is an amateur. As some distance will always open up between them, a political institution has to bridge the (existing, not newly created) gulf between them continuously. The name of this institution is the political party. Each party, for its own sake and success, tries to bridge the gulf between professional politics and amateur involvement, i.e. participation by party activists, party members, political donors and citizens at large. As a relevant source of political income state aid is given in specific ways and these include safeguards against potential abuse. Much will depend not on the principle, but on the details of its application.

3. Means to increase the legitimacy of public subsidies

If subsidies are given as flat grants from the general revenue fund, a parliament composed of party representatives makes decisions, which favour the parties and/or their candidates. The most important hazard inherent in this process, which some scholars see as some sort of "self-service" operation,[28] is the legitimacy of public subsidies, political parties and eventually the democratic process. By careless handling of public funds, individuals may learn that they do not have to care for party funds by dues or donations. Linkage between citizens and the political class may whither away. Trying

---

25 Landfried 1994a, pp. 14, 353.
26 Pinto-Duschinsky 1981, pp. 9, 292; see also ibid., p. 287.
27 For details see above in chapter VI, sub-section B1 (membership fees).
28 E.g. von Arnim 2001, p. 106.

to prevent a self-service attitude of the parties, to legitimise public funding of partisan efforts and to ensure the broadest possible participation by individual citizens, politicians need to implement well designed subsidy programmes.

Some jurisdictions stipulate partial approval by taxpayers or party supporters to legitimise public funding schemes. First, *mixed funding* can be safeguarded by an indirect subsidy, some kind of *tax benefit* for private contributions.[29] If individual taxpayers do not go along, no public support within this programme will be forthcoming. Second, a subsidy programme can stipulate that only a political competitor who has collected a certain amount of private donations is entitled to public subsidies (*matching funds*).[30] If politicians do not solicit in order to qualify and party supporters do not contribute, then there will be no public subsidy. Third, legitimacy will be enhanced if the taxpayer is asked to agree that part of her or his tax money be appropriated to party politics. Via the *tax check-off* option, citizens decide that a specific tiny portion of public revenue is set aside for that purpose.[31] Participating citizens do not dispose of their own funds. Rather, they assent to a public subsidy programme.

All serious efforts to operate the latter device occurred in the United States.[32] Public funding for presidential elections is based on an income tax check-off, by which individual American citizens can indicate on their tax return that a minute portion of their income tax ($1 until 1993 and $3 since 1994) be transferred to the Presidential Election Campaign Fund. Over time 11 to 29 percent of the American taxpayers have participated in the federal tax check-off programme. The participation rate was highest in 1981 and it has decreased with the growing distance from the Watergate scandal. Participants belong to the middle class and more frequently identify with the Democratic Party.[33]

In addition, several U.S. states introduced this instrument, mostly an income-tax check-off. From the start, the participation rates differed in individual states. When compared with the voter turnout, the participation rate in some states was acceptable in the beginning. However, all check-off systems suffered a decline in the participation rate during the 1980s: In New Jersey support dropped from 41 to 32 percent. The same happened in Michigan (26 to 14), Wisconsin (20 to 13), Minnesota (18 to 15), Iowa (16 to 9), Oregon and Kentucky (15 to 8).[34] In reaction to this, legislators increased the amount of money earmarked by the check-off. Minnesota's programme, which is based on income and property tax, hit the highest dollar amount ($5) in 1987. Political culture, the party system (one-party dominated North Carolina has the lowest, com-

---

29 See above in chapter VI, sub-section C2 (stimulating contributors).
30 See above in chapter VI, sub-section C1 (energising fundraisers) and below in this chapter, sub-section D2a (allocation of matching funds).
31 Jones 1980, p. 283, 287.
32 An Italian law of 1997, which offered a similar procedure, was nothing but a disguise to replace the flat grant that had been abolished by referendum (Bianco/ Gardini 1999, pp. 23/24).
33 Patterson 2006, p. 73; Wawzik 1991, pp. 87/88; Nassmacher/ Wawzik 1992, pp. 36, 38, 64.
34 Citizens Research Foundation 1990 (unpublished); participation rates in: Nassmacher/ Wawzik 1992, p. 45.

petitive New Jersey the highest rate), efforts to familiarise taxpayers with the programme and varying methods of placing the check-off option on the tax form cause deviating levels of participation. If other worthy causes are added to the income tax form, this does not improve participation. Data from Kentucky reveals no relationship between participation rate and local party organisation strength. In Oregon, however, participation was positively correlated with party registration and voter turnout.[35]

In sum, results of the U.S. check-off programmes are mixed. "When ample funds can be concentrated on only a few campaigns or a few candidates, as in New Jersey and Michigan, public funds have a significant impact on the election campaign process." In general, high hopes concerning the impact of public funds at an early stage of implementation (independence from large donors, more equal distribution of campaign funds) were not fulfilled.[36] This suggests a dual approach to such programmes. Probably the best bet is to use them solely to legitimise public funding. Additional intentions have to be addressed by different measures.

It should be added that state aid will not work wonders for the political process. Public funding is more than just a stop-gap measure but it is less than the white knight of political finance. A carefully designed programme that combines public entitlement and transparency duties is a practical device, which promotes the risk diversification of political funding and entices parties to co-operate voluntarily with political finance regulation. Mixed funding of politics and effective regulation of political money are important improvements to the democratic process.[37] Nevertheless a lot of practical problems come up when the variety of available subsidies and the specific rules attached to them are presented in detail.

B) Types of subsidies

The range of subsidies for political purposes is wide, from general grants to clandestine support. Public funding of the political process started indirectly. Administration of voting procedure led to subsidies-in-kind, which were followed by indirect support, e.g. tax privileges or funding of caucuses (parliamentary groups), and by a variety of reimbursements and grants, which are available to parties and candidates.[38] Today, different legal instruments provide access to public funding, e.g. electoral laws, party regulations, parliamentary caucus rules, or just a budget allocation. The U.S. and

---

35 Jones 1980, p. 288; Goldstein 1986, pp. 2, 9, 10; Nassmacher/ Wawzik 1992, pp. 43, 54.
36 Noragon 1981, p. 686; quote from Jones 1984, p. 203.
37 Regulatory options are presented by Nassmacher 2006, pp. 446-454 and Ewing 2007, pp. 37-62.
38 For cross-national overviews see Paltiel 1981, pp. 164-166; Nassmacher 1993, pp. 241-243; Casas-Zamora 2002, pp. 23/24; Austin/ Tjernström 2003, pp. 209-223; Casas-Zamora 2005a, p. 19.

Switzerland are the most restrictive cases, whereas the countries of continental Europe use multiple approaches, which are quite diverse in detail. Britain, which to this day most fiercely resisted the global trend towards direct public subsidies, "has been undergoing a quiet revolution ... of new forms of indirect state aid."[39]

1. Subsidies-in-kind

Governments pay for election material (voting slips and envelopes), election officers and polling station facilities. Preparation of the voters' list (roll, register) has become the sole responsibility of public authorities (state or local administration) in all European countries (as well as in Australia and Canada), thus rendering U.S. style voter registration drives unnecessary. Compulsory voting (as in Australia) can be another means of public support, however it is rare after the Netherlands, Belgium and Austria repealed it. Nowadays the most important campaign support given to political parties and their candidates is free media time, which is worth a considerable amount of money that parties do not have to spend for electioneering.

a) Access to media

TV and radio are needed to transmit political messages in campaigns. In general, established democracies (the traditional OECD member countries) apply balanced rules for fair political broadcasting.[40] Free media time is provided in all countries covered in this study, except the U.S. and Costa Rica.[41] Four countries in continental Europe signify the range of opportunities available to regulators. In Austria and the Netherlands parties, represented in parliament are allocated free air time on radio and TV on an ongoing basis. In Switzerland and Sweden parties cannot present their own advertising material in the electronic media, not even during campaigns. They may only participate in traditional style election debates.

Two countries in the Anglo-Saxon orbit represent the policy options for dealing with paid political advertising. An Australian statute prohibited parties from buying media time and required broadcasters to provide some free time for party advertisements. Without being tested in a general election, the High Court declared this law unconstitutional. The court held that it was interfering excessively with the freedom of speech necessary for free elections under a system of representative government.[42] A legal ban makes paid political advertising on radio or television unavailable to British parties, candidates or interest groups. The same applies for Belgium, Denmark, Finland,

---

39 Pinto-Duschinsky, Michael: "It's their party, and we pay for it", in: *The Sunday Times*, 22 October 2006.
40 Norris 2000, p. 153.
41 Casas-Zamora 2002, pp. 39/40; Casas-Zamora 2005a, pp. 30/31; for Poland see Walecki 2001, p. 205.
42 Amr/ Lisowski 2001, pp. 64/65.

France, Ireland, Norway and Spain. In Sweden paid political advertising by parties is allowed on local television and radio only.[43]

In most European countries, public broadcasters allocate free airtime to parties contesting an election in proportion to their performance in the previous general election. Major parties receive more time than smaller ones (in Belgium, France, Germany and India).[44] By way of contrast Denmark, the Netherlands and Norway provide equal time to all parties. All parties that have presented lists of candidates in all regions of the Netherlands may claim their equal share of free airtime on television and radio during the campaign period of seven weeks plus some of their production costs.[45] In Italy there exists a compromise between both methods (allocating equal shares to all parties and dividing time in proportion to the votes polled previously). In Israel each party, including those that were not represented in parliament, is given ten minutes TV time and 25 minutes radio time free of charge. Moreover, each party already represented in the outgoing parliament receives three additional minutes on TV and six minutes on radio for each MP. Parties „are not free to trade television time for radio time".[46]

In Japan political parties are entitled to a limited amount of TV campaign spots, which is determined by the number of candidates that the party fields in a region.[47] In addition, candidates may air one free TV spot and 10 free radio spots on public channels to introduce themselves to the voters. In Canada a Broadcasting Arbitrator allocates the time to contesting parties based on the quantity of seats held, popular support in the previous general election and the number of candidates nominated for the current election. No party may receive more than half of the total time allocation. In Ireland the allocation formula "takes account both of a party's current … representation and of the number of candidates nominated."[48]

In the U.K., the public network (BBC) and commercial channels allocate free broadcasting time to parties both for campaign periods and between elections. The commercial channels do this on a voluntary basis, and consider it to be a public duty. The ratio of broadcasting time allotted to the Labour Party, the Conservatives and the Liberal Democrats is 5:5:4. The formula corresponds neither to the parties' voting strength nor to their representation in the House of Commons. However, it gives a built-in lead to the parties in opposition, which partly balances the government's routine advantage in the news coverage.

In Britain free broadcasting saved the three major parties an estimated £7 million, i.e. almost half of their central spending for the 1987 general election.[49] In Austria the

---

43 Norris 2000, p. 153; Gidlund/ Koole 2001, pp. 124/125.
44 Miguet 1999, p. 47; Fromont 1992, p. 167-169; Schurig 2006, p. 114; Sridharan 2006a, p. 373.
45 Schmid 1990, p. 124; see also: Pedersen/ Bille 1991, p. 162; Vesterdorf 1992, p. 70; Koole 1999, p. 347.
46 Ridola 1992, p. 297/298; Blechinger/Nassmacher 2001, p. 171; quote in Levush 1997, p. 116.
47 Klein 1998, p. 250 (Candidates are banned from buying media time for campaigning).
48 Amr/Lisowski 2001, p. 65; quote in Laver/ Marsh 1999, p. 156.
49 Fisher 1996b, p. 159, estimate by Pinto-Duschinsky 1989, pp. 26/27; Pinto-Duschinsky 1994, pp. 14, 17, 21.

equivalent was ATS 55-60 million, almost a quarter of the major parties' federal cash outlay in 1980. In New Zealand the net value of free television and radio time was estimated at NZ-$2.3 million for the 1984 election campaign.[50] Other means of public in-kind support to parties and candidates are less important but they should be mentioned.

b)   Other support options

In Sweden and Israel public authorities cover expenses for *transportation* to and from polling stations. Municipal governments and local administrations in Belgium, France, Germany, Italy, the Netherlands and Spain offer free space for party *posters* during campaign periods. France even reimburses the costs of posters.[51] For campaign purposes, candidates in Japan are entitled to five newspaper advertisements free of charge. Additional options available are posters, a car, rent of assembly halls, and printing as well as mailing of campaign literature.

In Switzerland parties receive just one public support of monetary importance, a reduction in postage for mass *mailings* without address. A reduced postal rate is available in Belgium. Italy, Sweden and Spain (at increasing cost) mail campaign literature for free to each voter in national elections. The 1991 amendment to the Spanish electoral law granted considerable amounts of state funds for the costs of direct election mailings. In Ireland parties are entitled to send leaflets free of charge as well as 300 letters per week.[52] In Britain candidates in a nationwide election (to the Westminster or the European parliament) may send one letter free of charge to every elector within the constituency.

Free use of *public halls* (e.g. schools) for the purpose of election rallies is available to candidates standing for parliamentary and local elections in Britain as well as to parties in France and Spain. Italy permits the use of public buildings for party political purposes. Furthermore, rates for the use of public places as well as on public advertisements and billboards as well as the distribution of pamphlets are reduced by one third. The local rate for public places is also reduced in Israel. In Italy and Sweden political parties are allowed to organise *lotteries*. Furthermore, parties in Italy enjoy preferred treatment in terms of rental contracts for party premises, which are granted for a minimum of six years. Additionally, rents on party *premises* may not be increased by the same amount as rents on other property.[53] On top of such privileges party officers in some countries have been tempted to utilise public resources illegally for partisan ad-

---

50   Cf. Kofler 1981, p. 375; Commission on Election Finances (Ontario) 1988, p. 151.
51   Schurig 2006, p. 113. - The borderline to abuse of public resources is crossed when by tacit agreement some Danish "parties have their posters hung by municipal personnel" (Pedersen 2003, p. 253).
52   Drysch 1998, p. 117; Suetens 1990, p. 67; Kelly 1990, p. 363.
53   Ridola 1992, p. 296

vantage. The most notorious examples have been discussed already.[54] This is also true for indirect subsidies resulting from tax benefits for political donations.[55] We will therefore turn to those types of subsidies, which can be considered as direct state aid to parties, candidates and partisan purpose, all of them given in cash.

2. Reimbursement of costs incurred

In some countries, a clearly defined proportion of reported and receipted expenses actually incurred by candidates and/ or parties is reimbursed with public funds. Reimbursements ensure a mix of public and private funding, because recipient candidates and parties are forced to seek out additional donations as the subsidy covers only part of the actual expenditure. Despite an uninterrupted process of subsidisation, citizens continue to participate financially. In Canada registered political parties and constituency candidates are entitled to be reimbursed 50 percent of their declared election expenses up to the legal spending limit. In 2000 the Canadian government paid CAD 7,680,388 in election reimbursements.[56] The amount of reimbursements received by parties other than the major ones (i.e. three up to 1988, five 1993-2001, four since 2004) and independent constituency candidates has been insignificant.

In Ireland eligible parties are entitled to a campaign reimbursement up to IEP 5,000 (€ 6,350) for each candidate who has not lost his or her deposit, i.e. polled a minimum of votes.[57] In France campaign reimbursements are provided for elections of parliaments, administrative assemblies and the president. Candidates running for president are refunded one third of the spending limit. In legislative elections candidates are eligible to receive a flat-rate reimbursement up to 50 percent of the legal spending limit. A similar system is applied to all other elections.[58] All of these procedures make sure that subsidies are used for the purpose that has been determined by law. Some funding programmes use other methods towards this end.

3. Earmarked funds

The road from indirect support to direct funding of political parties has been difficult to travel for modern democracies. In many countries legislators hesitated to provide general flat grants to candidates and parties. Instead of funding party activities many programmes have preferred subsidies-in-kind, reimbursement of costs incurred or grants, which are earmarked for specific aspects of party work. Such prescriptions, meant to strengthen grass-root activity or to support (specific) campaigns, may be a

---

54 See above in chapter VII, sub-section D1 (abuse of public resources).
55 See above in chapter VI, sub-section C2 (stimulating contributors).
56 Smith 2005, pp. 101-102, citing Young 2003.
57 Laver/ Marsh 2004, pp. 157/158.
58 The regime for political parties (or groups) is quite different. See below in this chapter, section D (allocation of national party subsidies).

pretext of symbolic value, a proviso to improve legitimacy or a device to limit the amount of money distributed. Depending on the political system and the political situation at the time of inception, different labels have been applied. Training of voluntary party workers (Germany, 1959), support of the party press (Sweden, 1965) and provision for policy development (Britain, 2000) have been used early on or more recently.[59]

In the U.S. federal subsidies are earmarked for the presidential election. Each of the sub-grants for primaries, party conventions and general election campaigns aims at a specific purpose and recipient. During the primaries, each candidate running in the pre-nomination contests, raising campaign contributions in little sums and abiding by statutory spending limits may claim a matching grant.[60] Only parties are entitled to receive a grant for their national convention, which nominates the candidates for president and vice president. Once they are nominated, presidential candidates who claim a flat grant for their general election campaign have to refrain from raising private contributions (of individuals, PACs or party committees). New Zealand provides subsidies, "which can be used to buy advertising time on radio or television." In 2002 a total of NZD 2.08 million was distributed. "In 1996, some 20 parties received broadcasting funds, although only 12 qualified for free broadcasting time."[61]

Initially, party subsidies in the Netherlands were specifically geared towards research, training and youth.[62] State aid was distributed among party institutes serving one of these purposes only. Since 1999 the funds provided for parties continue to be goal-oriented, but grants are paid to the parties now and the list of goals has been broadened to include contacts with foreign sister parties and information to party members. Only minor portions of this direct subsidy are earmarked for youth organisations and research institutes. Campaign spending is explicitly excluded from public subsidies, because campaigns are very hard to control and state aid is intended to reinforce the intermediary position of political parties.[63]

In Latin America, e.g. Mexico,[64] like in some European countries, there is a tendency to provide part of the public funding for policy research and institutional development of partisan political groups. Sometimes additional funds are geared towards specific purposes, such as civic education campaigns or youth activity.[65] Funding of such activities is seen as essential for the strengthening of democratic political parties and is meant to ensure their continuous operation by becoming more than mere electoral machines.

---

59 Schleth 1973, pp. 409-429; Walter 1966, pp. 395, 398; Klee-Kruse 1993b, pp. 186/187; Ewing 2007, p. 191.
60 For details see above in chapter VI, sub-section C1 (energising fundraisers) and below in this chapter, sub-section C 2a (distribution of matching funds).
61 Miller 2005, pp. 96/97.
62 In addition Koole (1999, p. 347) mentions a subsidy for the intra-party support of women.
63 Van den Berg report 1991, p. 24; Koole 1999, p. 347.
64 Zovatto 2001, p. 375.
65 For all other countries see Nassmacher 2001a.

To this day grants to party affiliated but separate institutes earmarked for training and research have survived in Austria and Germany.[66] Such allocations are provided in addition to general grants for party activity in parliament and in the field, during election periods and beyond. In most countries legislators have abstained from defining the purpose because they feel that the items of political spending cannot be or should not be determined.

4. General grants

Today most of the countries that provide public subsidies prefer general purpose grants, even if publicity or campaigns are identified as the intended use of specific subsidies in individual cases. Germany is a quite instructive example. The party law, which is the legal basis for state aid, was amended after more than 25 years. Initially (1967) the public subsidy, due to a supreme court ruling, was "earmarked" for campaign purposes. Because the implementation of this intention was not pursued in any way or by anyone, it has remained just a pretext. When the court ruled in 1992 that general subsidies are constitutional, it was reacting to the problem that a demarcation line between on-going activities and campaigns cannot be drawn, and German parties were increasingly claiming that all of their activity was campaign-oriented. Without needing much time to realize the obvious, a minimum of 15 established democracies allocated general purpose grants (for all kinds of activity) to national party headquarters. Such subsidies are unknown only in Britain, India, New Zealand, Switzerland and the U.S.[67]

Policy analysis in other fields of public policy demonstrates that different options of public support, different rules for access and distribution as well as details of implementation contribute towards diverse kinds of impact. It would be most surprising if such findings did not apply to a field of public policy that has produced such variety of instruments and such wealth of experience in roughly five decades. Although parties may tailor subsidy programmes to suit their needs,[68] their politics is subject to unintended consequences, pressures from public opinion and decisions by supreme courts. Incumbents may be in control of the legislative process, but they cannot determine the effects of misperception and litigation, policy outcomes or policy impacts.[69] Under the circumstances no general hypothesis can predict the consequences of all public subsidy schemes, just like general predictions for membership or donor funding are inappropriate and fail reality by a wide margin. As democratic politics is a competitive process, even the variety of recipients may contribute towards some difference among the results of public subsidies to partisan activities.

---

66 See below in this chapter, sub-section C4 (party penumbra).
67 Many countries provide public subsidies practically without any obligation for the recipient, which may be exactly the problem that critics of public funding intend to raise without becoming so specific.
68 Cf. Ebbighausen et al. 1996, pp. 26-29; Casas-Zamora 2002, pp. 335-349.
69 For details see Nassmacher 2003d, pp. 139-141, 153/154.

C) Recipients of cash subsidies

Although the general aim of public subsidies is to support participants of political competition the specific recipient varies. Depending on the major institutions of the political system and specific electoral rules this may be a pre-eminent candidate, e.g. for the presidency, the group of parliamentary candidates, a caucus of elected representatives or the headquarters of a well-established organisation. Entitlement to public subsidies is derived from this selection. Occasionally legislators may shy away from such open preference and provide subsidies to organisations of the party penumbra.

1. Candidates (for parliament or the presidency)

In a presidential system, like the U.S. and Mexico, or a semi-presidential-system, like France and Poland, the presidential election is the most important arena of political competition. A logical consequence seems to be that candidates for the presidency are entitled to public funding. However, there are no specific subsidies to presidential candidates in Mexico and Poland.

In the U.S. the bulk of all public funding goes to the presidential candidates, not to their parties, and this happens to be the only campaign sponsored by federal funds. Whereas both major party candidates automatically qualify for a general election grant, pre-nomination candidates have to demonstrate their ability to fundraise. Candidates must solicit small contributions from a variety of individual donors in twenty different states to qualify for partial public funding. Whereas both major party candidates are allocated the same fixed amount for their general election presidential campaigns, a third party's candidate is entitled to a general election grant from public funds (in proportion to the votes polled), but only after the election was held, and only if he or she has won at least 5 percent of the popular vote.

The public purse distributes matching funds for presidential primaries. The first $250 of a donation to a qualifying candidate by any individual is matchable, i.e. the amount donated is doubled. Donations by PACs are not matched. In 2000 (1996) pre-convention subsidies from *primary matching payments* totalled $ 53.5 (56.8) million, which was 16 (23) percent of total pre-nomination spending, 26 (24) percent of the total subsidies distributed or $0.28 ($0.30) per registered voter.[70] Recently a leading U.S. newspaper noted a "gradual breakdown of the public funding system," which began in 2000 when George W. Bush was stupefied by the (unsuccessful) pre-nomination bid of a self-financing Steve Forbes and continued when both major party candidates (Bush Jr. and Kerry) passed up matching funds in order to avoid the statutory spending limit in the primaries.[71]

---

70 Alexander 1999, p. 18; Nelson 2002, p. 28; Green/ Bigelow 2002, pp. 54, 62, 70.
71 „Money's Going to Talk in 2008", in: Washington Post, 11 March 2006.

By way of contrast in France, where the president is embedded in a parliamentary system, the public purse subsidises not only the presidential election but also parliamentary campaigns. In accordance with electoral rules (second ballot majority system), the public purse reimburses candidates for part of their expenses. Specific thresholds apply for *parliamentary and presidential candidates*. All presidential candidates in France are entitled to a campaign subsidy. However, candidates have to win more than 5 percent of the national vote in the first round if they want to claim more than a token state contribution towards their campaign expenses.[72] The amounts of presidential campaign grants depend on the number of votes polled. No campaign grants are available for popularly elected presidents in Austria, Finland and Ireland.

In parliamentary political systems with plurality or majority voting, constituency candidates are entitled to campaign reimbursements. For instance, constituency candidates in Canada (a first-past-the-post system) have to obtain at least 10 percent of the votes cast in their riding to be reimbursed for half of their campaign expenses. About half of all candidates and roughly two thirds of the major party candidates qualify. The public purse reimbursed "a total of 739 candidates in 1988 (47 percent of 1,574), in 1993 a total of 714 candidates (33 percent of 2,155) and in 1997 a total of 801 candidates (48 percent of 1,672). .... Among candidates of the major parties (3 in 1988, 5 from 1993 to 2000 and 4 since 2004) the share is considerably higher: 82 percent in 1988, 61 percent in 1993 and 66 percent in 1997."[73] In the 2004 general election 844 candidates in 308 constituencies, which is about half of all candidates and a minimum of 3 candidates in most constituencies, were eligible for reimbursements.[74]

In France (a second ballot majority system) parliamentary candidates qualify for campaign subsidies if they win at least 5 percent of their constituency vote in the first round.[75] Eligible parliamentary candidates in Canada and France (as well as parties contesting a federal election in Canada) are partly reimbursed for campaign expenses, which they have incurred, provided that they comply with spending limits. In addition, parties may be entitled to subsidies, too, as they are in Canada and France. In Australia parties as well as independent candidates may qualify for a campaign subsidy. Single-member constituencies notwithstanding, the U.K. and Germany restrict their subsidies to parties without supporting individual candidates.

2. Party organisations

In parliamentary systems with proportional representation (despite recent efforts to put more emphasis on candidates, as in Sweden and Austria), parties are the relevant political competitors and thus the major recipients of public subsidies. However, funding the party organisation does not necessarily equate to support national party headquar-

---

[72] Kempf 2007, p. 35; Schurig 2006, pp. 115-117.
[73] Amr/ Lisowski 2001, p. 64.
[74] Chief Electoral Officer: Report on the 38th General Election, 2004, p. 66.
[75] Kempf 2007, p. 265; Miguet 1999, p. 63; Schurig 2006, pp. 104-108.

ters. For all sorts of revenue the distribution modalities empower those levels of a party organisation that initially collect money. Quite naturally this also applies for public subsidies. Some countries distribute party subsidies at the national level only. This contributes to the growing importance of party headquarters, a trend that many scholars working on parties have elaborated on.[76] Sometimes even new laws for the provision of public funds (e.g. in the Netherlands 1999 and in the U.K. 2000) have not paid attention to this problem.

In other countries, specific party financing rules for the sub-national level address the centralising effect of national subsidies. This is rather easy for regions in a federal system. All Canadian provinces and Austrian states, and – more moderately – some U.S. states,[77] Germany (for votes polled in state elections) and regions in Spain have enacted separate legislation. Among the 27 jurisdictions of the Swiss federation just two, the states (*Kantone*) of Geneva and Fribourg, grant subsidies for election campaigns (and ballot issues). In spite of devolution to a federal system, Belgium continues to provide party subsidies at the national level only.[78]

Even in centralised countries, such as Denmark, Israel, Norway, Sweden, and to some degree France and Uruguay, political finance regimes systematically take care of decentralised funding. In addition to national subsidies for party headquarters, nationwide aid is given to party sub-organisations, the municipal and/or provincial branches. In Denmark a subsidy for each vote polled in the most recent municipal election "will be awarded to the central party organization, which is then supposed to distribute the money" among its regional and local chapters.[79] "Overall, Denmark and Finland direct the greater part of their subsidies to central rather than to sub-national parties, though Finland (unlike Denmark) channels public funds to national party offices rather than parliamentary organisations." In 1975 (following the Swedish example) Norway started to distribute subsidies to provincial and local branches.[80]

The total amount of regional and local subsidies in Sweden is much higher than the total of the national subsidies. In 1999 sub-national subsidies totalled SEK 445 million, national grants only SEK 221 million. Contrary to the national parties, electoral defeats have very damaging effects on the sub-national organisations of Swedish parties. A party that has lost representation in a regional or a municipal council receives public funding for only one year after its defeat. On the other hand, the decentralised system of public funding has contributed to the maintenance of local party activity during non-election periods.[81] In France and Spain public subsidies at the national level, as well as financial aid towards campaign expenses incurred for regional and

---

76 Panebianco 1988; Katz/ Mair 1995, p. 20.
77 As of 2000 public funding was available in 22 states, only 14 provided party subsidies (Smith 2005, p. 72).
78 Wewer 1989, pp. 28/29; Drysch 1998, p. 121 Suetens 1992, p. 36.
79 Stegagnini 1989, p. 38; Strom 1990, p. 579; Pierre/ Widfeldt 1994, p. 345; Schurig 2006, p. 295; Casas-Zamora 2002, p. 134; Vesterdorf 1990, p. 137; quote in Pedersen/ Bille 1991, p. 159.
80 Svasand 1994, p. 322; quote in Sundberg 2002, p. 199.
81 Gidlund/Koole 2001, p. 121; Gidlund 1983, pp. 240/241, 277/278; Klee 1993b, p. 192.

municipal elections are available. In Israel there is a specific subsidy for each party list participating successfully in local elections; the public purse provides public funding for campaigns only, but new lists of candidates are eligible, too.[82]

On top of both federal subsidies (for parliamentary campaigns and national party organisations) in Austria each of the nine states (*Länder*) grants subsidies to political parties as well. Although each state has its own regulation, in general they are similar to those at the federal level. Most of the public money given to parties is provided at the sub-national level, which is quite similar to Sweden. Between them, the nine Austrian states distribute two to three times the total amount allocated for party purposes in the federal budget.[83] In Germany, the parties' regional (*Land*) organisations collected one third of the total public subsidy in their own right during the 1980s. The new legal basis, established in 1994, decreased this share. However, party headquarters have to compensate their regional branches via equalisation transfers.[84]

If the political finance regime does not include safeguards for an automatic distribution of public funds to different levels of the party organisation, the top level (party headquarters) will be able to provide extra-funding for local branches at will (or upon "good" behaviour). This centralising effect can be balanced by rules for redistribution, which are enshrined in the individual party's by-laws. Providing ample support for parliamentary parties can foster intra-party competition, but the additional power centre thus created may also be an agent of centralisation and bureaucratisation.[85]

3. Party caucuses (parliamentary groups)

Drawing a line between the parliamentary caucus and the party organisation will never be easy in practice because politicians usually act in two capacities, MP and party officer. Facilities available to an individual MP (e.g. franking privilege, travel allowance, personal assistant, and constituency office) can be used to support local party life.[86] The dividing line between extra-parliamentary parties on the one hand and caucuses and their members on the other hand, has not always been strict. Sometimes the public funds distributed to caucuses in parliament are routinely passed on to the extra-parliamentary parties (such as in Switzerland and Ireland, before the introduction of party subsidies),[87] sometimes the funding of party caucuses is treated as just one part

---

82   van Biezen/ Nassmacher 2001, p. 145; Schurig 2006, p. 295; Blechinger/ Nassmacher 2001, p. 168.
83   Dachs 1986, p. 451; Müller 1994, p. 55; Sickinger 1997, p. 27; Drysch 1998, pp. 116/117.
84   See above in chapter VI, sub-section D 2 (equalisation transfers).
85   For a discussion of impacts on intra-party power see below in chapter X, section B (Distribution of power).
86   Recently MPs in Britain have used public funding for office expenses partly to pay for services provided by their constituency party offices. As we are not dealing with the impacts of incumbency we shall neglect all such benefits and limit our discussion to parliamentary caucuses as collective bodies.
87   Weigelt 1988, p.34; cf. Ladner/ Brändle 1999, p. 20; Gallagher 1985, p. 130; Farrell 1992, p. 452.

of the regular party subsidy (Sweden), and sometimes caucus funds are used for indirect support of party organisations (Austria).[88] However, occasionally a transfer of funds from caucus to party is expressively banned (Germany). Whichever borderline towards party financing applies, much of the public funding to parliamentary groups (caucuses) is spent on intra-parliamentary business only.

Two thirds of the countries studied here support party caucuses via cash grants. This procedure seems to be characteristic in Europe.[89] The level of such grants per eligible voter differs considerably. In Switzerland the annual total of (state and federal) caucus subsidies was about €0.75, in Belgium some €1.50 for both houses of the national parliament. German party caucuses in federal and state parliaments received almost €2.00, Austrian federal and state budgets provided €5.00.[90] Rather moderate support to party caucuses in cash and kind is available in Norway. By the end of the 1980s parliamentary groups in Finland were granted about 15 percent of the total amount distributed among party organisations. In Denmark parliamentary caucuses received almost 1.5 times the amount allocated to national party organisations, which is a "proportion that far outweighs that found elsewhere in Scandinavia".[91] For the U.S. Congress "funds are authorized for congressional party committees and congressional operations under a variety of headings." Parties in Congress "conduct most of their business very independently" from their extra-parliamentary organisations.[92] In Europe parliamentary party groups as collective bodies are entitled to office assistance to hire staff for secretarial and research duties, e.g. in Spain, France and Sweden.[93]

Von Arnim has frequently pointed out that public subsidies to federal and state caucuses have exploded in Germany since 1966 and that for decades they lacked a proper legal basis. Now that adequate laws are in place, a shady area remains. Parliamentary groups are entitled to "publicity activities" funded by the caucus subsidy, which are necessarily extra-parliamentary. However, three differences to Austria should be noted. In Germany no part of the subsidy is earmarked for publicity; recipient parliamentary groups are obliged to file financial reports; this obligation applies to federal as well as to state funds.[94] In 2001 the share of federal caucus funds spent on publicity did not exceed 10 percent of the average budget, just about half of that share for the major parties, considerably more for the smaller ones.

---

88 Drysch 1998, p. 152. Pierre, Svasand and Widfeldt (2000, p. 6) offer details on the years of inception and the demarcation between subsidies to parliamentary parties and national party organisations in 12 democracies.
89 Among the non-European democracies, which provide caucus grants, are Costa Rica, New Zealand and Uruguay (Casas-Zamora 2002, pp. 39/40; Casas-Zamora 2005a, pp. 30/31).
90 Ladner/ Brändle 2001, pp. 150, 153/154; Suetens 1990, pp. 65/66; Suetens 1992, pp. 36/37.
91 Sundberg 2002, p. 199; cf. Wiberg 1991c, pp. 75, 78; Svasand 1991, p. 137; Svasand 1994, p. 323; Pedersen/ Bille 1991, pp. 157/158, 161; Vesterdorf 1992, p. 71.
92 Kolodny/ Katz 1992, p. 927 respectively Katz/ Kolodny 1994, p. 44.
93 New Zealand (Vowles 2002, p. 423) is closer to this than to the British procedure.
94 von Arnim 1993, pp. 211, 212; Nassmacher 2001c, pp. 104/105.

In the Netherlands [95] and Britain, both of which had no direct public subsidies for extra-parliamentary parties until the end of the 1990s, subsidies to caucuses and their staff have been important for quite a while. In Britain subsidies to parliamentary groups (as introduced in 1975), have always been restricted to opposition parties holding a minimum of two seats in the House of Commons.[96] The subsidies were intended to assist opposition parties in carrying out their parliamentary business. During the 1990s other funds have been added to this 'Short money,' including a specific allocation for the Leader of the Opposition's office, an allowance for travel and associated expenses of opposition frontbenchers and a subsidy to parties in the House of Lords, the 'Cranborne money.'[97] In several steps the current Labour government has increased the total amount for all such subsidies to £7.4 million in 2007-2008.

In some countries party groups in municipal assemblies are also eligible for public support. In Germany such support is common since the 1970s. The amount of money provided depends on individual cities and the state, to which they belong. In France the introduction of caucus grants for larger cities coincides with the process of devolution in recent decades.[98] Because parties perform linkage functions between governmental institutions (such as national parliaments, regional assemblies or municipal councils) and civil society a proper demarcation of activities will also affect party related bodies with NGO status.

4. Organisations of the party penumbra

There are four examples that suffice to illustrate the wide range of party related activities: organisation of youth groups, adult education, production of newspapers and foreign aid to assist democracy building. All of this can be done without any party being involved. However, in all these areas there are examples of party-affiliated bodies, which receive public subsidies because they provide such services. In some countries state funds support the work of youth and students organisations. Party *youth groups* are eligible along with religious, sports and other groups or they receive extra-grants due to their alleged role in civic education. This may relieve parties of a financial burden although not of a very onerous one.[99]

Financially more important are subsidies for the *party press*. From the 19th century on newspapers owned and operated by political parties were a powerful means to convey

---

95   Koole 1994, pp. 279, 291/292.
96   At present this is a total of 6 parties. For details see Ewing 1987, pp. 118-121; Ewing 2007, pp. 183-185.
97   The funds were named after the Leader of the House of Commons (respectively the Leader of the House of Lords) who introduced the subsidies in 1975 and 1996.
98   Schurig 2006, p. 293; Kempf 2007, p. 265.
99   For examples see Farrell 1994, p. 235; Lucardie/ Voerman 2001, p. 324 and Svasand 1994, p. 322.

the political message, as well as a source of extra-funding.[100] When the printing press declined, party papers became unable to break-even in the market. In order to preserve a variety of political opinions some countries decided to subsidise newspapers, including or even emphasising the party press. Considerable aid to party media is available in Austria, Finland, France, Italy, Norway and Sweden.[101] In Sweden press subsidies of SEK 487 million (€56 million) in 1994/95 were given to publishing houses directly not channelled via political parties. Italian legislation provides public subsidies to radio stations and newspapers that are owned by political parties. In 1996 *L'Unità*, the paper linked to *Democratici della sinistra* (the former PCI) received about €10 million. In order to be eligible for state aid, Italian media must have direct links to a party that is represented by at least two MPs or one MP plus one MEP.[102]

Within the realm of adult education, municipal institutions or "third sector" non-profit organisations may offer training courses for professional skills or seminars on a wide range of social issues. If public subsidies are available to such outfits it may be either difficult or undesirable to draw a line that precludes *training* of party workers or partisan debates of political issues. Some European countries have proceeded further from such practices in Scandinavia and set up a pluralistic set of party affiliated institutes (called foundations or academies).[103] In Belgium there are two different groups of recipients (one for each eligible party) for tax deductible donations and public subsidies. Most of these funds are spent on additional staff, possibly in affiliated study centres.[104] In Germany separate foundations were established for "political education" and they receive public funds, which up to 1966 had been collected by the parties represented in parliament. Formally the foundations offer courses in adult education that are open to all citizens and not only to party members. However, they are largely responsible for the training of party workers, candidates and municipal councillors. Besides that they provide political (although not necessarily policy) research for the parties. In the early 1970s Austria and the Netherlands followed suit and adapted this model to their needs. In Germany and Austria the party-affiliated foundations get substantial public subsidies. However, only part of their work is a direct service for the parties. The four *Parteiakademien* in Austria are more closely linked to their parties than the six foundations in Germany (*Politische Stiftungen*), which are more loosely related to the parties represented federally.[105] In the Netherlands (from 1970 to 1998) earmarked subsidies were given to specific bodies (called *stichting*), such as research institutes, educational

---

100 See above in chapter VII, section C (party enterprises).
101 Wiberg 1991c, p. 92; Svasand 1991, p. 138; Svasand 1994, pp. 322/323; Schurig 2006, p. 85/86.
102 Gidlund/ Koole 2001, p. 122; Bianco/ Gardini 1999, p.25; van Biezen/ Nassmacher 2001, p. 146.
103 Vesterdorf 1992, pp. 67/68; Svasand 1991, p. 139; Svasand 1994, pp. 311/312, 323; Pedersen/ Bille 1991, p. 162. Ireland has introduced similar budget allocations (Murphy/ Farrell 2002, p. 243).
104 Suetens 1992, pp. 33, 47; Deschouwer 1994, p. 104.
105 See Sickinger 2001, pp. 338/339, 342-349; for Germany see Pinto-Duschinsky 1991b, pp. 179-250.

institutes and youth organisations. Consequently, activities that had hitherto been carried out within the framework of the parties were transferred to the affiliates.[106]

Following a German precedent set in the 1970s, other countries have established agents for *international aid* to democracy building and transition from authoritarian rule. The Netherlands, Austria, Sweden, France, the U.S. (National Endowment for Democracy, International Republican Institute and National Democratic Institute) and Britain (Westminster Foundation for Democracy) are cases in point.[107] All key parties co-operate in the Netherlands Institute for Multiparty Democracy, which initially served as an instrument to support political parties in South Africa. The important difference between all tasks mentioned earlier and democracy building activities is that the latter will have no impact upon party competition within any of the established democracies. Therefore this field of party related activities can be neglected in our study of donor countries and considered for recipient democracies only.

As far as other purposes are concerned, a variety of subsidies and a multitude of recipients can be expected to support different fiefdoms within the party universe. Multiple power centres contribute towards intra-party competition and thus counterbalance the potential for centralised power inherent in a concentrated supply of cash subsidies. Occasionally the parliamentary leadership (e.g. the Dutch), well endowed with ample caucus funds, can build a power centre within the party.[108] Whereas the variety of recipients will influence intra-party power, the allocation of subsidies should have an impact on inter-party competition.

D) Allocation of national party subsidies

Public subsidies to political parties are granted and distributed according to statute law.[109] Without such laws all recipients of a subsidy would depend entirely on the whims of the government of the day. Critics of public subsidies have frequently claimed that the allocation of subsidies is unfair to minor parties and newcomers because the parties in power tailor the rules to suit their own needs.[110] Such suspicion cannot be proved or refuted in general. Procedures for access and distribution must be considered separately and closely before a conclusion on openness and fairness will be justified.

---

106 For details see Lucardie/ Voerman 2001, pp. 325-333.Since 1999 parties now receive a flat grant, which they may spend more freely. See above in this chapter, sub-section B3 (earmarked grants).
107 For details see Pinto-Duschinsky 1997 and Pinto-Duschinsky 2001c, pp. 299-303.
108 Koole 1999, p. 343.
109 Pierre, Svasand and Widfeldt (2000, pp. 8-12) discuss four dimensions of subsidies to national party organisations: recipients, eligibility (qualifying criteria), targeting and accountability. Because the democratic principle of fairness is at stake, this study puts emphasis on eligibility.
110 The „party cartel" is discussed below in this chapter, sub-section F1 (Influence of party competition), the „cartel party" in Chapter XI, sub-section B2.

1. Access to public funding

In democracies access to public subsidies depends on political finance regimes, which combine general stipulations, especially transparency standards, with thresholds of access. Parties that do not pass the barrier or meet the legal requirements are not entitled to a subsidy for campaign purposes or current operations. This may have serious implications on the strategic choices, which are open to party elites, especially if voting rules are amended.[111] Access to public funds can be defined in terms of vote and seat requirements, demand a minimum of candidates fielded or focus on successful fundraising.

a) Minimum of votes polled

Among the established democracies, Denmark has set the most moderate threshold for public funding: 1,000 votes in a national election, an extremely small share of the popular vote (0.03 percent). In Germany access is more restricted: 0.5 percent of the vote in a federal or a European election or 1.0 percent of all votes cast in any state election entitle parties to the national subsidy. Drawing more countries into the comparison increases the threshold considerably: 1.5 percent in Uruguay, 2 to 3 percent in Ireland, Sweden, Norway, Italy and Poland. In Canada a registered political party receives federal funds if it obtained at least 2 percent of the number of valid votes nationwide or 5 percent of the votes in those electoral districts where this party endorsed a candidate. In a comparative perspective, this positions Canada clearly beyond Germany and slightly below Italy. In Australia party or independent candidates qualify for entitlement in all constituencies where they receive at least 4 percent of all first preference votes cast. As the qualifying quota is based on constituencies the factual threshold for general elections in Australia is around 2 per cent of the national vote, for Senate elections even less (i.e. slightly above 1 per cent).

b) Minimum of seats held

Depending on the electoral system, the regional distribution of party support and the size of a parliament, the requirement of one seat can be transformed into the share of votes needed to win the first seat. For example, in first-past-the-post systems a party will need regionally concentrated voters to qualify for parliamentary representation. Some systems of proportional representation apply a specific threshold before seats are allocated thus making it more difficult to get represented.

In the Netherlands all parties represented in parliament are given an annual subsidy.[112]

---

111 Hooghe/ Maddens/ Noppe 2006, pp. 353, 366.
112 A recent court ruling has created an additional prerequisite for public subsidies: The Netherlands are not allowed to subsidise a party (i.e., the small Calvinist SGP), which discriminates against women, even if this is due to religious beliefs that are a core element of the party program. ("Keine Subventionen mehr für kalvinistische Partei", in: *Frankfurter Allgemeine*, 8 September 2005.

The actual minimum required is the number of votes cast divided by the total number of seats, i.e. 0.667 percent of the national vote. In Belgium a party is allowed a subsidy if it holds a seat in each of the two chambers of parliament. Parties with less than 1 percent of the national vote have been unable to pass this test. In Israel each party represented in the *Knesset* is entitled to state aid for current and campaign activity. The latter is paid to parties of the incoming as well as the outgoing parliament (if they field a list of candidates). The electoral threshold of 1.5 percent of all valid votes grants access to public funding. Subsidies in Finland require a minimum of one seat held in the national parliament, which will be allocated for 0.5 to 1.5 percent of the national vote. Compared to other countries, the Netherlands can be placed just beyond Germany. Belgium, Finland and Israel range between the Netherlands and Ireland. With 4 percent of the vote Costa Rica operates a much higher threshold.[113]

At first glance access to party subsidies in Austria looks rather complicated because different barriers (most of them defined in terms of seats held) apply to different parts of the subsidy. However, the electoral threshold of four percent of the vote is the most relevant. A higher barrier (of about six percent) is enforced for the subsidy linked to campaigns for the European parliament. A much lower threshold of one percent of the vote grants a token subsidy of less than one fifth of the regular entitlement.[114] For all practical purposes this seems to be the most restrictive rule among parliamentary democracies.

In Britain the policy development fund is distributed among registered political parties represented by a minimum of two MPs. Since 2002 this includes eight parties, some of them with regionally concentrated support of no more than 0.6 percent of the total vote.[115] Two parties with broadly distributed support (up to 1.5 percent) were unable to win representation (and thus admission to the subsidy). Parties in Spain may claim public funds if they are able to win at least one seat in one of the multi-candidate constituencies. This equals the electoral threshold in the largest regions (Madrid, Barcelona), which is about 3 percent of the regional vote. However, parties on the regional fringe have entered parliament with less than 0.8 percent whereas a party with 0.7 percent of the national vote, spread out over 8 provinces, was not successful. In practice, British access to public funds is slightly easier than the Canadian. Spain falls somewhere between Germany and Italy.

A slightly different policy option defines the threshold by using seats and votes as an alternative or in combination. In Japan parties are entitled to public funds if they hold an aggregate of five seats in either house of parliament or have won at least 2 percent of the vote in the most recent nationwide election.[116] In France there are two parts of

---

113 Casas-Zamora 2002, p. 322.
114 Sickinger 1997, pp. 148/149, 151, 153. Obviously this fairness is the showpiece of Austria's party law.
115 www.electoralcommission.gov.uk; www.legislation.hmso.gov.uk.
116 Blechinger/ Nassmacher 2001, pp. 170/171.

the annual subsidy for political parties. One part is distributed among parties, which have polled at least 1 percent of the vote in a minimum of fifty single member districts, and the other is paid to parties, to which at least one MP (deputy or senator) has declared affiliation. Whereas access to the second part is easier for regional parties, the first part is more accessible for parties with a broader distribution of activity and support.[117] Occasionally the legal barrier depends on other options than a minimum of votes or seats.

c)   Other options (fixed amount, successful fundraising)

Some cash subsidies to political competitors are granted without any reference to seats or votes. In each presidential year both major U.S. parties automatically qualify for a convention grant.[118] In France there is compensation for new political forces, such as special funds that are provided for small initiatives. If political groups fail to receive an annual grant, they may apply for a specific grant, which is based on the condition that a total of FRF 1 million (€152,000) has been solicited from 10,000 identified persons, provided that 500 elected officials scattered over 30 regional units are among them. A similar option is available in Italy; ethnic groups get special funds.[119]

The regulation of access to party subsidies shows different degrees of exclusiveness. Ten countries (Denmark, Germany, the Netherlands, Spain, Belgium, Finland, Israel, Uruguay, Australia and Britain) insist on *less* than 2 percent of the national vote and offer a varying degree of fair and open access to public funding. Four democracies (Canada, Italy, Ireland and Japan) stipulate a medium sized threshold of 2 percent for state aid to parties. Finally, no more than five countries (Norway, Poland, Sweden, Cost Rica and Austria) require *more* than 2 percent of the vote as a minimum and thus support the contention that established parties try to exclude newcomers from public funding.[120] France should be added to this group because each of the three different subsidies available in that country is saddled with specific restrictions (regionally concentrated vote, considerable number of candidates, minimum of elected officials and regions).[121] In general, high thresholds tend to favour major established parties and may contribute towards a petrifaction of the party system.[122] All rules for access are supplemented by procedures for the distribution of state aid.

---

117 Schurig 2006, pp. 65, 70; Kempf 2007, p. 264.
118 See above in this chapter, sub-section B3 (earmarked funds).
119 Doublet 1999, pp. 70, 73; Koole 2001, p. 82; Schurig 2006, pp. 76/77; von Beyme 2000, p. 143.
120 Different „effective subsidy thresholds" have been calculated by Casas-Zamora 2002, pp. 321/2 (table A).
121 Effective subsidy threshold calculated by Schurig 2006, pp. 68/69, 74/75.
122 This potential impact is discussed below, in chapter IX B (ossification of party system).

2. Distribution of subsidies

Not too many options are practical for the distribution of public subsidies.[123] Giving the same amount of money to each eligible recipient is rarely done. U.S. convention grants are the only example. Subsidising parties according to size prevails although details vary. This principle can be modified in favour of smaller parties. A completely different method ties public funding to each recipient's success in fundraising, favourably of small contributions.

a) Allocation of matching funds

The general idea of all matching fund programmes is to create a link between a legal entitlement to public subsidies and financial support provided by the voluntary giving of individual citizens. In just a few countries public funds are distributed in proportion to the amounts that parties (or candidates) have raised in little sums. This mode of allocation was first introduced for U.S. presidential primaries and in some state elections.[124] A modification of this method (although not limited to small contributions) is used for campaign reimbursements to parties in Canada.[125] New political groups in France, which do not receive a general subsidy on the basis of seats and votes, may collect a public matching grant of FRF 2 million (€305,000) if they have been able to solicit a total of FRF 1 million from 10,000 identified individuals.[126]

In Germany parties, which receive public subsidies, need to demonstrate their linkage to the grass-roots of society. The supreme court (*Bundesverfassungsgericht*) has mentioned three indicators of grass-roots linkage: voters, party members and political donors. Since 1994 distribution of public funds to political parties is partly based on successful fundraising. About half of the total subsidy is allocated as a matching grant of 38 percent of the sum of all small donations by individuals and membership fees lumped together per individual party. At first glance the programme looks quite promising. The details, however, reveal important weaknesses. The maximum contribution to be matched is set relatively high (at €3,300). Revenue from assessment of officeholders [127] is included in the matchable total. Although the grant is primarily based on fundraising by local sections of the party, the federal headquarters collects the subsidy. If the fundraising revenue of all parties declines, then each of them will keep its share of the allocation because a cap on the total subsidy has been set considerably lower than the current total of all contributions, which are matched. Finally, there is a

---

123 For the variety of distribution rules see Casas-Zamora 2002, pp. 39/40; Casas-Zamora 2005a, pp. 30/31.
124 See above in chapter VI, sub-section C1 (energizing fundraisers).
125 Nassmacher 1992a, pp. 167/168; Nassmacher 1994, pp. 152/153. For details see above in this chapter, sub-section B 2 (reimbursement).
126 Doublet 1999, pp. 70, 73.
127 For details see above in chapter VII, sub-section D 3 (assessments).

problem of fairness as new and small parties, which normally cannot rely on many members or donors, will find it hard to claim a considerable share of the matching grant.

In Japan a far-flung attempt at matching was short-lived. Initially public funding should not have exceeded two thirds of the amount that a party accumulated on its own during the previous year. This clause was meant to ensure that parties would not become entirely dependent on state aid. When the ceiling hurt two small parties, *Shakaitô* and *Sakigake*, which were coalition partners of the *Jimintô* (LDP) at the time, the provision was abolished.[128] Thus Japan re-entered the fold of countries, which distribute public subsidies more traditionally.

b)   Distribution by party size (number of seats held or votes polled)

In most countries party subsidies are distributed in proportion to size. Size of the recipient parties can be measured either in terms of parliamentary seats held or in terms of votes received,[129] or a combination of both. The amount of the subsidy is determined either by the budget allocation of an annual total or by the legal definition of a fixed amount per vote or per seat. In Finland the subsidy is distributed in proportion to the number of seats held,[130] which under a P.R. system does not make much of a difference. In Sweden the bulk of the party subsidy (*partistöd*) is based on the average number of seats won in the two most recent elections.[131] Countries with less proportional systems face harder decisions.

In France and Spain the total grant to national party organisations is split in two parts. Eligible parties are allocated their share of the first part (half or two thirds of the total) according to the proportion of the number of votes cast for first round candidates or deputies. The second part of the subsidy is distributed in line with the aggregate number of MPs (deputies plus senators in France, deputies only in Spain).[132] This allotment favours the major national parties over smaller groups without regional strongholds. An additional bias applies in Spain. Allocation per vote is not based on the aggregate at the national level, but on the number of votes polled in constituencies where the party has obtained a parliamentary seat. Insofar the distribution of subsidies is unfair to smaller parties.[133]

---

128   Blechinger/ Nassmacher 2001, p. 170.
129   On the proportionality of direct state funding see Casas-Zamora 2002, p. 54; Casas-Zamora 2005a, p. 41.
130   Casas-Zamora 2002, pp. 39/40; Casas-Zamora 2005a, pp. 30/31.
131   Eligible parties, which are not represented in parliament, receive a fixed amount per seat for each whole tenth of a % of the vote, obviously in an election year only. For details see Gidlund/ Koole 2001, p. 122.
132   Fromont 1992, pp. 176/177; Koole 2001, p. 82; Schurig 2006, pp. 67, 71, 73; van Biezen 2000, p. 331.
133   The discriminating effect inherent in this procedure is criticised by Blanco 1994; López 1994.

Many countries distribute their total subsidy in proportion to the number of votes polled, e.g. Australia, Canada, Denmark, Ireland, Italy, and Norway.[134] In Germany this applies to about half of the total disbursement. In Australia, Canada and Ireland the grants are indexed to the CPI, in Denmark, Germany, Italy and Norway they have to be adjusted by legislative measures. Although distribution of public funding by number of votes is the least discriminating procedure available, it may be hard for small or new parties to compete on a level playing field. The concept of providing an equal base amount (or a bonus) in combination with allocation by size attempts to deal with this problem.

c) Distribution of base amounts

The most generous application of this option has been adopted for the very moderate policy development grants in Britain. Half of the total is allocated equally among (currently eight) participating parties, the other half in proportion to the votes polled in the elections for the national, the European parliament and one of the three regional assemblies.[135]

In Belgium and the Netherlands some ten parties each are entitled to an annual grant, which consists of an equal base amount for each eligible party plus a fixed amount for each vote obtained respectively each seat held by the party in either chamber of parliament.[136] In Mexico 30 percent of the total subsidy (for current operations and for campaign purposes) is distributed in equal parts among the parties represented in congress (about five). Allocation of the remaining 70 percent is based on the number of votes received.[137]

In Austria each party represented by a minimum of 5 MPs receives a base amount (*Sockelbetrag*).[138] The rest of the appropriation in the annual budget is distributed among eligible parties in proportion to the votes polled in the most recent federal election. Non-parliamentary parties are entitled to their proportional share of the subsidy in an election year only. (In addition to the annual grant, parties receive campaign subsidies for the national and the European elections according to their share of the vote.)[139] Each year Swedish parties collect a small subsidy for office assistance (*kanslistöd*). This grant consists of a fixed amount for each party and an allocation per seat, which is smaller for governing than for opposition parties.

---

134 Amr/ Lisowski 2001, p. 62; www.aec.gov.au; Bill C-24; www.elections.ca; Pedersen/ Bille 1991, p. 159; Laver/ Marsh 2004, pp. 157/158; Bianco/ Gardini 1999, p. 23; Svasand 1994, p. 322.
135 www.electoralcommission.gov.uk; www.legislation.hmso.gov.uk. (28/02/05)
136 Lucardie/ Voerman 2001, pp. 323/324; Suetens 1992, pp. 45-47.
137 De Swaan et al. 1998, p. 162; Martinez 2005, pp.177-179. In election years about ten parties are subsidised.
138 In 1985 and 1987 a newly composed coalition changed the base amount, which had a considerable impact on the distribution of subsidies between smaller and larger parties (Nassmacher 2001c, p. 102).
139 Sickinger 1997, pp. 148/149, 151, 153.

In Israel subsidies are based on a "financing unit". After each election, all eligible parties are entitled to a grant of one financing unit for each MP to cover campaign expenses. In addition each party may collect a monthly grant to cover current expenses, which amounts to five percent of the financing unit for each MP. An extra bonus (base amount) of five percent of the financing unit is paid to each eligible party regardless of size.[140] Whereas subsidies in Austria, Belgium and Israel are indexed to the CPI, they have to be adjusted to inflation by legislative amendment in Britain, the Netherlands and Sweden.

Despite a lot of national peculiarities the allocation rules, as presented in this section, help identify some criteria when considering the fairness of distribution:

- Links to the number of candidates and to grassroots fundraising are rare, although desirable, not only as indicators of linkage but also as a reward for competitive effort.
- A distribution based on *all* votes polled rather than on the seats held precludes skewed apportionment of funds in non-proportional voting systems.
- Allocation of a base amount, equal to all eligible parties (probably less than the British and more than the Israeli) provides a floor for (small and new) competitors.

Access and distribution rules that have been discussed so far do not indicate the volume of effective revenue collected by individual parties. The importance of public subsidies for each party and different democracies varies considerably, and possibly in distinctive ways.

E)   Significance of public funding

In most democracies (although not in India, Switzerland, New Zealand, the U.S. and the U.K.) public funds seem to be a necessity.[141] Parties have found no other way to raise enough funds as the amounts provided by voluntary giving to political parties and candidates do not suffice. However, the need may be felt more heavily in some countries and by some parties.

1.   Contribution to party revenue (Income situation of parties)

If public funds do bridge a gap between expenses and donations, then different situations can be expected in old and new democracies, among various parties in specific

---

140 Boim 1979, p. 209; Kalchheim/ Rosevitch 1992, p. 218..
141 The introduction of public funding has been seriously discussed in Switzerland during the 1980s and 1990s, in India around the turn of the millennium. In New Zealand a subsidy is earmarked for media campaigns and survey research, in the U.S. it is limited to presidential campaigns. In the U.K. considerably increased public funding is discussed since the spring of 2006.

established democracies, and for individual parties (by size and by party family). Because *party families* traditionally differ by shares of grass-roots financing and plutocratic funding,[142] this may also be true for the share of total revenue that is raised by public subsidies. For parties in continental Europe, public subsidies provide the bulk of the money for national party headquarters.[143] In the 1970s and 1980s bourgeois (right-of-centre, conservative and liberal) parties received the largest share (on average 55 percent) from this source. On average, left-of-centre parties (Social Democratic, Labour, Socialist) (48 percent) and far left/ Communist parties (51 percent) stayed just slightly below this mark. More detailed estimates are given in Table 8-1. In the 1980s, Communist (50 percent), Socialist (42-65 per cent) and Agrarian parties (49 percent) received relatively more subsidies than the Conservatives (44 percent), Ecologists/ Greens (41 percent), Liberals (38 percent), Social Democratic (Labour) parties (33 percent), and Christian Democrats (31 percent).[144] On average 40 percent of the annual budget of national party organisations may be a fair estimate for the revenue share that originates from public subsidies.

Because of such data the assumption that parties' income structures differ traditionally by party families may be up for revision. Eventually, however, this is quite in line with the contrasting revenue shares of membership dues and interested money. Whereas left-of-centre parties relied on upward transfers of part of their membership dues, right-of-centre parties funded their party activity (headquarters' organisation and election campaigns) from the top down by soliciting donations from the business community. Each party used one source of revenue to compensate for a lack of the other. Nowadays income from either source has levelled off and public subsidies have come in as a useful substitute.[145] Nevertheless this process has not advanced at equal pace for all parties in all countries.

---

142 For details see above in chapter VI, sub-section B1c (revenue from membership dues) and in chapter VII, sub-section B1 (institutional fundraising) and B3 (corporate contributions).
143 Unfortunately data for sub-national party organisations are available just for individual countries or as estimates for individual years. Thus we have to limit the comparative effort to national party headquarters.
144 Estimates by Casas-Zamora 2002, p. 61; Casas-Zamora 2005a, p. 46 and Krouwel 1999, p. 83 (both using data from Katz/ Mair 1992). Findings confirmed by Nassmacher 1989b, 1992b, 1993, 2002.
145 The U.K. (Britain) offers a deviant case of some importance. Casas-Zamora (2002, pp. 64/65; Casas-Zamora 2005, p. 48) notes that in the absence of public subsidies both major parties have cushioned a decline in grass-roots funding of their central offices by (plutocratic) donations. The consequence have been various funding scandals. For details see Ewing 2007, p. 115-142.

Table 8-1: Public funding of party headquarters, by country and party family (averages in percent of headquarters' annual revenue, 1980s and 1990s)

Country	M/E Ratio	Com./ Left	Green/ Ecol.	Social. Labour	Centre	Chr. Dem	Liberal	Conservat.	Populist	Count. Ave.
Austria a)	18	-	52.6	22.4	-	37.0	-	-	48.6	30
b)		-	-	21.9	-	36.1	-	-	42.6	34
Canada b)	n.a.	-	-	3.9	-	-	6.9	5.9	-	5
Denmark	5	25.9	-	15.6	56.4	13.4	17.5	n.a.	66.8	20
Finland	10	56.0	-	59.4	58.8	-	60.0	60.8	-	57
France *	2	32.9	54.3	50.5	-	-	66.8	57.2	33.6	50
Germany a)	3	-	80.9	66.6	-	62.4	63.2	60.9	-	72
b)		-	80.0	49.3	-	43.8	45.5	49.1	-	50
Italy a)	4	25.1	89.8	32.7 / 59.7	-	47.9	79.5 / 65.3	-	85.7	34
b)		33.2	77.1	44.4 / 74.1	-	61.6	90.1 / 78.5	-	78.5	68
Japan *	n.a.	0.0	-	49.6	48.6	-	66.4	54.6	13.6	30
Netherlds.	3	10	25	14-17	-	17-21	25-31 / 31-37	27-37 / 38-52	-	26
Norway	7	51.9	-	78.0	31.0	53.2	44.5	46.4	81.5	60
Spain *	3	70.8	-	77.0	-	-	-	81.5	-	76
Sweden	6	71.9	45.6	49.0	70.9	-	68.4	50.7	-	52
Fam.average		40	69	47	53	46	56	56	56	46
Fam.range		0-72	25-90	4-78	31-71	13-77	7-90	6-88	14-86	-

Sources: a) Casas-Zamora 2002, pp. 63, 324/5 (for Austria, Denmark, Finland, Germany, Italy, Norway, and Sweden); Koole 1999, p. 347 (for the Netherlands); Blechinger/ Nassmacher 2001, p. 169 (for Japan); Knapp 2002, p. 127; Schurig 2006, pp. 400-405 (for France); van Biezen 2003, pp. 186/187, 189, 191 (for Spain).
b) data computed for Nassmacher 1992b and Nassmacher 1993; Krouwel 1999, pp. 82/83.
M/E (member-to-elector) ratio for the late 1990s see Table 6-1:
Legend: * = data for the 1990s (all other for the 1980s); n.a. = not available; Fam. = family; Count. = country; ave. = average.

Actually there is a significant difference among some party families, which in reality may result from different party types. Whereas traditional mass parties of the 19th century built an elaborate grass-roots organisation before they became successful electorally, in the age of media communication "new parties [of a more cadre type] frequently proceed the other way around: electoral success brings public subsidies, which in turn may be used to build a regular party organisation."[146]

State aid for German party headquarters is very important and only small parties in Italy and Sweden surpass it in importance.[147] Swedish political parties at the national

---
146 Pierre/ Svasand/ Widfeldt 2000, p. 15.
147 Nassmacher 1992b, p. 475.

level are rather dependent on public funding, which is now the dominating source of income for all of them although to a different degree. The Social Democrats depended on public money for 39 percent of its total income, but the Liberal Party and the Green Party (*Miljöpartiet*) for about 84 percent. The conservative Moderate Party (76 percent), the agrarian Centre Party (68 percent) and the (former) Communist Party (66 percent) fell into the medium range of income from public subsidies. On average, state support to political parties in France accounted for half of the national parties' revenue in the late 1990s. Smaller parties seem to depend on this source for up to 90 percent of their headquarters' income. For most of the recipient parties in Japan, public subsidies cover about 50 percent of the total annual budget of the national party headquarters. For smaller parties it is even more important. Only the Communist party, which has not claimed its statutory share of the subsidies, is the exception.[148]

An analysis of the income situation of party headquarters illustrates how small and new parties in most countries depend more on public funds. While the larger parties collect less than half of their national budgets from public funds, the major source of revenue for small parties is constantly public subsidies. Via a regression analysis Casas-Zamora observed an inverse relationship between party size and dependency on public subsidies. That is, the smaller the party, the more important revenue is from the public purse.[149] Many *small parties* (especially in Italy and Sweden) get three quarters (and more) of their total income from the public purse, some occasionally even up to 90 percent, such as the German Greens in the early 1980s and some small parties in France. During the 1980s the populist Progress Party in Norway, with a low member-to-voter-ratio and without links to major interest groups, received more than four fifths of its central revenue in state aid.[150] A comparison of old and *new parties* of the left (i.e. Social Democrats/ Labour vs. Socialist Left or Greens) in five countries (Austria, Denmark, Germany, Norway and Sweden) found "no clear-cut, universal pattern with regard to differences". However, "subsidies frequently play a fundamental role in the consolidation of new parties."[151] The Green Party in Germany was arguably the first party built on public funding.[152]

In the *course of time* this party's reliance on state aid has declined. While in 1983 public funds accounted for 94 percent of the budget of the Greens' party headquarters that share dropped to 41 percent in 2005.[153] This may be just a natural trend for a new party (oper-

---

148 Gidlund/ Koole 2001, p. 124; Koole 2001, p. 82; Schurig 2006, p. 79; Köllner 2000a, p. 123; Köllner 2000b, p. 152; Blechinger/ Nassmacher 2001, p. 169.
149 Casas-Zamora 2002, pp. 56, 278; Casas-Zamora 2005a, p. 42; confirmed by Walecki 2005, p. 140 (Poland).
150 Koole 2001, p. 82; Svasand 1994, p. 324; see Nassmacher 1989b, pp. 252- 254, and 1993, pp. 258-259.
151 Quotes from Pierre/ Svasand/ Widfeldt 2000, p. 15 respectively p. 16.
152 Fürst report 1983, p. 135. Australian Greens primarily rely on private sources (Young/ Tham 2006, p. 17).
153 *Deutscher Bundestag*, parliamentary paper, nos. 10/2172 and 16/5090 (comparing election years).

ating in a system of public funding largely based on electoral support), which gradually asserts itself in the national party system. For other, more established participants of political competition, critics of public subsidies would expect a trend of increasing dependence among parties, at least of party headquarters, on public funding.[154]

However, this trend has not materialised. The data for various established democracies (as presented in Table 8-2) do not display a general "pattern of continuously increasing financial dependency" on state aid.[155] The six countries studied by Pierre, Svasand and Widfeldt (Austria, Finland, Germany, Italy, Norway and Sweden) show different developments. Annual percentages establish neither a trend nor a pattern.[156] While in Austria the importance of public funds as a major source of income has increased, in France and Sweden it has declined.[157] Quite contrary to conventional wisdom, the share of public subsidies towards national party budgets has not increased across the board.

Table 8-2: Public funding of party headquarters, by country and time period

Country		1961-65	1966-70	1971-75	1976-80	1981-85	1986-90
Austria	a)	-	-	26.3	37.0	36.5	42.8
	b)	-	-	-	32.0	30.3	27.1
Denmark	a)	-	-	-	-	-	33.9
Finland	a)	-	86.9	55.2	44.9	47.8	46.1
	b)	-	97.5	69.0	72.4	82.7	84.3
France	a)	-	-	-	-	-	59.2
Germany	a)	47.5	32.9	21.7	15.8	19.7	19.1
	b)	-	54.2	47.1	53.2	60.5	68.4
Ireland	a)	35.4	29.4	19.1	18.9	15.4	-
Italy	a)	-	91.6	67.8	67.2	66.2	53.7
	b)	-	-	-	24.1	21.8	28.4
Netherlands	a)	1.9	1.3	1.7	1.2	0.8	1.8
Norway	a)	3.2	57.0	63.4	54.1	58.1	55.6
	b)	-	-	49.4	50.6	50.9	52.2
Sweden	a)	49.0	51.6	63.5	68.8	60.9	54.6
	b)	-	53.0	63.9	62.0	54.7	51.2
U.K. (Britain)	a)	-	-	13.8	10.8	9.4	10.5

Sources: a) Krouwel 1999, p. 82; b) Pierre/ Svasand/ Widfeldt 2000, p. 14; both referring to data reported by Katz/ Mair 1992.

---

154 Landfried 1994, pp. 20/21.
155 Pierre/ Svasand/ Widfeldt 2000, p. 14.
156 Data given for Germany and Italy are inconsistent with my own calculations (see Nassmacher 1992b, p. 476 and Nassmacher 1993, p. 257). Although the levels of subsidisation may be different, the trend identified by Pierre/ Svasand/ Widfeldt 2000 is quite consistend with my data.
157 Nassmacher 1992b, p. 475; cf. Knapp 2002, p. 127; Schurig 2006, pp. 400-405; Sundberg 2002, p. 198.

State aid seems to be a necessity for political parties in *new democracies*. Public financing of organisational routine activities is considerable in Spain, where most party headquarters are extremely dependent on public funding, which may contribute up to 90 percent of their annual budget. Between 1987 and 1992 the major parties in Spain reported that 74 to 96 percent of their headquarters' income (excluding parliamentary parties) was provided by national routine and election grants. Revenue shares ranged between 74 and 91 percent for the PSOE and 78 to 96 percent for the PP. The minor parties reported lower shares of subsidy income: CDS 65 to 95, PCE 56 to 84, CiU 49 to 74 and PNV 12 to 76 percent. On average the major parties collected more than four fifths of their funds from the public purse, most minor parties about two thirds and only the Basque PNV less than half.[158]

In the early years of democracy-building Poland shied away from public subsidies. Thus they covered only minor proportions (about 5 to 10 percent) of party revenue in the 1990s. Since 2000 higher amounts are available.[159] In Mexico state funding has facilitated the development of the major opposition parties (PAN, PRD) and contributed to the long-ruling PRI eventually losing presidential power in 2000.[160] For the three major parties subsidies cover 80 to 90 percent of headquarters' annual revenue.[161] For all such cases (small and new parties as well as new democracies) public funds are a means to make competition work. Thus it is not surprising that the major difference is not between party families but between countries, even among established democracies.

2. Level of the taxpayers' contribution

Because different situations occur in different countries we will also consider trends over time (Table 8-2). Although the data available are most likely not strictly comparable (due to a varying range of inclusion: party caucuses, party penumbra, tiers of party organisation), they give an impression of trends and levels. Subsidisation is quite high in Finland (on average 79 percent). Subsidy averages are slightly above half of the total annual revenue for France (50.2 percent), Norway (50.5 percent), Sweden (55.1 percent) and Germany (56.4 percent).[162] For Italy, von Beyme's data (more than half of national revenue) are more in line with my own research [163] than those given by Pierre, Svasand and Widfeldt (average of 24 percent). Data on Germany, as reported by von Beyme, may be related to the entire party organisation and thus it is not reliable for a comparison with data for national headquarters only. For Norway and Sweden the two sets of data in Table 8-2 are fairly similar. Therefore the level of

---

158 van Biezen 2000, pp. 333-335, 338.
159 Walecki 2001, p. 403; Walecki 2005a, pp. 118, 139.
160 Prud'home et al. 1993 give an overview for the run-up to future elections.
161 Lujambio 2003, p. 383; Martinez 2005, pp. 145, 181.
162 Averages from data given by Pierre/ Svasand/ Widfeldt 2000, p. 14 and Schurig 2006, p. 79.
163 Nassmacher 1992b, p. 476 and Nassmacher 1993, p. 257.

subsidisation in both countries is beyond doubt. Despite the difference in detail, Finnish data indicate a high level of state aid.

For Austria and Denmark information differs considerably. While Smith and Krouwel assume that on average public subsidies provide no less than one third of all national level party funds in both countries, Cordes and Pedersen indicate that about 60 per cent (two thirds in Austria, 58 percent in Denmark) originate from this source.[164] Data for the Netherlands, as reported by von Beyme, are not in line with those presented by Dutch authors. When public subsidies in this country were provided for specific activities only and given to party affiliated organisations, Elzinga estimated that public funding amounted to 35 percent of the total budget of parties, which means that parties were relieved of about one third of their total expenditure.[165] Koole states that on average one fourth of party revenue came from subsidies (Table 8-1).[166] Cordes reports an average of 18 percent for the 1990s.[167]

The very nature of public subsidies and their provision poses a major problem: public grants may cause an income pull.[168] Access to grants seems quite easy because the parties in parliament make decisions about the political finance regime and the amounts of state aid that are to be provided. However, none of the countries, which are presented in Table 8-2, demonstrates clear evidence to support the pre-empirical notion in mainstream media and academia that parties are able to steadily increase the income from public subsidies to national party organisations as an act of their own free will.

At this point, the level of subsidisation comes into focus. Although Pierre, Svasand and Widfeldt correctly state that "it is almost impossible to calculate how much money the state ... spends on political parties"[169] we suggest two approaches to determine the level of subsidisation. The taxpayers' contribution to party funding can be measured either by the share, which public subsidies contribute towards party revenue in a specific country (see Table 8-1 above) or by the amount of cash the average tax-paying citizen contributes to the funding of party activity (see Table 8-3 below).

Switzerland, India, New Zealand do not provide cash subsidies for national parties. On both counts the level of taxpayers' contribution is zero. In Canada, the U.S., Britain and the Netherlands the share of party income from the public purse is considerably below the European average. For parties in the Netherlands (without direct cash subsidies to national parties until 1999) the revenue share of state aid is still much smaller than their income from membership dues. Even in Britain the extremely low share of grassroots funding (membership subscriptions or constituency quotas) outnumbers

---

164 Krouwel 1999, p. 82; Smith 2005, p. 102; Cordes 2001, pp. 71-74; Pedersen 2003, p. 336. Differences may be due to changes during a decade or to inclusion of party academies.
165 Elzinga 1992, p. 383.
166 Gidlund/ Koole 2001, p. 116 (referring to Koole 1997, pp. 156-182).
167 Cordes 2001, pp. 99, 102/103, 106.
168 See above in chapter V, section C (cost push or demand pull).
169 Pierre/ Svasand/ Widfeldt 2000, p. 12.

the current policy development grants (introduced in 2002).[170] The almost constant level of subsidies given in Table 8-2 refers to opposition parties' caucus grants, which for other countries are not included in the data.

The highest amounts of public funding per citizen (as seen in Table 8-3, column 5) are provided to national party headquarters in Israel (€10.50), Norway (€4.40), France (€4.20), Ireland (€3.80), Austria (€3.30), Japan (€3.00) and Sweden (€2.40). The lowest amounts of state aid (per elector, i.e. person entitled to vote) are distributed in Britain (€0.05), the U.S. (€0.20), the Netherlands (€0.40), Australia (€0.60), Denmark (€0.60) and Poland (€0.75). Casas-Zamora's rank-order [171] is basically in line with the one presented here. However, he adds Mexico to the high-subsidy group. He does not rank Ireland among the high-subsidy and Australia among the low-subsidy countries. His medium level of subsidisation (US $ 1.00 to 1.90) includes Ireland, Australia, Spain, Italy, Uruguay and Costa Rica (see Table 8-3).

If public subsidies are more important for small parties than they are for major parties and parties in specific countries enjoy higher levels of subsidisation than do their counterparts, a stimulating idea from the 1980s comes to mind. In 1983 Gidlund proposed the term "political financing" for the subject that is called "public subsidies" or "state aid" among the international community of scholars.[172] Her proposal never gained recognition but she makes an important point. All state aid is established by political decision-making in specific democracies. Thus the politics of public funding must be discussed.

F) Politics of public subsidies

Obviously parties in some countries (such as Germany and Sweden) have been more hard pressed for funds than parties in others (like Britain, Canada, New Zealand and the U.S.). Looking at individual parties, we can observe that especially the smallest parties have been able to claim extremely high proportions of public funds to sustain their operations. At this point the structure of party competition comes into focus.

1. Influence of party competition on funding rules

In order to get access to public funds, parties become dependent on other parties, which help to create the majorities needed for a broad consensus. This results in the hypothesis that established parties behave like a cartel.[173] This hypothesis assumes that the established parties especially take advantage of public subsidies. Party finance legislation belongs to the major institutional set-ups, which new parties have to deal

---

170 Gidlund/ Koole 2001, p. 116; Neill report 1998, pp. 30/31.
171 Casas-Zamora 2002, p. 48; Casas-Zamora 2005a, p. 37.
172 Gidlund 1983, pp. 10, 29, 353.
173 Katz/ Mair 1995, p. 22.

with (because they are not involved in decision-making on the issue). It is supposed that, directly or indirectly, old parties (which set the rules) hinder new parties' access political competition. The governing parties are especially seen as gatekeepers. Because the political finance laws are often created in a consensual manner, the opposition parties are also accused of favouring a "closed shop". Some scholars have rejected these assumptions and given proof for their views.[174]

If the rules of access and distribution provide for a low threshold, a considerable base amount in favour of small parties and a variety of criteria (among them the number of all votes polled) even the cartel-like behaviour of legislators (i.e. the incumbent parties) will not be able to exclude new competitors from the political market. However, two democracies stand out as negative examples. In Spain the self-protective action of the established parties is most obvious:[175] Not counting the votes for candidates that had not been elected when distributing public subsidies is unfair to all parties that were less successful electorally. In Belgium the established parties confessed to their conduct[176] when they favoured a high threshold, because they did not want to contribute to the rise of more small parties (and especially populist fringe parties) in the extreme multiparty system.[177]

On the other hand, the institutionalisation of subsidies may be due to the importance of small parties for a parliamentary majority and relevant options of putting a majority together (due to coalition opportunities, toleration of a minority government or blackmail potential).[178] Thus countries with coalition governments or with a tradition of "hung parliaments" may provide more public funds than countries with plurality voting systems or manufactured majorities.[179]

An analysis of the decision-making process on the subject reveals that in most cases the institutionalisation of public subsidies did not result in discrimination against smaller parties. In most cases exactly the opposite is true. In order to make various minimum winning coalitions a realistic opportunity, the major parties have passed laws in favour of specific small parties, which one day could be approached to form a coalition or at least be relied on to tolerate a minority government. This has been the case in Sweden, where the threshold for access to public funding was lowered to 2.5 percent in two elections, following each other, to make the (former) Communists available for toleration if needed. In Austria the SPÖ favoured the FPÖ during the 1970s and early 1980s. In Germany the CDU/CSU supported legislation in favour of the FDP.[180] Moreover rulings by the Supreme Court favoured small and new parties.

---

174 Mendilow 1992, pp. 93, 99, 105, 107; Nassmacher/ Nassmacher 2001, pp. 191/192.
175 see van Biezen/ Nassmacher 2001, pp. 145-153.
176 Suetens 1992, p. 44; Weekers/ Maddens 2007, pp. 1/2.
177 Nevertheless this is exactly the change that took place: xenophobe parties (Volksunie, Vlaams Blok, Vlaams Belang) grew stronger. For details see below in chapter IX, sub-section B1 (access for new parties).
178 Sartori 1976, pp. 122-123.
179 Nassmacher 2002, p. 13; Nassmacher, H. 2004a, p. 48.
180 Klee-Kruse 1993a, p. 182; del Castillo 1985, pp. 88-89.

Even in countries, which traditionally are ruled by single party governments, the party that potentially may be needed to tolerate a minority government was favoured in new legislation. For example, in Canada the Liberals needed to attract the N.D.P. to tolerate their Liberal minority government. Therefore, in 2003 the legislature amended the political finance reform of 1974 (which was passed during a minority government) to include fixed rate party reimbursements, which replaced subsidies for postage and media expenses in 1980.[181]

The deviating cases of Belgium [182] and the Netherlands can be explained by the fact that in their extreme multi-party systems there are too many potential coalition partners. None of them has to be especially enticed. The experience of Italy set important precedents and issued a warning to all neighbouring countries. It demonstrates the ambivalence of referendums. In 1978 the initiative against public subsidies failed, but in 1993 it was successful, although in practice it remained inconsequential.[183]

One assumption may be plausible and also true: major parties provide public funding in their own favour. However, new candidates and small parties may also benefit from such regulation as an unintended consequence. To sum up the major findings from this comparison, it is obvious that wherever established parties tried to be grossly unfair to small competitors and newcomers, referenda, court rulings or political necessities (such as the need to find current or future majorities) stopped them. Thus a general rule of cartel politics cannot be established. Nevertheless, as can be expected from any result of politicking, none of the distribution procedures includes the full potential of fair allocation. However, contrary to expectations about any legislation produced by incumbents, only one of the political finance regimes (the Spanish) ignores all (even symbolic) contributions to a level playing field and intensifies the disproportional effects of the electoral system. This leads directly to the possibility that the level of subsidisation may depend on the mechanics of democratic government.

2. Public funding as a result of government structure

Earlier in this study, we discussed the mechanism of democratic decision-making and the level of public subsidies as potential cause of political spending.[184] Now it is time to change perspective and evaluate the democratic process as a trigger for high levels of state aid.[185] It may well be that looking for coalition partners or paying heed to

---

181 Ewing 1992, pp. 6/7; Smith 2005, p. 54.
182 For the formation of governments see de Winter et al.1997, p. 389.
183 Bianco/ Gardini 1999, pp. 23/24.
184 See above in chapter IV, sub-sections A3 (Routines of conflict resolution) and C1 (Unlimited sources of funding).
185 As about half of the countries studied in depth have introduced the single European currency we will measure the level of subsidisation by direct cash subsidies to the national parties in € per citizen (registered voter). For general orientation all € amounts can be read as roughly equivalent to US-$ figures.

significant minorities has a major influence on the politics of public subsidies. This should bring about more generous public funding in consensus than in majoritarian democracies.

To contrast both groups of established democracies we will use two of the indicators advanced by Lijphart in his comparison of 36 democracies (columns 3 and 4 in Table 8-3). The first measure is the majoritarian-consensus continuum summed up in Lijphart's "first (executives-parties) dimension" for the period from 1945 to 1996. Positive values represent a consensus orientation, the highest of which has Switzerland. Majoritarian systems receive negative scores. The U.K. is highest among the countries presented here. A second indicator, the frequency of "minimal winning one-party cabinets", is part of Lijphart's "first dimension". He argues that this "variable can be regarded as the most typical variable in the majoritarian-consensus contrast." The actual measure is "the percent of the whole time period governed by a minimal winning one-party cabinet".[186] In order to allow for some variance we have selected the values for the time period between 1971 and 1996.

Both variables should produce identical results. For most countries the contrast is quite clear. The U.S., Spain, Australia, France, Canada and the U.K. are majoritarian. Switzerland, Israel, Denmark, the Netherlands, Italy, Sweden, Japan, Germany and Norway are consensus democracies. By Lijphart's standards Austria and Ireland are hard to classify. As the literature (due to grand coalitions and corporatism) generally considers Austria among the major examples of consensus democracy,[187] we follow the mainstream as far as Austria is concerned.

a)   Level of public funding in consensus democracies

Among the ten countries identified as consensus democracies six (Israel, Norway, Austria, Japan, Sweden, Germany) fit the assumption that they provide higher levels of public subsidies than majoritarian democracies. A total of three countries cultivate doubt about the hypothesis: Although Switzerland and the Netherlands (due to the "magic formula" and a variety of coalition options) are undoubtedly consensus democracies, they do not follow the expected pattern. Ireland, which is not a consensus democracy, has a high level of party subsidies.

---

186   Lijphart 1999, quotes on pp. 90 and 109.
187   Lehmbruch 1967, pp. 20-26.

Table 8-3: Party subsidies and type of democracy

Country	Index of Party Spending (IPS)	Majoritarian – consensus continuum (Lijphart)	Minimal winning / one-party cabinets	National cash subsidy per year and voter (€)	Direct state funding per year and voter (US-$)	Total subsidy per capita in €
(1)	(2)	(3)	(4)	(5)	(6)	(7)
Switzerland	0.45	1.77	0.0	0.00	-	0.80
Israel	3.16	1.47	7.9	10.50	11.20	13.50
Denmark	0.36	1.25	23.9	0.60	0.20	0.60
Netherlands	0.23	1.23	37.3	0.40	0.40	0.40
Italy	2.47	1.07	9.2	1.20	1.40	1.20
Sweden	1.47	0.82	41.4	2.40	2.60	11.00
Japan	2.33	0.70	31.4	3.00	2.80	3.00
Germany	0.86	0.67	46.2	1.80	2.00	5.50
Norway	n.a.	0.63	45.1	4.40	n.a.	4.40
Austria	2.66	0.33	65.1	3.30	2.80	19.00
Ireland	0.55	0.01	57.3	3.80	1.10	3.80
Costa Rica	n.a.	-0.34	90.0	n.a.	1.90	n.a.
USA	0.46	-0.54	80.1	0.20	0.20	0.30
Spain	1.10	-0.59	73.0	1.50	1.60	1.50
Uruguay	n.a.	n.a.	n.a.	n.a.	1.70	n.a.
Mexico	2.99	n.a.	n.a.	1.90	3.30	1.90
Poland	1.46	n.a.	n.a.	0.75	n.a.	0.75
Australia	0.32	-0.78	85.3	0.60	1.90	0.60
France	0.76	-1.00	63.5	4.20	6.50	4.20
Canada	0.49	-1.12	95.2	1.20	0.20	1.20
Britain	0.28	-1.21	93.3	0.05	-	0.25

Sources: Party spending data (IPS) from Tables 3-3 and 3-4 above; for other data: Lijphart 1999, p. 312; subsidies (columns 5 and 7) from Nassmacher 2002, p. 16 (revised); direct state funding per year and registered voter in US-$ (column 6) from Casas-Zamora 2002, pp. 12, 48, 63, 65; Casas-Zamora 2005a, pp. 14, 37, 47.

There seems to be a correlation between *consensus governments* and high levels of public funding. In each of the six countries that support the hypothesis, the dependence on specific small parties as coalition partners or supporters of minority cabinets is obvious. Thus the governing parties are more generous in determining the rules of public funding. This ends up making more parties eligible and allocating larger sums, especially in Israel. In the multi-party system of Israel, the struggle for coalitions is extremely hard. The two "major" parties (in 2006 down to 23 and 17 percent of the national vote) are forced to make concessions to a multitude of small parties. The funds provided for them are a most striking enticement. During the 1980s the Israeli party system changed from one-party dominance, to close and fierce competition between the two leading parties (Labour and *Likud*), none of which has ever held a majority in parliament. A continuous search for coalition partners was the result. More than three decades of experience indicate that the amounts of public subsidies have grown permanently without restriction. Hyper-inflation provided a perfect pretext for a steady increase in public financing.[188]

The need to support minority cabinets in Norway fits very well into this picture. The total amount of subsidies to Norwegian parties has increased enormously from NOK 8 million in 1970 to NOK 121 million in 1997. This is an almost twelve-fold boost when we examine subsidies per voter on list from NOK 3.10 to NOK 35.60 (€ 4.40). Inflation has certainly taken its toll, but the growth, as well as the level, is still impressive. A further hint to this mechanism can be found in Denmark. For smaller parties income from public subsidies was so high that some of them had problems spending all the money they were entitled to.[189]

Austrian rules are a piece of bipartisan legislation, which came about after a general shortage of funds among all parties and led to a change of mind among SPÖ leaders. In 1975, the legislature introduced public subsidies to political parties and to the press (including the party press) simultaneously. They added more campaign grants in 1989 and 1996. The annual amount of direct cash subsidies to national parties was ATS 64 million (ATS 12.75 or €0.93 per voter) in 1976. In 1996/ 1997 the annual grant was ATS 202 million. At that time a quarter of the national election grant (ATS 138 million) and one fifth of the election grant for the European parliament (ATS 126 million)[190] had to be added to calculate a comparable total of ATS 45.40 (€3.30) per voter and year.

The dominance of one party in Italy and Japan over a period of many years (DC and *Jimintô*/ LDP) clouds the fact that strong inner-party factionalism creates a specific sort of "multi-party" situation. Although three referendums have dealt with public subsidy laws, these have not been entirely abolished in Italy. There is an annual subsidy of roughly €1.50 per voter on list, which is not in line with the rule of consensus politics. To support political parties, the Japanese government sets aside a fund of JPY 250 (€2.00) per citizen from tax revenue, in sum about JPY 30.9 billion (€248 million).

Concerning the amount of public subsidies, Sweden is an outstanding example. Different types of state aid (to national parties, to parliamentary parties and to two tiers of sub-national parties) added up to SEK 666 million in 1999. Of these no more than SEK 140 million were distributed to national party organisations. Whereas they collect no more than €2.40 per citizen, the average adult taxpayer contributes €11.60 to political competition. In 1972 national party organisations received less than SEK 31 million of state aid, i.e. SEK 5.40 (about €0.60) per eligible voter.[191] In Germany the overall total of direct party subsidies given to state and federal party organisations was

---

188 For details see Arian 1998, p. 155; Yishai 2000, p. 674
189 Svasand et al. 1997, p. 113; *Frankfurter Rundschau*, 28 January 2000; cf. Pedersen 2003, p. 326.
190 Sickinger 1997, pp. 149, 151, 153.
191 Gidlund/ Koole 2001, p. 123; Gidlund 1983, p. 240.

DEM 965 million (€493 million), i.e. about DEM 4.00 (€2.00) per year and individual citizen. No public subsidies are available for local party organisations or individual party candidates. The first round of federal aid for the 1966-1969 election cycle averaged DEM 24 million per year, DEM 0.63 (€0.32) per voter and year. The current annual grant of €133 million a year (€ 2.20 per voter on list) is divided between federal (€1.84 per voter) and state parties (€0.36 per voter).

The cases of Germany and Sweden demonstrate the consequences of creating boundaries for this kind of comparison. That is, if for the sake of comparability the indicator is limited ("cash subsidies to national party organisations"), then the amounts that measure the level of subsidies for both countries are pretty close to each other. If all cash subsidies to parties and parliamentary groups at all levels are included (column 7 in Table 8-3) a gap opens up between the two countries, despite the fact that both stay among the high subsidy cases. If all separate allocations were considered, too, Germany should make up for the difference. In that country additional subsidies go to party youth organisations, party associations of municipal councillors and party foundations. On top of all that the net value of tax benefits for political donations, free air time (on radio and television) and other in-kind services (mostly provided by municipal governments) have to be added.[192] Sweden would once again push ahead if subsidies to the party press were added to complete the evaluation. Unfortunately precise data for all these subsidies are not available, even an informed guess would not be possible. Nevertheless the patchy data base and a comparison of national cash subsidies will suffice to establish a significant difference between consensus and majoritarian democracies.

Despite their consensus tradition, the Netherlands and Switzerland have stayed aloof from the practice of high subsidies to national parties. Ireland, which shares the high level of subsidies and the quest for small coalition partners but not the consensus tradition, comes up as the other odd case. This makes all three countries exceptions to the rule, which have to be discussed in detail. In Switzerland public subsidies do not exist on the federal level and in the Netherlands the per capita amount is very low (€0.40).[193] This may be explained by different aspects of political culture. That is, the Calvinist tradition in the Netherlands and the permanent four-party government in Switzerland, both lead to the same thrifty budget management. In the Netherlands there are so many potential coalition partners. Thus nothing has to be done in favour of the small ones. In Switzerland there is no need to do something in favour of potential coalition partners. The major obstacle for the provision of public subsidies seems to be the possible threat of a popular initiative in a direct democracy. Because there are less veto-players in majoritarian democracies, input and outcome of the decision-making are different.

---

192 For details see above in this chapter, sub-section B1 (subsidies-in-kind) and chapter III (Germany).
193 Gidlund/ Koole 2001, p. 120.

b)   Level of public subsidies in majoritarian democracies

Contrary to the experience of consensus democracies, the level of per capita subsidies in majoritarian democracies is much lower. Among the six majoritarian democracies studied here, four live up to the rule and provide a low level of direct cash subsidies to national party organisations. In the U.S. federal aid is available only for presidential elections, and part of the subsidy is spent on intra-party competition. Canada, Australia and Britain are clearer cases in point. Even if additional subsidies to pre-nomination candidates (U.S.), parliamentary candidates (Canada) and parliamentary caucuses of opposition parties (U.K.) are included (see column 7 in Table 8-3), the level of state aid to national party politics remains extremely low. Not even anticipating the recent increase of party reimbursements and the addition of quarterly allowances in Canada will bring the annual subsidy to national parties per eligible voter too far beyond the Australian, and anywhere near the German level.

Two other majoritarian democracies, Spain and France, leave room for doubt and require further consideration. France with its presidential and parliamentary elections and subsidies for different elections, stands out as a deviant case. Two additional kinds of possible influences come to mind. First, there may be some spill-over from neighbouring Germany to France or German support to Spanish parties during the transition period, which may have caused this deviating path of action. Second, both democracies have experienced high pressure from corruption cases.[194] Either force may have caused the deviation from the majoritarian pattern. In Spain subsidies are rather generous. However, as a relatively young democracy it can be considered a special case that should be closer to Mexico.

c)   Countries, which do not fit (either the categories or the hypothesis)

Among the newer democracies, Poland has been mentioned already. After the 1997 general election the treasury allocated to participating parties a total of US-$ 4.1 million, i.e. US-$0.15 per voter on list. The two major parties at the time, the Solidarity Election Action (AWS) and the Democratic Left Alliance (SLD), received about 79 percent of this amount, four other parties had to divide among them about one fifth of the total. The political finance reform of 2001 introduced a system of considerable public financing. The new subsidies cost the national budget around US $ 14.5 million (about US $0.52 per eligible voter) in 2002.[195]

Until the 1990s even coalition governments in India had no impact on public funding because of the dominance of the Congress Party. In line with British tradition India may have been reluctant to provide any public subsidy in addition to subsidies-in-kind for candidate campaigns and free election broadcasts. Consideration of public funding

---

194 For details see above in chapter VII, sub-section D 2 (graft from business).
195 Walecki 2001, pp. 402/403.

has only led to proposals, which favour small amounts of public subsidies earmarked to special tasks in election campaigns, most of them as subsidies-in-kind.[196]

3. *Public funding in (comparative) perspective: parties and other organisations*

The amounts of public subsidies to political parties are very different in the countries covered in this study. State aid as a share of total party revenue is highest in Austria, followed by Sweden, Israel, France, Germany and Spain, while the lowest share is provided in Switzerland, Britain and the U.S. The level ranges from 0 (Switzerland) to 68 percent (Austria).[197] Before scholars start to criticise the amounts of public funds given to political parties they will have to consider that in many countries other non-profit-organisations (e.g. charities) and NGOs frequently are supported by public funds. Public support sums up to more than 50 percent of total funding in health and social organisations. It is extremely high in Germany, where public funds provide almost 70 percent of total outlay in these sectors. Also extremely high is the percentage of public funding for international activities (foreign aid) in Germany (77 percent), while the average for all (other) countries (U.S., France, U.K, Italy, Japan and Sweden) is only 37 percent.[198] Time and again a range of new services is created. Initially they are performed by people in need of the service, i.e. the voluntary help of active citizens or activity based on donors and sponsors. After some time has passed, the scope of duties, which are performed by a citizens' action group (NGO) is recognised as dealing with important problems of society. At that point, strong forces in the political arena demand support from the public purse for groups, which tackle such [new] tasks, e.g. to give a grant to employ staff. Once allocated the subsidies are expended as long as the recipient organisation is part of the game. By means of access to public money the organisation becomes more formal and finally an established organisation. This process has also occurred to political parties. Not only the organisation gets used to depend on public funding, but also the citizens accept that tax-paying will take care of everything. Exit becomes an option used by party members, as well as by those who give to the churches, which have been responsible for most non-profit organisations.

In summary, we can return to the questions asked in the very beginning of the chapter:

- Public subsidies are neither a mere stop-gap nor a problem-solving source of political revenue in general. As with any other kind of funding, specific problems accompany them (for example rules for access and distribution). However, in combination with other sources of revenue as well as rules to enforce its legitimacy (especially the matching principle), state aid is a means of political funding that no modern democracy should forgo.

---

196 Jain 2001, pp. 362/363.
197 Nassmacher 2002, p. 16.
198 Anheier 1997, p. 68; Salamon/ Anheier 1997, p. 167.

- Considering the variety of public funding programmes, which this chapter has presented, party organisations rather than party caucusses or party candidates should be the recipient of public support. Moreover no further strings should be attached except for a specified responsibility for transparency. In general indirect funding (i.e. subsidies-in-kind and tax benefits) should be preferred over cash aid. If subsidies in cash have to be allocated, access needs to be fair (preferably with a low threshold defined in terms of overall votes polled) and distribution should be unequal, mostly according to party size, preferably with a certain base amount given to all recipient parties.
- The significance of public subsidies can be judged from two points of view that of the party treasurer and that of the average taxpayer. From both angles, the level of subsidisation is almost impossible to calculate and to generalise. Taxpayers in Israel, Norway, Ireland, Austria, Japan, Sweden, Germany, France and Mexico provide the highest amounts towards party activity. Taxpayers in Anglo-Saxon countries (plus Denmark and the Netherlands) are much less generous. Many party headquarters cover between 40 and 60 percent of their annual budget via public grants. In Germany and Spain the share of national party revenue is higher, and in Canada, Denmark, Japan and the Netherlands it is considerably lower.

Now that all factual information on party spending and party revenue has been presented, we can turn to evaluate the impacts of funding on party organisation and party systems.

CHAPTER NINE

Impacts on Party Systems

The sustainable combination of fair competition and grass-roots democracy is a litmus test for good party government. Among other challenges political parties have to raise funds and to meet regulations of a (sometimes complex) political finance regime. In this area the most important innovation during the second half of the 20th century has been public funding for parties and candidates. Party financing happens to be a restless issue in all democracies, old and new. Although parties in power have the advantage of determining such laws, the watchful eyes of the media, public opinion and the judiciary may prevent parties in power from framing regulations exclusively for their own benefit.[1] In order to analyse the specific impacts of party funding we will turn to party organisation in the next chapter and deal with political competition in this one.[2] First, the question arises, whether money matters in political competition. Is the availability of specific resources significantly different among competitors? Is competition under the rules enshrined in political finance regimes open and fair? Does the provision of public subsidies foster or hinder political rivalry?

The focus of researchers has frequently been on the role of money in campaigns. That is, can you spend your way into public office, especially into a democratic parliament? If so, competition between the champions of the haves and the champions of the have-nots would not be fair. Furthermore the results of competition among parties can be studied by comparing *party systems*. Has there been any change within the party systems studied? Are there any indicators that such change (or non-change) has been caused or supported by party funding? Are there any indicators that an exclusion of parties from political competition may have been caused by party funding? If so, party competition would not be open and fair and the funding of politics may have contributed to that situation. The most obvious issue of fair competition is whether or not money will determine the outcome of an electoral contest.

A) Spend and win? – Money as a means of success

There are a lot of factors that influence political competition. Among them, money could possibly be the most important, as it is the only resource that may be used to

---

1 Katz and Mair (1995, pp. 15, 22) emphasise the former and tend to neglect the latter elements of political decision-making in established democracies.
2 See below in chapter X (Impacts on party organisation).

activate supporters. It can also be transformed into other resources,[3] thereby improving the performance of parties and candidates. Addressing the impact of the great potential of funds in the real world of politics is a task that will be pursued in a stepwise process:

- Is the influence of money strong enough to make the competitor who can dispose of the most funds the likely winner of a political contest?
- Will competitors who hold a financial edge continuously, or over a period of time, be successful more often than those who have fewer monetary resources?
- Does the availability of public subsidies infringe upon the opportunity of new and minor parties to compete?

Now let us turn to the first question, whether or not money matters in political competition.

1. (Campaign) Spending by individual candidates

Fairness in political competition is an important issue of elective politics. The metaphor of a "level playing field" is frequently transferred from sports to politics. However, no financial regime will prevent candidates and parties from having different amounts of cash at their disposal. Major parties will not only receive more votes but also raise and spend more money than minor competitors. Incumbents have an advantage over challengers. However, does this imply that contestants who raise and spend more funds will (as a consequence) have more electoral success? Quite obviously people who spend more and more money on political competition expect that this will have some sort of impact.

The question, whether money wins elections, suggests itself. Moreover journalists and scholars have considered it quite frequently. Because the media is more important in campaigns, which is leading to a commercial style of campaigning, the hypothesis that money wins elections seems much more relevant today than it used to be in the good old days of mass parties and machine politics. "The gap in expenditures ... suggests the electoral value of extensive funding."[4] Because no "neat correlation is found between campaign expenditures and campaign results," Heard stated rather inconclusively that "under some conditions the use of funds can be decisive. And under others no amount of money spent could alter the outcome." Thus the "old notion that the side with more money will for that reason win, or will usually do so, is not correct."[5] Contrary to this, other scholars have demonstrated that a candidate with superior resources has an improved chance of success at the polls, i.e. more money for a specific party

---

3   Alexander 1992b, pp. 362/363.
4   Crotty 1977, p. 116.
5   All quotes by Heard 1960, pp. 16, 6; cf. Fisher 1999a for national parties, Smith 2001 as general criticism.

correlates with more votes.[6] Money is also found to be important in local campaigns. Can the impact of political spending on the election outcome be measured? What are the major factors influencing the impact?

Statistical analysis in examining political finance has been greatly enhanced by two developments of the 1970s: the use of computers and the wealth of available data. As is well-known from other areas of social science, researchers in North America entered the field first. For candidate spending in the 1979 Canadian election, the first under the current political finance regime, Isenberg found a clear "relationship between spending and the number of votes obtained." There "was evidence of a relationship between coming first and spending most in a riding."[7] For the election in 1980 he confirmed this finding: on average winners spent three times more than losers. In order to investigate the transformation of economic power into political power, Welch evaluated data for the 1972 U.S. congressional election. His "model of the interaction between money and voting in American politics" revealed that "money influenced voting in U.S. House elections in 1972, although its effect was small." Most contributors prefer likely winners. Districts inhabited by more wealthy people with more years of schooling tend to provide more funds to political candidates.[8]

The weakest point of Welch's analysis has been identified by Heard, when he pointed out that "the flow of funds to a candidate might simply reflect his prior appeal rather than create it."[9] Using more data and different modelling Jacobson also found "a clear connection between campaign spending and election results" in the U.S.[10] For Canadian riding candidates Chapman and Palda observed "a substantial influence of campaign expenditures on voting behavior." Although the impact is not uniform across parties or elections, Eagles claims that "candidates' spending efforts can and do have an impact." However, when evaluating English constituencies (1951-83), Johnston found that the "evidence ... does not indicate that the level of spending is a major, let alone a dominant influence on the result."[11] This seems also true for India where spending big does not necessarily produce victory.[12] Obviously it is more important how the money is spent and who spends it.

---

6 Alexander 1970, p. 104; Palda 1975; Owens/ Olson 1977; Shepard 1977; Tucker 1986; Isenberg 1980; Isenberg 1981; Johnston 1986, p. 472; Johnston/ Pattie 1995, p. 271; Cox/ Thies 2000, pp. 37-57.
7 Quotes in Isenberg 1980, pp. 33, 35; cf. Isenberg 1981, p. 8.
8 Welch 1981, pp. 226/227 (including both quotes). – In passing this is another indication that political revenue may matter more than political spending; see above in chapter V, section C (cost push or demand pull).
9 Heard 1960, p. 16.
10 Jacobson 1980, p. 51; thus financial support by the candidate's party can be important (Medvic 2001, p. 207).
11 Chapman/ Palda 1984, p. 225; Eagles 2004, p. 133; Johnston 1987, p. 179; the latter confirmed for Australian state elections by Forrest 1992, p. 75, and Forrest/ Johnston/ Pattie 1999, p. 1127.
12 Sridharan 2006a, p. 376.

The previous findings do not imply the simple causality that spending gathers votes. "Spending by challengers has a substantial impact on election outcomes,"[13] whereas spending by incumbents has relatively little effect; "the more incumbents spend, the worse they do."[14] Marginal returns for campaign dollars are greater for challengers, money spent is more important to non-incumbents than it is to incumbents. The non-incumbents include candidates in open seats as well as challengers. Although spending is less important for House incumbents, they typically "spend 60 to 80 percent more than do their opponents. Candidates for open seats usually spend even more than incumbents,"[15] most likely in their primary campaigns.[16]

Rewieving such findings it occurs that a more general doubt with regard to the design of all these studies has to be raised: The whole set of analyses is based on spending data and election results. Frequently spending is analysed as the cause of voting. In such studies it may never have occurred to the researcher that donating is a means of support and spending is a consequence of cash-at-hand.[17] If this is true, spending may just be a bellwether of success, but not its cause. Thus I feel "that available evidence to date of spending effects ... [in constituencies] is an artefact of improper methodology."[18]

Many other studies have confirmed these findings or added specific details. On the fact that spending by challengers is more effective, previous research generally has been consistent. However, in specific elections other factors may also become relevant.[19] After examining the congressional elections of 1968 and 1970 in five U.S. states, Lott and Warner found that, next to incumbency, party strength is more important than campaign expenditure. Owens and Olson even observed a relative insignificance of incumbency as compared to other factors, especially party strength, in California.[20] Besides strength of a party in the district, Jacobson emphasises that national electoral forces and characteristics of the individual candidate are crucial as well.[21] Another finding for local elections is that spending in single member district elections is more important than in multiple seat situations.[22] However, an examination of the national level in Japan does not confirm this.

---

13 Jacobson 1978, p. 469. Palda/ Palda (1998, p. 170) confirm this for France; Johnston/ Pattie 1993, p. 147) for Britain.
14 Jacobson 1978, p. 469; Jacobson 1976, pp. 12/13; a similar, yet weaker relationship is identified by Cox/ Thies 2000, p. 41 (for Japan).
15 Jacobson 1980, pp. 38, 41, 49, quote on p. 52.
16 Oldopp 2001, p. 314.
17 For a detailed review of such factors see above in chapter VI, section A (cornerstoe of democracy) and chapter V, section C (cost push or demand pull?).
18 Eagles 2004, p. 122, referring to Cutler 1999, p. 14. For a summary of previous studies cf. Eagles 2004, pp. 118-120.
19 Giles/ Pritchard 1985, p. 71.
20 Lott/ Warner 1980; Owens/ Olson 1977, pp. 511.
21 Jacobson 1986, p. 605; see also Jacobson 1990 and Jacobson 1993.
22 Arrington/ Ingalls 1984, p. 125.

Whether money matters or not, also depends on the electoral system. In their multivariate model, which controls for many variables including candidate and district characteristics, Cox and Thies demonstrate that the impact of money in Japanese elections under single non-transferable vote is much higher than it is in the U.S. under a FPTP system.[23] Johnston and Pattie were the first to examine the issue more closely at the constituency level in Britain. Johnston found sufficient evidence from British constituency campaigns between 1951 and 1983 "that spending cannot be dismissed as irrelevant; the amount spent on ... campaigns is linked to the electoral outcome."[24] The impact of spending, even by challengers, was much less substantial in a two-party than in a three-party contest. Cash is especially significant for smaller parties.[25] That is, the level of spending reflects the constituency's marginality.[26] Pattie et al. examined constituency campaign spending in the 1983, 1987 and 1992 general election in England, Scotland and Wales, and found that "in general the more that a party spends the more votes and seats it gets."[27] However, the "money spent by a party on a constituency campaign reflects the strength and commitment in the local party organization there ..."[28] Spending is merely a surrogate of campaign effort in general.

In sum, these findings point out that a simple correlation (as well as causality) between political money and electoral success is obviously misleading. Campaign money is most productive where other factors (which have been given above) make winning possible. Denver and Hands, after a detailed analysis of U.K. constituency campaigns, concluded that swimming with the current has more effect than swimming against the tide. That is, Liberal campaigns had less effect, wherever the party started far behind the two major parties. Labour had to work harder to mobilise, while Conservative campaigns did not produce the same electoral benefits as stronger Labour and Liberal Democrat campaigns.[29] Obviously there is no causal relationship between money and votes in just one direction. This is also true for voter turnout.

A new problem arises when attention is shifted towards presidential campaigns and one specific question: Who is able to run? Staging a promising pre-nomination campaign has a price tag. For the U.S. presidential race in 2008, political pundits identify the total between USD 35 million (for an early candidate who enjoys national media attention) and USD 100 million (for a candidate who needs to build such name recognition by running successfully in Iowa, New Hampshire and other early primaries).

---

23 Depending on the perspective "spending effects for conservative candidates in Japan are about 10-25, times larger than for U.S. incumbents and 2-5, times larger than for U.S. challengers." (Cox/ Thies 2000, p. 53)
24 Johnston 1987, pp. 179, 185 (quotes in reverse order); see also Johnston 1986, pp. 469, 470; further information on elections in English constituencies see ibid., note 15.
25 Johnston 1986, p. 469; Johnston 1987, p. 96.
26 Johnston/ Pattie 1993, p. 147.
27 Pattie/ Johnston/ Fieldhouse 1995, p. 970. – The importance of constituency efforts in British campaigns was already established by Seyd/ Whiteley 1992.
28 Both quotes by Pattie/ Johnston/ Fieldhouse 1995, p. 981.
29 Denver/ Hands 1997, pp. 190/191.

Soliciting these amounts is no problem for candidates who are well-connected to the universe of interested money (PACs, corporate managers and wealthy individuals alike).[30] However, the odd candidate may encounter a couple of difficulties before he or she draws enough media attention to trigger "big money in little sums" via direct mail drives or the internet.[31] Thus, raising the necessary "seed-money" in a non-plutocratic manner may become a serious problem for the openness of elite competition in political systems where the party does not control the nomination of candidates.

This approach helps to focus on the real competitive edge. It is not the "unlimited" amount of money that has actually been spent but the capability to raise "money to burn." The real test of competitiveness is the "ability to put together a national organisation to raise money," to secure "the support of men and women who have proven effective ... at raising large sums – usually from a well-tended network of business associates, corporate subordinates and clients."[32] Once again, it is not spending but revenue that proves to be the most important issue of political finance.[33]

Despite all the details presented so far, the assumption prevails that the increasing use of high-cost modern technology will inevitably make money more decisive in the future. Money "buys access to the means of reaching voters – radio, television, newspapers, billboards, telephones, mailings ..."[34] and web blogs.[35] Incumbents are able to (and do) publicise themselves continuously. They deliver services to their constituents on a regular basis and they reach more voters more frequently. Only in the face of stiff opposition by a heavily spending challenger do incumbents really need to spend. Incumbents do most of their electioneering before the formal campaign period has even started. They can and will use the perquisites of office (staff, equipment, allowances and the franking privilege). All non-incumbents begin their bid in obscurity. Candidates, who do not find the attention of their constituents, will certainly not do well in any election.[36] However, Snyder et al. have determined that there is "no evidence of an important relationship between TV costs and the vote shares of incumbents."[37]

The most important question if money is a means of influence, must remain unsolved. In the U.S. (and quite rightly so) it has always been a big question, if interested money (e.g. money solicited by PACs) can buy politicians. In 1980 PACs gave USD 78.3 million more than in 1976. Of these additional funds USD 32.6 million were raised by congressional candidates, two thirds of it by House and one third by Senate candi-

---

30 "Money's Going to Talk in 2008", in: *Washington Post*, 11 March 2006.
31 Like Barry Goldwater, Eugene McCarthy, George Wallace, George McGovern or John McCain did in their presidential bid(s); see above in chapter VI, section A (Cornerstone of democracy).
32 Both quotes from: "Campaigns Turning More to Online Videos", in: *Washington Post*, 3 April 2006.
33 See above in chapter V, section C (Cost push or demand pull).
34 Jacobson 1980, p. 37.
35 "Campaigns Turning More to Online Videos", in: *Washington Post*, 3 April 2006.
36 Jacobson 1980, pp. 42, 146.
37 Ansolabehere/ Gerber/ Snyder 2001, in: www.mit.edu/faculty/snyder/files, p. 22.

dates.[38] In connection with the funding activity of U.S. political action committees (PACs) [39] empirical results are available,[40] e.g. PAC money causes the major difference between incumbents and challengers. However, the controversial debate about the impacts of money continues.

2. *Skewed competition between individual parties*

In most democracies one of the major parties will be better off financially than its counterpart. A minor party will most likely use fewer funds than a major one. How does traditional access to political funding influence the fairness of party competition? Affluent segments of a society favour conservative parties (with votes and contributions). Is this financial advantage "unfair" towards more progressive competitors? At this point it should be noted that some effects may counterbalance each other. Because there are many less affluent people in a democracy, parties that attract more funds will find it hard to be preferred by a large number of voters and vice versa. Established parties will have a pool of volunteers, experience in fundraising, some full-time staff, offices and assets. Such resources (especially money and volunteers) are not distributed evenly within any party system. Does a skewed distribution of funds indicate unfair competition? How much equality of funds, resources and opportunities is necessary to ensure fairness? Any normative answer to this question will most likely fire up a new round of arguments. Thus we attempt to establish descriptive data first and consequences afterwards.

Generally speaking, the inequality of money for competing parties cannot be avoided as long as political funding rests on voluntary donations by participating individuals and contributions by those who represent economic interests. Equal access to similar sources of funding is no realistic target because parties and party families have an individual history, which results in specific links to financial supporters.[41] Older parties enjoy competitive advantages over new ones because they have traditional resources. Especially on the left (and to a smaller degree also on the right) affiliated organisations stabilise cleavages and thus provide a permanent source of money and continuity.[42] This was extremely important in the Netherlands (*verzuiling*) and in Austria (*Lager*). Such "pillarised" linkage has become looser in recent decades. Parties may not have tended to their organisational links well enough and politicians may not have met the challenge of new value orientations. New rules and regulations (such as limits and bans on individual donations (e.g. in the U.S.) and specific donors (e.g. in Germany),

---

38 Alexander 1983, p. 127.
39 See above in chapter VII, sub-section B1c (political action committees - PACs).
40 E.g. Eismeier/ Pollock 1988.
41 It always strikes a scholar of political finance rather strange that in works dealing with party linkage to society (e.g. Poguntke 2000) the potential significance of political funding is not even mentioned.
42 On the related dimension of linkage see below in chapter X, A (linkage).

the deregulation of collective membership (e.g. in Sweden), restrictions for contributions by affiliated organisations (e.g. in the U.K.) and access to public funding) play a noteworthy role. At this point the main issue is, has all of this equalised the fiscal balance between parties of the haves and those of the have-nots.

Regarding their total revenue, major parties, small parties and new parties obviously compete from different levels of opportunity. Testing inequality as a hazard to fair competition requires three different sets of comparisons. First, what is the financial situation of one major party as compared to the other? Secondly, has the total amount of funds available to either competitor been balanced over time? Thirdly, the same questions have to be answered separately for small parties as well as for all parties running in a parliamentary election for the first time.

As Overacker stated decades ago, the U.S. Republicans traditionally have been better off financially at the national level than their Democratic competitors.[43] "Republicans outspend Democrats with regularity and … like it or not, the heavy spender usually won."[44] Although this inequality may have contributed to some prevalence it has not forestalled alternation of executive leadership and legislative majorities. In the 1990s "the gap between the two parties has narrowed during the last few years."[45] Sorauf assumes that the Democratic edge in non-cash contributions (e.g. labour-intensive campaign support) has offset the cash advantage of the Republicans.[46] A lot of U.S. states also provide some sort of financial aid to political competitors. "To date, it would appear that public funding plays a significant, consistent, and stabilising role in the financing of election campaigns in those states that allocate the money to political parties."[47] However, in 2000 this only applied to 14 of the 50 states. Matching funds for U.S. presidential elections and at the state level have reduced the influence of big donors and increased revenue in small amounts.[48]

Data from two European countries (see Table 9-1 below) below for a more systematic approach to the consequences of unequal revenue. In post-war Britain the two major parties have alternated in government. The Labour Party was in power from 1945-51, 1964-70, 1974-79, 1997-2010 (about 30 years) and the Conservatives were in office from 1951-64, 1970-74, and 1979-97 (or about 35 years). The total years in government since 1945 show a slight lead by the Conservatives. However, in financial terms, the Conservative Central Office has been able to outspend Labour headquarters in 25 of 33 (well documented) years since 1970, mostly by far (Table 9-1).[49] Although Pin-

---

43 Overacker 1932, pp. 131-135; Sorauf 1988, pp. 149-152.
44 Crotty 1977, p. 111.
45 Hrebenar et al. 1999, pp. 160, 159; Herrnson 1999, pp. 101/ 102.
46 Sorauf 1988, p. 25.
47 Jones 1984, p. 203.
48 Düselder 1992, pp. 106/107, 109; Smith 2005, pp. 71, 269.
49 The post-war years, which are not covered in Table 9-1, but included in Pinto-Duschinsky 1981, pp. 138, 163/164, add another 18 years to the Conservative advantage. A similar financial edge has prevailed and still prevails for constituency parties see Houghton report 1976, p. 34, Pinto-Duschinsky 1981, pp. 275-281 and Neill report 1998, p. 40.

to-Duschinsky's claim that "the Conservative advantage over Labour has been declining",[50] was twenty years to early, it did finally materialise after the turn of the century. Nevertheless, the financial resources of the two parties in non-election years (a total of some 63 million GBP in four consecutive years) had been more balanced than ever before. However, election years brought back the old pattern.

The U.K. Conservatives won the elections of 1979 to 1987, which corresponded to their financial edge. The same happened to Labour after 2000. The informed observer will recall the causes of the election outcome in 1979 to 1987 (the "winter of discontent", the Falklands war, and the "sleaze" factor respectively) and the fact that it was not campaign spending but the general mood of public opinion, which was in favour of change (1979, 1997) or in favour of continuity (1983, 1987, 1992). The losing party was fighting an uphill battle; no matter how much it was able to spend. Obviously the distribution of funds has not translated into outcomes of parliamentary elections. By and large the disadvantage in financial terms was balanced by other resources, which is quite a contrast to the initial argument that political funds play a central (or possibly dominant) role. The Conservatives lost by a landslide in 1997; their big financial advantage over Labour notwithstanding. During the 21st century, financial fortunes have changed completely. Recently Labour outspent the Conservatives (between 2001 and 2005). In both election years the financial lead was with the winner (see Table 9-1).

More comprehensive information on party funding is available for a shorter period of time from Germany. Party revenue data enables a comparison of the two major parties (CDU/CSU and SPD) for some 30 years (1970 to 2002) and of two minor parties (Liberals and Greens) for some 20 years (1981 to 2002). There were (long) periods of great imbalance and (short) periods of near-balance between pairs of parties. 1992 to 1997 the two major parties had a total of 1,730 million DEM each in six years. 1984 to 1989 each of the minor parties posessed a total 210 million DEM for a similar period. During most of the years covered the two right-of-centre parties (CDU/CSU and Liberals) held a competitive edge in financial terms.

---

50 Pinto-Duschinsky 1981, p. 276.

Table 9-1: Party revenue in Britain and Germany, 1970-2005 (million GBP resp. DEM)

Party/ Year	Britain – Central Office		Germany – Total party organisation			
	Conservatives	Labour	CDU/CSU	SPD	Liberals	Greens
1970	1.860	1.034	55.4	58.1	-	-
1971	0.930	0.585	57.3	56.4	-	-
1972	1.199	0.692	136.4	113.1	-	-
1973	2.819	0.842	82.8	76.7	-	-
1974	1.624	1.781	135.9	95.7	-	-
1975	1.889	1.371	131.3	118.8	-	-
1976	2.094	1.527	173.4	123.4	-	-
1977	2.794	1.536	117.0	93.1	-	-
1978	3.402	2.124	141.5	110.5	-	-
1979	5.292/5.6	3.113	232.6	197.4	-	-
1980	3.2	2.8	196.9	156.1	35.0	6.7
1981	4.1	3.7	135.6	120.0	23.5	2.8
1982	4.8	3.9	182.2	143.2	20.6	7.0
1983	9.4	6.2	320.2	233.5	40.7	19.4
1984	4.3	4.2	235.3	198.1	28.6	34.9
1985	5.0	4.9	216.2	193.7	30.3	26.8
1986	8.9	6.1	252.3	199.2	33.2	30.4
1987	15.0	10.0	241.3	214.0	44.6	44.4
1988	8.6	6.7	217.6	195.8	33.2	29.6
1989	9.2		255.4	241.3	42.8	41.8
1990	13.0	9.3	420.3	353.9	83.8	48.5
1991	22.0	12.4	264.5	339.6	52.2	32.5
1992	23.4	13.2/16.2	263.1	262.6	47.3	39.3
1993	11.6	12.8	281.9	280.8	49.5	37.7
1994	14.1	13.7	347.8	353.4	70.3	52.8
1995	15.3	15.1	271.2	285.2	45.9	48.4
1996	21.4	21.5	284.0	283.0	40.6	50.1
1997	42.5	24.1	274.3	281.0	41.6	51.3
1998			335.7	304.5	49.4	57.0
1999			322.8	306.0	45.9	51.4
2000			310.8	292.0	43.9	45.9
2001	25.0	44.5	323.9	312.9	50.3	46.6
2002	10.5	22.1	367.1	310.6	61.6	51.4
2003	16.0	24.3	365.9	351.7	54.3	51.2
2004	26.2	32.1	384.3	332.7	57.4	49.7
2005	39.2	49.8	399.0	330.7	63.5	52.0

Sources: Pinto-Duschinsky 1981, pp. 138, 163/164; Pinto-Duschinsky 1989, pp. 27, 31; Pinto-Duschinsky 1994, pp. 14, 17; Neill report 1998, pp. 30/31; Fisher, in: Neill report 1998, vol 2, Tables 1, 2; „Tory Money", in: *Business Age*, vol. 3, no, 32 (May) 1993, p. 42; Electoral Commission data as reported in: www.publications.parliament.uk/pa/cm200607/cm-select/cm…; *Deutscher Bundestag*, parliamentary paper, nos. 12/5575, 14/7979, 14/8022, 15/700, 15/2800, 16/1270, 16/5090.

The period of fiscal balance between the two major parties (CDU/CSU, SPD) between 1991 and 1997 did not lead to equal voting strength. When this finally happened in 2002, the financial advantage of the conservative parties returned to the level of 1986. The obvious difference in fundraising capacity does not mean that the left-of-centre parties have been unable to compete on an equal footing. As a consequence there have been four changes in government leadership in six decades. Two of them favoured the SPD (in 1969 and 1998), and two its major competitor, the CDU (in 1982 and 2005).[51]

In Germany and the U.K. financial fortunes may have influenced the electoral outcome. However, there is no evidence that it was determined by party revenue. Labour won by a landslide in 1997 despite a massive financial edge of the Conservatives. Furthermore, the SPD retained the Chancellor's office despite a considerable funding lag in 1972, 1976, 1980 and 2002. And in 1994 this party lost the federal election despite near-parity of funds and in 1998 it won despite the conservative advantage in money terms. The Greens achieved financial parity with the Liberals between 1984 and 1989, but failed to translate this into votes. The former became the leading minor party in 1994 despite being behind in financial terms.

Many people consider it valuable to strive for a level playing field in all factors that influence political competition (including financial resources). Although a competitor with very little money will be handicapped, perfect equity of funds available is neither a necessary nor a sufficient pre-condition for equal opportunities. A long-standing imbalance of financial resources does not conquer the underdog. Some aspects that go with it may even help him or her, because too much money from the wrong sources can tip the scales of public opinion towards the have-nots. Unfortunately strong evidence for this kind of impact is rather scarce.

The only major case was the breakdown of DC and PSI in Italy. Their illegal financing[52] has been identified as a major cause for the collapse of individual parties and the party system in the 1990s.[53] However, this may have been an exceptional case. In Japan the flow of funds from private (business) sources has never stopped. Private sponsors provide the politicians of the governing *Jimintô* (LDP) in Tokyo and in the constituencies with various means of organisational support (personnel, offices or cars) free of charge. The political fallout of the ensuing scandals has resulted in just one electoral defeat in 1993 and a short period in opposition for the dominant party.

Scandals in France and Spain indicated that parties needed more money than they could solicit legally. When the Socialists in both countries (*PS, PSOE*) were hit by the aftermath of major funding scandals,[54] each of them lost a national election (and the government) to its conservative competitor (*RPR, PP*). In the U.K. the "sleaze" factor, although not necessarily a matter of party funding, contributed to the fall of the Con-

---

51 For a detailed account see below in this chapter, sub-section B3 (transition of power).
52 For details see above in chapter VII, section D (income from graft).
53 Zohlnhöfer 2002, p. 272.
54 For details see above in chapter VII, sub-section D2 (graft from business sources).

servative government in 1997. When similar events occurred in Germany (e.g. ex-chancellor Kohl's slush fund) the *CDU* lost a few percent of the vote in two state elections (Schleswig-Holstein, North-Rhine Westphalia) and remained in opposition there.[55] Two local funding scandals cost the *SPD* the mayoral races in two major cities (Cologne in 1999 and Wuppertal in 2004). In the long run improper and illegal funds may contribute to de-legitimise parties in particular and the democratic political system in general. Such hazards are frequently used to argue in favour of public funding. This in turn holds different risks for a party system, especially the suggested trend of petrification, which may result from an unfair advantage for established parties over a recently created competing party or newly emerged challenger.

B) Ossification of the party system?

Since the 1970s a theory related to the impact of public funding on the party system has been repeated frequently and become widely accepted. Public funding is said to lead to a freezing (ossification or petrifaction) of party systems.[56] Subsidies are said to "give established parties a much stronger position than emerging party formations and hence petrify or cement the party system."[57] Or in the words of the Neill report: State funding "could cause ... any existing party system to ossify, with the existing parties handsomely supported out of the public purse."[58] If we look at opportunities of change within party systems more precisely, we see that the hypothesis is dealing with three different aspects that have to be considered separately.

First, the opportunity of new parties to win access to parliament by means of a fair chance to compete with "established" parties, i.e. the "openness" of a party system; second, the strength of established parties in comparison to other parties, large or small, may stop changing, i.e. a "freezing" of the party system; and third, the change of roles held within the system, especially the alternation of individual parties between the functions of government and opposition, can be halted by an "arrested" distribution of power within the party system. Either kind of change may relate to public subsidies. We shall address these various aspects separately as we try to answer three questions:

- Does the availability of public subsidies seriously infringe upon the opportunity of new parties to compete with their established counterparts?
- Have public funds undermined the volatility of party strength, the potential for change, which is the prime mover of democratic politics?

---

55   von Beyme 2000, p. 63.
56   Andren 1970, p. 67; Paltiel 1979b, p. 38; Paltiel 1980, p. 370; Seidle/ Paltiel 1981, p. 279; cf. Wiberg 1991c, pp. 108 and Mendilow 2003, p. 115.
57   Pierre/ Svasand/ Widfeldt 2000, p. 3.
58   Neill report 1998, p. 91.

- Can the transition of government power between (current) majority and minority be hindered by the allocation of public subsidies?

1. Access for new parties: Openness of the party system? [59]

The access of additional parties that win seats in parliament and establish themselves as a parliamentary party will change the format of the party system.[60] Based on experiences in Germany and Italy, grave doubts about the "closure" theory have been voiced rather early.[61] Comparing Austria, Germany and Switzerland, Drysch repeated this observation after a decade. He argued that in reality party systems have developed quite contrary to conventional wisdom. Switzerland, a country without public funding, had new entrants to the party system just like Austria and Germany, despite the distribution of public subsidies.[62] Any observer of European politics could easily find an even more contrasting pair by adding the U.K. with no subsidies and no new parties to one side and Sweden with high subsidies and two completely new parties to the other group of countries. Recent decades have offered further evidence for a wider range of democracies. To which of the groups (with public subsidies or without, with new parties or with a closed system) do the 20 other democracies of our sample belong?

Graph 9-1:   Model of analysis (most relevant variables) [63]

Antecedents (essentials of politics)	Independent variables (= potential objects of political engineering)	Dependent variables (objects of change)
Political system, i.e. institutions of government (frequently called the state)	Political finance regimes (regulation of party funding)	Political competition: Party system
Cleavages, associations and linkages of civil society	Election laws (detailed rules for electoral systems)	Party organisation, including party type(s)

In general, stability and change of party systems are caused by social developments and institutional arrangements. Traditional social cleavages (resulting from the age of modernisation) are supplemented by new ones. If a political entrepreneur intends to

---

59   This sub-section draws heavily on Nassmacher, H., 2004a, pp. 29-51.
60   Niedermayer 1992, p. 145.
61   Nassmacher 1989b, p. 248.
62   Drysch 1998, p. 256. All democracies of western Europe have incorporated "green" parties into their party systems (Stöss et al. 2006, pp. 19-22).
63   The analytical model is based on the landmark findings of Hermens 1941 and Duverger 1967, pp. 206-255, 281-351 (for electoral systems) as well as those of Lipset and Rokkan 1967 (for traditional cleavages).

start a new party and wants to establish it within the national party system she or he better look for a social cleavage that is not represented at present. Political issues and political leaders are important factors for the sustainability of a political party, even more so for its successful take-off.[64] Although social factors are more frequently discussed, institutional factors are influential, too. Among these, only the electoral system is usually taken into consideration whereas the impact of monetary resources and political finance regimes is widely neglected.[65] However, both can change the political opportunity structure and thus may have an impact on party systems (see Graph 9-1 above).

As our study deals with money in politics, we need to pursue the role of public funding on the rise of political parties. Parties in parliament may try to raise the threshold of access to public funding[66] in order to exclude non-incumbents from the benefits that the established parties (sometimes called "cartel parties") want to preserve for themselves.[67] For an analysis of effects caused by such policies, we assume that small amounts of total subsidies will not have a major impact. A token subsidy, for example those in the U.S. (established in the 1970s for presidential campaigns), in the U.K. (the recently created policy development fund), in Italy (during the 1980s) or in the Netherlands (before 1999), cannot be expected to influence access to the party system in any significant way. In order to evaluate the impacts on access (i.e. party system format) we will therefore lump together democracies without any party subsidy with those that provide minor or insignificant amounts of state aid only (see Graph 9-2 below).[68] Because Belgium, Denmark and Ireland were fairly late in introducing public subsidies, the absence of new parties in Ireland (prior to 1987), the populist addition(s) to the Belgian party system and the political earthquake of 1973 in Denmark cannot be related to the existence of state aid.[69]

The dynamics of party systems are too complex to be solely determined by funding regimes. Nevertheless it would be a mistake to dismiss the impacts of party funding without analysis. All regulations that provide easy access to public funds [70] contribute to more and fairer competition, because they enhance the opportunities of smaller parties to compete (and vice versa). Time and again new parties have successfully made their way into parliaments, even in countries with high electoral thresholds and despite

---

64 For details see Nassmacher, H. 1989, pp. 169-190 and Nassmacher, H. 1990, pp. 177-209.
65 Without much response among scholars Wildenmann (1968, pp. 71, 77) identified the political finance regime (in addition to the electoral system) as an important element of the „rules governing the quest for power", i.e. political competition. Recently Hooghe/ Maddens/ Noppe (2006, p. 353) have re-discovered the importance of both sets of competitive regimes.
66 See above in chapter VIII, sub-section D 1 (access to public funding).
67 Katz/ Mair 1995, pp. 17-23.
68 Two definitions for "significant" apply in Table 9-3: for parties 5 percent of the total vote in a nationwide election; for public subsidies 10 percent of total party revenue.
69 Pierre/ Svasand/ Widfeldt 2000, p. 20.
70 Denmark, Finland, Germany, Israel and the Netherlands; for details see above in chapter VIII D 1 (access to public funding). Due to its recent regulation the U.K. is neglected here.

high thresholds for public funding.[71] In Austria, Belgium, France, Germany and Switzerland post-materialist ("Green") parties, which on average poll at least 4 percent of the vote, have entered parliament.[72] Despite lower shares of the vote (e.g. in Finland and Sweden) the same applies to a few other democracies.[73] In a different group of countries (Britain, Spain, Canada and Japan), Green parties have not made the breakthrough to parliamentary representation. Obviously this is due to a lower share of the popular vote and a higher electoral threshold, not to the availability of public subsidies.

Among the countries with P.R. electoral systems some established public financing a long time before post-materialist ideas emerged (Austria, Finland, Germany, Norway and Sweden). Other countries introduced public subsidies to parties after this wave of new value orientation had created a new political cleavage (Belgium, Denmark and Italy). After 1957 political development in Germany tended toward a two-and-a-half party system, which was stable until the late 1970s. The different situation that now prevails began to develop in the 1980s. For the first time a new party, the Greens, was able to win seats in parliament, in Germany (in 1983), in Austria (in 1986) and in Sweden (in 1988). This means that party system change happened after the introduction of public funding for political parties, precisely more than two decades later in Germany and in Sweden and about one decade afterwards in Austria.

In Germany the unification process and its economic consequences favoured a new party representing the old Communist stalwarts and disappointed voters in East Germany. Whereas the impacts of a new social cleavage (de-industrialised East vs. post-materialist West) and the electoral threshold (five percent or three constituency seats) are obvious, any impact of public subsidies on this new party is doubtful.

Most right wing populist parties, a few of them calling themselves "progressive", entered the political arena in continental Western Europe after the wave of post-materialist parties: Front National (France), New Democracy (Sweden), Progressive Party (Denmark), Danish People's Party, Progressive Party (Norway), *Vlaams Blok* (now: *Vlaams Belang*, Belgium), *Lega Nord* (Italy) and *Lijst Pim Fortuyn* (Netherlands). Some of these are completely new, others simply followed in the footpath of another party. The Reform Party in Canada manifested a traditional progressive streak of politics on the prairie. In Austria and Switzerland traditional parties (FPÖ, SVP) have been able to utilize the populist wave and to recruit lots of new voters beyond their traditional clientele.

---

71 The example of Belgium indicates that the combined effects of electoral and funding rules are quite compelling (Hooghe/ Maddens/ Noppe 2006, pp. 353, 361-365).
72 Due to changes in the electoral system the Flemish Greens (Agalev) were defeated in the 2003 national election, but recovered in the reginal election of 2004. See Hooghe/ Maddens/ Noppe 2006, pp. 363-365.
73 *GroenLinks* (Netherlands) is rather a renamed old (Ex-Communist) party than a new entrant to the system.

Graph 9-2: Access to party systems (new parties since 1980)

Openness of Party System/ Availability of Public Subsidies	Party systems with significant new parties		Party systems without significant new parties
	Country	Parties	
Party systems **with** significant public subsidies (high electoral threshold)	Austria	Grüne, LiF	Australia
	Canada	Reform Party, B.Q.	Costa Rica
	France	FN, Verts	Mexico
	Germany	Grüne, (PDS)	Spain
	Japan	Democratic Party	
	Poland	PiS, PO, LPR, Samoobrona	
	Sweden	Miljöpartiet, KrFP	
	Uruguay	FrenteAmplio (now: ERP)	
Party systems **with** significant public subsidies (low electoral threshold)	Belgium	Groen/ Ecolo, Vlaams Belang	Finland
	Costa Rica	Partido del Progresso	
	Denmark	Fremskridtspartiet, DFP, Enhedslisten	
	Israel	Israel Beitenu, Kadima, Gil	
	Norway	FrP	
Party systems **without** significant public subsidies (high electoral threshold)	India	BJP	United Kingdom
			United States
Party systems **without** significant public subsidies (low electoral threshold)	Ireland	Progressive Democrats	
	Italy	Lega Nord, Forza Italia, Margherita	
	Netherlands	LPF	
	New Zealand (after electoral reform)	Greens, NZ First, ACT, United Future	
	Switzerland	Grüne, Autopartei	

Evidence from Costa Rica and Uruguay – as gathered and discussed in detail by Casas-Zamora – "has conspicuously failed to back the ... contention that subsidies bias the electoral arena in favour of established parties and prevent the entry of newcomers".[74] In Poland the party system is still in flux. Despite public funding there are passing combinations of post-communist and post-solidarity parties as well as new parties created by political entrepreneurs. Occasionally other newcomers (Christian Democrats

---

74 Casas-Zamora 2002, p. 292; Casas-Zamora 2005a, p. 227.

in Sweden; NZ First, ACT or United Future in New Zealand) were successful.[75] Some of them are of minor, others of major importance, for their respective party system. In Canada two major parties (Reform Party and Bloc Quebecois) came in after state aid had been available for more than a decade. Both new parties became well established in the House of Commons. Public money did not hinder this; in fact it may have even supported the rise of both newcomers. „In the 1993 federal election, the Reform Party ran 207 candidates, 52 of them were elected. It received 18.7 percent of the popular vote (versus 16.0 percent for the P.C. with 295 candidates)."[76]

In Israel, during the period with public subsidies in place, no less than 20 new parties made their way into the *Knesset*. About half of them „started from scratch."[77] Success of a new party may be merely due to new issues, which the older parties have neglected, among them the representation of Russian immigrants and of senior citizens. However, as the case of New Zealand demonstrates, a change of electoral law (with a new, lower threshold for access) can always play an important role. In Japan splits in the dominant party (LDP), both before and after reform of the electoral system and the political finance regime, were instrumental in creating the (new) Democratic Party of Japan. In Italy the decline of formerly established parties, especially *PSI* and *DC*, was quite dramatic and paved the way for *Forza Italia*. In both countries, clientelistic structures within the dominant party and the popular response towards corrupt exchanges have been influential. The leading party in Israel after the election of 2006, *Kadima*, was created by prime minister Sharon (after a policy dispute with his old *Likud* party) and it was led to political victory (although a moderate one) by his heir-apparent Olmert. Occasionally a political entrepreneur is able to shake up the party system. All these cases point to other potential variables beside public subsidies.

Contrary to assumptions proclaimed by politicians who supported state aid, as well as by academics who expected a closure of the party system, new parties have entered parliament in countries with and without public subsidies (see Graph 9-3 below). The widely held belief that state aid preserves the existing party system, frequently called "the petrification hypothesis, places an enormous weight" on the impact of subsidies and ignores many other intervening factors. Party system change is a "complex and multi-dimensional" process, which is "related to overarching changes in society. Public subsidies ... are too weak to make a decisive difference in any crucial aspect."[78] A low electoral threshold and the rise of new issues or the determination of political entrepreneurs to create their own party seem to be more important for access to the

---

75 We disregard the Dutch D66 because its first success dates back to the late 1960s and the German PDS because this post-communist party is a consequence of German unification rather than any other factor.
76 Stanbury 1996, p. 83.
77 Mendilow 1992, p. 100.
78 Pierre/ Svasand/ Widfeldt 2000, pp. 20, 22.

party system than the distribution of and threshold for public subsidies.[79] At least the hypothesis that state aid causes the closure of a party system can be refuted.

The countries with (significant) new parties outnumber those without them even if significant public subsidies are in place. The conclusion is that state aid does not open or close the party system to newcomers. However, public subsidies enable ideological factions within established parties to split a party successfully. Cases in point are Poland and Israel. Moreover state aid may enhance the survival of new parties.[80] In this respect public subsidies seem to be of some importance. Because public funding has no visible impact on the access of new parties, their sustainability and the fragmentation of party systems come to the fore.

2. Room for changing weight of individual parties: Freezing of the party system?

Easy access to a national party system turns out to be a matter of social engineering. Setting low thresholds for representation (in parliament), as well as for distribution (of public funding), are useful precautions in favour of openness. However, both thresholds do not secure sustainability of any party. Sufficient funds may not be at the disposal of the party leadership and initial voters may turn to other parties later. For the individual party a lack of funds and volatile citizens are embarrassing risks, for democratic party systems both are necessary elements of political freedom and competition. In his thoughtful evaluation Paltiel warned that public subsidies, "a regular, reliable, and predictable source of funds … may promote a … lack of responsiveness to demands for social change."[81] When party linkage with social groups loosens and parties fail to secure their monetary resources, they become vulnerable and most likely dependent on public subsidies. When parties ruin reliable funding from their grass-roots, they also lose electoral support from their traditional voting clientele.

Party systems can be described by the interaction of parties of different size, which are represented in parliament.[82] A cursory view on the party systems in a couple of countries shows not only a changing number of parties (a change in format), but as well a change of relative weight between various parties (a change in fragmentation).[83] Before we start to evaluate changes in fragmentation of democratic party systems, we need to identify intervening variables and organise our sample into groups of comparable cases (see Graph 9-3 below).

The analysis should concentrate on democracies that have provided *significant public subsidies* for a decade or more, as impacts will be visible only after some time has passed by. Among the countries discussed here, this excludes the "late comers" Japan,

---

79 For the thresholds that apply to public subsidies see above in chapter VIII D 1 (access to public funding).
80 Mendilow 1992, p. 100.
81 Paltiel 1979b, p. 38.
82 Sartori 1990, pp. 318, 320/321.
83 Niedermayer 1992, p. 145.

the Netherlands and Ireland as well as the U.K. and the U.S. that have only token subsidies respectively India, New Zealand and Switzerland, which are without any direct subsidies. All of them will be assigned to the control group, which is needed to distinguish between impact and non-impact. Furthermore public funding should be important for parties and not only be a minor aspect, as it was in Italy until the 1990s. Australia, Austria, Belgium, Canada, Costa Rica, Denmark, Finland, France, Germany, Israel, Mexico, Norway, Poland, Spain, Sweden and Uruguay, which is more than half of our sample, meet all three requirements: public funding, for more than a decade, which covers a significant share of party revenue.

Before a potential impact of public subsidies on the fragmentation of party systems can be established, we have to keep in mind a wide consensus among scholars. That is, *electoral systems* are important rules for party competition that shape party systems.[84] In order to control the impact of public funding for this variable, our comparison will contrast countries with similar electoral systems and funding rules. If countries have experienced significant changes of their electoral system (the major rule for the transformation of votes to seats), then they have to be dropped from the sample. The impact of this change cannot be separated from possible impacts of public subsidies. Thus we have to drop four cases (Italy, Japan, Mexico and New Zealand) with major changes in electoral rules from the sample and end with 21 cases, which belong to four different groups (see Graph 9-3 below).

Most democracies use a system of proportional representation (P.R.), which makes it easier for all parties of any size to win a considerable number of seats in parliament. However, some of these democracies require a minimum vote of two, four or five percent, in order to partially offset the devastating effects of multi-party systems on government majorities. In Europe only three countries rely on systems that result in manufactured majorities: Britain with traditional plurality voting ("first past the post"), France with two ballots in single member constituencies and Spain with P.R. in multi-member constituencies of different size – on average 7 seats). The U.S., India, Canada and Australia are the cases of majority voting (FPTP, alternative vote) outside Europe.

Our next step is to identify an indicator for ossification or change of a party system. According to Sartori there are two types of party systems: alternating governments without coalitions and multi-party systems, needing more parties to form a coalition government.[85] Among the latter there are systems with and without dominant parties. This classification is too vague to be useful here. A more precise analysis becomes possible by calculating an index. The "effective number of parties" as developed by Laakso and Taagepera is now widely used to measure the fragmentation (fractionalisation) of party systems (in parliaments or in the electorate).[86] "When the parties are not

---

84 Wildenmann 1968, p. 77.
85 Sartori 1976, pp. 122-123.
86 Laakso/ Taagepera 1979; for details see above in chapter IV, sub-section A3b (Anglo-Saxon vs. other traditions of polities).

equal in strength, the effective number of parties will be lower than the actual number."[87] If three parties hold 45, 40 and 15 percent of the vote or the seats in parliament, then N equals 2.6. A changing percentage of seats held by individual parties as related to all seats in parliament will immediately impact on the fragmentation of the party system (see Graph 9-3 and Table 9-2). Our analysis will focus on the composition of parliaments.

At first glance, the comparison of party systems between the 1950s and today demonstrates that direct public funding did neither foster nor hinder change. We can observe that fragmentation has tended to change as party systems have become more complex. Casas-Zamora observes that "volatility was higher in elections, in which DSF [i.e. state aid] was available."[88] Among the countries with manufactured majorities the most dynamic development has occurred in France and Canada (after the introduction of public funding) and India (without state aid). With or without public funding the party systems in Britain and the U.S., Australia and Spain (after the early phase of transformation) have changed much less.

In countries that use a combination of manufactured majorities and public funding, the party systems have experienced impressive stability, as well as significant changes in fragmentation. Among the P.R. democracies (mostly in continental Europe) that distribute considerable state aid to political parties all have undergone massive changes in the fragmentation of their party systems. Just one exception to this general rule stands out. Israel, the only non-European democracy in this group, has seen the most massive change in the fragmentation of its party system.

The "effective number of parties" in Israel grew to 8.7 in 1999. Despite two efforts of social engineering in favour of less fragmentation (permanently increased electoral threshold and popular election of the chief executive, although temporarily only) this country has experienced the highest rise in fragmentation. At the dissolution of the 5th *Knesset* (in 1969), the two major parties jointly held 71 percent of all seats. At the election of 1965, the last one without public subsidies, the effective number of parties was 4.7. Four decades later (and after 36 years of public subsidies) the combined share of seats held by the two major parties (after the 2006 election) is down to 39 percent, and the effective number of parties has gone up to 7.9. Political and social cleavages over peace with the Palestinians, immigration from Russia, consequences of demographic change and of a free market economy have had a much stronger impact upon the party system than the potentially "freezing" force of public subsidies.[89]

---

[87] Lijphart 1999, p. 69.
[88] Casas-Zamora 2002 p, 58; Casas-Zamora 2005a, pp. 43/44. For the mean number of effective parties see Casas-Zamora 2002, p. 59; Casas-Zamora 2005a, p. 45.
[89] Arian 1998, pp. 144/145.

Graph 9-3: Composition of party systems (change of fragmentation)

	Major change in Fragmentation		Minor change in Fragmentation	
With public funding & P.R.	Austria (2.1-3.7),	1.6		
	Belgium (3.4-5.5),	2.1		
	Denmark (3.9-5.5),	1.6		
	Finland (4.6-6.2),	1.6		
	Germany (2.4-3.4),	1.0		
	Israel (3.1-8.7),	5.6		
	Norway (3.0-4.4),	1.4		
	Poland (2.9-4.3),	1.4		
	Sweden (3.3-4.3),	1.0		
	Uruguay (2.5-3.4)	0.9		
With public funding & Manufactured majorities	Canada (1.5-3.2),	1.7	Australia (2.2-2.7),	0.5
	France (1.7-4.6)	2.9	Costa Rica (1.8-2.5),	0.7
			Spain (2.3-2.9)	0.6
without public funding & P.R.	Ireland (2.4-3.5),	1.1		
	Netherlands (3.7-6.5),	2.8		
	Switzerland (4.7-5.8)	1.1		
without public funding & manufactured majorities	India (3.7-5.1)	1.4	U.K. (2.0-2.5),	0.5
			U.S. (1.8-2.0)	0.2

Source for values of Laakso-Taagepera index: Nassmacher, H. 2004a, p. 40 (Dr Nassmacher kindly provided the values for countries, which were not included in her study).
Comments: Japan, Mexico and New Zealand are missing in this table.
Data for Belgium does not imply the separation between Flemish and Walloon (ethnic) wings.

In all established democracies the ranges of party system fragmentation presented in Graph 9-3 apply to the whole post-war period of more than fifty years. This may not be precise enough to test the potential "freezing" impact of public subsidies. In order to produce a control group, we have divided the period under study into two intervals (before and after the implementation of state aid, see Table 9-2). Minor changes in range and average occurred in Australia, Canada, Costa Rica, Denmark, Finland and Germany. Some change is obvious for the Netherlands and Sweden, some more for Austria, Ireland and Norway. The two time periods differ most impressively in Belgium (average) and Israel (maximum).

We have discussed the Israeli case already. In Belgium the higher fragmentation is not equally distinct if we take into account the division of the three major parties (left, right and centre) along ethnic lines (into Flemish and Walloon parties) and the rise of a populist and xenophobic party (*Vlaams Block, Vlaams Belang*). In sum, the data offer no evidence for any "freezing" of party systems caused by public subsidies. This leaves the third dimension of ossification, i.e. an arrested distribution of power among the major parties, open for discussion.

Table 9-2: Fragmentation of party systems (and the influence of public funding)

Country	Fragmentation **before** pub.subs.			Year of Introduction	Fragmentation **after** pub.subs.		
	Minimum	Maximum	Average		Minimum	Maximum	Average
Finland	4.6	6.2	5.2	1967	4.9	5.6	5.2
Denmark	3.8	6.8	5.1	1986	4.7	5.6	5.0
Switzerld	4.7	5.8	5.1	-	-	-	-
Israel	3.6	5.8	4.9	1969	3.1	8.7	5.1
Netherld	3.7	6.5	4.7	1999	4.8	5.8	5.1
India	3.7	5.1	4.4	-	-	-	-
Belgium	2.5	4.3	3.3	1989	3.9	7.0	5.0
France	1.7	4.6	3.3	1988	2.3	3.5	2.9
Sweden	3.1	3.2	3.2	1965	3.3	4.2	3.7
Norway	3.2	3.6	3.4	1970	3.1	4.9	4.1
Poland	-	-	-	1993	2.9	4.3	3.7
Uruguay	-	-	-	1928	2.5	3.4	2.9
Germany	2.4	3.5	2.8	1967	2.5	3.4	2.7
Ireland	2.4	3.0	2.7	1997	3.0	4.2	3.6
Spain	-	-	-	1977	2.5	2.9	2.6
Australia	2.5	2.7	2.6	1984	2.3	2.6	2.4
CostaRica	1.8	2.2	2.0	1956	2.2	2.5	2.3
Canada	1.5	2.8	2.4	1975	1.7	3.2	2.6
Austria	2.1	2.5	2.2	1975	2.2	3.7	2.9
U.K.	2.0	2.5	2.2	(2001)	-	-	-
U.S.	1.8	2.0	1.9	(1976)	-	-	-

Source: Data compiled by Dr Hiltrud Nassmacher from her own research (Nassmacher, H. 2004a, pp. 40/41). Cf. Casas-Zamora 2002, p. 59; Niedermayer, McBride, Zohlnhöfer, all in Niedermayer et al. 2006. pp. 114, 238, 278. Data for Costa Rica and Uruguay: Casas-Zamora 2002, pp. 262, 276.

3. Changing roles of political parties: Arrested distribution of power?

Changes in the format and fragmentation of a party system do not necessarily indicate that new or small parties have entered the centre of power. In democracies that rely on manufactured majorities, one major party may lose seats in parliament until the other major party will win a majority (and form the government). The breakdown of a governing party (like the Canadian P.C. or the Spanish UCD) simply meant that the party in opposition took over. The new minority may consist of a traditional party (like the Spanish PP) or of newcomers (like the Reform Party and the B.Q. in Canada).

Within a proportional representation system a coalition government is the most likely outcome. The composition of this coalition will first depend on numbers ("minimal winning coalition") and political traditions ("oversized majorities").[90] However, ideological distance between parties and personal aversion between leaders may also be a factor. While in the long run a change in government is an indicator of fair competition (and sustainable democracy), there is no obvious measurement that applies to all situations. Trying a minority government, recruiting new coalition partners or leaving the government completely are serious options for a governing party that has lost an election, unless another party (or a group of parties) has gained an outright majority. Sometimes parties in power are willing to accept coalition partners or be tolerated by parties, with which they have no common ideological background.[91]

In most countries, the participation of new parties in governments is not a common feature. The case of Israel may be an exception, just because small parties are of major importance in every coalition. In the case of a "hung parliament," such as in Britain and Canada, there is a tradition of one-party governments, formed by the strongest minority party. The participation of small or new parties in governments has not happened in Spain, although minority governments have relied on their support in parliament. In other countries new parties were included in governing majorities rather late, such as when the Greens in France (1997), Germany, Sweden (1998) and Belgium (1999) entered (or supported) a left-of-centre government.

In the Netherlands two new parties were able to join a government coalition just after entering parliament for the first time, the LPF (in 2002) and DS'70 (in 1971). Most of the time, the formation of substantially different oversized multi-party coalitions achieved a change in power. In contrast to this, in Switzerland, a coalition-like arrangement has been set up more than four decades ago to exclude newcomers from access to the government. Even changes in fragmentation have taken a long time to be reflected by changes of weight in government. It took the Swiss People's Party (SVP) three election victories in a row (1995, 1999, 2003), growing from the smallest to the largest party of the governing bloc, before the allocation of government positions (*Zauberformel*) was finally adjusted in its favour to reflect this change.

Because we do not want to discuss such details for all democracies in our sample, we will concentrate on the transfer of power between right-of-centre parties and left-of-centre parties or vice versa.[92] Such transitions (see Table 9-3 below) may suffice as an adequate indicator of fair competition. Our intention is to find out if a change in power has occurred more or less frequently after implementation of public funding. This must be tested especially in countries where a dominant party held a secure position over decades, e.g. Social Democrats in the Scandinavian countries, Gaullists (under various party labels) in France (Fifth Republic), CDU/CSU in Germany (between

---

90 Lijphart 1999, pp. 91-103.
91 von Beyme 2000, p. 86.
92 Cases, where changes of parties in coalition from the same spectrum (right or left) or change of the head of the government from these parties have taken place during the legislative period, are not paid attention to (quite contrary to Müller/ Strom 2000, p. 12). The classification of parties to either the right or the left, however, follows Mackie/ Rose 1991 and Müller/ Strom 2000.

1949 and 1966), Mapai in Israel (up to 1977) and PRI in Mexico until 2000. The LDP (*Jimintô*) in Japan is still dominant although a seriously competitive opposition party (DPJ) was observed in 2000.[93]

Table 9-3 indicates that ten democracies in Western Europe have regularly experienced a government turnover. The same applies to Poland, which expelled the governing party whenever a free election was held. An impact of public subsidies on this process cannot be established, because some of these countries have substantial state aid, others have not.

Table 9-3:   Changes of government composition (transition of power) [94]

Y.	AT	AU	CA	CR	DE	DK	ES	FI	FR	IN	IR	IL	IT	JP	ME	NL	NO	NZ	PL	SE	UK	UR	US
83	X			X					X								X						
84		X			X			X			X							X					
85						X														X			
86				X		X										X	X						
87						X			X														
88						X						X											
89									X								X	X					
90		X														X	X					X	
91									X										X				
92													X										X
93		X	X				X					X	X						X				
94			X	X						X		X		X									
95							X																
96	X				X		X			X	X	X											
97								X	X								X	X			X		
98			X	X			X																
99	X																	X					
00															X	X							X
01				X					X							X	X						
02						X								X									
03						X																	
04				X			X																
05			X														X				X		
06		X	X								X	X					X	X					

Among the non-European democracies, Australia, Canada, Costa Rica, India, Israel, Mexico, New Zealand, Uruguay and the U.S. have seen transitions of power (executive leadership) from centre-right to centre-left parties or vice versa. Whereas no im-

---

93 Kevenhörster 2003, p. 297.
94 Belgium and Switzerland are not included in our table because a tradition of oversized majorities renders the underlying category of analysis - change of government - inapplicable.

pact of public subsidies is obvious in five of them, Israel and Mexico stand out as exceptions. In Mexico the dominance of the PRI has been terminated after a massive increase of public subsidies. In Israel despite the initial dominance of the Labour party (*Mapai, Maarach, Avodah*), parties of the right (especially the *Likud*) were frequently able to form a government.

India, on the other hand, has not introduced public subsidies. Japan and New Zealand are the odd cases. In Japan public subsidies were introduced after the dominant party (LDP, *Jimintô*) temporarily lost its government position. In New Zealand the transformation of the electoral system from FPTP to MMP halted the traditional alternation of power.

Regular changes in government (i.e. alternation in power) are customary in countries with plurality voting, such as in Britain, Canada and the U.S. This happened also in Spain, with its manufactured majorities, three times and the total time governed by Socialists and Conservatives each is about equal. In France the first change of power occurred in 1981, when the Socialists took over from the Gaullists, which had been the leading party of government since 1958. This transpired years before the implementation of public subsidies (1988) and again after that.

In Canada the "government party", the Liberals, had an advantage.[95] After the introduction of the new political finance regime in 1974, a change of power has taken place more frequently. Even in this country the rise of a new party to the role of official opposition occurred after the implementation of reform legislation and a collapse of the former governing party, the P.C. A similar finding can be reported for countries with proportional voting systems and with high thresholds. In Germany the first change in power happened in 1969, ten years after the implementation of public funding. Meanwhile three more changes of government took place (1983, 1998 and 2005).

This is also true for Sweden: In 1976, after four decades of Social Democratic dominance, the right-of-centre parties took over. Since then four further changes of government have taken place. Norway already experienced shifts in government before the implementation of public subsidies (1963, 1965). Since the 1980s the alternation between governing parties has occurred more regularly.[96] Similar changes can be reported for Denmark. In 1982 and in 1993 the Social Democrats returned to power, which they had lost before. In 2001 this happened to the right-of-centre parties.

In general, the Scandinavian party systems, dominated by Social Democrats after 1945, changed to multi-party systems without the dominance of a single party. The former leading party lost votes continuously. Instead of the main party (thus the view of well informed scholars like Gidlund), other parties mostly benefited from public subsidies.[97] Before the implementation of state aid, these parties (mostly bourgeois)

---

95 Whitaker 1977.
96 Bergman 1997, p. 255; Narud/ Strom 1997, p. 216.
97 Gidlund/ Koole 2001, p. 124.

had always run into financial shortages. Thus they had to tap sources that were deemed undesirable by public opinion. Perhaps public money has made them less dependent on "dubious" funds and thereby made them more competitive and promoted them as a political alternative.

Even in countries with a tradition of oversized coalitions, such as Austria, the change in power may have been supported by public funding of political parties. Although between 1966 and 1983 just one of the two major parties (ÖVP, SPÖ) has governed alone, the years from 1947 to 1965 and 1987 to 1999 were dominated by an oversized (i.e. "grand") coalition of both parties. Two deviations from this pattern are noteworthy: First, an SPÖ-FPÖ government in 1983. Second, the ÖVP-FPÖ coalition in 1999. Public funds were among the factors that helped the FPÖ survive beyond 1980 and grow in the 1990s, and finally win even slightly more votes than the ÖVP. In all of these countries the party that was strongest when public subsidies were introduced has lost votes.

Despite these details we should not overrate the impact of public subsidies on the competitive potential of political parties as there are countries with and without such subsidies in our sample. There is no doubt that changes in government positions have taken place in countries without public subsidies, as well as in those with public subsidies. Therefore these funds cannot be considered to trigger change. However, new and old parties have welcomed additional funds washed into their coffers.

C) Summary of findings for party competition

The potential impact of political funds in the real world of politics has been addressed in two stepwise processes, aiming at the general impact of funds on party competition first and at the specific impact of public subsidies afterwards. If money is a means to success in political competition, then the candidate (or party) who is able to spend the most should be the winner;[98] at least most of the time. However, if enough data is available, this simple hypothesis does not stand the test of reality. In sum, it emerged that

- the influence of money is not strong enough to make the competitor who can dispose of the most funds the likely winner of a political contest.
- competitors who hold a financial edge continuously or over a period of time may be successful more often than those who have less money.

Nevertheless there is not sufficient evidence to prove that money is the only, or even the major cause for success. If the distribution of disposable funds between competitors is uneven, he who can spend more will not always win. Competing parties have

---

98   Forrest et al. 1999, p. 1127; Mandle 2003, p. 1; Maddens et al. 2006, pp. 161-167.

access to resources other than money that help them to contest elections on an equal footing. Right-of-centre parties (big or small), which enjoyed a traditional funding edge over left-of-centre rivals, were often unable to turn their financial advantage into a lead among voters. More generally spoken, money does not win elections; although sometimes it may help to do so, especially

- challengers more than incumbents,
- by spending with the tide rather than in uphill battles.

Thus it is definitely the voters' choice and not the politicians' cash that will decide the outcome of an election.[99]

Because the availability of public subsidies is said to infringe upon the opportunity of new and minor parties to compete, this dimension was discussed separately. The potential freezing (ossification or petrifaction) of party systems, i.e. reduced opportunities of change within a party system, also had to be explored more precisely. It emerged that the hypothesis is dealing with three different aspects:

- the "openness" of the party system,
- a "freezing" of the party system and
- an "arrested" distribution of power within the party system.

Because either kind of change may relate to public subsidies, the various aspects were addressed separately. Wherever enough data is available, the theory that public subsidies lead to an ossification of the party system does not stand the test of reality. New parties have entered the party system in many democracies. Established parties have lost and gained electoral support with and without state aid. An arrested distribution of power between parties of government and parties of opposition has occurred solely in Japan, but not in Austria, France, Germany, Israel, Italy, Mexico, Spain or Sweden, which (due to a high level and/or long duration of public subsidies) were the likeliest candidates for such suspicion.

The evidence presented in this chapter has substantiated that state aid for political parties and their candidates has not prevented various dimensions of change within party systems (such as access, volatility and government participation).[100] Nowhere have public subsidies contributed towards a closing or freezing (i.e. ossification/petrifaction) of the party system.[101] Quite frequently governing parties have lost voters, seats in parliament and the reins of government. We have empirically refuted the hypothesis that public subsidies are advantageous merely for established parties. The "subvention for democracy" does not simply preserve the party system or safeguard the governing

---

99   Quite in this line Casas-Zamora 2002, p. 19; Casas-Zamora 2005a, p. 13.
100 Nassmacher, H. 2006a, p. 516.
101 Quite to the contrary, in Post-Communist Europe „the provision of state money for campaign purposes seems to be associated with a dispersal of the vote" (quote by Kenneth Janda from Birch 2003, p. 90).

parties. Since the provision of public funds, competition among established parties has intensified, the number of parties has increased and new parties have used their access to money to seize seats and power.

At times windfall subsidies resulting from impressive results at the polls have contributed to the maintenance of parties, which had no funding base of their own (i.e. considerable revenue from members or donors). The FPÖ in Austria, which had been rather poor over decades, is a case in point. Public subsidies did neither prevent nor create parties, neither did they prevent or promote their entry to the party system. State aid did not help to make parties grow or enter governments. It did, however, underpin the process of party-building (respectively re-building), which has helped some parties survive. Mexico adds an example that the massive expansion of direct public funding to all major competitors has fostered the transition of power (possibly also the transition to democracy).

Mendilow has advanced the refined hypothesis "that public funding acts as a partial barrier, which may be overwhelmed only by other factors militating for change." His conclusion, drawn upon the example of Israel, is that "in none of the cases ... did public funding actually bring about the process ... However, in each case, public funding added to the impetus of such factors."[102] Parties in parliaments decide on the provision of public funds. Considerations concerning the potential for coalitions can be a cause for generosity with public money in order to help potential partners to survive or to become stronger. Easy access to public funding may encourage newcomers to participate in races for seats in parliament or may help them to run a successful campaign.

Although findings in this chapter concerning the influence of money on political competition are quite promising beyond the refutation of the frequently repeated prejudice that public subsidies will close and freeze the party system, the impact of political funds cannot be neglected or ignored. To make parties independent of unwanted influences "a regular flow of financial resources from a plurality of sources"[103] is a vital element in the institutionalisation of parties. In many countries public subsidies "have led to a stable flow of resources, but with less plurality than used to be the case..."[104] For many parties this kind of revenue has become important. However, the annual share of public subsidies for the individual party varies. When comparing the public share of total party income, there are great differences between parties that range between 20 and 90 percent. Because of the inherent risks, the flow of funds into the party system has to be observed continuously. In addition to this discussion of party competition, we still have to evaluate whether or not the distribution of power in party organisations is affected by political money.

---

[102] Mendilow 2003, pp. 116, 120 (one quote on each page).
[103] Panebianco 1988, pp. 58/59.
[104] Svasand 1991, p. 122.

CHAPTER TEN

Impacts on Party Organisation

Each party organisation is a Janus-like element of political competition. The inward-looking face concerns the political machine, the mechanisms of its operation and the efficiency of its political efforts. The outward-looking face is directed towards the party's supporters, the accessible part of civil society, which it represents in everyday politics. A regular flow of funds from a variety of sources,[1] e.g. specific sectors of society, into party coffers at any level of the organisation (most likely the political system, too) represents a link between politics and society and ensures the legitimacy of party activity.[2] The specific sectors of a society that support a party are usually called its grass-roots. Scholars expect parties to provide linkage between civil society and the political elite, more precisely between a part of civil society and a part of the political elite (hence the name political party). Among the environmental challenges parties currently have to face is their changing relationship with their supporters in the electorate at large. This is a result of changes in communication technology and institutional rules, among them new political finance regimes. In order to evaluate the impacts of such regulations we consider various inter-related questions in different sections of this chapter.

- Is money a means of or an obstacle to links with party supporters? Have specific routines of funding assisted parties in securing *linkage to their grass-roots*? Or have such routines contributed towards alienation between civil society and political elite?

For the sustainability of democratic government, it is important that grass-roots support and elite responsiveness do not whither away, however there are concerns that this may be happening. For example, most scholars expect that the volatility of voting behaviour will increase in the future. One option that can counteract this volatility is an adequate party organisation. Poguntke and Scarrow consider strong party organisations to be important for stable election results.[3] Because information about this inter-

---

1 Panebianco 1988, pp. 58/59.
2 For opinion polls on public subsidies see above in chapter VI, section A (cornerstone of democracy).
3 Poguntke 2000, pp. 253, 259, 265. The question, whether or not party organisation makes a difference, is answered in the affirmative by Scarrow 1996, pp. 10-11. It will not be addressed here.

action was scarce for a long time,[4] scholars have tried to fill in some of the blanks.[5] In order to address the potential impacts of political funds on the internal operation of individual parties (more precisely the extra-parliamentary structure) we will discuss several questions:

- Have political finance regimes caused (or enhanced) changes within individual party organisations?
- What have such changes meant for the *distribution of power between parts of the organisation*, especially national headquarters, regional branches and local chapters, individual candidates and party affiliated bodies?

More generally put, different sources of funding may have divergent impacts on party activity (Graph 10-1). Although such impacts seem evident they reflect assumptions rather than empirical knowledge. We will assemble all available data to test such hypotheses and address those, which concern grass-roots linkage first.

Graph 10-1: Selected impacts of funding strategies on party activity

Impact on/by	Grass-roots funding	Plutocratic funding	Public subsidies (flat grant)	Public subsidies (careful design)
1. relationship between party elite and grass-roots	linkage	dependency	autonomy	responsiveness
2. funding				
a) corruption	no corruption	corruption possible	neglect of private donors	neither neglect nor corruption
b) capitalisation or etatisation	no capitalisation	capitalisation	etatisation	etatisation unlikely
3. situation in local districts	scarcity of funds possible	waste of funds possible	waste of funds most likely	scarcity of funds unlikely
4. activity between elections	cutbacks possible	bureaucracy possible	bureaucracy most likely	cutbacks likely

A) Linkage between parties and their grass-roots

All parties face environmental challenges, which they have to meet if they do not want to risk failure. That is, each political party operates within an external framework of incentives, and it is restricted by an institutional setting. Among the institutional arrangements that influence intra-party structure, electoral legislation and party finance

---

4   Epstein 1993, pp. 2, 5.
5   Nassmacher/ Nassmacher 1988; Nassmacher 1992a; Katz/ Mair 1992 and 1994; Scarrow 1996; Cordes 2001; Carty/ Eagles 2005; Smith 2005.

regimes stand out because they define the rules of the game. Political parties are involved in creating the rules for party competition, and party politicians use these options to advance their goals. Especially governing parties are able to change such external institutional conditions. This occurs rarely or only marginally for the electoral system, as a trend towards more personalisation of P.R. systems indicates. France in the 1950s and 1980s, Italy, Japan and New Zealand in the 1990s are the exceptions. Quite contrary to this, the political finance regime is a restless issue. Its change follows some sort of negative experience (e.g. the shock of losing an election, or scandals caused by party funding) or diffusion forces, which induce neighbouring countries or sister parties to follow a similar path of reform. Political finance laws may constrain or empower actors of the political game. On the one hand, such laws foster or curb cost explosion as well as organisational development, which may end up in bureaucratisation of party structure as well as in party oligarchy, or lead to a commercialisation of campaign activities.[6] This may increase alienation between party elite and party members in particular, and between parties and voters in general. On the other hand, political finance regimes can establish access to new sources of funds (i.e. public subsidies) and/ or strengthen a party's link to its grass-roots.

Some advocates of state aid have claimed that public funds may prevent the use of corrupt or interested money. The examples of Italy, France, Japan and Spain, however, indicate that public funding of political parties did not ensure the "cleaner" financing of politics.[7] Moreover, public largesse has "not provided a substitute for corporate payments",[8] because private contributions may simply find a new focus. In the Israeli case "the funding of individual contests [i.e. intra-party competition for positions on the party list] came to depend on the source that the national party system has gradually eliminated since 1969."[9] Such observations warn against many excessive expectations, which are placed in public subsidies.

Traditionally parties maintain linkage to their grass-roots via branches. These local nuclei may comprise hundreds of card-carrying party members or a handful of local notables who represent the party label in their community whenever they feel challenged to do so, especially at the time of an election. A well-organised party is expected to communicate with its supporting sectors of (civil) society through local activists who volunteer to contact their fellow citizens wherever they meet them (in associations, in the neighbourhood or at the workplace), talk about politics, solicit donations and provide additional contributions (membership fees plus other cash and non-cash support) from their own funds.[10] The ideal assumption is that the linkage represented by a continuous flow of money from specific sectors of civil society to individual parties guarantees the legitimacy of party activity, as well as the sustainability of party

---

6   For the former see Nassmacher 1989b, for the latter Landfried 1994a.
7   See above in chapter VII, section D (income from graft).
8   Pinto-Duschinsky 1991b, p. 235; for further details see Leonard 1979, p. 63.
9   Hofnung 2005b, p. 66.
10 For some examples see Theis 2007.

democracy. A loss of card-carrying members, or of support by local notables, translates into a loss of potential party workers and a decline in party revenue; be it from dues or donations. In countries where party income from membership dues is (relatively) high, i.e. Switzerland, Sweden and Austria, the volatility of voters tended to be less.[11]

1. Changes of grassroots linkage via membership dues and small donations

Critics expect that public subsidies will change these long established routines of sustainable democracy, especially the funding of party activity by signed-up party members. In the late 1980s "the official attitude" in the Netherlands still assumed that state aid would increase "the distance between elite and grassroots ... because the parties would no longer have to rely financially on their members" (and small donors). Public funding of parties was expected to cause a decline in party membership and revenue from membership dues, to reduce the willingness of citizens to give and their readiness to join. Sometimes subsidies are still seen as a major step towards alienation between party elites and party supporters, because secure income from state aid was expected to harm the party elites' drive towards grass-roots funding.[12] Once again this development has been observed for the "cartel party," in which a party becomes part of the state and is no longer rooted in society.[13] In short, public subsidies endanger the inclination of supporters to give and the propensity of parties to solicit.

Casas-Zamora follows this line of argument, and has presented the view that direct state funding causes a reduction in membership dependence, i.e. a party's dependence on membership dues as a source of income. However, he continues by stating that he was unable to find a covariance between public subsidies and membership decline.[14] Although "party membership has declined [15] ... simultaneously with the expansion of the public subsidy schemes, it is unclear to what extent these two developments are related to each other." Thus, within his study there is little evidence to support any systematic cause-effect-relationship.

A broadly based empirical test (including verification or falsification) of this hypothesis is not easy, because both sources (Katz and Mair as well as Casas-Zamora) did not supply any statistical evidence. Moreover there is no simple correlation between the availability of public subsidies and the amount of revenue from grass-roots' support (membership dues and small donations). A comparison of membership figures by party families in a selection of European countries found little to suggest a systematic

---

11 von Beyme 2000, pp. 59/60. Recently Austrian and Swiss voters have drifted away from such traditions.
12 Pinto-Duschinsky 1981, p. 292. In the U.K. the opinion still prevails: Neill report 1998, p. 92. Quite in this line Landfried (1994a, p. 17 respectively 1994b, p. 133) has argued that "etatization" of party funding endangers linkage."
13 Katz/ Mair 1995, p. 18. Quote in this paragraph by Koole 1989, p. 210.
14 Casas-Zamora 2002, pp. 64, 65/66; Casas-Zamora 2005a, p. 48.
15 See above in chapter VI, sub-section B 1 a (number of party members).

impact of public subsidies on the development of party membership. The "patterns displayed ... indicate a very limited impact of the subsidies; party families, which had experienced a declining [or increasing] membership prior to the introduction of public subsidies largely continued to do so once they were implemented."[16]

A different test of the hypothesis can be based on a comparison between countries. The evidence that is most obviously inconsistent with the hypothesis hails from the two countries where it originated, the U.K. and the Netherlands. In the latter grass-roots linkage to all major parties in the form of pillarisation declined before public subsidies (albeit moderate and indirect) were introduced. To this day, membership fees that are collected by local chapters and funnelled upward within the organisation make up the major source of party funding despite the fact that membership figures and member-to-voter ratios have declined massively.[17] Obviously Dutch party elites have neither completely neglected the financial links that bind them to their supporters, nor have politicians tapped the public purse for sufficient funding.

Evidence from the U.K. is even more striking. Between 1950 and 1997 aggregate party enrolment shrunk from 3.4 million to 0.8 million. By the late 1990s the member-voter ratio had declined to less than 2 percent of the electorate.[18] Local support for all British parties has also decreased. By the mid-1970s constituency quotas (the U.K. embodiment of grass-roots funding) supplied more than a quarter of the total (non-election year) income for the Conservative Central Office, but in the 1980s it was barely 12 percent. For 1992-97 party headquarters received less than 5 percent of its total annual revenue from this source. At that time the Labour Head Office revenue from membership subscriptions was less than 15 percent of the total.[19] All of this has happened despite the absence of public funding.

Likewise it is generally assumed that leaders will be instrumental in devising and implementing strategies, which have a financial impact. In Britain the Thatcher era caused the most important change, which reduced membership figures for both major parties by different policies. Prime Minister Thatcher wanted to make a direct populist appeal to the voters and thus neglected her own party organisation and its funding base, while her treasurer turned to "fat cats" for funding. In addition, the Thatcher government tried to hit Labour Party funding via legislation on affiliated unions in the 1980s. The Labour Head Office tried to meet the challenge by encouraging constituency activists to collect donations, including permanent dues from individual members. "In 1993 the Conservative Party followed the examples of the Labour Party ... when it introduced its own fundraising credit card for members." However, Labour has been more active in 'cultivating' its membership, while the Conservatives have targeted mainly affluent financial backers. Nonetheless local party organisations of

---

16 Quotes in two paragraphs from Pierre/ Svasand/ Widfeldt 2000, pp. 17, 18 respectively.
17 Gidlund/ Koole 2001, p. 116.
18 Scarrow 2000, p. 89; Mair/ van Biezen 2001, p. 9. For details see above in chapter VI, subsection B1 (membership dues) and D 1 (constituency quotas).
19 Pinto-Duschinsky 1981, p. 138; Pinto-Duschinsky 1994, p. 15; Neill report 1998, pp. 30/31.

both major parties decline.[20] Cutting back the local influence of the unions on the selection of candidates (1992) and later on the financial support for individual candidates (since 1997), Blair may have contributed to the decline of grassroots labour organisations. At present, contrasting to such activities Labour has much less individual members than the Conservatives.

In all European countries there has been a decrease in party membership, whether the country provides public subsidies or not. The case of Germany is specifically telling. Public subsidies (moderate flat grants) were introduced in 1959, considerably increased during the early 1960s, formalised by legislation in 1967, and continuously increased throughout the 1970s and 1980s. All of this should have sufficed to trigger decline as predicted by the alienation hypothesis. However, aggregate party enrolment actually increased during the 1970s, hit a maximum in 1980, and has levelled off ever since, slowly at first and more heavily after a unification blip faded.[21] During the first 20 years of public funding German parties were able to recruit additional members. Only later on they were less successful in keeping their flock together.

When measured by numbers of citizens, all parties in Germany have lost grass-roots support during the most recent decades. In contrast to this, their fundraising effort has been considerably more successful. In 2006 (a post-election year) membership dues accounted for 27 to 29 percent of the two major parties' and 19 to 24 percent of three minor parties' total revenue. (The post-communist PDS is even more dependent on membership dues, which are 41 percent of total party revenue.) In 1970 (the first post-election year, for which data are available) comparable shares for the two major parties had been widely apart (22 percent for the CDU and 40 percent for the SPD), whereas for the two minor parties (existing at the time) the share was almost 14 percent each.[22] In 1981 (another post-election year), after more than two decades of public funding, membership dues contributed some 43 (CDU) to 57 (SPD) percent of total revenue for the major parties and 21-25 percent for the minor ones.

The conclusion to be drawn from this evidence is that in almost 50 years of public funding the major parties have become more similar to each other,[23] and that the minor parties have increased (although not recently) their reliance on grass-roots funding. Moreover the average amounts of membership fees (see Table 6-3 above) show that public funding in Germany has destroyed neither the members' willingness to give nor the leaderships' incentive to solicit.[24] Quite to the contrary, since 1994 the German approach to public subsidies is partially based on the "matching principle." This induces

---

20 Hamel et al.1995, p. 4; Scarrow 1996, pp. 120, 123 (quote ibid, p. 123); Webb 2002, p. 27.
21 Scarrow 2000, p. 89; Rudzio 2003, p. 189.
22 *Deutscher Bundestag*, parliamentary paper, no. 16/8400; Schindler 1983, pp. 96-103.
23 As anticipated by the „catch-all" party type; see below in chapterXI, sub-section B 1 (catch-all parties).
24 This result is contrary to pre-empirical beliefs among mainstream political scientists (e.g. Katz/ Mair 1995, p. 15) but quite in line with the empirical findings of Pierre/ Svasand/ Widfeldt 2000, pp. 3, 18.

parties to care for "big money in little sums" contributed by their signed-up party members in the form of regular dues.[25]

The evidence from the countries that have been discussed in some detail should suffice to falsify all general versions of the "public subsidies destroy grass-roots linkage" hypothesis. Quite the contrary, our examples support the hypothesis presented by Casas-Zamora that public subsidies do "not negatively affect the incentive structure for potential party members."[26] In support of his hypothesis, he reports Sundberg's finding who compared the relative stable membership rates in the Scandinavian countries. Membership rates of Sweden, Norway and Finland went up after introducing public subsidies. Only figures for Denmark show a substantial decrease. However, the fall in party membership rates in Western Europe pre-dates the advent of public funding. Sundberg argued that the absence of direct state funding in Denmark and the correlative obligation of party members to bear the cost of ever-more expensive campaigns, severely increased the costs attached to active participation and led to a reduction in membership rates.[27] In Sweden a changed relationship between labour unions and the social democratic party (SAP), resulting in a loss of collective members, had a great effect on this process of membership decrease.

Because public funds are distributed in different ways,[28] a more sophisticated version of the alienation hypothesis, however, would assume that political finance regimes are among the factors that have an impact upon the link between parties and their grass-roots. In order to test this hypothesis we will have to discuss different measures taken in democracies that operate different kinds of subsidy programs and different sets of public incentives (or disincentives) to improve relations between parties and average citizens.

For Austria, where public subsidies are provided in the form of a flat grant, the Houghton Commission could not confirm a decline in dues after subsidies were introduced.[29] The public may not have been aware of the total amount given to parties, because state aid is given through different channels and to different levels of the party organisation, as well as to party affiliated bodies (*politische Akademien, Parlamentsklubs*). Another assumption is that due to a specific political culture, Austrian citizens were used to paying party dues in order to get access to housing and jobs, whereas in other countries people have to be motivated to participate in political activities and political donations.[30] After a time it may be that party officials became used to the revenue from the public purse and stopped membership recruitment efforts. However,

---

25 See above in chapter VI, sub-section C 1 (energising fundraisers).
26 Casas-Zamora 2002, p. 66; Casas-Zamora 2005a, p. 49.
27 Sundberg 1987; Sundberg 2002, p. 196.
28 See above in chapter VIII, sections B (types), C (recipients) and D (allocation of subsidies). For a world-wide overview see Tjernström 2003, pp. 209-223 and Nassmacher 2006, pp. 448-450.
29 Houghton report 1976, p. 322.
30 Quite contrary to the *Austrian* practice such individual benefits for party members are not relevant in the *Netherlands* and therefore a high level of dues is not initiated by such need.

membership maintenance activities have increased via communication depending on full-time staff in party offices.

In times of overwhelming media importance, a party's link to civil society is often pursued by public relations and seen as the task of specialised, professional staff, including advisers for media performance, spin doctors and the like. However, this is not sufficient. Parties have to be vital in order to recruit candidates at all levels of the political system (national/ federal, regional/ state and local/ municipal). The vitality of the "party on the ground" may find its expression in a different strategy of individual fundraising.

2. Approaching members and supporters by direct mailings

As mentioned already, small donations are a general indicator of linkage between individual parties and specific strata of society. Even in European countries, which are said to have no fundraising tradition, non-governmental organisations (NGOs) demonstrate how effective efforts to solicit money for specific purposes can be.[31] However, NGOs have an advantage. Whereas parties must aggregate different policies, NGOs can address one specific topic. Even smaller parties that present only a small number of issues (due to a more specialised program and clientele) face a problem when collecting their funds by such means. Compared with activities of North American parties, the efforts of European parties are more or less limited.[32] This may be caused by reliance on membership as the major form of linkage, a lack of public incentives for party fundraisers and individual donors [33] or the absence of disincentives, i.e. rules that discourage big donors from giving.[34] Smith indicates that bans and limits, publicity of donors and donations also force parties to intensify their efforts in soliciting donations.[35]

In North America parties have reacted upon such incentives (tax benefits and matching programmes) and disincentives (especially limits) by going for small donations. In Canada the introduction of a tax credit for small donations to parties and candidates has caused a surge of fundraising activity, which has increased revenue from small donations as well as the donor base. In the U.S. disincentives for "fat cats" (especially contribution limits and disclosure rules) have contributed towards an increase in revenue from small donations without an enlarged donor base. Parties and other organisations closely linked to the parties, with (depending on the level)[36] volunteer or professional workers, have successfully applied direct mail and other means. Asking party supporters time and again for donations has mobilised the clientele and linked it

---

31 For experience in Austria and Germany see Smith 2005, pp. 195, 229, 240, 248.
32 Carty 1996, p. 200; Smith 2005, p. 173.
33 See above in chapter VI, section C (public incentives).
34 For details see Nassmacher 2003b, pp. 42-46 and Nassmacher 2006, pp. 449-451.
35 Smith 2005, p. 197.
36 For findings for the 1970s and 1980s see Jewell/ Olson 1978; Huckshorn 1984, pp. 103-105.

closer to the parties (or their penumbra). All of this has happened (with and without public incentives) due to a loss of "fat cat" contributions (before and after the introduction of public disincentives). The evidence available from both democracies may be inconclusive as far as cause and effect are concerned. However, all told new regulation has reinforced linkage between parties and their grass-roots in both countries.

In Canada parties turned towards individual supporters because big donations dried up. Apart from some basic similarities, the outputs and impacts of reform efforts were quite different. The success (of direct mail) not only created revenue for political parties but also intensified communication between various levels of the party organisation and party supporters among the general public. In addition the direct mail technique improved, and the style of standardised letters became more personal. Direct mail has also created more competition between levels, branches and actors within the same party of the U.S. and Canada. The implementation of new regulations in both Canada and the U.S. has encouraged party activity and closer links to party supporters. In particular, activity by U.S. state parties increased dramatically.[37]

Unlike the Liberal Party of Canada, the Progressive Conservatives started using direct mail techniques at the federal level early. The efficiency and success of this approach are mentioned frequently.[38] It even ushered in a new form of intra-party communication. Donors began to contact P.C. headquarters by writing letters, furnishing new ideas that the party leader might well consider. One of these ideas was party building in the provinces, and the leadership responded by providing well-calculated 'development aid'.[39]

Without strong public incentives such efforts will not be successful as the case of the U.K. has demonstrated. The headquarters of both major parties (with some additional staff) have experimented with direct mail. The Conservatives did so before the 1983 and 1987 elections, when Conservative Central Office sent out thousands of letters soliciting donations and recruiting new members. Labour tried the device in the run-up to the 1987 campaign. The results were not too encouraging, and the money raised was pocketed by party headquarters.

The dependency of both major parties on large contributions from businesses and trade unions (usually termed "institutional donations"[40]) may have caused the delay of reform legislation in Britain. However, both parties do not collect the same proportion of their revenue from this source that they raised in former days. Political finance reform, which occurred at the turn of the century, did not include incentives to encourage party fundraising. As disincentives for large donors (bans and disclosure regulation) are rather modest, recent reforms have not shown testable impacts on linkage as yet.

---

37 Rieken 2002, pp. 151-173; Smith 2005, pp. 174, 229/230, 232.
38 See, for example, Stanbury 1996, p. 80; Scarrow 1996, p. 104.
39 See below in this chapter, sub-section B 2 (national headquarters, regional branches, local chapters).
40 Koole 2001, p. 79; see above chapter VII, sub-sections B 1 a (affiliation fees) and B 3 (corporate contributions).

On the contrary, the Central Offices of both major parties have turned to a loophole in the new political finance regime and funded the 2005 campaign through loans from wealthy backers, which (unlike donations) were not liable to statutory disclosure. How the resulting mess will be cleaned up is still open to question.[41]

As we compare the fundraising activities of Austrian and German parties, the findings fit into the picture, which results from the comparison between North American and British parties. In Austria there are flat grant subsidies, no measures to energise fundraisers and no incentives for donors. As a consequence fundraising activity is lower than in Germany, where tax credits are available and subsidies (in part) are given as matching funds. Introduction of matching-subsidies "spurred the growth of fundraising in Germany after 1994",[42] but compared to the efforts in North America the technique is underdeveloped. The value of direct mail campaigns as a tool for linkage with the grass-roots is very limited. While in the U.S. and Canada contribution limits and disclosure requirements have encouraged political fundraisers to go for small donations, not least in order to show a wide range of support in civil society, the absence of such regulatory elements in Austria provides no incentive for similar moves.

However, there are exceptions to these findings on impacts. The Netherlands, where donations are tax deductible,[43] are a case in point. Because a public incentive is in place, it could be expected that parties, like their North American counterparts, would employ such devices when soliciting donations. Strangely enough no such effort has ever been mentioned in empirical studies. This may be explained by legacies of the past. As long as the relationship between parties, their members and affiliated organisations of each "pillar" was stable, the parties received sufficient financial support. Although these links (the traditional "pillars") have collapsed decades ago and traditional financial sources have dried up, party activists and party leaders have not changed their behaviour too much. Some public funding has been introduced but party organisations remained rather small.

Furthermore in U.S. states (e.g. Indiana) and some Canadian provinces (e.g. Quebec) flat rate subsidies did not hinder the development of fundraising. As Smith argues, the amount of money given to parties may be too small to cover their budgetary needs. Party organisers in the U.S. continue to believe that money is the only way to pursue other activities and that fundraising is the best means to this end.

3. *Measurement of and incentives for grass-roots linkage*

As we have discussed, what really counts for all parties in democracies is the linkage to civil society. However, measuring grass-roots linkage is not easy. In the old days of political mobilisation, high voter turnout was a good indicator; despite the fact that in general high turnout means an agitated electorate, which is not desirable in itself. More

---

41 see „Good intentions meet the bottom line," in: *The Economist*, 27 October 2007, p. 47.
42 Smith 2005, p. 197; cf. ibid., pp.182, 200 and Nassmacher 2001c, p. 109.
43 Elzinga 1992, p. 359.

recently party membership figures or member-to-voter ratios have been better substitutes because party membership definitely means linkage to those who care to be a member. However, a M/E ratio of 2 percent no longer serves the initial purpose, i.e. measuring linkage. Nowadays total income from the grass-roots or its percentage of total party revenue are possibly more suitable indicators, although neither of them should be overestimated. In principle the general problem of finding an adequate measure of linkage remains unsolved.

For political parties, funding from private sources indicates linkage (to the grass-roots and/ or interest organisations) and (if given in small amounts) direct legitimacy as well. Membership dues, as pointed out above, are shrinking and small donations are not too important for parties in western Europe these days. Ideological links of older parties (with their voting clientele) have weakened. Those with newer parties do not provide safe income. Party revenue from large and small donations is not a reliable source any more, as traditional links to financial supporters (business and its organisations, unions and other organisations of the penumbra) have loosened up. The special relationship of the unions with left wing parties is common in all political systems and does not change in relation to election results. However, union contributions in cash or kind are less reliable than in former times, as the British and the Swedish cases indicate. In systems with consensus/ consociational governments, the links between the parties and their associated organisations seem to be more stable. This is true for the links to business as well as to unions.

Large donations from other organisations are unknown in European countries. If firms provide large donations this includes the risk of corruption. Political income from the business community small or large is much more oriented towards the outcome of elections and the performance of governments. This is obvious in Canada, partially in the U.S. and recently also in Britain. The P.C. in Canada, which during the 1970s and 1980s were very successful in soliciting small donations, got into trouble when the popularity of Prime Minister Mulroney faded away, as the party had become more and more leader-oriented. Approaching the rank and file directly, while disregarding riding associations eroded the close relationship between supporters and their local organisations.[44] The successful start of organisational development at the grass-roots withered away. When supporters of the Conservatives in the U.K. were not content with the output of their party in government, this source of funding declined.[45] This indicates that democracies have to incorporate grass-roots organisations in the process of providing small contributions and to back up the efforts of local party fundraisers to solicit. Political finance regulation should be regarded as an opportunity to encourage this.

In Japan the reformed electoral rules and the political finance regime have encouraged politicians of the conservative LDP to transform personal support organisations

---

44 Woolstencroft 1996, pp. 289, 299.
45 For the U.K. see Fisher 1996b, p. 162.

(*koenkai*) into local party chapters.⁴⁶ It remains to be seen in the decades to come whether this is just a change of name or the beginning of a more formalised LDP organisation at the grass-roots that will survive the transition from the current generation of MPs to the next one. In Israel a resurgence of the parties on the ground was tried by a change in the non-financial rule of intra-party competition, the introduction of nominating "primaries" for the party lists by the major parties.⁴⁷ This happened after an impressive decline in party membership figures had occurred, possibly for the most part due to changes from a largely collectivist society to more individualistic patterns. But the distribution of public funds to party headquarters via flat grants may as well have contributed to destroy linkage to civil society. However, the significance of larger participation brought about by the primaries is hardly indicative of a grass-roots linkage and a revival of organisation. First, the new members have not increased membership dues as a percentage of total party revenue. Secondly, any informed observer of nomination processes will know that political contenders have to bring their personal supporters to vote for them for whatever reasons, and not necessarily those of political involvement. Thirdly, in Israel power-brokers have grabbed their opportunity to "sell" blocks of votes to the highest bidder.⁴⁸

B) Distribution of power within party organisations

Modern intra-party politics is a system of co-operation and confrontation between party strongmen (occasionally women take over a part of their own), where each of them controls his own power base. Similarities with feudalism in medieval Europe (and Japan) are most striking. Fiefs and vassals of the old days have been replaced by party coffers and party workers in our times. A squad of followers (paid staff as well as volunteers) and control of a separate war chest are the currencies of intra-party power.⁴⁹ The leader of a party faction or a party branch, or the holder of a public office or a top position on a party committee are the modern equivalents of a feudal lord.

The concept that is most adequate to describe such party structure (in North America as well as in Europe, in Japan as well as in Israel) is "loosely coupled anarchy" or "stratarchy".⁵⁰ The party boss in a U.S. metropolis, the head of a party faction in Italy and Japan, a "grandee" of the ÖVP and the CDU or a "baron of Gaullism" in France are examples of the type. Not only "the main German political parties may be seen as consisting of several baronies, ..." The same applies to other democracies. "The party barons and their forces ... work with each other for their common purpose, electoral victory."⁵¹ Besides this common purpose, party barons safeguard their own interests

---

46   Blechinger 2001, pp. 99/100; Köllner 2005, pp. 47/48, 55.
47   Hofnung 2005b, p. 72; Hofnung 2006, p. 372.
48   Hofnung 2005b, p. 75; cf. Hofnung 2006, p. 380; Hofnung 2004, p. 43.
49   The term "currency" as used by Deutsch 1966, pp. 120-123.
50   Quotes from: Lösche 1993 respectively Niedermayer 1993.
51   Both quotes from: Pinto-Duschinsky 1991b, p. 216.

and jockey for position within the party hierarchy. The availability of funds can be one of their resources, as any component of the political machine, which is called a "party", may be their power base.

According to a variety of observations, the power within political parties has been shifting

- from big donors (and party bagmen) to party leaders holding public office,
- from local branches to national headquarters (centralisation),
- from volunteer party workers to paid staff (bureaucratisation),
- from party apparatchiks to political consultants (professionalisation),
- from party organisation on the ground to parliamentary caucus.

Some of these observations may stand up to empirical tests. This does, however, not imply that the specific shift has been caused by a different handling of party funding or a new set of rules relating to the subject of our study (i.e. a political finance regime); let alone that such causality, if it has occurred, is a one-dimensional process. We will approach the interaction between political funding and intra-party power by looking at different networks:

- a party and its candidates,
- national headquarters, regional branches and local chapters,
- party organisation and party penumbra (especially caucus, affiliates and PACs).

1. Parties and their candidates

Candidates gain independence from their party whenever they run in a constituency or raise and spend their own money.[52] Candidates lose independence from their party whenever they rely on a party list for an election, party funds to pay for their campaign or party assistance in staff and expertise to make their campaign a success. Party leaders and party candidates live in a double-bind relationship. Money is among the strings that may pull one towards the other. On the one hand, candidates need

- access to the party label (via a party list, a letter of assent or a primary),
- campaign workers (volunteers or paid agents),
- campaign expertise (e.g. political consultants, accountants and financial agents),
- campaign funds (donations, transfers or subsidies).

On the other hand, party leaders need

- prospective winners (to campaign) and
- loyal supporters (to govern).

---

52 Cf. Japan (Blechinger 2001, p. 101), the U.S. and Israel, after implementation of intra-party primaries.

Over decades institutional structures of the political system (presidential or parliamentary, federal or centralized, P.R. or plurality voting) influence the organisational set-up of parties.

A widely accepted hypothesis stipulates that in P.R. systems voters choose parties rather than individuals. This competitive situation forces parties to increase their corporate identity. In contrast to this, constituency (plurality) electoral schemes encourage personalism and/ or localism in campaigning. On the basis of proportional representation, parties may have powerful incentives to develop strong, nation-wide organisations in order to maximise their overall vote. Wherever elections are decided in single-member-district contests, parties have strong incentives to target their organisational efforts to marginal districts.

In presidential systems the media give more attention to candidates than they do in parliamentary ones. Thus a parliamentary system may slow down the trend of candidate orientation. Other results indicate personalisation even in European democracies.[53] As P.R. systems are becoming more personalised, candidates running for public office rather than their party organisation may play a major role in future elections. All of these factors have to be taken into account if the power of different elements within a party organisation is to be assessed.

Parties in North America have been subject to numerous restrictions of party activity, such as non-partisanship stipulated for local council elections (U.S. and Canada), or primaries to select candidates for public office (U.S.). While U.S. parties lost control over nominations when primaries were introduced, parties in Canada and the U.K. exert significant influence on the selection of candidates.[54] Nevertheless parties in the U.S. survived by providing new services for candidates.[55]

For a long time the U.S., the U.K. and Canada neglected the role of parties. Just as in other democracies with plurality or majority voting systems and single-member constituencies, they concentrated their legislation on candidates. In 1974 Canada was the first country to move, when it passed legislation concerning party financing and tried to dampen rising campaign costs, which had driven individual politicians into not paying for their advertising.[56] Moreover it created the necessity to raise a large number of small donations.

In the U.S., following the FECA and Buckley v. Valeo (in the 1970s, too) parties "could engage in unlimited independent expenditures and issue advocacy."[57] This has encouraged the two major parties to raise as much money as possible, which state and local party organisations spent (without limit) on party-building activities. Thus the

---

53   Dalton et al. 2000, p. 51; Dalton/ Wattenberg 2000b, p. 12.
54   In Canada only in constituencies with no chance of winning the seat, and in the case of a few top candidates, does party headquarters influence the process (Carty/ Erickson 1991, pp. 97/98; Carty 2002, p.358.).
55   Jewell/ Olson 1978, p. 192; Bibby 1998, p. 26; Herrnson 1998, p. 55.
56   Nassmacher/ Nassmacher 1988, p. 33.
57   Bibby 1998, p. 43.

parties have developed extensive services to support their candidates indirectly, e.g. voter research and outreach. Surplus funds of the national party organisations are transfered to the state and local levels,[58] thus freeing them from spending restrictions imposed by the FECA. In the 1980s some scholars dared to predict that the significance of parties would rise, and they were proven correct. Just like PACs, parties now play a more important role in nominating procedure and campaign funding. However, even volunteers on the local level are partially replaced by paid professionals, "allied with, but not formally part of" the party organisation.[59]

Parties have "refocused their efforts by acting as centralized campaign fund-raisers, assisting candidates in raising money, and providing other electoral services."[60] Party expenditures may be limited in amount (some ten percent for congressional elections), but they are significant for the campaigns of challengers and in open-seats. While PACs tend to give most of their contributions to incumbents, party committees react by targeting most of their selective giving to challengers and open-seat elections.[61] Consequently, party committees have become a key source in the funding of such "neglected" campaigns. This new role for party politics has even increased competition, a major characteristic of democracies.

The goal of parties in Canada (just like in the U.S.) is to maximise seats in parliament. The largest amounts of money are spent in the most hotly contested constituencies. Reform legislation in Canada (just like the U.K.) prescribes tight expenditure limits for local candidates and national parties during the election period. Statutory campaign reimbursements and tax credits (both of them unlike the U.S. and the U.K.) stimulate fundraising activity at all tiers of the party organisation (local, regional, federal). Private donations collected by individual candidates are matched by public funds twice: a tax credit to the donor and a reimbursement to the spender (as long as he or she has spent within the legal limit). As candidate reimbursements frequently produce a surplus that remains with their constituency association, candidates and their "bagmen" also provide resources for party building at the grass-roots.[62]

The political finance regime of the U.S., consisting of statute law, Supreme Court rulings and FEC regulations, did not bring about streamlined party organisations but stratarchial structures with many nuclei, which solicit donations. Federal candidates (for President, Senate or House) and their support organisations sit in the centre, whereas their parties together with other PACs are among the supporters. By contrast, Canada's political finance regime centres on the activities of candidates as well as of parties. Nevertheless in Canada as well as in Britain the performance of the parliamentary party and/or its leader seems to be of major importance for the electoral success of the candidates and the party, due to the parliamentary system in both countries.

---

58 Katz/ Kolodny 1994, p. 35; Biersack 1996, pp. 108/109; Corrado 1999, p. 81.
59 Cotter et al. 1984; Kayden/ Mahe 1985; Sabato 1987; Green 2002, pp. 324, 326 (quote).
60 Gierzynski/ Breaux 1994, p. 183.
61 Hrebenar et al. 1999, p. 160; Herrnson 1999, pp. 103, 109.
62 Nassmacher/ Suckow 1992, p. 149; Carty 1996, p. 141.

Therefore candidate-oriented party organisations and politics should exist to an even lesser degree in the parliamentary democracies of continental Western Europe.

European countries with P.R. electoral systems share some similarities. Small countries show highly developed consensual decision-making (i.e. consociational democracies) because of their political culture. In Germany the same is true because of specific arrangements of the federal system. While in Germany the mixed member proportional (MMP) electoral system stimulates personalisation – to a degree –, in all small democracies of Europe demands for democratisation have led to increased focus on the individual candidates in P.R. party list systems. Such new rules, in turn, could have shifted the traditional party-oriented vote towards a more candidate-oriented vote. As a consequence, the emphasis (and funds) might have shifted to candidates and their individual races. Empirical research, however, indicates that no such tendencies have prevailed to this day. The number of MPs (which is the basis of parliamentary power) is determined by the party vote and this has remained the most important factor. Therefore, parties in these countries may show an increased centralisation of funds as well as a rising dominance of their headquarters and a depolitisation of their party organisation.

2. Different levels of the party organisation (headquarters, branches and chapters)

Analyses of organisational change within parties frequently focus on the impact of social and technological developments. Especially the challenge of the media is seen as most important to party organisations. In this age of media dominance, all parties have to coordinate their messages on the spot and brilliantly. Therefore professional communication has been established by the top level of all parties. Major developments in organisational change seem to be similar. That is, there is a strengthening at the top level and weakening at the lower levels of the party, because party leaders address party members directly without mediation by middle-level elites. This centralisation must not contradict a process that all parties have gone through since the 1970s, a movement towards democratisation, albeit to different degrees. These hypotheses require analysing the development of party organisations more closely.

Electoral systems are hardly ever taken into account as an important factor for the development and the structure of party organisations.[63] This is even truer for political finance regimes. As mentioned already party finance rules influence party building.[64] After all, the priorities of party building are access to improved funding and targeted advertising.[65] In a way, it was exactly these aims, which led to the inception of the mass party in the 19th century. The challenge, however, still exists.

---

63 An exception is Katz (1980), who discusses the impact of electoral systems on party structure from a specific viewpoint: the incumbent who is seeking re-election.
64 Nassmacher/ Nassmacher 1988, pp. 34-39; Smith 2005.
65 Appleton/ Ward 1996, p. 137; Farrell/ Webb 2000, p. 110.

Because volunteer work in parties has declined, expenditure data provide major indicators for the importance of sub-structures within political parties, especially

- party headquarters and the sub-national levels, measured in spending on staff and employees, as well as
- traditional and modern tasks, e.g. activities to strengthen field organisation vs. professionala dvertising.

Access to their own resources is expected to make actors stronger and independent from others. Applied to different levels of a party organisation, e.g. local chapters and regional branches, this principle gains additional weight when related to the more professionalised top level. If only party headquarters have access to public funding, this contributes to centralisation. If state aid is provided to each party level as well, this may cause problems to party tiers and contribute to bureaucratisation. Incentives for all levels to go after their own money can trigger organisational activities and development. Additionally internal transfers may improve local party organisations.

In both, the U.S. and Canada, the federal system has brought about parties with more or less independent organisations at different levels, which hardly influence or control each other. U.S. parties maintain contacts to supporters (donors, members and activists) in many ways. State parties use modern technology (e.g. electronic newspapers), as this provides parties with cheaper and more efficient alternatives to distributing inside information among party activists. The local parties are responsible for social events, but their frequency seems to depend on the efforts and the number of party activists on the ground.

"Costs of developing party policies or election strategies and costs of training candidates or election organisers would not be considered election expenses."[66] In the past, Canadian riding associations used to be weak, employing voluntary workers only. Meanwhile the local riding associations have become "a key link in the communication chain from party leader to members," as they organise all sorts of events and some mail their own newsletters. Recently parties are turning away from direct mail and use web-based means.[67]

New fundraising strategies (in various Anglo-Saxon democracies) and public subsidies (where available beyond the national level) have strengthened the grass-roots organisations considerably. Constituencies can now be active between elections. But even today, local parties are not active everywhere because volunteers sometimes prefer to stow away the campaign surplus into a bank account for the next election.[68] At least in constituency parties with a sitting MP, his or her staff can co-ordinate local party activity.[69]

---

66   Young 1998, pp. 348/349.
67   Smith 2005, pp. 238/239 (quote on p. 238); cf. Carty 1996
68   Nassmacher/ Suckow 1992, pp. 135, 145, 148; Carty/ Eagles 2005, p. 18.
69   Carty/ Eagles 2005, p. 26.

Because fundraising takes place at different levels of the organisation for both Canadian and U.S. parties, the results are organisational changes not only at the constituency level but at the higher levels (state/ province and federal) as well. The change of party structure in the U.S. may be characterised by the term centralisation. "National party committees assume the spending authority of state committees via agency agreements, and the party committees in Congress replace the local parties as the 'party' that incumbents and candidates deal with." At the state level, the legislative campaign committees "displace the local party units."[70] Obviously public finance laws in the U.S. had an impact on party building, too. Party organisations, especially at the county level, are staffed with permanent personnel now. At the end of the 1980s this organisational set-up already covered 57 percent of the electorate.[71]

When comparing the financial situation of parties in Canada with those in the U.S., it becomes obvious that political finance regulation has also had a severe impact on intra-party power. In Canada tax credits have improved fundraising potential at all levels, and reimbursements at the constituency level have contributed to its empowerment. (The impact of the recently introduced quarterly allowances cannot yet be assessed. It can be expected that they will help sustain party headquarters and their extended level of staff and activity.) All parties in North America have increased their spending on the party apparatus, with U.S. parties expanding most on the national level, in contrast to the Canadian parties, which also developed their constituency level.[72]

However, the strategies of individual parties differ. "Whereas the N.D.P. tried to boost campaign spending (in order to benefit from the national reimbursement), the P.C. [during the heyday of its fundraising power] increased pre-campaign publicity in order to stay within the spending limit for nation-wide campaigns."[73] At the local level party building depended more on political entrepreneurs and their ability to mobilise a funding base, than on their association with a specific party label. However, even "rich" riding associations in Canada (quite unlike their European counterparts) shrank away from employing full-time staff. Campaigns are organised by the candidates and the financial support of the party differs.[74]

The growing weakness at the grass-roots seems to be a problem for both major parties in Britain. While "political party headquarters appear fairly well endowed with staff compared to other countries," the picture begins to change when the country size is taken into account, that is, "parties ... seem relatively understaffed given the size of the population."[75] In the early 1970s the Houghton committee reported that over half of the Conservative constituency associations had a full-time agent, whereas no more than a quarter of all Labour associations were able to employ some sort of paid agent

---

70   Sorauf 1998, p. 239 (both quotes on this page).
71   Gibson et al. 1989, p. 87; Lösche 1989, p. 235.
72   Smith 2005, pp. 132, 136, 137, 139, 154.
73   Amr/ Lisowski 2001, pp. 66/67.
74   Carty/ Eagles 2005, pp. 73, 86, 90-92.
75   Webb 1995, p. 310.

(full-time, part-time or shared). Fisher's survey on behalf of the Neill committee pointed out an overall picture of decline at the constituency level. The same is observed by Webb.[76]

Constituency associations, which want to employ agents, have to pay for them.[77] The shortage of money became a problem for Labour after the influence of trade unions was cut back, which had provided (and still provide) most of the funds (political levies paid on behalf of indirect members by the trade unions).[78]

Whereas the Conservatives were a cadre party, Labour had never mobilised the working class through a network of its own but relied on its close links to the trade unions, which held collective memberships.[79] Therefore politics and policies were more or less determined by informal forces (the parliamentary party and the unions) not by party activity at the local level. To this day the major impact of funding on the internal operation of both major parties has resulted in the "plutocratic" rule of institutional donors and/ or "fat cats", which make the central party stronger at election times.

Parties in the U.K. concentrate their activities on winning a majority of parliamentary seats. All parties co-ordinate their resources and campaign strategies centrally, they target resources carefully, according to the challenges of the electoral system the money is funnelled to marginal or key seats. The regional offices staffed and paid by the Conservative Central Office and the Labour Head Office "are essentially provincial outposts of central party headquarters."[80] During election time, staff at the local level is supported by expertise from the national apparatus. Organisational change occurred after electoral defeats, e.g. after 1945, 1964/66 and 1997 with the Conservatives, after 1979 and 1992 with the Labour Party.[81]

Party activity does matter. That is, the more a party spends (relative to the maximum allowed) and the more active a party's local campaign is, then the better are its electoral performance and election outcome.[82] The result is that after an interlude the convergence of the major parties in the U.K. seems to be back on track. Both Labour and the Conservatives are trying to suppress the influence of corporate bodies such as parliamentary parties and unions in favour of individual members. However, the role of the parties in parliament is enlarged by the recently introduced public funds for research.

In sum, in the U.K. organisational decline at the grass-roots (mainly caused by dwindling traditional resources[83]) has been accompanied by a shift in organisational capac-

---

76 Houghton report 1976, p. 32; Neill report 1998, pp. 39-42; Webb 2000, p. 243.
77 Becker 1999, p. 65.
78 See Scarrow 1996, p. 71; more recently: "The real Labour funding crisis", in: *The Economist*, February 10, 2007, p. 40.
79 Webb 1994, p. 110.
80 Webb 1994, pp. 125, quote ibid. on p. 244; Scarrow 1996, p. 78.
81 Webb 1994, p. 125; Scarrow 1996, p. 78.
82 Johnston/ Pattie 1995, p. 271; Denver et al. 2003, pp. 555-557.
83 Koole 2001, pp. 78/79.

ity towards the centre,[84] creating an electoral-professional party type. While in the past the Conservative Central Office collected one fourth of its total revenue from the local level (in constituency quotas),[85] this share has collapsed, leaving the top level to survive on its own. Both major party headquarters have strengthened their leadership claim even further through changes in party organisation, policy competence and intra-party power.[86]

By comparing Canada and Britain no common trend for salary expenditures can be established. British parties spend the most at the national level, and these amounts are increasing (for the Conservatives including the costs of local agents). In Canada only one third of total party expenses is spent on the national level. In monetary terms a growing importance of the national level can not be proven. Despite a similar trend towards candidate-oriented campaigns caused by the electoral system for all parties in the U.S., Canada and the U.K., there are some differences. Due to federalism the centralisation of the major parties in the U.K. is not true for the U.S and Canada. In all three countries electoral law strengthened the candidates' position. In Canada and the U.K. the candidates are responsible for financial matters in their campaigns. In the U.K. only the candidates, not the parties, have to come forward and put down financial deposits. However, winning a seat depends heavily on the overall performance of the party and of its national leader.[87] This apparent contradiction has been largely due to the lack of any party finance regulation (until 2000) in the U.K., which increased the impact of the parliamentary system.

In general, "not one of the countries, for which we have been able to calculate national averages, shows decisive growth in sub-national staffing, although the Nordic countries come closest to achieving this: all other systems show staff shrinkage at the local level .... For the most part, the numbers of staff are related specifically to the level of state funding received by the party."[88] Hence the Netherlands and Switzerland, which had modest to no public funding until the late 1990s, should have the smallest staff numbers locally. In Austria and Sweden there is public funding not only on the national level but also on the sub-national (regional, local) level. Therefore Swedish parties as well as their Austrian counterparts, should be well staffed at all levels. The same can also be expected for German parties.

There are additional reasons that may explain differences between party organisations in Austria and Sweden on the one hand, the Netherlands (and possibly Switzerland) on the other. In the Netherlands individual patronage seems to be absent and party membership is by no means a prerequisite for a job in the public sector.[89] Thus there is no specific incentive for voluntary work in the constituencies. In contrast, during the

---

84 Webb 1995, p. 314; see above in chapter VI, sub-section D.1.
85 Paltiel 1981, p. 144.
86 Webb 2000, p. 42.
87 Katz 1980, p. 101.
88 Farrell/ Webb 2000, p. 118; although Smith (2005, pp. 131-134) finds that U.S. state parties are stronger due to public funding (in some states).
89 Andeweg 1999, p. 120.

classic period of consociationalism in Austria, political patronage was an important tool for the political mobilisation of the main political camps (*Lager*), the SPÖ slightly more so than the ÖVP. However, in both parties employees have become more important while the involvement of volunteers has decreased.[90] Despite generous public subsidies membership fees form a substantial share of party revenue in Sweden, Austria and Germany. Thus in these countries it may be necessary for parties to pay more attention to their members than an electoral-professional party with strong headquarters would need to do. This will have a substantial impact on party organisations.

Germany is the only country in Europe that (partially) provides public funding in the form of matching-funds. Furthermore, additional tax benefits for donors are available. Both rules should induce parties to care for their grass-roots in order to generate revenue from membership dues and small donations. Local party organisations, which are responsible for personal contacts to party members and potential donors, have not changed much in decades. There are ups and downs in activity and the number of activists between election and non-election times. However, the federal level of German parties is very strong.[91] The major parties have tinkered with direct mail since 1993 (SPD) respectively 1995 (CDU).[92] To a smaller degree this is also true for their larger regional organisations (state parties, *Landesverbände*), which have permanent offices as well as some full-time staff.[93] In recent years all parties have reduced their staff.

However, German parties are more active in recruiting new members than are their Austrian counterparts, which unlike the German parties receive public funds as flat grants.[94] As a consequence additional fund-raising is considered to be unimportant in Austria. Ever since public subsidies became available this kind of activity has decreased. Since 1975 even party organisations at the sub-national level (*Länder*) receive an amazing amount of public funding. Aided by this support the parties are able to sustain organisations in each municipality.[95] A lack of volunteers has brought about a shift towards professionalism even at the lower level, which has led to an increase in party staff and external services.

Also in Sweden state aid is available to parties at the regional and the local level. Each level operates relatively independently of the other levels. "Grants to local associations on the basis of votes or membership ... may even enhance labour intensity."[96] As membership declines, centralisation of the parties might be expected. But there was also "increasing organisational activity at the local level, with local organisations developing in number and activity during the period studied."[97] State aid completely

---

90 Luther 1999, pp. 54, 71; Smith 2005, pp. 150/151.
91 Nassmacher 2001c, p. 96; Smith 2005, pp. 137, 172.
92 Rieken 2002, pp. 98-102; Römmele 1999, pp. 304-315; Smith 2005, pp. 191/192.
93 Smith 2005, pp. 138, 183. Such efforts are less professional than in the U.S. and Canada. (ibid., p. 192).
94 Smith 2005, pp. 222/223.
95 Müller 1994, p. 60.
96 Strom 1990, p. 579.
97 Pierre/ Widfeldt, p. 345; cf. ibid, p. 349 and Gidlund/ Koole 2001, p. 124.

changed the framework of party activity. Because subsidies are distributed according to votes received, parties focus on election results. But as they depend on membership dues and lottery income as well, they have to bind members to the party by organising attractive events and thus vitalise local parties.

The size of routine spending by the parties in Sweden, Austria and the Netherlands is a good indicator for organisational strength. In Austria and Sweden such expenses are much higher than the costs of campaigning. For Austria, Sickinger estimates that, on average, total campaign costs (1991-1994, for all levels) ranged from a sixth (15-16 percent for SPÖ and ÖVP) to a fifth (20-22 percent for the Green party and the FPÖ) of the entire budget of a party. Average expenses on staff in all Austrian parties have been estimated at 25 percent.[98] In Sweden percentages of routine expenses differ between parties. However, "it is safe to conclude that annual routine spending is far more important than extra campaign expenses. But so-called routine activities are almost completely geared to campaigning in the period before the elections, and the importance of 'permanent campaigns' grows, ... All political parties (from sub-national to national level) set aside a lot of money from the public subsidies during non-election years."[99] Salaries form a large part of total expenses.

"Even if the amount for routine spending by Dutch parties is relatively low, the campaign expenditures are even more modest, stressing the importance of Dutch parties as inter-election organisations. Adjusted for inflation the campaign expenditures of the four major parties even decreased during the 1980s. In the 1990s budgets increased somewhat, but they are still modest."[100] Long ago Dutch parties contented themselves with a shortage of funds. Pursuing funds seems to be not a frequent activity on the various levels. Instead Dutch parties have turned to public money, although still on a modest scale.

In most European countries a process of organisational convergence among parties has been observed. For Scandinavian parties this owes "much to the new rules regarding state subventions,"[101] which "acted to fuel the process of organisational convergence"[102] and the progression of organisational development within all parties. However, a convergence of party structures is happening in the U.K. - as was pointed out above - and the Netherlands, as well, although public subsidies are modest. Therefore organisational development cannot be explained solely by particular details of the political finance regime. In Austria the decline of the farming industry and, as a consequence, the fading of former ÖVP strongholds have contributed to an organisational convergence of the major parties. State party organisations became more independent of the national party, and both levels became more independent of the rank and file.

---

98 Sickinger 1997, pp. 252, 257, 260.
99 Gidlund/ Koole 2001, pp. 114/ 115.
100 Gidlund/ Koole 2001, p. 114.
101 Mair 1994, p. 10, citing findings by Pierre and Widfeldt.
102 Pierre/ Widfeldt 1994, p. 338.

In the Netherlands, which offered no public funding directly to the parties until 1999, Koole has observed a "growing cross-party harmonisation of organisational structures". After a period of decentralisation, a re-centralisation took place in the 1990s, particularly in regard to nomination procedures. There is a "striking similarity in structure" between all major parties: a classic, three-level, membership party. Following the general decline in revenue, there has been a decrease in the number of branches, whereas party-affiliated organisations have grown due to public funding. Because there is hardly any paid staff at the sub-national levels, professionalisation may have taken place at the top level only, which, however, depends heavily on free expertise from (professional) party members. Permanent staffing is very modest even at the national level of Dutch parties.[103]

Different impacts of regulations come about in individual parties, as party officials have to use the instruments that financial regimes offer in order to seize or lose their opportunities. Concerning the parties' reaction to tax credits, there are striking parallels between U.S. Democrats and Canadian Liberals on the one hand, and U.S. Republicans and Canadian P.C. on the other. In the U.S., Republicans realised earlier than Democrats that building a party organisation was a major task. As a result, by the mid-1980s Republicans had created a more powerful organisation than the Democrats regarding budget and staff. "The RNC has developed multimillion-dollar programs to provide cash grants, professional staff, data processing services, and consulting services for organisational development, fund-raising, campaigning, media, and redistricting. Major investments of money and personnel have been made to assist state parties in voter list development and get-out-the-vote efforts."[104] This gave the RNC a sustained advantage over the Democrats. The Democrats, however, were the first to force democratisation.[105] Their focus was on more representativeness, openness and participation.[106] By mobilising voters the constituency level became better organised. In response the Republicans enlisted help from the national level. The national party organisation started to integrate state parties into national campaign strategies.[107]

The Liberal Party of Canada also concentrated its initial efforts on democratisation, when it advanced the representation of women in particular. Policy debate was another focus, policy conventions were held annually, but from 1972 onwards participation faded.[108] Financially the Liberals as "governing party" continued to rely on big donations. Their response to the reform legislation on political finance was decentralisation, which weakened the top level of the party. Like the Liberals provincial parties

---

103 Koole 1994b, pp. 279, 284-286, 288-291, 294; quotes on pp. 279, 284.
104 Bibby 1998, p. 41.
105 In four-year intervals the Democratic party launched regular waves of reform: after 1968, after 1972 and after 1976. In 1980 the 'Committee on Party Renewal' suggested procedural and organisational reforms (Harmel/ Janda 1982, p. 6). In 1984 a further re-arrangement took place. Eventually this entire process strengthened the national party authorities.
106 Herrnson 1998, p. 56.
107 Bibby 1998, p. 24.
108 Wearing 1981, pp. 162, 172.

of the Canadian P.C., especially those in power, relied heavily on their strong position and remained opposed to organisational innovation. Steps for reforms were introduced from the top level of the party. At the end of the 1980s the P.C. was the strongest party at the local level because some of the funds collected in the constituencies were returned to them.[109] Such organisational efforts may have secured Mulroney's victory in 1984. However, the fact that the organisation was strong once does not guarantee lasting success. When Mulroney lost the voters' favour the fight for political survival began right after the electoral disaster of 1993.

In a process of realignment and renewal of political conservatism the Reform Party recruited dues-paying members in western Canada first, which provided a modest but regular revenue. Since 2000, under its new name, the Canadian Alliance gathered dissident provincial conservatives in provinces where the P.C. had been very strong regionally during the 1980s.[110] Findings on intra-party activity point out that the Canadian Alliance looked very much like a European-style party,[111] when it finally merged with the remains of the P.C. to form the Conservative Party of Canada (CPC) and in 2006 took over federally as a minority government.[112]

In sum, public funds invigorate party organisations, and shape them by the procedure funds are distributed within the party and its penumbra. It is of major importance for party organisations how public funds are provided and collected. This applies especially to where they go. If public funding is channelled to national headquarters only, this does not support the links of local parties to members and supporters. Headquarters may communicate with individual members, activists and other supporters separately via the media or direct mail. As long as different sub-units, which include levels, factions, caucuses, cliques and groups, of a specific party can independently use resources (including money) for their own political purposes, a certain level of intra-party competition seems to be secured. However, sometimes individual parties counteract this set-up. In Sweden there are different arrangements within the various parties. Whereas each level of the Social Democrats and the Centre Party disposes of its own income, the bourgeois parties demand bottom-up transfers to prevent a loss of seats in the national parliament.

Intra-party top-down distribution is often combined with strategic considerations of the party leadership, which local parties have to accept, for example, central intervention in the fight for unsafe seats. Only in parties where the decentralisation of financial resources works there is a safeguard to prevent bureaucratisation or oligarchic structures. In sum, the hypothesis that public money will always strengthen the top level of a party[113] has to be modified.

---

109 Nassmacher/ Suckow 1992, pp. 143, 149.
110 see Nassmacher/ Suckow 1992, p. 149.
111 Clarke et al. 2000, pp. 84–85.
112 Amr 2000, pp. 19-21, 33-34 and Nassmacher, H. 2005, pp.10-11, 19-21.
113 Schleth 1973, pp. 346-348, citing various contributions to German political discourse.

3. Party organisation and party penumbra

Until the 1950s the U.K. experienced "a high degree of de facto similarity in the internal distribution of power within the major parties."[114] Power resided with the parliamentary elites. Afterwards the Labour Party, due to intra-party conflicts and left-wing leaders, became more decentralised and dependent on affiliated organisations.[115] During the 1990s internal reform and professionalisation streamlined the party until finally the dominance of the parliamentary elite was restored. Like in other countries, where politicians shy away or try to avoid direct public funding to extra-party organisations, e.g. New Zealand and the Netherlands, caucuses tend to be better funded and thus gain an advantage in political power. In Germany the parliamentary complex becomes a serious competitor of the extra-parliamentary party, if governing parties, bound by coalition compromise, are forced to accept decisions that are not in line with the beliefs of party members, activists and supporters.

In the U.S. new regulations (especially the FECA and the BCRA) have brought about innumerable support organisations. Parties at all levels, or groups with party links, have set up committees for campaign support. Although there is often no close connection between committees belonging to the same party label,[116] the efficient deployment of party resources at all levels has enabled parties to influence the selection of candidates at the national level and thus to have a say in campaign issues. The general effect has been a growth of party activity (party building) at all levels.[117]

At the same time, other FECA rules (especially the ban on donations by corporations and unions) have resulted in the rise of competing organisations that seem to dominate public opinion and thus threaten the parties. In an effort to evade FECA rules, PACs have mushroomed. According to the Federal Election Commission (FEC), a "multi-candidate committee," usually called PAC, is an organisation that receives donations from at least 50 individuals and supports at least 5 candidates. Covering the area between parties and interest groups PACs have been set up by business enterprises and associations, trade unions and all sorts of other organisations.[118] PACs support and influence candidates and incumbents through campaign funds, other types of assistance, and issue advocacy. Their organisational structure is very similar to that of parties. They have a treasurer, publish newsletters and organise political seminars, lectures or receptions. PACs seem to have more influence on election campaign strategies now than they did in the past.

Many PACs can easily be linked to political parties, whereas some PACs form close alliances with parties.[119] In 1976, more than 95 percent of all trade union funds went to Democrats, while almost 60 percent of all corporate donations were given to Re-

---

114 Webb 2000, p. 202.
115 See Scarrow 1996, pp. 77–78, 166; for a different view see Katz 1980, pp. 94–95.
116 Shea/ Hildreth 1996, p. 166.
117 See Herrnson 1998, pp. 60/61.
118 Herrnson 1999, p. 104. - See chapter VII above, sub-section B1c (PACs).
119 Herrnson 1998, p. 61.

publican candidates. This distribution pattern has been stable for the 1990s as well: "The corporate sector and trade associations have a closer affiliation to the Republicans than to the Democrats, while 96 (1994) respectively 94 (1996) percent of the donations by labour PACs went to the Democrats."[120] Both Democrats and Republicans seem to have adapted to the PAC phenomenon.[121] Parties try to encourage PACs to give money to candidates, especially those in close races. To that end, parties will offer PACs information about the closeness of a race, the general issue positions of their candidates and opportunities for backing a potential winner.[122] This has been very successful.[123] Thus PACs may be considered as run-up organisations of parties that use a modern approach to raise support and funds for issues and candidates. They are linked to parties, working and creating networks alongside the parties rather than destroying or weakening them.

Recent research reveals efforts to establish better links between congressional campaign committees and national party authorities. This initiative came from the Republican congressional side, which was seeking a majority and therefore asked for a united party message and funds for viable candidates.[124] The new "527" committees[125] have possibly given this process yet another spin and re-balanced the funding arrangements in favour of the Democratic party, the minority party of the time. Hitherto Canadian parties have not had to compete with powerful organisations such as PACs, which are still effectively held in check by the Canada Elections Act.[126]

In Austria, as well as in the Netherlands, public funding initially was provided for party-affiliated organisations, the so-called political foundations or political academies that, for example, offer training courses for party activists. In the Netherlands public funding was given only for certain activities. As a consequence the foundations are mainly youth organisations, and training or research institutes.[127] In Germany political foundations receive public money as well, but only a small part of it is used for purposes of party competition, e.g. the training of party workers.[128] Only in Austria the linkage to parties is much closer.

The overall result of this evaluation is that institutions matter. However, it is the actors who make organisations change. There is strong evidence that parties in opposition or after suffering defeat in an election are more active and creative at employing opportunities than a governing party is. Once again the bottom-line is that an international comparison is worthwhile, because it provides knowledge about regulatory impacts that legislators have to pay attention to in order to avoid unintended consequences

---

120 Herrnson 1999, p. 108.
121 Bibby 1987, p. 216.
122 Sorauf 1998, p. 229.
123 Kolodny/ Dwyre 1998, p. 287.
124 Kolodny/ Dwyre 1998, pp. 275-279, 291.
125 See above in chapter VII, sub-section B1c5 (stealth PACs).
126 Even more so since a „third party advertising" clause of the CEA is in place since 2004.
127 Gidlund/ Koole 2001, pp. 116, 120.
128 See above in chapter VIII, sub-section C 4 (party penumbra).

while offering opportunities to their party activists. Parties in government (mostly in co-operation with major parties of the opposition) have often failed to act well and timely on issues of political finance regulation. Such experience notwithstanding some conclusions have emerged from our analysis of funding impacts on party organisation.

C) Summary of findings for party organisation

Scholars have learned, and our effort confirms their view, to see parties as rather complex organisations with a multitude of more or less independent nuclei, including a wealth of loosely affiliated organisations, for which a patchwork structure is the appropriate model. A new term calls such organisations "network parties."[129] Many actors in various regions and on different levels have manifold resources (personnel, material and financial endowment) at their disposal. Party politicians and party activists use this network depending on their personal motives or organisational constraints. The political finance regime may provide monetary backing for different levels and activities, which can secure day-to-day activities. However, as soon as incentives to collect public subsidies exist (e.g. based on votes in regional and local elections, the number of members or matching funds tied to small contributions or membership dues) the sub-organisations become vulnerable and they must start activities for survival. Incentives for donors can have a similar impact. Bans and limits for donations helped to inflate the numbers and activities of associations (such as PACs). Sometimes such organisations compete with parties; sometimes they are more or less affiliated bodies. This development must be seen in connection with more professional approaches in the field of political fund-raising.

In the U.S. the patchwork structure of both major parties has led to competition among the fundraisers of candidates, party organisations at all levels and parliamentary branches (DCCC, DSCC, NRCC, NRSC). Motivating or de-motivating effects on activities performed by all these actors including those at the grass-roots cannot be foreseen. Moreover, conflicts within parties, among parties and (affiliated) associations as well as parties and constituency candidates are not only related to policies, but also to resources of power, which include available funds. Strong incentives fostering grass-roots efforts in party fundraising can be a counterweight against dominance by the top level of each and every party.

Wherever this strategy has been implemented in practice it does not show the dramatic effects that its advocates may have expected. After the reform legislation in the 1970s on the federal level and in some states impacts of such incentives have been studied in the U.S. Adamany concluded that only a few citizens participate for ideological reasons.[130] This is also true for people who would be able to support political

---

129 Heidar/ Saglie 2003, p. 235.
130 Adamany 1976.

competition because they are affluent. Studies focussed on specific instruments (tax check-off, tax add-on, matching grants, bans and limits) that were used to encourage more financial participation by citizens. The states were seen as laboratories for reform efforts.[131] In addition to investigations by Jones and Alexander, a German research group targeted specific instruments of political finance regimes in North America with emphasis on potential for cross-national transfer.[132] Intensifying participation by soliciting donations is hard work, even if there are public incentives for the donor and/or the fundraiser. Success may depend on political tradition and culture, as the case of the Netherlandsi ndicates.

Other institutional instruments seem to be more effective in binding party leaders to their grass-roots. Party by-laws, which assign a percentage of the funds raised to the disposal of organisational levels and, at the same time, oblige them to transfers are important organisational constraints. The general assumption that centralisation of power at the top cannot be avoided has to be regarded with care. Institutional structures of the political system (be they federal or centralised, parliamentary or presidential) have to be taken into account.[133] Furthermore the electoral system is a major device for centralisation or decentralisation of intra-party power. While in plurality (first-past-the-post) electoral systems the top level of parties concentrate their campaign efforts on marginal seats, in proportional systems the lower level is needed to win although it possesses some leeway. Last but not least, some party families, especially the left-of-centre (Socialist) parties, have shown resistance to top-down management.[134]

What makes sub-national levels of a party funnel their message to the top leadership successfully, is still an open question. Parties must select candidates for all levels of the political system. This means that enough suitable individuals have to be available. The aptitude test for such persons has to start with face-to-face communication, preferably in local party chapters, because candidates not only need the capability to use media for sending their message. If candidates are untried in personal contacts there is no reliable basis for their suitability. Parties must offer enough specific incentives to attract participation, especially at the sub-national levels. Thus they must recruit members and activists who in turn have the privilege of selecting candidates from the available pool of human resources. Recent studies point out that the loss of members has not been distributed equally over the regions and sub-units of all parties.[135] This brings in a reference to the financial resources, which are elaborated in this study. With enough money at the local level, parties are able to initiate highly distinguished forums for the discussion of specific issues that do not overstrain the commitment of individ-

---

131 Fling 1979, pp. 245, 247.
132 Nassmacher 1992a, passim.
133 Federalism may be reinforced by separate financial regimes on the regional (state/ province) level as in the U.S., Canada, Australia and Austria.
134 Gibson/ Römmele 2001, p. 37.
135 Aylott 2003, p. 376 for Sweden's Socialdemocraterna; Niedermayer 2002 for parties in Germany.

ual participants and give parties the opportunity for an adequate performance within the event-culture. Co-ordination of such activities will become complex, including the policy as well as the politics aspect, and must start at the local level organised by professional staff. Obviously the problem of party bureaucratisation has to be considered. Hitherto clientelistic structure, which integrated members by means of personal benefits (jobs, housing), is questioned everywhere. The event-centred approach offers the only way to combine recruiting and aggregating functions and to ensure the survival of local parties, which are able to perform both.

A convergence of parties may take place in the long run. Starting from different points of reference individual parties change to meet the competitive challenges (especially mass-communication under financial strain and unreliable sources of revenue). Additional power for one sector (the top level) will trigger a reaction from others, which use their funds and ideas in order to increase their own power. Thusfar Harmel et al. are correct in stating that internal decision-making is extremely important for change in general,[136] not only for the change of leaders. In order to perform their functions parties may move incrementally and gradually into the same direction. However, the impact of political cultures and institutional settings, including different political finance regimes, can be observed. Until now parties differ because of historical and institutional aspects. Candidate-orientation is dominant in the U.S. due to the presidential system and the FPTP electoral system. Both impacts are enforced by peculiarities of funding regulations. In parliamentary systems, party-orientation is stronger, although in combination with a first-past-the-post electoral system and specific finance legislation a development towards candidate-orientation can be observed. However, in P.R. systems the voters' option to give preference votes to candidates does not stimulate candidate-orientation sufficiently.

Traditional sources of political revenue like membership dues and small donations are expected to provide linkage between parties, candidates and their supporters at the grass-roots. The most important evidence on both sources of income is that public subsidies have not destroyed such linkage acrosss the board. Available data suggest that the present situation is more mixed than a simple cause-effect relationship suggests. In general a shift of party activity towards professional operation at the centre and in the field can be observed. As a consequence, the distribution of power within party organisations will continue to shift towards all those elements that wield the pursestrings, especially those which are able to raise additional funds (be it from individual supporters, corporate/ institutional donors, public funds, corrupt exchanges or by assessment of political office-holders). Such results offer a more realistic view of intraparty power than those advanced in many studies of party organisation, which tend to neglect the funding aspects. Thus our perception of money as a political resource may shed some new light on party analysis in general.

---

136 Harmel et al. 1995, p. 1; see also Panebianco 1988, pp. 239/240.

CHAPTER ELEVEN

Money as a Political Resource (Conclusion)

In concluding our study, we will sum up the major findings and consider ways to improve political analysis. Because the variety of political life that is covered by the term "party" seems so diverse, political scientists have tried to reduce complexity by describing types. Four types represent the universe of political parties operating in democracies: Neumann's mass party, Duverger's cadre party, Kirchheimer's catch-all party and – most recently – the "cartel party" created by Katz and Mair. We will complete our analysis by answering the question:

- What do the findings presented in this study mean for the current discourse *on party types* and the emergence of new ones in the future?

However, before we turn to this question that re-connects the sub-fields of party analysis and political finance, we will sum up the most important findings of this study.

A)   Summary of major findings

This summary of results, which emerged from this analysis, will follow the pattern that was applied to the presentation of research questions: Findings pertaining to spending are summed up first, revenue items come second and finally impacts are presented.

1.   Spending/ expenses [1]

The unifying concept of political party covers many facets of political competition. Although it is useful in identifying the manifold orbit of political competitors, the complete costs of political competition cannot be given in full or in detail for any one party or democracy. The categories of cost accounting (cost objects, cost centres, types of cost) facilitate the presentation of various dimensions of political expenses. The three systematic approaches to measuring the costs of democracy help aggregate total spending on party politics in a cross-national comparison. In order to gather such information, expenses at all the cost centres involved (party organisations with national headquarters and local chapters as well as all sorts of candidates) must be added up. Although most of these are common to all democracies, detailed features are quite specific and data is rather patchy. The approach by cost centres is more promising than

---

1   This sub-section sums up the findings of chapters II to V.

any attempt to aggregate the types of cost (e.g. for staff, offices, communication, publicity) or the cost objects, especially the variety of election campaigns and different patterns of organisational maintenance. However, all three approaches can help assess details and pursue comparative research of levels, trends and causes of political spending.

For party competition in the mid-20th century Heard, Heidenheimer and Penniman observed a considerable spread of per capita spending totals, which was still existent by 2000. Although data quality and reliability may be subject to doubt, high level spenders and low cost democracies can be identified as well as countries that fall in-between the two extremes. Among the 18 democracies, for which the costs of political competition can be established, five stand out as excessive spenders (Austria, Israel, Italy, Japan and Mexico). No more than four display a moderate level of party expenses (Australia, the U.K., Denmark, the Netherlands). A total of nine democracies operate at an intermediate level of political spending (Canada, France, Germany, Ireland, Poland, Spain, Sweden, Switzerland and the U.S.). In about five decades most countries have not changed much in their level of political spending.

For the level of political spending some features of the polity have a specific impact. The more a country can afford economically, the less likely it is to spend much on its democracy. Increasing experience in popular government (indicated by an earlier wave of democratisation) reduces the level of political spending, which also decreases as the size of the electorate increases, although the intensity of this impact differs. Party competition is less expensive in individualistic Anglo-Saxon style democracies than it is in the multiparty coalition governments of continental Western Europe and the clientelistic non-western democracies.

The impressive spread of spending levels noted in all comparative analyses is mainly caused by the impacts of public policy and the absence thereof. A practice of corrupt exchanges and generous public subsidies (as relevant sources of an – unlimited – supply of political funds) increase the level of political spending. Variables related to politics rarely apply to all countries in the sample. Nevertheless the most influential can be identified: Neither campaign-centred and organisation-oriented parties, nor ideological warfare, nor different forms and levels of intra-party competition increase or decrease spending on party politics. However, one-party dominance of political contests during more than two decades inflates the costs of democracy well beyond those in more competitive situations.

The evidence that is available at present supports some statements on spending trends. Our knowledge of political spending is still limited to a few countries, but it has improved during recent decades. More and better data may have caused increased spending totals as time went by. Growth of electorates and inflationary trends have made many observers believe that a cost explosion has occurred.[2] CPI-adjusted per capita data show a less dramatic picture – all the more so, if more comprehensive data are

---

2   Krouwel 1999, pp. 86/87 referring to Katz/ Mair 1992, tables E.6.

taken into account. Paid TV advertising, which is considered the principle villain far beyond the Anglo-Saxon orbit, is a symptom of political change rather than the unavoidable cause for financial needs. Neither is new campaign technology, which is applied – wherever the funds to pay for it are at hand, nor is the growing party apparatus staffed with highly skilled professionals and full-time staff. Into both areas competing parties sink a lot of money but this happens because parties can afford to do so, due to citizens' generosity, public subsidies or corrupt exchanges.

This supply-side theory of expenditure can be demonstrated in the U.S., the U.K., Canada, Germany, Japan and Austria. Per capita expenses for some decades reveal that current levels of political spending in all these countries fall short of earlier peaks, which is quite in line with earlier observations made by Pollock, Overacker and Heard.[3] If GDP deflated expenses for U.S. politics are compared for a period of some 90 years, they peak in 1912 and 1940. Following a trough between 1944 and 1964 political spending shows a lower and declining level since 1968. Similar trends can be demonstrated for four other countries. Political spending in Canada peaked in 1984, in Germany and Japan in 1983, in Austria in 1986 and in the U.K. in 1997. Current levels fall short of those peaks, in most cases by far. Obviously it is not spending needs but revenue possibilities that determine the current "costs of democracy."

2. Revenue/ income [4]

Among the three major sources of party revenue grass-roots funding is discussed first. Experience from countries as diverse as Britain, Germany, the Netherlands, Sweden and the U.S. supports the conclusion that a considerable amount of grass-roots revenue is available for political purposes. On average, individual donations in small amounts provide about half of the total revenue raised by federal parties in the U.S. and Canada. Only a few parties in Europe (most of them in the Netherlands and Switzerland) can collect a comparable share from signed-up party members. Even the traditional left-of-centre mass-membership parties (Social Democrats, Socialists, Post-Communists) collect on average less than a quarter of their funds from grass-roots income.

Popular financing can be an important source of political revenue but it is not a constant and reliable one. Just like voters, individual contributors (party members and small donors) are a volatile sort of citizens. Although grass-roots funding will never suffice in covering all the costs of politics, it can supply large amounts if parties and candidates put in some organisational effort. There is no general approach that will produce the best result under all circumstances. Various alleys have been explored successfully: recruiting party members, direct mail drives, neighbourhood solicitation, lotteries, and social events at the local level. Some sort of revenue sharing between different tiers of the same party will keep local chapters happy. A quota system may provide local support for party headquarters. A public benefit programme (preferably

---

3   Pollock 1926; Overacker 1932; Heard 1960.
4   This sub-section sums up the findings of chapters VI to VIII.

matching funds or tax credits rather than tax deductions) can ensure that political fundraising will not fall victim to competing solicitation (by NGOs or charities) and stimulate political funding that does not depend on flat grant (public) subsidies or plutocratic sources.

The analysis of plutocratic funding leads to a variety of important insights. First, the free flow of money into politics is both, a hazard and a necessity of democratic politics. The financial support of policies, politicians and parties is an expression of economic and political freedom, not necessarily the consequence of influence peddling or corrupt exchanges. However, as the latter may happen, the flow of funds into politics should be free, but transparent. Only then can the democratic sovereign, the voter, make informed choices. Second, among the various categories of interested money, contributions from personal wealth (i.e. by wealthy individuals) are the least dangerous if they are made transparent. Although buying honours and offices (both an Anglo-Saxon tradition in fundraising) has not ceased, it is in decline. If a candidate for public office pays for his or her campaign from personal wealth, the voters can decide whether they want to elect that person or not.

Money from the business community ("corporate donations" in most democracies) is no longer a real danger for democratic politics. Both alleys of raising such funds (direct contributions as well as institutional fundraising) have declined; mostly because their proceeds have been substituted by public subsidies. At the same time, public disincentives to discourage the flow of interested money into political competition (disclosure of large donations rather than limits or bans) have strengthened or preceded this trend.

However, there are still prevalent cases of political graft (corrupt exchanges). One of them is the abuse of public resources for partisan purposes, another the extortion of private business (toll-gating or kickbacks). The flow of such funds is always clandestine. Investigative journalism that occasionally uncovers scandals can serve to interrupt such felonies for a while, but not end it for sure. Systematic assessments of political officeholders (i.e. macing) is a kind of graft that will be much harder to uproot, as parties neither want to pass laws against "party taxes" nor to implement them if such laws have eventually made it into the statute book.

The most recent source of political funding are public subsidies. They are neither a mere stop-gap nor a problem-solving source of political revenue in general. As with any other kind of funding, specific problems accompany them (for example rules for access and distribution). However, in combination with other sources of revenue, as well as rules to enforce its legitimacy (especially the matching principle), state aid is a means of political funding that no modern democracy should forgo.

Considering the variety of public funding programmes that are available, party organisations rather than party caucuses or party candidates, should be the recipient of public support. Moreover no further strings ought to be attached except for a specified responsibility for transparency. In general indirect funding (i.e. subsidies-in-kind and tax benefits) are to be preferred over cash aid. If subsidies in cash have to be allocated, access needs to be fair (preferably with a low threshold defined in terms of overall votes polled) and distribution should be unequal, mostly according to party size; preferably with a certain base amount given to all recipient parties.

The significance of public subsidies can be judged from two points of view: that of the party treasurer and that of the average taxpayer. From both angles, the level of subsidisation is almost impossible to calculate and to generalise. Taxpayers in Israel, Norway, Ireland, Austria, Japan, Sweden, Germany, France and Mexico provide the highest amounts towards party activity. Taxpayers in Anglo-Saxon countries (plus Denmark and the Netherlands) are much less generous. Many party headquarters cover between 40 and 60 percent of their annual budget via public grants. In Germany and Spain the share of national party revenue is higher, in Canada, Denmark, Japan and the Netherlands it is considerably lower.

3. Impacts of political funding [5]

Following a tradition in party research the impacts of political funding are discussed separately for party systems and party organisation. The impacts on *party competition* start out with individual candidates and extend to the development of party systems. If money is a means to success in political competition, then the candidate (or party) who is able to spend the most should be the winner; at least most of the time. However, if enough data is available, this simple hypothesis does not stand the test of reality. Likewise a skewed distribution of disposible funds between the major parties in Britain and Germany and between two minor parties in Germany has not determined their ups and downs in voter support.

The more sophisticated theory that public subsidies lead to an ossification of the party system can also be refuted. New parties have successfully entered party competition in many democracies. Established parties have lost and gained electoral support with and without state aid. An arrested distribution of power between parties of government and parties of opposition has occurred solely in Japan, but not in Austria, France, Germany, Israel, Italy, Mexico, Spain or Sweden, which (due to a high level and/or long duration of public subsidies) were the likeliest candidates for such suspicion.

Finally, some impacts of political spending on *party organisation* can be reported. Traditional sources of political revenue like membership dues and small donations are expected to provide linkage between parties, candidates and their supporters at the grass-roots. The most important evidence on both sources of income is that public subsidies have not destroyed this link across the board. Available data suggest that the present situation is more mixed than a simple cause-effect relationship maintains. In general a shift of party activity towards a more professional operation at the centre and in the field can be observed. As a consequence, the distribution of power within party organisations will continue to shift towards all those elements that wield the purse-strings, especially those which are able to raise additional funds; be it from individual

---

5   This sub-section sums up the findings of chapters IX and X.

supporters, institutional/ corporate donors, public funds, corrupt exchanges or by assessment of political office-holders.

Such insights can be utilised best when they are confronted with the current analysis of political parties. A brief look at the state of party research is expected to be an additional stepping stone for the understanding of party politics and party development.

B) Consequences for the debate on party type(s)

In the early 1950s Duverger identified two types of democratic parties: *cadre parties* and *mass parties*.[6] This typology was rooted in a century of political development. Both types of party had a specific origin (inside vs. outside parliament), a specific power centre (parliamentary caucus vs. party bureaucracy) and a specific source of funds (campaign-centred donations from interested money vs. regular dues from a mass membership). Looking at both types of parties in the 1960s, Kirchheimer observed that the marked differences between them were fading. Cadre parties pursued more sustainable forms of organisation, whereas mass parties opened up towards the rest of society (beyond their original working class or catholic clientele) and addressed other organised interests. Parties that had originated from either of the old-fashioned types tended to become *catch-all parties*.[7]

1. Catch-all parties

Following an even more traditional line of thinking, which dates back to Ostrogorski, parties in North America (more precisely in the U.S.) are contrasted with European parties.[8] Patronage parties, customarily based on (local or regional) machine politics, are confronted with programmatic organisations. Party machines in New York, Boston and Chicago supported the impression that in North America everything was still different from western Europe; although the joint forces of political reform (especially nomination primaries), welfare programmes (especially the New Deal) and new media (especially television newscasts and talk-shows) had sucked away the lifeblood of the big city machines. The downfall of Richard Daley Sr., who was the last surviving dinosaur of the party bosses, closed the decade that had begun with John F. Kennedy's successful bid for the presidency against fierce opposition of the Democratic party establishment. U.S. parties were changing rapidly. As a consequence the hypothesis that "the party is over"[9] was widely accepted among scholars for quite a while.

---

6 Duverger 1967, pp. 63-67.
7 Kirchheimer 1966, pp. 177-200.
8 Ostrogorski 1902, vol. II, pp. 47-52, 84; for details see Epstein 1980, pp. 104-111.
9 Broder 1972; see also Crotty 1985, Meisel 1985; Wattenberg 1990.

In the late 1950s European parties began to change massively. The well-established tradition of cadre parties and mass parties gave way to Kirchheimer's new type of catch-all party.[10] Catch-all parties are characterised by a reduction of ideological baggage, a loose connection with the electorate, the mobilisation of voters on policy preferences and a drift towards the centre as well as the personalising of electoral appeal thereby strengthening the top leaders and downgrading the individual member.[11]

Since the 1970s party development has continued and scholars have become more creative in generalising their observations. Additional types of parties have sprung up throughout the political science literature. For many years after Kirchheimer's candid observation, the development of all parties was expected to pursue the same direction, i.e. a trend towards catch-all parties (*Volksparteien*).[12] In the late 1990s Krouwel observed that "not one of the eighty-three parties ... [that he has studied in depth] ... completely fulfils all the criteria of the catch-all party model. ... Nevertheless, some parties ... come relatively close."[13]

For the past two decades other scholars have advanced a unified view regarding the future of political parties: a convergence of party structure, based on the campaign practice of parties in elections. However, differences between U.S. parties as campaign-oriented organisations and European parties, classified as modern mass parties or modern cadre parties are stressed time and again as well. The former mass parties of Europe still have large numbers of members, but they have tended to develop into the direction of "modern cadre parties" that Koole characterises by a small membership and a democratic organisation.[14] The dominance of professional leaders is coupled with a "high degree of accountability to the lower strata in the party."[15] In the meantime empirical findings indicate that North American parties, not least due to financial regimes, are back in the political arena as stratarchical organisations. They perform functions like European parties; in particular they assist their candidates by employing consultants, staging registration campaigns and get-out-the-vote drives.[16] At the same time their European counterparts have become more patronage-oriented and less ideological than they had been before. Moreover they have started to regard their top candidates as a major resource in campaigning. Everywhere incumbents are using their support staff (provided to perform parliamentary duties) to strengthen their party organisation or to carry out functions, which party organisations did perform in the past.[17]

---

10 Kirchheimer 1966, pp. 188, 190, 192/193.
11 Krouwel 1999, pp. 36, 47, 59; Krouwel 2003, pp. 26-34.
12 Among the individual scholars studying this subject Mintzel (1978, pp. 316-322) prefers the term "major parties" (*Grossparteien*).
13 Krouwel 1999, p. 238.
14 Katz/ Mair 1995, p. 18; Koole 1994b, p. 279.
15 Koole 1994b, pp. 298-299.
16 Kolodny/ Dulio 2003, p. 730; Nassmacher, H. 1992, pp. 116/117 and Nassmacher, H. 2004b, p. 99.
17 Monroe (2001, pp. 65-67, 84, 96) argues that the permanent staff of office-holders has effectively replaced the party machines of a bygone era.

The process of assimilation between former cadre parties and former mass parties is best illustrated by the current funding situation of the two major parties in Germany (CDU and SPD). In 1970 both parties still were miles apart with respect to their share of membership funding (22 and 40 percent). In 2006 both parties raised almost the same share of their revenue (27 to 29 percent) from signed-up members. The former mass party (SPD) has lost its ability to keep the level of dues paid at equal pace with the rising income of its members. The former cadre party (CDU) has recruited more members and makes them pay an adequate level of dues.[18]

Kirchheimer's observation of a trend towards "catch-all parties" should be connected to the fact that dependence on specific funds was typical for each of the two traditional party types. The end of ideology, i.e. the process of moderation that has blurred the traditional ideological confrontation of market economy and socialism, has detached donors as well as members from the political battlefield, at least emotionally. Many parties of either type felt the need for additional funds and turned to the public purse to provide them.[19] This new kind of funding has smoothly replaced other sources and has led to a convergence of party revenue. In turn public subsidies have completed the alienation of catch-all parties to their original clienteles in civil society. Kirchheimer's analysis was too early to note or foresee that catch-all parties developed their own source of funding. Public subsidies granted freely by the parties' own representatives in parliament, became a major source of party income in many democracies since the 1970s. However, this does not mean that the members of different party families in financial terms already look like each other. But there are doubts, whether party families still cause a major difference with respect to funding.[20] Koole considers the age of the individual party to be more important.[21] The evidence, which has been presented in this study, confirms this assumption, as younger and newer parties depend much more on public subsidies than do their older competitors.[22]

The catch-all party is a scintillating but still functional type of party. As "the instruments of democratic government"[23] modern political parties combine features from all five types, which preceded them, the cadre party, the mass party, the patronage party,

---

18 See above in chapter X, sub-section A1 (grass-roots linkage).
19 It should not go unnoticed that major political decisions (in Sweden 1965 and in Germany 1967) were taken shortly after Kirchheimer (1966) had published his landmark study, which first appeared in the leading German political science journal (*PVS*) in 1965.
    Mendilow (1992, p. 105) presumes that "Austria and Germany had introduced PPF [= public party funding] several years before Kirchheimer published" the catch-all party hypothesis. This statement refers to the years 1959 and 1963 (ibid., p. 93), which saw minor grants to parties in Germany and parliamentary caucuses in Austria. Viewed from the 1990s these grants may look like the inception of public funding, which was converted to massive support on a statutory basis not before 1967 in Germany and 1975 in Austria.
20 Krouwel 1999, pp. 45/46, 71, 76, 78.
21 Koole 1996, pp. 519-521.
22 See above in chapter VIII, sub-section E 1 (party revenue).
23 Hermens 1958, p. 162.

the brokerage party[24] and the programmatic party. The catch-all party preserves a belief system that helps to anchor party policies in the cleavages of society. It determines policies by brokering the interests of lobby groups, and hands out patronage jobs and favourable deals to core supporters, which are not necessarily party members. It recruits signed-up members (although the party does not rely entirely on their dues for funding) and, finally it counts on elite activism for current operations as well as (local) campaigning. The catch-all party offers specific privileges to those who join and/or support it:

- participation in the political process for the new (social/ political) elite of people who can dispose of (free) time,
- membership rights to meet with leading politicians and to select party candidates for public office,
- ideology-based planks in campaign manifestos, "contracts with the people/ country" or labels of identification (e.g. the "small guy" or the "reborn Christian"),
- access to a vast range of government jobs or government contracts wherever and whenever the party holds or shares power.

As an adequate party type should do, the term "catch-all party" addresses the relationship between party leaders and party supporters. Kirchheimer observes the decomposition of the exclusive linkage between a party and specific groups.[25] In principle the party has opened up for all social groups, although it may not necessarily reach all of them in equal proportion. Party leaders become more important than party members for the day-to-day communication with voters and get-out-the-vote drives. As Katz and Mair have argued, the "party competes for access to non-party channels of communication."[26] Thus the cadre party and the mass party, the brokerage party and the patronage party have converged without completely shedding their specific roots. It is not at all surprising that the end of the "special relationship" (between a party and its core supporters) has endangered, sometimes even terminated, financial contributions by the traditional clientele, be they membership subscriptions, institutional contributions, corporate or other periodical donations.

Whereas Kirchheimer does not even mention the funding aspect of party activity, recent authors overemphasise party financing. "The sources and uses of funds are among the key features distinguishing types of parties."[27] Katz and Mair identify a (new) party type by a term that is derived from the access to public funding: "The state guarantees the provision of parties much as it guarantees the provision of hospitals and schools."[28] Access to public funding has solved the catch-all party's funding problem,

---

[24] Epstein 1980, p. 357; Thorburn 1985b, p. 21.
[25] Kirchheimer 1966, pp. 186/187.
[26] Katz/ Mair 1995, p. 18.
[27] Katz 1996, p. 124. For Switzerland Ladner and Brändle (2001, p. 323) reject this assumption because parties do not receive public funding in that country.
[28] Katz 1996, p. 122.

but at the same time it imperils a continuing interest of the party leadership in the more traditional means of fund-raising.[29] Observing this process scholars have concluded that parties operate in a cartel-like manner.

2. Cartel parties

In the 1990s Katz und Mair identified a new type of party and named it the "cartel party." They emphasise that the "party in public office" has gained advantage over the (extra-parliamentary) "party on the ground." Observing negotiations on party funding from the public purse has led Katz and Mair to the hypothesis that in the future parties will converge to represent this new type.[30] The major essentials of the "cartel party" type are

- (first of all) party leaders have to secure financial privileges, as
- financial dependency on public subsidies is high,
- professional management is capital-intensive,
- access to votes uses state regulated channels of communication,
- competition is about managerial competence, not about ideology and issues.[31]

To safeguard privileges and to perform the new style of communication, the party-in-office and the central party headquarters become more important.

However, headquarters must not act cartel-like as Dettelbeck points out for Britain.[32] Some parties that depend on public funds have tried to revitalise their membership organisations.[33] Strangely enough the given name of this new party type refers to the behaviour of party leaders towards each other (despite the competitive mission of their organisation) rather than to a dimension of the internal operation of the party.

Another shortcoming occurred to one of the inventors rather early. That is, the type of cartel party does not explain all parties operating under similar conditions. As differences among party systems in some countries became obvious over time, Mair consequently subsumed the Greens (in various European countries), *Front National* (in France) and *Forza Italia* (in Italy) under the new category of anti-system-parties,[34] obviously in order to preserve the recently developed type of cartel party.

There is, however, one general observation to be applied to all such efforts. Each of the newly created party types overemphasises one aspect of modern party politics, most of them not entirely new but more important recently:

---

29 See above in chapter X, sub-section A 1 (revenue from membership dues/ local fundraising).
30 Katz/ Mair 1995, p. 18.
31 Katz 1996, p. 121.
32 Dettelbeck 2005, pp. 182/183.
33 Nassmacher, H. 2004b, p. 105 (for Austria and Sweden); Dettelbeck 2005, p. 184 (for Denmark).
34 Katz 1996, p. 132.

- the ambivalent behaviour of established parties, which cooperate and compete simultaneously.
- the enhanced role of professional activity (by pollsters and consultants) in the age of media-centred communication.
- the loosely coupled anarchy of party sub-units operating under a common label, which hides intra-party strife as it enables partisan competition.

The new type of cartel party assumes that the top level has become more important. While Janda's investigation (for 1950 to 1962) found two major modes of collecting and disbursing money: decentralised (19) versus centralised (15) parties,[35] currently there seems to be a general shift towards a centralised routine of soliciting political donations. Public funds, mostly given to the top level of a party, reinforce this direction.[36] The centralised party as a professionalised body has to stand its test during elections. "As politicians of all parties have become more similar sociologically (middle class) and politically (moderate), there may appear to be less point in electoral competition."[37] This fits in with Mendilow's observation that public subsidies have enabled "the large competitors to conduct campaigns geared to exchange width for depth of support." Funded from the public purse "catch-all parties ... perpetuate their non-ideological bid to maintain or to gain power."[38] In this situation three major differences prevail. Parties and politicians differ in the policies they pursue, the managerial skills they offer and the leadership they support.

Between campaigns a permanent communication with voters, supporters and members takes place via the media. Such observations result in a hierarchical model, called the electoral-professional party, as introduced by Panebianco. In this party type the central role of the professionals is combined with a personalised leadership, while vertical ties within the organisation are weak.[39] The major support to affirm this type of party is found in the party environment.

The debate on new types continues. There are tendencies to overemphasise the mass media in new models. For example, Jun observes a change from organisational logic to media logic, which makes it the major task of a political party to gain opinion leadership in the media. This implies professional communication management. Issues and personnel have to be chosen with regard to media logic, strategically managed by the party centre, while party members become less important. For such reasons Jun calls his new type "professionalised media communications party".[40]

Meanwhile a growing number of party types seem increasingly incapable of capturing diversity as well as common ground of party development. The question arises wheth-

---

35 Janda 1980, p. 113. - Details computed from ICPSR data (Janda 1979, pp. 189/190).
36 For Israel see Mendilow 1996, p. 334.
37 Katz 1996, p. 132.
38 Mendilow 2003, p. 118.
39 Panebianco 1988, p. 264.
40 Jun 2004.

er a new party type for the new century is emerging. Even Katz and Mair reject this assumption, although currently they see the cartel party type at "an early stage" of its development.[41] Some scholars advocate an increase in the number of party types.[42] Others propose a new type, the franchise party, in which a centralised organisation determines the product line and sets standards for production and labelling of policies and politics, while the local organisations perform according to their own style.[43] What about the communication between the sub-units and the centre? Are there only top-down channels of information? As analyses of the direct-mail approach have pointed out, this is not true and the same can be said for websites.[44] Does the party leadership communicate only with individual members, who are empowered to decision-making, and supporters, who are not, thus excluding all sub-units of the party? The franchise model describes the relationship between central (national, federal) organisation and its local field agencies as varying enormously even within the same organisation. "The local partners will be more attuned to local community perspectives, practices and market demands than those in a remote headquarters, an advantage in attracting support in a changing environment. Individual franchises can also test market product innovations and delivery of services, producing valuable ground-level information feedback of the centre."[45]

Such observations suggest that party still is a multi-tier type of political organisation, which combines central government roles with outreach on "the ground." This leads directly back to Kirchheimer's discovery of the bi-focussed nature of "cadre parties", operating in parliament and the constituencies. Nothing seems to have changed in this respect; parties operate centrally and locally. Their emphasis of weight to either kind of sub-units may change, but the bifurcated structure stays. Taking all this into account it occurs that the more recently created party types have not remarkably enriched the substance of party analysis. Much as the camel is a horse designed by a committee, the cartel party is a catch-all party re-labelled by two novelty seeking scholars.

What Katz and Mair discovered is not a new type of political parties but a new, more solid state of parties, which mediate between social movements and government actors. Parties that used to be voluntary associations of the civil society have become necessary institutions of the political system. There is no doubt that they are "the instruments of democratic government" (Hermens).[46] In becoming such institutions individual parties have shed some traditional characteristics, which did accompany their development from mass suffrage to majority rule (Kirchheimer).[47] Party activity has been fenced in by public law, which has turned them into public utilities (Epstein).[48]

---

41 Katz/ Mair 1995, p. 17; see also Katz/ Mair 1996, p. 532.
42 Gunther/ Diamond 2003, p. 171.
43 Carty 2004, p. 10.
44 Norris 2003, p. 43.
45 Carty 2004, pp. 10-12, quote on p. 11.
46 Hermens 1958, p. 162.
47 Kirchheimer 1966, pp. 178, 183-185, 191/192.
48 Epstein 1986, pp. 155-157.

Parties perform the civic duties of presenting candidates, offering policies and mobilising voters. As a consequence their financial needs have also become the subject of public policy (Paltiel).[49] Nowadays parties are partly funded by the taxpayer, whom they serve and whose avarice scares their treasurers (Linz).[50] Like Columbus, who never reached India but discovered America, Katz and Mair did not discover a new type of party. They just attached a catchy label to a process of changing emphasis in describing the fundamental role of political parties. They integrated various details that Hermens, Kirchheimer, Epstein, Paltiel and Linz had identified long ago.

---

49 Paltiel 1976, p. 109.
50 Linz 2003, p. 307.

Bibliography

Adamany, David W. (1972): *Campaign Finance in America*. North Scituate MA: Wadsworth-Duxbury,1972.

Adamany, David W. (1976): The Sources of Money. An Overview. In: *The Annals of the American Academy of Political and Social Science*, 425 (1976) May, pp. 17-32.

Adamany, David W. (1978): The Failure of Tax Incentives for Political Giving. In: *Tax Notes*, 3 July 1978, pp. 3-5.

Adams, Karl-Heinz (2005): *Parteienfinanzierung in Deutschland: Entwicklung der Einnahmestrukturen politischer Parteien oder eine Sittengeschichte über Parteien, Geld und Macht*. Marburg: Tectum, 2005.

Aguiar, Roberto (1994): The Cost of Election Campaigns in Brazil. In: Alexander, Herbert E./ Shiratori, Rei (eds.), 1994a, pp. 77-84.

Alemann, Ulrich von (ed.) (2005a): *Dimensionen politischer Korruption: Beiträge zum Stand der internationalen Forschung*. Wiesbaden: VS, 2005.

Alemann, Ulrich von (2005b): Politische Korruption: Ein Wegweiser zum Stand der Forschung. In: Alemann, Ulrich von (ed.), 2005a, pp. 13-49.

Alexander, Herbert E. (1961): *Tax Incentives for Political Contributions*. Princeton NJ: Citizens' Research Foundation, 1961.

Alexander, Herbert E. (1962): *Financing the 1960 Election*. Princeton, NJ: Citizens' Research Foundation,1962.

Alexander, Herbert E. (1963): *Responsibility in Party Finance*. Princeton NJ: Citizens' Research Foundation, 1963.

Alexander, Herbert E. (1966): *Financing the 1964 Election*. Princeton, NJ: Citizens' Research Foundation,1966.

Alexander, Herbert E. (1970): Links and Contrasts Among American Parties and Party Subsystems. In: Heidenheimer, Arnold J. (ed.), 1970a, pp. 73-106.

Alexander, Herbert E. (1971): *Financing the 1968 Election*. Lexington MA: D.C. Heath, 1971.

Alexander, Herbert E. (1972): *Money in Politics*. Washington DC: Public Affairs, 1972.

Alexander, Herbert E. (1976): *Financing the 1972 Election*. Lexington MA: D.C. Heath, 1976.

Alexander, Herbert E. (ed.) (1979a): *Political Finance*. Beverly Hills and London: Sage, 1979.

Alexander, Herbert E. (1979b): *Financing the 1976 Election*. Washington DC: Congressional Quarterly,1979.

Alexander, Herbert E. (1983): *Financing the 1980 Election*. Lexington MA: Lexington Books, 1983.

Alexander, Herbert E. (1984): *Financing Politics. Money, Elections, and Political Reform*. Washington DC: Congressional Quarterly, 3rd ed. 1984.

Alexander, Herbert E. (1987): *Financing the 1984 Election*. Lexington MA: Lexington Books, 1987.

Alexander, Herbert E. (ed.) (1989a): *Comparative Political Finance in the 1980s*. Cambridge, UK: Cambridge University, 1989.

Alexander, Herbert E. (1989b): Money and Politics. Rethinking a Conceptual Framework. In: Alexander, Herbert E. (ed.), 1989a, pp. 9-23.

Alexander, Herbert E. (1989c): American Presidential Elections Since Public Funding 1976-84. In: Alexander, Herbert E. (ed.), 1989a, pp. 95-123.

Alexander, Herbert E. (1992a): *Financing Politics. Money, Elections and Political Reform*. Washington DC: Congressional Quarterly. 4rd ed. 1992 (1st ed. 1976; 2nd ed. 1980; 3rd ed. 1984).

Alexander, Herbert E. (1992b): Khayyam Zev Paltiel and Theories of Public Financing. In: Gagnon, Alain G./ Tanguay, A. Brian (eds.), 1992, pp. 355-369.

Alexander, Herbert E. (1994): American Presidential Elections, 1976-1992. In: Alexander, Herbert E./ Shiratori, Rei (eds.), 1994a, pp. 41-56.

Alexander, Herbert E. (1999): Spending in the 1996 Elections. In: Green, John C. (ed.), 1999a, pp. 11-36.

Alexander, Herbert E./ Bauer, Monica (1991): *Financing the 1988 Election*. Boulder et al.: Westview, 1991.

Alexander, Herbert E./ Corrado, Anthony (1995): *Financing the 1992 Election*. Armonk NY: M.E. Sharpe, 1995.

Alexander, Herbert E./ Haggerty, Brian A. (1987): *Financing the 1984 Election*. Lexington MA: D.C Heath, 1987.

Alexander, Herbert E. et al. (eds.) (1992): *Public Financing of State Elections. A Data Book on Tax-Assisted Funding of Political Parties and Candidates in Twenty-Five States*. Los Angeles CA: Citizens' Research Foundation, 1992.

Alexander, Herbert E./ Frutig, Jennifer W. (eds.) (1982): *Public Financing of State Elections. A Data Book and Election Guide to Public Funding of Political Parties and Candidates in Seventeen States*. Los Angeles CA: Citizens' Research Foundation, 1982.

Alexander, Herbert E./ Shiratori, Rei (eds.) (1994a): *Comparative Political Finance Among the Democracies*. Boulder CO: Westview, 1994.

Alexander, Herbert E./ Shiratori, Rei (1994b): Introduction. In: Alexander, Herbert E./ Shiratori, Rei (eds.), 1994a, pp. 1-11.

Alvarez-Conde, Enrique (1994): *La Financiacion de los Partidos Politicos*. Madrid: Centro de Estudios Constitucionales, 1994.

Amr, Dima (2000): Auf dem Weg zu einem Zweiparteiensystem? Die kanadische Unterhauswahl 2000. In: *Zeitschrift für Kanada-Studien*, 20 (2000) 2, pp. 10-34.

Amr, Dima/ Lisowski, Rainer (2001): Political Finance in Old Dominions: Australia and Canada. In: Nassmacher, Karl-Heinz (ed.), 2001a, pp. 53-72.

Andeweg, Rudy B. (1999): Parties, Pillars and the Politics of Accommodation: Weak or Weakening Linkages? The Case of Dutch Consociationalism. In: Luther, Kurt Richard/ Deschouwer, Kris (eds.), 1999, pp. 108-133.

Andren, Nils (1970): Partisan Motivations and Concern for System Legitimacy in the Scandinavian Deliberations on Public Subsidies. In: Heidenheimer, Arnold J. (ed.), 1970a, pp. 50-67.

Angell, Harold M. (1987): Duverger, Epstein and the Problem of the Mass Party. The Case of the Parti Quebecois. In: *Canadian Journal of Political Science*, 20 (1987) 2, pp. 363-378.

Angell, Harald M. (1996): *Provincial Party Financing in Quebec*. Lanham MD: University Press of America, 1996.

Angell, Harald M. (2001): The Parti Quebecois: Financing a Mass Party to Quebec Independence. In: Nassmacher, Karl-Heinz (ed.), 2001a, pp. 252-266.

Anheier, Helmut K. et al. (eds.) (1997): *Der Dritte Sektor in Deutschland. Organisationen zwischen Staat und Markt im gesellschaftlichen Wandel*. Berlin: Rainer Bohn, 1997.

Ansolabehere, Stephen/ Gerber, Alan S./ Snyder, James M. (2001): Does TV Advertising Explain the Rise of Campaign Spending? A Study of Campaign Spending and Broadcast Advertising Prices in US House Elections the 1990s and the 1970s. In: www.mit.edu/faculty/snyder/files.

Ansolabehere, Stephen/ Figueiredo, John M./ Snyder, James M. (2003): Why is There so Little Money in U.S. Politics? In: *Journal of Economic Perspectives*, 17 (2003) 1, pp. 105-130.

Appleton, Andrew M./ Ward, Daniel S. (1996): How We Are Doing: Party Leaders Evaluate Performance of the 1994 Elections. In: Green, John C./ Shea, Daniel M. (eds.), 1996, pp. 125-139.

Archer, Keith (1991): Leadership Selection in the New Democratic Party. In: Bakvis, Herman (ed.), 1991, pp. 3-56.

Arian, Asher (1998): *The Second Republic. Politics in Israel*. Chatham NJ: Chatham House, 1998.

Arnim, Hans Herbert von (1993): Campaign and Party Finance in Germany. In: Gunlicks, Arthur B. (ed.), 1993, pp. 201-218.

Arnim, Hans Herbert von (1996): *Die Partei, der Abgeordnete und das Geld. Parteienfinanzierung in Deutschland*. München: Droemer Knaur, 2nd ed. 1996.

Arnim, Hans Herbert von (2001): *Das System. Die Machenschaften der Macht*. München: Doemer, 2001.

Arrington, Theodor S./ Ingalls, Gerald L. (1984): Effects of Campaign Spending on Local Elections. In: *American Politics Quarterly*, 12 (1984) 1, pp. 117-127.

Ashworth, Scott (2006): Campaign Finance and Voter Welfare with Entrenched Incumbents. In: *American Political Science Review*, 100 (2006) 1, pp. 55-68.

Austen-Smith, David (1995): Campaign Contributions and Access. In: *American Political Science Review*, 89 (1995) 3, pp. 566-581.

Austin, Reginald/ Tjernström, Maja (eds.) (2003): *Funding of Political Parties and Election Campaigns*. Stockholm: International IDEA, 2003.

Avril, Pierre (1994): Regulation of Political Finance in France. In: Alexander, Herbert E./ Shiratori, Rei (eds.), 1994a, pp. 85-96.

Aylott, Nicholas (2003): After the Divorce. Social Democrats and Trade Unions in Sweden. In: *Party Politics*, 9 (2003) 3, pp. 369-390.

Baker, Ross K. (1989): *The New Fat Cats. Members of Congress as Political Benefactors*. New York: Priority, 1989.

Bakvis, Herman (ed.) (1991): *Canadian Political Parties. Leaders, Candidates and Organization*. Toronto: Dundurn, 1991.

Barbeau Report (Committee on Election Expenses) (1966): *Report*. Ottawa: Queen's Printer, 1966.

Bardi, Luciano (2002): Italian Parties: Change and Functionality. In: Webb, Paul et al. (eds.), 2002, pp. 46-76.

Bardi, Luciano/ Morlino, Leonardo (1992): Italy. In: Katz, Richard S./ Mair, Peter (eds.), 1992, pp. 604-606.

Bardi, Luciano/ Morlino, Leonardo (1994): Italy: Tracing the Roots of the Great Transformation. In: Katz, Richard S./ Mair, Peter (eds.), 1994, pp. 242-277.

Bartolini, Stefano (1983): The Membership of Mass Parties: The Social Democratic Experience, 1889-1978. In: Daalder, Hans/ Mair, Peter (eds.), 1983, pp. 139-175.

Becker, Bernd (1999): *Mitgliederbeteiligung und innerparteiliche Demokratie in britischen Parteien - Modelle für die deutschen Parteien?* Baden-Baden: Nomos, 1999.

Becker, Bernd (2002): *Politik in Großbritannien.* Paderborn et al.: Schöningh, 2002.

Benoit, Kenneth/ Marsh, Michael (2003): For a Few Euros More: Campaign Spending Effects in the Irish Local Elections. In: *Party Politics*, 9 (2003) 5, pp. 561-582.

Bedlington, Anne H./ Malbin, Michael J. (2003): The Party as an Extended Network.: Members Giving to Each Other and to their Parties. In: Malbin, Michael J (ed.), 2003, pp. 121-137.

Bergman, Torbjörn (1997): Schweden: Minderheitsregierungen als Regel und Mehrheitskoalitionen als Ausnahme. In: Müller, Wolfgang C./ Strøm, Kaare (eds.), 1997, pp. 239-288.

Beyme, Klaus von (2000): *Parteien im Wandel. Von den Volksparteien zu den professionalisierten Wählerparteien.* Wiesbaden: Westdeutscher, 2000.

Bianco, Alessandro/ Gardini, Gianluca (1999): The Funding of Political Parties in Italy. In: Ewing, Keith D. (1999), pp. 19-30.

Bibby, John F. (1987): *Politics, Parties and Elections in America.* Chicago Ill.: Nelson-Hall, 1987.

Bibby, John F. (1998): State Party Organizations: Coping and Adapting to Candidate-Centered Politics and Nationalization. In: Maisel, L. Sandy (ed.), 1998, pp. 23-49.

Biersack, Robert (1996): The Nationalization of Party Finance. In: Green, John C./ Shea, Daniel M. (eds.), 1996, pp. 108-124.

Biersack, Robert/ Haskell, Melanie (1999): Spitting on the Umpire: Political Parties, the Federal Election Campaign Act, and the 1996 Campaigns. In: Green, John C. (ed.), 1999a, pp. 155-185.

Biezen, Ingrid van (1998): Building Party Organisations and the Relevance of Past Models: The Communist and Socialist Parties in Portugal and Spain. In: *West European Politics*, 21 (1998) 2, pp. 32-62.

Biezen, Ingrid van (2000a): Party Financing in New Democracies. Portugal and Spain. In: *Party Politics,* 6 (2000) 3, pp. 329-342.

Biezen, Ingrid van (2000b): On the Internal Balance of Party Power: Party Organizations in New Democracies. In: *Party Politics,* 6 (2000) 4, pp. 395-417.

Biezen, Ingrid van (2003): *Political Parties in New Democracies: Party Organization in Southern and East-Central Europe.* Basingstoke and New York: Palgrave Macmillan, 2003.

Biezen, Ingrid van (2004): Political Parties as Public Utilities. In: *Party Politics*, 10 (2004) 6, pp. 701-722.

Biezen, Ingrid van/ Nassmacher, Karl-Heinz (2001): Political Finance in Southern Europe: Italy, Portugal, Spain. In: Nassmacher, Karl-Heinz (ed.), 2001a, pp. 131-154.

Bille, Lars (1992): Denmark. In: Katz, Richard S./ Mair, Peter (eds.), 1992, pp. 199-272.

Bille, Lars (1994): The Decline of the Membership Party? In: Katz, Richard S./ Mair, Peter (eds.), 1994, pp. 134-157.

Bille, Lars (1997): *Partier i Forandring*. Odense: Odense Universitetsforlag, 1997.

Blackwell, Richard/ Terry, Michael (1987): Analysing the Political Fund Ballots. A Remarkable Victory or the Triumph of the Status Quo. In: *Political Studies*, 35 (1987) 4, pp. 623-642.

Blake, Donald E. et al. (1996): Coming and Going. Leadership Selection and Removal. In: Tanguay, Brian/ Gagnon, Alan G. (eds.), 1996, pp. 213-237.

Blankenburg, Erhard et al. (1989): Political Scandals and Corruption Issues in West Germany. In: Heidenheimer, Arnold et al. (eds.): *Political Corruption. A Handbook*. New Brunswick NJ: Transaction Publications, 1989, pp. 913-931.

Blanco Valdes, Roberto (1994): Consideratione sobre la Necesaria Reforma del Sisterna Espanol des Financiation de los Partidos Politicos. In: *La Financiacion de los Partidos Politicos*. Madrid: Centro des Estudies Constitutitionales, 1994, pp. 37-52.

Blechinger, Verena (1998): *Politische Korruption in Japan. Ursachen, Hintergründe und Reformversuche*. Hamburg: Institut für Asienkunde, 1998.

Blechinger, Verena (1999): Changes in the Handling of Corruption Scandals in Japan since 1994. In: *Asia-Pacific Review*, 6 (1999) 2, pp. 42-64.

Blechinger, Verena (2001): Politische Reformen in Japan - Auswirkungen und Perspektiven. In: Bosse, Friederike/ Köllner, Patrick (eds.): *Reformen in Japan*. Hamburg: Institut für Asienkunde, 2001, pp. 89-110.

Blechinger, Verena/ Nassmacher, Karl-Heinz (2001): Political Finance in Non-Western Democracies: Japan and Israel. In: Nassmacher, Karl-Heinz (ed.), 2001a, pp. 155-180.

Blechinger-Talcott, Verena (2005): Japan. In: Grant, Thomas D. (ed.), 2005, pp. 297-318.

Bloom, Arnold (1956): Tax Results of Political Contributions. In: *Boston University Law Review*, 36 (1956), pp. 170-189.

Boatright, Robert C./ Malbin, Michael J. (2003): *Political Contribution Tax Credits and Citizen Participation*. Paper, prepared for the 2003 Annual Meeting of the American Political Science Association(unpublished).

Bogdanor, Vernon (1982): Reflections on British Political Finance. In: *Parliamentary Affairs*, 35 (1982) 4, pp. 367-380.

Boim, Leon (1979): The Financing of Elections. In: Penniman, Howard R. (ed.), 1979, pp. 199-225.

Bolleyer, Nicole (2007): *Indirect State Funding of Political Parties in Western Democracies: Party-State Relations and the Strength of Party Organization*. Party Politics Working Group, EUI (European University Institute), Florence, November 20, 2007 (unpublished).

Borchert, Jens (ed.)(1999): *Politik als Beruf*. Opladen: Leske & Budrich, 1999.

Borchert, Jens/ Golsch, Lutz (1999): Deutschland: Von der "Honoratiorenzunft" zur politischen Klasse. In: Borchert, Jens (ed.), 1999, pp. 114-140.

Bouissou, Jean-Marie (1997): Gifts, Networks and Clienteles: Corruption in Japan as a Redistributive System. In: Della Porta, Donatella/ Mény, Yves (eds.) 1997a, pp. 132-147.

Boyken, Friedhelm (1998): *Die Neuordnung der Parteienfinanzierung. Entscheidungsprozeßanalyse und Wirkungskontrolle*. Baden-Baden: Nomos, 1998.

Brändle, Michael (2002): *Strategien der Förderung politischer Parteien. Eine vergleichende Untersuchung der Parteienförderung in der Schweiz, Großbritannien und den Niederlanden.* Bern et al.: Paul Haupt, 2002.

Broder, David S. (1972): *The Party's Over: The Failure of Politics in America.* New York: Harper & Row, 1972.

Brunken-Bahr, Werner (1990): *Bürgerbeteiligung und Steuervorteil in der Parteienfinanzierung. Ein Vergleich zwischen Deutschland und Nordamerika.* Oldenburg: M.A. thesis, 1990.

Burnell, Peter (1998): Introduction: Money and Politics in Emerging Democracies. In: Burnell, Peter/ Ware, Alan (eds.), 1998, pp. 1-21.

Burnell, Peter/ Ware, Alan (eds.) (1998): *Funding Democratization.* Manchester and New York: Manchester University, 1998.

Butler, David/ Butler, Gareth (1994): *British Political Facts since 1979.* Basingstoke: Macmillan, 7th. ed. 1994.

Butler, David/ Kavanagh, Dennis (1988): *The British General Election of 1987.* Houndmills et al.: Macmillan, 1988 (reprint: *The British General Elections 1945-92.* Houndmills: Macmillan, 1999).

Butler, David/ Kavanagh, Dennis (eds.) (1997): *The British General Election of 1997.* Houndmills et al.: Macmillan, 1997.

Butler, David A./ King, Anthony: (1965): *The British General Election of 1964.* Houndmills et al.: Macmillan (reprint: *The British General Elections 1945-92.* Houndmills: Macmillan, 1999).

Butler, David/ Pinto-Duschinsky, Michael (1971): *The British General Election of 1970.* London: Macmillan, 1971, (reprint: *The British General Elections 1945-92.* Houndmills: Macmillan, 1999).

Butler, David E./ Rose, Richard (1960): *The British General Election of 1959.* Houndmills et al.: Macmillan, 1960 (reprint: *The British General Elections 1945-92.* Basingstoke et al.: Macmillan, 1999).

Butler, David/ Ranney, Austin (eds.) (1992): *Electioneering. A Comparative Study of Continuity and Change.* Oxford: Clarendon, 1992.

Butler, David et al. (eds.) (1981): *Democracy at the Polls.* Washington DC: American Enterprise Institute, 1981.

Cahill, Kevin et al. (1993): Tory Money. The unexpected Millions that elected tree Governments. In: *Business Age,* 3 (1993) 32, pp. 40-48.

Cain, Matt/ Taylor, Matthew (2002): *Keeping it Clean: The Way Forward to State Funding of Political Parties.* London: Institute for Public Policy Research, 2002.

Camby, Jean-Pierre (1995): *Le financement de la vie politique en France.* Paris: Montchrestien, 1995.

Carrillo, Manuel et al. (eds.) (2003): *Dinero y contienda político-electoral. Reto de la democracia.* México: Fondo de Cultura económica, 2003.

Carty, R. Kenneth (1991): *Canadian Political Parties in the Constituencies.* Toronto: Dundurn, 1991.

Carty, R. Kenneth (1996a): An Interpretation of the Development of National Politics. In: Thorburn, Hugh G. (ed.), 1996, pp. 128-145.

Carty, R. Kenneth (1996b): Party Organisation and Activity on the Ground. In: Tanguay, Brian/ Gagnon, Alan G. (eds.), 1996, pp.190-212.

Carty, R. Kenneth (2002): Canada's Nineteenth-Century Cadre Parties at the Millenium. In: Webb, Paul et al. (eds.), 2002, pp. 345-378.

Carty, R. Kenneth (2004): Parties as Franchise Systems. The Stratarchical Organizational Imperative. In: *Party Politics*, 10 (2004) 1, pp. 5-24.

Carty, R. Kenneth/ Eagles, Munroe D. (2005): *Politics is Local. National Politics at the Grassroots*. Oxford: Oxford University, 2005.

Carty, R. Kenneth/ Erickson, Lynda (1991): Candidate Nomination in Canada's National Political Parties. In: Bakvis, Herman (ed.), 1991, pp. 97-189.

Casas-Zamora, Kevin (2002): *Paying the Democracy in Latin America: Political Finance and State Funding for Parties in Costa Rica and Uruguay*. University of Oxford, 2002.

Casas-Zamora, Kevin (2005a): *Paying for Democracy: Political Finance and State Funding of Parties*. Colchester: ECPR, 2005.

Casas-Zamora, Kevin (2005b): State Funding and Campaign Finance Practices in Uruguay. In: Malamud, Carlos/ Posada-Carbó, Eduardo (eds.), 2005, pp. 189-266.

Castillo, Pilar del (1985): *La Financiation de los Partidos y Candidatos en las Democracias Occidentales*. Madrid: Centro de Investigaciones Sociologicas, 1985.

Castillo, Pilar del (1989): Financing of Spanish Political Parties. In: Alexander, Herbert E. (ed.), 1989a, pp. 172-199.

Castillo, Pilar del (1994): Problems in Spanish Party Financing. In: Alexander, Herbert E./ Shiratori, Rei (eds.), 1994a, pp. 97-104.

Castillo, Pilar del/ Zovatto, Daniel G. (eds.) (1998): *La Financiacion de la Politica en Iberoamerika*. San Jose CR: Instituto Interamericano de Derechos Humanos, 1998.

Chang, Shih-Hsien (2005): Taiwan. In: Grant, Thomas D. (ed.), 2005, pp. 497-512.

Chaples, Ernest A. (1988a): Campaign Donations: The Real Issues. In: *Current Affairs Bulletin*, 64 (1988) March, pp. 30-31.

Chaples, Ernest A. (1988b): *The Evolution of Public Funding of Elections in Australia*. Paper presented to the World Congress of the International Political Science Association, Washington DC, 1988 (unpublished).

Chaples, Ernest A. (1989): Public Funding of Elections in Australia. In: Alexander, Herbert E. (ed.), 1989a, pp. 76-94.

Chaples, Ernest A. (1994): Developments in Australian Election Finance. In: Alexander, Herbert E./ Shiratori, Rei (eds.), 1994a, pp. 29-40.

Chapman, Randall G./ Palda, Kristian S. (1984): Adressing the Influence of Campaign Expenditures on Voting Behavior with a Comprehensive Electoral Market Model. In: *Marketing Science*, 3 (1984) 3, pp. 207-236.

Ciaurro, Gian Franco (1989): Public Financing of Parties in Italy. In: Alexander, Herbert E. (ed.), 1989a, pp. 153-171.

Cigler, Allan C. (2002): Interest Groups and Financing the 2000 Elections. In: Magleby, David B. (ed.), 2002a, pp. 163-187.

Clarke, Harold D. et al. (2000): Not for Fame or Fortune: A Note on Membership and Activity in the Canadian Reform Party. In: *Party Politics,* 6 (2000) 1, pp. 75-93.

Coignard, Sophie/ Lacun, Jean-Francois (1989): *La République bananière*. Paris: P. Belfond, 1989.

Commission on Election Finances, Ontario (1988): *A Comparative Survey of Election Finance Legislation 1988,* Toronto 1988.

Compendium of Election Administration in Canada (2003), www.elections.ca/loi/com2003.

Congleton, Roger D. (1989): Campaign Finances and Political Platforms. The Economics of Political Controversy. In: *Public Choice,* 62 (1989) 2, pp. 101-118.

Cordes, Doris (2001): *Die Finanzierung der politischen Parteien Deutschlands, Österreichs und der Niederlande.* Carl-von-Ossietzky Universität Oldenburg: dissertation, 2001 (www.uni-oldenburg.de/.docserver.bis.uni-Oldenburg/publikationen/dissertation/2002/cor..-corfin01.htm).

Cordes, Doris/ Nassmacher, Karl-Heinz (2001): Mission Impossible: Can anyone control the unlimited increase of political spending? In: Nassmacher, Karl-Heinz (ed.), 2001a, pp. 267-286.

Cordes, Doris/ Rieken, Marion (1997): Rückkehr zur Normalität? Die kanadische Unterhauswahl von 1997. In: *Zeitschrift für Kanada-Studien,* 17 (1997) 2, pp. 126-141.

Corrado, Anthony (1999): Financing the 1996 Presidential General Election. In: Green, John C. (ed.), 1999a, pp. 63-93.

Corrado, Anthony (2002): Financing the 2000 Presidential General Election. In: Magleby, David B. (ed.), 2002a, pp. 79-105.

Corrado, Anthony (2006): „The Regulatory Environment: Uncertainty in the Wake of Change". In: Magleby, David B.et al. (eds.), 2006, pp. 30-67.

Corrado, Anthony et al. (eds.) (1997): *Campaign Finance Reform: a Sourcebook.* Washington DC: Brookings Institution, 1997.

Cotter, C. P. et al. (1984): *Party Organizations in American Politics.* New York: Praeger, 1984.

Cowley, Philip/ Fisher, Justin (2000): The Conservativ Party. In: *Politics Review,* 10 (2000) 2, pp. 2-5.

Cox, Gary W./ McCall Rosenbluth, Frances/ Thies, Michael F. (1999): Electoral Reform and the Fate of Factions: The Case of Japan's Liberal Democratic Party. In: *British Journal of Political Science,* 29 (1999) 1, pp. 33-56.

Cox, Gary W./ Thies, Michael F. (2000): How Much Does Money Matter? "Buying" Votes in Japan, 1967-1990. In: *Comparative Political Studies,* 33 (2000) 1, pp. 37-57.

Crotty, William J. (1977): *Political Reform and the American Experiment.* New York: Thomas Y. Crowell Company, 1977.

Crotty, William J. (1985): *The Party Game.* New York: W. F. Freeman, 1985.

Daalder, Hans (ed.) (1987a): *Party Systems in Denmark, Austria, Switzerland, The Netherlands and Belgium.* New York: St. Martin's, 1987.

Daalder, Hans (1987b): The Dutch Party System: From Segmentation to Polarization. In: Daalder, Hans (ed.), 1987a, pp. 193-284.

Dachs, Herbert (1986): Öffentliche Parteienfinanzierung in den österreichischen Bundesländern. In: Khol, Andreas et al. (eds.): *Österreichisches Jahrbuch für Politik 1985.* München and Wien: Oldenbourg, 1986, pp. 439-454.

Dahl, Robert A. (1971): *Polyarchie. Participation and Opposition.* New Haven and London: Yale University, 1971.

Dahl, Robert A. (1972): *Who Governs? Democracy and Power in an American City.* New Haven and London: Yale University, 1972.

Dahl, Robert A. (1982): *Dilemmas of Pluralist Democracy. Autonomy vs. Control.* New Haven and London: Yale University, 1982.

Dalton, Russell J./ Wattenberg, Martin P. (eds.) (2000a): *Parties without Partisans.* Oxford: Oxford University, 2000.

Dalton, Russell J./ Wattenberg, Martin P. (2000b): Unthinkable Democracy: Political Change in Advanced Industrial Democracies. In: Dalton, Russell J./ Wattenberg Martin P. (eds.), 2000a, pp. 3-18.

Dalton, Russell J./ Wattenberg, Martin P. (2000c): Partisan Change and the Democratic Process. In: Dalton, Russell J./ Wattenberg Martin P. (eds.), 2000a, pp. 261-285.

Dalton, Russell J. et al. (2000d): The Consequences of Partisan Dealignment. In: Dalton, Russell J./ Wattenberg, Martin P. (eds.), 2000a, pp. 37-63.

Dekker, Paul/ van den Broek, Andries (1998): Civil Society in Comparative Perspective: Involvement in Voluntary Associations in North and Western Europe. In: *International Journal of Voluntary and Nonprofit Organization,* 9 (1998) 1, pp. 11-38.

Della Porta, Donatella (1997): The Vicious Circles of Corruption in Italy. In: Della Porta, Donatella/ Mény, Yves (eds.), 1997a, pp. 35-49.

Della Porta, Donatella (2000): *Political Parties and Political Corruption.* San Domenico: European University Institute, 2000.

Della Porta, Donatella/ Mény, Yves (eds.) (1997a): *Democracy and Corruption in Europe.* London and Washington: Pinter, 1997.

Della Porta, Donatella/ Mény, Yves (1997b): Introduction: Democacy and Corruption. In: Della Porta, Donatella/ Mény, Yves (eds.), 1997a, pp. 1-6.

Della Porta, Donatella/ Mény, Yves (1997c): Conclusion: Democracy and Corruption: Towards a Comparative Analysis. In: Della Porta, Donatella/ Mény, Yves (eds.), 1997a, pp. 166-180.

Della Porta, Donatella/ Vannucci, Albert (1999): *Corrupt Exchanges. Actors, Resources, and Mechanisms of Political Corruption.* New York: Aldine de Gruyter, 1999.

Denemark, David (2003): Electoral Change, Inertia and Campaigns in New Zealand: The First Modern FPTP Campaign in 1987 and the First MMP Campaign in 1996. In: *Party Politics,* 9 (2003) 5, pp. 601-618.

Denver, David/ Hands, Gordon (1997): Challengers, Incumbents and the Impact of Constituency Campaigning in Britain. In: *Electoral Studies,* 16 (1997) 2, pp. 175-193.

Denver, David/ Hands, Gordon/ Fisher, Justin/ McAllister, Iain (2003): Constituency Campaigning in Britain 1992-2001. Centralization and Modernization. In: *Party Politics,* 9 (2003) 5, pp. 541-559.

Deschouwer, Kris (1994): The Decline of Consociationalism and the Reluctant Modernization of Belgian Mass Parties. In: Katz, Richard S./ Mair, Peter (eds.), 1994, pp. 80-108.

Deschouwer, Kris (2002): The Colour Purple: The End of Predictable Politics in the Low Countries. In: Webb, Paul et al. (eds.), 2002, pp. 151-180.

De Sousa, Luis Manuel Macedo Pinto (1999): *Corruption and Parties in Portugal.* Working Paper: European University Institute Florence, 1999.

De Sousa, Marcelo Rebelo (1992): Parteienfinanzierung in Portugal. Tsatsos, Dimitris Th. (eds.), 1992, pp. 399-419.

Deth, Jan W. van et al. (eds.) (1999): *Social Capital and European Democracy.* London and New York: Routledge, 1999.

Dettelbeck, Klaus (2005): Cartel Parties in Western Europe? In: *Party Politics*, 11 (2005) 2, pp. 173-191.

Deutsch, Karl W (1966): *The Nerves of Government. Models of Political Communication and Control*, New York: The Free Press, and London: Collier-Macmillan, 1966.

Dewachter, Wilfried (1987): Changes in a Particratie: The Belgian Party System from 1944 to 1986. In: Daalder, Hans (ed.), 1987a, pp. 285-355.

Dipper, Christof (1997): *Deutsche Geschichte 1648-1789.* Frankfurt a. M.: Suhrkamp, 1991 (reprint: Darmstadt: Wissenschaftliche Buchgesellschaft, 1997).

Doron, Gideon (1986): Party Financing. In: Arian, Asher/ Shamir, Michal (eds.): *The Election in Israel, 1984.* New Brunswick and Oxford: Transaction Books, 1986, pp. 37-53.

Doublet, Yves-Marie (1997): *L'argent et la politique en France.* Paris: Economica, 1997.

Doublet, Yves-Marie (1999): Party Funding in France. In: Ewing, Keith D. (ed.), 1999, pp. 67-79.

Doublet, Yves-Marie (2003): Is there a Crisis of Party Finance and Political Parties Among Industrial Countries? In: *Participation*, 27 (2003) 2, pp. 12-14.

Doublet, Yves-Marie (2005): France. In: Grant, Thomas D. (ed.), 2005, pp. 113-122.

Downs, Anthony (1957): *An Economic Theory of Democracy.* New York: Harper&Brothers, 1957, reprint 1986.

Drew, Elizabeth (1983): *Politics and Money. The New Road to Corruption.* New York: Macmillan, 1983.

Drew, Elizabeth (1998): *Whatever It Takes. The Real Struggle for Political Power in America.* New York: Viking, 1998.

Drew, Elizabeth (1999): *The Corruption of American Politics. What Went Wrong and Why.* Secaucus NJ: Carol Publishing Group, 1999.

Drury, Colin (2000): *Management and Cost Accounting.* London: Business Press, 5th ed. 2000.

Drysch, Thomas (1998): *Parteienfinanzierung. Österreich, Schweiz, Bundesrepublik Deutschland.* Opladen: Leske & Budrich, 1998.

Drysch, Thomas (o.J.): *Wahlkampf- und Parteienfinanzierung in Frankreich* (unpublished).

Dübber, Ulrich (1962): *Parteienfinanzierung in Deutschland: eine Untersuchung über das Problem der Rechenschaftslegung in einem künftigen Parteiengesetz.* Köln et al.: Westdeutscher, 1962.

Dübber, Ulrich (1964): Zur öffentlichen Finanzierung politischer Parteien. In: *Die Neue Gesellschaft,* 11 (1964) 2, pp. 105-111.

Dübber, Ulrich (1970a): *Geld und Politik. Die Finanzwirtschaft der Parteien.* Freudenstadt: Eurobuch, 1970.

Dübber, Ulrich (1970b): Parteienfinanzierung. In: *Staatslexikon,* Volume 10, 2nd. Additional Volume. Freiburg: Herder, 1970, pp. 855-860.

Dübber, Ulrich/ Braunthal, Gerhard (1963): West Germany. In: *Journal of Politics*, 25 (1963) 4, pp. 774-789.

Düselder, Heike (1992): Institutionalisierte Garantien der Mischfinanzierung. Matching Funds and Reimbursement als Programmelemente. In: Nassmacher, Karl-Heinz, 1992a, pp. 99-129.

Dunleavy, Patrick/ Weir, Stuart (1995): Media, Opinion and the Constitution. In: Ridley, Frederik F./ Doig, Alan (eds.): *Sleaze*, Oxford: Oxford University, 1995, pp. 54-68.

Duverger, Maurice (1967): *Political Parties. Their Organization and Activity in the Modern State*. 3rd ed., London: Methuen & Co., 1967 (first published: Paris: Armond Colin, 1951).

Dwyre, Diana (1999): Interest Groups and Issue Advocacy in 1996. In: Green, John C. (ed.), 1999a, pp. 187-214.

Eagles, Munroe D. (2005): The Effectiveness of Local Campaign Spending in the 1993 and 1997 Federal Elections in Canada. In: *Canadian Journal of Political Science*, 37 (2005) 1, pp. 17-136.

Easton, David et al. (1995): Introduction: Democracy as a Regime Type and the Development of Political Science. In: Easton, David et al. (eds.): *Regime and Discipline: Democracy and the Development of Political Science*. Ann Arbor: University of Michigan, 1995, pp. 1-26.

Ebbighausen, Rolf et al. (1996): *Die Kosten der Parteiendemokratie. Studien und Materialien zu einer Bilanz staatlicher Parteienfinanzierung in der Bundesrepublik Deutschland*. Opladen: Westdeutscher,1996.

Eismeier, Theodore J./ Pollock, Philip H. (1988): *Business, Money and the Rise of Corporate PACs in American Elections*. New York: Quorum Books, 1988.

Elections Canada (ed.) (2003): *Compendium of Election Administration in Canada*. (www.elections.ca/loi/com2003).

Electoral Commission (U.K.) (2004): *The Funding of Political Parties*, December 2004 (www.electoralcommission.org.uk/files/dms/partyfundingFINALproofs........pdf).

Elkins, David J. (1991): Parties as National Institutions: A Comparative Study. In: Bakvis, Herman (ed.), 1991, pp. 3-62.

Elzinga, Dowe J. (1992): Parteienfinanzierung in den Niederlanden. In: Tsatsos, Dimitris Th. (ed.), 1992, pp. 333-398.

Engelhardt, Klaus et al. (eds.) (1997): *Fremde Heimat Kirche. Die Dritte EKD-Erhebung über Kirchengemeinschaft*. Gütersloh: Verlagshaus, 1997.

Epstein, Edwin M. (1976): Corporations and Labor Unions in Electoral Politics. In: *The Annals of the American Academy of Political and Social Science*, 425 (1976) May, pp. 33-58.

Epstein, Leon D. (1980): *Political Parties in Western Democracies*. New Brunswick NJ: Transaction, 2nd. ed. 1980.

Epstein, Leon D. (1986): *Political Parties in the American Mold*. Madison WI: University of Wisconsin, 1986.

Epstein, Leon D. (1993): Overview of Research on Party Organizations. In: Margolis, Michael/ Green, John C. (eds.), 1993, pp. 1-6.

Etzioni, Amitai (1984): *Capital Corruption*. San Diego CA: Harcourt Brace Jovanovitch Publishers, 1984, pp. 227-231.

Ewing, Keith D. (1982): *Trade Unions, the Labour Party and the Law. A Study of the Trade Union Act 1913*. Edingburgh: Edinburgh University, 1982.

Ewing, Keith D. (1987): *The Funding of Political Parties in Britain*. Cambridge and New York: Cambridge University, 1987.

Ewing, Keith D. (1992): *Money, Politics and Law. A Study of Electoral Campaign Finance Reform in Canada*. Oxford: Clarendon and New York: Oxford University, 1992.

Ewing, Keith D. (1999) (ed.): *The Funding of Political Parties. Europe and Beyond*. Bologna: CLUEB, 1999.

Ewing, Keith (2001): „Corruption in Party Financing. The Case for Global Standards". In: Hodess, Robin et al. (eds.): *Global Corruption Report 2001*, Berlin: Transparency International, 2001, pp. 186-188.

Ewing, Keith D. (2007): *The Cost of Democracy. Party Funding in British Politics*. Oxford and Portland OR: Hart, 2007.

Fabiano, Laura (2005): Italy. In: Grant, Thomas D. (ed.), 2005, pp. 281-296.

Farrell, Brian/ Farrell, David M. (1987): The General Election of 1987. In: Penniman, Howard R./ Farrell, Brian (eds.): *Ireland at the Polls 1981, 1982, and 1987. A Study of Four Genenal Elections*. Washington DC: American Enterprise Institute, 1987, pp. 233-244.

Farrell, David M. (1992): Ireland. In: Katz, Richard S./ Mair, Peter (eds.), 1992, pp. 389-457.

Farrell, David M. (1993): Campaign Strategies. In: Gallagher, Michael/ Lever, Michael (eds.): *How Ireland Voted 1992*. Dublin: Folens PSAI, 1993, pp. 21-38.

Farrell, David M. (1994): Ireland: Centralization, Professionalization and Competitive Pressures. Katz, Richard S./ Mair, Peter (eds.), 1994, 216-241.

Farrell, David M./ Webb, Paul (2000): Political Parties as Campaign Organizations. In: Dalton, Russell J./ Wattenberg, Martin P. (eds.), 2000a, pp. 102-128.

Ferdinand, Peter (1998): Building democracy on the basis of capitalism: towards an east Asian model of party funding. Burnell, Peter/ Ware, Alan (eds.): *Funding Democratization*. Manchester and New York: Manchester University, 1998, pp. 180-201.

Ferguson, Thomas (1995): *Golden Rule. The Investment Theory of Party Competition and the Logic of Money-Driven Political Systems*. Chicago and London: University of Chicago, 1995.

Fieschi, Catherine/ Gaffney, John (2004): French Think Tanks in Comparative Perspective. In: Stone, Diane/ Denham, Andrew (eds.), 2004, pp. 105-120.

Fisher, Justin (1994a): Why do Companies Make Donations to Political Parties? In: *Political Studies*, 42 (1994) 4, pp. 690-700.

Fisher, Justin (1994b): Political Donations to the Conservative Party. In: *Parliamentary Affairs*, 47 (1994) 1, pp. 61-72.

Fisher, Justin (1995): The Institutional Funding of British Parties. In: Broughton, David et al. (eds.): *British Elections and Parties Yearbook 1994*. London: Frank Cass, 1995, pp. 181-196.

Fisher, Justin (1996a): *British Political Parties*. London at al.: Prentice Hall/Harvester Wheatsheaf, 1996.

Fisher, Justin (1996b): Party Finance. In: Norton, Philip (ed.), 1996, pp. 157-169.

Fisher, Justin (1997): Donations to Political Parties [UK]. In: *Parliamentary Affairs*, 50 (1997) 2, pp. 235-246.

Fisher, Justin (1998): Local Party Income and Expenditure Survey. *Fourth Report of the Committee on Standards in Public Life*. Written Evidence and other Material 16/426. London (Volume 2).

Fisher, Justin (1999): Party Expenditure and Electoral Prospects: A National Level Analyses of Britain.I n: *Electoral Studies*, 18 (1999) 4, pp. 519-532.

Fisher, Justin (2000): Party Finance and Corruption in Britain. In: Williams, Robert (ed.), 2000a, pp. 15-36.

Fisher, Justin (2002): Next Step: State Funding for the Parties? In: *The Political Quarterly*, 73 (2002) 4, pp. 392-399.

Fisher, Justin (2005): Financing Party Politics in Britain. In: Malamud, Carlos/ Posada-Carbó, Eduardo (eds.), 2005, pp. 104-121.

Fisher, Justin/ Eisenstadt, Todd A. (2004): Introduction: Comparative Party Finance. What has to be done? In: *Party Politics*, 10 (2004) 6, pp. 619-626.

Fleischer, David (2000): Reforma Politica e Financiamento das Campanhas Eleitorais. In: Speck, Bruno Wilhelm et al., 2000, pp.79-103.

Forrest, James (1991): Campaign Spending in the New South Wales Legislative Assembly Elections of 1984. In: *Australien Journal of Political Science*, 26 (1991) March, pp. 526-534.

Forrest, James (1991): The Geography of Campaign Funding, Campaign Spending and Voting at the New South Wales Legislative Assembly Election of 1984. In: *Australien Geographer,* 23 (1991) 1, pp. 66-76.

Forrest, Jim/ Johnston, Ronald J./ Pattie, Charles J. (1999): The Effectivness of Constituency Campaign Spending in Australian State Elections during Times of Electoral Volatility: The New South Wales Case, 1988-95. In: *Environment and Planning*, 31 (1999) 6, pp. 1119-1128.

Francia, Peter L. et. al. (1999): Individual Donars in the 1996 Federal Elections. Green, John C. (ed.), 1999a, pp. 127-153.

Frendreis, John P./ Gitelson, Alan R. (1993): Local Parties in an Age of Change. In: *American Review of Politics*, 14 (1993) Winter, pp. 533-547.

Fromont, Michel (1992): Parteienfinanzierung in Frankreich. In: Tsatsos, Dimitris Th. (ed.), 1992, pp. 149-195.

Fürst report (1983): *Bericht zur Neuordnung der Parteienfinanzierung*. Vorschläge der von Bundespräsidenten berufenen Sachverständigen-Kommission. Köln: Bundesanzeiger, 1983.

Gagnon, Alain G./ Tanguay, A. Brian (eds.) (1992): *Democracy with Justice. Essays in Honour of Khayyam Zev Paltiel*. Ottawa: Carleton University, 1992.

Geddis, Andrew (2005): New Zealand. In: Grant, Thomas D. (ed.), 2005, pp. 355-372.

Gehne, David H./ Holtkamp, Lars (2002): Wahlkampf: Nicht ohne meine Partei? In: Andersen, Uwe/ Bovermann, Rainer (eds.): *Im Westen was Neues. Kommunalwahl 1999 in NRW*, Opladen: Leske+ Budrich, 2002, pp. 89-113.

Genckaya, Ömer Fraruk (2005): Turkey. In: Grant, Thomas D. (ed.), 2005, pp. 513-530.

Gibson, James L. et al. (1985): Whither the Local Parties? A Cross-Sectional and Longitudinal Analysis of Strength of Party Organizations. In: *American Journal of Political Science,* 29 (1985) 1, pp. 139-160.

Gibson, James L. et al. (1989): Party Dynamics in the 1980s: Change in Country Party Organizational Strength 1980-1984. In: *American Journal of Political Science,* 33 (1989), pp. 67-90.

Gibson, Rachel/ Römmele, Andrea (2001): A Party-Centered Theory of Professionalized Campaigning.I n: *Party Politics,* 6 (2001) 4, pp. 31-43.

Gidlund, Gullan M. (1991a): Public Investments in Swedish Democracy. In: Wiberg, Matti (ed.), 1991a, pp. 13-54.

Gidlund, Gullan M. (1991b): Conclusions. The Nature of Public Financing in the Nordic States. In: Wiberg, Matti (ed.), 1991a, pp. 173-186.

Gidlund, Gullan/ Koole, Ruud A. (2001): Political Finance in the North of Europe: The Netherlands and Sweden. In: Nassmacher, Karl-Heinz (ed.), 2001a, pp. 112-130.

Gidlund, Gullan M./ Möller, Tommy (1999): *Finansiering av personavalskampanjer i riksdagsvalet 1998.* SOU 1999: 92, pp. 53-59.

Gibbons, Kenneth M./ Rowat, Donald C. (eds.) (1976): *Political Corruption in Canada. Cases, Causes and Cures.* Toronto: McClelland & Stewart. 1976.

Gielen, Jos (1981): *Verkiezingscampagnes blijven een Miljoenen-aangelegenheid.* Leuven: Katholieke Universiteit te Leuven, 1981.

Gierzynsky, Anthony/ Breaux, David (1994): The Role of Parties in Legislative Campaigning Financing.I n: *American Review of Politics,* 15 (1994) Sommer, pp. 171-189.

Giles, Michael W./ Pritchard, Anita (1985): Campaign Expenditures and Legislative Elections in Florida. In: *Legislative Studies Quarterly,* 10 (1985) 1, pp. 71-88.

Gillespie, Richard (1990): The Break-up of the ‚Socialist Family': Party-Union Relations in Spain, 1982-1989. In: *West European Politics,* 13 (1990) 1, pp. 47-62.

Girvin, Brian (1999): Political Competition, 1992-1997. In: Marsh, Michael/ Mitchell, Paul (eds.), 1999, pp. 3-28.

Girvin, Brian/ Jay, Richard (eds.) (1998): *Irish Political Studies. Yearbook of the Political Studies Association of Ireland,* 12: Dublin: PSAI, 1998.

Godwin, Kenneth. R. (1988): *One Billion Dollars of Influence. The Direct Marketing of Politics.* Chatham NJ: Chatham House, 1988.

Goldstein, Ken/ Freedman, Paul (2002): Campaign Advertising and Voter Turnout: New Evidence for a Stimulation Effect. In: *The Journal of Politics,* 64 (2002) 3, pp. 721-740.

Goodhart, Lord/ Razzall, Lord (1999): The Funding of Political Parties in the United Kingdom: The Case for Cherry-picking. In: *Public Law,* 43 (1999) 1, pp. 43-50.

Grant, Thomas D. (ed.) (2005): *Lobbying. Government Relations and Campaign Finance Worldwide.* Navigating the Laws, Regulations and Practices of National Regimes. Oxford: Oceana Publications 2005.

Grasmück, Damian (2005): *Die Forza Italia Silvio Berlusconis.* Geburt, Entwicklung, Regierungstätigkeit und Strukturen einer charismatischen Partei. Frankfurt a. M. et al.: Peter Lang, 2005.

Green, John C. (ed.) (1999a): *Financing the 1996 Election.* Armonk NY and London: M. E. Sharpe, 1999.

Green, John C. (1999b): The End of an Area. In: Green, John C. (ed.), 1999a, pp. 3-9.

Green, John C. (2002): Still Functional After All These Years: Parties in the United States, 1960-2000. In: Webb, Paul et al. (eds.), 2002, pp. 310-344.

Green, John C./ Bigelow, Nathan S. (2002): The 2000 Presidential Nominations: The Costs of Innovation. In: Magleby, David B. (ed.), 2002a, pp. 49-78.

Green, John C./ Shea, Daniel M. (eds.) (1996): *The State of the Parties*. Lanham et al.: Rowman & Littlefield, 2nd ed. 1996.

Green, Matthew (2008): The 2006 Race for Democratic Majority Leader: Money, Policy, and the Personal Loyality. In: *PS: Political Science and Politics*, XLI (2008) 1, pp. 63-67.

Greene, Kenneth F. (2002): Opposition Party Strategy and Spatial Competition in Dominant Party Regimes. A Theory and the Case of Mexico. In: *Comparative Political Studies*, 35 (2002) 7, pp. 755-783.

Gross, Donald A. et al. (2002): State Campaign Finance Regulations and Electoral Competition. In: *American Politics Research*, 30 (2002) 2, pp. 143-165.

Gunlicks, Arthur B. (ed.) (1993): *Campaign and Party Finance in North America and Western Europe*. Boulder CO: Westview, 1993.

Gunther, Richard/ Ramon-Montero, Rose/ Lintz, Juan (eds.) (2002): *Political Parties: Old Concepts and New Challenges*. Oxford: Oxford University, 2002.

Gunther, Richard/ Diamond, Larry (2003): Species of Political Parties. A New Typology. In: *Party Politics*, 9 (2003) 2, pp. 167-199.

Guthmann Wolfgang (2007): *Demokratisierung in Afrika: Muster der Entwicklung in den SADC-Staaten*. Oldenburg: dissertation, 2007.

Gutmann, Emanuel (1963): Israel. In: *Journal of Politics*, 25 (1963) 4, pp. 703-717.

Gwyn, William B. (1962): *Democracy and the Cost of Politics in Britain*. London: Athlone, 1962.

Hall, Richard L./ Wayman, Frank W. (1990): Bying Time: Moneyed Interests and the Mobilization of Bias in Congressional Committees. In: *American Political Science Review*, 84 (1990) 3, pp. 797-820.

Harmel, Robert/ Janda, Kenneth (1982): *Parties and their Environments. Limits to Reform?* New York: Longman, 1982.

Harmel, Robert et al. (1995): Performance, Leadership, Factions and Party Change: An Empirical Analysis. In: *West European Politics*, 18 (1995) 1, pp. 1-33.

Harrison, Martin (1963): Britain. In: *Journal of Politics*, 25 (1963) 3, pp. 664-685.

Hart, Joep de/ Dekker, Paul (1999): Civic Engagement und Volunteering in the Netherlands: a ‚Putnamian' Analysis. In: Deth, Jan W. van et al. (eds.), 1999, pp. 75-107.

Heard, Alexander (1960): *The Cost of Democracy*. Chapel Hill NC: University of North Carolina, 1960.

Heard, Alexander (1968): Political Financing. In: Sills, David L. (ed.): *International Encyclopedia of the Social Sciences*, vol. 12. New York: Free Press - Macmillan, 1968, pp. 235-241.

Heidar, Knut/ Saglie, Jo (2003): Predestined Parties? Organizational Change in Norwegian Political Parties. In: *Party Politics*, 9 (2003) 2, pp. 219-239.

Heidar, Knut/ Saglie, Jo (2004): A Decline of Linkage? Intra-Party Participation in Norway, 1991- 2000. In: *European Journal of Political Research*, 42 (2004) 6, pp. 761-786.

Heidenheimer, Arnold J. (1963): Comparative Party Finance - Notes on Practices and Towards a Theory. In: *Journal of Politics*, 25 (1963) 4, pp. 790-811.

Heidenheimer, Arnold J. (ed.) (1970a): *Comparative Political Finance. The Financing of Party Organizations and Election Campaigns*. Lexington MA: D.C. Heath, 1970.

Heidenheimer, Arnold J. (1970b): The Major Modes of Raising, Spending and Controlling Political Funds During and Between Election Campaigns. In: Heidenheimer, Arnold J. (ed.), 1970a, pp. 3-18.

Heidenheimer, Arnold J. (2002): Parties, Campaign Finance and Political Corruption: Tracing Long-Term Comparative Dynamics. In: Heidenheimer, Arnold J./ Johnston, Michael (eds.), 2002, pp. 761-776.

Heidenheimer, Arnold J./ Johnston, Michael (eds.) (2002): *Political Corruption. Concepts and Contexts*. New Brunswick NJ and London UK: Transaction Publishers, 2002.

Heidenheimer, Arnold J./ Langdon, Frank C. (1968): *Business Associations and the Financing of Political Parties. A Comparative Study of the Evaluation of Practices in Germany, Norway and Japan*. The Hague: Martinus Nijhoff, 1968.

Helms, Ludger (ed.) (1999): *Parteien und Fraktionen. Ein internationaler Vergleich*. Opladen: Leske+ Budrich, 1999.

Hermens, Ferdinand A. (1941): *Democracy or Anarchy?* Notre Dame IN: University of Notre Dame, 1941.

Hermens, Ferdinand A. (1958): *The Representative Republic*, Notre Dame: University of Notre Dame, 1958.

Herrnson, Paul S. (1993a): The High Finance of American Politics. Campaign Spending and Reform in Federal Elections. In: Gunlicks, Arthur B. (ed.), 1993, pp. 17-40.

Herrnson, Paul S. (1993b): Political Parties and Congressional Elections: Out of the Eighties and into the Nineties. In: Margolis, Michael/ Green, John C. (eds.), 1993, pp. 7-19.

Herrnson, Paul S. (1998): National Party Organizations at the Century's End. In: Maisel, L. Sandy (ed.), 1998, pp. 50-82.

Herrnson, Paul S. (1999): Financing the 1996 Congressional Elections. In: Green, John C. (ed.), 1999a, pp. 95-125.

Herz, John H./ Carter, Gwendolen M. (1964): *Regierungsformen des 20. Jahrhunderts*. Stuttgart: Kohlhammer, 3rd. ed. 1964.

Heywood, Paul (1995): Sleaze in Spain. In: *Parliamentary Affairs*, 48 (1995) 4, pp. 726-737.

Heywood, Paul (1996): Continuity and Change: Analysing Political Corruption in Modern Spain. In: Little, Walter/ Posada-Carbo, Eduardo (eds.), 1996, pp. 115-136.

Heywood, Paul (1997): From Dictatorship to Democracy: Changing Forms of Corruption in Spain. In: Della Porta, Donatella/ Mény, Yves (eds.), 1997a, pp. 65-83.

Hine, David (1996): Political Corruption in Italy. In: Little, Walter/ Posada-Carbo, Eduardo (eds.), 1996, pp. 137-157.

Hjorth, Helga/ Nygard, Beate (2005): Norway. In: Grant, Thomas D. (ed.), 2005, pp. 373-386.

Höpner, Martin (2006): Beiträge der Unternehmen zur Parteienfinanzierung. Wer spendet an wen? Und warum? In: *Zeitschrift für Parlamentsfragen*, 37 (2006) 2, pp. 293-312.

Hofmann, Stefan (1998): *Parteienfinanzierung im Autonomiestaat Spanien.* Baden-Baden: Nomos, 1998.

Hofnung, Menachem (1996a): Public Financing, Party Membership and Internal Party Competition. In: *European Journal of Political Research,* 29 (1996) 1, pp. 73-86.

Hofnung, Menachem (1996b): Political Finance in Israel. In: Levi, Michael/ Nelken, David (eds.): *The Corruption of Politics and the Politics of Corruption.* Cambridge: Blackwell, 1996, pp. 132-148.

Hofnung, Menachem (2005): Fat Parties - Lean Candidates: Funding Israeli Internal Party Contests. In: Arian, Asher/ Shamir, Michal (eds.), *Elections in Israel - 2003.* New Brunswick (USA) and London (UK): Transaction, 2005, pp. 63-83.

Hofnung, Menachem (2006): Financing Internal Party Races in Non-Majoritarian Political Systems: Lessons from the Israeli Experience. In: *Election Law Journal,* 5 (2006) 4, pp. 372-383.

Holliday, Ian (2002): Spain: Buildung a Parties State in a New Democracy. In: Webb, Paul et al. (eds.), 2002, pp. 248-279.

Holmes, Leslie T./ Roszkowski, Wojciech (eds.) (1997): *Changing Rules – Polish Political and Economic Transformation in Comparative Perspective.* Warsaw: Institute of Political Studies - Polish Academy of Science, 1997.

Holtz-Bacha, Christina/ Kaid, Lynda Lee (1995): A Comparative Perspective on Political Advertising. Media and Political System Characteristics. In: Kaid, Lynda Lee/ Holtz-Bacha, Christina (eds.): *Political Advertising in Western Democracies.* Thousand Oaks et al.: Sage, 1995, pp. 8-18.

Holtz-Bacha, Christina/ Kaid, Linda-Lee (2006): Political Advertising in International Comparison. In: Kaid, Linda Lee/ Holtz-Bacha, Christina (eds.): *The Sage Handbook of Political Advertising.* Thousand Oaks: Sage, 2006, pp. 3-13.

Hooghe, Marc/ Maddens, Bart/ Noppe, Jo (2006): Why parties adapt: Electoral reform, party finance and party strategy in Belgium. In: *Electoral Studies,* 25 (2006) 2, pp. 351-368.

Horngren, Charles T./ Foster, George (1987): *Cost Accounting. A Managerial Emphasis.* Englewood Cliffs NJ: Prentice-Hall, 6th ed. 1987.

Houghton report (Lord Houghton of Sowerby) (1976): *Report of the Committee on Financial Aid to Political Parties.* London: H.M.S.O, 1976.

Hrebenar, Ronald J. et al. (1999): *Political Parties, Interest Groups, and Political Campaigns.* Boulder CO: Westview, 1999.

Huckshorn, Robert J. (1984): *Political Parties in America.* Monerey CA: Brooks/ Cole, 1984.

Huckshorn, Robert J. (1985): Who Gave It? Who Got It? The Enforcement of Campaign Finance Laws in the States. In: *Journal of Politics,* 47 (1985) 3, pp. 773-789.

Huntington, Samuel P. (1991): *The Third Wave.* Norman: University of Oklahoma, 1991.

Ikstens, Janis et al. (2002): Political Finance in Central Eastern Europe: An Interim Report. In: *Österreichische Zeitschrift für Politikwissenschaft,* 31 (2002) 1, pp. 21-39.

International IDEA (ed.) (1997): *Voter Turnout from 1945 to 1997: A Global Report on Political Participation.* Stockholm: International IDEA, 1997.

Isenberg, Seymour (1980): Can You Spend Your Way into House of Commens? In: *Optimum,* 11 (1980) 1, pp. 28-39.

Isenberg, Seymour (1981): Spend and Win? Another Look at Federal Elections Expenses. In: *Optimum*, 12 (1981) 4, pp. 5-15.

Jackson, Brooks (1997): Financing the 1996 Campaign: The Law of the Jungle. In: Sabato, Larry J. (ed.): *Toward the Millennium. The Election of 1996*. Boston: Allyn and Bacon, 1997, pp. 225-260.

Jacobson, Gary C. (1976): Practical Consequences of Campaign Finance Reform. An Incumbent Protection Act? In: *Public Policy*, 24 (1976) 1, pp. 1-32.

Jacobson, Gary C. (1978): The Effects of Campaign Spending in Congressional Elections. In: *American Political Science Review*, 72 (1978) 2, pp. 469-491.

Jacobson, Gary C. (1980): *Money in Congressional Elections*. New Haven: Yale University, 980.

Jacobson, Gary C. (1986): Party Organization and Distribution of Campaign Resources. Republicans and Democrats in 1982. In: *Political Science Quarterly*, 100 (1985/86) 4, pp. 603-625.

Jacobson, Gary C. (1990): The Effects of Campaign Spending in House Elections: New Evidence for Old Arguments. In: *American Journal of Political Science*, 34 (1990) May, pp. 334-362.

Jacobson, Gary C. (1993): The Misallocation of Resources in House Campaigns. In: Dodd, Lawrence C./ Oppenheimer, Bruce I. (eds.): *Congress Reconsidered*. Washington DC: Congressional Quarterly, 5th ed. 1993, pp. 115-139.

Jain, Randhir B. (2001): Electoral Financing in India. In: Nassmacher, Karl-Heinz (ed.), 2001a, pp. 350-368.

Jain, Randhir B. (2003): Asia. In: Carrillo, Manuel et al. (eds.), 2003, pp. 97-118.

Janda, Kenneth (1979): *Comparative Political Parties Data, 1950-1962*. Ann Arbor MI: Inter-University Consortium for Political and Social Research, 1979.

Janda, Kenneth (1980): *Political Parties. A Cross National Survey*. London: Macmillan, 1980.

Janda, Kenneth/ Birch, Sarah (2003): *Electoral Systems and Political Transformation in Post-Communist Europe*. Basingstoke and New York: Palgrave Macmillan, 2003.

Jardim, Torquato (1998): O Financiamento dos Partidos Politicos no Brasil. In: Castillo, Pilar del/ Zovatto G., Daniel (eds.), 1998, pp. 53-67.

Jewell, Malcolm E./ Olson, Davis M. (1978): *American State Political Parties and Elections*. Homewood 1978.

Jewell, Malcolm E./ Olson, Davis M. (1988): *Political Parties and Elections in American States*. Chicago: Dorsey, 3rd. 1988.

Joe, Wesley/ Wilcox, Clyde (1999): Financing the 1996 Presidential Nominations: The Last Regulated Campaign? In: Green, John C. (ed.), 1999a, pp. 37-62.

Johnston, Ronald J. (1986): A Further Look at British Political Finance. In: *Political Studies*, 34 (1986) 3, pp. 466-473.

Johnston, Ronald J. (1987): *Money and Votes. Constituancy Campaign Spending and Election Results*. London: Croom Helm, 1987.

Johnston, Ronald J./ Pattie, Charles J. (1993): Great Britain. Twentieth Century Parties Operating Under Nineteenth Century Regulations. In: Gunlicks, Arthur B. (ed.), 1993, pp. 123-154.

Johnston, Ronald J./ Pattie, Charles J. (1995): The Impact of Spending on Party Constituency Campaigns at Recent British General Elections. In: *Party Politics*, 1 (1995) 2, pp. 261-273.

Jones, Ruth S. (1984): Financing State Elections. In: Malbin, Michael J. (ed.), 1984, pp. 172-213.

Jones, Ruth S. (1988): *The U.S. Experience with Public Campaign Financing*. The Popular Base of Contributing. Paper presented to the World Congress of the International Political Science Association, Washington, 1988 (unpublished).

Jones, Ruth S. (1990): Contributing as Participation. In: Nugent, Margaret Latus/ Johannes, John R. (eds.), 1990, pp. 27-46.

Jones, Ruth S. (1993): Campaign and Party Finance in the American States. In: Gunlicks, Arthur B. (ed.), 1993, pp. 41-67.

Jones, Ruth S./ Borris, Thomas J. (1985): Strategic Contributing in Legislative Campaigns: The Case of Minnesota. In: *Legislative Studies Quarterly*, 10 (1985) 1, pp. 89-105.

Jones, Ruth S./ Hopkins, Anne H. (1985): State Campaign Fund Raising. Targets and Response. In: *Journal of Politics*, 47 (1985) 2, pp. 427-449.

Judt, Tony (2002): *Postwar. A History of Europe since 1945*. Harmondsworth: Penguin, 2002.

Jun, Uwe (2004): *Der Wandel von Parteien in der Mediendemokratie. SPD und Labour Party im Vergleich*. Frankfurt and New York: Campus, 2004.

Kalchheim, Chaim/ Rosevitch, Shimon (1992): The Financing of Elections and Parties. In: Elazar, Daniel J./ Sandler, Shmuel (eds.): *Who's the Boss in Israel. Israel at the Polls, 1988-89*. Detroit: Wayne State University, 1992, pp. 212-229.

Kaltefleiter, Werner (1968): *Wirtschaft und Politik in Deutschland*. Konjunktur als Bestimmungsfaktor des Parteiensystems, 2nd ed., Köln and Opladen: Westdeutscher, 1968.

Katz, Richard S. (1980): *A Theory of Parties and Electoral Systems*. Baltimore and London: Johns Hopkins University, 1980.

Katz, Richard S. (1990): Party as Linkage: A Vestigial Function? In: *European Journal of Political Research*, 18 (1990) 1, pp. 143-161.

Katz, Richard S. (1996): Party Organizations and Finance. In: LeDuc, Lawrence et al. (eds.), 1996a, pp. 107-133.

Katz, Richard S./ Crotty, William (eds.) (2006): *Handbook of Party Politics*, London: Sage, 2006.

Katz, Richard S./ Kolodny, Robin (1994): Party Organization as an Empty Vessel: Parties in American Politics. In: Katz, Richard S./ Mair, Peter (eds.), 1994, pp. 23-50.

Katz, Richard S./ Mair, Peter (eds.) (1992): *Party Organizations. A Data Handbook on Party Organizations in Western Democracies. 1960-90*. London: Sage, 1992.

Katz, Richard S./ Mair, Peter (eds.) (1994): *How Parties Organize. Change and Adaptation in Party Organizations in Western Democracies*. London et al.: Sage, 1994.

Katz, Richard S./ Mair, Peter (1995): Changing Models of Party Organization and Party Democracy: The Emergence of the Cartel Party. In: *Party Politics*, 1 (1995) 1, pp. 5-28.

Katz, Richard S./ Mair, Peter (1996): Cadre, Catch-all or Cartel? A Rejoinder. In: *Party Politics*, 2 (1996) 4, pp. 525-548.

Katz, Richard S./ Mair, Peter (2002): The Ascendency of the Party in Public Office: Party Organizational Change in Twentieth-Century Democracies. In: Gunther, Richard et al. (eds.), 2002, pp. 113-134.

Kayden, Xandra/ Mahe, Eddie (1985): *The Party Goes on: The Persistence of the Two Party System in the United States.* New York: Basic Books, 1985.

Kelly, John M. (1990): Die Institution der politischen Partei in Irland. In: Tsatsos, Dimitris Th. et al. (ed.), 1990, pp. 337-365.

Kelly, John M. (1992): Parteienfinanzierung in Irland. In: Tsatsos, Dimitris Th. (ed.), 1992, pp. 259-272.

Kempf, Thomas (1989): Organisation der Fraktionsarbeit. In: Kempf, Thomas/ Kodolitsch, Paul von/ Nassmacher, Hiltrud: *Die Arbeitssituation von Ratsmitgliedern.* Berlin: Difu, 1989, pp. 111-157.

Kempf, Udo (1997): *Von de Gaulle bis Chirac. Das politische System Frankreichs.* Opladen: Westdeutscher Verlag, 3 rd. ed. 1997.

Kempf, Udo (2007): *Das politische System Frankreichs.* Wiesbaden: VS Verlag für Sozialwissenschaften, 4th. ed. 2007.

Kerbusch, Ernst J. (1971): *Das uruguayische Regierungssystem.* Berlin: Carl Heymanns, 1971.

Kerde, Ortrud (1998): Geld und Politik. Grauzonen der Parteienfinanzierung in Japan. In: Ernst, Angelika/ Poertner, Peter (eds.): *Die Rolle des Geldes in Japans Gesellschaft, Wirtschaft und Politik.* Hamburg: Institut für Asienkunde, 1998, pp. 163-192.

Kevenhörster, Paul (1969): *Das politische System Japans.* Köln and Opladen: Westdeutscher, 1969.

Kevenhörster, Paul (1973): *Wirtschaft und Politik in Japan. Interessengruppen, politische Meinungsbildung und wirtschaftliche Entscheidungen.* Wiesbaden: Otto Harrassowitz, 1973.

Kevenhörster, Paul (1993): *Politik und Gesellschaft in Japan.* Mannheim et al.: Brockhaus, 1993.

Kevenhörster, Paul (2003): Politik. In: Kevenhörster, Paul et al.: *Japan.* Opladen: Leske + Budrich, 2003, pp. 259-391.

Kirchheimer, Otto (1966): The Transformation of Western European Party Systems. In: LaPalombara, Joseph/ Weiner; Myron (eds.) (1966): *The Political Parties and the Political Development.* Princeton: Princeton University, pp. 177-200.

Klee-Kruse, Gudrun (1992): Kosten der Demokratie in Österreich und Schweden. In: *Zeitschrift für Parlamentsfragen,* 23 (1992) 3, pp. 455-462.

Klee-Kruse, Gudrun (1993a): *Öffentliche Parteienfinanzierung in westlichen Demokratien. Schweden und Österreich.* Ein Vergleich. Frankfurt a. M. and New York: P. Lang, 1993.

Klee, Gudrun (1993b): Financing Parties and Elections in Small European Democracies. Austria and Sweden. In: Gunlicks, Arthur B. (ed.), 1993, pp. 178-200.

Klein, Axel (1998): *Das Wahlsystem als Reformobjekt,* Bonn: Bier'sche Verlagsanstalt, 1998.

Knapp, Andrew (2002): France: Never a Golden Age. In: Webb, Paul et al. (eds.), 2002, pp. 107-150.

Köllner, Patrick (2000a): Japan unter Reformdruck. In: *Japan aktuell,* 8 (2000) 1, pp. 54-146.

Köllner, Patrick (2000b): Parteienfinanzierung in Japan: Regulierungsmechanismen und Anpassungsstrategien.I n: *Japan aktuell*, 8 (2000) 2, pp. 147-158.

Köllner, Patrick (2005): Informelle Parteistrukturen und institutioneller Wandel: Japanische Erfahrungen nach den politischen Reformen des Jahres 1994. In: *Politische Vierteljahresschrift*, 46 (2005) 1, pp. 39-61.

Kofler, Anton (1981): Parteienfinanzierung und deren Auswirkungen auf innerparteiliche Strukturen, dargestellt am Beispiel der ÖVP. In: Khol, Andreas/ Stirnemann, Alfred (eds.): *Österreichisches Jahrbuch für Politik 1980*. München and Wien: Oldenbourg, 1981, pp. 361-389.

Kolodny, Robin/ Dulio, David A. (2003): Political Party Adoption in US Congressional Campaigns. Why Political Parties Use Coordinated Expenditure to Hire Political Consultants. In: *Party Politics*, 9 (2003) 6, pp. 729-746.

Kolodny, Robin/ Dwyre, Diana (1998): Party-orchestrated Activities for Legislative Party Goals: Campaigns for Majorities in the US House of Representatives in the 1990s. In: *Party Politics*, 4 (1998) 3, pp. 275-295.

Koole, Ruud A. (1988): De Transformatie van Nederlandse politieke Partijen. In: *Jaarboek 1988 DNPP*. Groningen: Rijksuniversiteit Groningen, 1988, pp. 198-223.

Koole, Ruud A. (1989): The 'Modesty' of Dutch Party Finance. In: Alexander, Herbert E. (eds.), 1989a, pp. 200-219.

Koole, Ruud A. (1992): *De opkomst von de moderne kaderpartij: veranderende partijorganisatie in Nederland 1960-1990*. Utrecht: Het Sectrum, 1992.

Koole, Ruud A. (1994a): Dutch Political Parties. Money and the Message. In: Alexander, Herbert E./ Shiratori, Rei (eds.), 1994a, pp. 115-132.

Koole, Ruud A. (1994b): The Vulnerability of the Modern Cadre Party in the Netherlands. In: Katz, Richard S./ Mair, Peter (eds.), 1994, pp. 278-303.

Koole, Ruud A. (1996): Cadre, Catch-all or Cartel? A Comment on the Notion of the Cartel Party. In: *Party Politics*, 2 (1996) 4, pp. 507-524.

Koole, Ruud A. (1997): Ledenpartijen of staatspartijen? Financien von Nederlandse politieke partijen in vergelijkend en historisch perspectief. In: *Jaarboek 1996. Dokumentatiecentrum Niederlandse Politieke Partijen*. Groningen: University of Groningen, 1997, pp. 156-182.

Koole, Ruud A. (1999): Die Antwort der niederländischen Parteien auf die wahlpolitischen Herausforderungen. In: Mair, Peter et al. (eds.), 1999, pp. 315-352.

Koole, Ruud A. (2001): Political Finance in Western Europe: Britain and France. In: Nassmacher, Karl-Heinz (ed.), 2001a, pp. 73-91.

Koole, Ruud A./ Nassmacher, Karl-Heinz (2001): Political Finance in the United States. In: Nassmacher, Karl-Heinz (ed.), 2001a, pp. 34-52.

Kreutz-Gers, Waltraud (1988): *Die Reform der Wahlkampf- und Parteienfinanzierung in Kanada. Problemlage, Programmgestaltung, Implementation und Wirkungen*. Oldenburg: BIS, 1988.

Krouwel, Andrae (1999): *The Catch-all Party in Western Europe 1945-1990. A Study in Arrested Development*. Amsterdam: Vrije Universiteit, dissertation, 1999.

Krouwel, Andrae (2003): Otto Kirchheimer and the Catch-All Party. In: *West European Politics*, 26 (2003) 2, pp. 23-40.

Kumado, Kofi (ed.) (1996): *Funding Political Parties in West Afrika*. Accra: Friedrich Ebert Foundation,1996.

Laakso, Markku/ Taagepera, Rein (1979): 'Efffective' Number of Parties: A Measure with Application to West Europe. In: *Comparative Political Studies*, 12 (1979) 1, pp. 3-27.

Ladner, Andreas/ Brändle, Michael (1999): *Parteienförderung in der Schweiz. Analysen und Vorschläge. Schlussbericht.* Bern: Institut für Politikwissenschaft, 1999.

Ladner, Andreas/ Brändle, Michael (2001): *Die Schweizer Parteien im Wandel. Von Mitgliederparteien zu professionalisierten Wählerorganisationen?* Zürich: Seismo, 2001.

Ladrech, Robert (1990): *The French Socialist Party as a „Party of Government".* APSA Paper 1990 (unpublished).

Ladrech, Robert (2006): "The European Union and Political Parties". In: Katz, Richard S./ Crotty, William (eds.), 2006, pp. 492-498.

Landfried, Christine (1994a): *Parteifinanzen und politische Macht. Eine vergleichende Studie zur Bundesrepublik Deutschland, zu Italien und den USA.* Baden-Baden: Nomos, 2nd. 1994.

Landfried, Christine (1994b): Political Finance in West Germany. In: Alexander, Herbert E./ Shiratori, Rei (eds.), 1994a, pp. 133-144.

Lane, Jan-Erik/ Ersson, Svante O. (1996): *European Politics.* London et al.: Sage, 1996.

Laver, Michael/ Marsh, Michael (1999): Parties and Voters. In: Coakley, John/ Gallagher, Michael (eds.): *Politics in the Republic of Ireland.* London and New York: Routledge, 3rd. ed. 1999, pp. 152-176.

LeDuc, Lawrence/ Niemi, Richard G./ Norris, Pippa (eds.) (1996a): *Camparing Democracies: Elections and Voting in Global Perspective.* Thousand Oaks: Sage, 1996.

LeDuc, Lawrence et al. (1996b): Introduction: The Present and Future of Democratic Elections. In: LeDuc, Lawrence et al. (eds.), 1996a, pp. 1-48.

Lehmbruch, Gerhard (1967): *Proporzdemokratie.* Tübingen: Mohr, 1967.

Leibholz, Gerhard (1965): *Politics and Law.* Leyden, NL: A.W. Sythoff, 1965.

Leonard, Dick (1975): Paying for Party Politics: The Case for Public Subsidies. In: *PEP Broadsheet No. 555.* London: PEP, 1975.

Leonard, Dick (1975): Contrasts in Selected Western Democracies: Germany, Sweden and Britain. In: Alexander, Herbert E. (ed.), 1979a, pp. 41-73.

Leopold, John W. (1997): Trade Unions, Political Fund Ballots and the Labour Party. In: *British Journal of Industrial Relations*, 35 (1997) 1, pp. 22-38.

Levit, Kenneth J. (1993): Campaign Finance Reform and the Return of Buckley v. Valeo. In: *Yale Law Review*, 103 (1993) 5, pp. 469-503.

Levush, Ruth et al. (1997): *Campaign Financing of National Elections in Selected Foreign Countries.* Washington DC: Law Library. Library of Congress, 1997.

Lewis, Paul G. (1998): Party Funding in Post-Communist East-Central Europe. In: Burnell, Peter/ Ware, Alan (eds.), 1998, pp. 137-157.

Linz, Juan (2002): Parties in Contemporary Democracies: Problems and Paradoxes, In: Gunther, Richard et al. (eds.), 2002, pp. 291-317.

Lijphart, Arend (1984): *Democracies. Patterns of Majoritarian and Consensus Government in Twenty-One Countries.* New Haven and London: Yale University, 1984.

Lijphart, Arend (1999): *Patterns of Democracy. Government Forms and Performance in Thirty-Six Countries.* New Haven and Londen:Yale University, 1999.

Lipset, Seymor Martin/ Rokkan, Stein (eds.) (1967): *Party Systems and Voter Alignments: Cross-National Perspectives.* New York/ London: Free Press & Collier Macmillan, 1967.

Lisowski, Rainer (2006): *Die strategische Planung politischer Kampagnen in Wirtschaft und Politik.* Oldenburg: Isensee, 2006.

Little, Walter/ Posada-Carbo, Eduardo (eds.) (1996): *Political Corruption in Europe and Latin America.* Basingstoke and London: Macmillan, 1996.

Lösche, Peter (1984): *Wovon leben die Parteien? Über das Geld in der Politik.* Frankfurt a. M.: Fischer Taschenbuch, 1984.

Lösche, Peter (1989): *Amerika in Perspektive. Politik und Gesellschaft der Vereinigten Staaten.* Darmstadt: Wissenschaftliche Buchgesellschaft, 1989.

Lösche, Peter (1993): 'Lose verkoppelte Anarchie'. Zur aktuellen Situation der Volksparteien am Beispiel der SPD. In: *Aus Politik und Zeitgeschichte,* 43 (1993), pp. 34-45.

Lösche, Peter/ Franz Walter (1992): *Die SPD: Klassenpartei – Volkspartei – Quotenpartei.* Darmstadt: Wissenschaftliche Buchgesellschaft, 1992.

Lopez Garrido, Diego (1994): La Financiacion de los Partidos Politicos: Diez Propuestas de Reforma. In: *La Financiacion de los Partidos Politicos.* Madrid: Centro des Estudies Constitutitionales, 1994, pp. 65-72.

Lortie report (Royal Commission on Electoral Reform and Party Financing) (1991): *Final Report. Reforming Electoral Democracy,* 4 Volumes. Ottawa: Canada Communications Group – Publishing, 1991, Volume 3.

Lott, William F./ Warner, P. D. (1974): The Relative Importance of Congressional Expenditures: An Application of Production Theory. In: *Quantity and Quality,* 8 (1974) 1, pp. 99-105.

Lowry, Robert C. et al. (2003): *Leadership PACs and Campaign Contributions in the U.S. House of Representatives.* Paper, prepared for the 2003 Annual Meeting of the American Political Science Association (unpublished).

Lucardie, Paul/ Voerman, Gerrit (2001): Party Foundations in the Netherlands. In: Nassmacher, Karl-Heinz (ed.), 2001a, pp. 321-337.

Lucarelli, Sonia/ Radaelli, Claudio M. (2004): Italy: Think Tanks and the Political System. In: Stone, Diane/ Denham, Andrew (eds.), 2004, pp. 89-104.

Lujambio, Alonso (2003): Experiencias nacionales representativas - México. In: Carrillo, Manuel et al. (eds.), 2003, pp. 368-386.

Luther, Kurt Richard (1999): Must what goes up always come down? Of Pillars and Arches in Austria's Political Architecture. In: Luther, Kurt Richard/ Deschouwer, Kris (eds.), 1999, pp. 43-73.

Luther, Kurt Richard/ Deschouwer, Kris (eds.) (1999): *Party Elites in Divided Societies.* London and New York: Routledge, 1999.

MacIvor, Heather (1994): The Leadership Convention. An Institution under Stress. In: Mancuso, Maureen et al. (eds.): *Leaders and Leadership in Canada.* Toronto: Oxford University, 1994, pp. 13-27.

Mackie, Thomas T./ Rose, Richard (1991): *The International Almanac of Electoral History.* Houndsmills et al.: Macmillan, 3rd. ed. 1991.

Maddens, Bart/ Noppe, Jo (2005): Belgium. In: Grant, Thomas D. (ed.), 2005, pp. 39-56.

Maddens, Bart/ Wauters, Bram/ Noppe, Jo/ Fiers, Stefaan (2006): Effects of Campaign Spending in an Open List PR System: The 2003 Legislative Elections in Flanders/Belgium. In: *West European Politics,* 29 (2006) 1, pp. 161-168.

Magleby, David B. (ed.) (2002a): *Financing the 2000 Election*, Washington, DC: Brookings Institution, 2002.

Magleby, David B. (2002b): A High-Stakes Election. In: Magleby, David B. (ed.), 2002a, pp. 1-21.

Magleby, David B. (2006): Change and Continuity in the Financing of Federal Elections. In: Magleby, David B. et al. (eds.), 2006, pp. 1-29.

Magleby, David B./ Corrado, Anthony/ Patterson, Kelly D. (eds.) (2006): *Financing the 2004 Election*, Washington, DC: Brookings Institution, 2006.

Mahler, Gregory S. (1990): *Israel – Government and Politics in a Maturing State*. San Diego CA: Harcourt Brace Jovanovich, 1990.

Mair, Peter/ Müller, Wolfgang C./ Plasser, Fritz (eds.) (1999): *Parteien auf komplexen Wählermärkten. Reaktionsstrategien in Westeuropa*, Wien: Signum, 1999.

Mair, Peter/ Biezen, Ingrid van (2001): Party Membership in Twenty European Democracies, 1980-2000. In: *Party Politics*, 7 (2001) 1, pp. 5-22.

Maisel, L. Sandy (ed.) (1998): The Parties Respond: Changes in American Parties and Campaigns. Boulder CO: Westview, 1998.

Malamud, Carlos/ Posada-Carbó, Eduardo (eds.) (2005): *The Financing of Politics: Latin American and European Perspectives*. London: The Institute for the Studies of Americas 2005.

Malbin, Michael J. (1979): Campaign Financing and the Special Interest. In: *Public Interest*, 56 (1979) 2, pp. 23-25.

Malbin, Michael J. (ed.) (1980a): *Parties, Interest Groups, and Campaign Finance Laws*. Washington DC: American Enterprise Institute, 1980.

Malbin, Michael J. (1980b): Of Mountains and Molehills. PAC's, Campaigns, and Public Policy. In: Malbin, Michael J. (ed.), 1980a, pp. 152-184.

Malbin, Michael J. (ed.) (1984): *Money and Politics in the United States. Financing Elections in the 1980s*. Washington DC: American Enterprise Institute, 1984.

Malbin, Michael J. (ed.) (2003): *Life after Reform: When the Bipartisan Campaign Reform Act meets Politics*. Lanham MD: Rowman & Littlefield, 2003.

Maloney, William A. (1999): Contracting Out the Participation Function: Social Capital and Chequebook Participation. In: Deth, Jan W. van et al. (eds.), 1999, pp. 108-119.

Mandle, Jay (2003): *The Politics of Democracy: An Empirical Analysis*. Colgate University: Department of Economics (Discussion Paper No. 103-10 2003).

Mann, Thomas E. (2003): Linking Knowledge and Action: Political Science and Campaign Finance Reform. In: *American Political Science Association*, 1 (2003)1, pp. 69-83.

Margolis, Michael/ Green, John C. (eds.) (1993): *Machine Politics, Sound Bites, and Nostalgia: On Studying Political Parties*. Lanham MD: University Press of America, 1993.

Marsh, Ian/ Stone, Diane (2004): Australian Think Tanks. In: Stone, Diane/ Denham, Andrew (eds.), 2004, pp. 247-263.

Marsh, Michael (1999): The Making of the Eighth President. In: Marsh, Michael/ Mitchel, Paul (eds.), 1999, pp. 215-242.

Marsh, Michael/ Mitchell, Paul (1999) (eds.) : *How Ireland Voted 1997*. Boulder CO: Westview, 1999.

Martinez Cardenas, Tania M. (2005): *El Financiamento Publico a los Partidos Politicos. El Caso de Mexico: Causas y Consequencias*. Mexico, D.F.: U.N.A.M., Master's thesis, 2005.

Massicotte, Louis (1992): Popular Financing of Parties in Quebec: An Analysis of the Financial Reports of Parties, 1978-1989. In: Gagnon, Alain G./ Tanguay, A. Brian (eds.), 1992, pp. 383-390.

Mayntz, Renate (1988): Funktionelle Teilsysteme in der Theorie der sozialen Differenzierung. In: Mayntz, Renate et al. (eds.): *Differenzierung und Verselbständigung: Zur Entwicklung gesellschaftlicher Teilsysteme.* Franfurt/Main and New York: Campus, 1988, pp. 11-44.

McAllister, Ion (2002): Political Parties in Australia: Party Stability in a Utilitarian Society. In: Webb, Paul et al. (eds.), 2002, pp. 379-408.

McAlpine, Alastair (1998): *Once a Jolly Bagman,* London: Phoenix, 1998.

McKenzie, Robert T. (1963): *British Political Parties. The Distribution of Power within the Conservative and Labour Parties.* New York and London: Praeger, 1963.

Medvic, Stephen K. (2001): The Impact of Party Financial Support on Electoral Success of US House Candidates. In: *Party Politics,* 7 (2001) 2, pp. 191-212.

Melchionda, Enrico (1997): *Il finanziamento della politica.* Rom: Riuniti, 1997.

Mendilow, Jonathan (1989): Party Financing in Israel. Experience and Experimentation, 1968-85. In: Alexander, Herbert E. (ed.), 1989a, pp. 124-152.

Mendilow, Jonathan (1992): Public Party Funding and Party Transformation in Multi-Party Systems. In: *Comparative Political Studies,* 25 (1992) 1, pp. 90-117.

Mendilow, Jonathan (1996): Public Party Funding and the Schemes of Mice and Men. The 1992 Elections in Israel. In: *Party Politics,* 2 (1996) 3, pp. 329-354.

Mendilow, Jonathan (2003): Public Campaign Funding and Party System Change: The Israeli Experience.I n: *Israel Studies Forum,* 19 (2003) Fall, pp. 115-122.

Mendilow, Jonathan/ Rusciano, Frank (2001): The Effects of Public Funding on Party Participation. In: Nassmacher, Karl-Heinz (ed.), 2001a, pp. 222-239.

Mény, Yves (1996): Corruption French Style. In: Little, Walter/ Posada-Carbo, Eduardo (eds.), 1996, pp. 159-172.

Mény, Yves (1997): France: the End of the Republican Ethic? In: Della Porta, Donatella/ Mény, Yves (eds.), 1997a, pp. 7-20.

Merkel, Wolfgang (1999): *Systemtransformation. Eine Einführung in die Theorie und Empirie der Transformationsforschung.* Opladen: Leske + Budrich, 1999.

Meseznikov, Grigorij (2005): Slovakia. In: Grant, Thomas D. (ed.), 2005, pp. 439-448.

Michaud, Pascale/ Laferriere, Pierre (1991): Economic Analysis of the Funding of Political Parties in Canada. In: Seidle, Leslie F. (ed.), 1991c, pp. 369-398.

Michels, Robert (1968): *Political Parties: A Sociological Study of the Oligarchical Tendencies of Modern Democracy.* 2nd ed., New York: Free Press, 1968.

Miguet, Arnauld (1999): Funding of Political Life in the Fifth Republic. In: Ewing, Keith D. (ed.), 1999, pp. 45-79.

Miller, Raymond (2005): *Party Politics in New Zealand.* Oxford and New York: Oxford University, 2005.

Mintzel, Alf (1978): *Die CSU: Anatomie einer konservativen Partei.* Opladen: Westdeutscher, 1978.

Mitchell, Brian Redman (2003a): *International Historical Statistics. Europe 1950-2000.* Houndmills et al.: Palgrave Macmillan, 5th. ed. 2003.

Mitchell, Brian Redman (2003b): *International Historical Statistics. The Americas 1950-2000.* Houndmills et al.: Palgrave Macmillan, 5th. ed. 2003.

Mitchell, Brian Redman (2003c): *International Historical Statistics. Africa, Asia & Oceania 1950-2000.* Houndmills et al.: Palgrave Macmillan, 5th. ed. 2003.

Mockler, Frank (1994): Organisational Change in Fianna Fáil and Fine Gael. In: *Irish Political Studies,* 9 (1994), pp. 165-171.

Monroe, J. P. (2001): *The Political Party Matrix: The Persistence of Organization.* Albany NY: State University of New York, 2001.

Morlok, Martin/ von Alemann, Ulrich/ Streit, Thilo (eds.) (2006): *Sponsoring – ein neuer Königsweg der Parteienfinanzierung?* Baden-Baden: Nomos, 2006.

Müller, Wolfgang C. (1989): Party Patronage in Austria. In: Pelinka, Anton/ Plasser, Fritz (eds.), 1989, pp. 327-356.

Müller, Wolfgang C. (1994): The Development of Austrian Party Organizations in the Post-war Period. In: Katz, Richard S./ Mair, Peter (eds.), 1994, pp. 51-79.

Müller, Wolfgang C./ Strøm, Kaare (1997): Koalitionsregierungen in Westeuropa – eine Einleitung. In: Müller, Wolfgang C./ Strøm, Kaare (eds.): *Koalitionsregierungen in Westeuropa.* Wien: Signum, 1997, pp. 9-46.

Müller, Wolfgang C./ Strøm, Kaare (eds.) (2000): *Coalition Governments in Western Europe.* Oxford: Oxford University, 2000.

Mulé, Rosa (1998): Financial Uncertainties of Party Formation and Consolidation in Britain, Germany and Italy: The Early Years in Theoretical Perspective. In: Burnell, Peter/ Ware, Alan (eds.), 1998, pp. 47-72.

Munné, Rodolfo (2003): Argentina. In: Carrillo, Manuel et al. (eds.), 2003, pp.387-397.

Murphy, Ronan J./ Farrell, David M. (2002): Party Politics in Ireland: Regularizing a Volatile System. In: Webb, Paul et al. (eds.), 2002, pp. 217-247.

Narud, Hanne Marthe/ Strøm, Kaare (1997): Norwegen. Eine fragile Koalitionsordnung. In: Müller, Wolfgang C./ Strøm, Kaare (eds.): *Koalitionsregierungen in Westeuropa.* Wien: Signum, 1997, pp. 199-238.

Nassmacher, Hiltrud (1989): Auf- und Abstieg von Parteien. Ansätze zur vergleichenden Betrachtung von Etablierung und Niedergang von Parteien im Wettbewerb. In: *Zeitschrift für Politik,* 36 (1989 2, pp. 169-190 (republished in: Schmitt, Karl (ed.) (1990): *Wahlen, Parteieliten, politische Einstellungen.* Frankfurt a. M.: Lang, 1990, pp. 177-209).

Nassmacher, Hiltrud (1992): Parteien in Nordamerika: Apparatparteien "neuen Typs"?. In: *Zeitschrift für Parlamentsfragen,* 23 (1992) 1, pp. 110-130.

Nassmacher, Hiltrud (1999): Politische Führung auf Zeit: Zur Struktur und Bedeutung von Parteien und Fraktionen im politischen System Kanadas. In: Helms, Ludger (ed.), 1999, pp. 265-286.

Nassmacher, Hiltrud (2003): Und führe uns nicht in Versuchung! Neue Gefahren in der Kommunalpolitik: Eine Ursachensuche. In: *Verwaltungsrundschau,* 49 (2003) 5, pp. 158-160.

Nassmacher, Hiltrud (2004a): Parteiensysteme und Parteifinanzen in West-Europa. In: *Zeitschrift für Politik,* 51 (2004) 1, pp. 29-51.

Nassmacher, Hiltrud (2004b): Finanzen und Demokratie, dargestellt an der Parteienfinanzierung. In: Baringhorst, Sigrid/ Broer, Ingo (eds.): *Grenzgänge(r). Beiträge zu Politik, Kultur und Religion.* Siegen: Universitätsverlag, 2004, S. 94-114.

Nassmacher, Hiltrud (2005): Noch einmal davongekommen? Die kanadische Unterhauswahl vom 28. Juni 2004. In: *Zeitschrift für Kanada-Studien,* 25 (2005) 1, pp. 7-22.

Nassmacher, Hiltrud (2006a): Parteiensysteme und Parteienfinanzierung in Europa. In: Niedermayer, Oskar et al. (eds.), 2006, pp. 507-519.

Nassmacher, Hiltrud (2006b): The Prospects of the Grand Coalition in Germany. In: *Polish Political Science Yearbook,* 35 (2006), pp. 65-83.

Nassmacher, Hiltrud/ Lemke, Ina-Maja (1992): Steuerliche Anreize für private Zuwendungen. Tax Deduction and Tax Credit in drei Ländern. In: Nassmacher, Karl-Heinz, 1992a, pp. 69-97.

Nassmacher, Hiltrud/ Nassmacher, Karl-Heinz (1988): Von der Wahlkampfmaschine zur Apparatpartei. Party-Building in Canada. In: *Zeitschrift der Gesellschaft für Kanada-Studien,* 8 (1988) 14, pp. 29-41.

Nassmacher, Hiltrud/ Nassmacher, Karl-Heinz (2001): Major Impacts of Political Finance Regimes (Introduction). In: Nassmacher, Karl-Heinz (ed.), 2001a, pp. 181-196.

Nassmacher, Karl-Heinz (1982a): Öffentliche Rechenschaft und Parteifinanzierung. Erfahrungen in Deutschland, Kanada und in den Vereinigten Staaten. In: *Aus Politik und Zeitgeschichte,* 32 (1982) 14-15, pp. 3-18.

Nassmacher, Karl-Heinz (1982b): Parteifinanzierung in Kanada. Modell für Deutschland?. In: *Zeitschrift für Parlamentsfragen,* 13 (1982) 3, pp. 338-359.

Nassmacher, Karl-Heinz (1986): Die Kosten der Demokratie in Kanada. In: Chandler, William M. (ed.): *Perspektiven kanadischer Politik.* Oldenburg: BIS, 1986, pp. 91-115.

Nassmacher, Karl-Heinz (1987): Öffentliche Parteienfinanzierung in Westeuropa. Implementationsstrategien und Problembestand in der Bundesrepublik Deutschland, Italien, Österreich und Schweden. In: *Politische Vierteljahresschrift,* 28 (1987) 1, S. 101-125.

Nassmacher, Karl-Heinz (1989a): *Parteien im Abstieg.* Wiederbegründung und Niedergang der Bauern- und Bürgerparteien in Niedersachsen, Opladen: Westdeutscher, 1989.

Nassmacher, Karl-Heinz (1989b): Structure and Impact of Public Subsidies to Political Parties in Europe: the Examples of Austria, Italy, Sweden and West Germany. In: Alexander, Herbert E. (ed.), 1989a, pp. 236-267.

Nassmacher, Karl-Heinz (1989c): The Costs of Party Democracy in Canada: Preliminary Findings for a Federal System. In: *Corruption and Reform,* 4 (1989) 4, pp. 217-243.

Nassmacher, Karl-Heinz (1989d): Parteienfinanzierung im Wandel. Einnahmenentwicklung, Ausgabenstruktur und Vermögenslage der deutschen Parteien. In: *Der Bürger im Staat,* 39 (1989) 4, pp. 271-278.

Nassmacher, Karl-Heinz (1992a): *Bürger finanzieren Wahlkämpfe. Anregungen aus Nordamerika für die Parteienfinanzierung in Deutschland.* Baden-Baden: Nomos, 1992.

Nassmacher, Karl-Heinz (1992b): Parteifinanzen im westeuropäischen Vergleich. In: *Zeitschrift für Parlamentsfragen,* 23 (1992) 3, pp. 462-488.

Nassmacher, Karl-Heinz (1993): Comparing Party and Campaign Finance in Western Democracies. In: Gunlicks, Arthur B. (ed.), 1993, pp. 233-267.

Nassmacher, Karl-Heinz (1994): ‚Citizens' Cash in Canada and the United States. In: Alexander, Herbert E./ Shiratori, Rei (eds.), 1994a, pp. 145-158.

Nassmacher, Karl-Heinz (1997a): Ordnungsrahmen für eine plurale Parteiendemokratie. Das Beispiel des politischen Geldes. In: Keynes, Edward/ Schumacher, Ulrike (eds.): *Denken in Ordnungen in der Politik. Herausforderungen an eine anwendungsbezogene politische Wissenschaft.* Frankfurt a. M.: P. Lang, 1997, pp. 37-62.

Nassmacher, Karl-Heinz (1997b): Parteienfinanzierung in Deutschland. In: Gabriel, Oscar W. et al. (eds.): *Parteiendemokratie in Deutschland.* Opladen: Westdeutscher, 1997, pp. 157-176.

Nassmacher, Karl-Heinz (2000): Parteienfinanzierung in der Bewährung. In: *Aus Politik und Zeitgeschichte,* 50 (2000) 16, pp. 15-22. (O Financiamento de Partidos na Alemanha Posto a Prova. In: Speck, Bruno Wilhelm et al., 2000, pp. 105-126.)
(see: www.bpb.de/publikationen/J0QBRT,0,0,Parteienfinanzierung_in_der_Bewähru..)

Nassmacher, Karl-Heinz (ed.) (2001a): *Foundations for Democracy: Approaches to Comparative Political Finance.* Baden-Baden: Nomos, 2001.

Nassmacher, Karl-Heinz (2001b): Comparative Political Finance in Established Democracies (Introduction). In: Nassmacher, Karl-Heinz (ed.), 2001a, pp. 9-33.

Nassmacher, Karl-Heinz (2001c): Political Finance in West Central Europe: Austria, Germany, Switzerland. In: Nassmacher, Karl-Heinz (ed.), 2001a, pp. 92-111.

Nassmacher, Karl-Heinz (2001d): Parteienfinanzierung in Deutschland. In: Gabriel, Oscar W. et al. (eds.): *Parteiendemokratie in Deutschland.* 2nd ed., Bonn: Bundeszentrale für politische Bildung, 2001, pp. 159-178.

Nassmacher, Karl-Heinz (2002): Die Kosten der Parteitätigkeit in westlichen Demokratien. In: *Österreichische Zeitschrift für Politikwissenschaft,* 31 (2002) 1, pp. 7-20 (www.members. chello.at/ politikwissenschaft/aktuell/2002_1_nassmacher.htm).

Nassmacher, Karl-Heinz (2003a): Introduction: Political Parties, Funding and Democracy. In: Austin, Reginald/ Tjernström, Maja (eds.), 2003, pp. 1-19, www.idea.int/publications/funding_parties

Nassmacher, Karl-Heinz (2003b): The Funding of Political Parties in the Anglo-Saxon Orbit. In: Austin, Reginald/ Tjernström, Maja (eds.), 2003, pp. 33-52, www.idea.int/publications/ funding_parties

Nassmacher, Karl-Heinz (2003c): Party Funding in Continental Western Europe. In: Austin, Reginald/ Tjernström, Maja (eds.), 2003, pp. 117-137, www.idea.int/publications/funding_parties

Nassmacher, Karl-Heinz (2003d): Monitoring, Control and Enforcement of Political Finance Regulation. In: Austin, Reginald/ Tjernström, Maja (eds.), 2003, pp. 139-155, www.idea.int/ publications/ funding_parties

Nassmacher, Karl-Heinz (2003e): Fiscalization, Control y Cumplimiento de la Normatividad Sobre Financiamiento Politico. In: Carrillo, Manuel et al. (eds.), 2003, pp. 246-278.

Nassmacher, Karl-Heinz (2004): Ist unsere Demokratie zu teuer? In: *Einblicke. Forschungsmaagazin der Universität Oldenburg,* 18 (2004) 39, pp. 22-25.

Nassmacher, Karl-Heinz (2006): Regulation of Party Finance. In: Katz, Richard S./ Crotty, William (eds.), 2006, pp. 446-455.

Nassmacher, Karl-Heinz/ Nassmacher, Hiltrud (2009): *Nachhaltige Wirtschaftspolitik in der parlamentarischen Demokratie. Das britische Beispiel.* Wiesbaden: VS, 2009 (forthcoming).

Nassmacher, Karl-Heinz/ Suckow, Achim (1992): Parteienfinanzierung ganz unten. Ressourcen kanadischer Wahlkreisparteien. In: Nassmacher, Karl-Heinz, 1992a, pp. 131-151.

Nassmacher, Karl-Heinz/ Wawzik, Thomas (1992): Bürgerbeitrag und Finanzstimme in den USA. Evaluation and Programmwirkungen beim Tax-Check-Off. In: Nassmacher, Karl-Heinz, 1992a, pp. 27-67.

Nehmelman, Remco (2005): Netherlands. In: Grant, Thomas D. (ed.), 2005, pp. 345-354.

Neill Report (Committee on the Standards in Public Life) (1998): *The Funding of Political Parties. Issues and Questions.* London: The Committee on Standard in Public Life, 1998.

Nelson, Candice J. (2002): Spending in the 2000 Election. In: Magleby, David B. (ed.), 2002a, 22-48.

Nergelius, Joakim (2005): Sweden. In: Grant, Thomas D. (ed.), 2005, pp. 467-478.

Neugebauer, Gero/ Stöss, Richard (1996): *Die PDS. Geschichte. Organisation. Wähler. Konkurrenten.* Opladen: Leske & Budrich, 1996.

Newman, Bruce J./ Perloff, Richard M. (2004): Political Marketing: Theory, Research, and Applications. In: Kaid, Linda Lee (ed.): *Handbook of Political Communication Research*, Mahwah NJ et al.: Lawrence Erlbaum Assoc., 2004, pp. 17-44.

Nick, Rainer/ Sickinger, Hubert (1987): *Variations of Political Party Financing in Austria. A Comprehensive Examination.* Paper presented to the Conference of the Research Committee on Political Finance and Political Corruption, International Political Science Association, Mennagio, Italy, 1987 (unpublished).

Nick, Rainer/ Sickinger, Hubert (1989): *Current Scandals as an Accelerator of Political Change in Austria. Under Special Consideration of Party Finances.* Paper presented to the Roundtable of the Research Committee on Political Finance and Political Corruption, International Political Science Association, Kasimierz, Poland, 1989 (unpublished).

Niedermayer, Oskar (1992): Entwicklungstendenzen der westeuropäischen Parteiensysteme: eine quantitative Analyse. In: *Politische Vierteljahresschrift-Sonderheft*, Opladen: Westdeutscher, 1992, pp. 143-159.

Niedermayer, Oskar (1993): Innerparteiliche Demokratie. In: Niedermayer, Oskar/ Stöss, Richard (eds.): *Stand und Perspektiven der Parteienforschung in Deutschland.* Opladen: Leske & Budrich, 1993, pp. 230-250.

Niedermayer, Oskar (2002): www.polwissfuberlin.de/osi/dokumente/PDF/mitglieder.pdf

Niedermayer, Oskar et al. (eds.) (2006): *Die Parteiensysteme Westeuropas.* Wiesbaden: VS, 2006.

Nohlen, Dieter (2000): *Wahlrecht und Parteiensystem.* Opladen: Leske & Budrich, 3rd. ed. 2000.

Noragon, Jack L. (1981): Political Finance and Political Reform. The Experience with State Income Tax Checkoffs. In: *American Political Science Review*, 75 (1981) 3, pp. 667-687.

Norris, Pippa (2000): *A Virtuous Circle: Political Communications in Postindustrial Democracies.* New York: Cambridge University, 2000.

Norris, Pippa (2003): Preaching to the Converted? Pluralism, Participation and Party Websides. In: *Party Politics*, 9 (2003) 1, pp. 21-45.

Norton, Philip (1996) (ed.): *The Conservative Party*. Prentice Hall and Harvester Wheatsheaf: Simon & Schuster, 1996.

Nugent, Margaret Latus/ Johannes, John R. (eds.) (1990): *Money, Elections, and Democracy. Reforming Congressional Campaign Finance*. Boulder CO: Westview, 1990.

O'Dowd, John (2005): Ireland. In: Grant, Thomas D. (ed.), 2005, pp. 201-260.

O'Leary, Cornelius (1962): *The Elimination of Currupt Practices in British Elections, 1868-1911*. Oxford: Oxford University, 1962.

Oldopp, Birgit (2001): *Auf dem Weg ins Parlament. Auswahl und Wahlkampffinanzierung der Kandidaten in Deutschland, Kanada und den USA*. Frankfurt a. M. et al.: Campus, 2001.

Olson, Mancor (1971): *The Logic of Collective Action. Public Goods and the Theory of Groups*. Cambridge MA and London: Harvard University, 2nd 1971.

O'Shaughnessy, Nicholas/ Peele, Gillian (1985): Money, Mail and Markets. Reflections on Direct Mail in American Politics. In: *Electoral Studies*, 4 (1985) 2, pp. 115-124.

Osler, David (2002): *Labour Party PLC. Party of Business*, Edinburgh: Mainstream Publishing, 2002.

Orr, Graeme (2005): Australia. In: Grant, Thomas D. (ed.), 2005, pp. 1-14.

Ostrogorski, Mosei (1902): *Democracy and the Organization of Political Parties*. London: Macmillan, 1902.

Overacker, Louise (1932): *Money in Elections*. New York: Macmillan, 1932.

Overacker, Louise (1933): American Government and Politics. In: *The American Political Science Review*, 2 (1933) October, pp. 769-783.

Overacker, Louise (1937): American Government and Politics. In: *American Political Science Review*, 31 (1937) June, pp. 473-499.

Overacker, Louise (1941): Campaign Finance in the Presidential Election of 1940. In: *The American Political Science Review*, 35 (1941) 4, pp. 701-727.

Overacker, Louise (1945): Presidential Campaign Funds. In: *American Political Science Review*, 39 (1945), pp. 899-901.

Owens, John R./ Olson, Edward C. (1977): Campaign Spending and the Electoral Process in California, 1966-1974. In: *Western Political Quarterly*, 30 (1977) 4, pp. 493-512.

Pacifici, Giorgio (1983): *Il costo della democrazia. I partiti Italiani attraverso i loro bilanci*. Roma: Cadmo, 1983.

Padget, Donald (1991): Large Contributions to Candidates in the 1988 Federal Election and the Issue of Undue Influence. In: Seidle, F. Leslie (ed.), 1991d, pp. 319-367.

Palda, Filip/ Palda, Kristian (1998): The Impact of Campaign Expenditures on Political Competition in the French Legislative Elections of 1993. In: *Public Choice,* 94 (1998) 1/2, pp. 157-174.

Palda, Kristian S. (1975): The Effect of Expenditure on Political Success. In: *Journal of Law and Economics*, 18 (1975) 3, pp. 745-780.

Paltiel, Khayyam Z. (ed.) (1966): *Studies in Canadian Party Finance*, Committee on Election Expenses, Ottawa: Queen's, 1966.

Paltiel, Khayyam Z. (1967): The Proposed Reform of Canadian Election Finance - A Study and Critique.I n: *Jahrbuch des öffentlichen Rechts der Gegenwart*, NF 16 (1967), pp. 379-409.

Paltiel, Khayyam Z. (1970a): *Political Party Financing in Canada*. Toronto: Mc Graw-Hill, 1970.

Paltiel, Khayyam Z. (1970b): Contrasts among the Several Canadian Political Finance Cultures. In: Heidenheimer, Arnold J. (ed.), 1970a, pp. 107-134.

Paltiel, Khayyam Z. (1974): Party and Candidate Expenditures in the Canadian General Election of 1972. In: *Canadian Journal of Political Science*, 3 (1974) 2, pp. 341-352.

Paltiel, Khayyam Z. (1975): Campaign Financing in Canada and Its Reform. In: Penniman, Howard R. (ed.): *Canada at the Polls. The General Election of 1974*. Washington DC: American Enterprise Institute, 1975, pp. 181-208.

Paltiel, Khayyam Z. (1976): *Party, Candidate and Election Finance. A Background Report*. Study No. 22. Ottawa: Royal Commission on Corporate Concentration: Queens Printer, 1976.

Paltiel, Khayyam Z. (1979): The Impact of Election Expenses Legislation in Canada, Western Europe, and Israel. In: Alexander, Herbert E. (ed.), 1979a, pp. 15-39.

Paltiel, Khayyam Z. (1980): Public Financing Abroad. Contrasts and Effects. In: Malbin, Michael J (ed.), 1980a, pp. 354-370.

Paltiel, Khayyam Z. (1981): Campaign Finance. Contrasting Practices and Reforms. In: Butler, David et al. (eds.), 1981, pp. 138-172.

Paltiel, Khayyam Z. (1987): Political Finance. In: Bogdanor, Vernon (ed.): *The Blackwell Encyclopedia of Political Institutions*. Oxford and New York: Blackwell, 1987, pp. 454-456.

Paltiel, Khayyam Z. (1988a): The 1984 Federal General Election and Developments in Canadian Party Finance. In: Penniman, Howard R. (ed.): *Canada at the Polls, 1984. A Study of the Federal General Elections*. Durham NC: Duke University, 1988, pp. 137-160.

Paltiel, Khayyam Z. (1988b): Party Financing. In: *The Canadian Encyclopedia*, vol. 3. Edmonton: Hurtig, 2nd ed. 1988, pp. 1625-1626.

Paltiel, Khayyam Z. (1989): Canadian Election Expense Legislation 1963-1985. A Critical Appraisal or Was the Effort Worth it? In: Alexander, Herbert E.(ed.), 1989a, pp. 51-75.

Paltiel, Khayyam Z./ Seidle, F. Leslie (1981) see Seidle, F. Leslie/ Paltiel, Khayyam Z. (1981).

Panebianco, Angelo (1988): *Political Parties: Organization and Power*. Cambridge, UK: Cambridge University, 1988.

Papadimitriou, Georgios (1992): Parteienfinanzierung in Griechenland. In: Tsatsos, Dimitris Th. (ed.), 1992, pp. 197-230.

Pappin, J. Maureen (1976): Tax Relief For Political Contributions. In: *Canadian Tax Journal*, 24 (1976) 3, pp. 298-305.

Park, Chan Wook (1994): Financing Political Parties in South Korea: 1988-1991. In: Alexander, Herbert E./ Shiratori, Rei (eds.), 1994a, pp. 173-186.

Park, Cheol Hee (2001): Factional Dynamics in Japan's LDP since Political Reform. Continuity and Change. In: *Asian Survey*, 41 (2001) 3, pp. 428-461.

Pasquino, Gian Franco (1990): Party Elites and Democratic Consolidation: Cross-national Comparison of Southern European Experience. In: Pridham, Geoffrey (ed.): *Securing Democracy: Political Parties and Democratic Consolidation in Southern Europe*. Routledge, 1990, pp. 42-61.

Pasquino, Gian Franco (1996): *Political Corruption, Voters' Discontent, Institutional Change: Italy in Transition.* Bologna: Bologna Centre of the Johns Hopkins University, 1996.

Passigli, Stefano (1963): Italy. In: *The Journal of Politics*, 25 (1963) 3, pp. 718-736.

Patterson, Kelly D. (2006): Spending in the 2004 Election. In: Magleby, David B. et al. (eds.), 2006, pp. 68-92.

Pattie, Charles J./ Johnston, Ronald J. (1996): Paying their Way: Local Associations, the Constituency Quota Scheme and Conservative Party Finance. In: *Political Studies*, XLIV (1996), S. 921-935.

Pattie, Charles J./ Johnston, Ronald J./ Fieldhouse, Edward A. (1995): Winning the Local Vote: The Effectiveness of Constituency Spending in Great Britain, 1983-1992. In: *American Political Science Review*, 89 (1995) 4, pp. 969-983.

Payne, J. Mark/ Zovatto G., Daniel et al. (2002): *Democracies in Development. Politics and Reform in Latin America.* Washington, DC: Inter-American Development Bank, 2002.

Pedersen, Karina (2003): *Party Membership Linkage. The Danish Case.* Copenhagen: Copenhagen University, 2003.

Pedersen, Karina (2005): Denmark. In: Grant, Thomas D. (ed.), 2005, pp. 97-104.

Pedersen, Mogens N. (1979): *Dansk politik i 1970'erne – studier og arbejdspapirer.* (Copenhagen): Samfundsvidenskabeligt, 1979.

Pedersen, Mogens N. (1987): Party Finance. In: Daalder, Hans (ed.), 1987a, pp. 1-60.

Pedersen, Mogens N./ Bille, Lars (1991): Public Financing and Public Control of Political Parties in Denmark. In: Wiberg, Matti (ed.), 1991a, pp. 147-172.

Pelinka, Anton (1978): Parteienfinanzierung im Parteienstaat. In: *Österreichisches Jahrbuch für Politik*, 1977. Wien: Verlag für Geschichte und Politik, München: Oldenbourg, 1978, pp. 225-241.

Pelinka, Anton (1981): Parteienfinanzierung und Korruption. In: Brünner, Christian (ed.): *Korruption und Kontrolle*. Wien et al.: Böhlau, 1981, pp. 265-280.

Pelinka, Anton/ Plasser, Fritz (eds.) (1988): *Das österreichische Parteiensystem*. Wien et al.: Böhlau, 1988.

Pelinka, Anton/ Plasser, Fritz (eds.) (1989): *The Austrian Party System*. Boulder: Westview, 1989.

Pelletier, Rejean (1996): The Structures of Canadian Political Parties. In: Tanguay, A. Brian/ Gagnon, Alain G. (eds.): *Canadian Parties in Transition*. Toronto et al.: Nelson, 2nd ed. 1996, pp. 136-159.

Penniman, Howard R. (1984): 'U.S. Elections: Really a Bargain!'. In: *Public Opinion*, 7 (1984) 2, pp. 51-53.

Pennings, Paul (1998): Party Responsiveness and Socio-economic Problem-solving in Western Democracies.I n: *Party Politics*, 4 (1998) 3, pp. 393-404.

Peretz, Don/ Doron, Gideon (1997): *The Government and Politics of Israel*. Boulder CO: Westview, 3rd ed. 1997.

Pesonen, Pertti (1987): *Impact of Public Financing of Political Parties: The Finnish Experience*. Paper for the Conference of the Research Committee on Political Finance and Political Corruption, Villa Serbelloni (Rockefeller Foundation), May 1987 (unpublished).

Phillips report (Sir Hayden Phillips) (2007): *Strenghtening Democracy: Fair and Sustainable Funding of Political Parties*. Norwich: HMSO, 2007.

Piattoni, Simona (2001): Clientelism, Interests, and Democratic Representation. In: Piattoni, Simona (ed.): *Clientelism, Interests, and Democratic Representation: the European Experience in Historical and Comparative Perspective.* Cambridge University, 2001, pp. 193-212.

Pierre, Jon/ Svasand, Lars/ Widfeldt, Anders (2000): State Subsidies to Political Parties: Confronting Rhetoric with Reality. In: *West European Politics,* 23 (2000) 3, pp. 1-24.

Pierre, Jon/ Widfeldt, Anders (1992): Sweden. In: Katz, Richard S./ Mair, Peter (eds.), 1992, pp. 781-836.

Pierre, Jon/ Widfeldt, Anders (1994): Party Organizations in Sweden: Colossuses with Feet of Clay or Flexible Pillars of Government? In: Katz, Richard S./ Mair, Peter (eds.), 1994, pp. 332-356.

Pinto-Duschinsky, Michael (1981): *British Political Finance, 1830 – 1980.* Washington DC: American Enterprise Institute, 1981.

Pinto-Duschinsky, Michael (1985): Trends in British Political Funding 1979-1983. In: *Parliamentary Affairs,* 38 (1985) Summer, pp. 328-347.

Pinto-Duschinsky, Michael (1986): Financing the General Election of 1983. In: Crewe, Ivor/ Harrop, Martin (eds.): *Political Communications: The General Election Campaign of 1983,* Cambridge, UK: Cambridge University, 1986, pp. 283-293.

Pinto-Duschinsky, Michael (1989): Trends in British Political Funding, 1979-84. In: Alexander, Herbert E. (ed.), 1989a, pp. 24-50.

Pinto-Duschinsky, Michael (1991a): Foreign Political Aid: The German Political Foundations and their US Counterparts. In: *International Affairs,* 67 (1991) 1, pp. 33-63.

Pinto-Duschinsky, Michael (1991b): The Party Foundations and Political Finance in Germany. In: Seidle, Leslie F. (ed.), 1991c, pp. 179-250.

Pinto-Duschinsky, Michael (1994): British Party Funding, 1983-1988. In: Alexander, Herbert E./ Shiratori, Rei (eds.), 1994a, pp. 13-28.

Pinto-Duschinsky, Michael (1997): The Rise of "Public Aid". In: Diamond, Larry et al. (eds.): *Consolidating the Third Wave Democracies: Trends and Challanges.* Volume 2. Baltimore: John Hopkins University, 1997, pp. 295-324.

Pinto-Duschinsky, Michael (1998): Power to the Center. How the Neill Report Will Revolutionize the Funding of Political Parties. In: *The Times Literary Supplement,* December 25 1998.

Pinto-Duschinsky, Michael (2001a): *Political Financing in the Commonwealth.* London: Commonwealth Secretariat, 2001.

Pinto-Duschinsky, Michael (2001b): *Handbook on Funding of Parties and Election Campaigns – Overview.* Stockholm: International IDEA, 2001.

Pinto-Duschinsky, Michael (2001c): Supporting New Democracies. In: Nassmacher, Karl-Heinz (ed.), 2001a, pp. 297-320.

Pinto-Duschinsky, Michael (2002): Financing Politics: A Global View. In: *Journal of Democracy,* 13 (2002) 4, pp.69-86.

Pinto-Duschinsky, Michael (2003): Gran Bretana. In: Carrillo, Manuel et al. (eds.), 2003, pp. 321-331.

Pinto-Duschinsky, Michael (2005): The Funding of Political Parties and Election Campaigns: The Experience from Western Europe. In: Malamud, Carlos/ Posada-Carbó, Eduardo (eds.), 2005, pp. 54-67.

Pinto-Duschinsky, Michael/ Schleth, Uwe (1970): Why Public Subsidies Have Become the Major Source of Party Funds in West Germany, but Not in Great Britain. In: Heidenheimer, Arnold J. (ed.), 1970a, pp. 23-49.

Plasser, Fritz (1987): *Parteien unter Streß. Zur Dynamik der Parteiensysteme in Österreich, der Bundesrepublik Deutschland und den Vereinigten Staaten.* Wien et al.: Böhlau, 1987.

Poguntke, Thomas (2000): *Parteiorganisation im Wandel. Gesellschaftliche Verankerung und organisatorische Anpassung im europäischen Vergleich.* Wiesbaden: Westdeutscher, 2000.

Poguntke, Thomas/ Boll, Bernhard (1992): Germany. In: Katz, Richard S./ Mair, Peter (eds.), 1992, pp. 317-388.

Pollock, James K. (1926): *Party Campaign Funds.* New York: Knopf, 1926.

Polsby, Nelson W. (1980): Community Power and Political Theory. A Further Look at Problems of Evidence and Interference. New Haven and London: Yale University, 2nd. ed., 1980.

Potter, Trevor/ Ryan, Paul S. (2005): United States. In: Grant, Thomas D. (ed.), 2005, pp. 557-594.

Praag, Philip van/ Brants, Kees (eds.) (2000): *Tussen beeld en inhoud: Politiek en media in de verkiezingen van 1998.* Amsterdam: Het Spinhuis, 2000.

Prud'home, Jean Francois et al. (1993): *Dinero y Partidos. Propuestas para regular los ingresos y gastos de los partiodos politicos. Investigacion.* Mexico: CEPNA: Nuevo Horizonte Editores. Fundacion Friedrich Ebert, 1993.

Pujas, Veronique/ Rhodes, Martin (1999): Party Finance and Political Scandal in Italy, Spain and France. In: *West European Politics,* 22 (1999) 3, pp. 41-63.

Pulch, Michael W. E. (1987): *Parteienfinanzierung in Frankreich und Großbritannien.* Bonn: dissertation,1987.

Purcal, Christiane (1993): *Kommunalparteien. Eine Untersuchung von Struktur und Funktionen politischer Vereinigungen in der kanadischen Stadt Vancouver.* Oldenburg: BIS, 1993.

Raschke, Joachim (1993) : *Die Grünen. Wie sie wurden, was sie sind.* Köln: Bund, 1993.

Reif, Karlheinz (1983): Die ‚Nebenwahlen': Einbußen der französischen Linken seit ihren Siegen von 1981. In: *Zeitschrift für Parlamentsfragen,* 14 (1983) 2, pp. 195-209.

Reif, Karlheinz (1986): Parlamentswahlen in Frankreich 1986: Neues Wahlrecht, neue Partei, neue Koalitionsmuster. In: *Zeitschrift für Parlamentsfragen,* 17 (1986) 4, pp. 484-502.

Rhodes, Martin (1997): Financing Party Politics in Italy. A Case of Systemic Corruption. In: *West European Politics,* 20 (1997) 1, pp. 54-81.

Rich, Andrew (2001): United States. In: Weaver, R. Kent/ Stares, Paul B. (eds.), 2001, pp. 31-70.

Richardson, Bradley/ Patterson, Dennis (2001): Political Traditions and Political Change: The Significance of Postwar Japanese Politics for Political Science. In: *Annual Reviews of Political Science,* (2001) 4, pp. 93-115.

Ridola, Paolo (1992): Parteienfinanzierung in Italien. In: Tsatsos, Dimitris Th. (ed.), 1992, pp. 273-307.

Rieken, Marion (1991): *Frankophonie in der Parteienfinanzierung? Ein Vergleich zwischen Frankreich und Quebec.* Oldenburg: M.A. thesis, 1991.

Rieken, Marion (1993): Ein ganz normaler Machtwechsel? Die kanadische Unterhauswahl von 1993. In: *Zeitschrift für Kanada-Studien,* 24 (1993) 2, pp. 7-20.

Rieken, Marion (2002): *Direct Mail als Fund Raising-Instrument in der Politik.* University of Oldenburg: dissertation, 2002.

Rieken, Marion/ Römmele, Andrea (1997): Erste Wirkungen in der neuen Parteienfinanzierung? In: *Zeitschrift für Parlamentsfragen,* 28 (1997) 2, pp. 254-266.

Ringena, Take (2000): *Die Finanzen der Grünen.* Oldenburg: M.A. thesis, 2000.

Römmele, Andrea (1992): Unternehmenszuwendungen in der amerikanischen Wahlkampffinanzierung. Zur Rolle der Corporate PACs in Kongreßwahlen 1980-1988. In: *Zeitschrift für Parlamentsfragen,* 23 (1992) 3, pp. 488-496.

Römmele, Andrea (1995a): *Unternehmensspenden in der Parteien- und Wahlkampffinanzierung: Die USA, Kanada, die Bundesrepublik Deutschland und Großbritannien im internationalen Vergleich.* Baden-Baden: Nomos, 1995.

Römmele, Andrea (1995b): Politikfinanzierung. Welche Rolle spielen Unternehmenspenden? In: *Journal für Sozialforschung,* 35 (1995) 1, pp. 51-66.

Römmele, Andrea (1997): Communicating with Their Voters: The Use of Direct Mailing by the SPD and the CDU. In: *German Politics,* 6 (1997) 3, pp. 120-131.

Römmele, Andrea (1999): Direkte Kommunikation zwischen Parteien und Wählern – der Einsatz von direct mailing bei SPD und CDU. In: *Zeitschrift für Parlamentsfragen,* 30 (1999) 2, pp. 304-315.

Römmele, Andrea (2001): Direct Mailing as a New Form of Party Linkage. In: Nassmacher, Karl-Heinz (ed.), 2001a, pp. 240-266.

Römmele, Andrea (1999/ 2002): *Direkte Kommunikation zwischen Parteien und Wählern. Postmoderne Wahlkampftechnologien in den USA und der BRD.* Habilschrift FU Berlin 1999/ Wiesbaden: Westdeutscher, 2002.

Römmele, Andrea (2005): Partei- und Wahlkampfspenden aus der BRD und den USA. In: Alemann, Ulrich von (ed.), 2005a, pp. 384-394.

Rose, Richard (1965): Pre-Election Public Relations and Advertising. In: Butler, David A./ King, Anthony (eds.): *The British General Election of 1964.* Houndmills et al.: Macmillan (reprint: *The British General Elections 1945-92.* Houndmills: Macmillan, 1999, pp. 369-380).

Rose, Richard (1976): *The Problem of Party Government.* Harmondsworth: Penguin, 1976.

Rose, Richard/ Heidenheimer, Arnold J. (1963): Comparative Political Finance: A Symposium. In: *Journal of Politics,* 25 (1963) 4, pp. 648-811.

Rose-Ackermann, Susan (1999): *Corruption and Government.* Cambridge: Cambridge University, 1999.

Roth, Norbert (1998): ‚Wie wird man Bürgermeister und warum? Motivationen, Erkenntnisse, Hinweise, Handlungsanleitungen zum Wahlkampf'. In: Roth, Norbert (ed.): *Position und Situation der Bürgermeister in Baden-Württemberg,* Stuttgart: Kohlhammer, 1998, pp. 110-139.

Rothstein, Bo (1996): Political Institutions: An Overview. In: Goodin, Robert E./ Klingemann, Hans-Dieter (eds.): *A New Handbook of Political Science.* Oxford: Oxford University, 1996, pp. 133-166.

Rudzio, Wolfgang (2000/ 2003/ 2006): *Das politische System der Bundesrepublik.* Opladen: Leske & Budrich, 5th ed. 2000, 6th ed. 2003, 7th ed. 2006.

Rundswick, Alexandra (2004): *Life Support for Local Parties. An Analysis of the Decline of Local Political Parties and the Case for State Support of Local Activism.* London: New Politics Network, 2004.

Russ, Sabine (2005): Analytische Schattenspiele: Konturen der Korruption in Frankreich. In: Alemann, Ulrich von (ed.), 2005a, pp. 365-383.

Saalfeld, Thomas (2000): Court and Parties: Evolution and Problems of Political Funding in Germany. In: Williams, Robert (ed.), 2000a, pp. 89-121.

Sabato, Larry J. (1981): *The Rise of Political Consultants: New Ways of Winning Elections.* New York: Basic Books, 1981.

Sabato, Larry J. (1987): *PAC Power.*, New York: Norton, 2nd. ed. 1987.

Sabato, Larry J. (1988): *The Party's Just Begun.* Boston MA: Scott, Foresman et al., 1988.

Sabsay, Daniel (1998): El Financiamiento de los Partidos Politicos en Argentina. In: Castillo, Pilar del/ Zavatto G., Daniel (eds.), 1998, pp. 1-31.

Sahr, Robert (2004): Using Inflation-Adjusted Dollars in Analyzing Political Developments. In: *PS: Political Science & Politics*, 37 (2004) 2, pp. 273-284.

Salamon, Lester M./ Anheier, Helmut K. (1997): Der Dritte Sektor in internationaler Perspektive. In: Anheier, Helmut K. et al. (eds.): *Der Dritte Sektor in Deutschland. Organisationen zwischen Staat und Markt im gesellschaftlichen Wandel.* Berlin: Rainer Bohn, 1997, pp. 153-174.

Sangita, S.N. (2005): India. In: Grant, Thomas D. (ed.), 2005, pp. 169-200.

Sartori, Giovanni (1976): *Parties and Party Systems: A Framework for Analysis.* Cambridge: Cambridge University, 1976.

Sartori, Giovanni (1990): Structering the Party System. In: Mair, Peter (ed.): *The West European Party System.* Oxford: Oxford University, 1990, pp. 75-77.

Sayers, Anthony M. (1999): *Parties, Candidates, and Constituency Campaigns in Canadian Elections.* Vancouver: UBC, 1999.

Scarrow, Susan E. (1996): *Parties and their Members.* Oxford: Oxford University, 1996.

Scarrow, Susan E. (2000): Parties without Members? Party Organization and the Changing Electoral Environement. In: Dalton, Russell J./ Wattenberg, Martin P. (eds.), 2000a, pp. 79-101.

Scarrow, Susan E. (2002): Party Decline in the Parties State? The Changing Environement of German Politics. In: Webb, Paul et al. (eds.), 2002, pp. 77-106.

Scarrow, Susan E. (2006): Party Subsidies and the Freezing of Party Competition. In: *West European Politics*, 29 (2006) 4, pp. 619-639.

Scarrow, Susan E. (2007): Political Finance in Comparative Perspective. In: *Annual Review of Political Science*, 10 (2007), pp. 193-210.

Schaller, Roland (1994): Die Kommunalparteien und das Geld. In: Geser, Hans/ Ladner, Andreas et al. (eds.): *Die Schweizer Lokalparteien.* Zürich: Seismo, 1994, 225-249.

Scheer, Hermann (1979): *Parteien kontra Bürger? Die Zukunft der Parteiendemokratie.* München and Zürich: Piper, 1979.

Schefold, Dian (1996): *Background and Basic Principles of the Financing of Political Parties.* Johannisburg: Konrad-Adenauer-Stiftung, 1996.

Schindler, Peter (ed.) (1983): *Datenhandbuch zur Geschichte des Deutschen Bundestages 1949 bis 1982*. Bonn: Deutscher Bundestag, 1983.

Schindler, Peter (ed.) (1994): *Datenhandbuch zur Geschichte des Deutschen Bundestages 1983 bis 1991*. Baden-Baden: Nomos, 1994.

Schläpfer, Martina (2003): *Budget und Wahlkampfausgaben der Lokalparteien in der Schweiz*. Bern: Institut für Politikwissenschaft, 2003 (Seminararbeit).

Schlesinger, Joseph A./ Schlesinger, Mildred S. (1995): French Parties and the Legislative Elections of 1993: A Research Note. In: *Party Politics,* 1 (1995) 3, pp. 369-380.

Schleth, Uwe (1970) see Pinto-Duschinsky/ Schleth (1970).

Schleth, Uwe (1973): *Parteifinanzen. Eine Studie über Kosten und Finanzierung der Parteitätigkeit, zu deren politischer Problematik und zu den Möglichkeiten der Reform*. Meisenheim am Glan: Anton Hain, 1973.

Schmid, Gerhard (1981): *Politische Parteien, Verfassung und Gesetze. Zu den Möglichkeiten und Problemen einer Parteiengesetzgebung in der Schweiz*. Basel and Frankfurt a. M.: Helbing and Lichtenhahn, 1981.

Schmid, Josef (1990): Die Finanzen der CDU. In: Wewer, Göttrik (ed.), 1990, pp. 235-255.

Schmitt, Karl (1993): Die Neuregelung der Parteienfinanzierung in Frankreich. Chancen einer späten Geburt? In: *Zeitschrift für Parlamentsfragen,* 24 (1993) 1, pp. 73-103.

Schmitt, Uwe (1992): Japans Pate steht über dem Gesetz. In: *FAZ,* 28.09.1992.

Schneider, Hans-Peter (1989): The New German System of Party Funding. The Presidential Committee Report of 1983 and Its Realization. In: Alexander, Herbert E. (ed.), 1989a, pp. 220-235.

Schumpeter, Joseph A. (1950): *Capitalism, Socialism and Democracy*. New York: Harper & Row, 1950.

Schurig, Martin (2006): *Politikfinanzierung in Frankreich*. Berlin: Duncker & Humblot, 2006.

Sciarini, Pascal/ Hardmeier, Sibylle/ Vatter, Adrian (eds.) (2003): *Schweizer Wahlen 1999 - Elections fédérales 1999*. Bern et al.: Paul Haupt, 2003.

Seidle, F. Leslie (ed.) (1991a): *Interest Groups and Elections in Canada. Research Studies*. Royal Commission on Electoral Reform and Party Financing [Canada], Volume 2. Toronto and Oxford: Dundurn, 1991.

Seidle, F. Leslie (ed.) (1991b): *Provincial Party and Election Finance in Canada. Research Studies*. Royal Commission on Electoral Reform and Party Financing [Canada], Volume 3. Toronto and Oxford: Dundurn, 1991.

Seidle, F. Leslie (ed.) (1991c): *Comparative Issues in Party and Election Financing. Research Studies*. Royal Commission on Electoral Reform and Party Financing [Canada], Volume 4. Toronto and Oxford: Dundurn, 1991.

Seidle, F. Leslie (ed.) (1991d): *Issues in Party and Election Financing. Research Studies*. Royal Commission on Electoral Reform and Party Financing [Canada], Volume 5. Toronto and Oxford: Dundurn, 1991.

Seidle, Leslie F. (1996): *Canadian Political Finance Regulation and the Democratic Process: Established Rules on a Dynamic System*. Prepared for the Round Table on Discontent and Reform in the Mature Democracies, Tokyo, Januar 1996 (unpublished).

Seidle, F. Leslie/ Paltiel, Khayyam Z. (1981): Party Finance, the Election Expenses Act and Campaign Spending in 1979 and 1980. In: Penniman, Howard R. (ed.): *Canada at the Polls,*

1979 and 1980. A Study of the General Elections. Washington DC and London: American Enterprise Institute, 1981, pp. 226-279.

Seyd, Patrick/ Witheley, Paul (1992): *Labour's Grass Roots. The Politics of Party Membership.* Oxford: Clarendon, 1992.

Seyd, Patrick/ Witheley, Paul (2002): New Labour's Grassroots: The Transformation of the Labour Party Membership. Basingstoke et al.: Palgrave Macmillan, 2002.

Shea, Daniel M./ Hildreth, Andrew K.G. (1996): Where's the Party? A Second Look at Party Structure in New York State. In: Green, John C./ Shea, Daniel M. (eds.), 1996, pp. 163-177.

Shefter, Martin (1994): *Political Parties and the State: The American Historical Experience.* Princeton NJ: Princeton University, 1994.

Shepard, Lawrence (1977): Does Campaign Spending Really Matter? In: *Public Opinion Quarterly,* 41 (1977) 2, pp. 196-205.

Shiratori, Rei (1994): Political Finance and Scandal in Japan. In: Alexander, Herbert E./ Shiratori, Rei (eds.), 1994a, pp. 187-206.

Sickinger, Hubert (1997): *Politisches Geld: Politikfinanzierung in Österreich – ein Handbuch.* Taur, 1997.

Sickinger, Hubert (1999): Parteien- und Wahlkampffinanzierung in den 90er Jahren. In: Mair, Peter et. al. (eds.), 1999, pp. 305-331.

Sickinger, Hubert (2000): Parteien- und Wahlkampffinanzierung in den 90er Jahren. In: Plasser, Fritz/ Ulram, Peter A./ Sommer, Franz (eds.): *Das österreichische Wahlverhalten.* Wien: Signum, 2000, pp. 305-331.

Sickinger, Hubert (2001): The Austrian Party Academies. In: Nassmacher, Karl-Heinz (ed.), 2001a, pp. 338-349.

Sickinger, Hubert (2002): Überlegungen zur Reform der österreichischen Parteienfinanzierung. In: *Österreichische Zeitschrift für Politikwissenschaft,* 31 (2002) 1, pp. 73-90.

Sickinger, Hubert (2005): Austria. In: Grant, Thomas D. (ed.), 2005, pp. 15-38.

Sickinger, Hubert/ Nick, Rainer (1990): *Politisches Geld. Parteienfinanzierung in Österreich.* Thaur: Kulturverlag, 1990.

Smith, Anthony (1981): Mass Communications. In: Butler, David et al. (eds.), 1981, pp. 173-195.

Smith, Bradley A. (2001): *Unfree Speech. The Folly of Campaign Finance Reform.* Princeton NJ and Oxford UK: Princeton University, 2001.

Smith, Claire M. (2005): *Money to Burn: Party Finance and Party Organization in Federal Countries,* Ph.D. Thesis, Notre Dame Graduate School, 2005.

Smith, Gordon (1992): Parteienfinanzierung in Großbritannien. In: Tsatsos, Dimitris Th. (ed.), 1992, pp. 231-257.

Somes, Teresa (1998): Political Parties and Financial Disclosure Laws. In: *Griffith Law Review,* 7 (1998) 2, pp. 174-184.

Somjee, A. H./ Somjee, G. (1963): India. In: *The Journal of Politics,* 25 (1963) 3, pp. 686-702.

Sorauf, Frank J. (1988): *Money in American Elections.* Glenview IL et al.: Scott, Foresman and Company, 1988.

Sorauf, Frank J. (1990): Public Opinion and Campaign Finance. In: Nugent, Margaret Latus/ Johannes, John R. (eds.), 1990, pp. 207-224.

Sorauf, Frank J. (1998): Political Parties and the New World of Campaign Finance. In: Maisel, L. Sandy (ed.), 1998, pp. 225-242.

Speck, Bruno Wilhelm et al. (2000): *Os Custos da Corrupcao*. Sao Paulo: Fundacao Konrad Adenauer,2000.

Sridharan, E. (1999): Toward State Funding of Elections in India? A Comparative Perspective on Possible Options. In: *Policy Reform*, 3 (1999), pp. 229-254.

Sridharan, E. (2006a): Electoral Finance Reform: The Relevance of International Experience. In: Chand, Vikram K. (ed.): *Reinventing Public Service Delivery in India. Selected Case Studies*. New Delhi et al: Sage, 2006, pp. 363-387.

Sridharan, E. (2006b): Parties, the Party System and Collective Action for State Funding of Elections: A Comparative Perspective on Possible Options. In: de Sousa, Peter Ronald/ Sridharan, E. (eds.): *Indian's Political Parties*. New Delhi et al.: Sage, 2006, pp. 311-339.

Stanbury, William T. (1986): *Business - Government Relations in Canada. Grappling with Leviathan*. Toronto: Methuen, 1986.

Stanbury, William T. (1991): *Money in Politics. Financing Federal Parties and Candidates in Canada. Research Studies*. Royal Commission on Electoral Reform and Party Financing [Canada], Volume 1. Toronto and Oxford: Dundurn, 1991.

Stanbury, William T. (1993): Financing Federal Politics in Canada in an Era of Reform. Gunlicks, Arthur B. (ed.) (1993), pp. 68-120.

Stanbury, William T. (1996): The Effect of Federal Regulations on Financing Political Parties and Candidates in Canada. In: Thorburn, Hugh G. (ed.), 1996, pp. 72-95.

Steen, Jennifer A. (2003): The Millionaires' Amendment. In: Malbin, J. Michael (ed.), 2003, pp. 159-173.

Steen, Jennifer A. (2006): *Self-financed Candidates in Congressional Elections*. Ann Arbor: University of Michigan, 2006.

Stegagnini, Bruno (1989): Financing of Political Parties: A Cornerstone of Pluralist Democracies. In: *Council of Europe*, Strasbourg 1989.

Stöss, Richard et al. (2006): Parteiensysteme in Westeuropa: Stabilität und Wandel. In: Niedermayer, Oskar et al. (eds.), 2006, pp. 7-37.

Stone, Diane (2004): Introduction: Think Tanks, Policy Advice and Governance. In: Stone, Diane/ Denham, Andrew (eds.), 2004, pp. 1-18.

Stone, Diane/ Denham, Andrew (eds.) (2004): *Think Tank Traditions. Policy Research and the Politics of Ideas*. Manchester and New York: Manchester University, 2004.

Strøm, Kaare/ Svåsand, Lars (1997): Political Parties in Norway. Facing the Challenges of a New Society. In: Strøm, Kaare/ Svåsand, Lars (eds.): *Challenges to Political Parties. The Case of Norway*. Ann Arbor: The University of Michigan, 1997, pp. 1-32.

Sturm, Roland (1997): Die britischen Parteien vor der Wahl. In: *Aus Politik und Zeitgeschichte*, 47 (1997), pp. 3-9.

Sturm, Roland (2003): Das politische System Großbritanniens. In: Ismayr, Wolfgang (ed.): *Die politischen Systeme Westeuropas*. Opladen: Leske+Budrich, 3rd. ed. 2003, pp. 225-262.

Suetens, Louis P. (1990): Die Institution der politischen Partei in Belgien. In: Tsatsos, Dimitris Th. et al. (eds.), 1990, pp. 27-72.

Suetens, Louis P. (1992): Parteienfinanzierung in Belgien. In: Tsatsos, Dimitris Th. (ed.), 1992, pp. 19-60.

Sundberg, Jan (1987): Exploring the Basis of Declining Party Membership in Denmark: A Scandinavian Comparision. In: *Scandinavian Political Studies*. 10 (1987) 1.

Sundberg, Jan (1994): Finland: Nationalized Parties, Professionalized Organizations. In: Katz, Richard S./ Mair, Peter (eds.), 1994, pp. 158-184.

Sundberg, Jan (2002): The Scandinavian Party Modell at the Crossroads. In: Webb, Paul et al. (eds.), 2002, pp. 181-216.

Sung, Nak In (2005): Korea. In: Grant, Thomas D. (ed.), 2005, pp. 319-332.

Svasand, Lars (1991): State Subventions for Political Parties in Norway. In: Wiberg, Matti (ed.), 1991a, pp. 119-146.

Svasand, Lars (1992): Norway. In: Katz, Richard S./ Mair, Peter (eds.), 1992, pp. 732-780.

Svasand, Lars (1994a): Change and Adoption in Norvegian Party Organizations. In: Katz, Richard S./ Mair, Peter (eds.), 1994, pp. 304-331.

Svasand, Lars (1994b): Partiernes finansieringsmonster: Fra medlemmenes Iommebroker til statsbudsjettet. In: Svasand, Lars/ Heidar, Knut (eds.): *Partierne i en Brytningstid*. Bergen: Alma Mater, 1994, 180-212.

Svasand, Lars et al. (1997): Change and Adoption in Party Organization. In: Strøm, Kaare/ Svåsand, Lars (eds.): *Challenges to Political Parties. The Case of Norway*. Ann Arbor: The University of Michigan, 1997, pp. 91-124.

Swaan, Mony de/ Martorelli, Paola/ Molinar Horcasitas, Juan (1998): Public Financing of Political Parties and Electoral Expenditures in Mexico. In: Serrano, Monica (ed.): *Governing Mexico. Political Parties and Elections*. London: Institute of Latin American Studies, 1998, pp. 156-169.

Tadashi, Yamamoto (2001): Japan. In: Weaver, R. Kent/ Stares, Paul B. (eds.), 2001, pp. 71-88.

Tanguay, Brian/ Gagnon, Alan G. (eds.) (1996): *Canadian Parties in Transition*. Toronto: Nelson, 2nd ed. 1996.

Tham, Joo-Cheong (2007): *Lessons from a 'Relaxed and Comfortable' Country: Money and Politics in Australia (or How to regulate Political Finance)*. Paper for Symposium on 'The Funding of Political Parties and Election Campaings', Victoria University of Wellington, 15 June 2007.

Theis, Carmen (2007): *Die lokale Basis der FDP. Ihre Bedeutung für die Gesamtpartei*. Oldenburg: BIS, 2007.

Thorarensen, Björg/ Hardarson, Olafur Th. (2005): Iceland. In: Grant, Thomas D. (ed.), 2005, pp. 153-168.

Thorburn, Hugh G. (ed.) (1972): *Party Politics in Canada*. Scarborough: Prentice Hall, 3rd. ed. 1972.

Thorburn, Hugh G. (ed.) (1979): *Party Politics in Canada*. Scarborough: Prentice Hall, 4th ed. 1979,

Thorburn, Hugh G. (ed.) (1996): *Party Politics in Canada*. Scarborough, Ont. et al.: Prentice Hall, 7th ed. 1996.

Thunert, Martin (2001): Germany. In: Weaver, R. Kent/ Stares, Paul B. (eds.), 2001, pp. 157-206.

Thunert, Martin (2004): Think Tanks in Germany. In: Stone, Diane/ Denham, Andrew (eds.), 2004, pp. 71-88.

Timmermann, Heinz (1971): *Probleme der Parteienfinanzierung bei den Italienischen und Französischen Kommunisten*. Köln: Bundesinstitut für Ostwissenschaftliche Studien, 1971.

Titzck, Karl-Reinhard (1999): *Verfassungsfragen der Wahlkampfkostenerstattung*. Baden-Baden: Nomos, 1999.

Tjernström, Maja (2003): Matrix on Political Finance Laws and Regulations. In: Austin, Reginald/ Tjernström, Maja (eds.), 2003, pp. 181-223.

Trautmann, Günter/ Ulrich, Hartmut (1997/ 2003): Das politische System Italiens. In: Ismayr, Wolfgang (ed.): *Die politischen Systeme Westeuropas*. Opladen: Leske & Budrich, 3rd. ed. 2003, pp. 553-607.

Treisman, Daniel (1998): Dollars and Democratisation: The Role and Power of Money in Russia's Transitional Elections. In: *Comparative Politics*, 31 (1998) 1.

Tsatsos, Dimitris Th. (ed.) (1992): *Parteienfinanzierung im europäischen Vergleich. Die Finanzierung der politischen Parteien in den Staaten der Europäischen Gemeinschaft*. Baden-Baden: Nomos, 1992.

Tsatsos, Dimitris Th. et al. (eds.) (1990): *Parteienrecht im europäischen Vergleich. Die Parteien in den demokratischen Ordnungen der Staaten der Europäischen Gemeinschaften*. Baden-Baden: Nomos, 1990.

Tucker, Harvey J. (1986): Contextual Models of Participation in U.S. State Legislative Elections. In: *Western Political Quarterly*, 39 (1986) 1, pp. 67-78.

Van den Berg Report (1991): Rapport van de Commissie subsidiering Politieke Partijen. *Waarborg van Kwaliteit*. 's Gravenhage: Ministerie van Binnenlandse Zaken, 1991.

Vannucci, Alberto (1997): Politicians and Godfathers: Mafia and Political Corruption. In: Della Porta, Donatella/ Mény, Yves (eds.), 1997a, pp. 50-64.

Vesterdorf, Peter L. (1990): Die Institution der politischen Parteien in Dänemark. In: Tsatsos, Dimitris Th. et al. (eds.), 1990, pp. 73-150.

Vesterdorf, Peter L. (1992): Parteienfinanzierung in Dänemark. In: Tsatsos, Dimitris Th. (ed.), 1992, pp. 61-86.

Vieira, Tarcisio (2003): Brasil. In: Carrillo, Manuel et al. (eds.), 2003, pp. 425-434.

Voerman, Gerrit (1996): Politieke Partijen in Nederland: en Inleiding. In: Jansen, Eddi M. Habben/ Stolwijk, Lilian/ Voerman, Gerrit (eds.): *Gids Politieke Partijen*. Amsterdam/Groningen: Instituut voor Publiek en Polititiek, 1996, pp. 11-25.

Vowles, Jack (2002): Parties and Society in New Zealand. In: Webb, Paul et al. (eds.), 2002, pp. 409-437.

Walecki, Marcin (2001): Political Finance in Central Eastern Europe. In: Nassmacher, Karl-Heinz (ed.), 2001a, pp. 393-416.

Walecki, Marcin (2005a): *Money and Politics in Poland*. Warszawa: Institute of Public Affairs, 2005.

Walecki, Marcin (2005b): Poland. In: Grant, Thomas D. (ed.), 2005, pp. 387-422.

Walter, Hannfried (1996): Staatliche Parteienfinanzierung in Schweden seit dem Reichstagsbeschluß vom 15. Dezember 1965. In: *Zeitschrift für ausländisches öffentliches Recht und Völkerrecht,* 26 (1966) 2, pp. 371-404.

Ward, Ion (2003): Localizing the National: The Rediscovery and Reshaping of Local Campaigning in Australia. In: *Party Politics,* 9 (2003) 5, pp. 583-600.

Ware, Alan (2006): American Exceptionalism. In: Katz, Richard S./ Crotty, William (eds.), 2006, pp. 270-277.

Wattenberg, Martin P. (1990): *The Decline of American Political Parties, 1952-1988.* Cambridge, MA: Harvard University, 1990.

Wawzik, Thomas U. (1991): *Großes Geld in kleiner Münze. Amerikanische Erfahrungen mit der Finanzstimme zur Wahlkampf- und Parteienfinanzierung.* Oldenburg: BIS, 1991.

Wearing, Joseph (1981): *The L-Shaped Party: The Liberal Party of Canada: 1958-1980.* Toronto and New York: Mc Graw-Hill Ryerson, 1981.

Weaver, R. Kent/ Stares, Paul B. (eds.) (2001): *Guidance for Governance. Comparing Alternative Sources of Public Policy Advice.* Tokyo and New York: Japan Center for International Exchange, 2001.

Webb, Paul D. (1992): The United Kingdom. In: Katz, Richard S./ Mair, Peter (eds.), 1992, pp. 837-870.

Webb, Paul D. (1994): Party Organizational Change in Britain: The Iron Law of Centralization? In: Katz, Richard S./ Mair, Peter (eds.), 1994, pp. 109-133.

Webb, Paul D. (1995): Are British Political Parties in Decline? In: *Party Politics,* 1 (1995) 3, pp. 299-322.

Webb, Paul (2000): *The Modern British Party System.* London: Sage, 2000.

Webb, Paul (2002a): Political Parties in Advanced Industrial Democracies. In: Webb, Paul et al. (eds.), 2002, pp. 1-15.

Webb, Paul (2002b): Political Parties in Britain: Secular Decline or Adaptive Resilience?. In: Webb, Paul et al. (eds.), 2002, pp. 16-45.

Webb, Paul/ Farrell, David/ Holliday, Ian (eds.) (2002): *Political Parties in Advanced Industrial Democracies.* Oxford: University, 2002.

Weber, Max (1925): *Wirtschaft und Gesellschaft.* 2nd ed. Tübingen: J.C.B. Mohr, 1925.

Weber, Peter (2000): Parteienfinanzierung in Italien. Ein Menetekel ohne Wirkung. In: *Das Parlament,* 11./18.02.2000.

Weekers, Karolien/ Maddens, Bart (2007): *Explaining the Evolution of the Party Funding Regime in Belgium.* Paper presented at the 57th Political Studies Association Annual Conference, Bath UK, 11-13 April 2007.

Weggeman, Johan (1999): Zwischen Unabhängigkeit und Verflechtung: Parteiorganisationen und Fraktionen in den Niederlanden. In: Helms, Ludger (ed.), 1999, pp. 197-217.

Weigelt, Kurt (1988): *Staatliche Parteienfinanzierung. Zu den Möglichkeiten einer staatlichen Parteienfinanzierung in der Schweiz unter vergleichender Berücksichtigung der Gesetzgebung in Frankreich, der Bundesrepublik Deutschland und den Vereinigten Staaten von Amerika.* Grüsch, CH: Rüegger, 1988.

Welch, William P. (1974): The Economics of Campaign Funds. In: *Public Choice,* 20 (1974) 1, pp. 83-97.

Welch, William P. (1979): Patterns of Contributions: Economic Interest and Ideological Groups. In: Alexander, Herbert E. (ed.), 1979, pp. 199-220.

Welch, William P. (1980): The Allocation of Political Monies: Economic Interest Groups. In: *Public Choice*, 35 (1980) 1, pp. 97-120.

Welch, William P. (1981): Money and Votes: A Simultaneous Equation Model. In: *Public Choice,* 36 (1981) 2, pp. 209-234.

Wells, Henry (1961): *Goverment Financing of Political Parties in Puerto Rico.* Princeton NJ: Citizens' Research Foundation, 1961.

Wewer, Göttrik (1986): Kommunistische Unternehmungen in der Bundesrepublik Deutschland. Wissenschaftliche Fragestellungen nach österreichischen Erfahrungen. In: *Beiträge zur Konfliktforschung,* 16 (1986) 1, pp. 87-109.

Wewer, Göttrik (ed.) (1990): *Parteienfinanzierung und politischer Wettbewerb.* Rechtsnormen, Realanalysen, Reformvorschläge. Opladen: Westdeutscher, 1999.

Whitaker, Reginald (1977): *The Government Party: Organizing and Financing the Liberal Party of Canada 1930-58.* Toronto et al.: University of Toronto, 1977.

White, Theodore H. (1982): *America in Search of Itself. The Making of the President 1956-1980.* New York: Harper and Row, 1982.

Whiteley, Paul (1983): *The Labour Party in Crisis.* London and New York: Methuen, 1983.

Whiteley, Paul/ Seyd, Patrick/ Richardson, Jeremy (1994): *True Blues. The Politics of Conservative Party Membership.* New York: Oxford University, 1994.

Wiberg, Matti (1988): *Public Financing of Political Parties as a Guarantee for Political Pluralism in Finland.* Paper presented at the Workshop on „Money and Politics", European Consortium for Political Research, Rimini 1988.

Wiberg, Matti (ed.) (1991a): *The Public Purse and Political Parties. Public Financing of Political Parties in Nordic Countries.* Jyväskylä, Finland: Gummerus Printing, 1991.

Wiberg, Matti (1991b): Introduction. In: Wiberg, Matti (ed.), 1991a, pp. 7-11.

Wiberg, Matti (1991c): Public Financing of Parties as Arcana Imperii in Finland. In: Wiberg, Matti (ed.), 1991a, pp. 55-118.

Wicha, Barbara (1988): Parteienfinanzierung in Österreich. In: Pelinka, Anton/ Plasser, Fritz (eds.), 1988, pp. 489-525.

Wiesendahl, Elmar (1980): *Parteien und Demokratie. Eine soziologische Analyse paradigmatischer Ansätze der Parteienforschung.* Opladen: Leske+Budrich 1980.

Wiesli, Reto (1999): Schweiz: Miliz-Mythos und unvollkommene Professionalisierung. In: Borchert, Jens (ed.), 1999, pp. 415-438.

Wilcox, Clyde (1988): I Owe it All to Me. Candidates' Investments in Their Own Campaigns. In: *American Politics Quarterly,* (1988) 3, pp. 266-279.

Wildenmann, Rudolf (1968): *Gutachten zur Frage der Subventionierung politischer Parteien aus öffentlichen Mitteln.* Meisenheim a.G.: Hain, 1968.

Wildenmann, Rudolf et al. (Kaltefleiter/ Schleth) (1965): Auswirkungen von Wahlsystemen auf das Parteien- und Regierungssystem der Bundesrepublik. In: Scheuch, Erwin K./ Wildenmann, Rudolf (eds.): *Zur Soziologie der Wahl.* Köln and Opladen: Westdeutscher, 1965, pp. 74-112.

Williams, Robert (ed.) (2000a): *Party Finance and Political Corruption.* Houndmills et al. and London: Macmillan; New York: St. Martin's, 2000.

Williams, Robert (2000b): Aspects of Party Finance and Political Corruption. In: Williams, Robert (ed.), 2000a, pp. 1-13.

Wilson, John (2004): *Donations to Political Parties: Disclosure Regimes*. www.clerk. parliament.govt.nz/ Contents/ResearchPapers/04-4DonationstoPoliticalParties.pdf, 2004.

Winczorek, Piotr (1990): Problemy ustawowej regulacji pocenia parttii politycznych w Polsce. In: *Panstwo i Prawo*, 1990/1, p. 13.

Winkelmann, Rolf (2007): *Politik und Wirtschaft im Baltikum*. Saarbrücken: VDM-Dr. Müller, 2007.

Winkelmann, Rolf (2008): *Tabaklobbyismus. Einflußmöglichkeiten und -techniken der Zigarettenindustrie in Deutschland*. Saarbrücken: VDM-Dr. Müller, 2008.

Winkler, Karlheinz (1978): *Die Geldquellen der DKP*. Köln: Edition Agrippa, 1978.

Winter, Lieven de/ Timmermans, Arco/ Dumont, Patrick (1997): Belgien: Über Regierungsabkommen, Evangelisten, Gläubige und Häretiker. In: Müller, Wolfgang C./ Strøm, Kaare (eds.): *Koalitionsregierungen in Westeuropa*. Wien: Signum, 1997, pp. 371-442.

Wivenes, G. (1992): Fraktions- und Parteienfinanzierung durch das Europäische Parlament. In: Tsatsos, Dimitris Th. (ed.), 1992, pp. 455- 480.

Woolstencroft, Peter (1997): On the Ropes again? The Campaign of the Progressive Conservative Party in the 1997 Federal Election. In: Frizzell, Alan/ Pammet, John H. (eds.): *The Canadian General Election of 1997*. Toronto: Dundurn, 1997, pp. 71-90.

Yishai; Yael (2000): Bringing Society Back In Post-Cartel Parties in Israel. In: *Party Politics*, 7 (2000) 6, p. 667-687.

Ysmal, Colette (1989): *Les partis politiques sous la Ve République*. Paris: Montchrestien, 1989.

Young, Lisa (1998): Party, State and Political Competition in Canada: The Cartel Model Reconsidered.I n: *Canadian Journal of Political Science*, 31 (1998) 2, pp. 339-357.

Young, Lisa (2004): Regulating Campaign Finance in Canada: Strengths and Weaknesses. In: *Election Law Journal*, 3 (2004) 3, pp. 444-462.

Young, Sally/ Tham, Joo-Cheong (2006): *Political Finance in Australia: A skewed and secret System?* Draft Audit Report No. 7, March 2006. Political Finance & Government Advertising Workshop - 25 February 2006.

Zelle, Carsten (1996): Parteien und Politiker in den USA: Personalisierung trotz „party revival". In: *Zeitschrift für Parlamentsfragen*, 1996, pp. 317-335.

Zohlnhöfer, Raimut (2002): Das italienische Parteiensystem nach den Wahlen: Stabilisierung des fragmentierten Bipolarismus oder Rückkehr zur „ersten Republik"? In: *Zeitschrift für Parlamentsfragen*, 33 (2002) 2, pp. 271-290.

Zovatto G., Daniel (2001): Political Finance in Latin America. In: Nassmacher, Karl-Heinz (ed.), 2001a, pp. 369-392.

Index

abuse of public resources 277-9, 288
access to media 168-70, 297-9
access to party system
   see openness (of party system)
access to public funding
   see public funding (access to)
accountants, certified 64, 375
accounting, terms of 47-8, 60-1, 73-4
administration, (demarcation to) public 35, 84, 296-7
advertising, political
   see communication, media
advertising, publicity
affiliated organisations 49-50, 55-8, 308-10, 330, 341, 369, 371, 372, 373, 375, 385, 387-9
   see also collective membership
Africa 39, 310
agrarian sector 245, 276, 318
airtime charges 170-1, 176, 187
allocation of public subsidies
   see public funding
allowances (to MPs) 35-6, 59, 93-4, 134, 182
allowances (to parties)
   see grant, public funding
alternation of power 175, 322, 342-3, 345-6, 356-60, 362
Anglo-Saxon orbit 120, 131-2, 151, 176-8, 200, 205-6, 209, 222, 297, 333, 379, 396, 397
annual (routine) spending
   see routine spending
Argentina 33
assessment (of officeholders) 228, 277, 284-8, 314, 396
association quota 231-3
Australia 33
– impacts of political money 353, 354, 355, 356, 358

– revenue, political 201-2, 205-6, 220, 223, 227, 247, 266, 267, 289, 297, 311, 313, 316, 324, 328, 331
– spending, political 67, 75-6, 79-80, 102-3, 111, 117-9, 128, 178
Austria 33, 394, 395, 397
– impacts of political money 341, 350, 353, 355, 356, 358, 360, 361, 362, 372, 382-4, 388
– revenue, political 196, 201-2, 205, 206-7, 210, 211, 212, 214, 220, 233, 246, 268, 269, 274, 275-6, 283, 285-6, 289, 297, 298-9, 302, 304-5, 306, 307, 309, 310, 312, 313, 316, 319, 320-1, 323-4, 325, 328, 329, 332-3
– spending, political 56, 57-8, 59, 105, 117-9, 129, 134, 137-8, 158-62, 164, 168, 180-1, 188-9
autonomy (of parties) 244, 291
   see also public utilities

balances, annual (party)
   see reporting
bans (in party funding), legal 34, 243-4, 247, 252, 260-1, 266-70, 288, 291, 297, 307, 370, 371, 387, 389
Belgium 33-4
– impacts of political money 348-50, 353, 355-6, 357
– revenue, political 201-2, 204-6, 211, 228, 278-9, 285-6, 289, 297-8, 305, 307, 309, 312-3, 316, 325, 326
– spending, political 77-9, 111
blind trust 55, 274
B.Q. (*Bloc Quebecois*, Canada) 62, 70, 80, 165, 209, 351, 356
branches, (regional) party 50, 53, 64, 106, 181-3, 233-5, 305-6, 330, 374-8, 381, 385-6
Brazil 33

Britain
    see United Kingdom
broadcasting
    see airtime charges, media advertising, publicity expenses
bureaucratisation   45, 177-8, 306, 364-5, 375, 379, 386, 391, 398
business associations
    see organised interests
business contributions
    see donations (corporate)
buying honours (or offices)   257-8, 288, 396

cadre parties   41, 105, 203, 209, 231, 233, 319, 381, 393, 398-400, 404
campaign expenditure   74-9, 184, 258, 292, 336-8, 242-3, 377, 380-2
    see also election campaign(s)
campaign finance regulation
    see regime (political finance)
campaign funds   32, 218, 247, 249-54, 258-62, 302-3, 335-6, 375-6, 398-9
    see also party revenue
campaign-oriented democracies   156, 173-4, 176-8, 189
campaign period, official   70, 72, 88, 174, 224
campaign routines/ strategy   75, 136, 381, 387-8
campaign spending
    see campaign expenditure, election campaigns
Canada   33, 394-5, 397
– impacts of political money   349-51, 353, 355-6, 357, 359, 371-3, 376-8, 382, 385-6
– revenue, political   200, 202, 209, 216, 218-9, 223, 224, 229-30, 233-6, 247, 254, 259, 261-4, 270, 289, 297-300, 303-5, 311, 312, 313, 316, 323-6, 331, 333
– spending, political   30-1, 54-5, 62-3, 64, 66-8, 70, 72, 75, 77-9, 80-2, 101-2, 117-9, 137-8, 140, 158-62, 164-5, 169, 173, 175-6, 177-8, 187-90
candidate campaigns   97, 99, 101, 140, 197, 235, 237, 258-9, 375-8, 389
candidate competition   291, 336-8, 361, 377 –
challengers   256, 258
– incumbents   191, 340, 387, 399
– marginal seats   133, 172
candidate promotion/ selection   201, 203, 248, 250, 252, 257, 267, 281
candidate spending, impact of
    see spend and win
candidates, subsidies to   303-4
capital-intensive campaigning   133-5, 169, 186, 364-5
cartel parties   25, 324, 326, 348, 366, 393, 402-5
catch-all parties   198, 209, 393, 398-402, 404
caucus
    see grant (caucus), parliamentary party
CDU (*Christlich-Demokratische Union*, Germany)   53-4, 56, 62, 180, 205-8, 214, 223, 234, 250, 259, 263-5, 275, 283, 286-7, 325, 343-4, 368, 374, 383, 400
CEA (Canada Elections Act, 1974)   67, 73, 236, 326
central eastern Europe   268-9, 272, 275, 289
    see also individual countries
centralisation   183, 377-82, 383-6, 389-90, 403
    see also intra-party power
central office
    see headquarters (national party)
centre parties (of Scandinavia)   201, 213, 214, 319, 320
change of government see alternation of power
chapters, (local) party   51, 53-4, 65, 79, 82-3, 91, 106, 181-3, 219, 221-3,

231-6, 246-8, 305, 330, 346, 364-9, 373-6, 378-80, 382-4, 386, 390, 393, 404
Christian Democratic parties 207, 213-4, 235, 319
circumventing the rules
    see enforcement (of funding rules)
civil society
    see interested money, issue advocacy, linkage, NGOs
cleavages (of civil society) 128-9, 136, 190-1, 401
clientelism 132, 138-9, 151, 165, 203, 212, 277, 279-80, 284-5
cluster analysis 126-7, 149-52
coalition government/ politics 128, 132, 325, 328-9, 356-7, 360, 362
collective membership 175, 204, 212, 246-9, 369
committees of inquiry, reports by 28, 67, 69, 98, 161
communication expenses 66-8, 76, 242, 275, 298-9
communication, professional 167-71, 174, 186, 378-9, 386, 401-3
communication technology
    see technology
Communist parties 201, 207, 211, 212-3, 234-5, 236, 246, 273-4, 285-6, 318, 319, 320
comparative studies (of party funding)
    see cross-national analysis
competition among parties 359-60, 362, 393-4
competition within parties
    see intra-party competition
congresssional campaigns/ candidates 166, 177, 186, 258-9
Congress Party (India) 205, 268, 331-2
consensus democracy 34, 128-31, 327-30, 378
conservative parties 180, 207, 211-3, 250, 260, 318, 319
    see also Christian Democratic parties

Conservatives (U.K.) 52, 62, 82, 135, 136, 174-5, 179, 190, 201, 205, 207, 208-9, 214, 220-1, 223, 231-2, 256, 257, 258, 262-3, 273, 276, 298, 342-5, 367, 371-3, 380-1
constituency associations 50-1, 98, 189, 218-9, 382, 385-6
    see also chapters (local party)
constituency campaigns/ candidates 54, 69, 74-5, 304, 339, 375, 377
constituency office (of MP) 36, 93-4, 106-7, 306
consultants, media/ political 64, 255, 375
Consumer Price Index (CPI) 159-61, 173
contracts, public/ tendered 144, 146, 179-83
contributions (to party coffers)
    see collective membership, donations, membership dues
control (of political funds), public
    see bans, disclosure, enforcement, limits, regime, reporting
conventions, party 67, 69, 84, 314
convergence of parties 391, 399-401
conveyor organisations 245-6, 249-51
corrupt and illegal practices 257, 267, 268, 270, 273, 274, 291
    see also regime (political finance)
corruption 20, 21, 42, 139, 141-4, 151-3, 196, 201, 239-41, 259-60, 277, 279-83, 288, 364-5, 394, 396
Corruption Perceptions Index (TI) 142-4, 150
Costa Rica 33-4
 – impacts of political money 350, 353, 355, 356, 358
 – revenue, political 200, 268, 273, 289, 291, 297, 312, 313, 324, 238
 – spending, political 112, 168
cost explosion 40, 155-92, 394
cost push, impact of 145, 181, 183-92
costs of democracy,

453

- general   20-1, 24, 31, 36, 85, 394-5
- level (by countries)   38-9, 87-120
- causes of level   39, 121-54
- trends (over time)   155-92

court rulings
   see supreme courts

CPC (Conservative Party of Canada)   70, 209, 386

CPI deflated   83, 159-60, 168, 173-4, 176, 183, 191

cross-national analysis (of party funding)   26-9, 88, 110-20, 121-52

CSU (*Christlich-Soziale Union*, Germany)   62, 205-8, 214, 263-5, 275, 286, 325, 243-5

currency exchange rates   111-3, 114-5

Czech Republic   33

D66 (Netherlands)   103, 215

data, quality and quantity   40, 47-9, 52, 59-60, 74, 76, 150, 156, 161-4, 191

DC (*Democrazia Cristiana*, Italy)   55, 137-8, 201, 202, 214, 235, 245, 278, 281, 329, 351

demand pull
   see income pull

democracy, consensus/ majoritarian
   see consensus, majoritarian democracy

democracy, theory of   20, 23, 30-1, 34, 36, 37, 41, 44-5, 136, 195, 239-44, 290-4, 302, 332
   see also party theory

democratic experience/ tradition, impact on spending   123-4, 150

democratisation, waves of   33-4, 123-4, 127, 145-6, 152, 186, 289-90

Democrats, U.S.   49, 80, 217-8, 224, 233, 247, 252, 254, 295, 342, 385, 387-8, 398

Denmark   34, 394, 397
- impacts of political money   348-9, 353, 355-6, 358, 359, 369

- revenue, political   201-2, 206, 207, 210-3, 227, 245, 246, 260-1, 266, 275, 289, 297-8, 305, 307, 311, 313, 316, 319, 320-1, 323, 328-9, 333
- spending, political   59, 62, 107-8, 118-9, 181

developing nations   119, 122

direct mail/ marketing   68, 171, 175, 187, 191, 216-9, 220-1, 253, 280, 370-1, 386, 395, 404

disclosure of
- donor's identity   25, 243, 267, 271-2
- political funds   260-1, 266, 268, 271, 288, 291, 370-1
   see also reporting

disincentives, public
   see public disincentives

distribution of power (within party organisations)
   see intra-party power

distribution of public funding see public funding (distribution of)

DKP (*Deutsche Kommunistische Partei*, Germany)   273-4, 276

dominant party   34, 137-8, 151, 165

donating/ donations   41, 218-9, 227, 250-1, 338, 341-3

donations (share of revenue)   218-22

donations,
- big/ large   215, 218, 220-1, 223, 225-6, 236, 240-4, 254-6, 260-1, 266-9, 282, 318, 370-3
- business/ corporate   34, 139, 176, 193, 228-9, 239-43, 249-53, 260-8, 269-70, 273-4, 281, 318, 365, 371, 373, 387-8, 396, 398
- small   193-4, 197-8, 215-30, 236, 241, 251, 301, 303, 314, 342, 365-6, 369, 370-3, 376, 391, 395, 397

donations in-kind   106, 172, 216-7, 247, 251, 266, 274-5

donors, individual   198, 217-8, 225-8, 229-30, 255, 256, 259, 261-2, 268-9, 283-4

dues paid by party members
  see membership dues

economic development/ growth, impact on political spending   114, 122-3, 183-90, 192
economies of scale   123-7, 151-2
education, political
  see training
election campaign(s)   20, 38-9, 44, 68-9, 74-9, 164-5, 174-5, 183-4, 187, 303-4, 318, 376
  see also campaign expenditure, constituency campaigns
election cycle   76, 109-10, 164-5, 180
election law
  see electoral system(s), regime (political finance)
election years, spending in   63, 187-9
electoral-professional party   178, 382, 383, 403
electoral system(s)   131, 133, 139, 140, 166, 178, 303-4, 311-2, 315, 326, 339, 347-8, 353-5, 364, 373, 375-7, 381
enforcement (of funding rules)   26, 80, 103, 162, 176, 243, 270, 291, 396
  see also FEC
enterprises, party owned (commercial)   50, 193, 266, 274-6
enrolment (of party members)
  see M/E ratio, party membership
entitlement of MPs
  see allowances (to MPs)
entitlement of parties
  see grants, public funding
equality   30-1, 241, 242, 244
Estonia   33
Europe
  see central eastern Europe, western Europe, individual countries
European style parties   178-9, 399, 400
expenditure, categories of (types of cost)
  see goods and services

factions   55, 91, 138, 203, 235, 246, 267, 329, 374
fairness (of political competition)   32, 43, 44, 230, 242, 291, 298, 310, 313, 316, 325-6, 333, 335, 341, 348
fat cats (wealthy donors)
  see wealthy individuals
FDP (*Freie Demokratische Partei*, Germany)   62, 180, 207, 208, 215, 234, 250, 263-5, 275, 286-7, 343-4, 345
FDP (*Freisinnig-demokratische Partei*, Switzerland)   211, 213, 268, 287
FEC (Federal Election Commission)   49, 76, 90, 176, 271, 377, 387
FECA (Federal Election Campaign Act, 1976)   251, 261, 387
federalism/ federal system   34, 95-6, 101-2, 128-9, 135
fees
  – for accountants, consultants, fundraisers, lawyers
    see professional fees
  – paid by party members
    see membership dues
FF (*Fianna Fàil*, Ireland)   137, 213, 267
FG (*Fine Gael*, Ireland)   208, 267
field agencies/ organisers, local (party)
  see chapters (party), party agents
finance regime
  see regime (political finance)
financial laws, decision-making on   324-32
Finland   33
  – impacts of political money   349-50, 353, 355, 356, 369
  – revenue, political   196, 201, 204, 205, 210, 212-4, 222, 234, 265-6, 285, 289, 297, 304, 305, 307, 312, 313, 315, 319, 321-2
  – spending, political   181
FN (*Front National*, France)   62, 287, 349
foreign funds (for parties)   139, 269, 272-3, 275, 308

455

foundations, party
  see party institutes
FPÖ (*Freiheitliche Partei Österreichs*, Austria) 166, 180, 206, 215, 268, 325, 349, 360
France 33, 394, 397
– impacts of political money 345, 349, 350, 353, 354-6, 357-8, 361, 365, 374
– revenue, political 200-3, 207-8, 212-3, 214, 223, 227-8, 240, 260, 269, 271-2, 273, 275, 276, 277, 281-2, 285, 286, 287, 289, 291, 298, 303-4, 307, 308-10, 312-5, 319-22, 324, 328, 331-3
– spending, political 62, 65, 68-9, 72, 98-9, 110, 113, 115, 117-9, 135, 137, 143-4, 151, 172
franchise party 49, 404
freedom 30, 242, 244, 250, 288
freedom of speech 34, 242, 297
free-rider 197, 198
freezing (of party system) 346, 356, 361, 362
funding (of political competition) see party revenue, public funding
funding laws, party
  see public funding, regime;
  see also CEA, FECA, *PartG*, PPERA
fundraising
– costs 71, 195, 222, 253
– efforts 171, 196-7, 216-7, 218-23, 225, 235-7, 239-50, 256, 257-8, 284, 294, 303, 314, 341, 370, 372-3, 377, 379-80, 385, 389, 395
– events 194, 199, 222-3, 231, 391
– potential 183, 188, 190-1, 380
– strategies 193, 260, 281, 288
  see also grass-roots, plutocratic or public funding

Gaullist party (France) see RPR
GDP deflated 183-8, 189
Germany 33-4, 394-5, 397

– impacts of political money 343-5, 347, 353, 355-6, 357-9, 368, 372, 378, 382, 387, 388
– revenue, political 195-6, 200, 201-4, 205-6, 210-3, 215, 220, 221, 223, 225-6, 228-9, 234, 236, 245-6, 249-50, 259, 260, 261, 263-5, 269, 271, 272-3, 275, 285, 286-7, 289, 299, 301, 302, 304-5, 306-7, 309-14, 319-22, 325, 327-33
– spending, political 51-4, 56-8, 59-60, 62-3, 65, 67, 77, 79, 91-5, 117-8, 134, 136-8, 151, 158, 160-2, 164, 166, 168, 172, 180, 181-2, 188-9
gift, political
  see donations
goods and services (types of cost) 38, 47, 60-73, 394
governing parties 196, 198, 242, 257, 260, 277, 280-3, 284-5
  see also fairness (of political competition)
government advertising 35-6, 75
government contracts
  see contracts
government (expenditure/ spending, regulation of the economy) 146-9
graft, political 42, 142-4, 193, 203, 235, 276-88, 296
grant, caucus 58-60, 92-3, 296, 306-8
  see also parliamentary party
grant, flat/ general 169, 294, 302, 307, 369, 372, 374, 383
grants to MPs (incumbents)
  see allowances
grass-roots funding 41, 193-237, 239, 291-2, 314, 317, 323-4, 363-6, 373, 394-6
grass-roots funding
  (general evaluation/ discussion) 194-8, 209-10, 215-6, 221-2, 229-32, 236-7, 294
grass-roots linkage
  see constituency/ local campaign(s),

linkage
Greece 33
Green parties 62, 166, 207, 212, 213, 234, 286-7, 318-9, 320, 249-50, 357, 384
GroenLinks (Netherlands) 103, 213, 287
Gross Domestic Product (GDP) 114-5, 122-3, 150, 185-6
Grünen, Die (Green party, Germany) 53, 62, 166, 180, 208, 213, 245, 265, 275, 286-7, 320, 343-4, 345

headquarters, national party 50, 53-4, 63, 65, 67, 81-2, 98, 133-4, 168, 174, 178-80, 206, 209, 211, 213, 217, 218, 219, 221, 223, 230-5, 236, 247, 256, 261, 262, 265-6, 273, 274, 279, 286, 302, 304-5, 306, 314, 318-24, 329-30, 374-5, 378-9, 384-6, 389-91, 393
honours (as a source of party funds)
 see buying honours
hourly wage, average 113-4
Human Development Index (HDI) 123, 125, 150
Hungary 33

Iceland 33
ideology, political (and funding) 136, 198, 203, 245, 275, 399-400, 403
implementation of party regulation
 see enforcement
incentives for
– donations/ donors 195, 222, 225-30, 241, 255, 257, 291, 377
– fundraisers/ fundraising 224-5
 see public incentives
– grass-roots linkage 197, 224-30, 370-4, 379-80, 382-3, 388-90
– party membership 195, 201, 203, 205
income from
– assessments ("party taxes") 284-8

– corporate contributions 260-9, 288
– donations
 see donations (share of revenue)
– graft/ illegal practices
 see graft (political)
– membership dues
 see membership dues (share of revenue)
– party enterprises
 see returns on investment
– public funding 317-24
– trade unions 246-9
income of political parties
 see party revenue
income pull 145, 183-91, 323
independent expenditures 90, 256, 261, 270, 276-7
Index of Economic Freedom (IEF) 147-8
Index of Political Spending (IPS) 114-5, 118-20, 125-7, 143, 147
India 33
– impacts of political money 350, 353, 355, 356, 358-9
– revenue, political 201, 205, 260, 268, 273, 283, 285, 289, 298, 302, 317, 323, 331
– spending, political 75, 88, 117, 118, 122
inflation, impact on spending 39-40, 114-5, 158-61, 168, 179, 187-9
inflation, measurement of (deflator)
 see CPI
innovations, campaign
 see campaign routines, technology
institutional fundraising
 see collective membership, conveyor organisations, PACs
interested money 146, 193, 195, 197-8, 239-44, 249-54, 260-1, 268, 283, 288, 318, 340, 365
 see also organised interests
international aid 57, 84, 310
internet 68, 76, 79, 404

457

intra-party competition 54-5, 58, 74, 84, 107, 138-41, 153, 218, 278, 306, 310, 331, 371, 374, 389, 394
see also factions
intra-party organisations 50, 56, 203, 206
intra-party power 53-4, 98. 233-4, 304-6, 309-10, 314-5, 364, 373-80, 382-3
see also distribution of power
intra-party (financial) transfers see association quota, transfers (intra-party)
Ireland 33, 394, 397
– impacts of political money 348, 350, 353, 355-6, 358
– revenue, political 206, 208, 209, 212-3, 267, 289, 298, 299, 300, 304, 306, 311-3, 327-8, 330, 333
– spending, political 108-9, 118, 137
Israel 33, 394, 397
– impacts of political money 350, 351, 352, 353-9, 361-2, 365, 374-5
– revenue, political 196, 201-3, 205-7, 246, 266-7, 270, 272, 274, 279, 282, 289, 299, 305, 312-3, 317, 324, 328-9, 332, 333
– spending, political 78, 83, 88, 106-7, 117-8, 129, 134, 137, 139-40, 144, 146
issue advocacy/groups 162, 252-3, 266, 332
Italy 33, 34, 394, 397
– impacts of political money 345, 347, 349, 350-1, 358, 365, 374
– revenue, political 201-3, 206, 210-3, 229, 235, 245, 260, 266, 269, 272-6, 278, 289, 298-9, 309, 311, 313, 316, 319, 324, 327-8, 329, 332
– spending, political 88, 96-7, 111, 117-8, 137-8, 143, 144, 145, 181
Japan 33, 34, 394, 395, 397
– impacts of political money 339, 345, 349, 350, 358-9, 361, 365, 373-4

– revenue, political 201-3, 209, 212, 213, 214, 225, 228, 240, 245, 250-1, 267, 270, 276, 281, 289, 298, 312, 315, 319, 324, 327-8, 332, 333
– spending, political 50, 72, 91, 117, 118, 119, 129, 137, 138, 144, 158, 160-1, 163, 165, 172, 187, 188

kickbacks 279, 280, 281, 282, 283, 288
see also graft (political) Korea 33

labour parties 211, 246-9, 256-7, 318, 320
see also Social Democratic parties
Labour Party (U.K.) 52, 62-3, 82, 135, 174-5, 179, 190, 205, 208, 212-3, 220, 223, 231-2, 233, 247-8, 249, 256-7, 262, 270, 273, 298, 342-5, 367-8, 371-2, 380-1, 387
labour unions
see trade unions
Latin America 200, 258, 268, 272, 284, 290, 291, 301
see also individual countries
Latvia 33
LDP (Liberal Democratic Party, Jimintô, Japan) 50, 55, 137, 138, 251, 267, 315, 329, 345, 351, 358, 374
leadership contests 54, 74, 102, 136, 140
leader's tour 70, 175
legal restrictions (for parties)
see bans, disclosure, limits, reporting
legislation on funding
see regime (political finance)
legitimacy 194, 239, 242, 243, 296, 332
levels of party organisation see branches, chapters, headquarters, spending units
levels of political spending
see costs of democracy, spending levels

458

Liberal Democrats (U.K.) 52, 62, 81, 179, 215, 233, 256, 298
liberal parties 207, 212, 213, 215, 318, 319
Liberal Party of Australia 80, 267
Liberal Party of Canada 62, 70, 80-1, 233, 236, 254, 262-4, 319, 326, 359, 385
Liberals (*Folkpartiet*, Sweden) 266, 319-20
Likud (Unity, Israel) 206, 328, 359
limits, (legal)
– contribution 25, 270, 274, 288, 370, 389, 390
– spending 25, 244, 274, 300, 303, 304, 377, 380
linkage (between parties and supporters) 25, 30, 194, 196, 198, 201, 234, 240, 242, 245, 252, 259, 261, 268, 277, 290-4, 308, 314, 317, 325, 341, 352, 363-74, 379, 386, 388-91, 397, 401
Lithuania 33
local campaign(s) 133, 162, 172, 199, 338-9, 381
see also constituency campaigns
local (party) organisations
see chapters (local party), constituency associations
lotteries 194, 216, 222, 237, 299, 384, 395
Luxembourg 33

machine, political
see party machine(s), party organisation
majoritarian democracy 34, 129-31, 327, 328, 331
manifesto, campaign/election/party 84-5, 401
Mapai (*Mifleget Poale Erez Jisrael*) 137, 328-9, 359
marketing, political
see direct mail, internet, publicity

mass media
see media, newspapers
mass (membership) parties 61, 133, 180, 198, 200, 209, 214, 230, 319, 385, 398, 399, 400
matching funds 224-5, 237, 295, 301, 303, 314, 332, 368, 372, 377, 383, 390, 396
mayoral campaigns
see municipal campaigns
media 23, 85, 260, 265, 293, 336, 340, 370, 385, 386, 390, 395, 403
media advertising 67, 68-9, 75-6, 140, 167-71, 172, 174, 259, 279, 297-8, 319, 331
see also airtime charges, publicity expenses
media consultants
see professional fees
media mix/ strategy 167-71
meetings, party 67-8, 79, 85
membership drives 194, 198, 205, 237, 395
membership dues/ fees
– general infomation 41, 61, 193-4, 199-215, 228-9, 233, 234-5, 314, 318, 323, 366-70, 373, 383, 397, 403
– annual averages 206-8
– share of revenue 200, 202, 205-6, 208-11, 212-5, 248-9, 371-2, 382-3
membership party
see mass parties, party members
membership services 67, 79
member-to-voter (M/E) ratios 200-6, 210
merchandising 223, 274, 276
Mexico 33, 34, 394, 397
– impacts of political money 350, 353-5, 358-9, 361
– revenue, political 200, 273, 289, 301, 303, 316, 322, 324, 328, 331, 333
– spending, political 85, 118, 119-20, 123, 124, 128, 129, 137, 143-4

459

minor parties, performance of 336, 341, 343
  see also freezing (of party system), small parties
minority governments 325, 329
Moderaterna (conservatives, Sweden) 104, 210, 214, 266, 320
modern campaigning/ electioneering 121-2, 156, 168, 172, 174
money (as a political resource) 336-41
money in politics
  see party revenue, political spending
motives (for political contributions)
  see incentives for donors
multi-party system(s) 130, 326
municipal campaigns 75, 94, 100, 101, 107, 108
municipal subsidies 100, 308, 330 nationalised industries see patronage, public enterprises

N.D.P. (New Democratic Party, Canada) 62, 70, 80-1, 209, 219, 233, 236, 247, 255, 259, 326, 380
Netherlands 33, 34, 394, 395, 397
– impacts of political money 341, 348, 350, 353, 355, 356, 357, 358, 366-7, 382, 384, 385, 387, 388
– revenue, political 201, 204, 205, 206-7, 210, 229, 235, 236, 246, 260, 270, 271, 285, 287, 289, 297-8, 299, 301, 305, 308, 309, 312, 313, 316, 319, 321, 323, 327-8, 330, 333
– spending, political 57, 59-60, 103, 117-9, 129, 134, 181
new democracies 321, 322, 331
  see also Mexico, Poland, Spain
new parties 310, 315, 316, 319, 320, 322, 336, 342, 346-52, 356-7
  see also openness (of party system) newspapers
  see media advertising, party press, publicity expenses
New Zealand 33

– impacts of political money 350, 351, 353, 358, 365, 387
– revenue, political 201, 205, 216, 240, 242, 247, 289, 317
– spending, political 56, 133, 155
NGOs (non-governmental organisations) 34, 272, 308, 332, 370, 396
nomination contests/ procedure/ process 138, 146, 387-8
  see also primaries
non-partisan elections 74, 101
non-party groups
  see issue advocy, NGOs
North America 25, 32, 243, 255, 258, 370, 374, 376, 398, 399
  see also Canada, U.S.
Norway 33, 34, 397
– impacts of political money 349, 350, 353, 355, 356, 358, 359, 369
– revenue, political 201-2, 204, 205, 210, 212-3, 222, 246, 260, 266, 275, 289, 298, 305, 307, 309, 311, 313, 316, 319, 320, 321-4, 327-9, 333
– spending, political 181

office expenses 64-6, 67
official reports
  see reporting
openness (of party system) 43, 44, 310, 313, 340, 347, 348, 352, 361
opinion, public
  see polling
opportunity structure (for party funding)
  see regime (political finance)
opposition parties
  see fairness (of political competition), parties in opposition
organisation maintenance 64-8, 70, 79-84, 177-83
organisation, nuclei of party
  see spending units
organised interests 34, 105, 106, 131, 146, 196, 269

organisers, local (party)/ permanent
see party agents
ossification (of party system) 346, 361, 397
see also freezing, openness
ÖVP (*Österreichische Volkspartei*, Austria) 56, 138, 201, 206, 211, 217, 233, 259, 268, 360, 374, 384
paid labour see staff expenses
paid media
see media advertising, publicity expenses
parliamentary party (party-in-public-office) 50, 58, 285-8, 296, 306-8, 375, 377, 381, 387, 396
see also grant (caucus)
parliamentary systems 34, 75, 120, 131, 304-5, 376, 377-8
PartG (*Parteiengesetz*, parties's law, 1967) 52-3, 73, 91-3, 163-4, 182-3, 302
participation 19, 40, 41, 111, 193, 196, 205, 229, 239, 248, 294-5, 385, 390, 401
parties in government
see governing parties
parties in opposition 196, 198, 277, 285, 293, 298, 308, 322, 325, 346, 388
parties, small
see small parties
party activists 50, 65, 72, 79, 84, 89, 172, 177, 194, 216, 375
party activity 187, 223, 364-5, 376-7
party agents 32, 64-5, 82, 135, 178-80, 375
see also staff expenses, chapters (local party), constituency associations
party analysis
see party functions, party theory, party types
party apparatus 48, 50, 183, 380, 395
see also party organisation party branches, regional

see branches (regional party)
party-building 178-9, 180, 186, 272, 310, 320, 362, 371, 376-7, 378, 380, 385, 387
party caucus
see parliamentary party
party chapters, local
see chapters (local party) party competition, modes of 135-41
party enterprises 193, 274-6
see also returns on investment
party factions
see factions
party families 41, 43, 62, 208-9, 211-5, 245, 318-9, 322, 400
see also Christian Democrats, Communists, conservatives, Greens, liberals, populists, Social Democrats, Socialists
party functions 24, 31-2, 34, 66, 73, 79, 194-8, 290, 292, 293, 294, 404-5
party funding laws
see CEA, FECA, *PartG*, PPERA, regime (political finance)
party headquarters, national
see headquarters (national party)
party institutes 50, 57-8, 84-5, 93, 180, 272-3, 301-2, 309-10, 330, 388
party label 259, 375, 403
party machine(s) 140, 280, 398
see also party organisation
party members/ membership 139, 193, 194, 196, 198, 199-206, 209, 234-5, 236, 369, 373, 381, 383, 386, 395, 401
see also collective membership, M/E ratios
party on the ground 32, 79, 82, 178, 402
see also chapters (party), constituency associations, party agents
party or ganisation(extra-parliamentary) 133-5, 177-81, 198, 292, 347, 363, 374-88, 389-91, 397, 399, 403

461

see also branches, chapters, headquarters, party apparatus, spending units
party penumbra see affiliated organisations, party institutes, youth organisations
party press 32, 67, 308-9, 330
party revenue (funding, income) 40-3, 193-4, 239-40, 395-7, 400-2, 405
party revenue, impact on spending 142-6, 150, 186-92
party revenue, share(s) of sources 246-7, 260, 261-2, 263, 286-7, 317-23
see also donations, graft, income, membership dues, public funding
party spending (factual pattern/ overview) 38-40, 47-86, 120, 393-5
see also goods and services, political spending, purposes (of party activity), spending units
party spending, rank order (of countries) 88, 115, 116, 118, 120
party system, change of 44, 165, 187,345-6, 347, 348, 350-9, 361
see also freezing, openness
party theory 28-9, 38, 49-50, 60-1, 375, 397, 398-405
see also party functions, party types
party types 393, 398-405 see also cadre parties, cartel parties, catch-all parties, mass parties
patronage (as a source of party funds) see buying honours
patronage, political 20, 36, 57, 139, 196, 274, 282, 284, 285, 382-3, 399
patronage party 398, 400
P.C. (Progressive Conservatives, Canada) 62, 80-1, 165, 196, 209, 219, 223, 233, 236, 254, 259, 262-4, 356, 359, 373, 380, 386
PCE (*Partido Communista de Espana*, Spain) 234, 260, 322
PCF (*Parti Communiste Français*, France) 62, 203, 273, 275, 282, 286

PCI (*Partido Comunista Italiano*, Italy) 275, 285-6
PDS (*Partei des Demokratischen Sozialismus*, Germany) 53, 62, 166, 207-8, 275, 286
petrification (of party system) 25-6, 313, 346
see also ossification
Philippines 88, 117, 118, 119, 121
pluralism 128-9, 131
plutocratic funding 41-2, 194, 225, 239-88, 290, 291, 318, 364, 381, 396
plutocratic funding (general evalution/ discussion) 240-4
Poland 33, 34, 394
– impacts of political money 350, 352, 353, 355-7, 358
– revenue, political 204, 206, 255, 268-9, 276, 279, 285, 289-90, 303, 311, 313, 322, 324, 328, 331
– spending, political 100-1, 118-9, 123, 124, 128, 151
policy development (research) 57-8, 73, 84-5
policy, impacts on spending levels 141-9
political action committees (PACs) 33, 49, 162-3, 166, 176, 191, 218, 246, 247, 251-4, 270, 301, 303, 340, 375, 377, 387-8, 389
political culture (heritage, tradition) 132, 151-3, 209-11, 216, 269-70, 288, 203, 295-6, 330, 331
political finance laws/ regulation
see regime (political finance)
political funds/ income/ revenue
see party revenue
political research
see party institutes, policy development, research (political)
political spending see candidate spending, costs of democracy, party spending, spending

politics, impacts on spending level 132-41

polity, impacts on spending level 121-32
see also electoral system(s), consensus/ majoritarian democracy

polling (of public opinion) 58, 71, 72, 84-5, 168, 172, 174, 175, 302, 343
see also professional fees

populist parties 207, 213, 319, 320, 325, 349-50, 357

pork barrel legislation, costs of 31, 36

Portugal 33, 272, 289

post-communist countries see central eastern Europe, Poland

PP (*Partido Popular*, Spain) 210, 214

PPERA (Political Parties, Elections and Referendums Act, 2000) 24, 27, 85, 270, 301, 312, 316, 323, 371-2

pre-campaign spending 70, 77, 172-5

pre-nomination campaigns/ spending 54-5, 74, 107, 166, 197, 256, 258, 301, 303, 331, 339

presidential campaigns 169-70, 184-7, 255-6, 257-8, 258, 261, 303, 339-40, 348

presidential candidates 54, 166, 303

presidential elections 74, 99, 100, 109, 197, 224, 295, 301, 342

presidential primaries 303, 314

presidential systems 34, 303, 376, 377

press
see media advertising, party press, publicity expenses

pressure groups
see organised interests

PRI (*Partido Revolucionario Institucional*, Mexico) 322

primaries, nomination by 55, 139, 203, 259, 261, 301, 303, 314, 374, 376

print media
see media advertising, party press, publicity expenses

privacy (of parties) see autonomy (of parties) private contributions (to party coffers)
see donations/ donors, membership dues

professional fees/ services 64, 72, 85, 172, 174, 175, 177-8, 383

professionalisation 172, 177-83, 294, 375, 385, 389, 391, 395, 397, 402-3
see also staff expenses

propaganda see publicity expenses

provincial parties
see branches (regional party)

PS (*Parti Socialiste*, France) 55, 62, 208, 212, 273, 282, 286

PSI (*Partido Socialista Italiano*, Italy) 139, 203, 212, 278, 280, 281, 345, 351

PSOE (*Partido Socialista Obrero Español*, Spain) 210, 212, 234, 275, 282, 322, 345

public contracts
see contracts

public control (of party funding)
see regime (political finance)

public disincentives 269-72, 288
see also bans, disclosure, limits

public enterprises (publicly owned corporations) 134, 266, 276-7

public funding 42-3, 95, 104, 106-7, 143, 289-333, 388, 400-2
see also candidates (subsidies to), grant, matching funds, reimbursements, subsidies in-kind, tax benefits
– access to 311-3
– distribution of 300-2, 314-7
– general evaluation/ discussion 23-5, 290-6, 322-3, 331-3, 396-7
– impacts 144-6, 265-6, 302, 342, 346, 348-52, 354-60, 361-2, 364-70, 372, 379, 382, 383-4
see also income pull
– politics of see subsidies (public)
– recipients 303-10, 375

- significance of
  see income from public funding, taxpayers' contribution
public incentives
  see matching funds, tax benefits
publicity expenses   67, 68-71, 75-6, 140-1, 169-71, 172-6, 274-5, 307
publicity, political/ professional   122, 167-8, 169-70, 266
public office (as a source of graft)
  see assessments, buying honours
public opinion see polling
public subsidies/ support
  see public funding, subsidies in-kind
public utilities, parties as   23-4, 191, 193, 204-5
Puerto Rico   284, 289
purposes of party activity (cost objects)   47, 73-85, 89
  see also party functions
PvdA (*Partij van de Arbeid*, Netherlands) 103, 212, 287

Quebec   209, 289, 372

radio see airtime charges, media advertising, publicity expenses
recipients of public subsidies   303-10, 332-3
referendum   105, 107-8, 326, 330
Reform Party (Canada)   62, 80, 165, 209, 351, 356, 386
regime, political finance
- general discussion/ evaluation   22-4, 25-6, 32, 239-40, 242-3, 260-1, 269-72, 289-90, 292-6, 302, 308-17, 323, 326-33, 335, 347, 351-2, 364, 368-9, 379, 396-400
  see also enforcement
- individual countries/ examples   162-3, 169, 176, 179, 255-6, 268-9, 305, 349, 359-60, 370-4, 376-7, 382-91
  see also CEA, corrupt and illegal practices, FECA, PartG, PPERA

regional (party) branches
  see branches (party)
regression analysis   126-7, 148-51, 189
regulation (of party funding)
  see regime (political finance)
regulatory agency
  see enforcement
reimbursement(s)   175, 224, 236, 296, 300, 304, 314, 326, 331, 377, 380
remuneration (of MPs/ politicians)   35, 59 reporting of
- assets   26, 274, 275
- expenditure   26, 47, 64, 77, 91-2, 102, 107, 162, 243
- income/ revenue   26, 47, 91-2, 107, 215-6, 220, 221, 243-4, 283, 291, 307
Republicans, U.S.   49, 71, 80, 209, 217-8, 224, 233, 252, 342, 385, 388
research, political   84-5, 301, 309
  see also party institutes, policy development
responsiveness (of political elite)
  see democracy (theory)
Retail Price Index (RPI) see CPI, inflation
returns on investment (as a source of party funding)   274-6
revenue sharing   230-6, 305-6, 386, 397
rise of political spending see cost explosion, spending trends
routine spending, annual   62, 96-7, 101, 106, 108, 165, 182, 187
royal commissions (reports by)
  see committees of inquiry
RPR (*Rassemblement pour la République*, France)   62, 137, 208, 214, 279, 282, 287, 357, 374
rule of law   22, 141
rules for political competition/ funding, see electoral system(s), public utilities, regime (political finance)

salaries
  see staff expenses, remuneration of MPs
SAP (*Socialdemokratiska Arbetareparti*, Sweden) 104, 137, 201, 204, 210, 222, 246-7, 286, 319, 369, 386
  scandals 20, 21, 24, 33, 145, 239, 260, 261, 267, 268, 270, 281, 282, 283, 288, 289, 295, 345, 365
Scandinavia (Nordic countries) 204, 222, 246, 266, 307
  see also Denmark, Finland, Norway, Sweden
SD (*Socialdemokratiet i Danmark*) 62, 212, 260
seed money 256, 340
self-financing (by wealthy candidates) 258-9, 303
service institutions
  see party institutes
service of experts see professional fees
services for party leaders 73, 84-5, 274
shadow economy 114, 141
single issue groups 196, 204
  see also issue advocacy, NGOs
size of country (electorate) 111, 124-7, 156-9, 168, 184
Slovakia 33
small parties 214-5, 249-50, 293, 310, 313, 314, 316-7, 320, 324-6, 328-9, 342, 348-9 social activities/ events (organised by parties)
  see fundraising events
Social Democratic (labour) parties 61, 134, 180, 199, 204-5, 206, 210-1, 212, 213, 220-1, 222, 236, 242, 245, 246-9, 286, 318, 319-20, 357, 359, 395, 400
Socialist parties 207, 212, 236, 246, 318, 319, 320
  see also Communist parties, Social Democratic parties
soft money 90, 162-3, 186, 255, 261

solicitation (of political funds)
  see fundraising
Solidarnosc (Solidarity, Poland) 255, 289, 331
sources of funding
  see party revenue
Spain 33, 34, 394, 397
  – impacts of political money 345, 349, 350, 353, 354-8, 361, 365
  – revenue, political 195, 200-2, 209-10, 246, 260, 269, 271, 277, 282, 285, 289, 299, 305, 307, 312, 313, 315, 319, 322, 324, 325, 328, 331, 332-3
  – spending, political 83, 100, 117, 118, 119, 124, 144, 151
SPD (*Sozialdemokratische Partei Deutschlands*, Germany) 49, 53, 54, 56, 62, 71, 180, 196, 205, 207, 208, 212, 223, 234, 250, 259, 273, 275, 286, 287, 343, 344-6, 368, 383
specific costs
  see goods and services
spend and win 258-9, 336-40, 342-3, 344, 360-1, 397
spending, increase of political
  see cost explosion, spending trends
spending, routine
  see routine spending
spending levels/ totals 38-9, 89-109, 110-20, 394
spending levels, causes for different 39-40, 121-54, 394
spending trends 40, 155-6, 158, 160-1, 173, 182, 185, 188, 191-5, 394-5
  see also cost explosion
spending units (cost centres) 47-60, 89, 393-4
sponsoring, private see donations in-kind
SPÖ (*Sozialdemokratische Partei Österreichs*, Austria) 138, 180, 201, 206, 211-2, 234, 268, 286, 325, 329, 360, 384

SPS (*Sozialdemokratische Partei der Schweiz*, Switzerland) 212, 287
staff expenses (full- or part-time staff) 59, 61-4, 133-5, 177-83, 370, 375, 377, 379, 380, 381, 382, 385, 391, 395
state aid
   see public funding
state parties
   see branches (regional party)
statutory rules for party competition
   see electoral system(s), public utilities, regime (political finance)
subsidies in-kind 99, 226, 233, 278-9, 297-300, 330, 331, 333, 396
subsidies, public
   see public funding
subsidies, public (politics of) 324-33, 403
supreme courts (and political funding) 87, 92, 190, 228, 242-3, 269, 297, 302, 311, 314, 325-6, 376
Sweden 33-4, 395, 397
– impacts of political money 342, 349-51, 355-6, 358-9, 366, 369, 373, 382, 383-4, 386
– revenue, political 201-2, 204, 206, 210, 212-4, 222, 246-7, 265-6, 270, 271, 275, 289, 297, 299, 301, 305, 307, 309-11, 313, 316, 319-22, 324, 327-9
– spending, political 104, 115-9, 137, 181 Switzerland 33-4, 394, 395
– impacts of political money 347, 349-50, 353, 355-7, 382
– revenue, political 201-2, 206, 210-3, 227, 235, 268, 270, 283, 285, 287, 289, 297, 299, 305-7, 323, 327-8, 330, 332
– spending, political 83, 105-6, 115-9, 125, 129, 135

Taiwan 33
tax add-on 226, 390

tax benefits/ incentives 25-6, 225-30, 236-7, 261, 286, 300, 330, 333, 383, 395-6
tax check-off 226, 295-6, 390
tax credit 227-30, 377, 380, 385
tax deduction 226-8, 309, 372
tax-payers' contribution (to party revenue) 143, 322-4, 327-33
technology 65, 72, 76, 79, 133, 171-7, 179, 181, 183, 191, 192
theories
   see democracy (theory), party theory
tiers of party organisation 50-4
   see also levels of party organisation
time series analysis (of political funding) 27, 29, 39, 52, 154, 155-92
toll-gating 279-80, 281-2, 283, 288, 396
   see also graft
trade unions 34, 105, 107, 190, 196, 204, 212, 242, 245-9, 251-2, 262, 269-70, 274, 369, 371, 373, 381, 387
traditions, political see political culture (heritage, tradition)
training of party activists 57-8, 84, 92-3, 301-2, 308-9, 379, 388
transfers, intra-party 53, 214, 230-6, 306-7, 318, 379, 381, 391, 395-6
transparency 244, 270, 283, 288, 291, 293, 296, 311, 333, 396
   see also disclosure, reporting
Turkey 33
TV advertising
   see airtime charges, media advertising, publicity expenses

UDF (*Union pour la Démocratie Francaise*, France) 62, 71, 211, 215, 287
union contributions see collective membership
United Kingdom (U.K.) 33, 394, 395, 402
– impacts of political money 339, 342-6, 347, 350, 355-6, 358-9, 367-8, 371-3, 376, 377-8, 380-2, 384

- revenue, political 195, 199, 200-2, 205, 206-14, 220-1, 223, 231-3, 236, 240, 247-9, 256-7, 258, 260, 261-4, 270-1, 273, 283, 289, 298-9, 301, 305, 308, 310, 312, 316, 317, 321, 323-4, 327, 328, 331, 332
- spending, political 52, 55, 59, 61-2, 65, 67, 75, 77-9, 81-2, 85, 97-8, 117-20, 128, 129, 135, 137, 158, 159-61, 164-5, 168, 171, 173-5, 177-80, 188, 189, 190, 192

United States (U.S.) 33-4, 394, 395, 398
- impacts of political money 339, 342, 348, 354-6, 358-9, 370-1, 372, 376-7, 379-80, 385, 389-90
- revenue, political 197, 209, 216-8, 222-5, 226, 227, 236, 240, 242, 247, 251-4, 255-6, 257-9, 260-1, 270-1, 273, 279-80, 284, 289, 295-6, 301, 302, 303, 307, 310, 313, 314, 317, 323-4, 327-8, 331, 332
- spending, political 49, 51, 67, 74, 76, 77-80, 90, 117-20, 137-8, 140, 153, 156-8, 159-63, 164, 166-71, 173-4, 176, 177-8, 184-7, 188-92

units of party organisation (cost centres) see spending units

Uruguay 33-4
- impacts of political money 350, 353, 355-6, 358
- revenue, political 200, 268, 273, 285,

289, 291, 305, 311, 313, 324, 328
- spending, political 54, 111, 167

V (*Venstre*, liberal party in Denmark) 62, 201, 245
Venezuela 88, 118, 119
Verts, Les (France) 62, 287
volatility (of voting behaviour) 236, 366, 395
volunteer labour 198, 199, 209, 216, 233, 235, 301, 332, 365, 370, 374, 375, 377, 379, 382
see also participation, party activists
vote buying, traditional 72, 75, 121, 134, 138-40, 165
voter turnout 111, 157, 297, 339, 372
VVD (*Volkspartij voor Vrijheid en Democratie*, Netherlands) 103, 215

wealthy individuals, contributions by 122, 228, 230, 240, 255-9, 268-9, 271, 273, 288, 340, 341, 372, 381
western Europe 25-6, 32, 132, 133, 152, 180, 181, 199, 205, 210-2, 243, 285, 297, 307, 318, 378
see also individual countries
Westminster tradition see Anglo-Saxon orbit, parliamentary systems

youth organisations, party 92, 301, 308, 330, 388